BREAKING

EXPOSING
THE HIDDEN FORCES
AND SECRET
MONEY MACHINE
BEHIND JOE BIDEN,
HIS FAMILY, AND
HIS ADMINISTRATION

BIDEN

ALEX MARLOW

THRESHOLD EDITIONS

New York   London   Toronto   Sydney   New Delhi

Threshold Editions
An Imprint of Simon & Schuster, Inc.
1230 Avenue of the Americas
New York, NY 10020

First Threshold Editions hardcover edition October 2023

THRESHOLD EDITIONS and colophon are trademarks of Simon & Schuster, Inc.

For information about special discounts for bulk purchases,
please contact Simon & Schuster Special Sales at 1-866-506-1949
or business@simonandschuster.com.

The Simon & Schuster Speakers Bureau can bring authors to your live event. For more information, or to book an event, contact the Simon & Schuster Speakers Bureau at 1-866-248-3049 or visit our website at www.simonspeakers.com.

Interior design by Davina Mock-Maniscalco

Manufactured in the United States of America

10 9 8 7 6 5 4 3 2 1

Library of Congress Cataloging-in-Publication Data is available.

ISBN 978-1-6680-2300-6
ISBN 978-1-6680-2302-0 (ebook)

To Robert, Wynn, and Molly

CONTENTS

INTRODUCTION

J oseph Robinette Biden was born in Scranton, Pennsylvania, on November 20, 1942, to Catherine Eugenia "Jean" Biden (née Finnegan) and Joseph R. Biden Sr. Jean was homecoming queen and belonged to a big and close-knit, boisterous Irish-Catholic family from Scranton.[1] Joe Jr. would capitalize on his Irish roots and Catholic upbringing, building a constituency of Irish-Catholic voters.

The man who would be president boasts less about the rest of his heritage, which is presumed to be mostly English. It's easy to understand why. Claims circulated online at the climax of the presidential race in the summer of 2020 that Biden's ancestors on his father's side owned slaves.

America's racial tensions had been simmering for years and finally hit a boiling point with the death of George Floyd in late May of that year. Far-left demonstrators rioted throughout what Seattle mayor Jenny Durkan called the "Summer of Love."[2] They toppled and defaced statues, torched buildings and businesses—many owned by other blacks—and injured more than two thousand police officers,[3] all in the name of racial justice. In what may have been the lowest moment, a twenty-six-year-old looter named Stephan Cannon killed a seventy-seven-year-old retired St. Louis police captain named David Dorn while Dorn tried to defend a friend's business.[4] Dorn himself was black.

For such a public family, relatively little has been written about the Bidens, particularly those not named Joe or Hunter, so this apparent revelation that they are direct descendants of slaveholders had all the hallmarks of a bombshell. It was also particularly bad timing for Joe, who was on the verge of fulfilling his lifelong goal of becoming president of the United States.

But then a miracle happened—a miracle if you are a fan of Joe Biden, that is. The establishment media bailed him out. *USA Today*, Snopes, and PolitiFact determined that the claims that Joe was heir to slave owners were unfounded. Despite evidence submitted by readers, Snopes held firm that it was "unproven," effectively, and erroneously, exonerating the Bidens.

Not until after Biden won the election did a genealogist make it official: one of Joe's ancestors, Thomas Randle, did in fact own slaves.[5]

Biden had gotten away with it.

Over his eight decades on the planet, he's gotten away with plenty, and this book explores many of those examples.

The oldest of four, Joe often found himself responsible for his younger siblings, thrusting him into a leadership position at an early age. Joe was scrappy and athletic; he was a talented football player in high school and played briefly in college. He developed a level of charisma that he had not come by easily because he grew up with a serious stutter. The story goes that it was so bad, even a nun mocked him during a seventh-grade class, referring to young Joe as "Mr. Buh-buh-buh Biden."[6] He overcame it, though, partially by reciting poetry. (He claimed he tried to learn to speak by putting pebbles in his mouth, but that method failed.[7]) Through adversity, the power of speech and well-delivered oratory were instilled in Biden at an early age.[8]

Despite the stutter and the fact that he was undersized in his youth, Joe was elected class president his junior and senior years at the prestigious Archmere Academy.[9]

He did not enjoy a similar level of accomplishment in the classroom. There is no sugarcoating it: Joe was a bad student. He left the University of Delaware football team after his first year to focus on his grades after pulling a mere 1.9 GPA. He managed to get into law school at Syracuse, attending in no small part to pursue a young woman there, Neilia Hunter, whom he met cute on a spring break trip to the Bahamas in 1964. She would become his first wife.[10] In 1968, he graduated 76th out of 85 in his class at Syracuse University College of Law.[11]

By then he already knew he wanted to be president of the United States, and he probably had for some time. Biden claims in one of his memoirs that he wrote a paper in grade school saying that he wanted to be president, though he also fibbed quite a bit, then and now, so it's hard to verify that detail.

Joe Biden's grandiosity began to translate into a career in politics two years after law school, when he ran successfully for county council in 1970. He miraculously won his first race for U.S. Senate at the age of twenty-nine and ran for president for the first time in 1988, when he was forty-five. It wasn't until more than thirty years later, when he was seventy-eight years old, that he finally landed his dream job.

The centerpiece of his 2020 campaign for the highest office in the land was composed of three key promises: he would shut down the Chinese coronavirus (dubbed "COVID-19" by the World Health Organization), the economy would roar back from the pandemic-induced economic collapse, and he would unify the country. Nearly three years into his presidency, he has not achieved any of these goals. The Delta and Omicron variants, along with apparent waning vaccine efficacy, ensured that the COVID-19 death toll under President Joe Biden surged past that of his presidential predecessor,[12] Donald Trump. Inflation hit a forty-plus-year high, and economic confidence fell to levels unseen in recent decades aside from during the 2008 financial crisis.[13] He forged an agenda focused on strictly partisan legislation and delivered a series of speeches demonizing his political opponents, so it quickly became apparent that there would be no actual effort to unify the country, unless, of course, all Americans spontaneously decided to agree with Joe Biden on everything.

Indeed, Joe Biden has gone to great lengths to deepen our political divides. Not only has he acknowledged that political tensions have risen during his administration, but he has attempted to use that fact to his political benefit, laying the blame squarely on the "extreme MAGA" movement.[14]

Throughout his career, Biden had emphasized how important it is for the president to trust his own gut. He has certainly abided by that, and by one objective measure, it has worked for him. He got the career he always wanted. Still, Joe's gut often tells him to insult and demean Americans with whom he differs, if he even chooses to acknowledge them at all.

This is not a classy look, especially for a U.S. president.

Biden's public image is that of "Lunch Bucket Joe," champion of the blue-collar worker and the middle class. But his policies have more often served the ruling classes both in the U.S. and abroad. His domestic agenda has included the importation of more foreign workers to compete with Americans, inflationary spending, and a steady opposition to affordable abundant energy. On a personal level, he lived for two decades in a ten-thousand-square-foot mansion formerly owned by the fabulously wealthy du Pont family.[15]

Nothing says "man of the people" quite like having your own ballroom.[16]

Thus, it follows that there would be a disconnect between his everyman public persona and his governing priorities. After all, Joe Biden's entire adult life has been spent as a politician. After thirty-six years in the Senate, eight as vice president under Barack Obama, and now as president of the United States, there is no one in America who more clearly embodies the *establishment* than Joe Biden.

Without Joe Biden and the ideas that have driven his career, our system of governance would not be what it is today.

He has benefited greatly from the protection of our partisan media establishment, which has spent far more time over the last half century running interference for Biden than challenging him. For example, an air of corruption has swirled around his family over the last decade, especially his son Hunter, who has appeared to have scored numerous lucrative business deals off the family's name. Hunter even lost track of the infamous "Laptop from Hell," which revealed numerous personal and family secrets, including troubling insights into their business dealings. Yet none of it was enough to keep Joe out of the White House.

He also has had some high-profile personal failings. Joe flunked a law school class in 1965 for lifting, without attribution, five pages from a published law review. He dropped out of the 1988 presidential race after a plagiarism scandal. He was caught copying entire passages of stump speeches from the likes of Robert F. Kennedy, again without attribution.[17]

President Barack Obama reportedly said, "Don't underestimate Joe's ability to fuck things up."[18] Former defense secretary Robert Gates said in 2014 that "he has been wrong on nearly every major foreign policy and national security issue over the past four decades." You'd be hard-pressed to find examples of Biden international successes since. In this book, we'll examine new, extravagant failures.

Yet Yet Joe Biden rose to the top, despite it all.

Prior to the presidency, the places where he made indelible marks on American society were rarely positive ones.

He played a pivotal role in the deal that gave the U.S. access to the

Chinese box office—and ultimately led to Hollywood outsourcing our know-how to the Chinese Communist Party (CCP).

He ushered in the era of politicized judicial confirmations, starting with the "borking" of Judge Robert Bork and then the "high-tech lynching" of black conservative Clarence Thomas. (My late friend and mentor Andrew Breitbart cited the Thomas hearings as one of the key moments that caused him to renounce his "factory setting" Los Angeles liberalism and become a conservative Republican.)

Biden said that busing would create "a racial jungle," among other insensitive comments about minorities in America. He has also spoken fondly of segregationist senators.[19]

Before Biden began complaining about institutional racism in our society[20]—which is ironic coming from someone who has been in control of those same institutions for half a century—he was responsible for a crime bill in 1994 that led to the mass incarceration of black men.[21] (He would go on to make Kamala Harris his vice president, who also built a career on jailing the nonviolent.) In 2020, Biden said the bill was a mistake,[22] but it was convenient that his change of heart after more than twenty-five years occurred while he was in the midst of a presidential run.

When he was a U.S. senator from Delaware, it was well known that the train was his preferred mode of transportation, which he emphasized presumably to present a populist image to the masses. Yet Biden was known to hold up the Amtrak Acela when he was running late, even if that meant delaying the lives of all the other souls on board. (In actuality, the Acela is one of the least populist modes of transportation; tickets from Union Station in Washington, DC, to Wilmington, Delaware, can cost upward of three hundred dollars per seat in 2023 dollars and are typically booked by people with substantial corporate or government expense accounts.)

There are also all those gaffes. *"Let me start off with two words— Made in America."*[23]

And the brain freezes. *"There are more corporations incorporated in America than every other state in America combined."*[24]

And the fibs. *"I used to drive an eighteen-wheeler, man."*

And the absurd embellishments. *"I had the great honor of being arrested with our UN ambassador on the streets of Soweto trying to get to see [Nelson Mandela] on Robbens [sic] Island."* (He was stopped at an airport in South Africa, neither he nor the ambassador was arrested, and Biden was not "on the streets.")[25]

And the light racism. *"Poor kids are just as bright and just as talented as white kids."*[26]

And the heavy racism. *"If you have a problem figuring out whether you're for me or Trump then you ain't black."*[27] He even casually slurred Jews during a public speech, referring to them as "Shylocks who took advantage of these women and men" by issuing bad loans that lead to foreclosures.[28]

He has stolen valor. *"I say this as a father of a man [who] . . . lost his life in Iraq."*[29] (This is 100 percent false.)

There are also the schoolyard taunts. *"You're a lying dog-faced pony soldier."*[30]

And the occasional invitations to violence. *"I'd beat the hell out of him."*[31] (This comment was in reference to the president of the United States at the time, Donald Trump.)

All of these examples paint the picture of a man with a not particularly facile mind. Colloquially, Joe Biden has always been a little *off*. A shameless, mildly racist bullshitter with a vindictive streak and no apparent expertise beyond being the familiar face of the government itself.

Yet in my view, this makes his rise all the more fascinating. It is tempting to marginalize Joe Biden as someone who has simply failed upward. He has, after all, climbed the career ladder as high as any human can go, and he's done so without striking political gifts, a dazzling record, or any other innate or inherited advantage.

Perhaps the sheer volume of the cringe-inducing moments of Joe Biden's career might help explain his rise to power, not belie it. As it turns out, integrity, accomplishment, and a history of excellence might not make the prototypical president in these modern times. Maybe it's the exact opposite.

Yes, Joe Biden does have a set of skills and character traits that have aided his rise.

For example, he's an egotist, which is a true advantage in the age of social media and cable news, where the political discourse is constantly overwhelmed by vitriol. He tends to recruit and appoint allies who have a similar nature: potentially incompetent but with a preternatural and undeserved self-confidence (I'm looking at you, Secretary Pete.) While running for president for the first time in 1987, then senator Biden was asked by a reporter,

"What law school did you attend and where did you place in that class?" Biden's response needs to be read in its entirety to be believed[32] (fact-checks in brackets and italics):

> I think I probably have a much higher IQ than you do, I suspect. I went to law school on a full academic scholarship, the only one in my in my class to have a full academic scholarship. *[Records show Biden received an $800 scholarship based on financial need; tuition was $1,620.]*
>
> The first year in law school I decided I didn't want to be in law school and ended up in the bottom two-thirds of my class *[he was in the bottom quarter of his class his first year]*, and then decided I wanted to stay, went back to law school, and in fact ended up in the top half of my class. *[Biden graduated law school near the bottom of his class.]*
>
> I won the international moot court competition. *[There is no known record of this specific victory.]* I was the outstanding student in the political science department at the end of my year. *[He graduated from the University of Delaware in 1961, ranking 506th in a class of 688; he carried a C average.]* I graduated with three degrees from undergraduate school and 165 credits; I only needed 123 credits. *[He graduated with two degrees.]*
>
> And I'd be delighted to sit down and compare my IQ to yours if you'd like. *[This might be true, and it's fun to picture this "sit-down" actually taking place.]*[33]

A thirty-second torrent of lies and delusions, and C-SPAN's cameras were rolling to capture it all. The footage has the feel of a black comedy, i.e., it's vaguely humorous and tremendously uncomfortable. The footage, immortalized on YouTube, is priceless. It provides a crystal-clear view into an unclear mind. Yet it is the mind of someone who has "what it takes" to become the most powerful person in the world.

Over his life, Joe Biden has, to his credit, built up an unusual amount of rhinoceros skin. In common parlance, he DGAF. He has mastered the ability to suffer life's indignities with the whole world looking on and act as though everything is going according to plan. This trait might not have mattered quite so much in 1988, but it would be utterly essential decades later, in a time when a candidate needs to run the gauntlet of cable news and Twitter and dank memes in order to get to 1600 Pennsylvania Avenue.

Besides, he's never much cared for the media.

For Joe Biden, family is everything. This suits Joe's personality, but it has been an even greater benefit to the rest of the Bidens. Though Joe pledged "an absolute" wall between himself and his family's financial dealings, history has shown his commitment to keeping the cash flowing—and his willingness to use his office to protect it. The most obvious recent example of this is perhaps how he has used the White House ethics office to implement a plan to keep the buyers of his son Hunter's art anonymous.[34]

Is it possible that those willing to pay big money for the president's son's amateur drawings might want special consideration or a favor in return? Americans deserve to know basic details about these purchases, but Joe Biden clearly disagrees and, as the pattern goes, doesn't care.

There are many similarly shocking examples. During an interview, Peter Schweizer, head of the Government Accountability Institute, informed the House Oversight Committee about a private global cell phone that Hunter Biden's business allegedly provided to Joe Biden while he was vice president. Schweizer shared the phone number and account information, hoping the committee would subpoena the records to determine the extent of communication between Hunter Biden, his business partners, and Joe Biden. Additionally, Hunter claimed that he was expected to give up to 50 percent of his earnings to Joe while also covering his father's household expenses during Joe Biden's vice presidency.[35] Hunter is certainly exaggerating here, but still, wow. Read enough examples like this and you might begin to wonder if the system is rigged.

I have spent fifteen years in journalism, more than half of that inside the Beltway, and during that time the most powerful American has been Joe Biden. Donald Trump and Barack Obama changed the world in their respective ways, are larger-than-life figures, and are much easier to root for and against. They also burst onto the political scene and summited the political power structure basically all at once. Joe Biden, on the other hand, is the embodiment of the permanent political class. He's held office for nearly two-thirds of his life with minimal interruption. He also, as he is fond of saying, gets stuff done.

There are lessons to be learned in this fact, even though his successes are often to my chagrin.

Breaking Biden was researched over hundreds of hours with a small group of some of the best investigators in all of journalism.

Upon embarking on this project well over a year before the date of publication, it was clear to me that even at eighty years old, already the oldest president in U.S. history, Joe Biden would run again. He has been a candidate, at least in his own mind, since he was a boy. The presidency—first coveting it, then living it—has defined his life. And Joe Biden has always attempted to live his life to the fullest.

So I started digging, and the facts and patterns that I've uncovered, I believe, are extraordinary, and I think you will agree. It is my sincere hope that *Breaking Biden* paints the most vivid and complete picture to date of the sum total of Joe Biden's career, who made it possible, who has benefited from it most; how his legacy will be viewed; and what his rise to power says about our republic.

Over the course of researching and writing this book, I came to believe that though he does appear to be deteriorating both physically and mentally, that has led his critics to underestimate him, which has not served them well. Marginalizing him as unintelligent and incompetent is not only lazy, reductionist thinking, but it has been a colossal waste of time. The evidence is that Joe Biden continues, as of this writing, to accumulate unfathomable levels of power and influence that have enriched his family, benefited our geopolitical adversaries, and, in the end, made America a weaker and more divided place.

Joe Biden is neither a visionary nor an ideologue; he is an operator. He knows where the levers of power are, who controls them, and how to work them himself. He wasn't always this way, but considering the sheer length of time and variety of responsibilities he has had in Washington, it's hardly a surprise that he eventually figured things out. Modern Washington, DC, is run by a vast network of bureaucrats, consultants, donors, government officials, lobbyists, "dark money" philanthropists, and information gatekeepers in Big Tech and the establishment media. Collectively, they form the engine that keeps our capital running. Biden helped build this apparatus, and it is constantly working for his benefit, and his family's.

But Joe Biden didn't merely create *the system* over fifty years: he is *the system* incarnate. To understand him is to understand America's present and our recent past.

And unless there is a course correction, he is a window into our future.

PART I

THE BIDEN BUSINESS

CHAPTER 1

Joe Biden Can Do Anything

Before Joe Biden Jr. was born, his father had a taste of the good life, courtesy of his wealthy "uncle" Bill Sheene Jr., an Irishman who had amassed success selling sealants for coffins.

For the first five years of Joe Jr.'s life, his father, Joe Biden Sr., was in business with the Sheenes. During World War II, the Sheenes' company received a lucrative deal with the U.S. government to supply their patented sealant for armor plates; Joe Sr. moved north to helm the company's Boston branch. For a time, the family didn't want for anything. They moved into a big home. His father and uncle would pilot company planes, hang out on the Sheenes' yacht, and hunt pheasant together. For the first few years of his existence, Joe Biden Jr. was pampered, too, getting presents like fancy toys and even a pony.[1] (Perhaps Joe was the original "dog-faced pony soldier.")

As it is now, the business of unstabilizing geopolitical turmoil was a good one in the 1940s.

But the war ended, and in time, Sheene's access to vast sums of government funds dried up. Thus, so did the Bidens', at least for the time being.

Uncle "Big Bill" Sheene had a reputation as a philanderer and a gambler. He was also an alcoholic and was said to go on benders that could last for weeks. All of this vice might have been his method of coping with a debilitating stutter that caused him setbacks throughout his life. He did, however, dote lavishly on his "nephew," Joe, whose own father also abused alcohol but had not struck the same luck in business.[2]

Bill Sheene's son, Bill III, was Joe Biden Jr.'s pal, so Joe was invited to share in his favorite cousin's largesse. He spent summers with the Sheenes through early adulthood. He rode horses with them and played on their golf course. They visited the dog races together. Joey absorbed the fashion, mien, and etiquette of their social strata, without actually belonging to it. His uncle supplied him a job, money, and even wheels.

Reporter Adam Entous, who has enjoyed direct access to the Biden family for several stories on their history and struggles, suggested Sheene's business was crooked from the start. Uncle Bill relied on scary, mobbed-up dudes to get where he was going. Sheene had a professional relationship with Arthur Briscoe, a bootlegger who served stints in a mental hospital. He was diagnosed with "psychopathic personality." Right after Briscoe began a relationship with a woman who had connections to the mob, his second wife was scalded to death in a bathtub, clearing the way for him to marry his mistress. "There was no autopsy and the death was declared an accident. . . . They couldn't pin anything on him." When his and Sheene's new venture, the Maritime Welding & Repair Company, faced increasing gripes from maritime unions, he elicited the help of notorious mobster Frank Costello, and the picketing soon ceased.[3]

Joe Biden Sr. made one last grandiose bet with Bill Jr.: they bought an airport. But mere months into the venture, it failed, too. Bill Sheene took back the car he had given Joe Jr., and the Bidens moved in with Jean's parents and siblings, the Finnegans, in Scranton.

This fall from grace presumably had an effect on Joe Jr., though the rest of his siblings—Valerie (born 1945), James (born 1949), and Frank (born 1953)—did not bask in luxury for much of their childhoods.

Joe's earliest years would have overlapped with his father's loss of the family's previous status. This certainly proved to be a driving influence on the rest of Joe's life, which is marked by constant striving to take his family to the next echelon of American society.

MORE BALLS THAN BRAINS

To hear Biden's friends tell it, young Joe didn't think, he just did—especially when it came to dares or fights. Locals still talk about it in Scranton. In his epic-length book on the 1988 presidential election, *What It Takes: The Way to the White House*, Pulitzer Prize winner Richard Ben Cramer illustrates this bravado with a couple of anecdotes. In 1953, ten-year-old Joey and his buddies would wander around town looking for something to do. One day, another youngster bet Joey and another kid five bucks that they wouldn't be able to climb the town culm dump. Culm is the residual debris left over from coal mines that, in those days, was piled high as mountains and burned over the course of years, "lava-hot on the surface, except where it burned out underneath, and then there'd be a pocket of ash where you could fall right into the mountain, if you stepped on it." While the other child chickened out, Joe, in a reckless dismissal of fate, took the dare and climbed up it, roughly two hundred feet to the top, covering millions of tons of fiery soot. According to Cramer, Joe never saw the five bucks, but he did catch a fleeting glimpse of immortality.[4]

In another incident, an older kid named Jimmy Kennedy (who later became a judge in Scranton) dared Joe to run under the wheels of a moving dump truck. He said later that he never thought that Joe would do it. But Joe did, so the story goes. He was small and ran between the front and back wheels, letting one of the axles go over him. As Cramer puts it, "Joe Biden had balls. Lot of times more balls than sense."[5]

Poetic.

It was this reckless moxie at inappropriate moments that made young Joey Biden the talk of Scranton and stayed with him into older age. Those who knew him there were probably unsurprised when, for instance, in 2019, he challenged one prospective voter to a push-up contest after the man, himself eighty-three years old, dared to question him about his old age.[6]

Joe was scrappy as a youth, and he needed to be. After all, the family was struggling.

They finally were able to escape the cramped house with their extended family in it when he was eleven years old for (marginally) greener pastures: the tenements of Delaware. Joe repeated the third grade after moving to Wilmington. He claims in his memoirs that it was to have his tonsils and adenoids out, but there is certainly reason to speculate it could have been that he simply wasn't keeping up.

Joe Sr. tried work cleaning boilers, selling doodads on a farm, and finally, selling cars, a profession that embarrassed him. According to Entous, even though the Bidens lived a "comfortable middle-class existence" and had that taste of the good life, Joe Sr. couldn't shake the sense of failure, and that, in turn, instilled in the Biden children a desire to move up in the world.[7] Joe Sr. had been *someone* once, and the Bidens identified as a feisty family of modest means fighting for a better life. This perspective typified the down-home culture of Delaware in the 1950s and '60s, and Joe Biden Jr. had internalized it.

Even when Joe Jr. was still a boy, he started putting that philosophy into action.

For several years the Biden family lived across the street from Archmere Academy, one of the most prestigious Catholic schools in Delaware.[8] Archmere occupies the former estate of John J. Raskob, a famous industrialist who was an executive for DuPont and General Motors, ran the Democratic National Committee (DNC), and is credited with building the Empire State Building. The school represents the pinnacle of the upper-crust Delaware identity to which Joe Biden aspired. Staring across the street at that impressive estate made an impression on the young Biden: he called it his "Oz."[9]

By this time, however, Archmere was above the means and status of the family. Still, Joe's grandiose vision that the Bidens would one day be among the elite had already taken hold. He needed Archmere. Joe was eventually admitted, even though his attendance at the school strained his family's finances.

Biden, who was undersized at five feet one and 100 pounds, entered the school with a number of obstacles in his path. Aside from the socioeconomic realities and the fact that he was not (nor would he ever be) an academic all-star, he still had that stutter, which was severe enough that he was excused from having to stand up for requisite public speaking exercises. Though Joe himself said that he had begun to overcome the affliction by then, he still was nicknamed "Joe Impedimenta" by cruel peers.

The nicknames and bullying didn't stop there. He was given another moniker by classmates: "Dash." This wasn't a reference to his speed on the football field, either. It was "like Morse code—dot dot dot, dash dash dash dash," according to Biden himself.[10]

In case you're searching for the origin of why adult Joe Biden seems to constantly fantasize about fistfighting people, I believe we've found the answer.

Nonetheless, he was ambitious and gradually harnessed some natural charisma, which propelled him to become class president;[11] he was ineligible to be president of the entire student body due to too many demerits. He also was a standout on a dominant Archmere football team. Joe was already ascending to legendary status in his own mind both on and off the field. According to Biden family lore, Joe led eight football players in a walkout of the Charcoal Pit restaurant when they refused to serve a black team member inside.[12] This was a relatively minor gesture in the scheme of the civil rights movement, but it became an indelible part of Joe's political narrative. He even made sure to return to the restaurant as vice president with President Barack Obama. They made sure to eat indoors.

To listen or read Joe wax on about his high school glory days, you would have thought he grew into a studly character out of a Hollywood movie. Archmere still occupies a special place in his heart—he sent all three of his kids there and eventually brought the football team to the White House.[13]

Next up for Joe was the University of Delaware. During these years, Biden was a "teetotaling semi-jock with a sweater around his neck— the type who seemed more consumed with date nights than civil rights," according to a 2020 *New York Times* profile. Biden played on football team during his freshman year, but left after one season ostensibly to focus on his lackluster grades.[14] Biden eventually did graduate in 1965, ranking near the bottom of his class.

It was on a spring break trip in the Bahamas that he met the woman who would become his first wife, a Syracuse student named Neilia Hunter. She was at a pool party Joe crashed at a Nassau resort. They went out for hamburgers, which Joe claims were pricier than what he could afford, so she helped him pay for the tab. The way he describes it, the typically cocksure Joe was charmingly befuddled the entire date. He kept embarrassing himself while she fell in love with him. He believed by the end of the first date that they would be married. It's a romantic story, if a bit saccharine.

Joe pursued his JD at Syracuse law school, but he really appeared to be pursuing Neilia. Joe's academic record was pathetic, but that did not stop him from claiming he was on a full-ride scholarship.[15] Though he was an academic dud, his political skills continued to develop. The only class he aced was legislation,[16] garnering praise from his professor for his "presence" in the classroom.[17] These were rare bright spots on his academic record.

Biden nearly flunked a course in law school when he was caught plagiarizing five(!) pages from a law review article published years earlier. Joe begged for forgiveness in a letter defending his name that, in retrospect, looks entirely unmoored from reality: "My intent was not to deceive anyone. For if it were, I would not have been so blatant," he wrote in a letter to law school faculty. "If I had intended to cheat, would I have been so stupid?"[18]

Passages of the letter read like the lunatic ravings of a desperate man.

"I value my word above all else," Biden pleaded. "This is a fact which is known to all those who are or have been acquainted with my character."

Years later we would know for certain that his pleas were all a put-on to try to avoid more humiliation and maybe even expulsion, as this would not be the last time he was busted plagiarizing.

He didn't so much graduate from law school as he did survive it. But he did marry Neilia during this time, so it wasn't entirely unproductive.

Newlywed Joe even bought his new bride a dog. He named it Senator.[19]

THE ROAD TO THE SENATE

After leaving law school, Joe Biden worked at a corporate law firm in Wilmington and as a public defender. Though this stint would later be used to claim progressive bona fides, it didn't last long.[20] He was mere moments away from entering politics, a field where he would remain for the next half century.

It was clear early in his professional career that Joe did not have a defined political ideology. He was less interested in issues than image. Politics was a channel to get respect and elevate his family. In 1970, at twenty-seven years old, armed with youth, ambition, and an intuitive sense of which ways the political winds were blowing, he officially entered the political arena, running a successful campaign for the New Castle County Council.[21]

During this time, Joe and Neilia were rapidly expanding the Biden family. Joseph Robinette "Beau" Biden III was born on February 3, 1969;

Robert Hunter Biden came almost exactly a year later on February 4, 1970; and Naomi Christina "Amy" Biden was brought into the world on November 8, 1971.

In 1972, Joe mounted his first campaign for the U.S. Senate, successfully defeating former governor and two-term senator J. Caleb Boggs in a major upset. Boggs, who was sixty-three, got outmaneuvered by the fresh-faced, twenty-nine-year-old Joe. Biden effectively portrayed himself as a high-energy, forward-thinking outsider, tuned in to hip issues like civil rights, ending the Vietnam War, and protecting the environment.

Meanwhile, the Biden family machine was being assembled. The family shrewdly operated as a single unit during the campaign, modeling themselves after the Kennedys. During the run, they acted as if they all were on the ballot, answering questions in the first-person plural, using language like "We haven't decided what our position is on that" or "We aren't running for president."[22] Joe's twenty-seven-year-old sister, Valerie, a former homecoming queen at the University of Delaware, broke a glass ceiling by running the campaign.[23] Biden kinfolk would organize coffee klatches and canvas door-to-door, Joe's brother James "Jim" Biden served as finance chairman for the campaign, and brother Frank Biden organized student volunteers on campuses.

The clannish mentality of the Finnegans, Jean's family, profoundly influenced how she raised her own children. Growing up, they already thought of themselves as a dynasty; the world just didn't know it yet. His mother would say, "There's nothing in life but family," and "You're a Biden. You can do anything. There's nobody, anywhere, better than you. Maybe just as good, in a different way . . . but not any goddamn better."[24]

Biden also benefited from something during this Senate run that might seem familiar: an information blackout. Boggs, his Republican opponent and long-standing Delaware incumbent, was set to release a slew of damning political ads against Biden in the week leading up to the election. In a stroke of good fortune for Joe, the unions staged a strike the night before the ads ran and the paper shut down. The ads didn't reach the public on a wide scale.

It reminds me of a recent presidential election.

Biden's ads in 1972, unlike the oppo research against him, did hit a vast audience and were apparently quite effective. The Biden campaign stressed how he, and not the aging Boggs, was in touch with the real issues facing voters. The strategy, coupled with the oppression of Boggs's attack ads, was enough to give Joe Biden a three-thousand-vote victory on November 7, 1972.

The full story of the suppression of those Boggs ads remains a mystery. At the time, it seemed like Joe simply got tremendously lucky, but prosecutor Charles Brandt later insinuated there was foul play involved in the episode, in his book *I Heard You Paint Houses,* on mafia hitman Frank Sheeran. (The book would later be adapted into the movie *The Irishman,* directed by Martin Scorsese and starring Robert De Niro, Al Pacino, and Joe Pesci.) Sheeran was an infamous Teamsters union official. Brandt claims that someone visited Sheeran to ask if he could prevent the evening and morning papers from running Caleb Boggs's campaign advertisements. "I told him I would hire some people and put them on the picket line for him. They were people nobody would mess with," Sheeran is quoted as saying.

Was Joe Biden aware of any of this? Brandt claims he has no way of knowing.[25]

The world may never know for certain if Biden's 1972 Senate election was rigged, or if Joe knew what measures organized crime had taken on his behalf.

Biden would be only thirty years and forty-four days old when he was sworn in, making him one of the youngest senators in U.S. history. Yet his life would be immeasurably different that day than it was on election night, because Joe Biden was about to experience ineffable tragedy.

JOE GETS KNOCKED DOWN

One of Joe Biden's favorite lines is one he attributes to his father: "[T]he measure of a man wasn't how many times or how hard he got knocked down, but how fast he got back up."[26] That wisdom never mattered more than after the events of December 18, 1972.

Just days before he was to be sworn in following his Senate win, Joe's first wife, Neilia Hunter Biden, age thirty, and their infant daughter, Naomi, were killed in a car crash when their station wagon collided with a hay truck while they were out shopping for Christmas presents. His two young sons, Hunter and Beau, were badly injured in the accident, requiring extended hospitalization, but survived. Hunter suffered from head injuries and Beau from multiple fractures. The accident, unsurprisingly, took an incalculable toll on Joe.

He contemplated quitting the Senate before he even got started, but Majority Leader Mike Mansfield (D-MT) dangled prestigious committee assignments in front of him to encourage him to stay. The Senate passed a resolution in order to allow Joe to be sworn in bedside to Beau and Hunter while they were still hospitalized.[27]

Joe said in his memoir, *Promise Me, Dad*, that he contemplated suicide,[28] but ultimately his boys saved his life.

Young and handsome and a newly elected senator who'd won in upset fashion, he was already becoming a celebrity, but it became a media frenzy when tragedy befell Joe Biden. These circumstances enhanced his public image, but it also made him wary of the press. He was reluctant to be open with journalists, but he decided to sit with Kitty Kelley for a *Washingtonian* magazine profile in 1974, a decision that would poison the media for him forever.

The senator's openness about the tragedy led to some uncomfortable—and, frankly, inappropriate—moments. "My beautiful millionaire wife," he called Neilia, bizarrely. (Neilia's parents owned a diner.)[29] Joe repeatedly spoke of Neilia in lustful tones. "Neilia was my very best friend, my greatest ally, my sensuous lover. The longer we lived together the more we enjoyed everything from sex to sports," he told the journalist, for no apparent reason. "She had the best body of any woman I ever saw. She looks better than a *Playboy* bunny, doesn't she?" he said, showing Kelley a photo of Neilia in a bikini. No matter how long and arduous the campaigning days could be, Joe boasted, he still would be able to "satisfy" Neilia "in bed."

Do you get it, ladies? Joe isn't just an elected leader. He's a tiger in the sack and he wants you to know it.

Perhaps he was trying to impress the young reporter because she was blond. Maybe he was cribbing off the Kennedys again.

"I know I could have easily made the White House with Neilia," Joe crowed during the interview. "And my family still expects me to be there one of these days." I guess he got that one right.

Whatever the explanation for his forthrightness, heavy pervert vibes came through in the published article.

After the interview, in which Kelley compared him to Jay Gatsby (not a compliment), he blamed the journalist for making him seem "slightly unhinged."[30]

The interview has haunted Joe ever since, causing him to hate the press. Biden was apparently so spooked that he wouldn't do another interview for fifteen years, when he spoke to the *Washington Post*'s Lois Romano during his first presidential run in 1987. This is a statistic that sounds fake in the era of the modern 24/7 news cycle, but it isn't.[31]

There is no doubt a straight line from the *Washingtonian* article to his unwillingness to engage with the media as president nearly fifty years later.

Biden would recall his infamous chat with Kitty Kelley, claiming that the young journalist "cried at my desk" after the intense reaction to the piece. "I found myself consoling her, saying, 'Don't worry. It's OK. I'm doing fine.' I was such a sucker," Joe said.[32]

To his credit, Biden does occasionally have a way of cutting to the quick.

Part of Biden's grieving process, it appears, was to embellish elements of the story of Neilia and Amy's death to enhance his own personal narrative. In several speeches years later, he not only attributed the accident to the other driver, but he also falsely claimed that the man was drinking. At one point he said that "a guy who allegedly—and I never pursued it—drank his lunch instead of eating it, broadsided my family." In another instance he said, "It was an errant driver who stopped to drink instead of drive and hit—a tractor trailer—hit my children and my wife and killed them." This statement was as dishonest as it was self-serving. The driver in question was not drinking, and was, in fact, not even responsible for the accident. Neilia had veered into his lane and did not heed a stop sign. Later, the driver's family publicly stated that Biden's statements were "hurtful and untrue." Biden called and apologized to them after CNN "exonerated" the driver in an independent report.[33]

JOE GETS BACK UP

In his telling, the first time Joe Biden saw Jill Jacobs, the future Dr. Jill Biden, was in an ad for tourism at Wilmington Airport in March 1975. "She was blond and gorgeous," he wrote in his memoir *Promises to Keep*.

"That's the kind of woman I'd like to meet," Joe thought to himself.[34] Jill, whose first marriage ended in 1975, had befriended Frank Biden years earlier at the University of Delaware. Frank gave the newly available Joe her phone number, and, according to author Ben Schreckinger in his book *The Bidens*, Joe "sweet-talked her into breaking a date" so they could go to dinner and a movie. Jill, a twenty-three-year-old college student who went through her divorce that very year, was a bit overwhelmed going out with a senator, particularly one who was a "natty dresser." Still, Joe won her over at the dinner.

Jill had actually met Biden's first wife, Neilia, in the 1970s. When Jill was a college student at the University of Delaware, she was married to Bill Stevenson, a Wilmington nightclub owner. He was an early supporter of Joe's, and he and Jill attended the Bidens' party on election night in 1972 at the Hotel Du Pont. After noticing how calm and staid Neilia was all night, Jill introduced herself.[35]

Jill was the daughter of a homemaker and a banker from Philadelphia. She was also the eldest of five sisters, and, like the Bidens, the Jacobs prized family loyalty. Schreckinger writes that she still "found the Biden clan intimidating."[36] But Jill turned out to be a natural fit and would eventually become the matriarch of the family we know today. When she and Joe tied the knot in 1977, she became a stepmother to Beau, then eight, and Hunter, seven, before she gave birth to Ashley Biden on June 8, 1981.

Intriguing biographical details in the ensuing years are few and far between. Joe had the job he wanted and was rebuilding his family. He tried to find ways to put a bit more money into his pocket, but unfortunately for him, he inherited his father's willingness to engage in suboptimal business ventures. This is, as it turns out, a family trait.

In an effort to officially join Delaware's elite society, Joe purchased a compound-like home that maybe one day would be the Biden dynasty's equivalent of the Kennedys' summer retreat in Hyannis Port, Massachusetts. This would be the culmination of decades of Biden family striving.

When it came to the house, Joe's vision has teetered on the verge of obsession. "The first thing you've got to know about Joe is the house. Probably the first thing he'd show you anyway," begins Richard Ben Cramer's profile of Biden in his 1992 political classic, *What It Takes*. The house in question was a sprawling, 1930s-era du Pont mansion Joe rescued from demolition in 1975. Joe's dreams for that property never quite materialized, but he did manage to sell it, at a tidy profit, twenty years later, to an executive from MBNA, a bank that had been a major supporter of Biden's.[37]

Things appeared to be on a relatively even keel for Biden, at least compared to his whirlwind first three decades. They got much more exciting in the summer of 1987.

THE WILDEST YEAR OF JOE'S LIFE

People wanted Joe Biden to run for president in 1987—smart people. Jill wanted him to run, too; even in moments when he got cold feet, Jill encouraged him to continue. "He wouldn't leave the podium until he knew he had the connect," Cramer wrote in *What It Takes*. He lived for "the connect." That is the moment in the big speech when the orator has the audience eating out the palm of his hands. The statesman—now a showman—was making the audience feel exactly how they wanted to feel. Joe was hooked on that sensation like it was heroin, and he would chase that dragon all day long.

There was a big problem, though: he didn't have a message, and everyone around him knew it. He decried the materialism and individualism of the Reagan era, which was drawing to a close, while trying to channel John F. Kennedy, according to the *New York Times*.[38] This was a sensible approach. After all, Biden was a Democrat and only forty-four years old, just a year older than JFK when he was elected president. And they shared, to some degree, a certain preppy, youthful, Irish-American appeal.

Reagan bad. Kennedy good. Simple.

But what was his platform? His staff constantly quarreled over what the energetic and ambitious Biden should say when he was on the trail trying to make that connect.

They never found their answer.

By all accounts, the campaign was a hot mess.

Joe Biden claimed that he marched for the civil rights movement, which never happened. He claimed he was at Selma, which he wasn't. In the very speech in which he announced his run, he quoted Bobby Kennedy—without actually attributing the quote to him.[39] All of this is Bidenesque.

In 1987, the *New York Times* reported that in an August speech Biden made in Iowa, he plagiarized the words of the British Labour Party leader Neil Kinnock. Kinnock began his speech: "Why am I the first Kinnock in a thousand generations to be able to get to university?" Then, pointing to his wife in the audience, he continued: "Why is Glenys the first woman in her family in a thousand generations to be able to get to university? Was it because all our predecessors were thick?" Biden began his speech by saying, "I started thinking as I was coming over here, why is it that Joe Biden is the first in his family ever to go to a university?" Then, pointing to his wife, he continued: "Why is it that my wife who is sitting out there in the audience is the first in her family to ever go to college? Is it because our fathers and mothers were not bright? Is it because I'm the first Biden in a thousand generations to get a college and a graduate degree that I was smarter than the rest?"[40]

Cringe-inducing.

Biden mirrored Kinnock's words, lifting lines verbatim, right down to the conclusion.

Kinnock ended his speech with the words, "Does anybody really think that they didn't get what we had because they didn't have the talent or the strength or the endurance or the commitment? Of course not. It was because there was no platform upon which they could stand."

And Biden: "No, it's not because they weren't as smart. It's not because they didn't work as hard. It's because they didn't have a platform upon which to stand."[41]

Joe Biden speaks endlessly about the importance of his integrity as if the Bidens have an outsized amount of it. But he was living a lie. Now he had another plagiarism scandal. However, unlike at Syracuse Law, there would be consequences this time.[42] His chaotic campaign was doomed. To make matters worse, his law school plagiarism had hit the news cycle at this point, making it all the clearer that it was time to exit the race.[43]

Yet this first presidential run was not without its silver linings. The most important of which is that had this presidential bid ever developed any "Joementum," he probably would be dead.

Joe Biden suffered *two* brain aneurysms in February 1988.[44] Biden wrote in his memoir, *Promises to Keep,* that he was giving a speech at the University of Rochester when he began to feel sick and lost his train of thought (more than usual). He later passed out in a hotel after feeling "lightning flashing inside my head, a powerful electrical surge—and then a rip of pain like I'd never felt before."[45] He returned home but was rushed to the hospital the next day.

He underwent two surgeries at what is now Walter Reed National Military Medical Center to treat the aneurysms, one in February and one in May. Doctors told him his chances of dying on the operating table were a coin toss, and if he were to survive, a full recovery was not guaranteed. A priest even read him his last rites. A doctor said that "the side of the brain that the first aneurysm is on controls your ability to speak,"[46] which meant permanent loss of speech was a risk with surgery. After the ordeal, Biden's face was partly paralyzed, but by August, he had recovered and returned to work.[47]

Had Joe continued on the campaign trail and had success, had he pursued that "connect" with audiences while traveling up and down the country for months on end, it may well have been a death sentence.

Ever since he was a boy, his family had imbued him with the mantra that there was a plan for Joey Biden. He had a destiny. In this moment at least, it's hard to say they were wrong.

Joe Biden had saved his own life with his incompetent campaign.

The first presidential run was successful in at least one other regard as well: it solidified the political foundation that would undergird Biden for his entire career.

His sister, Valerie, managed the campaign, as she had his earlier Senate campaigns,[48] but Biden's political operation had also scaled up to include a number of bona fide professionals, many of whom are with Biden to this day. The 1988 campaign staff included future White House staffers Ron Klain and Mike Donilon, as well as Ted Kaufman and Mark Gitenstein, two of Biden's closest confidants outside the White House.[49] Polling prodigy Pat Caddell, who had burst onto the political scene as a twenty-one-year-old during Biden's first Senate race in 1972, was also on the Biden bus. (Toward the end of his life, Caddell, who had a wide populist streak, would become a daily guest on my radio show, *Breitbart News Daily*.)

By 1988, Biden was a national brand with the professional political machinery to match his ambition, but it would be twenty years before he would try another run.

THE BORKING AND THE HIGH-TECH LYNCHING

Back on the campaign trail in 1987, Joe Biden had a major distraction that no doubt interfered with his ability to run for president: his day job. Biden was the chairman of the Senate Judiciary Committee at the time, and President Ronald Reagan had just nominated Judge Robert Bork to replace retiring Supreme Court justice Lewis Powell. Biden would have to lead the confirmation hearings.

This was going to be awkward.

First of all, Biden had been in the presidential race for only three weeks when the nomination came down. But more importantly, legally speaking, Joe Biden wasn't fit to carry Robert Bork's powdered wig.

Biden was a famously dreadful law student and an unaccomplished lawyer. His academic and professional careers are plagued by intellectual dishonesty. He barely even used the law degree he barely even earned. Nonetheless, he would seize the opportunity to become one of the most influential persons shaping the Supreme Court in the last fifty years.

Biden spearheaded the Democrats' effort to stop Bork from getting confirmed. Biden initially indicated that he could possibly be convinced to vote to confirm Bork, but after meeting with the Federation of Women Lawyers and other interest groups, he changed his position. He would focus his attack on Bork's positions on abortion and alleged civil rights illiberalism, but the true rationale for rejecting his nomination was that he was just too conservative. Liberal Harvard Law professor Laurence Tribe suggested a new criterion: "not fitness as an individual, but balance of the court as a whole."[50]

"Balance on the court as a whole." There is no constitutional mandate for a balanced court, but this baseless standard provided a rationale to torpedo Bork's nomination.

The Democrats were successful in stopping Bork's ascent to the court, making history by preventing the confirmation of a Supreme Court justice, according to *Washington Post* columnist George Will, "on naked political grounds."[51]

Ultimately, Anthony Kennedy was confirmed to the court in Bork's place. In a vacuum, it was a historic win for Democrats; Kennedy often broke with conservatives throughout his Supreme Court career, including as the deciding vote in 2015's landmark *Obergefell* decision, which legalized same-sex marriage across the country.[52]

Still, the victory certainly had its drawbacks. *Borking* became a slang term for smearing a nominee to the court and has become the go-to tactic to hold up conservative nominees ever since.

But Biden wasn't at all troubled by his role in politicizing the court, as evidenced by the fact that he would try the exact same approach in 1991, this time with different results, when he led the infamous effort to keep Clarence Thomas from getting confirmed.

During that confirmation hearing, the Senate Judiciary Committee, chaired by Biden, heard the testimony of Anita Hill, a former Thomas adviser who accused him of sexual harassment. The saga brought forth many embarrassing allegations used to humiliate and smear Thomas, a black conservative. Under Biden's questioning, Hill testified that Thomas once mentioned a pornographic film star named "Long Dong Silver" to her and, at one point, asked her who had put a pubic hair on his can of cola.[53]

The claims were likely apocryphal—and even if true, they were hardly grounds for destroying a man's name—but the images were lodged firmly in the public's minds. That Thomas had overcome an impoverished childhood in Jim Crow–era Savannah, Georgia, to become one of the country's most prominent jurists was no longer of interest. Who has time to talk about a man's character and accomplishments when we haven't solved the mystery of the rogue pube?

When Thomas finally had the chance to defend himself, he delivered one of the most searing statements in modern American history:

> From my standpoint, as a black American, as far as I'm concerned,
> it is a high-tech lynching for uppity blacks who in any way deign to
> think for themselves, to do for themselves, to have different ideas.
> And it is a message that unless you kowtow to an old order, this is
> what will happen to you. You will be lynched, destroyed, caricatured
> by a committee of the U.S. Senate, rather than hung from a tree.

Thomas was confirmed, but largely thanks to Biden's "high-tech lynching," he has been in the crosshairs of the Left ever since. The tactics Biden deployed against Bork and Thomas have become commonplace. They are designed not just to stop the confirmation of conservative and originalist jurists, but to personally humiliate them. Andrew Breit-bart referred to this tactic as "the politics of personal destruction."

In recent years, Biden has stated that he believed Hill, but Thomas and his wife claimed Biden called them after reading subsequent FBI investigative reports and stated that there was "no merit" to Hill's claims.[54] Of course, Biden would prove to be more skeptical of similar accusations later made against himself.

Biden's playbook has been an enduring stain on the court. The same scheme was trotted out against Kennedy's successor, Brett Kavanaugh, leading to an even bigger media circus than the one surrounding Thomas. When Senate Republicans blocked then president Obama's nomination of Merrick Garland in 2016, Democrats cried that Senate Majority Leader Mitch McConnell was playing politics with the court. But Biden and the Democrats had beaten them to it by decades. What's more, the Republicans never turned Garland into an object of personal hatred in the way Democrats have done with Thomas and Kavanaugh.

Biden served thirty-six years in the Senate, and these twin Supreme Court nomination spectacles were certainly the most essential part of his legacy. The only close second would be the Violent Crime Control and Law Enforcement Act, which was debated and passed in the mid-1990s. I explain and discuss the legacy of that controversial law in the final chapter of this book.

Biden himself would prefer if he were known for the Violence Against Women Act (passed in 1994 and renewed in 2022) or his role in progress toward peace in the Balkans (which he catalogs in excruciating detail in his second memoir, *Promise Me, Dad*). But those did not have nearly the practical nor cultural effect as the *borking* of Bork and the high-tech lynching of Thomas.

Joe Biden came into the Senate as a show pony. Though he never became a workhorse, he did learn the machinations of Washington while he was there. This put him in a prime position to make that apparatus work for him, both politically and for the financial benefit of his family.

CHAPTER 2

The Biden Dynasty

B
eginning in that first Senate campaign when he was twenty-nine years old, Joe Biden's political inner circle, when possible, has been his family. Having spent nearly a decade in Washington myself, I can tell you that is the correct instinct. Political loyalties are fickle, and most everyone surrounding powerful people wants something from them— or many things. Generally speaking, family members will have your best interest at heart more often than strangers will. It is no wonder that large, tight-knit families have dominated American politics since our nation's founding. The Kennedys and Bushes come most quickly to mind, but families like the Trumps, the Clintons, the Roosevelts, the Rockefellers, the Adamses, and Delaware's own du Ponts will dot American history books forever. Joe believes that the Biden name is worthy of that rarefied air.

Since his early political days, he has envisioned a Biden family dynasty. He has brought in siblings to staff campaigns. He fantasized about Beau as president and Hunter as Beau's most trusted adviser and speechwriter. He even attempted to cure cancer with his son-in-law (as Joe would say, not a joke!).

If I'm being charitable, this is an ambitious vision. In all honesty, it's ludicrous. He was never going to get his dynasty. Once you get to know the Bidens, I think you'll agree.

JOE BIDEN

The patriarch of the Biden clan and the leader of a dynasty in his own mind, Joe Biden has had more moments of public humiliation than any other living American. Aside from the personal failings that derailed his 1988 presidential campaign, or the aforementioned "I probably have a much higher IQ than you" rant directed at a journalist—a low-IQ attack, if there ever was one—Joe's career in the public eye has featured cringeworthy moments throughout.

The best argument that President Biden does not have rapidly diminishing mental function is that he has consistently had cognitive lapses.

In fact, Biden claimed that he was "constantly tested" for cognitive decline when on the campaign trail in 2020.[1] Yet just a month later, Joe said he hadn't taken any cognitive tests and lashed out when asked if he had. "No, I haven't taken a test. Why the hell would I take a test?" Biden told a reporter representing the National Association of Black Journalists and National Association of Hispanic Journalists. "Come on, man. That's like saying you, before you got on this program, you take a test where you're taking cocaine or not. What do you think? Huh? Are you a junkie?"[2]

Asking a BIPOC journalist if he or she is a junkie would have been grounds for cancellation from public life if Biden were a conservative, but this attack came and went from the news cycle rather quickly. The perks of being a Democrat.

What's more, forgetting if you've ever taken a mental acuity test might be a sign of waning mental acuity, but I'm not a doctor, so who am I to say?

Now on the other side of eighty, it is clear that Joe Biden is not of sound body and mind, but his doctors have not been forthcoming with us. As with most things, Biden denies the obvious truth about his health until he has no other option. Based on a physical exam conducted in early 2023, his afflictions are merely acid reflux and a stiff gait. This beggars belief. Dr. Neal Kassel, the doctor who performed both aneurysm surgeries on Biden in 1988, told *Politico* that Biden fully recovered and, by the 2020 campaign, was "every bit as sharp as he was 31 years ago."[3]

That's great news. Now can we see the results of the mental acuity tests? Oh, right, we don't know if he has actually taken any.

In a telling incident in June of 2023, Biden was photographed with clear indentations on his face from a CPAP machine, a medical device used to treat sleep apnea. His official checkups had not disclosed sleep apnea or any similar condition. The face imprints forced the White House to again acknowledge that Biden's health was not so perfect. A White House spokesman admitted that the president had been using a

CPAP machine in "recent weeks," but also confusingly asserted that he had disclosed his issues with sleep apnea since 2008. The problem is new and fleeting, but also old news because he mentioned it fifteen years ago.[4]

That's enough spin to make a figure skater dizzy. If Biden World goes to this much effort to conceal the true nature of a common disorder, imagine what else they might be hiding.

There is just about as much solid information about Joe Biden's metamorphosing physical body as there is about his mind, which is to say, not a lot. His hair certainly looked thinner in 1987 than it does as president. His teeth are considerably whiter as well. The particular tint of his porcelain veneers he sports as of 2023 is closer to Benjamin Moore "Chantilly Lace" house paint than it is to the hue of actual human teeth. Neither Biden nor White House spokespeople publicly address these things.

In 2022, Graydon Carter's *Air Mail* newsletter quoted Dr. Marc Lowenberg, a cosmetic dentist, who unfurled a brutal dis at Biden's chompers: "1 out of 10 says, 'I don't want my teeth to look like Joe Biden's.' I'm not kidding."[5]

Other doctors told *Air Mail* that they believed that Biden had undergone cosmetic procedures on his eyelids and neckline—just not recently enough to be terribly effective. "If you look at old photos, he does seem to have had a tighter neckline than would be expected," one of the doctors told *Air Mail*. "I don't think it was within the last 10 or 15 years because it looks like it's worn off a bit."[6]

I asked the White House specifically which procedures the president has undergone and why he insists on making this particular element of his very public life a mystery. I did not get a response.

That said, I am much less interested in presidential nips and tucks than I am in the true explanation for why Joe Biden says some of the outlandish things he says. At a March 2, 2020, campaign event, Joe went off-script and started to quote from the Declaration of Independence, only he was unable to retrieve the actual words from the recesses of his mind. Instead, he freestyled: "We hold these truths to be self-evident, all men and women created by, go, you know you know the thing," the future president of the United States scatted.

Here's "the thing" that we all know: "We hold these truths to be self-evident, that all men are created equal, that they are endowed by their Creator with certain unalienable Rights, that among these are Life, Liberty and the pursuit of Happiness."

Biden added an extraneous "women" to the immortal words that shaped our nation, as if to subtly imply that our Founding Fathers were sexist. It's a nice little woke update for our modern times.

My favorite Biden tall tale was perhaps his most haughty. It occurred on what was assuredly a big day for Joe. It was June 26, 2017, and he was addressing a small group in Wilmington, Delaware. The former vice president, surrounded by children and their parents, was celebrating the dedication of the Joseph Biden Jr. Aquatic Center. Biden's remarks went on for more than twelve minutes, which was at least eleven longer than necessary. Joe was savoring the moment. At one point, he actually seemed to bring his speech to a dramatic close, only to give himself a curtain call no one asked for, continuing to regale the audience for yet another minute. The highlights of the remarks were two of the most sur-real stories told by any American, ever. They might be familiar to you:

Corn Pop was a bad dude, and he ran a bunch of bad boys.

And I did, yeah he—and back in those days—you—to show how things have changed—one of the things you had to use, if you used pomade in your hair, you had to wear a bathing cap. And so, he was up on the board, wouldn't listen to me.

I said, "Hey, Esther, you! Off the board or I'll come up and drag you off." Well, he came off. And he said, "I'll meet you outside."

My car [pointing off-screen]—this was mostly—these were all public housing behind you. My car—there was a gate out here. I parked my car outside the gate. And I—he said, "I'll be waiting for ya." He was waiting there with three guys in straight razors. Not a joke.

There was a guy named Bill Wright, Mouse. The only white guy, and he did all the pools. He was the mechanic. And I said, "What am I gonna do?" And he said, "Come down here in the basement where all the mechanics—where all the pool filter is." You know the chain—there used to be a chain that went across the deep end. He cut off a six-foot length chain, he fold[ed] it up, he said. "You walk out with that chain. And you walk to the car and say, 'You may cut me, man, but I'm gonna wrap this chain around your head.'" I said, "You're kidding me." And he said, "No if you don't, don't come back," and he was right.

So, I walked out with the chain. And I walked up to my car—and in those days remember the straight razors you'd bang on the curb, gettin' 'em rusty and puttin' 'em in a rain barrel, get 'em rusty? And I looked at him, but I was smart, then. I said, "First of all," I said, "when I tell you to get off the board, you get off the board, and I'll kick you out again, but I shouldn't have called you Esther Williams, and I apologize for that. I apologize." But I didn't know that apology was gonna work.

He said, "You apologize to me?" I said, "I apologize but not for throwing you out, but I apologize for what I said." He said, "OK," closed that straight razor, and my heart began to beat again.[7]

I'm tempted to spend the rest of this book analyzing just this single passage. The text is that rich. Biden's (almost assuredly fictional) swimming pool race war story has it all: a rusty razor blade, old-timey hair product, goofy but charming nicknames, DIY weaponry, arcane references, a happy ending, and a heroic arc for our protagonist, young Joey Biden. Perfection.

The speech somehow got wackier from there: "I got hairy legs that turn blond in the sun," Joe told the crowd of children and parents. "And the kids used to come up and reach in the pool and rub my leg down so it was straight and watch the hair come back up again. They'd look at it. And so, I learned about roaches, I learned about kids jumping on my lap. And I've loved kids jumping on my lap."[8]

Picturing Biden letting children rub down his hairy legs, then relishing the youngsters in his lap, is revolting. Yet the most outrageous part of this quote is Biden's reference to "roaches," which is a racial slur against black people.[9]

Yes, Joe Biden called black children "roaches" while giving a speech surrounded by black children. In 2017.

The media completely ignored this remark, just as they had ignored so many other racially insensitive comments by Biden over the decades.

In 2006 he said, "In Delaware, the largest growth of population is Indian Americans, moving from India. You cannot go to a 7-11 or a Dunkin' Donuts unless you have a slight Indian accent."[10] I know that sounds like a bad joke that didn't land, but Joe implored the audience that "I'm not joking."

He called Obama "the first mainstream African American who is articulate and bright and clean" on the same day he filed official paperwork to run for president in 2008.[11] In August 2012, just months before he and Obama faced reelection, he told a crowd of Virginia voters that Mitt Romney's Republican Party would "put y'all back in chains."[12]

Insane.

Responding to a question about segregation during the Democrat presidential debate in 2019, Biden implored parents, "Play the radio, make sure the television, excuse me, make sure you have a record player on at night, make sure that kids hear words, a kid coming from a very poor school, or a very poor background, will hear four million fewer words spoken by the time they get there."[13]

After 250 years of racial division, who knew America's solution was right in front of our noses? Record players.

To list and analyze all of Joe Biden's inexplicable brain freezes would fill volumes. In 2008, he told a paraplegic man to stand up during a campaign rally.[14] He said in 2020 that his campaign attorneys were visiting with "voter registration physicians."[15] He called future second gentleman Doug Emhoff Kamala Harris's wife.[16] While giving a speech in 2022, he called out to recently deceased congresswoman Jackie Walorski as if she were in the audience.[17] (Maybe that wasn't a gaffe; maybe Joe is actually a medium.)

He claimed that "more than half of the women on the—in my administration are women."[18] This is true, though I hope that number is a lot closer to 100 percent than 50 percent.

He even once bizarrely and inappropriately started to laugh while discussing a woman who had lost two children to fentanyl overdoses in 2023.[19]

Also in 2023, near the end of a rambling speech in an Irish pub, President Biden was standing next to star rugby player Rob Kearney, whom he referred to as "a hell of a rugby player, and he beat the hell out of the Black and Tans." He meant to say the Ireland team beat the All Blacks, which is the name of the internationally renowned New Zealand rugby team. The "Black and Tans" were British security forces who fought the Irish Republican Army nearly one hundred years ago. Also on that trip to Ireland, Biden encouraged an audience to "go lick the world."[20]

If I had to summarize Joe Biden's fifty years in politics in one of his quotes, it would be this one from the Iowa State Fair in 2019: "We choose truth over facts."[21]

Ponder that one long enough and you can actually feel your own brain hurt.

Joe Biden's words have gotten him into trouble plenty of times, but so have his hands . . . and his nose. Throughout his career, he has been seen engaging in unambiguously creepy behavior. Though he has evaded any consequences for this pattern, it does cause him his fair share of public embarrassment. Take, for example, the interview with Kitty Kelley where he repeatedly told the journalist about hot sex with Neilia.

Joe never changed.

In a May 2020 interview with *Wired*, Joe descried his sister Valerie as "the love of my life." The comment is ridiculously off-putting, yet there was a complete media blackout of that story. I couldn't find this quote in Google or another major search engine and had to rewatch the interview just to make sure I hadn't hallucinated it.[22]

Videos abound on the Internet of Joe holding on to women and girls, seeming to savor them. Touches that linger beyond an appropriate interval. Occasionally he'll brush back a girl's hair. At a swearing-in ceremony in 2015, Joe appeared to whisper into the ear of Democrat senator Chris Coons's thirteen-year-old daughter.[23] What is it that Joe could have possibly been saying to this poor girl?

Then . . . *oh, no . . . no, Joe, please no! . . .* the then vice president went in for a little kiss.

In 2016, a hug with a purple-pantsuit-clad Hillary Clinton lasted for seventeen seconds, even though she literally tried to tap out of the embrace twice as if she were in a mixed martial arts cage fight.[24]

The most infamous example of surprise PDA inflicted on unexpecting women while cameras were rolling was when he caressed the shoulders of Secretary of Defense Ash Carter's wife while her husband delivered a speech. Biden put his nose in her hair and drew in a breath, seeming to indulge in the aroma. All this with her husband standing right there next to them!

Ick.

There are other examples. Many of them, in fact.

On a trip to Europe in the summer of 2023, Biden was videoed attempting to nibble a baby girl. It's the type of behavior that would be considered odd if he had done it to his own flesh and blood.[25]

No wonder he ended up campaigning from his basement in 2020. What campaign manager worth his or her salt would let him out in public?

If this is what he does in front of the cameras, what is Joe like in private?

He's certainly behaved inappropriately and abused his power, but none of the aforementioned instances are violent, and, let's be honest, many of them are kinda funny. What is not funny is what is alleged by Tara Reade.

Reade (who legally changed her name to McCabe in 1998 after experiencing harassment throughout her life[26]) was a congressional aide to Biden in 1992 and 1993. In March 2020, she alleged that Biden had sexually assaulted her during that time.

As Reade tells it, during the nine months she worked for him, Biden harassed her in multiple ways.[27] She claimed there were multiple instances of inappropriate touching on her shoulders and her neck, as well as unwanted senatorial fingers run through her hair.[28] She also claims he made her serve drinks at a fundraiser because he liked her legs.[29]

However, the most serious allegation is that in one instance, the then senator pushed her up against a wall and kissed her, and then, according to Reade, "[h]is hands went underneath my clothing and he was touching me in my private areas and without my consent." She told NPR that Biden penetrated her vagina with his fingers. Reade said she was unable to recall the exact location of the event but said it was likely in the basement of the Senate building in 1993.[30]

Reade said she filed a formal complaint to the Senate personnel office, but no police report was filed. While employment records confirm she did work in Biden's Senate office, the alleged complaint has not surfaced.[31] A Freedom of Information Act request has been filed, but at the time of this writing, it had returned no answers. She eventually filed a police report in Washington, DC, in 2020.

The establishment media was, yet again, uninterested in the story. After all, there is a dearth of solid evidence supporting Reade's claims, and despite Joe's pattern of creepiness, he'd never before been publicly accused of a violent molestation. But the media didn't merely move on, they attacked Reade. *Politico*, for example, ran an article in which Joe's accuser was descried as a "[m]anipulative, deceitful, user."[32]

So much for the #MeToo-era slogan "Believe all women."

There is still one allegation against Joe that might be the most disturbing, yet it is the one that is the most uncomfortable to discuss.

In 2020, two people obtained a copy of his daughter Ashley Biden's diary from a rehab facility in South Florida.[33] The entries, according to media reports, were written while at the recovery center the previous year, making her thirty-seven or thirty-eight at the time.[34] Prosecutors said the individuals had hoped to sell it to the Trump campaign, but they failed to do so. They found a buyer in Project Veritas, the activist conservative journalism outfit then helmed by James O'Keefe. Project Veritas told Congress that they believed the diary had been left in a room where Ashley was staying. The price was reportedly $40,000.[35] The full diary was ultimately published by the conservative National File website in October 2020, just days before the election.[36]

The entries were written by a woman who identifies herself as Ashley Blazer Biden, the full name of Biden's eldest daughter, and they appear to have been scrawled as part of therapy for sex addiction. The author details her own alleged drug use and "hypersexualized" life.

The details were shocking, disturbing, illicitly obtained, and perhaps most significantly, potentially damaging to the political prospects of the Democrat nominee for president. Predictably, with the election just days away, much of the press took a "wait and see" approach, if they even covered it at all.

One portion of the diary that did find its way into at least a few publications details alleged showers the author took with her father that made her uncomfortable.

"Was I molested," the author writes. "I think so—I can't remember specifics but I do remember trauma. Hyper-sexualized @ a young age . . . I remember being somewhat sexualized with Caroline [Biden, Ashley's younger cousin]; I remember having sex with friends @ a young age; showers w/my dad (probably not appropriate)."

That final statement is undeniably newsworthy—regardless of how it was obtained—not necessarily because of what it reveals about the author, who is in many ways an innocent bystander, but because of what it details about the alleged behavior of her father.

The saga drew the attention of the Department of Justice, which began investigating how the diary was obtained—not what was alleged in the diary.[37] The FBI staged a predawn raid of Project Veritas founder O'Keefe's home as part of their probe into the diary.[38] The DOJ's pursuit of Project Veritas was met with objections across the conservative media, as well as from groups like the American Civil Liberties Union and the Reporters Committee for Freedom of the Press.[39]

The entries may be sensationalized or even outright fictitious, but Ashley has not denied that the diary is hers. The intensity of the reaction of the federal government's response certainly suggests the diary is legit.

Nevertheless, what is indisputable is that Joe Biden has said foolish if not downright awful things. He also has been inappropriate with women and girls, to one degree or another.

Yet neither of these attributes is necessarily a dynastic deal breaker.

Just ask the Kennedys.

ASHLEY BIDEN AND HOWARD KREIN

Born Ashley Blazer Biden on June 1981, Joe Biden's surviving daughter studied anthropology at Tulane University, received her master's from the University of Pennsylvania in 2010, and then began a career in social work. She avoids the press more than most of the other Bidens do, but like others in her family, a history of substance abuse has made her life occasional tabloid fodder.

In 2009, a decade before details of the aforementioned diary surfaced, a reported "friend" of Ashley's attempted to sell a video to the *New York Post* depicting the then vice president's daughter appearing to snort cocaine.[40]

In 2012, she joined the Delaware Center for Justice, a criminal justice reform group, where she worked until 2017, when she started a sustainable-fashion brand called Livelihood. According to a profile by *Elle* magazine, it was conceived in connection to "American laborers and more recently to Black Lives Matter."[41] She is tormented and woke, but she does not appear to be corrupt.

Yet Ashley did greatly benefit from her father's position of power via her husband, the surgeon and businessman Dr. Howard Krein.

Krein married Ashley in 2012, but in 2011, Joe Biden arranged a meeting for him in the Oval Office with then president Obama mere weeks after the founding of his business, StartUp Health. Krein is chief medical officer for the company, which he runs with his brother, Steven Krein. The meeting proved fruitful for the Kreins, who landed big business soon after.[42]

When Joe Biden ran for president in 2020, Krein was hired by Biden's campaign to advise the candidate on health care–related matters, including Biden's cancer moon shot initiative. Yes, Biden has absurdly promised on multiple occasions that he is going to find a "cure" for cancer, apparently with the help of Ashley Biden's boo. (I have several oncologists in my family, and none of them has ever used the words "cure" and "cancer" in the same sentence, other than to point out Joe Biden's political shamelessness. That is to say, Biden's claim that he can and will achieve this medical miracle is purely political and without scientific basis.[43]) In 2016, Krein traveled with Vice President Biden to the Vatican, where the two met with Pope Francis to discuss the cancer moon shot.[44] Krein also accompanied Biden on a trip to the World Economic Forum in Davos, Switzerland, a well-known gathering of rich and powerful advocates of expanding governments and supranational bureaucracies.[45]

Meanwhile, StartUp Health began investing in businesses that allegedly supply solutions for COVID-19.[46]

StartUp Health is funded by Ping An, among other groups.[47] Ping An is one of China's largest insurance companies. The firm made a killing during the pandemic. The company's Good Doctor app, which allows patients to access medical advice online, rose 900 percent in January 2020 alone.[48] Revenue surged soon after.[49]

Krein and StartUp are linked to another health care company called Henry Schein, which scored a $53.4 million contract for personal protective equipment (PPE) with Biden's U.S. Department of Health and Human Services.[50]

In May 2022, the White House listed Henry Schein as a company that has shown its commitment to helping "vaccinate the world" and "build better health security."

Yes, Ashley Biden's husband advised Joe Biden on the China virus while making money off the China virus and using funds from China.

And once he helps us beat COVID-19, he's going to get back to curing cancer with President Joe.

The White House has denied that these business dealings have anything to do with Biden's family ties.[51]

Riiiiighhhhhtttttt.

In September 2022, StartUp launched yet another "moon shot," called the Health Equity Moon Shot at the Clinton Global Initiative,[52] with the goal of making the health care system less racist. In July of 2023, Biden would state that "we ended cancer as we know it."[53]

Curing cancer while defeating racism. Howard Krein is like a modern Hippocrates and Fredrick Douglass rolled into one, and we're lucky enough he happened to marry Joe Biden's daughter.

BEAU BIDEN

There is a deeply personal and tragic reason President Biden makes irrational proclamations about cancer: the disease wreaked havoc on his life by taking his first-born son.

Joseph Robinette "Beau" Biden III was born in February 1969. He was the eldest of Joe's children. He went to law school at his father's alma mater, Syracuse University College of Law, and then clerked for Judge Steven McAuliffe of the U.S. District Court of New Hampshire. From 1995 to 2004, he worked at the U.S. Department of Justice in Philadelphia, first as counsel to the Office of Policy Development and later as a federal prosecutor in the U.S. attorney's office. He helped train judges in Kosovo after the 1998–99 Balkans war ended.[54]

Beau married Hallie Olivere in 2002, and the couple had two children.

For several years, Beau was a partner at a law firm before he was elected Delaware's attorney general in 2006.[55] He served in Iraq for a year in 2008 in an administrative post in a combat zone with the 261st Signal Brigade, earning him a Bronze Star.

On multiple occasions, Joe Biden has claimed that Beau died in Iraq.[56] He did not.

Beau flirted with running for the Senate seat his father vacated when he became the vice president, but instead successfully ran for reelection as attorney general in 2010.[57]

Beau was the good son. He was the linchpin to the Biden family future. The hopes of a dynasty were on his shoulders even more than on Joe's. Whether the Bidens could one day rival the Kennedys and the Bushes would depend on Beau.

He was all but guaranteed to win the governorship of Delaware in 2016, but he wouldn't live to see Election Day.

In August 2013, Beau was diagnosed with a glioblastoma, which is a particularly vicious type of brain cancer, and he passed away on May 30, 2015, at the age of forty-six.

The process was agonizing for Joe, who sought to maintain a composed public appearance while serving as vice president, even as his son and the rest of his family suffered. Beau's death was yet another major tragedy to befall Joe Biden in addition to the loss of his first wife and daughter.

Joe says that Beau wanted him to run for president in 2016 despite the cancer diagnosis. The elder Biden decided against it at the time, but he opted to take his late son's advice in 2020. "We should be introducing him as president," Joe said of Beau in January 2021, mere hours before he would be sworn in himself.

One of Joe's political gifts is that he speaks to audiences like they are all enduring a psychological or emotional trauma, and that he has a unique understanding of what they are going through. Living through losses of this magnitude might be why.

Whereas Bill Clinton is famous for saying "I feel your pain," Joe Biden actually might.

VALERIE BIDEN OWENS

Perhaps of all the Biden family members, Joe's sister, Valerie, is his closest advisor. (Remember, she's also "the love of [his] life.") Valerie, born November 5, 1945, briefly worked as a schoolteacher before becoming a full-time political consultant, yet she never stepped far outside of her brother's shadow. She managed all of Joe's Senate campaigns as well as his presidential bids in 1988 and 2008. These collaborations were financial boons for her. Her communication firm was paid $2.5 million by organizations supporting Biden's 2008 presidential bid, for instance.[58] When she wasn't working for her brother's campaigns, she was executive vice president of Joe Slade White & Company, a media consulting firm.[59]

She married John Owens, a friend and law school classmate of Joe's. Owens, who runs a Delaware-based telemedicine company, hosted Joe Biden as a speaker in 2017 and promptly used the affiliation for marketing purposes.[60] Under Obama, Val served as an alternate representative to the United Nations, and she now vice-chairs the Biden Institute at the University of Delaware.[61]

Like their mother, Valerie Biden Owens's three children have, for the most part, enjoyed relatively tame professional careers that nonetheless appear to have been buoyed by access to Joe. Daughter Missy Owens worked in the Obama administration, and, more recently, in high-level government-affairs positions at General Motors and Coca-Cola. While Missy was at Coke, the company lobbied against the Uyghur Forced Labor Prevention Act, a bill meant to ban the import of products made via forced labor of imprisoned Uyghur Muslims in China.[62] The bill ultimately passed and was a blow to China's economy.

Missy's sister, Casey Castello, also enjoyed a stint at the Treasury Department under Obama and became a Starbucks executive.[63]

Val's family proves that being related to Joe Biden is a jobs program in and of itself.

Cuffe, Valerie's only son, is an entertainment attorney who had fifteen minutes of fame when he married *Real Housewives of Orange County* star Meghan King.[64] At times the Biden family can literally seem like a cast of characters.

JAMES BIDEN

From the beginning, James "Jim" Biden's professional life has been a whirlwind. Campaign finance maven, nightclub owner, hedge fund mastermind—Jim has done it all, though "it all" rarely strays far from the influence of his big brother, Joe. So, it follows that Jim's commercial opportunities really began to ramp up after Joe became vice president.

On November 4, 2010, a longtime Biden family friend from Delaware, Kevin Justice, had a meeting in DC with the Office of the Vice President.[65] At the time, Justice was the president of a construction company called HillStone International.[66] A couple of weeks after the meeting, HillStone hired James as an executive vice president, despite the fact that James had no experience in the housing construction industry.[67] James's profile on the company website touted his only experience that really mattered: "James Biden was the finance chairman of his . . . brother's bid for a U.S. Senate seat in Delaware and successfully enlisted the support of national unions, political leaders and financiers across the country."[68]

James joined HillStone at a fortuitous time: the firm was negotiating a massive contract in war-torn Iraq to build 100,000 homes. This was part of a $35 billion, 500,000-unit project, as Peter Schweizer reported in his book *Profiles in Corruption*.[69] HillStone also got a $22 million construction contract from the State Department. The company's founder, David Richter, told investors at a private meeting that it really helps to have "the brother of the Vice President as partner."[70] For the years James worked with HillStone, the firm "accumulated contracts from the federal government for dozens of projects, including projects in the United States, Puerto Rico, Mozambique, and elsewhere."[71]

On February 14, 2023, the *Daily Mail* reported that Jim Biden admitted in legal filings that he was hired by Hill International, the parent company of HillStone, to "negotiate with Saudis over a secret $140 million deal" because of his relationship to Vice President Joe Biden, who at the time was leading delegations to Saudi Arabia.[72] The case documents reveal that on at least two occasions, "Jim told a former senior U.S. Treasury official working as a private investigator" that he was "often sent to meetings to represent Hill because 'of course, the [Biden] name didn't hurt.'" Hill CEO Irvin Richter further confided "that he selected Biden because KSA [the Kingdom of Saudi Arabia]would not dare stiff the brother of the Vice-President who would be instrumental to the deal."[73]

Jim's wife, Sara, also claimed in official affidavits that "Joe and his brother 'told each other everything.'"

Lamentably, this influence peddling is as legal as it is flagrant.

Despite being able to book gigs all over the world thanks to his last name, James is constantly in and out of financial trouble. James fell deeply into debt to the Internal Revenue Service,[74] but conveniently received a half-million-dollar loan in 2015 from Biden donor and Ukrainian-American car dealer John Hynansky. Three years earlier, Hynansky's company had received a $20 million federal loan to build a new dealership—near Kyiv, Ukraine.[75]

It's good to have friends in high places, especially if they are Bidens.

FRANCIS W. "FRANK" BIDEN

Born in November 1953, Joe's other little brother, Frank Biden, is also in the Joe Biden business. From being involved with various philanthropies associated with his brother's name to working in the Clinton administration, his career highlights are all on the periphery of Democrat politics. Frank has achieved few accolades on his own outside of his brother's shadow, and he seems fine with that. He touted his familial ties in an ad for his law firm:[76] "The two Biden brothers have long held a commitment to pushing environmental issues to the forefront," the ad says, implying that the new president endorses working with his brother's firm.

This ad came out on Inauguration Day 2021, the day Joe became president.

Placing the ad on that particular day is a little on the nose, even for the Bidens.

The short bio listed on the Berman Law Group, where Frank serves as a "Senior Advisor (Non-Attorney)," claims he has been an "advisor and unpaid campaign coordinator over many years" for his brother's campaigns.[77] A year after Joe Biden became president, Frank told a medical professional group in Boston that he could help them get "federal dollars."

Frank tested Joe's loyalty in dramatic fashion after events that occurred late one evening in July 1999. Frank Biden let a young friend named Jason Turton drive his Jaguar to a concert at a tavern in Cardiff, California. Frank's Florida driving license had been suspended, so he rode shotgun during the trip, controlling the stick shift himself while giving Turton instructions. At one point, they had the Jaguar humming along at over 70 mph in a 35 mph zone when they slammed into a pedestrian crossing the street. They drove off, leaving the victim to die at the scene. Two witnesses who were in the back seat during the crash claim that Frank Biden told Turton to "keep driving" after the fatal collision. The victim, Michael Albano, was a single father whose death left behind two young daughters.

Turton eventually pleaded guilty to "felony hit and run" charges, while Frank was hit with a wrongful-death lawsuit in August 2000 by the guardians of the Albano daughters. Frank never showed up to the courthouse for any hearings, and he refused to reply to "any legal correspondence from the court, including a court final judgment in September 2002 that Frank owed each of the girls $275,000 for his role in the tragedy,"

Schweizer reported.[78] The Albano girls eventually hired a private investigator to track down where Frank was hiding so he could accept service of documents. Investigators said they had received information that Frank occasionally lived at his brother Joe's house in Delaware, but they were unable to locate a bank account for Frank, who had become evasive.

Eight years later, in 2008, attorneys for the Albano sisters reached out to the soon-to-be vice president, Joe Biden, in the hopes that he could help them collect the money Frank owed them.[79] Even though Joe Biden's own wife and daughter were killed in an automobile accident, he seemed to show no sympathy for the Albanos and did not respond to them. His chief of staff replied callously: "Senator Biden has received your letter of September 16 regarding a judgment by your clients against his brother Frank. The Senator wishes to express his deep sympathy with the Albano daughters over their loss. . . . Frank has no assets with which to satisfy the judgment. The Senator regrets that this is where matters stand and that he cannot be more helpful."[80]

Joe had Frank's back, even when it meant denying orphaned girls what was rightfully theirs.

Schweizer believes that Joe was being dishonest about Frank's ability to compensate the victims. "Frank Biden was earning money," he reported. "Indeed, seven days before Joe Biden's office sent that letter, his brother was slapped with a tax lien from the IRS for $23,638.59 in unpaid taxes. In total, he owed more than $32,000 at the time, a clear indication that Frank had income. In 2013, he paid off the tax lien in full."

With interest, Frank owed them a debt of $900,000 in 2019.[81] Less than a year after Schweizer published the letter, the *Daily Mail* reported that after two decades, Frank Biden had finally agreed to pay the Albano family some of the money.[82]

Meanwhile, as he avoided this particular financial obligation, Frank was out hustling using the family name. Throughout Joe's vice presidency (2009–2017), for example, Frank was a dealmaker in several complex international real estate development schemes in Costa Rica and Jamaica, putting himself in a position to get access to substantial U.S. government funding dedicated to those countries.[83]

Another industry Frank delved into without any qualifications or experience is education. Also in 2009, Joe's first year as VP, the Obama/Biden federal stimulus package allotted $5 billion for innovative educational models, which included charter schools. Frank's eyes turned into dollar signs. Federal grants and taxpayer dollars could be used by charter schools, which he saw as a way to generate reliable profit. Frank became president and director of development for a Florida company called Mavericks in Education Florida LLC, more commonly known as Mavericks. Frank called himself "the big cheese" of the company.[84] As Schweizer points out in *Profiles in Corruption*, before long "Frank was flying around Florida in a private jet, lobbying local politicians and school officials," all ostensibly on behalf of Mavericks. Naturally, his ties to the president were an essential part of his business pitch.[85]

Mavericks eventually opened eight schools in Florida, including one in Fort Lauderdale, where Frank acquired a building from a scandal-ridden power broker named Jesse Gaddis, who'd gained notoriety as "Fort Lauderdale's Taxi King."[86] At the time Gaddis had known ties to mobsters and drug smugglers, including his brother and business partner, Donald Gaddis, who was killed during a drug-smuggling operation for double-crossing his mob boss.[87] Frank's deal turned out to be extraordinarily lucrative for Gaddis, who began collecting high-interest-rate payments every month on the public dime. The charter schools themselves, however, were an extraordinary failure: several posted graduation rates lower than 10 percent.

Long story short, Frank Biden flew around in PJs, a mobbed-up guy made a lot of money, and children got screwed.

Florida's auditor general investigated Mavericks in 2013 and 2014 and accused them of illegally collecting tax dollars for students who did not fully attend the school.[88]

Mavericks had received more than $70 million in state funding by 2014, and all along the way "Frank enjoyed access to the highest levels of the White House," Schweizer reported, even attending exclusive meetings with education officials.[89]

While on the campaign trail in 2020, Joe Biden told a Texas crowd that he did "not support any federal money . . . for for-profit charter schools—period. The bottom line is it siphons off money from public schools, which are already in enough trouble."[90] Shamelessly, Joe acted as though his own brother's scandalous for-profit charter school business didn't exist.[91]

It certainly wouldn't have existed if not for Joe Biden.

There is one essential person in the Biden dynasty whom I've left off the list until this point. In fact, according to Joe, he might be the smartest Biden of them all.[92] He gets his own chapter.

CHAPTER 3

Hunter Biden and the Classified Documents

In terms of sheer newsworthiness, there is one Biden who stands above the rest, perhaps even his presidential pop, and that is Robert "Hunter" Biden. Hunter has been mentioned in over 2,000 stories at Breitbart News since I have been editor in chief.[1] His exploits are so wild it's hard to believe he is a real flesh-and-blood human being. They invoke the full range of emotion. They are maddening, saddening, hilarious, and impressive, often interchangeably, sometimes all at once. At times I think he must be the most corrupt, soulless man in our country. Other times I think he might be the only cool Democrat and one of the few "fully realized" Americans who are openly living their lives as their true selves.

Yet the stories highlighted in this chapter are, as Joe has been known to put it, not a joke. He has found loophole after loophole to make illicit cash off his family name, occasionally with a crack pipe in his mouth. These examples represent the worst America has to offer. They erode our national culture and our respect for our institutions.

This makes Hunter the quintessential Biden.

Hunter Biden was born on February 4, 1970, almost a year to the day after his brother. He took up drinking at a young age, beginning a decades-long pattern of substance abuse that would bring personal shame to himself and his family. By their own admission, addiction runs in the family. Hunter, Ashley, and Frank have all spent time in rehab. Joe himself has sworn off alcohol after witnessing its effects on his relatives growing up.[2]

Shortly after Hunter Biden graduated from Yale Law School in 1996, MBNA signed the Biden scion to a six-figure consulting contract—while Joe was pushing bankruptcy reform legislation strongly supported by the bank. Hunter continued to receive payment from the Delaware-based bank until 2005, the year the bill passed with Joe's support.[3] Hunter cofounded his own lobbying shop, Oldaker, Biden & Belair, in 2002 with William Oldaker, an attorney who had worked for Joe's campaigns, and former Biden Senate staffer Robert Belair. Hunter and assorted allies repeatedly claimed that the son never lobbied the father. His partner Oldaker, however, has acknowledged that he has worked Biden's staff about some clients.[4]

Next, Hunter formed a partnership with Uncle Jim Biden, the former nightclub owner. In August 2006, just months before Joe would become chairman of the Senate Foreign Relations Committee and launch his second presidential campaign, Jim and Hunter purchased a Manhattan hedge fund called Paradigm Global Advisors.[5] A source told *Politico's* Ben Schreckinger that Hunter, Jim, and Beau showed up to fire the president of the company with two large men. It was at that point that James reportedly laid out a disquieting vision for the business: "Don't worry about investors," he said, according to an executive. "We've got people all around the world who want to invest in Joe Biden. . . . We've got investors lined up in a line of 747s filled with cash ready to invest in this company."[6]

Did Scorsese write Jim's dialogue?

The mafia wiseguy routine reportedly embarrassed Beau.[7]

Jim and Hunter deny these episodes ever took place, but the story is consistent with accounts made by others at the firm, and it fits with the family's extensive history of finding ways, as Schreckinger put it, to "take money from rich foreigners who could not legally give money" to Joe.[8]

As a registered lobbyist, Hunter was going to be subject to onerous disclosure requirements. He was going to go along with those types of constraints for only so long.

So, Hunter found a new line of work, and he largely had Joe to thank. He would become a "consultant." In modern Washington, consultants are allowed to peddle influence without facing the disclosure requirements to which lobbyists must adhere.

Soon, Hunter would be jet-setting around the world, often aboard Air Force Two, scrounging up business from various foreign interests. Secret Service records show that between 2009 and mid-2014, Hunter took twenty-three flights into or out of Joint Base Andrews, which houses Air Force Two,[9] all the while launching new ventures that would be almost entirely concealed from public scrutiny (I was first to report that detail in *Breaking the News*).

With "consulting," Hunter had found his sweet spot. It was business time.

The younger Biden son stayed busy while his father was vice president, and I'm not just talking about with girls and drugs. In 2013, he sealed a deal to launch a multibillion-dollar private equity fund in partnership with the Chinese government.[10] That company, BHR Partners, quickly began gobbling up strategically important assets around the world, including a cobalt mine in Africa, a Chinese nuclear firm charged with spying in the U.S., and an American manufacturer—but only after that acquisition was reviewed and approved by the Obama administration.[11] In 2014, Hunter scored a lucrative board seat at shady Ukrainian energy company Burisma, which paid him as much as $83,000 a month.[12]

In 2015, Hunter briefly worked with investors who defrauded public employee pension funds and the Oglala Sioux, one of the nation's poorest Native American tribes.[13]

He was consigliere to both an embattled Romanian businessman and a Chinese energy executive who has since been jailed for corruption.[14]

His qualifications for all of these jobs were nonexistent, and he kept teaming up with the least savory people imaginable. Yet due to lax disclosure rules, there is only so much that will ever become public about these arrangements.

Somehow during all this wheeling and dealing, he managed to budget enough time to do an inordinate quantity of drugs.

He made one attempt at a clean life in May 2013. At forty-three years old, he was commissioned as an ensign in the Navy Reserve. This was a part-time position, but he still needed two waivers to join: one for his advanced age and another because of "a drug-related incident when he was a young man," sources told the *Wall Street Journal*.[15] His brief stint in the navy came to a calamitous end when he tested positive for cocaine in 2014.[16]

It was during this time that Beau was going through treatment for the brain cancer that would kill him in 2015. By all accounts, Beau and Hunter were extremely close. Joe describes Hunter as Beau's rock as his elder son suffered from his illness.

When Beau passed away, Hunter grieved in the most unthinkable way: by sleeping with his brother's widow. Hunter and Hallie Biden's mutual pain "turned into a hope for a love that maybe could replace what we lost," Hunter told CBS, as if the grotesque affair were something far more innocent.

Hallie was not free from scandal herself. First, she apparently assisted Hunter with disposing of a firearm by throwing the weapon away in a dumpster behind a grocery store. Hunter had lied to get the gun, answering "no" to an application question about whether he had a history of drug use.[17] The weapon eventually ended up in the hands of a dumpster diver.

At least one high-profile Democrat believes in the Second Amendment.

In 2023, the Republican-led House Oversight Committee revealed that Hallie had received $35,000 in 2017 from a Biden family associate who had banked $3 million from a state-run Chinese energy company that had close ties to Hunter.[18] Committee lead James Comer (R-KY) suggested that the pile of money paid to Hallie did in fact come from China.

So, maybe she was a good match for Hunter after all. Hunter certainly has a type—it's not girls next door—and got increasingly indulgent in this regard after his brother passed away.

Somehow his affair with his deceased brother's wife isn't the most scandalous relationship Hunter Biden has had in recent years. While he was dating Hallie, Hunter had a fling with a stripper named Lunden Roberts. In August 2018 she gave birth to his daughter.[19] Initially Hunter left open the possibility that he never had had sex with her, boldly claiming in his memoir, *Beautiful Things*, that he had "no recollection" of any such encounter with Roberts. However, legal records reveal Hunter had Roberts on his company's payroll during the duration of her pregnancy.[20]

While compiling research for this book, I was unable to ascertain exactly how many strippers Hunter typically keeps on his books.

Roberts quickly filed a paternity suit, and eventually DNA proved "with scientific certainty" that Hunter was indeed the father. He agreed to pay Roberts $20,000 a month in child support payments.[21]

In response to a March 2022 subpoena from federal prosecutors working on the IRS probe into Hunter's unpaid taxes, Roberts gave over ten gigabytes of Hunter's financial data—obtained through the paternity suit—to the authorities.

On May 1, 2023, Hunter appeared before an Arkansas judge to try to reduce his monthly child support payments. At that time, his lawyers revealed that he'd paid Roberts only $750,000 of the $2.5 million settlement he owed her.[22] Despite living a famously lavish lifestyle, he claimed financial difficulties. This was going to be a tough sell considering that he flew to at least one of these hearings via private jet. Aviation experts told the *New York Post* that the round trip "likely cost between $55,000 to $117,000—or the value of up to six months in child support payments to Hunter Biden's baby mama."[23]

As of early 2023, Hunter had never met his four-year-old daughter, who goes by the name Navy Joan Roberts. Roberts wanted their daughter to have the last name Biden, claiming that it had become "synonymous with being well-educated, successful, financially acute, and politically powerful." Hunter tried to deny her that. In January 2023, he petitioned a judge to prevent her from taking the family name. He suggested it was in the girl's best interest.[24]

Only an idiot would think Hunter has the small child's best interest at heart.

Yet somehow, deadbeat-dad Hunter isn't the only male Biden to let little Navy Joan down: her grandfather, the president of the United States, shamelessly refuses to acknowledge her as well. In what is arguably the coldest and most callous detail I reviewed while researching for this book, doting grandfather and family man Joe Biden acts as though this particular granddaughter doesn't even exist.

During a March 2023 "take your child to work day" event at the White House, President Biden was quoted as saying, "I have six grandchildren. And I'm crazy about them. And I speak to them every single day. Not a joke . . . they're crazy about me because I pay so much attention to them."[25] He says things like this a lot.[26] President Biden has refused even to offer basic security services for granddaughter Navy Joan after she and her mother were violently threatened multiple times.[27] During the Christmas season of 2021, First Lady Jill hung stockings honoring six Biden grandchildren in the White House State Dining Room. Even then, twenty-seven-year-old Naomi got one with her name on it. But not Navy Joan, who was ignored, rejected by the First Family—her family.[28]

"There is no such thing as someone else's child. No such thing as someone else's child. Our nation's children are all our children," Joe Biden said, quoting a former teacher during a speech honoring teachers in the White House Rose Garden in 2023.[29] This is a lovely sentiment. It also makes him a hypocrite and a deadbeat grandpa.

In 2020, Joe tweeted a message so dishonest and uncaring that you almost have to marvel at it: "No matter what's happening, no matter how important the meeting, I'll always answer a call from my grandchildren." First of all, this should be the standard for any grandparent and nothing to brag about, and second of all, it's not even true, especially for Navy Joan.[30]

You don't get to choose your family. Joe Biden knows that better than most. You do, however, get to choose how you treat people. Joe has made his choice, and he chose cruelty.

THE LAPTOP FROM HELL

In one video that was apparently recorded in 2018—one of the oddest videos you will ever see in your life—first reported by the *Daily Mail*, Hunter Biden can be seen slipping down a water slide naked at a Malibu, California, rental property that reportedly cost more than four thousand dollars a night. As he emerges from the water, he can be seen pulling his penis. This is apparently the same home where almost all of Hunter's classic tabloid photos were snapped, including the one of him sleeping with a crack pipe in his mouth, the one where a grinning Hunter is pulling a woman's hair while she poses on all fours, and the one where he displays his signature look: the Biden-style aviators, white tennis shoes, tighty whities, and an impeccably tied red scarf.[31]

All of this content could be found on the laptop that Hunter Biden abandoned at a Delaware repair shop in April 2019. The FBI seized the device that year, but a copy of the material didn't become public until October 2020, just prior to the presidential election.

What might have been rock bottom for Hunter (who am I kidding? I have no idea what rock bottom looks like for a guy like that) was documented in a video obtained by British tabloid newspaper the *Sun* that appeared online in 2022. In the footage, under the green glow of an infrared camera, Hunter is seen in a float tank at a detox clinic, smoking drugs and drinking a White Claw hard seltzer. At one point he wanders up to the camera, as if daring whoever might one day see the footage to stare into his sunken, glassy eyes. It's typically hard to feel much sympathy for Hunter, but if there was ever a moment, this would be it.

The big, obvious question was, Where did this laptop come from?

In late September 2020, the *New York Post* was notified of the existence of an external hard drive holding the contents of a laptop belonging to Joe Biden's son. Two points of contact were made with the *Post* by two sources in possession of the hard drive. Steve Bannon, who had been executive chairman of Breitbart News and chief strategist for Donald Trump, approached then deputy politics editor Emma-Jo Morris. Rudy Giuliani approached reporter Jon Levine.

At the time, Levine and Morris worked on different desks and did not know each other.

They spoke for the first time on a conference call with Bannon's publicist, Alexandra Preate, after both sources were insisting on giving the *Post* cherry-picked documents but refusing to hand over the full hard drive. The pitch to Levine focused on the lasciviousness of the content. Giuliani had initially offered the tabloid nude photos of the First Son.

After an extended back-and-forth with Preate, Levine shouted into the phone: "This is too heavy a lift for porn!" He was out.

But Bannon had given Morris a different pitch, that there were never-before-seen documents on the device detailing the Bidens' deals with Chinese Communist Party–linked entities. That would be worth the lift.

Morris eventually obtained the full hard drive.

On October 14, 2020, the *Post* went to print with the first tranche of stories that would come to be known colloquially as the "Laptop from Hell" series. The articles—which did not include any porn—detailed what appeared to be involvement by Joe Biden in his son's foreign business, which included dealings in corruption-ridden countries on almost every continent.

The initial stories detailed the family's business in Ukraine. The main takeaway was that Hunter had been leveraging his family ties to boost his pay from Burisma.[32]

One story showed Hunter referring to the upcoming visit of "my guy" to Ukraine, which he would use to entice Ukrainian clients to pay a $25,000/month retainer for his consulting services.

Another story showed that the Obama administration let Democrat PR company Blue Star Strategies, which had been retained by Burisma, take part in a conference call about an upcoming visit to Ukraine by then vice president Biden. "The trip, in December 2015, turned out to be the one during which Biden later bragged about forcing Ukrainian officials to fire a state prosecutor who was investigating Burisma by threatening to withhold a $1 billion US loan guarantee," according to the *Post*'s report.[33]

A bombshell story revealed an email from Burisma executive Vadym Pozharskyi to Hunter, thanking him "for inviting me to DC and giving an opportunity to meet your father and spent [*sic*] some time together." All of a sudden, Biden family happy talk about Joe not knowing about Hunter's business endeavors was nuked into the stratosphere.

Now everyone would know the truth about the Bidens.

Or would they? When the stories appeared on social media that morning, within hours, they were censored on all major platforms. Twitter slapped a "hacked materials" policy violation on the *Post*'s content, refusing to allow users to share the link to the stories. Facebook said it would curb distribution and reach of the links on its platform as precaution against "Russian disinformation."

Twitter went so far as to even ban the links from being shared in private messages, which is a policy typically used to clamp down on child porn distribution. Twitter locked the *Post* out of its verified account for days on end without even giving the paper a heads-up that they were going to do so. (The material was in no way "hacked," as the paper clearly explained in the articles themselves.)

Meanwhile, the *Post* was working on what would become the signature story of the series, wherein an email was revealed to show a remuneration package in a deal between the Biden family and CEFC China Energy Company, in which there was 10 percent equity "held by H for the big guy."[34]

"H" clearly represented Hunter, and "the big guy" was indubitably Joe Biden himself.

All of this info was legit. Not hacked. Not disinformation. Not good for the Bidens.

The Deep State had to think fast, and they did.

On October 19, 2020, *Politico*'s Natasha Bertrand—who has since failed upward to CNN—published a story headlined "Hunter Biden Story Is Russian Disinfo, Dozens of Former Intel Officials Say." Bertrand's reporting said former members of the U.S. intelligence services claimed in a letter that the *Post* exposé "has all the classic earmarks of a Russian information operation." Most notable among the signatories of the letter were Jim Clapper, former director of national intelligence; Mike Hayden, former director of the CIA; and John Brennan, also former director of the CIA.[35]

Apparently we are all supposed to take America's spy chieftains at their word.

The letter was an op: purely political, rooted in nothing, no more substantial than fairy dust. The signatories even admitted that "we do not have evidence of Russian involvement."[36]

It was another variation on the Russian collusion hoax theme. Yet the Democrats, establishment media, and, more importantly in this case, the Silicon Valley Masters of the Universe had their talking points.

On October 22, 2020, just before the final presidential debate, a business partner in the CEFC deal named Tony Bobulinski held a press conference in which he went on the record to confirm that the "big guy" is Joe Biden, and that he was involved in deals with entities linked to the Chinese Communist Party.[37] "I have heard Joe Biden say he has never discussed his dealings with Hunter. That is false. I have firsthand knowledge about this because I directly dealt with the Biden family, including Joe Biden," Bobulinski said.

He recalled meeting Joe Biden in Beverly Hills, California, in 2017: "That night, we discussed the Bidens' history, the Biden family's plans with the Chinese, with which he was plainly familiar, at least at a high level."

But when Biden went up onstage that night in one of only two presidential election debates with Trump, he insisted that all of what (some of) the American people had just read and heard with their own eyes and ears was a "Russian plot." "Fifty former national intelligence professionals said this: what he's accusing me of is a Russian plot," the future president said, inarticulately.[38]

The level of coordinated effort that went into that false narrative—a conspiracy among the highest levels of power in politics, media, government, and especially social media—would be revealed only years later.

It was a master class in information warfare, and it worked like a charm.

In April 2023, former CIA acting director Michael Morell testified to the House Judiciary Committee that Obama/Biden State Department alumnus Antony Blinken called him about the "Laptop from Hell" reporting days after the *New York Post* published it. That call, according to

Morell's closed-door testimony to Congress, catalyzed the infamous letter published by *Politico* and referenced by Biden.

Yes, the future secretary of state, Blinken, gave a past acting CIA director the idea to draft the hoax letter, and then they rounded up all their Deep State buddies and got them to sign it.[39] It was instantly touted in establishment media and by Biden himself as it were a papal bull.

Somehow it gets worse. In May 2023, House investigative committees alleged that at least one current CIA employee helped obtain signatures for the farcical statement, and that formalities of the CIA's Prepublication Classification Review Board were jettisoned so that person could do so.

In a tranche of internal communications released by Elon Musk as part of the "Twitter Files" series, documents show that the FBI and other intelligence community members directed the censorship operation by working with top management. Social media companies hire eye-popping numbers of alphabet-agency alumni, so it is no wonder the Deep State's request was quickly honored.[40]

Journalist Michael Shellenberger reported, based on documents he obtained from Musk, that federal agents "discredited factual information about Hunter Biden's foreign business dealings both after and *before* *The New York Post* revealed the contents of his laptop on October 14, 2020." Shellenberger noted "an organized effort by representatives of the intelligence community (IC), aimed at senior executives at news and social media companies," to smear factual and accurate stories based on a hard drive belonging to Hunter Biden, which the FBI had in its possession almost a year before the *Post*'s reporting and knew was authentic.

This is bombshell information. The IC was running interference for Hunter and Joe even before the contents of the laptop were revealed to the public.

There was such intimate cooperation by mid-September 2020, weeks before the *Post* would begin publishing the "Laptop from Hell" series, that FBI, Office of the Director of National Intelligence (ODNI), and Twitter executives had an encrypted messaging network set up, which they dubbed a "virtual war room."

Joe Biden, as of July 2023, has not acknowledged or commented on anything regarding his son's laptop or the censorship conspiracy surrounding the reporting of it.

Following the 2020 election, *Atlantic* journalist Edward-Isaac Dovere published a book, *Battle for the Soul: Inside the Democrats' Campaigns to Defeat Trump*, which covers the Democrats' 2020 campaigns. There is a short passage in the book that gives the reader a small glimpse into the Biden campaign at the time the "Laptop from Hell" series was published. It describes Joe as basically unfazed by the coverage, insisting, as he does in public, that he loves his son and that he did nothing wrong.[41]

Based on my impression of Joe Biden, this is exactly how I would have expected him to react.

But there is one line, somewhat buried in this section of Dovere's book, where Biden appears to concede that the contents of the laptop are real: "*[T]he Post* kept chopping, publishing photos of Hunter getting high and a long text message exchange purporting to be between Biden and Hunter that revealed an angry son snapping back at a father struggling to be loving," Dovere writes. "The texts were real: Hunter writing from rehab . . . Their pain and grief were splayed in a tabloid spread. Biden tried to keep himself steeled against it."

I've long wondered why Hunter would leave a laptop at a Delaware repair shop and supposedly forget about it, especially knowing what contents were on it. By far the most logical explanation, in my opinion, is that it was a cry for help. He wanted to get caught. And when he was, the government, the media, and even his own father, the future president, acted like it was all a fake story planted by Vladimir Putin. This worked politically for Joe, and it certainly set up Hunter to cut beaucoup deals once his dad was sworn in as president.

But maybe that wasn't what Hunter really wanted.

It surely wasn't what he needed.

THE ART LIFE

After the events infamously documented in the "Laptop from Hell" series, Hunter managed to straighten himself out long enough to pull off a con that is nothing short of genius.

With Joe running for the presidential nomination, Hunter had positioned himself to get a limitless flow of foreign cash into his bank account, and he got the *New York Times* to help him do it. In February

2020, the Gray Lady ran a story headlined "There's a New Artist in Town. The Name Is Biden." The very top of the article, as it appears online, shows Hunter looking hip, handsome, and happy, surrounded by mediocre paintings he sells at a premium price. Yes, after his stint in rehab, Joe's son set off to become an artist, and the *Times* was right there with a puff piece to give him publicity that no other fifty-year-old budding painter could have gotten in their wildest dreams.

Scrolling through the article, you will see a photo of Hunter, leaning over a table with his lips around a hollow glass cylinder. No, he wasn't doing drugs—he was puffing on paint.

It was as clear as crystal meth: Hunter was trolling the whole world with an homage to his past life as a junkie.

And the *Times* turned it into an advertisement for Biden and Son, Inc.

"His process with alcohol ink—it can take 14 layers for the material to adhere—includes blowing it with a metal straw," read the caption underneath the photo. "You have to be really focused in order to be able to alter it to your own imagination," he said.

Alcohol ink. "Altering your imagination." "Painting" with an instrument that looks like a cocaine straw or maybe a crack pipe. It was all a colossal joke, made by Hunter, on the rest of us.

There was artistry to what he was doing, but it wasn't on the canvas: it was his performance.

A consensus among art critics emerged that these paintings should not fetch a high price, but that did not stop Hunter for asking as much as $500,000 for a single piece. That number would be shocking for any newcomer to the art scene,[42] but Biden was in such hot demand that he sold five prints—not even original pieces—for $75,000 apiece before he even had his first show in 2021.[43]

"It is absolutely, 100 percent certain that what is being sold is the Biden name and story," art critic Ben Davis told *Politico*.[44] I don't think you need to be an authority on art to have figured that out.

The planned sale sparked outrage from the public as well as ethics experts. How could the Biden administration, after promising to finally address Hunter's ethical problems, allow him to hawk overpriced paintings (that is, his name) to the notoriously shady art world? The White House had to intervene.

Intervene they did, but not in the way you would have hoped. Instead of stopping the sale, the White House worked with Hunter's art dealer to concoct a scheme that would keep the buyers secret, theoretically keeping Hunter and the White House from showing any possible favor that would be done for those who stroked the checks.[45] Nothing in the arrangement keeps the buyer from informing Hunter after the fact; the only secrecy it guarantees is from the public.

In case there was any doubt that Hunter's art was a gigantic hoax so he could sell the family's name, his art dealer refused to turn over the buyers' identities to the House Oversight Committee.[46]

Former Obama White House ethics chief Walter Shaub offered up the following summary in a tweet: "So instead of disclosing who is paying outrageous sums for Hunter Biden's artwork so that we could monitor whether the purchasers are gaining access to government, the WH tried to make sure we will never know who they are. That's very disappointing."[47]

What little we know about Hunter's patrons is from gallery documents obtained by Business Insider in 2023. Up until that point, Hunter had raked in at least $1,379,000 from selling his art, according to the documents, with one anonymous buyer paying $875,000.[48] There is no reason to believe that the Bidens don't know his or her identity. After all, despite the White House's promises, Hunter learned the names of at least two other buyers, one of whom was his own attorney, Kevin Morris. Biden donor Elizabeth Hirsh Naftali also is apparently a big fan of Hunter's paintings. It is not clear when exactly Naftali made her purchase, but she visited the White House on more than a dozen occasions since Hunter's first art show in 2021.[49] In 2022, Biden appointed her to the Commission for the Preservation of America's Heritage Abroad.[50] The dots practically connect themselves.

Whether these people want a quid pro quo, are cleaning dirty money, or honestly believe Hunter is a modern Renoir, the result is the same: easy cash for the president's son.

I have a contrarian take on Hunter Biden's entrée into the art world. I think Hunter and Joe Biden formulated an immaculate heist. Now everyone knows that if you want to do a favor for Hunter and the Big Guy, here is how you do it: buy some of Hunter's prints and privately let him know you did so. The public will be none the wiser, the Biden family will be quite a bit richer, and they'll know exactly who their friends are. It was clearly unethical, and thanks to a tweak to the law from Joe's administration, it all appeared to be legal. It wasn't merely done in plain sight: it was done with a highly publicized media campaign.

It is the strongest bit of evidence yet that Hunter really is the smartest guy Joe knows.

Hunter wasn't done cashing in on the perks of being a Biden while his dad is in office. He never is. It was revealed in 2022 that the Secret Service detail tasked with protecting him had been paying upward of $30,000 a month to rent out a mansion in Malibu.

It must have been a really peaceful place to paint.[51]

The constellation of facts paints a vivid picture of influence peddling by Joe Biden's family. Their ability to capitalize on America's crises is uncanny. Yet all of it (aside from the gun violations and crack binges) appears to be legal. Not only has the establishment media avoided many of the stories, but they colluded with the government to suppress them.

DR. JOE BIDEN, THE PENN BIDEN CENTER, AND THE BIDEN INSTITUTE

Given all the stories already highlighted in this chapter, and many others that don't show up in these pages, it's hardly a surprise that there is a Hunter Biden connection to the high-profile scandals of Joe Biden's presidency to date.

First, a little history:

In February 2017, the University of Pennsylvania announced that Joe Biden had been appointed as Benjamin Franklin Presidential Practice Professor (who doesn't see Joe Biden as cut from the same cloth as the First American?) and would lead the newly created Penn Biden Center for Diplomacy and Global Engagement.[52] We were told for years that Dr. Jill Biden was the real educator of the family—after all, she had gotten her EdD from the University of Delaware (UD) when she was fifty-five years old. Now it was Joe, who had spent his lifetime in politics, who would be a full-blown professor.

The Penn Biden Center's website states that it is focused on "strengthening American global leadership" by "advancing dialogue on internationalism" and "addressing threats to the liberal international order."[53] The website also features photos of Biden meeting with Chinese president Xi Jinping.[54] Since its founding, the Penn Biden Center has served as a landing pad for Biden aides who were later appointed to White House positions.

Critics have noted its lack of financial transparency, refusing to disclose its sources of funding. The University of Pennsylvania itself has received tens of millions in anonymous donations from China since founding the Biden Center.[55] These same criticisms can also be leveled against the Biden Institute at the University of Delaware, which was launched the same day as the Penn Biden Center but has received far less attention. In February 2023, Breitbart News broke the story that secret donations to UD soared after the opening of the Biden Institute, including more than $1 million from the Chinese government itself.[56]

Joe Biden announced the founding of the Biden Institute at UD as part of Biden's "vision for the institute . . . an annual conference at UD, similar to the World Economic Forum or the Aspen Institute."[57] Both are incubators for Biden's globalist and elitist views.

These entities didn't receive this level of funding because Chinese financiers consider Biden a swell guy. They wanted a quo.

The Penn Biden Center: From its founding, the Penn Biden Center became a pipeline of longtime aides and advisors who would join Joe Biden when he became president.[58] As of early 2023, at least twelve staffers have been appointed by Biden to White House positions, including Secretary of State Antony Blinken and Counselor to the President Steven J. Ricchetti.

UPenn does not publish the delineated financials for various entities within the university, so funding sources are mostly a mystery. We do know some details from Peter Schweizer's reporting in *Red-Handed*. For instance, we know from U.S. Department of Education records that the university received $950,000 from China Merchant Bank, a "state-owned enterprise under the direct supervision of the State Council," mere weeks after the Biden Center opened.[59] They also received $1 million from a Chinese company called Cathay Fortune, which is headed up by a "secretive Chinese billionaire" named Yu Yong, who has ties to the Communist Party.[60] Cathay Fortune is the controlling shareholder of a Chinese company called China Molybdenum, which is involved in a joint venture with Hunter Biden's BHR investment fund.[61]

According to records kept by the Department of Education, between 2014 and 2017, UPenn received thirty-eight gifts/contracts from China totaling nearly $23.5 million. Only three of these gifts ($1.3 million, altogether) were from anonymous sources. But once the Penn Biden Center opened its DC office in February 2018, anonymous funding from China started flooding in at a steady clip.[62]

A total of $75 million has been given by Chinese sources since the Penn Biden Center opened its DC office, amounting to roughly 75 percent of UPenn's total funding from China since 2013. More than $40 million of these funds has come from Chinese sources that UPenn has never publicly disclosed.

We know what this looks like: an influence play by the Chinese. It's not in the interest of UPenn, Joe Biden, or the CCP to disclose more details about these gifts than absolutely necessary.

University of Delaware Biden Institute: While media reports have focused primarily on UPenn's Biden Center, less attention has been paid to UD's Biden Institute, even though these two "institutes" were meant to serve a shared goal. Emails from Hunter Biden's Laptop from Hell reveal that Hunter himself and several of his business partners began planning the venture at UD and UPenn in early 2016, with a forthcoming Penn Biden office in DC that would be the public-facing "stage" for the "Biden Brand.[63]

On December 11, 2018, UD announced that it was naming its public policy school after Vice President Biden. Emails show that this move was orchestrated by members of UD's Biden Institute.[64] Also, on the day of the announcement, Hunter Biden received a text message from his aunt, Valerie Owens, saying: "Bravo Hunter—UD was your baby and you made sure I was part of it."[65]

The University of Delaware Biden Institute was "Hunter's baby." And this was the type of baby the family most certainly was not going to ignore.

The emails show that in March 2016, Hunter and his colleagues met with incoming UD president Dennis Assanis to discuss plans for the UD/UPenn venture months before Assanis was officially instated. Assanis has deep and long-standing ties to China. In addition to serving as the founding director of the U.S.-China Clean Energy Research Center—Clean Vehicle Consortium (CERC-CVC)[66] since 2003, Assanis has been a guest professor (2003–2008) and advisory professor (2009–present) at Shanghai Jiao Tong University (SJTU).[67] This fact alone raises concern given that SJTU has signed cooperative agreements with China's People's Liberation Army (PLA). What's more, cyberattacks on American companies such as Google have been traced to computers at SJTU.[68]

Like UPenn, the UD Biden Institute was quickly stocked with twelve future Biden appointees, including soon-to-be senior Biden advisor Mike Donilon[69] and Surgeon General Vivek Murthy.[70] Assanis himself would be named to Biden's President's Council of Advisors on Science and Technology.[71]

The University of Delaware had never disclosed receiving funds from China until April 2018, when it accepted over $3.2 million for a contract with an unnamed Chinese entity. This came two months after the Penn Biden Center opened its DC office. Then, in December 2018, UD received $1.9 million from an unnamed Chinese entity. In 2019, UD received another $625,000 from China.[72] In 2020, UD initiated three contracts with the Chinese entities and received over $1 million in funds. In sum, UD has received over $6.7 million from unnamed Chinese sources, including a substantial amount from the Chinese government.[73]

All these funds started flowing to UD after the Biden Institute was announced and increased immediately after the launch of the Penn Biden Center.

This money from China is cause for alarm given that UD has thirty-seven international partnerships with Chinese universities, including several that support the development of Chinese military technologies.[74] The most logical reasons for the Chinese to engage in these partnerships are that they want to influence American institutions, acquire American intellectual property, or both.

On February 8, 2022, Senator Marco Rubio (R-FL) wrote a letter to UD president Dennis Assanis urging him to terminate UD's academic and research partnership with Xiamen University, which actively supports Beijing's military-industrial complex[75] and which allegedly conspired with Huawei to steal trade secrets from an American semiconductor startup.[76] Yet according to the International Cyber Policy Centre's China Defence Universities Tracker database, that partnership with Xiamen University is only a "medium" risk.

The University of Delaware has worked with at least four other universities linked to Chinese defense laboratories.[77]

In April 2016, Hunter exchanged emails and had at least one meeting with Craig Gering, a talent agent for the legendary Creative Artists Agency, about Vice President Biden's future after he leaves office. Gering took "confidential notes" from the meeting that describe details about the plans for the UD/UPenn operation, including the possibility of Hunter serving in the

Penn Biden Center DC office. Gering fantasized about an entity that "operates like The Clinton Global Initiative (CGI) without the money raise."[78]

CGI claims it convenes "established and emerging global leaders to create and implement solutions to the world's most pressing challenges," according to its website,[79] but functionally, it was an easy way for the Clintons to reap donor funds and leverage relationships with celebrities and major corporations to boost their profiles all the while promoting their own cultural and political agenda items. Donations to CGI dried up when it came under media scrutiny from Schweizer and others for soliciting millions of dollars from foreign governments and businesses—the same governments and businesses that received favorable treatment from the Obama administration during Hillary's tenure as secretary of state.[80]

The Clinton Global Initiative was shut down in 2016[81] and revived in 2022. It was always meant to be an influence-peddling operation by the Clintons; this was clear to anyone paying attention. It was shuttered at the specific moment when Hillary Clinton could no longer do anything substantial for the donors.

It dawned on the Bidens, Hunter in particular, that they could step in and fill the void.

It was clear from the Laptop from Hell emails that Biden World fantasized about such an entity for Joe. It could be a means for influential figures around the world to boost the Biden brand. After all, the UD/UPenn/Biden venture is ultimately about "wealth creation," according to Gering.

It could be used for philanthropy, bettering the world, and advancing the Biden name. But most importantly, "wealth creation."

A stunning admission.

The degree to which the Bidens were able to leverage these new entities to benefit themselves financially is unclear, but we do know, thanks to the laptop, that the vision was in place to create a secret money machine that could be relevant for generations.

It was Hunter's baby.

THE CLASSIFIED DOCUMENTS

Like so many others in the political establishment, even when Joe Biden wasn't in the government, he was in the business of government. Never was that more clear than in November 2022, when classified documents from his time as vice president were discovered by attorneys at the Penn Biden Center's office in Washington, DC. Documents were later discovered in Biden's personal residences, as well.[82]

It was known that Biden family politics and the Biden family business are deeply intertwined, but never had that been quite this overt.

The second crop of documents was found stashed in the garage that houses Joe's green 1967 Corvette 327 Stingray convertible. The exact contents of the documents or Biden's intended purpose for them is yet unknown, though the president's special counsel Richard Sauber suggested they were from the Obama/Biden administration and some of them were of a classified nature. This is significant because while the president of the United States can declassify any document he wants at any time, a vice president cannot.

It also remains a mystery why Biden's attorneys were looking for these documents and why they alerted the National Archives and Records Administration (NARA)—and thus the public—specifically when they did.

The scandal's timeline is suspicious: whether coincidental or not, it minimized the political fallout for the president. The first batch of documents was discovered just prior to the November 8, 2022, elections, in a locked closet at the Penn Biden Center; Biden's lawyers say they were found when cleaning out the Washington, DC, office. They claim they immediately turned over the classified materials to NARA.[83] The FBI began their assessment of whether classified materials were mishandled the day after the election, on November 9. Attorney General Merrick Garland assigned a U.S. attorney to look into whether a special counsel should be convened in mid-November. A second batch of documents, the ones in the garage near the classic roadster, were found in late December.[84]

Yet news of the scandal did not break until January 9, 2023. This was good timing for Biden (relatively speaking). While the government gathered information and equivocated outside of the public eye, the Democrats were overperforming in the midterm elections, giving Joe Biden a big political boost. It missed the 2022 election news cycle entirely. The news finally emerged well before the 2024 election season got under way, so when America goes to the polls next, it will be a distant memory for most voters.

What's more, classified documents found in the possession of Donald Trump and his former vice president, Mike Pence, ate into Joe's negative news cycle and minimized the fallout. In fact, Biden actually scored points with the media by cooperating with authorities relative to Trump. Establishment media reports often ignored that Trump had the ability to declassify all the documents in his possession whereas Biden did not.

If you must be part of a scandal, this is the best-case scenario.

Biden himself said he was "surprised" to learn the records were discovered.[85] This explanation strains credulity. The pattern throughout Joe Biden's life in Washington is that access to government information and relationships has been his currency. Perhaps Joe was holding on to these materials so that he could write more memoirs, perhaps he was using them to peddle influence, but he pled to the world that it was just a simple mix-up. If we learned that he was monetizing our nation's secrets, it wouldn't shock anyone. If we learned it was actually the fault of staffers' carelessness, as Biden claimed,[86] that would be a far greater surprise.

Joe Biden, and many of the people he has elevated to the top of his administration, publicly flaunt their virtue while undermining the substance of their own edicts. They write the rules, then flagrantly break them, either directly or via loopholes. Even if Biden's illegal possession of classified documents was an innocent mistake, as he has publicly claimed, the scandal proves that separation between the personal and political in modern Washington—a Washington that Joe Biden himself created—does not exist.

In June of 2023, Donald Trump was indicted on charges that related to his handling of classified documents that he had retained at his Mar-a-Lago club in Palm Beach after his presidency. This makes Trump the first former president in U.S. history to face federal charges. He is also the current president's most popular political rival. Biden could shut down the investigation at any time, but he would never do that. President Biden, after all, has never cared about unity or democracy or equal justice under the law, but he does care mightily about satisfying the left-wing base of the Democrat Party, which badly wants to see the Bad Orange Man in a collared orange jumpsuit. The hypocrisy is breathtaking, but it's also a double-dog dare to Republicans and everyone else in Washington: Joe Biden is confident that no one will ever hold him accountable for his mishandling of classified documents. This is a partisan advantage afforded only to Democrats.

Joe Biden knows this better than most. After all, he built the system.

CHAPTER 4

American Corporatism

THE BIDEN BENEFICIARIES

Publicly, Joe Biden has been outspoken about standing up to big business. His campaign swore off donations from lobbyists.[1] His executive orders have urged more scrutiny of tech giants.[2] He is a staunch advocate for corporate tax hikes.

But these are half measures—a smoke screen to cover up decades of ties to big business.

For thirty-six years, Joe Biden represented the state of Delaware as a senator. He is their prodigal son. Delaware, while being the second-smallest state in the union, has been dubbed "the sexiest place in America to incorporate a company."[3] According to the Delaware Division of Corporations, more than two-thirds of Fortune 500 companies are domiciled in the state of Delaware.[4] For decades, the state was in the pocket of the du Pont family, which dominated state politics for generations. You've heard of company towns; Delaware was a company state.[5]

Delaware is the biggest tax shelter in the United States, with corporate privacy laws that would give notorious havens like Panama and Luxembourg a run for their money.[6]

"Today, there are nearly twice as many Delaware-incorporated companies as there are Delaware voters, and incorporation fees constitute the second-largest share of the state's annual revenue," according to a 2019 profile in *Mother Jones*.[7]

Delaware is so friendly to corporations that, in a number of cities and towns throughout the state, limited liability companies (LLCs) are allowed to vote in local elections. Mitt Romney once said, "Corporations are people, my friend,"[8] and in Delaware, that's actually true. In one instance, a single property owner—who managed his holdings through thirty-one LLCs—was able to vote thirty-one times in a local race.[9]

Columnist Byron York once dubbed Biden "the Senator from MBNA" over his cozy ties with the financial institution formerly known as Maryland Bank National Association. Despite its name, the bank was founded in 1982 in Delaware, where its headquarters remained until it was acquired by Bank of America in 2006. MBNA was the biggest issuer of credit cards in the country and donated generously to Joe Biden's campaigns. In fact, one of its top executives even purchased Biden's former home—once a du Pont mansion—for an amount comfortably over its apparent market value.[10] Can you say "windfall"?! Shortly after Hunter Biden graduated from Yale Law School in 1996, MBNA signed him to a six-figure lobbying contract at the same time Joe was championing bankruptcy reform legislation that would have served the interest of the bank.[11] The bank seemed to have bought the Biden family off. This would prove to be a harbinger for what was in store for young Hunter.

President Biden came into office pledging to curb corporate influence over the White House.[12] That's a welcome sentiment, but corporatism has thrived within the Democrat Party for most of the century, with Hollywood, Silicon Valley, and increasingly Wall Street and big-business boardrooms catalyzing cultural change in America, rarely for the better. What's more, no administration has had deeper ties to the lobbying and consultant classes than Biden's.

The Biden Inaugural Committee raised $62 million, much of it from a who's who of corporate America.[13] Donors from Microsoft, Google, Qualcomm, AT&T, Comcast, Anthem, and Boeing headlined the list, the *Wall Street Journal* reported.

According to OpenSecrets, federal lobbying spending surged to $3.77 billion in 2021, almost a quarter-billion-dollar increase compared to 2020.[14] Adjusted for inflation, more money is being spent lobbying the federal government than at any other time since the 2008 financial crisis.[15]

An incestuous relationship between business and government is something Delaware and Washington have in common. Something else they have in common is Joe Biden.

BAGGING BIDEN BUCKS

It isn't only Joe Biden's family members who have taken advantage of his policies. His friends have also made a mint, thanks to the Big Guy.

Ricchetti Inc., the lobbying outfit cofounded by Biden advisor Steve Ricchetti and still operated by his brother Jeff, saw its lobbying revenue nearly double when Biden launched his presidential bid, from $625,000 in 2019 to $1.25 million in 2020. When Biden won the election, Ricchetti Inc.'s billings surged again, to $3.1 million in 2021—a fivefold increase over 2019.[16]

Ricchetti Inc., which had not signed a new client since 2016, signed sixteen between the beginning of 2019 and early 2023, among those Amazon, Canadian gas pipeline operator TC Energy, and a variety of pharmaceutical companies.[17]

Steve Ricchetti's son JJ also landed a gig in the Biden Treasury Department's Office of Legislative Affairs.[18]

Ricchetti Inc.'s story isn't unique.

Putala Strategies, a firm run by longtime Biden aide Chris Putala, saw its revenue triple from $1.3 million in 2020 to $4 million in 2021, according to *Politico*. TheGROUP DC, which employs Biden's former legislative affairs director Sudafi Henry as a partner, saw its revenue spike from $3.6 million to $7.5 million over the same period.[19]

It pays to be in the Biden business.

More problematic, though, is the administration's close ties with secretive "consulting" companies that don't face strict disclosure requirements like lobbying firms. By 2022, more than three dozen Biden administration staffers came from a small group of extremely influential consulting firms.

Thirteen former employees of the Albright Stonebridge Group (ASG), the consulting firm founded by the late former secretary of state Madeleine Albright, have joined the Biden administration as of early 2023. This list includes powerful people within the administration such as Undersecretary of State for Political Affairs Victoria Nuland, one of the architects of Biden's Ukraine policy. According to financial disclosures, ASG alumni entering the administration represented corporate giants like Amazon, Microsoft, Lyft, Merck, Discovery, Pfizer, and more.

In 2018, Michèle Flournoy, former undersecretary of defense for defense policy and cofounder of the Center for a New American Security, and Antony Blinken, then managing director of the Penn Biden Center and future secretary of state, founded the consultancy WestExec Advisors with the aim of "advising companies on geopolitical risk and emerging opportunities."[20] At least sixteen Biden administration officials have come from WestExec, including Director of National Intelligence Avril Haines and former White House press secretary Jen Psaki. The firm served as a sort of "government-in-waiting." Its staff is largely composed of former Obama administration officials.

WestExec ultimately provided much of Biden's foreign policy thinking power.[21] This is troubling considering that the consultancy claimed to help American universities seek funding and partnerships in Communist China; they scrambled to hide this fact in the months leading up to the 2020 election.[22]

Upon its founding, WestExec quickly partnered with Jigsaw, a branch of Google that "explores threats to open societies," one of which is disinformation.[23] This is coded language for censoring online speech in the name of fighting "online trolls." Critics immediately saw Jigsaw as a potential antidemocratic tool that authoritarian regimes could use to tamp down dissent. It's not a coincidence that WestExec's Blinken helped execute the "Russian disinfo" hoax that got the Laptop from Hell censored before the 2020 election.

WestExec also works closely with a firm called Pine Island Capital Partners. Its team is composed almost entirely of former congresspeople, military high-ups, and other former White House staff, Flournoy included.[24]

Days after Biden's election, Pine Island Acquisition Corporation, a blank-check investment firm focused on asset acquisition, IPO'd, touting its ability to offer access to DC partnerships as a strength.[25] The firm was mainly focused on aerospace and defense assets. At the time, the company's leadership included Flournoy and Blinken along with a host of other powerful government-connected people like General Lloyd Austin, who would become Biden's defense secretary. For perhaps the first time in history, a future secretary of state and a future secretary of defense were business partners. Former House majority leader Dick Gephardt as well as three other former senators were also high up in the firm. Investors from Goldman Sachs, Merrill Lynch, and other major corporations got in on the action. Rob Walker, a known Hunter Biden associate, was also listed as an advisor on the Pine Island website but was later removed.[26]

This is the defense industry at its swampiest and most brazen: powerful people grabbing whatever cash they could before returning to public service.

WestExec employees turned Biden administration officials disclosed that their clients include Lyft, Boeing, SoftBank, JPMorgan Chase, Microsoft, Open Philanthropy, Blackstone, FedEx, GLG, Lazard, Royal Bank of Canada, AT&T, Discovery, Facebook, LinkedIn, Sotheby's, Gilead Sciences, and Uber. Once they entered the Biden administration, they were supposed to provide oversight of these exact companies.

Sounds legit. *Psych.*

Macro Advisory Partners is another feeder system into Biden World. At least six administration officials worked for the "strategic business consultancy," including National Security Advisor Jake Sullivan[27] and Secretary of Veterans Affairs Denis McDonough (who was Obama's former chief of staff).[28] Macro Advisory's clients include Apple, GlaxoSmithKline (now GSK), Mastercard, PWC, and Deutsche Telekom.[29]

The list of Biden officials with conflicts of interests when it comes to policy that affects major corporations seems endless. It would take a long (and probably boring) book to enumerate all of the business ties. For example, Pete Buttigieg and Susan Rice previously worked for mega-firm McKinsey & Company, arguably the most prestigious consultancy in the world. To get a sense of McKinsey's business model, consider that the firm advises both governments and the corporations those governments regulate. That is a system that normalizes the appearance of pay-to-play. Yet this is exactly how business is done in the DC swamp, and throughout much of the world.

The new consulting class is the latest evolution of the model pioneered by the Clinton machine. In fact, Teneo, the mega-consultancy launched by former Bill Clinton aide Doug Band, purchased a majority stake in WestExec in 2022.[30] Oddly, the Clintons' nonprofit activities have endured much more scrutiny than Democrat-establishment-connected consulting firms.

While using nonprofit status to make illicit money offends our moral sensibilities, turning our government over to stakeholders in multi-national, self-interested corporations has had a much more profound effect on the culture of Washington, and thus the way our nation is governed.

ETHICS, BIDEN-STYLE

In January 2021, Joe Biden unveiled his new White House ethics policy via executive order. It was designed to rein in the alleged sleaze of the Trump years. His stated goal was to "restore and maintain public trust in government." "I commit myself to conduct consistent with that plan," Biden wrote. "I commit to decision-making on the merits and exclusively in the public interest, without regard to private gain or personal benefit."[31] Lovely words.

Biden suggested that he intended to target influence peddling by members of his administration. Under the policy, lobbyists who have lobbied the administration within the last year are barred from taking positions in the Biden administration, and former officials are barred from lobbying the White House for two years after leaving the administration. However, he left open a loophole big enough to drive an eighteen-wheeler through: because they are not technically lobbyists, consultants are not subject to the administration's restrictions.[32] This meant the aforementioned consultancies that double as slush funds and farm systems for current and future Biden administration officials can operate with impunity.

Thus Biden can talk tough on ethics and still benefit from the system of influence peddling that has been exploited by his family and many of his closest allies.

Tony Blinken's clients included companies such as Boeing, Microsoft, and AT&T. Blinken has attempted to recuse himself from foreign policy that relates to Boeing, but to completely disqualify himself from this part of his portfolio would leave him little left to do as secretary of state. Boeing's products are crucial in diplomacy with China, Israel, the Middle East, and, Ukraine. For example, the U.S. sent Ukraine GPS-guided bombs in February 2023 made by . . . wait for it . . . Boeing![33] The company's CEO later said he hoped Blinken's 2023 visit to China would lead to more orders for planes.[34] If Blinken were serious about recusing himself from all matters Boeing, he would have to resign. There is no other ethical alternative.

Blinken has reached the height of power in the consultant class and the federal government bureaucracy. *Forbes* said that Blinken amassed "a small fortune" (an estimated eight-figure net worth) thanks to West-

Exec.[35] His decisions as secretary of state directly affect the bottom lines of his current (and likely future) clients. These are substantial conflicts of interest that were deemed insignificant by President Biden, despite his pontifications about integrity.

In Biden World, some types of self-enrichment are frowned upon, but others are résumé enhancements.

Make no mistake, the consulting business is the place to be in Biden's America.

Blinken initially valued his stake in WestExec at between $500,000 and $1 million, but he sold it back to the firm for between $1 million and $5 million—up to ten times its initial reported value.[36] And that's not counting the nearly $1.2 million he was paid by WestExec prior to taking office.[37] Perhaps the original value estimate turned out to be a little off. Or perhaps the prospect of having its partners staff the incoming administration inflated WestExec's value even further.

Testifying before the Senate Intelligence Committee, fellow West-Exec consultant and incoming director of national intelligence Avril Haines characterized her employment with WestExec as being contract work amounting to less than one day per month. But she disclosed nearly $55,000 in income from WestExec in 2020—a nice payday for the equivalent of two weeks' work.[38] Additionally, Haines was paid $330,000 in consulting fees by Palantir Technologies and the Johns Hopkins Applied Physics Laboratory.[39]

The goal with the consultancy grift is clear: get all the power of public office and all the wealth and the secrecy of private life.

It's not just WestExec that is structured this way. Anita Dunn, who cofounded the DNC-aligned consulting firm SKDKnickerbocker (now SKDK), joined the Biden administration as a "special government employee," allowing her to dodge disclosure requirements. (Democrats have used this loophole in the past; Huma Abedin had "SGE" status as well, allowing her to work for the Clinton Foundation and the State Department simultaneously.) Dunn became a White House senior advisor, and after months of dodging disclosure, eventually divested a portfolio worth between roughly $17 million and $48 million.[40]

One family that seems to have mastered using the nexus of government and business to make exorbitant amounts of money is the Podestas.

After years of living in political disgrace, Biden welcomed the Podesta family back into mainstream politics. John, the Center for American Progress (CAP) founder and 2016 Hillary Clinton campaign chairman, suffered dual humiliations by having personal secrets exposed by WikiLeaks and botching the campaign that was lost to Donald Trump. His brother, Tony Podesta, founder of the Podesta Group, was forced out of his own lobbying firm when he came under scrutiny during the Robert Mueller probe for his deep ties to Ukraine.

Yet Biden redeemed John by tapping him to lead the new White House Office on Clean Energy Innovation and Implementation, which oversees the $370 billion in green investments earmarked by the Inflation Reduction Act.[41] This decision might have been geared more toward trolling conservative critics than efficiently distributing government funds.

Andrew Breitbart famously told a journalist, "Fuck. You. John. Podesta."[42] Andrew was on a rant about "the politics of personal destruction," which was his expression for trying to score political victories by assassinating your ideological opponent's character rather than debating the merit of their ideas. He believed Podesta's Center for American Progress, which is funded by George Soros, normalized that approach to public (non-)debate. Andrew was right (as usual) about Podesta's CAP, which certainly is part of the lineage of modern cancel culture.

During his most recent stint in government prior to joining the Biden administration, John Podesta became personally involved in Joule Unlimited, a now-defunct green energy company backed by the Russian government. Podesta failed to disclose his board seat at the company when he joined the Obama administration in 2014.[43] When his emails were published by WikiLeaks in 2016, it became apparent that Podesta had sidestepped disclosure rules by transferring his stake in the company to an LLC controlled by his daughter.[44]

Since then, Podesta's net worth has soared, according to financial disclosures, largely due to consulting gigs with green energy outfits— exactly the sort of entities that stand to benefit from the billions Podesta now oversees.[45]

In the Biden era of political ethics, who better to control climate spending?

Podesta was a paid advisor to Galvanize Climate Solutions, a green investment fund backed by Tom Steyer and Laurene Powell Jobs's Emerson Collective.[46] He was also on the payroll as an advisor to Hansjörg Wyss's HJW Foundation.[47] Wyss, a Swiss billionaire, had launched the controversial Hub Project, which is designed to influence U.S. elections, primarily through media coverage.[48] Podesta sat on the board of Climate Power, a Wyss-backed climate organization that looks to influence the Biden agenda.[49] Why not help a foreigner interfere in our elections and manipulate our leaders? What's the worst that could happen? Besides, he's rich.

Wyss has been a megadonor to the Clinton Foundation;[50] his money flows freely into the Democrat ecosystem through the banally named Berger Action Fund.[51]

Wyss made a $680 million bid to buy Tribune Publishing in 2021, but it fell through.

He's another major donor to Podesta's CAP.

Meanwhile, his mega-lobbyist brother Tony Podesta's fall from grace occurred when his firm attracted Special Counsel Mueller's attention for work representing the ousted pro-Russian president Viktor Yanukovych's party in Ukraine. Yet he is back in the game as well, having raked in $1 million in 2021 lobbying for Huawei, the embattled Chinese telecom firm that Biden himself has targeted as a threat to national security.[52]

If you are a connected Democrat and your dignity has a price, there are a lot of buyers in Joe Biden's Washington.

THE DONOR CLASS

There are two sides to the influence-peddling coin: the person in power who needs/wants cash and the wealthy person who has interests to advance. The individuals cutting the checks are most often framed in media as "philanthropists." That's neither entirely accurate nor inaccurate. They do give, and not necessarily to ignoble causes, but in Joe Biden's America, the giving is rarely for a donor's proverbial health. It is said that money talks, and that is particularly true in Washington. The donor class have agendas of their own—personal, political, and financial—and they are adroit at getting what they want.

The Democrat Party donor class in particular has attained unprecedented levels of influence during the Biden era of politics. Despite Joe's public pining for a politics outside the influence of the donor class, the gravy train has kept flowing.

How could it not? To hear allies describe it, cutting off high-net-worth individuals from buying political influence would be the equivalent of surrendering in a war. "We weren't going to unilaterally disarm against Trump and the right-wing forces that enabled him," Guy Cecil, the chairman of Priorities USA, a pro-Biden PAC, told Bloomberg News in 2021.[53] This specific language has been in use since the Obama/Biden administration. "Democrats can't be unilaterally disarmed," Obama's campaign manager Jim Messina said in a 2012 interview. This was a signal to wealthy donors that they should support Obama/Biden's reelection bid via super PAC contributions.[54] "We're not going to fight this fight with one hand tied behind our back," he said.

In other words, show me the money!

That's a scary worldview and certainly paves the way for corruption, much of which, as previously noted, is free from the scrutiny that comes with public disclosure requirements.

The figures bankrolling the grassroots foundation of Joe Biden's America are among the wealthiest and most powerful people on the planet. Here are a few of them:

George Soros (estimated net worth: $6.7 billion)[55]: The Hungarian-born hedge fund tycoon founded Open Society Foundations (OSF), the world's largest funder of special interest groups.[56] He transferred $18 billion of personal wealth to the OSF as of 2018, according to *Forbes*.[57] While the OSF claims that promoting democracy and individual rights is its main mission, it has consistently provided all political contributions to left-wing candidates and causes. Throughout 2021 and 2022, Tom Perriello, an executive director at OSF and former Democrat member of the House of Representatives, has been a regular at the White House, appearing on visitation logs thirteen times.[58] As of May 2023, Soros's activist son Alexander had visited Biden's White House at least seventeen times.[59]

Soros gave $170 million toward the 2022 midterm elections, according to CNBC,[60] making him the top individual funder of American politics. In addition, a nonprofit backed by Soros invested a minimum of $140 million in left-wing political causes in 2021.[61] Individuals from Soros Fund Management contributed more than $10.5 million during the 2020 presidential election[62] and over $20.2 million in the 2018 election cycle.[63] Soros has also given heavily to the aforementioned pro-Biden Priorities USA PAC.[64]

Soros is a regular "agenda contributor" to the World Economic Forum (WEF).[65]

He seems to fund nearly every leftist, globalist, and anti-American cause imaginable. It would take volumes to document it all.

Tom Steyer (estimated net worth: $1.5 billion)[66]: Steyer, a San Francisco–based former hedge fund manager and climate activist, spent $73 million on left-leaning causes during the 2020 cycle.[67] Biden hired Steyer to advise him on climate change.[68] Steyer has advocated for halting of drilling permits and the blocking of pipelines,[69] and thus shares responsibility for the skyrocketing gas prices during Biden's first term, as well as other downstream effects that I examine in subsequent chapters.

Though Steyer plays the part of climate change combatant in public, his Farallon Capital Management had large investments in a four-thousand-acre Australian coal mine that is expected to pump carbon into the atmosphere for decades. In addition, the fund has invested vast sums in companies with coal-fired power plants and coal mines in China and Indonesia.[70]

At least four appointed Biden White House staff have financial disclosures tying them to Steyer's businesses.[71]

Laurene Powell Jobs (estimated net worth: $13.7 billion)[72]: Apple cofounder Steve Jobs's widow is one of the richest women in the world and one of the most powerful people in Democrat politics and media. She is nearly as much a part of the Democrat machine as Joe Biden himself. The heiress's primary vehicle for spreading her wealth around is the Emerson Collective, which is a core subject of my book *Breaking the News*. Through the Emerson Collective, she gives lavishly to globalist social justice causes and candidates, funds establishment and alternative left-wing media,[73] and provides jobs for Biden and Obama administration officials. Unsurprisingly, her media outlets tend to report favorably on her other causes.

Jobs accepted the Presidential Medal of Freedom from President Biden on behalf of Steve Jobs in July 2022.[74] She attended a state dinner held by Biden in December 2022.[75]

Reid Hoffman (estimated net worth: \$2.1 billion)[76]: Hoffman, who made his billions from helping launch PayPal and cofounding LinkedIn, has become one of the most prolific funders of Democrats in the country. He uses nonprofits and takes advantage of lenient disclosure laws to make large contributions in relative obscurity.

Hoffman is said to be the "most connected man in Silicon Valley."[77] He was an early investor in Facebook, had big bucks in Airbnb, and sits on the board of Chan Zuckerberg Biohub, the biomedical arm of the Chan Zuckerberg Initiative, which is named for Facebook cofounder Mark Zuckerberg and his wife, Priscilla Chan.

Hoffman's venture capital firm, Greylock Partners, has made eight-figure contributions to Democrat PACs and interest groups in recent elections.[78] LinkedIn and Microsoft donate almost exclusively to Democrats.[79]

Hoffman was responsible for a "false flag" operation in Alabama that planted the idea that the Roy Moore U.S. Senate campaign in 2018 "was amplified on social media by a Russian botnet," according to an internal report on the scheme reviewed by the *New York Times*.[80] Hoffman apologized for the deception after it had become public knowledge.[81]

All the evidence suggests he's not an ethical guy, so he's an ideal person to bankroll the institutional Democrat Party in the Biden era.

Even among the myriad unethical guys in politics, Hoffman still stands out. He has stated that the U.S. should emulate the Chinese communist regime and occasionally collaborates with the CCP. He advises the left-wing Berggruen Institute, which runs an artificial intelligence (AI) research center at Peking University and regularly has summit meetings with Xi Jinping to help the world better understand China.[82] As Peter Schweizer reported in his book *Red-Handed*, LinkedIn managed to stay in compliance with Chinese censorship rules until 2021 (Facebook and Twitter were banned by 2009). Hoffman has been the "go-to guy" when it comes to helping all other Silicon Valley firms cut foreign deals, particularly with China, according to the *New York Times*.[83]

To put it bluntly, this guy really loves Communist China.

Hoffman funds Courier Newsroom and ACRONYM with Laurene Powell Jobs as well as the Good Information Foundation with George Soros, all of which are organizations that push left-wing ideology on social media. Attorney and legal commentator Preston Moore claimed he was offered money from the Good Information Foundation to make videos attacking Donald Trump and "Trump Republicans," which is a no-no as far as federal tax law is concerned when it comes to 501(c)(3) organizations.[84] It is unclear whether the IRS has taken action against the group; I personally filed a complaint against it in 2022.[85]

Eric Schmidt (net worth: $20.5 billion)[86]: Eric Schmidt spent twenty years heading Google and its holding company, Alphabet, holding titles like CEO and executive chairman. During his tenure, the company proudly exercised every tactic possible to avoid paying taxes domestically and abroad.[87] He left the company in 2020[88] and has turned his focus to his philanthropic foundation, Schmidt Futures, which is run by former Clinton Foundation financier Eric Braverman.[89] Futures paid the salaries for two employees in Joe Biden's Office of Science and Technology Policy. This raised ethics concerns, as there were "a large number of staff with financial connections to Schmidt Futures," according to the office's then general counsel, Rachel Wallace.[90]

Schmidt helps fund the AI tech companies Abacus.AI[91] and Civis Analytics, which aided Democrat campaigns, including Biden's 2020 effort to target voters.[92]

During Schmidt's tenure at Google, he partnered with WestExec on the AI project Jigsaw, which was designed to crack down on free speech on the Internet.[93]

Political contributions Schmidt and related organizations have made over the years have been large and numerous. Google has given more than $11 million to mostly Democrat political causes and has a $75 million lobbying record.[94] Since its founding, Alphabet has given $59 million, again to mostly Democrats, and lobbied the government with upward of $119 million,[95] Joe Biden being the largest recipient of the 2020 cycle at just under $4.5 million. Schmidt gave $775,000 to the Future Forward PAC, which is discussed in detail in the chapter of this book on energy policy; it has been funded by other top Democrat donors from Big Tech like disgraced crypto "entrepreneur" Sam Bankman-Fried ($10 million) and Facebook's Dustin Moskovitz ($91.78 million).

Dustin Moskovitz (net worth: $11.6 billion)[96]: Moskovitz, a co-founder of Facebook, has emerged as one of the absolute biggest players in Democrat politics. After separating from the social media giant, he went on to found a tech company called Asana and became one of Biden's (and the Democrat Party's) largest donors.[97]

He gave $20 million in 2020 to the Future Forward PAC, another one of Biden's biggest donors.[98] The PAC was relatively unknown but was able to raise tens of millions of dollars rapidly thanks to tech elites like Eric Schmidt and FTX's Sam Bankman-Fried. Future Forward spent more than $180 million across the 2020 and 2022 elections.[99]

Moskovitz gave roughly $50 million total in the 2020 election cycle.[100] Asana employees, including Moskovitz, contributed $6.1 million in 2022.[101]

Hoffman, Moskovitz, Laurene Powell Jobs, and Schmidt all worked on technological modernization of Biden's campaign to help boost turnout to defeat Donald Trump.[102]

Yet this is only a partial list of high-net-worth donors who provide the funding for the instructional left.

For example, Bankman-Fried donated $39.2 million in 2022, overwhelmingly to Democrats.[103]

Businessman and former New York City mayor Michael Bloomberg, whom I profiled in *Breaking the News*, was another of the top donors of the 2020 cycle. He spent a jaw-dropping $1.1 billion on his own stillborn presidential campaign, but the spending did not stop there. He spent another $150 million supporting Democrat candidates and causes.[104] He even spent $15 million on TV ads for Biden in Texas (Trump won the state by 6 percent).[105]

Democrats have been innovative in the ways they collect and distribute funds that make left-wing politics powerful and profitable in Joe Biden's America. Arabella Advisors, a centralized hub of nonprofits and astroturf activist organizations, for example, is effectively a billion-dollar ATM for the hard left.[106] It collected $2.4 billion during the 2020 election cycle, which *Tablet* magazine notes is "nearly twice as much as the Republican and Democrat national committees combined."[107] Arabella operates four different funds, one of which is the Sixteen Thirty Fund. Sixteen Thirty gave grants to more than two hundred different groups in 2020.[108] Nonprofits connected to Swiss billionaire Hansjörg Wyss, discussed previously in this chapter because of his close ties to John Podesta, donated $135 million to the Sixteen Thirty Fund in 2016 and 2020, according to the *New York Times*.[109] The League of Conservation Voters (LCV), an environmental nonprofit, received massive sums from Arabella: $77.7 million in 2020 and $114.7 million in 2021, all to advance the climate change idealism that is already ubiquitous in Washington and Democrat circles.[110] LCV also received millions directly from Dustin Moskovitz and his wife.[111]

This is a complex web of money flowing every which way, and that is part of the design. It is easy to lose track of how much is being spent, by whom, and what the agenda is behind each expenditure. Yet the goal is clear and consistent: buy votes and buy influence, at least in the figurative sense. For example, "Moskovitz's North Star is a desire to nail the lowest 'cost-per-net-Democratic-vote,'" Vox has reported.[112]

Why win votes, when you can purchase them?

Needless to say, all of this money isn't "well spent." It doesn't need to be. There is so much of it. Yet nothing is truly wasted. Anything that doesn't directly contribute to a political victory still becomes chum for current and future Democrat Party sharks.

Until recently, the Right has had nothing like this. Conservative donors gravitate toward candidates and think tanks. Only recently have they begun to cut big checks to try to compete with the Moskowitzes and the Arabellas.

It is this class—the consultants and billionaire financiers—who ensured that Joe Biden won in 2020.

In the process, these financiers are assured that the government prioritizes their favorite causes and endeavors. Whether it be through direct funding, tax incentives, favorable legislation, or simply by leaving them alone, establishment Washington protects the business interests of the wealthy elite. In return, the wealthy elite provide money, resources, and credibility to the administration.

Yes, they are all in the Biden business, and business is good.

PART II

THE BIDEN DOCTRINE:

SPEAK LOUDLY AND CARRY A SMALL STICK

CHAPTER 5

Withdrawn, but Not Forgotten

THE AFGHANISTAN CALAMITY

One of the most repeated phrases about Joe Biden is from former defense secretary Robert Gates, who said of the vice president in 2014, "I think he has been wrong on nearly every major foreign policy and national security issue over the past four decades."

His decision-making when it comes to Afghanistan was certainly not an exception. He was even skeptical that the late-night raid on Osama bin Laden's Abbottabad, Pakistan, compound would be successful (according to Obama himself).[1]

It has been another decade since Gates uttered those immortal words, and somehow, Joe Biden's record has only gotten worse.

The clearest example of this phenomenon since he has been president was his mismanagement of America's withdrawal from Afghanistan in 2021.

The hours and days immediately following America's pullout on August 15, 2021, were marked by chaos, horror, and death. Panicked U.S. embassy staff tried desperately to leave the country, but they weren't alone. Afghans streamed into the airports by the thousands, penetrating any possible gap in fencing and security, trying to circumvent the Taliban and somehow get on a flight out of the country.[2]

The media quickly declared the Afghanistan debacle Joe Biden's "Saigon moment," drawing comparisons to the fall of Saigon at the end of the Vietnam War in 1975. This time, instead of images of U.S. helicopters plucking people from the roof of an apartment building, we watched people fall from evacuation planes.[3]

The establishment media had protected Joe Biden to this point in his term, but there was nothing nice to say about what was unfolding before our eyes.

The world collectively gasped at video footage of Afghans trampling over one another as they flooded runways and tried to mount the outside of C-17 military transport aircraft, gripping the sides of the plane, literally holding on for dear life. Some of them managed to cling to the aircraft even after takeoff. Minutes later, they would plummet to their deaths. The remains of one person who must have had a particularly strong grip were found four miles from where the plane took off.[4] Rarely has there been a picture of desperation so vivid.

An Afghani American who advised four four-star U.S. generals told Breitbart News, "The people didn't know what to do. There was no control. The airport was completely open. There was no security left. Everybody took off their uniform. They were scared."[5]

U.S. and Turkish forces, who were previously in charge of airport security, shot at some of the Afghans overwhelming the airport. At least one U.S. service member fired what was supposed to be a warning shot that killed a man. The Turks took a far more extreme tack: they opened fire into a crowd of civilians including women and children, killing as many as twenty of them.[6]

One American service member described how Taliban factions were openly executing Afghans in broad daylight, forcing many evacuees to escape secretly in the dead of the night. "We had these 18-, 19-, 20-year-old [American] kids witness these Taliban dudes just schwacking people . . . just taking a rifle, grabbing it by the barrel and just swinging for the fences and cracking people in the body and on the head, whatever, trying to push people back," the service member said.[7] A distraught American citizen whose daughter was trampled to death during the airport stampede was heard crying and screaming: "Fuck, I'm not going to America. Fuck America, my child is gone. I'm not going anywhere. Fuck America."[8]

One plane was briefly hijacked.[9]

It was anarchy.

Reports indicate that Afghan women and girls who were attempting to make their way through the crowds at the airport were beaten, shot, sexually assaulted, trampled, and forced to stand in wastewater for extended periods of time.[10]

Despite allegedly prioritizing the evacuation of high-risk women, data from the Departments of State and Homeland Security reveal that only 25 percent of those evacuated from Afghanistan were women or girls, significantly lower than the historical female average for emergency refugee outflows.[11] That means women and girls were disproportionately left behind.

Next came the reprisal killings. The Taliban went door-to-door looking for Afghan security members the U.S. government had left behind. The jihadi group vowed to govern in an equitable manner, at least relative to what the world had come to expect from them. They had promised an amnesty for Afghan security forces and government workers, for instance. But this proved to be a lie. A *New York Times* analysis reveals that nearly five hundred former government officials and members of the Afghan security forces were killed or forcibly disappeared during the Taliban's first six months back in power.[12]

But the most frightening yet predictable result of America's precipitous withdrawal was that terrorists of the region would mobilize.[13] Biden had entrusted the security of the capital, Kabul, to the Taliban. The Taliban is deeply aligned with the Haqqani Network, which is a hybrid terrorist organization and organized crime syndicate. The Haqqani Network is deeply tied to al-Qaeda.[14] Taliban's Kabul security chief is Khalil Ur-Rahman Haqqani, a key member of the family at the center of the network.

Though the Biden administration tried to portray ISIS and the Taliban as rival entities, the Pentagon admitted that one of the first moves the Taliban made upon seizing power was to release thousands of ISIS terrorists from prisons.[15] ISIS's presence in the country would spread like wildfire as the Taliban rose.[16]

Afghanistan was a powder keg.

IT SOMEHOW GETS WORSE: THE DEADLY DRONE ATTACK

On August 26, suicide bombings outside Hamid Karzai International Airport and the Baron Hotel in Kabul killed more than 170 people, including thirteen U.S. service members.[17] ISIS-K claimed responsibility for the attack. (The *K* in *ISIS-K* refers to "Khorasan," which is a region that includes parts of Afghanistan, Iran, and other Central Asian countries.) One Afghan witness told the *Washington Post*: "People were burning alive, people could not breathe."[18]

A desperate President Biden vowed revenge: "I've ordered my commanders to develop operational plans to strike ISIS-K assets, leadership, and facilities. We will respond with force and precision at our time at the place we choose in a moment of our choosing."[19] Beginning two days later, the U.S. military spent its final days in the country conducting drone strikes against individuals alleged to have been responsible for the airport bombing. On August 28, the U.S. claimed that an "over-the-horizon" counterterrorism strike (aka an aerial attack with an unmanned drone) killed two high-profile ISIS-K targets in Nangarhar Province in eastern Afghanistan with no civilian casualties.[20]

The next day a second drone strike targeted a white Toyota Corolla in Kabul driven by a suspected ISIS-K threat. U.S. Army general Mark Milley celebrated the second attack as a "righteous strike," and for days the Pentagon insisted it had been conducted properly.

It was soon revealed that the drone strike was a catastrophic error.

Ten Afghan civilians were killed, including seven children.[21] U.S. Central Command (CENTCOM) confirmed that "no Isis fighters are believed to have been killed in the attack."[22]

As of mid-2023, no one has been publicly held accountable for the deadly mistake, or anything else that occurred during the entire calamitous operation.[23]

A year later, Representative James Comer (R-TN) summed it up starkly but accurately: "[T]he American people have not received any answers about this national security and humanitarian catastrophe. U.S. servicemen and women lost their lives, thousands of Americans were abandoned, billions of taxpayer dollars are still unaccounted for, military equipment fell into the hands of the Taliban, progress for Afghan women has stalled, and the entire region is under hostile Taliban control."[24]

As they so often do, the Chinese government used Biden's failings as a propaganda coup. From their "Report on Human Rights Violations in the United States in 2021"[25]:

Washington has a history of ignoring basic humanitarianism for its own selfish ends. In the chaos at Kabul airport, a U.S. C-17 transport plane forcibly took off regardless of the safety of Afghan civilians, with someone crushed to death in the wheel well while the plane retracted its landing gear, and others falling to their deaths from the air. Even in the last minutes of the frantic evacuation, U.S. army's air strikes caused heavy civilian casualties. However, the U.S. Defense Department publicly said that no U.S. military personnel would be punished for the deaths of civilians in drone strikes.

What was already a devastating loss instantly became a tool to weaken America's reputation abroad.

BIDEN LIED, PEOPLE DIED

By the time of the withdrawal, the war in Afghanistan—the longest in American history—had become deeply unpopular. Though the nation was divided on seemingly everything else, Democrats, Republicans, and Independents all agreed on this issue.[26]

According to the Associated Press, 2,448 American service members and 3,846 U.S. contractors were killed in the war in Afghanistan through April 2021.[27] The war cost $2.3 trillion, according to a report from Brown University's Watson Institute.[28]

Biden, who had put faith in his political instincts for the last half century, knew he had to get out. But how?

In retrospect, we now know he had no idea.

On April 12, 2021, Biden gave a speech announcing a U.S. unconditional pullout from Afghanistan by September 11, 2021. Circling any specific date on the calendar for ending a hostile conflict is a dubious (read: idiotic) strategy. It allows the enemy to plan and calibrate. Biden clearly chose this specific date, September 11, for symbolic reasons. But that symbolism would benefit our jihadi enemies far more than Americans. Biden sent a signal that they could declare victory over our country on exactly the twentieth anniversary of when their predecessors committed the greatest act of terrorism on American soil in history. This was bound to become a propaganda tool for radical Islamic terrorists.

During Biden's speech and in the months that followed, he gave several reasons for withdrawal, and as is often the case, they were inaccurate or misleading.[29] Here are some of the most noteworthy falsehoods:

It Was All Trump's Fault

As was the case with other parts of Joe Biden's agenda that were failing, Joe Biden attempted to blame the Afghanistan debacle on former president Donald Trump. The substance of his claim was that Trump's Doha Agreement, forged in February 2020, had left Biden in an impossible position, and he had to choose between horrific options.[30] The accord, which was named for the Qatari city in which it was signed, required certain conditions to be met by the Taliban before a complete withdrawal could take place, most notably that the jihadi group had to cut ties with al-Qaeda.[31] Trump had promised that the U.S. would be out of Afghanistan by May 2021, months before Biden's withdrawal deadline, but only if all the conditions were met, including that there would be no attacks plotted against Americans on Afghan soil. The Taliban would also need to participate in "intra-Afghan dialogue" to pursue a lasting peace.

The Biden administration heavily criticized Trump's deal as weak; it also suffered from relying on the quintessentially unreliable Taliban as a peace partner.[32]

But that's why the Trump administration insisted that commitments needed to be met for withdrawal. He maintained that the "withdrawal would be guided by facts on the ground."[33]

Biden misrepresented Trump's position, but more importantly, he didn't bother to renegotiate the deal or forge a new one himself (he did push back the deadline of the Doha Agreement several months, but that clearly didn't do any good).

When Biden took over, his administration removed the conditions, conceding that he would have withdrawn from Afghanistan regardless of what the Doha Agreement stipulated.[34] Even still, that did not stop him from pleading that it was Doha that was the real reason America's exit from the region went so badly.[35]

Even establishment media outlets like the Associated Press[36] and the *Wall Street Journal*, as well as the liberal Brookings Institution,[37] faulted Biden's approach.[38] Yet he stuck to his guns. In April 2023, more than a year and a half later, and, more relevantly, two weeks before he announced his run for reelection in 2024, Joe Biden and his National Security Council released a report laying the blame squarely at the feet of Donald Trump.[39]

The Taliban Will Not Take Afghanistan

In July 2021, amid growing fears that we weren't prepared for the massive evacuation that was coming, Biden made a statement that would become infamous: "There's going to be no circumstance where you see people being lifted off the roof of an embassy . . . the likelihood there's going to be Taliban overrunning everything and owning the whole country is highly unlikely."[40] This claim would age poorly, but that didn't stop Biden from doubling down on this false promise on national TV. Speaking with George Stephanopoulos on August 18, right as Kabul was descending into chaos, Biden claimed, without evidence, that U.S. personnel had taken back control of the airport. Then he promised that "if there's American citizens left, we're gonna stay to get them all out."

The Taliban quickly overran and took control of everything, and we didn't stay to get everyone out. Though there were no rooftop evacuations, as previously noted, far worse things happened involving desperate people and aircraft.

Thousands of Americans were left to fend for themselves.[41]

Biden's secretary of state, Antony Blinken, also served up false promises, claiming during a June 2021 House Foreign Affairs Committee hearing that there would be no urgent need to evacuate the U.S. embassy in Afghanistan: "We're staying, our embassy's staying . . . if there is a significant deterioration in security, I don't think it's going to be something that happens from a Friday to a Monday."[42] But two months later, in mid-August, a "Friday-to-Monday" disaster is literally what happened when the Taliban violently and swiftly swept through Kabul over the course of a weekend, forcing a dramatic acceleration of embassy evacuations.[43]

Afghan Forces Could Defend the Country Without American Troops

The claim that Afghan forces were prepared to defend themselves was either the most embarrassingly naïve opinion Biden offered up or the most blatant lie of them all. The premise proved to be absurd the instant Americans began to evacuate the country. The Taliban immediately overwhelmed the Afghani government and seized control. President Mohammad Ashraf Ghani quickly fled the country himself. According to BBC reporter Kawoon Khamoosh, "Ghani escaped with bags full of 169 million U.S. dollars."[44]

That's a lot of cash for someone who intends to return to a country and lead it to glory.

Ghani would still lay claim to being the head of state, despite the fact that he took up residence in the United Arab Emirates.[45]

Within days, the Taliban appeared to be firmly in control, yet Biden and his team continued to optimistically prognosticate that Afghan forces could win out in the end. This was nonsense. In actuality, during the days leading up to the fall of Kabul on August 16, 2021, Biden had received "numerous intelligence assessments that a partial or total collapse of Afghan government forces was the most likely scenario," according to a House Foreign Affairs Committee report.[46]

John Sopko, who serves as special inspector general for Afghan reconstruction (SIGAR), told an NPR reporter that he testified a stunning "50 or 60 times" that "the Afghans couldn't sustain what we were giving them."[47] He warned of everything from poor logistics to "ghost soldiers," who are nonexistent personnel, fictional employees fabricated specifically to draw more American funding. The Pentagon inspector general confirmed their existence—rather, nonexistence—as part of schemes to grift the American taxpayers.[48]

"Afghanistan political leaders gave up and fled the country," Biden said matter-of-factly in a White House speech on August 16. "The Afghan military collapsed, sometimes without trying to fight."[49]

He said this as if he hadn't been warned countless times that exactly this would happen.

Advisors Supported the Full Withdrawal

Two days after Biden's speech, *Politico* published an article citing multiple sources claiming that even some of Biden's closest advisors at the Pentagon disagreed with his withdrawal strategy. "The Pentagon is not making these decisions," sources said, reporting that it was Antony Blinken and National Security Advisor Jake Sullivan who were truly "running the Pentagon."[50]

Biden told Stephanopoulos in the same August 18 interview that he could not recall any military advisor counseling him to keep 2,500 troops

in Afghanistan to maintain stability and conduct counterterrorism efforts.[51] However, the commander of CENTCOM in the run-up to the
evacuation, General Kenneth "Frank" McKenzie, specifically testified, "My
concern was that if we withdrew below 2,500 and went to zero, that the Afghan military and government would collapse."[52] Chairman of the Joint
Chiefs of Staff Army general Mark Milley agreed with his colleague, testifying: "My assessment was, back in the fall of '20 and it remained consistent throughout, that we should keep a steady state of 2,500."[53]

Military commanders expressed deep concern that a Taliban takeover would make the country a safe harbor for terrorists similar to what
it was before September 11, 2001.[54] Biden didn't think a Taliban takeover
would happen. We instantly found out who was right.

The U.S. Would Need "a Hell of a Lot" More Troops to Stay in Afghanistan

Biden introduced another (almost assuredly false) justification for a full
and immediate pullout, regardless of downstream consequences: the
alternative would be to drastically increase America's presence in the region. During an August 2021 speech, Biden said, "We were left with a
simple decision: Either follow through on the commitment made by the
last administration and leave Afghanistan, or say we weren't leaving and
commit another tens of thousands more troops. Going back to war. That
was the choice, the real choice."[55]

This was a false dichotomy. There were, of course, other options,
including those put forward by Biden's most trusted military advisors.
An example is the aforementioned recommendations of Secretary of
Defense Austin, General Milley, and General McKenzie to reduce troop
levels to 2,500.[56]

Biden would repeat this bogus argument well into 2022,[57] which did
not make it any more true.

Biden's Plan Had the Support of America's Allies

"I have seen no question of credibility from our allies around the world.
I have spoken with our NATO allies. . . . [T]his is about America leading
the world, and our allies have agreed with that," Biden said on August 20,

2021.[58] However, this was, yet again, entirely false. According to an official interviewed by the House Foreign Affairs Committee, crucial allies "favored a conditions-based approach but the President at the end did not."[59] "The Biden government have just come in and, without looking at what is happening on the ground, have taken a unilateral decision, throwing us and everybody else to the fire," Parliament member and former British defense minister Khalid Mahmood said.

It didn't stop there. Officials and diplomats from American allies all around the world eviscerated Biden:

"Withdrawal under these circumstances would be perceived as a strategic victory for the Taliban, which would weaken the Alliance and embolden extremists the world over."
—General Nick Carter, British chief of defense staff, 2021

"The reason the United States pulled all of its forces out was that President Biden was following a political agenda."
—Australian Foreign Affairs, Defence, and Trade References Committee, January 2022

"I say this with a heavy heart and with horror over what is happening, but the early withdrawal was a serious and far-reaching miscalculation by the current administration. This does fundamental damage to the political and moral credibility of the West."
—Norbert Röttgen, chairman of the Foreign Affairs Committee of Germany's Bundestag, August 2021

"He hasn't just humiliated America's Afghan allies. He's humiliated his Western allies by demonstrating their impotence."[60]
—Rory Stewart, former British cabinet minister

Dishonesty, excuses, and buck passing defined Biden's response to what was arguably the worst decision of his presidency. The lack of humility is quintessential Biden. Yet all the lying and all the excuses could not change the devastating reality about what happened on the ground.

THE HORRIFYING NUMBERS

Overall, 124,000 people were evacuated by the U.S. during the "military evacuation phase" of the withdrawal, according to the Biden administration. This included 2,000 U.S. embassy personnel, 5,530 U.S. citizens, and 3,335 "third-country nationals."[61]

The U.S. Department of Homeland Security claims that of those evacuated, more than 82,000 were not U.S. citizens. In fact, more than 36,000 of these evacuees had no history of working with the U.S. and were not supposed to be prioritized.[62] These numbers become more outrageous when put into context. The Biden administration officially abandoned more than 800 Americans in Afghanistan; initially, they falsely claimed only 100–200 were left behind enemy lines.[63] Even the State Department itself failed to evacuate all its locally employed Afghan staff.[64]

But many in the media believed that number was wildly underestimated. In the *Washington Post*, Josh Rogin wrote that a Biden official told him that number was closer to ten thousand. Sources in Afghanistan told the *Daily Mail* the number might be four times that.[65]

Nearly fifty American children were trapped in terrorist territory for longer than a month.[66]

Why were so many non-Americans prioritized over Americans? Why was anyone prioritized by our federal government over American children?

Afghan security personnel were instrumental to the limited success America had in the region, yet only six hundred of those security personnel were officially evacuated.[67]

Many Afghan children, 1,450 in fact, were evacuated without their parents. Efforts to reunite many of these separated children with their relatives took months after they arrived in the U.S.[68]

Senator Jim Risch (R-ID) testified to Congress in October 2021 that the State Department had received 16,668 evacuation requests, but only 110 of those people had been successfully evacuated. In other words, the "U.S. State Department was 99.3% non-responsive to these members' requests."[69]

In addition to the thirteen U.S. soldiers who were killed during the evacuation process,[70] forty-five U.S. service members were injured and

160 Afghans were killed, according to a House Foreign Affairs Committee report.[71]

The Pentagon reported that the U.S. left $7.12 billion of military equipment in Afghanistan upon our departure. This includes aircraft, air-to-ground weaponry, other military vehicles, munitions, and communications equipment.[72]

The Biden administration simply dropped a $7.12 billion windfall of U.S. military equipment in the Taliban's lap, including:[73]

- 208 aircraft, including UH-60 Black Hawks and M-17 helicopters, between 2003 and 2016[74]

- 61,000 military vehicles of all types,[75] including more than 2,000 armored vehicles and Mine-Resistant, Ambush-Protected (MRAP) vehicles

- 258,000 rifles, including M-16s and AK-47s

- 56,000 machine guns

- 31,000 rocket-propelled and handheld grenade launchers

- 18,000 "gravity" bombs

- 16,000 aviation rockets

- 1,845 D-30 mortar systems with more than a million mortar rounds

- 224 D-130 howitzer artillery guns

- 30 million rounds of ammunition

- 17,400 night-vision devices

- 95 small drones

- body armor

- biometric security equipment

There were likely other beneficiaries of this bounty besides the Taliban. Our sophisticated weaponry and convoys of military vehicles could easily have fallen into the hands of Iran's Islamic Revolutionary Guards Corps or other hostile actors in the region. Two months after the evacuation, in October 2021, U.S. supplies were already for sale by Afghani gun dealers.[76]

THE ABANDONED AIRFIELDS

The fall of Kabul got immense media attention, and for good reason, but it wasn't the only strategic blunder involving an important Afghan air base. In fact, it wasn't even the first.

Bagram Air Base (also known as Bagram Airfield) sits twenty-five miles north of Kabul and was known for being the "crown jewel of U.S. Intelligence Operations in the region." It was a "key hub for air support for everything that we were doing over there for the last 20 years."[77] On July 2, 2021, the U.S. abandoned the base in the middle of the night without even notifying the Afghan commander in charge. "In one night, they lost all the goodwill of 20 years by leaving the way they did, in the night, without telling the Afghan soldiers who were outside patrolling the area," said one Afghan soldier.[78] Within twenty minutes of the U.S.'s departure, Bagram's electricity was shut off, which caused "sudden darkness" of the surrounding areas. Next, according to Afghan military officials, was looting, ransacking, and destruction.[79]

Former intelligence officer Khushal Safi, an Afghan native, called the evacuation of Bagram "the original sin of the evacuation" and "the dumbest thing anybody could have ever done. At what point do you believe abandoning one of the largest airfields in the world is a good thing?"[80] The loss of access to a secure, technically advanced airfield made it impossible for key personnel and American citizens to be evacuated safely. Losing Bagram also meant losing the only staging area for drones and other special operations aircraft needed for counterterrorism efforts.[81]

There were also five thousand prisoners who were being detained at the base. These weren't petty criminals; there were heavy hitters from the Taliban, al-Qaeda, and ISIS, who were ultimately released when the Taliban eventually took control over Bagram.[82] When the U.S. left, thousands of offenders in all were let free.[83]

In retrospect, this was all a precursor to what would occur weeks later in Kabul, and it would provide the Taliban a strategic advantage that would be ruinous for America's chances for a successful withdrawal.

The Biden strategy of precipitous withdrawal was coming into focus, and it would be solidified when America let Kabul fall to the Taliban.

As hard as it is to believe, the Taliban initially offered the Biden administration the opportunity to secure Kabul, but U.S. generals declined the offer.[84] Here is an exasperating passage from a House Foreign Affairs Committee report on the "strategic" failure of the Afghanistan withdrawal:

> On August 15, 2021, Taliban representatives met with the Special Envoy [Zalmay] Khalilzad and Gen. Frank McKenzie in Doha, Qatar. There, they discussed who would maintain security of Kabul during the evacuation. Kabul is Afghanistan's capital and most populous city, being the home to one out of every ten Afghans.
>
> The Taliban reportedly offered the U.S. the opportunity to secure Kabul, telling them, "we want you to have it," Special Envoy Khalilzad told the Committee Minority. The offer was first reported by *The Washington Post* and subsequently confirmed by Special Envoy Khalilzad and Gen. McKenzie.
>
> While still serving the Biden administration, Special Envoy Khalilzad told a reporter the Taliban were willing to stay out of Kabul and allow the U.S. to secure the city, telling the Americans, "we want you to take it."
>
> But Gen. McKenzie declined the offer. In testimony to Congress in September 2021, Gen. McKenzie explained his response, saying, "That was not why I was there, that was not my instruction, and we did not have the resources to undertake that mission."[85]

The report would go on to say that if the U.S. had secured Kabul, "it would not have needed the Taliban to secure the outer perimeter of the airport—a task the Taliban proved incapable of performing."[86]

We were given the option to not walk the plank, and we didn't take it.

The White House press secretary echoed McKenzie's fatal sentiment:

"Our objective has never been—and the President has been very clear about this—having a military presence to control Kabul. So, that's never been our objective."[87] At least their messaging was consistent.

Members of the House Foreign Affairs Committee concluded that ceding the Kabul airport was the key security failure that allowed for ISIS-K to commit the terror attack that led to the widespread death of Americans and our allies.

THE COST OF WAR

Since the invasion of Afghanistan in 2001, the war has cost the U.S. a staggering $2.46 trillion.[88] According to an analysis by *Forbes*, that comes out to "$300 million per day, every day, for two decades. Or $50,000 for each of Afghanistan's 40 million people.[89] We spent $800 billion on direct war fighting costs. The rest was allocated to things like training and payroll for Afghan soldiers, and of course, feeding the military-industrial complex."[90]

For nonenlisted men and women, war is incredibly good business. Since 2001, when the Afghanistan war began, payments to military contractors by the Department of Defense has risen more than 160 percent, and by 2020 were taking up nearly half of DOD's entire budget.[91] Despite concerns from critics who have long warned against "the concentration of defense contracts among just a handful of large firms," the majority of these contracts have been awarded to "five major corporations: Lockheed Martin, Boeing, General Dynamics, Raytheon, and Northrop Grumman."[92] The "$75 billion in Pentagon contracts received by Lockheed Martin in FY 2020 is well over one and one-half times the entire budget for the State Department and Agency for International Development for that year, which totaled $44 billion,"[93] according to a report from Brown University's Watson Institute.

During the twenty years of the war, the federal government spent nearly a trillion dollars more on Afghanistan than it spent on education programs in the U.S.[94] (Though, to be fair, both budget items have proven to be epically wasteful.)

What's more, financial expenditures don't end when a war is over. The U.S. government will provide a lifetime of medical and disability care to American veterans of all the post-9/11 wars, with estimated future costs of around $2.2 trillion through the year 2050.[95] Interest on money borrowed to fund the war continues to accrue.

Yet, as is always the case, the human cost of war is more severe than the financial cost. In total, there were approximately 2,500 U.S. military deaths in Afghanistan, and nearly 4,000 more U.S. civilian contractors were killed. The Afghan death total was far greater: 69,000 Afghan military police and 47,000 Afghan civilians perished. (An estimated 53,000 opposition fighters died during the conflict.[96])

In 2001, before the war started, 62 percent of Afghans faced food insecurity; by 2022, that number had increased to 92 percent.[97] Prior to the war, only 9 percent of Afghan children under five experienced malnutrition. In today's Afghanistan, 50 percent of children now suffer from the debilitating effects of undernourishment.[98] Roughly 80 percent of Afghans were living in poverty before the war. Now that the war has ended, nearly the entire country (97 percent) is living below the poverty line.[99] It remains one of the poorest countries in the world. In other words, things got immeasurably worse for the people of Afghanistan during this time.

It wasn't Joe Biden who caused the extent of the morass, but it was his shortfalls as a leader that assured we salvaged nothing of value from the wreckage. Unless, of course, you held one of those defense contracts.

All this for a war that failed, proving accurate the worst perceptions of America's twenty-first-century foreign policy. Freedom and democracy were not exported (was that ever really the point?), but billions of dollars were allocated to the ever-expanding war industry. There is no chance of a lasting peace in the region, especially with America long gone.

AFTERMATH

Upon America's withdrawal from Afghanistan, the void was filled by the worst actors on the planet. The Taliban, al-Qaeda, and ISIS all became stronger. Russia and China got to savor watching their primary geopolitical foe suffer a humiliation on the world stage. CCP state media immediately declared that China was the real winner of the Afghanistan debacle.[100] China shares a small section of border with Afghanistan and saw America's pullout as a business opportunity. Naturally, this excited the Taliban as well, which accepted Beijing's offer to help "rebuild" Afghanistan.[101]

In early 2023, the Taliban and China's Xinjiang Central Asia Petroleum and Gas Company signed an oil extraction deal.[102] China and the Taliban's partnership is bound to deepen.

As the world's largest opium producer, Afghanistan profits greatly from the narcotics that are made from it. Though the United States spent billions trying to eradicate opium poppy fields, Reuters still describes the illegal drug trade as a "boon" for the Taliban.[103] They'll only produce more, now that we're gone.

In the months following America's withdrawal, starving Afghans sold their young daughters to old men for as little as one thousand dollars.[104]

In Afghanistan, the rise of the Taliban proved to be utterly devastating for the women of the region. Less than ten days after the Taliban took over the country, their official spokesman, Zabihullah Mujahid, ordered females to stay home until further notice. The rationale as presented to the public was that their soldiers were not trained to respect women.[105] Apparently any training that has been done since has not been effective, as the semi-lockdown has not been revoked at the time of this writing. In fact, things have gotten worse.

Women have been barred from gyms and parks. They are ordered to cover their face in public. They are not allowed to work in most industries. Their travel is heavily restricted.[106]

Amnesty International published a report in 2022 claiming that women were being arbitrarily detained for minor infractions of the Taliban's rules, leading to harassment, arrest, and even forcible disappearance and torture.[107]

Kelley Curie, former ambassador-at-large for the State Department's Office of Global Women's Issues, blamed one man in particular: Joe Biden. "This is the legacy of the Biden administration in Afghanistan: failing to listen to the Afghan women who warned that the Taliban still were the same monsters, and who instead partnered with those monsters on a botched evacuation that cost Afghan women everything and shamed our nation," she wrote.[108]

The withdrawal from Afghanistan was a 360-degree disaster. So much blood and treasure lost, yet the region became even more perilous. It was a resounding defeat for the concept of American nation-building and Western globalism. Even though they made billions of dollars in the process, the military-industrial complex had never looked more dastardly and ineffectual.

It was also the most resounding failure of Joe Biden's fifty-year political career.

So surely heads rolled?

On the contrary.

That's not how Joe Biden's Washington works.

In our nation's capital, the more egregious the error, the fewer people get held to account. So, in this case, every individual responsible for the disastrous decision making was still in a position of power at the time this book was written. In retrospect, the lack of accountability was inevitable.

The Biden administration continues to be opaque, obstructing efforts to obtain greater details about the debacle, all the while blaming his top political rival, Donald Trump, who was out of power when the relevant events occurred. SIGAR John Sopko claims that in many cases the Biden administration "simply ignored our communications, refused to make staff available for interviews, or refused to permit SIGAR to travel internationally to conduct research."[109] President Biden himself has been resistant to a thorough review.[110]

Calls for impeachment ricocheted around the conservative ecosystem in the immediate aftermath, but Republicans didn't have the votes in the Democrat-controlled Congress.

Though Biden's presidency survived the catastrophic withdrawal of American forces from Afghanistan, many American and Afghani innocents did not.

Only time will tell if his reputation—or America's—will fully recover.

CHAPTER 6

Joe Biden's Undeniable Role in Ukraine's Invasion of Russia

The conflict in Ukraine occurred at the hands of anti-Western strong-man and Russian president Vladimir Putin when he invaded the country on February 24, 2022, but President Joe Biden and his administration failed to contain it and, perhaps more importantly, missed opportunities to avoid it completely.

Any good foreign policy requires both strength and diplomacy. When it comes to Russia and Ukraine, Biden did not have much of either. This should hardly be a surprise, particularly if you are familiar with Gates's quote about Biden's abysmal international record.[1]

In the time leading up to Russia's invasion and throughout the conflict in Ukraine, Biden has consistently shown weakness in areas where he should have shown strength, while showing reckless obstinance in places where he should have shown diplomatic prudence. His approach has not only proven inelegant, it has also been wasteful. Joe Biden's decisions played an undeniable role in Putin's invasion of Ukraine, a situation that has brought the U.S. to its closest proximity to nuclear war in decades.

Russia's relationship with Ukraine is long, complex, and bloody. Russian forces had been fighting in eastern Ukraine since 2014, after Ukraine's pro-Russia government was ousted in favor of a new, Western-backed administration. Russia sees Ukraine as part of itself and has long taken a dim view of Ukrainian nationalism.[2] On top of that, Ukraine is a vital energy corridor and provides access to the Black Sea.[3]

Ukraine, of course, doesn't care about any of that. It sees itself as an independent nation and culture—a nation and culture that was the victim of the Soviet-orchestrated genocide under Joseph Stalin.[4]

The conflict doesn't just speak to practical political and economic concerns, but both nations' basic sense of identity. More modern concerns about energy and military alliances only exacerbated these long-running divides.

Just over a year after Biden took office, the conflict in Ukraine became a full-scale war. It also became a domestic political obsession. Leaked U.S. military assessments estimated that, as of February 2023, as many as 354,000 soldiers had been killed or injured fighting in Ukraine.[5] The U.S. devoted $75 billion in assistance to Ukraine, including $46.6 billion in military aid, in the first thirteen months of fighting.[6] Those numbers will have gone up substantially by the time you read this book. The cost on the Russian side is impossible to determine.

The outbreak of war has supercharged that divide, with the Ukrainian cause becoming a rallying cry for American establishment liberals and neoconservatives, and anathema to antiwar populists and libertarians. The discussion in the U.S. quickly became polarized. The establishment media framed it as though either we write a blank check to Ukraine president Volodymyr Zelensky, or we are with Putin. I'm oversimplifying a bit for emphasis, but not by much. Yes, it is possible to support Ukraine's cause and even loathe Putin and not believe the U.S. should involve ourselves in a border dispute halfway around the world.

But now is not the time for nuance! We are all rallying around the blue and yellow flag!

Ukraine instantly became a cause célèbre, literally. Ben Stiller, Bono, Angelina Jolie, and Sean Penn were among the Hollywood stars parading through the country to signal their virtue—and Zelensky's.

At first blush, it was a David-and-Goliath story on a grand scale. The charismatic and energetic Zelensky, a sitcom star turned politician, somehow managed to hold the line against international supervillain Vladimir Putin.

What was not to love? As it turns out, plenty. Both sides are master propagandists, so it immediately became difficult to sort out what was true and what was fake news. The conflict quickly got expensive for America, and there was little accountability for where the money was being spent.

It remains exasperatingly illogical that Ukraine's border with Russia is a bigger obsession in American media than our border with Mexico.

Then, of course, there is the elephant in the room: Russia has the most nuclear weapons in the world.

America was suddenly thrust into an international conflict of extreme magnitude, yet we blew past what I believe is an essential question: How did we get here?

Whether we should have funded Ukraine at all or if Zelensky is an amazing guy, Joe Biden's inconsistency, indecisiveness, and mismanagement of crucial diplomatic relationships played an indisputable role in the escalation of the Ukraine-Russia conflict.

We were promised that under President Biden, a supposed foreign relations expert, the U.S. and the world would once again have a steady hand guiding geopolitics, especially in Eastern Europe. Instead, the world is at its most tense moment in decades.

A HISTORY OF WEAKNESS

Biden has made America weaker on the world stage. This is well known by our hostile foreign governments, including Russia. First, by canceling the Keystone XL pipeline, he hobbled American energy production, intentionally making our nation less energy independent.

Other countries such as Germany had already ceded their energy independence to Russia by shutting down their nuclear power plants.[7] Germany had embraced Russia's Nord Stream pipeline as their main source of natural gas; they also get roughly half of their coal from Russia and more than a third of their oil.[8] Biden and Secretary of State Tony Blinken knew Germany's dependence on Russia was a huge liability for our ally.[9] Yet they failed to show leadership and convince the Germans that they were making a mistake that allowed Putin immense leverage.

In the early days of the Russian invasion, the U.S. was importing nearly 600,000 barrels of Russian oil per day. The Keystone XL pipeline would have brought in more than 800,000 barrels of oil per day, which would have allowed Biden to immediately ban Russian oil imports from the U.S. But Biden's energy strategy, as documented thoroughly later in this book, avoided tapping our own natural resources, which is horrific strategy when one of your chief rivals (Russia) is an energy powerhouse.

Initially, Biden's rhetoric wasn't even tough. When speaking about a potential Russian invasion of Ukraine at a White House news conference on January 19, 2022, Biden said, "Russia will be held accountable if it invades and it depends on what it does." "It's one thing if it's a minor incursion and we end up having to fight about what to do and not do, but if they actually do what they're capable of doing with the forces amassed on the border, it is going to be a disaster for Russia if they further invade Ukraine."[10]

These comments signaled that the U.S. would tolerate a "minor incursion," which was almost certainly seen as a green light for Putin. Biden's prattle about "fighting about what to do and not do" also signaled that members of the North Atlantic Treaty Organization (NATO) were not aligned on how they would handle such an incursion given that Ukraine is not part of NATO.[11]

Biden showed more weakness still when he tried to work with the Russians on an Iranian nuclear deal in the midst of Russia's Ukraine invasion. Donald Trump had abandoned the nuclear agreement with Iran that was cut during the second half of the Obama/Biden administration in 2018.[12]

The Joint Comprehensive Plan of Action (JCPOA) of 2015, or as it is colloquially known, the Iran nuclear deal, was one of Obama/Biden's signature foreign policy accomplishments, despite the fact that the deal was never sent to the Senate for ratification (or even scrutiny). Hundreds of retired generals and admirals warned that the pact was "defective," and they were correct.[13] The crux of the agreement was that the West would drop economic sanctions on Iran so long as Iran accepted restrictions on their nuclear program, including inspections. Critics rightly argued the accountability mechanisms were nonexistent and it was highly likely that Iran would use the infusion of cash for (you guessed it) their own nuclear development.[14]

Russia was essential to brokering the deal and, theoretically, enforcing it. Russian president Vladimir Putin was so necessary to the JCPOA's success that Obama singled him out for praise.[15] Reviving it empowers Putin on the world stage, yet Biden chose to do exactly that at the most inopportune time.[16] While Biden publicly talked tough, calling Putin "a butcher" in March 2022,[17] he was privately engaging with Russia on the new Iran nuclear agreement.

Details of the proposed deal that leaked mere weeks after Putin's invasion of Ukraine were frightening. "It reportedly offers the regime access to $90 billion in foreign currency; $7 billion in effective ransom for U.S. captives; and sanctions relief for the Iran Revolutionary Guard Corps and other notorious terrorists," Breitbart News' resident Middle East expert, Joel Pollak, wrote at the time.[18]

The deal was unpopular, even among Democrats.[19] Two officials who were a part of the U.S. negotiating group resigned after expressing concerns that the U.S. was about to give up far more sanctions relief with little gains in the realm of security.[20]

In November 2022, Iran acknowledged that they were supplying Russia with drones.[21]

As of December 2022, the Iran nuclear deal was no longer being pursued by Biden.[22] But for how long?

LIBERATING THE MERCHANT OF DEATH

There has been no weaker moment for Biden during the Ukraine-Russia conflict than in May 2022, when he traded Russian arms dealer Viktor Bout ("The Merchant of Death") in a one-to-one prisoner exchange for WNBA player Brittney Griner.[23] Griner was a thirty-one-year-old, two-time U.S. Olympic champion and a member of the WNBA's Phoenix Mercury. She was in Russia to play in their women's basketball league during the WNBA's off-season. Griner would earn a salary of more than $1 million from the Russian team, nearly five times as much as she makes in the U.S. each season.[24]

Griner was arrested in February 2022 for possessing hash oil at Sheremetyevo International Airport in Moscow. Hash oil is a marijuana concentrate that has high levels of THC. The punishments for pot crimes in Russia are far more severe than in the United States.[25]

She claimed she packed the cartridges accidentally.[26] Griner was convicted of possession and smuggling in August of that year,[27] received a sentence of nine years in prison, and would remain there until December, when Joe Biden swooped in and traded her for the man known as the Merchant of Death.

Viktor Bout is a former Soviet military translator who got into arms dealing in the 1990s after the fall of the Soviet Union.[28] He ran Cold War–era weapons and equipment to warlords, terrorists, and drug cartels in Africa and the Middle East. One of Bout's clients was a West African Liberian warlord named Charles Taylor, who was convicted of war crimes in connection with his role in the Sierra Leone Civil War of 1991–2002, including sexual slavery, rape, murder, child conscription, and other inhumane acts.[29]

Bout had obtained sixty large aircraft cargo planes that could deploy weapons to almost any given location with pinpoint accuracy.[30] He became a supplier of the Taliban in the mid-1990s after negotiating a deal with its founder, Mullah Omar.[31] The Taliban used Bout's weapons to take control of the southern and western regions of Afghanistan; he reportedly made $50 million from his dealings with them.

Bout is also a strong supporter of Putin's invasion of Ukraine.[32]

Moscow had been considering the idea of a prisoner swap involving Bout and U.S. Marine Corps veteran Paul Whelan in the summer of 2020.[33] The Russians claimed Whelan was arrested over a USB storage drive with a list of names of current employees at a classified Russian agency. He was charged with "espionage" in 2018 and sentenced to sixteen years in prison.

In July it was reported that the U.S. had offered to swap Bout for both Griner and Whelan, but in December 2022, it was revealed that Biden had managed to free only Griner and that Whelan would not be included in the exchange. Whelan's family labeled the trade a "catastrophe"[34] and criticized the U.S. government for not being "more assertive."[35] The failure to free Whelan received widespread criticism.[36]

The decision to focus on Griner was obviously political. Griner had as many woke points as a person could possibly have. She is black, a lesbian, a celebrity, and a left-wing activist (she protested during America's national anthem at WNBA games). She was also one of the top female basketball players in the country. "If it was LeBron [James], he'd be home, right?" Griner's coach on the Phoenix Mercury, Vanessa Nygaard, told reporters prior to her release. This was fundamentally true and impossible to ignore.

Whelan, on the other hand, was a middle-aged white male veteran. Total woke point tally: zero. Russian state TV lampooned the U.S. president for choosing to free a celebrity over an American hero.

This deal wasn't just gross; it sent a signal to the world that any traveling American abroad is potential trade bait for adversarial regimes. Former Drug Enforcement Administration agent Robert Zachariasiewicz summed up the Griner-Bout deal well: "Today's actions just placed a target on back of every United States citizen travelling throughout the world and they just became a commodity. . . . I think we just sent the message that it's really good business to illegally detain and if not kidnap American citizens, and it's really great to have one in your back pocket if you need them for a trade at some point."[37]

Biden sent a clear message to the world: Abduct Americans —especially woke ones—and we will cut a deal with you. You might even get back warmongers who want to kill us, if that's what it takes.

Several months after Griner's release, Russian authorities detained Evan Gershkovich, a reporter for the *Wall Street Journal* based in Russia. Like Whelan, Gershkovich, who covered issues related to the war in Ukraine, was accused of accessing classified information related to a Russian arms factory.[38] Following the arrest, Russian officials announced they would be open to discussing a prisoner swap following the trial.[39] Gershkovich doesn't have nearly as many woke points as Griner, so make sure to say a prayer for him.

Nonetheless, so long as our rivals feel like they can get what they want out of the current administration, expect the abductions to continue.

TALKING TOUGH, ACTING MEEK

Biden's history with Russia has been relatively consistent: he has talked tough and acted meekly.

In 2005, when the George W. Bush administration supported Russia entering the World Trade Organization (WTO), Senator Biden accused Bush of acting as a "friend" and "partner" of Putin. "You're being silent on Russia. They are bad guys," Biden exclaimed. Biden trashed Russia in the *Wall Street Journal* in 2009: "They have a shrinking population base, they have a withering economy, they have a banking sector and structure that is not likely to be able to withstand the next 15 years, they're in a situation where the world is changing before them and they're clinging to something in the past that is not sustainable," Biden told the paper.[40]

Powerful words, but as a point of policy, Biden's Russia doctrine has always been to try to maintain good relations. And there's only one way to keep good relations with Putin: give him things that he wants. The Obama/Biden administration helped Russia build up its economy and military and offered unprecedented concessions, including gifting the Russians advanced military technology. As previously noted, they relied on Russia to help broker their nuclear deal with Iran.[41] All this emboldened Putin.

In 2009, Obama/Biden told Russia's placeholder president Dmitri Medvedev via secret letter that the U.S. would abandon plans to deploy a new missile defense system in Eastern Europe.[42]

In 2010, Obama/Biden's New START arms control treaty severely limited the U.S.'s own missile defense options while conceding advantages to Russia's nuclear capabilities.[43] It did not put any limits on tactical nuclear weapons, an area where Russia holds a significant advantage, it did not limit Russia's rail-mobile intercontinental ballistic missiles (ICBMs), and it imposed severe limitations on the U.S. by reducing U.S. missile defense capabilities.

Obama/Biden negotiated a so-called 123 Agreement with Russia allowing the Russian government to sell nuclear materials directly to U.S. companies. A top Obama Foundation donor, Exelon Corporation, benefited from this policy.[44]

The Obama/Biden administration allowed Russia to gain a larger foothold in America's uranium supply, as famously documented in Peter Schweizer's book *Clinton Cash*. About 20 percent of America's uranium was allowed to fall under Russian ownership when they approved the sale of Uranium One, a Canadian firm that mined uranium throughout the world, to Russia's state-owned energy company Rosatom. "Few could have imagined in the past that we would own 20 percent of U.S. reserves," Rosatom's chief executive, Sergei Kiriyenko, once told Putin.[45]

As part of the so-called Russian reset, Obama/Biden helped Russia construct a Silicon Valley–style "innovation city" called Skolkovo. The project ended up resembling more of a military tech-transfer hub than a home for entrepreneurs. The DOD found that "Skolkovo is arguably an overt alternative to clandestine industrial espionage" and that Russia's first hypersonic missiles were developed through research done there.[46]

In the wake of these deals, Russia's gross domestic product (GDP) growth shot up from minus 7.8 percent in 2009 to 4 percent in 2012.[47] The result was clear: Biden and Obama had strengthened the very geopolitical foe Joe loved to trash-talk.

This dynamic painted the backdrop for what was to be a string of unprecedented concessions that were laid at the feet of Putin.[48]

THE BRIGHTEST OF RED LINES

From the 1990s, Biden has been a believer in NATO expansion, saying there is a "powerful moral argument" for it.[49] In essence, the argument was that a stronger NATO means there are fewer states vulnerable to Russian influence.[50] This viewpoint puts Biden at loggerheads with Putin.

Russian leaders have long indicated that the issue of NATO expansion to countries like Ukraine and Georgia is the brightest of red lines for Russia. It is understandable why. If Ukraine entered NATO, it would likely host American ballistic missiles and troops, which would be a direct threat.[51] Any conflict with Ukraine from then on would risk Russia's annihilation. Thus, Putin has viewed Ukraine and Georgia's exclusion from NATO as a top strategic objective.

At the Bucharest Summit in 2008, NATO agreed that Ukraine and Georgia "will become members of NATO," though they did not provide a timeline or circumstances for how and when it would happen.[52] Putin made clear that this was unacceptable to Russia[53] and proceeded to invade Georgia.[54]

In 2014, during the Obama/Biden administration, Ukrainian protesters overthrew the pro-Russian Viktor Yanukovych (who absconded to Russia)[55]; pro-Western Arseniy Yatsenyuk was installed in his stead. Putin saw the situation as a coup backed by NATO and the United States.[56]

At that point, the White House began looking toward Ukraine for leverage over Putin. At the vanguard of this campaign was Victoria Nuland, an ambitious Deep State official who now serves as President Biden's undersecretary of state for political affairs. At the time, Nuland was seen as a rising political star in DC, having served as chief of staff to Bill Clinton's deputy secretary of state Strobe Talbott in the mid-1990s and principal deputy foreign policy advisor to Vice President Dick Cheney during the early days of the Iraq War (2003–2005). After advising the vice president, Nuland was confirmed as U.S. ambassador to NATO, a position she held until 2008, when she joined Obama's State Department, eventually rising up through the ranks to assistant secretary of state for European and Eurasian affairs.

After Yanukovych won the Ukrainian elections in 2010, Nuland went to work supporting his opposition through various nongovernmental organizations (NGOs) in Ukraine that were funded by the U.S. State Department.[57] One such organization, the National Endowment for Democracy (Nuland is on their board as of early 2023), had reportedly established sixty-five projects in Ukraine aimed at training activists, supporting journalists, and mobilizing business organizations.[58] As award-winning journalist Robert Parry pointed out, the vast network of NGOs in Ukraine backed by the State Department were used by Nuland and others as a "shadow political structure" geared toward destabilizing governments in the name of "Democracy."[59]

Incidentally, destabilization is exactly what occurred to Yanukovych's government. In the fall of 2013, antigovernment demonstrations and rowdy protests engulfed Ukraine in chaos.[60] Nuland herself attended an opposition event where she reportedly handed out cookies to protesters.[61]

After Yanukovych was ousted, a leaked phone call between Nuland and the U.S. ambassador to Ukraine, Geoffrey Pyatt, revealed the extent of U.S. involvement within the organizational structure of the opposition leadership.[62] During the call, Pyatt indicated that the U.S. should bring someone with an "international personality" to Ukraine to "midwife this thing." Nuland indicated that the vice president would be the ideal candidate and that "Biden's willing."[63]

Nuland and thus the Obama/Biden administration had encouraged the ousting of Yanukovych, Russia's loyal ally and supporter. Russia subsequently invaded Crimea later that month and would succeed in taking it from Ukraine.

Whatever midwifing was done or not done was not a great success.

"DIPLOMATIC FINESSE"

Biden and Ukraine have a deep and complicated relationship. Ukraine is typically ranked as the most corrupt country in Europe, save Russia.[64] Fraud and bribery abound within all sectors of Ukraine, including the country's business industry,[65] political environment,[66] justice system,[67] health care system,[68] and higher education.[69] This would not be news to Hunter Biden, the president's perpetually embattled son, who made as much as $83,000 a month while sitting on the board of the Ukrainian energy company Burisma.[70] Hunter had no experience with the energy sector or Ukraine when he booked the gig, but his father, then the vice president of the United States, was in charge of Ukraine policy for the Obama administration at the time. Joe Biden, while vice president, told the Council on Foreign Relations that he threatened to withhold $1 billion of aide to Ukraine if they didn't fire Viktor Shokin, a prosecutor tasked with investigating Burisma.[71] "Well, son of a bitch. He got fired," Joe told the rapt audience of globalists.

In January 2021, the Brookings Institution published an article that highlighted key challenges that Biden would need to overcome in order to successfully navigate the ongoing conflict between Russia and Ukraine. One was that Biden would have to exhibit "diplomatic finesse" when maneuvering around the issue of Ukraine joining NATO, which, Brookings acknowledged, was a key motivating factor for Russia's conflict with Ukraine.[72]

Finesse has never been Biden's strong suit, particularly with regard to Russia and Ukraine.

Upon entering office, Biden had assembled a who's who of the military-industrial complex for his foreign policy team. Biden stacked the State Department with saber-rattlers who had already bungled relations with the Russians during the Obama era.

If "finesse" was Biden's strategy, he certainly wouldn't have tapped Victoria Nuland as undersecretary of state for political affairs.[73] She gained international notoriety for saying "Fuck the EU" on the aforementioned call with Ambassador Pyatt.[74] This is a perfectly legitimate sentiment, but it is the phraseology of an anonymous online "reply guy," not a diplomat. Nuland is widely believed to be the driving force behind the pugnacious side of Biden's Russia diplomacy.[75]

"Her popularity in Washington stems in part from the aggressive rhetoric she employs to castigate the Russians," according to a *Foreign Policy* profile on Nuland from 2015. "In Europe, Nuland is widely presumed to be the leading advocate for shipping weapons to Kiev—a proposal bitterly opposed by the Germans, Hungarians, Italians, and Greeks who fear setting off a wider conflict with Moscow," according to the profile.

The Russians banned Nuland from entering Russian territory due to her apparent role in orchestrating the Ukraine coup. This makes diplomatic exchanges with the Kremlin not only highly awkward but logistically cumbersome.[76] Even so, Biden made the decidedly undiplomatic Nuland his number three diplomat at the State Department.[77] It was a slap in the face to Putin before any negotiations had even begun. As thuggish as Putin is, it was needlessly contentious to have Nuland involved at all in the crafting of our Russia or Ukraine policy.

If it wasn't clear enough that the Biden administration's relationship with Russia was doomed from the start, in March 2021, Biden gave Ukraine lethal weapons and ran joint military drills on Russia's borders. "This action reaffirms the U.S. commitment to providing defensive lethal weapons to enable Ukraine to more effectively defend itself against Russian aggression," the Pentagon said.[78] It wasn't enough just to give Ukraine the weapons: the Biden administration had to rub it in Putin's face that they were cutting-edge. This was part of a DOD-announced $125 million financial package for Ukraine that would cover training and other equipment.[79]

That same month, Blinken traveled to NATO headquarters in Brussels, Belgium, to deliver a speech in which he sought to "revitalize" the U.S.'s relationship with NATO.[80] In his speech, Blinken took several shots at Russia and added that "we must expand our ability to address transnational threats."[81]

In an April 2, 2021, phone call with Zelensky, Biden pledged "unwavering support for Ukraine's sovereignty and territorial integrity in the face of Russia's ongoing aggression in the Donbas and Crimea," according to a readout of the conversation.[82] Two weeks after Zelensky's call with Biden, the Russians began amassing a large amount of military troops near the Ukrainian border. According to the Russians, the action was taken partially in response to the NATO exercise that was executed a month prior.[83]

Tensions ran high, with Blinken firing a verbal warning shot pledging consequences for Russia if it acted recklessly or aggressively.[84]

Then the Biden administration appeared to back off quite a bit. In May, Biden lifted Trump-imposed sanctions on Gazprom, the Russian-owned company overseeing construction of the Nord Stream 2 gas pipeline.[85] Zelensky said the move surprised and disappointed him, equating it to Biden providing "bullets" for "a weapon, a real weapon . . . in the hands of the Russian Federation."

The increasingly desperate Zelensky tried some premium diplomatic ass-kissing by comparing President Biden to basketball legend Michael Jordan.[86] It did not improve his situation; things were about to get worse for Ukraine.

On June 14, two days before a scheduled meeting between Biden and Putin, Zelensky shocked and confused the world by tweeting that NATO would accept Ukraine as a member. Secretary Blinken shot down the claim.[87] Biden himself was asked about NATO membership for Ukraine during a press conference in Brussels on June 14; he punted on an answer but did mention Ukraine's history of corruption.[88] Biden had stepped back from Russia's red line, which was a big win for Putin.

The U.S. and Russian presidents met in Geneva two days later in hopes of further de-escalating tensions. It seemed to be minimally productive for Biden and maximally productive for Putin. Biden had yet to meet with Zelensky or many of our allies at that point of his presidency, so this was terrific optics for Vlad. Russia agreed to draw down some troops at the Ukraine border (which proved to be quite temporary), so Biden basically got nothing. At a press event tied to the meeting, Putin deflected human rights abuse questions by mentioning the Black Lives Matter movement. (Naturally, there was no pushback from the media in the room.[89]) It was a good day that capped off a great week for Putin.

After the Geneva summit, Putin praised the result and complimented Biden, saying, "I think we managed to understand each other," and suggesting that the American president is a shrewd negotiator. This was all lip service to play to Biden's ego; if Biden negotiated anything of note for America, it wasn't reported by the White House or in the press.[90]

The drama died down until September 2021, when Biden hosted Zelensky, marking the first such visit from Ukraine's head of state to the White House.[91] Following the meeting, the U.S. and Ukraine made a joint statement that America fully supported Ukraine's "aspirations" to join NATO. This is a weasely statement by Biden. It's not a hard yes or a hard no on the question of NATO membership. He merely supports Ukraine's "aspirations," whatever that means.

But that wasn't the only news made that day: "The United States is announcing a new $60 million security assistance package, including additional Javelin anti-armor systems and other defensive lethal and non-lethal capabilities, to enable Ukraine to more effectively defend itself against Russian aggression," according to joint statement from the two countries.[92]

This wasn't diplomatic finesse. This was a lot closer to a diplomatic "fuck you" to Russia, and at a time of relative peace.

The Russians were infuriated and responded by reiterating their stance that Russia views NATO membership for Ukraine as a red line. Belarusian president Alexander Lukashenko, a close ally of Putin, told reporters after speaking with Putin that they intended "to take some kind of measures in response."[93]

In October 2021, Nuland traveled to Moscow to meet with Russian counterparts amid the coarsening geopolitical atmosphere. Again it was time for diplomatic finesse, and an ideal time to put in a pinch hitter for Nuland. Russia had to lift the ban on Nuland's entry just to even have the talks. Upon arrival, Nuland immediately goaded the Russians with informal dress, which the Russians regarded as a sign of deliberate disrespect.

The goal for Nuland was ostensibly to dissuade Russia from invading Ukraine. A few months later, we would learn that the meeting was not a success.[94]

The following month, despite Putin's objections, Biden signed a strategic partnership with Ukraine that stated, again, that the U.S. would support Ukraine's NATO "aspirations" and more collaboration between the two.[95] As had been the pattern, the angered Russian president issued a threat: this time that he would deploy hypersonic missiles if NATO made Ukraine a formal member.[96]

Russian troops returned to Ukraine's borders days after the U.S.-Ukraine agreement was signed.

It became apparent that Biden had doubted Russia's red line was literal. According to Emily Horne, who was spokesperson for the National Security Council, the White House's goal was not to actually negotiate but rather to "test whether the Russians were serious about the substance of the concerns." This was a critical blunder. The precedent set by Putin with the Georgia invasion of 2008 and the Crimea invasion of 2014 is that when he feels like NATO might expand into his backyard, he invades.[97]

Ahead of a phone call with Biden on December 6, 2021, it was expected that Putin would demand that the U.S. provide written guarantees that NATO would never allow Ukraine to join.[98] Biden reportedly wanted the call for the purposes of "de-escalation and a return to diplomacy." It was at that precise moment that Nuland burst into the conversation like a Russophobe in a China shop: she declared the U.S. was preparing a military response to Russia if Putin invaded Ukraine. "The Russians will have a very big fight on their hands, there will be severe casualties for them, and frankly it's hard to comprehend," she said, before recommending Putin focus on "building back better inside Russia" after the pandemic.[99]

This language is deliberately provocative. She may as well have screamed obscenities right at him.

After a couple of months of ineffectual multilateral negotiations,[100] the invasion occurred in February 2022.[101] Inexplicably, despite the ample evidence that it was coming sooner rather than later, Biden appeared caught flat-footed and was left with limited options. He put sanctions back on the Nord Stream 2, which had been built and was waiting for regulatory review before it would become operational.[102] Even still, there was only so much that could be done to target Russia's energy industry. Germany, for example, was reliant on Russia for energy. America, already in an energy crunch at home, did not want to make global energy markets any worse. With gas prices already up more than a dollar a gallon in America since Biden took office, he had political concerns he had to manage.[103] If America cut off Russian oil, there would be other buyers, namely China and India, who would buy at a reduced rate while prices went up for the West.

Advantage, Russia.

Even Biden's own staff were convinced that the imposed sanctions would have only marginal effect; dozens of officials allegedly told Bloomberg that they believed they were a "tired tool."[104] (NPR would declare in a headline in December 2022 that "sanctions against Russia aren't working,"[105] though other globalist publications have insisted that their full effect has not been felt yet.[106])

Biden had few moves he could make. He could continue to aid Ukraine by sending more supplies and/or weapons, or he could enforce a no-fly zone over Ukraine. The former would help Ukraine, but it was not a true deterrent; after all, Biden had already been supplying the country with materials and training prior to the invasion. The latter would have brought a hot war with nuclear Russia into the realm of possibility. He chose the former.

In April 2022, with the war raging, Zelensky told CNN's Fareed Zakaria that the Biden administration never intended to truly support Ukraine's membership bid for NATO. The Ukrainian president stated that throughout 2021, Biden officials privately told him that NATO membership was never truly on the table but that "publicly, the doors would remain open."[107]

Then why did the Biden administration continue to engage in all the NATO "aspirations" happy talk? Why not try to temper Zelensky's public ambitions for NATO membership? And why not reassure Putin that his "red line" was not going to be crossed? Biden could have continued to arm Ukraine so that they could resist an invasion, but also tried to make sure no one said or did anything that set Putin off. I asked the White House if they attempted that approach, and I did not get a response.

I also asked if, in retrospect, it would have been safer for the planet if they found Victoria Nuland a teaching job somewhere instead of letting her antagonize a nuclear power that had a history of invading neighboring countries.

They ignored that question, too.

WAR DOGS

Putin's invasion led to mass deaths, financial instability in the global markets, and widespread crises of food production and energy distribution across the globe. Battlefield losses quickly piled up due to troop mismanagement and deepening social distrust.[108]

Ukraine, meanwhile, was developing a not-so-secret weapon to deploy against Putin: a blank check (actually, multiple checks) from the

U.S. government. It started with a $40 billion(!) aid package in May 2022. Only eleven Senate Republicans voted to defy the Democrat establishment on the bill. Senator Rand Paul (R-KY) noted that we would have to borrow from China to pay Ukraine. Others like Senator Marsha Blackburn (R-TN) objected to the total lack of accountability as to where the money was going.[109] I opined on radio at the time that the lack of oversight for where and how the resources would be allocated indicated that the U.S. government would grant funds to the Ukraine military in perpetuity. Unfortunately, I appear to have been prescient.[110] There were other associated costs as well.

By 2023, Biden, straight-faced as ever, explained to the American people that some of the money would be going to pay for pensions for Ukrainian retirees.[111]

(Is it any wonder why our debt is astronomical?)

The war in Ukraine exacerbated a global food shortage that was already present from the pandemic.[112] A few months after the war began, Ukraine, a massive supplier of agricultural commodities, was exporting only 15–20 percent of what it normally sends through the Danube River. Russia and Ukraine also account for a large amount of global distribution of cereals (Russia 7.8 percent, Ukraine 11.3 percent in 2020–21). Prices for these products skyrocketed, which disproportionately impacted poorer countries like those in Africa and the Middle East.

Fertilizer exports have been severely constricted, given that Russia accounts for nearly 20 percent of nitrogen exports and 10 percent of phosphate exports. This decreases supply, which raises costs. Along with Belarus (a close ally of Putin and Russia), Russia accounts for nearly 40 percent of global production of potash fertilizers.[113]

Western sanctions on Russia have placed pressure on energy companies and oil and gas suppliers. Natural gas prices were driven to an all-time high. Countries like South Africa and Sri Lanka were devastated by power cuts and fuel shortages, a direct downstream effect of the war.[114]

The global financial fallout was significant.[115] But as is often the case with Joe Biden's policies, his allies have seen financial opportunity.

The war has been a gold mine for the military-industrial complex. Defense contractors such as Raytheon, Lockheed Martin, General Dynamics, and Northrop Grumman have all bagged cash thanks to Biden's policies on Ukraine and Russia. Biden's new National Defense Authorization Act (NDAA), which provides more than $816 billion to the DOD, removed restrictions on contracts for munitions related to Ukraine.[116]

As of February 2023, Lockheed Martin has scored over $950 million in contracts for missiles and missile systems in order to refill Ukraine's stockpiles. Raytheon won $2 billion to replenish or expand missile systems used in Ukraine.

Look for these numbers to go up over time.

Defense contractors are among the biggest lobbyists in DC. They try to buy up every politician who is for sale—and even some who aren't. They also spend exorbitant sums lobbying for bills like the NDAA. And why not? Each time America spends more on defense or subsidizes another military conflict somewhere on earth, these companies' bottom lines explode.

"Military spending next year is on track to reach its highest level in inflation-adjusted terms since the peaks in the costs of the Iraq and Afghanistan wars between 2008 and 2011, and the second highest in inflation-adjusted terms since World War II—a level that is more than the budgets for the next 10 largest cabinet agencies combined," the *New York\Times* reported in December 2022.[117]

The Biden administration has glaring conflicts of interests with some of these defense contractors, as discussed herein in the chapter on American corporatism. Secretary of Defense Lloyd Austin, for example, sat on the board of Raytheon.[118] William Hartung, director of the Arms and Security Project at the Center for International Policy, offered this analysis: "If General Austin were to recuse himself from decisions on programs and policies involving Raytheon, he could not carry out large parts of his job as defense secretary." That's my exact analysis when it comes to Blinken and Boeing. These types of conflicts of interest are commonplace in Biden's swamp.

BlackRock, the world's largest asset management firm, was also ready to take advantage of the world's perilous predicament. Chairman and CEO Larry Fink declared, "The Russian invasion of Ukraine has put an end to the globalization we have experienced over the last three decades,"[119] but BlackRock's global chief investment strategist, Wei Li, said that "there are opportunities created that we're evaluating very thoughtfully."[120]

A week after Biden announced a $45 billion financial aid package for Ukraine, Zelensky revealed that BlackRock would help rebuild Ukraine after the war.[121] According to the announcement, Fink and Zelensky "agreed to focus in the near term on coordinating the efforts of all potential investors and participants in the reconstruction of our country, channeling investment into the most relevant and impactful sectors of the Ukrainian economy." BlackRock also agreed to "provide advisory support for designing an investment framework, with a goal of creating opportunities for both public and private investors to participate in the future reconstruction and recovery of the Ukrainian economy."

According to the World Bank and the European Commission, the costs of rebuilding in Ukraine could amount to nearly $350 billion.[122] Fink told the World Economic Forum at Davos that he thinks the number will be closer to $750 billion, adding that he believes Ukraine "can be a beacon to the rest of the world about the power of capitalism." "We are creating a new Ukraine," he said. It doesn't get more grandiose than that.

According to senior U.S. officials, both the Russians and the Ukrainians have suffered 100,000 or more casualties. The Russian toll might be closer to 200,000 as of February 2023.[123] Also as of that time, General Milley estimated that 40,000 civilians had been killed because of combat in the region.[124]

As of December 2022, the U.S. had allocated $113 billion for the Ukraine war effort. This number eclipsed the military budget of every country in the world except the U.S. and China—including Russia. It is also more federal aid than most states receive from the federal government.[125] In June of 2023, the Pentagon confessed to an alleged "accounting error" that had overestimated the value of the weapons sent to Ukraine by $6.2 billion over two years. This isn't just an oopsie; America's largest government agency, which meticulously calculates our military budget, confirmed we gave Ukraine several extra bil worth of stuff. Why am I not surprised we didn't err on the side where Zelensky gets less?[126]

The American media and Democrat Party provided billions of dollars of propaganda for Zelensky as well. In December 2022, "Z" presented Nancy Pelosi and Kamala Harris a Ukrainian flag at a joint session of Congress, which they proudly displayed. The media lapped it up. "The symbolism was unmistakable—the American vice president and House speaker holding up before both chambers of Congress the blue and yellow Ukrainian flag," ABC News wrote in a celebratory piece.[127] It would have been more shocking to see the House Speaker and vice president waving the Star-Spangled Banner in the House chamber. Zelensky addressed the world's most powerful legislators in his signature green tracksuit while he asked for more resources. As usual, we obliged.[128] The irony is palpable: the same Congress that shut down in December 2018 for thirty-four days because Trump wanted $5 billion for a wall at our border seemingly can't stop sending Ukraine money to defend theirs.[129]

The evidence is clear that Joe Biden's failed diplomacy was an essential factor in Putin's decisions to invade Ukraine. Putin may have knocked over all these dominoes, but Joe Biden helped line them up. So why has Joe Biden gotten a pass to this point?

The obvious answer is that the establishment media tends to protect Joe, but there are exceptions to that rule, in particular after the Afghanistan withdrawal debacle.

I think the more compelling explanation is that so many of his allies have benefited from the chaos that followed Putin's invasion. The government and bureaucracy have gotten to grow a little bit. The defense industry and the big banks have cashed in on the war and will again during the forthcoming cleanup. The celebrity class and garden-variety Democrats have a safe and easy cause to champion. And the establishment media has something to cover other than problems facing Americans: inflation, crime, the border invasion, and deteriorating schools.

Even when Joe Biden fails, his best friends benefit.

That's something you just can't teach.

CHAPTER 7

China Joe and the Beijing Bidens

The Bidens' legacy will always be linked to China. To this point, both sides have indisputably benefited from one another. The Biden family has scored millions' worth of deals with Chinese businessmen, Chinese Communist Party–connected entities, and even individuals linked to the highest levels of Chinese intelligence.[1] These businesses have opaque structures and limited disclosures. These deals are often reliant on lax government regulation and enforcement. But most important is the willingness by America's most powerful family to take advantage of the country that gave them everything.

To fully understand the extent to which the Biden family has worked with the world's communist superpower to enrich themselves, it would take a really big evidence board and a lot of red yarn.

It would also take more pages than this entire book, never mind this chapter. What's more, this phenomenon is not isolated to the Biden family. Many in Biden's orbit, including donors or people in his cabinet, benefit from the same loopholes in our system that the Biden family has.

Thus I've chosen to isolate a few lowlights.

FIVE DEALS WITH THE DEVIL

Biden made his first overseas trip to China in 1979 when he was chairman of the Senate Foreign Relations Committee. He met with Chairman Deng Xiaoping just as the U.S. and China had formalized the new ties that Henry Kissinger had secretly begun to craft nearly a decade earlier.[2] Biden recalled fond memories of the trip, admitting that he has always

maintained a "long interest in the evolving nature of the Chinese Communist Party" since the days when he was just "a kid in the Senate."

Biden would continue to lavish encouragement on China's rise. When Joe traveled to China again in the early 2000s, this time to meet with Chinese president Jiang Zemin, he told the CCP leadership that he welcomed China's ascendance "as a great power." It follows that Biden was one of the politicians who wanted to admit China into the World Trade Organization. He argued that China's inclusion would inevitably "encourage China's development as a productive, responsible member of the world community."

"Responsible member of the world community" is about the last way any responsible person would describe China. China would go on to dominate global trade, all the while continuing to engage in human rights abuses. Biden promised Delawareans that normalizing trade relations with China would benefit General Motors and Chrysler, which had plants operating within the state.[3] Ten years later, those plants would be shuttered.

Still, in 2011, Biden said, "[I] believed then what I believe now: that a rising China is a positive, positive development, not only for China but for America and the world writ large."[4]

Before long, Biden himself would start feeling the weight of China's admission into the WTO. There were numerous examples of trade infractions,[5] forced technology transfers,[6] intellectual property (IP) theft,[7] human rights abuses,[8] and aggression toward their neighbors in the South China Sea.[9] While his policies put Americans in a weaker position in relation to China, Biden's family business entanglements with the Chinese communists grew ever stronger. The Bidens have done at least five deals with key players in the China's military, intelligence, and government. Not only did tens of millions of dollars change hands during these deals, but they brought the family into proximity with China's spy agency. Many of the details have been thoroughly documented by my friend and colleague Peter Schweizer, particularly in his bestselling book *Red-Handed*.[10] Here are some essentials:

The Dragon Head: Hunter Biden sold Rosemont Realty to a Hong Kong–based company called Gemini in 2014.[11] Gemini is owned by Sino-Ocean Land, an entity affiliated with the China Ocean Shipping Corporation (COSCO),[12] which congressional leaders have accused of being a front for China's military-industrial complex. In 1996, COSCO

was caught smuggling two thousand assault rifles into the U.S. on board their own ships. The House Task Force on Terrorism and Unconventional Warfare labeled COSCO "an arm of the Chinese military establishment."[13] Xi Jinping himself refers to COSCO as "the Dragon Head" due to its strategic importance.[14] In 2020, the company would go on to acquire part ownership of China Communications Construction Company (CCCC),[15] which constructed parts of China's artificial military islands in the South China Sea.[16]

While no one knows how much Hunter Biden bagged in the sale, he kept a stake in Rosemont Realty, and emails show that he was given at least one payment of $188,000 from the firm.[17]

Key takeaway: Hunter Biden sold his business to the Chinese "Dragon Head" for an untold sum that appears to be at least $188,000, plus he retained equity. Given the nature and scope of COSCO's business, this number is likely far lower than what he was actually paid.

Bohai Harvest RST (BHR) Partners: In 2013, Hunter Biden and his business partners were able to create a joint venture called Bohai Harvest RST in partnership with a number of state-backed financial institutions in China. Early negotiations for the fund involved Che Feng, a Chinese tycoon. Hunter referred to Che as the "the super chairman" in an email to his business partner Devon Archer. He was the son of a People's Liberation Army (PLA) soldier, and his father-in-law was governor of the People's Bank of China. Che had close business ties to Ma Jian, the CCP's vice minister of state security. As part of his role, Ma Jian oversaw North American intelligence operations that identified foreigners who could be used for counterintelligence purposes.[18] Che, who later became the target of an anti-corruption investigation in China, was not named as a partner in the final deal, but Hunter's partners in the new firm include the state-owned Bohai Industrial Investment Fund[19] and Harvest Fund Management, a major investment firm based in China.[20]

Key takeaway: According to Schweizer, Hunter Biden's BHR was the result of an effort to "fuse Chinese financial might to those with access to the highest levels of power in the Western world."[21] It succeeded.

Burnham Asset Management: One of Hunter's closest Chinese associates is Henry Zhao, a major figure in mainland China's financial indus-

try. Zhao has deep ties to China's ruling elite. Zhao had cofounded Harvest Global Investments with Jia Liqing. Jia is the daughter of China's former minister of state security (Jia Chunwang)[22] and is married to the son of another Chinese official named Liu Yunshun.[23] Liu is a former member of China's most powerful committee, the CCP Politburo Standing Committee. Liu's role was that of secretariat, overseeing China's propaganda and ideological indoctrination programs.[24] He served from 2012 to 2017.

Harvest Global Investments sent $5 million to Burnham Asset Management, another business associated with Hunter Biden.[25]

Key takeaway: Hunter's company received an investment from the spouse of China's top propagandist.

CEFC China Energy: Hunter Biden developed what seemed to be a close working relationship with Ye Jianming, who was chairman of a Chinese energy company called CEFC China Energy.[26] Ye was a former official at a Chinese organization called the Chinese Association for International Friendly Contact, which is bankrolled by China's military intelligence.[27] Hunter even served as an advisor to Ye;[28] they started numerous businesses together.[29]

According to a Senate investigation, Ye gave $6 million to a company associated with Hunter and James Biden, $5 million of which was received in the form of a loan, which suggests that Ye had significant leverage over the Biden family. A portion of those funds curiously found their way to Joe Biden's brother, James Biden.[30]

In a May 2013 email found on Hunter Biden's laptop, a provisional agreement was made between Hunter, his business associate Tony Bobulinski, and CEFC in which 10 percent of the money went to a "Jim" and another 10 percent was to be "held by H for the big guy."[31] As previously noted, "H" almost certainly stands for Hunter, and "the big guy" is Joe.

In 2017, Ye gave Hunter a 3.17-carat diamond that was believed to be worth $80,000. A photo of the appraisal from the diamond was found on the Laptop from Hell. Hunter insisted the diamond was not a bribe.[32]

Key takeaway: A man with close ties to the Chinese government and military sent Biden family companies millions of dollars. He and Hunter have been frequent collaborators. The energy executive also hooked Hunter up with some ice.

CEFC and Patrick Ho: In 2017, Patrick Ho, a top associate of Ye Jianming, was arrested by the FBI for offering bribes to African leaders. Hunter Biden's company, Owasco, was paid $1 million to "represent" Ho.[33] Hunter, who referred to Ho as "the fucking spy chief of China" in a leaked recording obtained by RealClearPolitics,[34] was entirely unqualified for whatever role he was actually playing. According to a U.S. Senate investigation, Joe's brother James received more than $1 million from Ho.[35]

Yes, Hunter Biden was in business with, in his own words, "the fucking spy chief of China."

Full stop.

Joe likely benefited as well. Schweizer notes that Hunter implied that he was giving half the money to "Pop." Even if Hunter wasn't being literal (it's Hunter, after all), it has been documented that Hunter had covered Joe's bills for a period of time, so perhaps that's what he meant.

Key takeaway: "The fucking spy chief of China" hired Hunter for no apparent reason. Jim Biden also cashed in on the relationship.

Collectively, these details portray a family business that operates in the shadows, in places where regulation and laws are sparse. That business has a name: influence peddling.

"There is also the curious fact that in 2014, Hunter Biden took the unusual step of telling the Secret Service that he did not want protection when he traveled overseas," Schweizer reported, noting that the request happened just after Hunter began expanding his business portfolio into China.[36]

If Occam's razor applies in this case, and it usually does, we know why Hunter preferred to be without government minders while he was on his grind.

This is how Hunter made his money: major international deals with the most powerful and connected people on earth, even when he had seemingly little to offer them. Except, of course, his name. What service did Hunter provide these individuals with deep ties to the Chinese power structure? The world may never know, but we certainly have our suspicions.[37]

"THEY'RE NOT COMPETITION": BIDEN'S CHINA POLICY

When Biden was on the campaign trail, he initially downplayed the threat of China. "China is going to eat our lunch? Come on, man. They're not competition for us," Biden said during a 2019 campaign stop in Iowa.[38] "I mean, you know, they're not bad folks, folks. But guess what? They're not competition for us," he said.

That's a lot of happy talk, and you can bet the CCP loved to hear it.

However, the American public is in strong disagreement with the position Biden articulated. As of 2022, 82 percent of Americans had a negative view of China, with 40 percent holding a "very unfavorable" opinion.[39] These numbers are trending even more negative. A soft stance on China would be a political liability. Huge shout-out to Schweizer, GAI, Breitbart News, and others in anti-establishment media who have done terrific reporting to educate the public on China.

Polls like this make it politically idiotic to be weak on China.

Joe Biden has many faults, but his political instincts are typically strong, so he has managed to not be as terrible on China during the early stages of his presidency as critics (me included) probably anticipated. He certainly hasn't been excellent, or even good, but there are a number of positions he has taken that could have been worse.

For example, he not only kept many of the Trump administration's China policies intact but also proposed beefing some of them up. Given the numerous Chinese deals that have enriched the Biden family, this is a pleasant surprise.

In the first two years of his administration, Biden mostly maintained Trump's "Entity List" that banned 184 Chinese individuals and corporations from U.S. investment.[40] Biden added 43 more by the end of his first year in office.[41]

Despite pressure from his corporate allies, as of early 2023, he has resisted efforts from the business sector to do away with Trump's tariffs on Chinese goods. Many Wall Street firms and Big Tech companies are represented by groups like the U.S.-China Business Council and Americans for Free Trade (AFT).[42] They would do well if the tariffs were taken off, but the Biden administration has stayed the course.[43]

President Biden has strengthened the Committee on Foreign Investment in the United States (CFIUS), a government interagency that

reviews (and can block) foreign investors who seek to invest in U.S. companies.[44] With advances in technology, AI, 5G, biotechnology, and more, many U.S. officials want CFIUS's role to be expanded so they are better able to block the transfer of U.S. technology to Chinese firms.[45] Biden has moved slowly in this regard, but in the right direction.

However, President Biden has thus far failed at what I believe is the most critical task: uncoupling America's economy from China. In fact, Biden doesn't even agree that being deeply intertwined with the communist superpower is such a bad thing. How do I know that? Because in May 2023 at the G7 Summit in Hiroshima, Japan, he said, "We're not looking to decouple from China" and "we are not decoupling."[46]

You could almost hear the sound of high-fiving coming across the East China Sea.

The reality is that America is dependent on China for consumer goods, generic pharmaceuticals, medical supplies, manufacturing, raw materials, and seemingly everything else we need for the basic necessities of life. Part of the supply chain for each goes through China before it gets to American businesses and consumers.

You like EV cars? Try making those without China. (Especially after Hunter Biden helped a Chinese company secure a $3.8 billion purchase of a mammoth cobalt deposit.[47])

If Chinese companies control our supply chain, it means the CCP has immeasurable power over American businesses.

China benefits financially from American capital flowing into their country, and they are able to siphon American know-how from our businesses that choose to set up shop in their country, which we often do. After all, Chinese workers' wages are on average about a quarter of what Americans make as of 2023.[48]

If Biden were to boldly challenge China, and the CCP retaliated by flexing their economic might, it would strain the U.S. economy. Prices would balloon in the short term. We would then scramble to find new high-volume trade partners while ramping up production ourselves. If we failed in the short term, the medium- and long-term effects could be devastating.

China can start toppling over these dominoes whenever they want just by cutting us off.

As of today, it would probably hurt China just as much as it would hurt us to do so, but that might not always be the case.

America is vulnerable, and we have politicians like Joe Biden to thank. The U.S. was the number one manufacturer in the world until the Obama/Biden administration; China overtook the U.S. in 2010 and has since dominated the globe. As of 2023, China tops the list of manufacturing countries, with 28.4 percent of global manufacturing output compared to the U.S. at 16.6 percent,[49] and that trend is going in the wrong direction for Americans. Chinese producers also gained export share in both low- and high-tech industries.

Though President Biden awkwardly (but appropriately) expressed support for the concept of "Buy American," America is faced with the ironic reality that we no longer even manufacture the literal tools needed to make many products here. In January 2023, the Department of Transportation denied requests from U.S. ports to use federal funds to buy equipment such as cranes, trucks, and other materials from foreign sources. According to the $1.2 trillion Infrastructure Investment and Jobs Act that Biden passed in 2021, American materials must be used for such ports. But industry workers and officials claimed that no domestic manufacturers exist for the equipment they need. The Biden administration issues waivers when domestic alternatives are not available or are too costly.[50]

This is an epic Made in America fail.

The spirit of "Buy American" is noble, but it would have been nice if Biden had prepared more for this problem in the previous five decades he spent in the federal government.

THE SWIRLY SUMMIT

It did not take long after his inauguration for the Biden administration to strike a pathetic tone with Communist China. In March 2021, Secretary of State Antony Blinken and National Security Advisor Jake Sullivan humiliated the entire country in front of the world by allowing the Chinese to mock America to our faces on our own soil at a summit in Anchorage, Alaska. Blinken mildly criticized the Chinese for their crackdown on Uyghur Muslims and cyberattacks on the U.S., but he had walked into a trap. The CCP foreign affairs chief, Yang Jiechi, responded

with a lecture that took seventeen minutes to translate back to Blinken. The contents must have been surreal to people who do not read Chinese media. Some essential moments:

> China is firmly opposed to U.S. interference in China's internal affairs. . . . On human rights, we hope the United States will do better on human rights. China has made steady progress in human rights, and the fact is that there are many problems within the United States regarding human rights, which is admitted by the U.S. itself as well. . . . The challenges facing the United States in human rights are deep-seated. They did not just emerge over the past four years, such as "Black Lives Matter." It did not come up only recently.[51]

The CCP, which harvests organs, interns Muslims in concentration camps, persecutes Christians, bans blacks from restaurants, has no free speech, and jails political dissidents, lectured the U.S. on our own supposed human rights abuses while they were guests in our country. They even cited Black Lives Matter, implying that the protesters and rioters who had torched American cities in the summer of 2020 actually had a legitimate point about America's racism.

Blinken was in a deep hole, but he kept digging. He meekly stated that other allies tell him with "deep satisfaction that the United States is back" because Joe Biden is president and that our allies and partners have "deep concern about some of the actions [the CCP] is taking." The secretary added that America is willing to admit our mistakes and engages in "a constant quest to form a more perfect union."[52]

In other words, America's top diplomat agrees with China's premise that we live in a racist country, but we're working on it!

Journalist Charles Hurt summed up the exchange when he was my guest on *Breitbart News Daily*: Blinken "got a swirly in the toilet."[53]

That Blinken did not forcefully defend our country against the CCP's verbal attack was as unsurprising as it was unacceptable.

"I don't think Tony Blinken reads Chinese media, because this is exactly how they talk about America every day," I noted at the time. "They call us racist every day, they echo what Black Lives Matter says about America every day, and that's how they use us against us."[54]

CHINESE FARMS—IN AMERICA

When Fufeng Group, a Chinese food manufacturer with links to the Chinese Communist Party, sought to purchase farmland in North Dakota near a U.S. Air Force base in 2021, Secretary of the Treasury Janet Yellen had the opportunity to block the deal. Fufeng Group's chairman, Li Xuechun, is a member of the CCP who has been recognized by the party as a "model laborer" and politician.[55] Due to the close proximity of the farmlands to Grand Forks Air Force Base, concerns were raised, including by Florida senator Marco Rubio and others. Rubio wrote to Yellen and Secretary of Defense Lloyd Austin urging them to review the deal.[56] Yellen didn't stop it.[57]

Grand Forks is known for world-class intelligence, surveillance, and reconnaissance capabilities. It is the definition of a high-capability base. There is no reason why a CCP-affiliated entity should be anywhere nearby. If China hoped to do espionage, now they had a commercial auspice for being in the region.

Why are we making things this easy for the CCP?

A California-based company called General Atomics, which manufactures unmanned aircraft at one of its locations in Grand Forks, says it opposed the Fufeng project because it "represents a major vulnerability for maintaining the necessary secrecy and integrity of classified weapons, communications frequencies, satellite connectivity and many other technologies vital to global security." General Atomics spokesman C. Mark Brinkley said that "[Fufeng's] foreign ownership and control mean there is no simple way to ensure the facility does not someday play host to electronic surveillance or other activities that pose security risks to American and allied unmanned aviation."[58]

Chinese ownership of U.S. farmland increased fourteenfold from 13,720 acres in 2010 to 192,000 acres in 2020. According to the latest available data, three-quarters of all Chinese-owned U.S. farmland is currently owned by Smithfield Foods, a company directly tied to the Chinese government. Smithfield was acquired by the Chinese Shuanghui Group, which eventually changed its name to WH Group. The acquisition took place in 2013, during the Obama/Biden administration. To date, the $7.1 billion acquisition of Smithfield Foods is the largest purchase of a U.S. company by the Chinese ever recorded, transferring ownership of 460 individual U.S.

farms to China. The result was that more than one out of every four hogs in the United States is now owned by China.

Another revolting part of the deal was that Smithfield allowed China to offshore its hog herds to the United States, which means the Chinese were able to transfer the toxic impact of steaming pits of hog waste to our country.[59] Yes, China sent us their hog shit. And the Obama/Biden administration signed off on it. WH Group was doubly happy about this because U.S. farms are subject to less stringent regulations than Chinese-based farms.[60]

U.S. government supervision of the deal was so limited that the U.S. Department of Agriculture (USDA) was left out of the Shuanghui/Smithfield discussion entirely. This was a conspicuous omission given it was the largest-ever U.S. agricultural acquisition by a foreign entity.[61] A U.S. government report released during the Biden administration acknowledged that "China's efforts to gain access to data on U.S. genetically modified (GM) grains present serious concerns for U.S. economic competitiveness as Chinese firms illicitly acquire U.S. IP. China relies heavily on grain imports from the United States to feed its growing livestock inventory." "Chinese scientists have in certain cases chosen to simply steal U.S. agriculture IP and technology rather than try to research and develop them themselves," the report continues.[62]

Despite the Biden administration's publishing this report, it is unclear whether the "concern" has led to any changes in policy.

Stealing America's IP is common practice for the Chinese, whether it is agriculture, engineering, or even entertainment. They try to acquire American knowledge and proficiency, and we enable it.

On January 2022, Chinese national Xiang Haitao was charged by the DOJ with conspiracy to commit economic espionage by stealing a trade secret from U.S.-based agricultural company Monsanto for the purpose of benefiting the People's Republic of China.[63]

Another Chinese scientist, Robert Mo, was convicted of stealing genetically modified seeds from cornfields in Iowa owned by Monsanto and then shipping them to China "through innovative means such as packing them in popcorn bags and smuggling them in luggage."[64] The goal was to create "a new hybrid for Beijing's use."[65]

"The American worker suffers when adversaries, like the Government of China, steal technology to grow their economies," said Assistant Director Alan E. Kohler Jr. of the FBI's Counterintelligence Division. "It's not just military technology developed in secret labs that adversaries want; in this case, it was agricultural technology used by American farmers to improve crop yields."[66]

What's more, GMOs can also be used in modern warfare, as Biden's government has acknowledged. A 2022 United States–China Economic and Security Review Commission (USCC) report detailing China's interest in U.S. agriculture states that "the potential weaponization of GMOs, like GM seeds, also poses a threat to U.S. economic and food security, which could be at risk if GM seed code is used to create a bioweapon." The report explains that "using the genetic code data it has obtained on U.S. crops, China can strengthen its agricultural output by replicating years of U.S. research on its own farms."[67] With technological innovation in gene editing, the potential danger is enormous.

China does not allow America to buy Chinese companies, yet we allow our companies to be sold to the Chinese with minimal oversight. Why do we give them this strategic advantage?

We are either too stupid or too corrupt to put a stop to it. Maybe both.

CHINA—AND HUNTER—GET AMERICA'S STRATEGIC OIL

Biden committed another grave and embarrassing error that benefited the Chinese when he failed to use the U.S.'s Strategic Petroleum Reserve strategically. In February 2022, as oil and gas prices soared to unprecedented heights in the U.S. (more on that later in the book), Joe Biden sent more than five million barrels of oil from the reserve to foreign nations, including China. In the summer of 2022, it was revealed that about one million barrels of petroleum went directly to the Chinese.

Naturally, China's Xinhua news agency announced that gasoline and diesel retail prices dropped soon after the sale.[68]

How could reserves that Biden tapped to relieve pain at the pump for struggling Americans go to our top economic rival? If there is a (highly strained) logic to the decision, it is that released U.S. oil reserves increase oil supply throughout the global economy, which does drive prices down. Experts agreed that such a move would lead to only a marginal decrease of gas prices for Americans, especially when compared to simply using the oil at home.

There was briefly hope that China, inspired by Biden's proactive approach to the skyrocketing prices, would release their own oil reserves to help bring global prices down as well.[69] That never happened. In fact, China started hoarding their own reserves, in what was a clear snub of Biden.[70]

It appeared to be another swirly administered by the CCP, yet there was more to the story: the Biden family may have profited financially from the supply of strategic oil sent to China.

Reports show that a Chinese company linked to Hunter Biden managed to get hold of some of the reserves sent by Biden. According to the *Washington Free Beacon*, the Biden Department of Energy released 950,000 barrels to Chinese state-owned firm Unipec in April 2022.[71] Unipec, the trading arm of China Petroleum and Chemical Corporation (also known as Sinopec Group), is affiliated with Hunter Biden's BHR Partners. BHR had purchased a $1.7 billion stake in Sinopec in 2014.[72] BHR specifically invested in the marketing arm of Sinopec, which manages distribution and sales of refined petroleum. The *Washington Examiner* reported in 2022 that a firm called Skaneateles was listed as a co-owner of BHR in March 2022, and that Hunter Biden is the sole owner of Skaneateles according to DC business records.[73] An attorney for Hunter had told the *New York Times* in 2021 that he "no longer holds any interest, directly or indirectly, in either BHR or Skaneateles," which could be inaccurate.

Oil prices dipped, Biden's Democrats outperformed the polls in the midterm elections, and it appears his family got a bit richer. A win-win for the big guy.

Later that summer, House Democrats blocked a bill that would prohibit Biden from selling oil drawn from our reserves to the CCP.[74]

BEFUDDLED BY THE BALLOON

The Biden family is tied to China for business, his secretary of state was degraded at the Swirly Summit, and President Joe did nothing to investigate the origin of the Chinese coronavirus pandemic or suggest any consequences for the CCP. Yet none of that is quite as humiliating for Biden as what happened when a Chinese spy balloon was spotted over the United States in early 2023.

The balloon, which was seemingly surveilling strategic sites within the U.S., was observed at an altitude of about 60,000 feet by civilians on February 1. The *Billings Gazette* published amateur video of the balloon, floating above Montana, on February 2.[75] The images broke the Internet (figuratively speaking). Biden would later claim that he had been made aware of the balloon on January 28 but apparently did nothing for days.[76] The president was clearly aware that this was a setback for already strained relations with China, because a trip Tony Blinken had planned to Beijing was quickly postponed.[77]

It is believed that the balloon drifted from China to Alaska, then southwest across Canada, entering the lower forty-eight states over Montana. If the balloon's entry point was some sort of coincidence, it is a wild one. Though it is difficult to know the exact flight path of the craft, it is reasonable to conclude that the goal was to surveil Malmstrom Air Force Base in Montana, which is a nuclear weapons base.[78] One hundred fifty warheads in all are located at Malmstrom AFB, making it one of the most important strategic locations in our country.[79]

Surveillance balloons like these are filled with helium and equipped with a payload that includes solar panels for power and instruments that could include cameras, radar, sensors, and other communications equipment.[80]

Biden claimed that he authorized shooting the balloon on February 1,[81] but it wasn't until February 4 that the inflatable was actually downed off the coast of South Carolina in U.S. territorial waters.

The administration claimed that they delayed blasting the vessel out of the sky as a safety precaution, but this was not a popular position. Everyone from former president Donald Trump to Leon Panetta, defense secretary under President Obama, said it needed to be intercepted expeditiously. Panetta even suggested it was continuing to gather intelligence as the news cycle played out eleven miles below. Meanwhile, Biden waited.[82] A Harvard/Harris poll showed that more than 60 percent of Americans believed the presence of the balloon was a "challenge to U.S. sovereignty by China," "an espionage threat," and "a threat to commercial aircraft," respectively. Sixty-three percent said they believed Biden acted too slowly in taking it down.[83]

The White House was more decisive in shooting down three additional unidentified airborne objects in the few days following the balloon fiasco, though they later admitted those aircraft were not part of the Chinese spy program.[84] An Illinois-based club, the Northern Illinois Bottlecap Balloon Brigade, began to believe one of those objects eviscerated by Biden was one of their balloons. The hobbyists' party-style "pico balloon" had gone off the grid off the coast of Alaska a few days earlier. Pico balloons are ultra-lightweight (about six pounds), carry a transmitter, reach altitudes of 40,000 feet, and are not particularly dangerous if they fall on you.[85] These balloons can circle the world several times, bringing delight to the enthusiasts who launched them.

Unless, of course, they get blasted out of the sky by the U.S. government.

"I tried contacting our military and the FBI—and just got the runaround—to try to enlighten them on what a lot of these things probably are," Ron Meadows, the founder of Scientific Balloon Solutions, told *Aviation Week*.[86] His Silicon Valley–based company supplies pico balloons to hobbyists and educators. "And they're going to look not too intelligent to be shooting them down," he continued.

Too late. The feds were on the verge of a very expensive humiliation.

On February 11, the leaders of the U.S. and Canada ordered a U.S. F-22 Raptor pilot to fire an AIM-9X Sidewinder missile at a mystery object over the Yukon Territory. (The missile likely cost more than $400,000.[87])

After the kill shot was delivered, The Royal Canadian Mounted Police attempted to retrieve debris from the suspected balloon, but it was swallowed up by the vast Yukon, likely gone forever.[88]

That fact is not so bad for Joe Biden, who was slow to shoot down the Chinese spy balloon but quick to blow some teenager's amateur radio craft to smithereens.

Two weeks later, China's top diplomat, Wang Yi, met with Secretary Blinken in Munich, Germany, only to scold him for Joe Biden's "hysterical" response to the balloon. Blinken supposedly told his Chinese counterpart that China's clandestine surveillance was an "unacceptable violation of U.S. sovereignty and international law" (as he wiped the toilet water out of his eyes).

The saga had a poetry to it. It summed up Biden's China policy better than words ever could. It was alarming, semi-frightening, cringe-inducing, and in the end a colossal embarrassment for Americans everywhere, especially Biden himself.

CHAPTER 8

How Joe Biden Sold Hollywood to China

O f all the brilliant points Andrew Breitbart made over the years, the one most often associated with him is that "politics is downstream from culture." This means that it is the artists, social influencers, media figures, and thought leaders who guide our politics more so than the actual politicians. With the rise of Barack Obama and then Donald Trump, America proved his thesis by literally electing pop culture superstars to the highest office in the land, regardless of gaps in their political résumés.

Yes, culture is king, and over the last hundred years, there has been no bigger cultural influence than the movies. In fact, there is nothing more American than the movies. Since the early twentieth century, film has been America's quintessential art form. Movies entertain you, they challenge you, they move a society forward, and occasionally, when bad values are glorified, they move it backward. And though there are many terrific films made elsewhere on earth, Hollywood built an industry producing them on a massive scale. Then we reaped the rewards.

We began exporting Americanism around the globe via the silver screen, and we had fun doing it. We told the world who we are as a people—our values and our style—by way of our stories playing out in celluloid.

If all that sounds a little romantic, that's because it is.

As a Hollywood native, it has given me little pleasure to track the film industry's slow and agonizing decline since we at Breitbart News launched Big Hollywood in 2009, the first original news website in Andrew's digital media empire.

The global box office went up significantly in that time up to the pandemic. Moviegoers spent $29.4 billion at the ticket counter in 2009 compared to $42.3 billion in 2019,[1] the last full year before COVID-19. Yet during that time, the domestic haul flatlined; yearly box-office receipts were $10.6 billion in 2009 and had ticked up to only $11.4 billion in 2019, which represents a slight gross decline when adjusted for inflation.[2] The price of an average ticket also rose during that time, from $7.50 to $9.16, which means that those mediocre returns were based on fewer butts in seats that prior years.[3]

Certainly, Hollywood has had to make considerable adjustments during this time. Advances in streaming and the widespread adaptation of smartphones offered more competition. There were more television shows with higher production value than ever. The Wuhan virus outbreak itself was devastating to production companies' bottom lines. It became more difficult to make movies, which is challenging enough in the best of circumstances. Undeniably, the lifelong habit of spending part of your weekend at the cinema was broken for many people by the lockdowns.

But those aren't the main causes of the decline of the movie business. If only those reasons were to blame, it would be impossible to explain how three of the seven highest-grossing films at the domestic box office of all time have been released since 2021 (*Spider-Man: No Way Home, Top Gun: Maverick*, and *Avatar: The Way of Water*).

So, clearly, Americans are willing to go to the theater for a certain type of movie. Just not the type of movies that Hollywood tends to make these days.

We can track the movie business's regression to when Tinsel Town started to put out a different type of product: a product made with a more global audience in mind. And the centerpiece of the "global" audience was China.

After all, they call it "show business," not "show art."

(The aforementioned tentpole blockbusters also dominated the international box office, but China wasn't driving that success. The CCP blocked the release of *Spider-Man: No Way Home* and *Top Gun: Maverick* altogether. The *Avatar* sequel hauled $245,996,272 from China, a big number, but that represented only about 10 percent of the film's total gross.[4])

It has been well over a decade since the beginning of this experiment. During that time, we have seen Americans vote (with their dollars), and we have made it abundantly clear: we think movies stink now.

Not all movies, of course. But most of them. The vast, vast majority of them.

And perhaps more than any other person in the country, Joe Biden is to blame.

Yes, Joe Biden destroyed American movies. And he did it by selling out to China.

KUNG FU PANDA-MONIUM

From 1994 to 2001, China had a policy that only ten non-Chinese movies could be shown in theaters in the country each year. That number was increased to twenty in 2002, with that quota remaining in place until 2012.[5] In order to be one of those chosen few, Hollywood executives were forced to go through the Chinese government and obtain CCP approval before they could sell their products to Chinese consumers.

Needless to say, this was severely limiting to American production companies and distributors, who saw the expanding Chinese movie market as a gold mine. Beginning in 2008, a deal began to come together between the vice presidents of the two countries, Joe Biden and Xi Jinping, to expand the presence of America's movies within China.

The person who gets the most credit—or blame—for initiating the process was Jeffrey Katzenberg. Katzenberg founded DreamWorks with director Stephen Spielberg and music mogul David Geffen; these are three of the most influential entertainment executives in the world. He also was instrumental to the rise of Barack Obama (and thus Joe Biden). The Hollywood hot shot supported the half-term senator when most of the entertainment industry was firmly behind Hillary Clinton.[6] As early in Obama's rise as February 20, 2007, Katzenberg, Spielberg, and Geffen raised over $1.3 million in campaign contributions for the then senator at a star-studded Hollywood event.[7]

With the general election campaign in full flight, on September 16, 2008, Katzenberg, Spielberg, and Geffen hosted another fundraiser during a record-breaking night in which Obama received nearly $11 million from top-level entertainment media donors. Leonardo DiCaprio, Jodie Foster, Will Ferrell, Eddie Murphy, Chris Rock, and Renee Zellweger were among those who stroked checks.[8]

Katzenberg went on to become one of Obama/Biden's biggest funders. And it was Katzenberg who was perhaps the first major player in Hollywood to home in on the Chinese market as the way to grow the entertainment business.

Katzenberg's working relationship to China goes back as far as 2008, when DreamWorks premiered the first film of the Kung Fu Panda series. The characters in the cartoon movie were voiced by Jack Black, Angelina Jolie, Jackie Chan, Dustin Hoffman, Seth Rogen, Lucy Liu, and other stars. It made $631 million worldwide, including $26 million in China, which was a record for an animated film.[9]

Katzenberg led a DreamWorks team of animators to Chengdu in 2008 before the launch of the first Kung Fu Panda movie at the invitation of the Chinese State Administration for Radio, Television and Film (SARFT).[10] SARFT originally tried to seize a monopoly of Chinese-themed movies, but that failed. So, they instead changed strategies: try to seduce Hollywood into including more pro-Chinese elements in their films in exchange for greater access to the Chinese consumer.

Spoiler alert: it worked.

Chengdu is said to be the home of the Kung Fu Panda and is featured extensively in the Kung Fu Panda series. When Katzenberg met with Chinese officials, he quickly and directly told the Chinese he would incorporate elements of Chengdu into the film, which surprised officials, who thought they would have to pay a large amount for those elements to be included.[11]

Give to get, as the expression goes.

"The subtle incorporation of Chinese culture has become a stepping stone for Hollywood to enter the Chinese market," Katzenberg said during a press conference in Los Angeles. "The Chinese elements in Kung Fu Panda were well-received by Chinese audiences," he boasted. Katzenberg reportedly said that he viewed *Kung Fu Panda* as a love letter from Hollywood to China.[12]

Gross.

In 2011, DreamWorks made *Kung Fu Panda 2*. As promised, Katzenberg increased the Chinese themes and cut out slightly humorous digs at ancient Chinese wisdom to appease the CCP.[13] According to one Chinese publication, the changes reflect an effort from the producers to overcome the shortcomings of the first film by incorporating more traditional Chinese elements.[14] The film would gross over $90 million at the Chinese box office.[15]

The floodgates were open.

The following year, Oriental DreamWorks would launch an operation in Shanghai (it would eventually be renamed Pearl Studio) with a new $330 million animation studio.

In 2016, Oriental DreamWorks' *Kung Fu Panda 3* would gross over $154 million in China despite significantly underperforming its two predecessors elsewhere around the world and in the U.S.[16]

XI, WHO HAS THE GOLD, MAKES THE RULES

In August 2009, the World Trade Organization (of which the U.S. and China are a part) ruled that China had violated international policies by limiting film imports/distribution into mainland China.[17] This sent a signal to Hollywood that widespread access to the Chinese market was imminent.[18]

In December of that year, Vice President Joe Biden met with movie and media executives, ostensibly to address the issue of piracy. In attendance were Attorney General Eric Holder, Secretary of Commerce Gary Locke (who would later become ambassador to China and accompany Biden on a trip there), FBI director Robert Mueller, Secretary of Homeland Security Janet Napolitano, and many others from the Obama administration.[19] But the true VIPs were a who's who of Hollywood. Executives from Sony, Warner Bros., Time Warner, Viacom, NBCUniversal, Disney, News Corporation, the Directors Guild, the Screen Actors Guild, the Motion Picture Association of America, and many other media enterprises were in attendance.

The meeting was said to be one-sided, including only the voices of the "privileged special interest group"[20] of film and media bigwigs. The directors of the FBI and Secret Service were present, as well as A.G. Holder, which raised suspicion.[21]

Talks between Obama/Biden and China continued into 2010. It was at this point that Obama's Hollywood cohort deployed their not-so-secret weapon: A-list celebrities who were willing to engage with China to gin up business.

From a seemingly limitless array of examples:

- Kevin Spacey traveled to Guangzhou to promote a film.

- Hugh Jackman went to Shanghai to learn Mandarin.

- Will Smith and son Jaden Smith traveled to Beijing and Shanghai to promote *The Karate Kid* remake, a coproduction between China Film Group and Sony.

- Olga Kurylenko ("Bond girl" from *Quantum of Solace*) worked on the film *Empires of the Deep* in Beijing (another U.S.-China coproduction).

- Christian Bale traveled to the mainland to work on a totally Chinese-financed film made by Chinese director Zhang Yimou.

- In November 2010, Leonardo DiCaprio traveled to St. Petersburg, Russia, as part of a campaign to save tigers. At the event, he met not only with Vladimir Putin but also China's premier, Wen Jiabao. Wen controls billions of dollars of assets and has aspired to be a Hollywood financier.[22]

In December 2010, WikiLeaks released cables showing that then vice president Xi Jinping had become quite interested in Hollywood. Quotes from Xi reveal that he admired World War II films due to their "grand and truthful" tales of good and evil and that he longed for Chinese entertainment to promote such values. Some of the movies that he liked most were *Saving Private Ryan* and *The Departed*. Xi surprisingly said that, in contrast to American cinema, Chinese movies were too confusing and too focused on palace intrigues and kung fu. He criticized Chinese directors for neglecting to use film to promote certain values.[23]

Xi wanted to learn how to make more effective propaganda in the style of the Hollywood blockbuster. As is so often the case with communists, his primary interest wasn't financial. It was ideological. Xi wanted to mimic U.S. "soft power": the ability to attract people and thus influence culture on a grand scale. His overarching goal was to have complete control over the way Chinese audiences—and eventually the world—perceived China. Once he had that control, he would convey a "grand and truthful" depiction of China and its allies and enemies alike.

In January 2011, the Obama Biden White House hosted its third state dinner in honor of Chinese president Hu Jintao.[24] Those in attendance included Jackie Chan, Disney CEO Bob Iger, Elaine Chao, Wendi Deng Murdoch, Barbra Streisand, James Brolin, and Robert Roche (member of American Chamber of Commerce Shanghai, appointed by Obama to the Advisory Committee for Trade Policy and Negotiations).[25]

(Peter Schweizer's GAI revealed in 2012 that Roche was no stranger to the idea of foreign influence peddling. He owned Obama.com, which did not have any apparent mechanism to prevent foreigners from contributing to the Obama campaign; a stunning 68 percent of the traffic going to Obama.com was foreign.[26])

In August 2011, Vice President Joe Biden traveled to Beijing to meet his Chinese counterpart. Biden, speaking with Xi about bilateral relations,[27] expressed his admiration for China's history and contributions to the world, including the country's "great achievements since the reform and opening up" of the late twentieth century. He also said that the U.S. welcomes China's rise and was committed to working closely with China. He articulated his view that history would prove that it was the right decision for the U.S. to establish a close relationship with China. He also conveyed that the U.S. fully understands Taiwan's and Tibet's importance to China's core interests and that the U.S. will continue to pursue the "one China policy."[28] Under "one China," territories like Tibet, Hong Kong, and especially the country of Taiwan do not have sovereignty apart from China itself. This is most awkward and geopolitically complicated with regard to Taiwan, which has never been under communist rule. Yet the CCP still maintains that "reunification" is inevitable.

As part of his trip, Biden visited the heart of *Kung Fu Panda* country: Sichuan University in the city of Chengdu,[29] where Katzenberg and DreamWorks first capitulated to China in 2008.

In May 2011, three months before Biden's trip, DreamWorks representatives including *Kung Fu Panda* art director Raymond Zibach had traveled to Chengdu at the invitation of the municipal Chinese government there.[30]

Biden pressed his Hollywood agenda in a speech by preaching about the importance of intellectual property protections and antipiracy.[31] These are certainly valid issues for Biden to raise, but it all seems incredibly naïve in retrospect.

It was clear that the Chinese film industry (backed by the CCP) had a deep interest in cutting deals with Hollywood in no small measure because they lacked talent, creativity, and expertise in producing movies. Joe Biden made it clear to Xi Jinping that it was all for sale. Xi was a willing buyer.

Meanwhile, China and Hollywood were cutting massive deals. Chinese media conglomerate DMG Entertainment created a $300 million film fund to help bring U.S. movies to China, as well as a $230 million theater chain investment for the Chinese market.[32] DMG had already been working with Endgame Entertainment to show the movie *Looper* starring Bruce Willis, Joseph Gordon Levitt, and Emily Blunt on the mainland. This was accomplished when a Chinese actress, Xu Qing, was added to the main cast.[33] According to *China Daily*, *Looper* was "the only Hollywood epic to be screened in China during this year's lucrative National Day Holiday slot."[34]

Also in 2011, Relativity Media, founded by Ryan Kavanaugh, launched a strategic partnership joint venture with Chinese film distribution companies Huaxia Film Distribution Company and Skyland (Beijing) Film-Television Culture Development that would handle distribution and film production in China and the U.S.[35]

In 2012, DMG would go on to score a deal with Marvel to cofinance, coproduce, and codistribute *Iron Man 3*.[36]

The communist cash would keep flowing for years to come. In 2017, DMG announced another $300 million for the China film fund.[37]

It was like a fire sale. Deals were constantly cut between American companies and Chinese ones, which are controlled by the CCP. And with each deal, China got a little more control over American movies.

JOE EXPANDS THE QUOTA

Biden emerged as Hollywood's point person in a bitter battle over the Stop Online Piracy Act (SOPA). Proponents argued the bill was necessary to protect the IP market in their industries, especially against "foreign-owned" and -operated websites (that is, China). Opponents, including many individuals from the tech world, left-leaning politicians, and libertarians like Rand Paul, argued that the proposed legislation would stifle free speech and innovation.[38]

On January 14, 2012, the White House released a statement on SOPA saying that while Obama supported antipiracy principles, he did not support legislation that could stifle innovation and lead to possible censorship online. Thus he would not support this bill. It died in the House less than a week later.[39]

That put Joe Biden in a challenging spot. He had to keep Hollywood happy even though their Frankenstein's monster (Obama) had killed their bill. If he failed, the endless campaign contributions to the Obama/Biden war chest from the Hollywood elite might be in jeopardy. Lo and behold, he found a way to save face for Hollywood: broker big deals with China.

As hopes for SOPA's passage died, Biden closed the deal with Xi Jinping and the Chinese government to increase the infamous film quota. On February 2, DreamWorks' Katzenberg announced that he would be hosting President Obama for a campaign fundraiser event at Katzenberg's $35 million home in the ultraexclusive Trousdale Estates neighborhood of Los Angeles. Spielberg, Geffen, filmmaker J. J. Abrams, and Tom Hanks, among others, were likely to attend. Ticket prices were reported to be $35,800.[40]

The season of blockbuster Hollywood fundraising was just beginning.[41]

On February 14, 2012, Xi Jinping traveled to Washington, DC, to meet with Joe Biden. Xi attended a White House visit that morning at the invitation of Biden and later dined with the vice president at a State Department lunch hosted by Hillary Clinton. Next Biden accompanied Xi to LA, where the Chinese VP had a meeting with DreamWorks cofounder Katzenberg and other Hollywood executives.[42]

Xi came to LA with an agenda to kick-start the Chinese film industry. The very same day that Xi and Biden struck the deal on film distribution in China, DreamWorks announced it had finalized its partnership with Shanghai Media Group, China Media Capital, and Shanghai Alliance Investment Limited to build a joint film studio in Shanghai.[43] Biden's office claimed the deals were unrelated and it was merely a wild coincidence they closed simultaneously. DreamWorks' government affairs consultant (apparently they have one of those) Andy Spahn, who was also an Obama bundler, told the *Washington Post* that the White House did not play a role in their deal.[44]

Very convenient, and highly suspicious.

In the final moments of Xi's U.S. visit, Biden was able to get the job done for his Hollywood patrons. China agreed to increase the film quota from 20 per year to 34 so long as 14 of the films were IMAX or 3-D. Additionally, the distribution fee for non-Chinese distributors would increase from 13 percent to 25 percent.[45] According to the Sunlight Foundation, Biden consulted with Iger and Katzenberg before landing on the 25 percent figure.[46]

This was the official narrative, according to the then deputy assistant to the president and national security advisor, Tony Blinken: "The two vice presidents sat next to each other at lunch and Biden said, 'We need 25 percent. It's a good deal—let's get it done today.'" Then, according to Blinken, Xi ran the details by the three agencies in China, and a memorandum of understanding was signed by dinnertime that night.[47]

However, there were nonpublic portions of the deal that remain a mystery.

Reports claimed that Katzenberg advised Biden on America's deal with Xi to open up the Chinese market; he would have been doing this while simultaneously cutting his own deal directly with Xi on behalf of DreamWorks.[48]

Months after the agreement with Xi, the Securities and Exchange Commission launched an investigation into DreamWorks Animation, the Walt Disney Company, and 20th Century Fox (among other corporations) for potential violations of the Foreign Corrupt Practices Act. The SEC inquired into possibly illegal payments to Chinese officials in exchange for the right to film and present movies in the mainland, but ultimately, nothing significant came from the investigation. Functionally, it might have been a warning shot to Hollywood on future conduct.

It must have been a celebratory moment for Biden, and one the Hollywood hotshots would not soon forget.

Yet it was Xi and the communists who would have the last laugh.

THE RED FLOOD

It is axiomatic in America's current political climate that if no one is held accountable for less-than-ethical behavior, that behavior will continue and probably escalate. This is precisely what happened after Joe Biden brokered the deal with Beijing.

He might not have known it at the time, but he had sold Hollywood's soul to China. Within just a couple of years, the CCP propagandists had spread their tentacles throughout all of Hollywood.

In March 2014, Shanghai Media Group (SMG) partnered with Disney to develop stories and scripts that incorporate Chinese themes in Disney movies.[49] SMG also partnered with Chinese tech giant Alibaba, which assumed a stake in Amblin Partners in 2016. Amblin, which was founded by Steven Spielberg, is connected to Katzenberg: the company is subdivided into Amblin Entertainment, Amblin Television, and DreamWorks Pictures.[50] Like Katzenberg, Geffen is a kingmaker in both Hollywood and Democrat politics. Comcast/NBCUniversal, another international conglomerate that does huge business in China, is one of Amblin's investment partners.

It's an impressive web of the most powerful media companies in the world, now all with deepening ties to Communist China.

(In 2020, SMG's subsidiary Yicai Global was designated by the State Department as a Chinese government entity designed to disseminate Chinese propaganda to the U.S.[51])

With the new agreement in place, Hollywood began to self-censor their content in anticipation of trying to comply with the CCP ministers of information. When the films did not meet China's standards, they could either get edited or simply withdrawn from consideration for entering the Chinese market.

The censorship contagion was spreading.

The reasons China would block a film are extensive and shockingly comprehensive. Nudity, drugs, drinking, smoking, violence, and blood were not going to get past the Chinese censors, nor were stories about rebellion, gay characters, time travel, or even ghosts.

Yes, mainland China is a ghost-free zone.[52]

China's regulators griped that far too many imported films "casually make up myths, have monstrous and weird plots, use absurd tactics, and even promote feudalism, superstition, fatalism and reincarnation."[53] American companies knew this, and began to make art as if the Chinese communists were looking over their shoulder.

Naturally, movies got worse. Much worse.

THE OPPOSITE OF LEGENDARY

There are enough examples to fill a book evidencing the deterioration of films under the new self-censorship protocol, but let's consider the catalog put out by Legendary Entertainment to illustrate the point. The production company launched with *Batman Begins* (2005), the first of the three Christopher Nolan Batman films Legendary would produce. All of them are darkly realistic, question authority, and glorify rebellion and vigilantism. They also were critically lauded and massive box-office successes.

Other films Legendary would produce over the next few years:

- *300* (celebrates Western civilization, intense gore, nudity, massive box-office success)

- *Watchmen* (thematically rich, dark realism, the government fails its citizens, intense violence, sexuality)

- The Hangover series (funny, wildly inappropriate, unrestricted, nudity, vulgarity, euphoric levels of fun, massive box-office returns)

Also in the Legendary canon are movies like *Inception* and *The Town*, where criminals are the protagonists, a no-no in China. Both films received critical acclaim in America.

Legendary also produced films about American icons like Steve Jobs, Jackie Robinson, Superman, and more from 2006 to 2016. These movies were often edgy, raw, and reflective of the concept of the "American spirit."

In 2016, Legendary Entertainment was acquired by Chinese conglomerate Dalian Wanda for $3.5 billion.[54] Since that date, the films have been . . . different. Some examples:

- *The Great Wall* (big-budget flop in the U.S. *and* China; star Matt Damon said he knew the movie was bad while they were making it)

- *Kong: Skull Island* (American military depicted as the bad guy during the Vietnam War era; Kong himself is seen as a metaphor for America's past colonial sins)

- *Pacific Rim: Uprising* (has been described as "China bait")

- *Jurassic World: Fallen Kingdom* (again, the American military are the bad guys)

- *Godzilla vs. Kong* (the villain in this one, as Breitbart's John Nolte put it, is "Corporate Whitey")[55]

Hollywood's self-censorship was widespread and often done in plain sight. In other words, it was no secret. Producers began cutting certain scenes, replacing dialogue, and removing background images that did not align with CCP values. A few examples from another seemingly infinite list:

- *Skyfall* (Sony Pictures, 2012): Censors of the James Bond film in China told Sony to cut a scene where a Chinese security guard is killed; they also demanded the removal of a portrayal of sex work and police torture in Macau.[56]

- *Cloud Atlas* (Warner Bros., 2013): Producers removed forty minutes, including gay and straight love scenes.[57]

- *Alien: Covenant* (20th Century Fox, 2017): Producers removed a scene in which a same-sex couple kiss.[58]

- *Bohemian Rhapsody* (20th Century Fox, 2018): Producers removed several scenes that delved into Freddie Mercury's sexuality.[59]

- *Minions: The Rise of Gru* (Illumination, 2022): The film got an alternate ending because an animated villain gets away with despicable deeds, which is verboten in China.[60]

Sometimes the pandering got downright silly. Eric Schwartzel of the *Wall Street Journal* reported a rise in Chinese product placement in American movies, observing that an ATM for China Construction Bank can be seen in a scene in a Transformers movie set in Texas. Also in the film, a character goes to a convenience store in Chicago—to buy Chinese protein power.[61]

Marvel Studios made a massive edit to *Doctor Strange* in 2016 by altering a major character who was Tibetan in the comic books. Screenwriter C. Robert Cargill stunningly cited Chinese censorship when defending the decision: "If you acknowledge that Tibet is a place and that [the character is] Tibetan, you risk alienating one billion people who think that that's bullshit and risk the Chinese government going, 'Hey, you know one of the biggest film-watching countries in the world? We're not going to show your movie because you decided to get political.'"[62]

This is the ultimate gaslighting. Cargill argues that it is political to present the original source material and that it is less political to alter it to appease totalitarian communists' draconian censorship regime. It is a morally idiotic position.

Studios will even conduct informal communications with Chinese regulators[63] in order to avoid the risk and uncertainty of getting slapped with a rejection. In fact, an entire industry of American and Chinese consultants, fixers, and lobbyists has emerged to back-channel communications with Chinese officials to get the most seamless outcome possible.

A burgeoning new global culture of censorship all of a sudden sprouted from a deal cut between Joe Biden and Xi Jinping when they were their countries' respective seconds-in-command.

Things appear to be getting worse. Perhaps the most egregious example of all is from Disney's live-action *Mulan* (2020). Not only was the movie partly shot in the region of China's Xinjiang Province where there are mass concentration camps for imprisoned Uyghur Muslims who endure forced labor, but Disney actually thanked an official Chinese government security bureau connected to the camps in the film's end credits.[64]

In May 2021, pro wrestler, Fast & Furious star, and giant weenus John Cena prostrated himself to Xi and the communists by apologizing —in Mandarin—for (accurately) calling Taiwan a country.[65]

Rarely does anyone in Hollywood take bold public stands against the censorship, but there are a few noteworthy exceptions. Director Quentin Tarantino, for example, refused to remove a negative portrayal of martial artist and actor Bruce Lee from his masterpiece *Once Upon a Time in Hollywood*.[66] He opted to preserve the integrity of his art over cash from the communists. But sadly, these cases are few and far between.

The Biden/Xi/Katzenberg deal, which was originally seen as a massive windfall for Hollywood, put the industry in a horrific position to constantly negotiate with the CCP the rules in which they can make art. China continued to ramp up censorship for cultural, economic, and diplomatic reasons. Hollywood continued to alter their films in order to appease the CCP censors, often in vain.

China's regulatory process allows for censors to take their time when reviewing films. They don't work on Hollywood studios' timetables. Any delays cost U.S. filmmakers money and can wreck a film's Chinese debut.[67] In 2018, China centralized its film regulatory and censorship apparatus and formally introduced its China Film Administration, officially shifting movie censorship oversight responsibilities directly to the State Council (aka the Communist Party and Xi Jinping).[68]

Outright blacklisting of films became more common.[69]

Thanks to recently acquired know-how from America, China no longer needs American movies. They are doing their best to rival us with their own.[70] This was all happening in plain sight, and the (typically pro-China) U.S. media hasn't seemed to care. In 2015, Chinese media reported that the government was on a hiring spree of veterans from Hollywood, including from studios like DreamWorks. The plan was to build up its own operations, essentially buying off talent that would otherwise be making movies in the U.S.[71]

By 2016, the Chinese were already progressing at making movies for the Chinese audience. Even though *Kung Fu Panda 3* had a big box-office haul that year, it was outperformed by two lower-budget Chinese films, *The Monkey King 2* and *The Mermaid*.[72] Neither of those films performed well outside of China, but Beijing could easily view this as progress. It was "soft power" in action.

In 2021, only twenty-one revenue-sharing Hollywood films were released in China, far fewer than the thirty-four-title quota set out by Biden and Xi in the 2012 agreement. Chinese films were gaining market share partly due to the reduced number of Hollywood films released in their country.

Biden had gotten rolled.

According to Chris Fenton, a Hollywood producer who used to work for DMG Entertainment, "Beijing offered up access to its market in exchange for a decade-long tutorial from Hollywood on how to replicate its filmmaking process."[73]

Oftentimes the Chinese censors made unreasonable requests that could cost a studio tens or even hundreds of millions of dollars. For example, regulators objected to Sony's *Spider-Man: No Way Home* for featuring a scene that showed the Statue of Liberty. The movie had already been shot, and the scene could not be edited out because Lady Liberty was integral to the plot. So, the movie was banned.[74]

For a town that claims to hate blacklisting so much, you would have thought that Hollywood's activist class would have raised a bigger stink about this phenomenon.

But they don't, because that would poke the panda.

Relations between Hollywood and China have further deteriorated in recent years, with Hollywood's share of Chinese ticket sales decreasing and studios struggling to get movies on the calendar in China. Even Disney, the ultimate CCP sellout with theme parks across China, has had releases canceled by the censors. And hope is not necessarily on the horizon. The 2012 film agreement was supposed to be renegotiated in 2017, but talks stalled out.

Voice of America reported in 2022 that Chinese censorship was expanding. For twenty-five years, the American studios could cut or edit scenes that ran afoul of the CCP censors and still get the rest of the movie approved. "Now it's kind of escalated," according to Stanley Rosen, a University of Southern California professor who tracks China's film industry. "They're much more direct in banning films outright rather than just tampering or asking for scenes to be removed."[75]

In March 2023, *Winnie the Pooh: Blood and Honey* was blocked by the CCP, and not for being in poor taste. The reason is that images of Winnie the Pooh are banned in China because they are often used to mock Xi Jinping.[76] The American media treated the blacklisting like it was a joke. "Oh, bother. Winnie the Pooh has found himself in another sticky situation," read one line in *Time* magazine.

Censorship is funny when the commies do it!

The CCP has even thumbed their nose at Hollywood by using American movies in their own military propaganda videos.[77] The Chinese video "The God of War H-6K Attack!" includes scenes from American films *The Rock, The Hurt Locker,* and *Transformers: Revenge of the Fallen,* for example. The video also includes satellite footage of the U.S. military's Andersen Air Force Base on Guam in what appears to be a not-so-veiled threat against the base. The video was released in September 2020, a time of high tension between the U.S. and China, with a recent visit to Taiwan by high-level U.S. diplomats angering the Chinese government.

"Hollywood's share of the China box office market in 2021 has collapsed to a shocking 9.5%, according to data from consultancy Artisan Gateway," *Variety* reported in August 2021.

Despite being the instigator of Hollywood's decline, Joe Biden has avoided the ire of the entertainment establishment. In fact, he continues to bag mountains of their cash. In the summer of 2020, Katzenberg and George Clooney held a virtual event for Biden and his vice presidential running mate, Kamala Harris, costing $100,000 per ticket.[78] The following week, Tom Hanks held a fundraising event for Biden.[79] By late August, Katzenberg had held events for Biden that had raised a reported $13 million that election cycle.[80] In May 2023, Katzenberg told the *Financial Times* that he would pledge Biden "all the resources" he needs to win reelection in 2024.[81]

The Hollywood oligarchy sold out to China, and it backfired. China was able to up their propaganda skills while neutering our greatest cultural asset. Now the CCP is squeezing us out of their country altogether.

A genius plot twist, if there ever was one.

It was also a stunning accomplishment in cultural warfare.

And this disaster epic has a clear villain: Joe Biden.

THE APOTHEOSIS OF AMERICANA

It is a perilous moment for the movie business. Movies are no longer at the center of the conversation culturally, and this has left a vacuum that has been filled seemingly by TV and thirty-six-second videos posted to TikTok (a Chinese company). Even politics now dominates the national dialogue more than the movies. Hollywood itself deserves much of the blame, but so does Joe Biden.

There are significant headwinds if we want to revitalize the medium. High-quality television sets and endless streaming options make it unnecessary to drive to the theater, pay for parking, buy a ticket and maybe some overpriced concessions, then sit captive for ninety minutes or more, perhaps surrounded by talking and texting strangers. This is not a fun proposition unless the movie is really good.

And most of them simply aren't really good.

Award season tends to elevate prestige films that very few people see (such as recent Academy Award Best Picture winners *Moonlight*, *Spotlight*, *Nomadland*, and *Coda*).

Then there are the big-budget, sexless, bloodless, China-friendly blockbusters that are more like theme park rides assembled by engineers than art created by auteurs. These are entirely disposable cash grabs, one barely distinguishable from the next, and many of them don't even grab all that much cash.

And of course, there is all that woke. Wokeness is box-office poison, yet Hollywood still can't help themselves from forcing their preferred social justice rhetoric into their films, squandering audience goodwill and box-office spoils. Unnecessary woke themes can be found in Pixar's *Lightyear*, Spielberg's *West Side Story*, and *Terminator: Dark Fate*, three of the biggest flops of the last decade.[82] DC's *Shazam! Fury of the Gods*, a family movie with a shoehorned LGBTQQIAAP2S+ character story line, is another recent example of a major box-office bust.[83] In-your-face propaganda like the critically acclaimed same-sex romantic comedy *Bros* is financially disastrous (almost no one saw that flick, including gays, despite a 90 percent Rotten Tomatoes score).[84]

There is nothing better than a movie that says something about what society is like right now, but wokeness tries to mold us into something we're not. Audiences hate that.

Unfortunately, I don't think this trend will get any better in the short term. Enforced diversity quotas are now the industry standard. This means a certain number of women and "BIPOCs" will need to be attached to a project for it to go forward.[85] This is anathema to the creative process. It is also pure racism and sexism, so hopefully a class-action lawsuit will end that trend. (Imagine if there were affirmative action for conservatives and Christians in writers' rooms and on movie sets. Hollywood and the establishment media would melt down.)

Between 2018 and 2022, movie theater attendance dropped 48 percent,[86] and the trade media has tried to blame flagging domestic box-office hauls squarely on the coronavirus (which was caused by China, a fact they typically omit in their reports). But that is willful ignorance. That theory provides no explanation for why some movies are performing like gangbusters in a post-COVID world. Films without a left-wing political agenda—or any agenda at all—are still bringing audiences out to the theater. The aforementioned *Spider-Man: No Way Home*, *Super Mario Bros.*, and the entire John Wick franchise are testament to this.[87] The lightly jingoistic crowd-pleaser *Top Gun: Maverick* was a historic success.

And best of all: none of these movies needed the Chinese market to be financially successful.

The lesson: ignore China and cut out the woke, and audiences will come back.

The magic of the movies still remains, and just because the quality of our films seems to be getting worse on average, it doesn't mean they *all* are getting worse, and it doesn't mean they can't get better again.

Hollywood, from my vantage point, is at its best when its goals are simple: reflect society at large (some exaggeration for emphasis is okay), inspire the audience, and above all else, entertain us. This is my perspective as a journalist, (erstwhile) movie lover, and someone who grew up in Tinsel Town.

Yet I can't speak for the studios that make these films. It's clear that ever since Joe Biden, Xi Jinping, and Jeffrey Katzenberg brokered those deals all those years ago, the strategy has been to bet the entire American film industry on a foreign country with a hostile authoritarian government.

Hollywood sold their soul to China, and now China is in the process of cutting Hollywood off. But this could be a good thing. We got addicted to that sweet, sweet commie cash, and now it is time to go cold turkey.

If we can do that, the movies can be great again, no thanks to China and Joe Biden.

PART III

AMERICA TRANSITIONS

JOE BIDEN'S MANAGED DECLINE

CHAPTER 9

Sneaky Joe's Low-Energy Energy Policy

O n the first day of Biden's Administration, according to the Intergovernmental Panel on Climate Change, there will only be 9 years left to stop the worst consequences of climate change. This premise was introduced by the Joe Biden/Kamala Harris campaign's "9 Key Elements of Joe Biden's Plan for a Clean Energy Revolution." (There was one "key element" for each year left until certain death.) This would be the duo's blueprint for how to achieve "climate and environmental justice."[1]

The pursuit of "climate and environmental justice," a term more about emotions and values than about science or law, has become the cornerstone of Biden's domestic agenda.

Though the concept of "environmental justice" dates back decades, according to *National Geographic*, it had never gotten the "attention it deserves," if the establishment media is to be believed. Perhaps they missed their own obsessive coverage of the subject in recent years.[2] America's most senior statesmen assumed not only that the American people were familiar with the term, but they were committed to confronting it, in all of its "heartbreaking forms."[3]

The sum total of this effort would lead to one of the most expensive public spending efforts in the history of the United States of America.

Here are a few of the principles that undergird Joe Biden's energy and environmental policies:

- The climate is changing for the worse and it is the fault of human beings,[4] and Americans are not exempt. (Naturally, he ignores the fact that the earth has gotten significantly greener over the last couple of decades.)[5]

- The effects of the changing climate are disproportionately felt by certain races and ethnicities.

- Man ought to try to rein in "global warming" through bigger government and more regulation.

- If we don't act quickly, that is, during the Biden presidency, we are probably dead. (In fact, we might already be dead. Andrew Yang, a businessman who challenged Biden in the 2020 Democrat primary, said that it is actually "too late to stop the warming," and we must all move to "higher ground.")[6]

- It is preferable for mankind to limit the ability to produce and utilize cheap and abundant energy sources, regardless of the benefits they provide mankind today, in order to pursue the goal of making things better for Mother Earth in the long term.

How much can he actually accomplish in his brief time as president? If I'm being charitable, not much. A study from the University of California, Berkeley, published in 2000 said the earth already needs 10 million years to recover from the damage humans have already wrought, and we presumably have continued to injure the planet in the twenty-three years hence. Professors and academics, most notably Paul Ehrlich of *Population Bomb* fame, have for decades asserted that the ideal number of humans on earth is somewhere between 1.5 billion and 2 billion.[7] We have approximately 8 billion at the time of this writing, and that number is rising.

The simplest way to achieve a massive global reduction in people—aside from the largest genocide in the history of the world (just to be safe, please, no one give Mr. Ehrlich control of any large fighting forces)—is to pit man against nature and undermine humanity's ability to prosper.

It is this godless and antihuman premise that has been accepted by much of the globalist left.

"Climate change" was among the top issues for Democrats in the 2020 election, with 68 percent of registered voters saying the issue is "very important" to them, according to an August 2020 Pew Research Center survey. Only 11 percent of Republicans agreed, which made "climate change" their lowest priority of any major issue surveyed by Pew and the single most divisive.[8]

Yet despite campaigning to unify the country, immediately upon taking office, Biden issued executive actions on energy and the environment that reversed the significant deregulation that took place under President Trump and greatly expanded the federal government's effort to control the temperature of the earth. Biden wasn't exactly subtle about his goals, stating that "on Day 1" he planned "to not just reverse all of the damage Trump has done, but go further and faster," according to the campaign material.

In fact, Biden issued more executive actions in the first week of his administration than any prior president.[9] Many of those executive actions expanded his powers on energy and climate.

One of Biden's objectives was the limiting of methane pollution from oil and gas companies. In November 2021, the Environmental Protection Agency (EPA) announced plans to regulate methane wells for the first time. This is expected to cost the oil and gas industry north of a billion dollars; stricter regulations on new well construction is also expected.[10] According to government data, methane emissions have declined 17 percent since 1990 anyway.[11] Over the same time period, emissions are up from agriculture operations and livestock management, both of which are significant sources of methane production. This reveals that Biden's true agenda is more about targeting the oil and gas industry—a favorite political target of the Left—than actually saving the planet.

While taking on the beef industry has not yet been an overt priority of Biden's, it remains to be seen how we will achieve his stated goal of cutting U.S. net emissions to zero by 2050 while not devastating that portion of the economy.[12] I don't think he wants his legacy to be as the president who encouraged Americans to eat bugs, which is probably a disappointment to some of the globalist elite. (Biden himself might not be around to see if his goal is realized, as he would be 108 years old when it is time to check how his grandiose vision is playing out.)

Other priorities on the Biden energy agenda include:

- Allocating massive amounts of federal funding toward electric vehicle initiatives. This includes a $600 million effort to replace hundreds of thousands of federal vehicles and more than $174 billion worth of funding for electric transit ve-hicles, school bus electrification, and EV charging stations across the nation.[13]

- Committing hundreds of billions of dollars toward energy innovation aimed at fighting climate change.[14]

- Banning new oil and gas leases on public lands. (These leases were eventually restarted when gas prices soared in the first half of 2022.)[15]

- Suspending drilling in the Arctic National Wildlife Refuge (ANWR). Even though gas prices were already on the rise as Biden took office, he canceled all oil and gas leases in the re-mote portion of northern Alaska. Trump had opened up the area for drilling in 2017 over the long-standing objections of environmental groups.[16]

- Rejoining the Paris Climate Accord. (In 2022, the United Nations announced "Finance for Climate Action," a financial blueprint to achieve the Paris treaty's global temperatures goals; the estimated costs are expected to exceed $2 trillion per year by 2030.)

- Implementing 500,000 new public charging outlets for elec-tric vehicles by 2030.[17]

- Financially incentivizing U.S. farmers to become the first zero-emission agricultural industry in the world.

- Pursuing the aforementioned "environmental justice." "Biden will make it a priority for all federal agencies—and hold them accountable for results—to engage in community-driven approaches to develop solutions for environmental injustices affecting communities of color, low-income communities, and indigenous communities," according to Team Biden.[18] In other words, "environmental justice" is something that is achieved through Zoom meet-ings with local officials, not with cutting-edge science.

- Imposing penalties on the excessive emitters via the EPA and DOJ.[19]

- Creating million of new jobs in the green infrastructure sector, largely via government grants and other various incentives.[20]

If—and only if—we follow these specific instructions, we can adjust the climate of the planet to Joe Biden's liking, or something.

His ideas won't make the lives of average American citizens any better, but they do align with those of green environmentalists and globalists at the World Economic Forum in Davos and CEOs of America's ESG (environmental, social, and governance) corporations. These are his most important political allies.

PRESIDENT MOTORS: JOE BIDEN, GM, AND KARMA

One of Joe Biden's all-time favorite corporations is no doubt General Motors.

Biden's history with GM has been long and romantic. When Joe Biden married Neilia, Joe Sr. gifted the couple a 1967 Corvette 327 Stingray convertible. Joe still owns the car (finished in Goodwood Green Metallic with a saddle tan leather interior, a combination evoking classic British race cars) to this day. The car was featured, along with the president himself, on an episode of *Jay Leno's Garage* in November 2022.[21]

Joe and Hunter Biden appeared in the car for a 2016 profile and photo shoot with *Popular Mechanics*.[22] His sister, Valerie, wrote fondly of "borrowing" Joe's Corvette to drive to her first day working as a history teacher.[23]

The Corvette went from famous to infamous when America learned that it was parked in the Delaware garage where Joe stashed classified documents.[24]

He has shown unwavering political support for GM throughout his career. During Biden's vice presidency, the Obama/Biden administration bailed out the struggling automaker for $50 billion. The taxpayers lost a staggering $11.2 billion on the deal,[25] but the iconic carmaker was able to stave off extinction.

A $50 million investment from the Delaware-based du Ponts into GM helped the company surpass Ford to become America's largest automobile manufacturer. The family maintained deep ties to the car company for the next half century. Ralph Nader, a prominent left-wing political activist and perpetual automobile critic, once wrote of GM's ties to Biden's home state that "General Motors could buy Delaware if the Du Ponts were willing to sell it."[26]

While GM never did buy Delaware, the company has always received special attention from the state's most famous politician. This even means promoting GM over more forward-thinking and environmentally sustainable automakers.

GM would also become a tent pole of Joe Biden's radical climate agenda.

Joe wasn't just nostalgic about that Corvette. He was nostalgic about all things GM. The culture surrounding the brand was deeply tied to his own roots. There was an iconic assembly plant that stood on Boxwood Road in Wilmington that had survived highs and lows since it opened its doors in 1947. There were the "malaise years" of the late 1970s and early '80s, during which emissions and safety regulations laid waste to the American auto industry, paving the way for European and Japanese rivals. A major retooling in the early 1990s nearly shuttered the plant entirely. Yet the Wilmington Assembly continued churning out cars until 2009, when the financial crisis and GM's ensuing bankruptcy finally put it out to pasture.

It was the end of an era. Or was it? Not if Vice President Joey Biden had anything to say about it.

In 2009, Obama's Energy Department extended roughly a billion dollars in loan guarantees to two electric vehicle start-ups: Fisker Automotive, backed by legendary automobile designer Henrik Fisker, and Tesla.[27]

In October 2009, Biden, in his first term as vice president, announced that Fisker would be buying the legendary GM plant on Boxwood Road in Wilmington, where it would produce its new all-electric sports car, the Orwellian-named Karma.[28] The company received more than half a billion dollars in loans through the Energy Department, where Biden's niece, Missy Owens, was working as deputy chief of staff at the time. Hunter Biden's "Rosemont" business partners were among the company's investors.[29]

Fisker went bankrupt within five years. Hunter, who had bought a Fisker using money transferred by Kazakh oligarch Kenes Rakishev, was named as a bankruptcy creditor.[30]

Only about two thousand Karmas were actually sold.[31]

Karma, I suppose.

The brand was sold off to the Chinese and has since been reintroduced, to limited success.[32]

Meanwhile, Tesla paid off its federal loans nine years early and went on to become the world's largest producer of electric vehicles and one of the world's most valuable companies.

Despite its success, Tesla has gotten the cold shoulder from Biden since he became president. Meanwhile, GM raked in big government dollars. One key example came in 2021 when it was announced that GM Defense would build an electrified military Hummer.[33]

Take that, Putin, Xi, and ISIS! The USA is gonna kick your butt while we fight carbon emissions!

The Department of Defense announced in 2022 that it selected GM Defense's Ultium platform to develop a battery pack for electric military vehicles.[34] In December 2022, the Department of Energy announced a $2.5 billion loan to Ultium Cells LLC (a joint venture of GM and LG Energy Solutions) to develop multiple consumer battery manufacturing facilities.[35]

Biden's favorable policy toward GM and the EV industry in general has paid financial dividends for his family, and even himself.

In February 2022, GM announced it was hiring Missy Owens—the same Biden niece who had worked in the Energy Department during the Fisker years—as director of environmental, social, and governance (ESG) policy, putting her at the forefront of the company's efforts to court Washington support for its EV product line.[36]

Biden continued to pursue favorable policies to funnel government and taxpayer dollars to GM, but only after significant lobbying by GM.[37] Open Secrets lists General Motors among the country's top ten lobbying entities; their top priority in 2022 was, unsurprisingly, the Inflation Reduction Act (IRA). The company and its executive also donate vast sums to Democrats, Joe Biden especially.[38]

The GM/Joe Biden backscratching must have been very satisfying.

GM, pivoting its business model to trendy environmentalism, announced plans to sell only electric vehicles by 2035.[39] This is a bold move, given limited evidence that the public will be willing to fully abandon gas and diesel cars by that time. This statement, however, would please Democrat voters and consumers.

Biden's IRA made GM's electric models eligible for a $7,500 federal tax credit. Conveniently, GM (and Ford) raised their prices on their electric trucks by $6,000 to $8,000 shortly after the legislation passed, though they claimed the move was not related to the tax credits.[40] How stupid do they think we are?

The crony connections continue: Jeff Ricchetti was tapped to lobby on GM's behalf just days after Joe Biden was sworn in.[41] He's a perfect choice for the job, considering that Jeff's brother, Steve Ricchetti, is counselor to President Biden and the former chairman of his 2020 presidential campaign.[42] Three of Steve's children also work in the Biden government, prompting *Politico* to refer to it as the "Ricchetti administration."[43]

EV prices are skyrocketing. The average price paid leapt from around $44,000 to about $54,000 from 2021 to 2022. That's an increase of 22 percent, which far outpaced the (still very high) 14 percent inflation for nonelectric vehicles.[44]

EVs remain a luxury, and Biden's policies did little to address that. If anything, he seemed to embrace it. In November 2021, he took a 999-horsepower electric Hummer for a spin while he was on a GM factory tour.[45] It looked pretty cool (aside from the fact that the president chose to wear a ridiculous, antiscience cloth mask during the test drive). It should have looked cool, considering the car's base model caries a $108,700 price tag. However, that number is irrelevant for most people because the car instantly sold out, likely for years.[46]

The U.S. government falsely bills electric vehicles as cost savers. Energy.gov claims that "prices for electricity are stable."[47] Yet a report released in January 2023 by the Anderson Economic Group showed that driving a gas-powered car one hundred miles costs an average of $11.29, while people who charge up their EVs at home paid $11.60 per hundred miles. A little more expensive than gas, and way more expensive than your lying, EV-obsessed government claims.[48]

Welcome to the new green future. Enjoy the expensive new cars you can't even buy.

But maybe we don't even want them.

As of June 2022, 140,000 all-electric Chevy Bolts had been recalled from all model years, due to batteries catching on fire.[49] Apparently, wide adoption of the technology of the future involves risking that your car will spontaneously erupt into an inferno. As one website put it, "Don't Park Your Chevy Bolt Inside Where It Might Burn Down Your Home."[50]

No wonder it's so easy to get nostalgic for classic American muscle cars.

CHINA'S EV DOMINATION, BROUGHT TO YOU BY THE BIDENS

Back in Wilmington, the GM/Fisker plant was torn down and became what was at the time the largest Amazon fulfillment center in the U.S. It used to be a place where Americans built American cars. Now it's where robots haul made-in-China products across a soulless warehouse.[51]

This is another terrible irony considering that China is dominating the EV market. Some facts:

- One of out every two EVs sold in 2021 was bought in China.[52]

- China has become the largest exporter of EVs overall.[53]

- China is currently the world's largest EV growth market.[54]

- Tesla, the world's biggest manufacturer of EVs, sells more cars in China than any other country.[55]

- China could hit 60 percent of global EV sales.[56]

- China's CATL is the world's largest supplier of lithium-ion batteries, servicing companies like Volkswagen, BMW, Tesla, and, of course, GM.[57]

China's path to global domination in this industry was massively accelerated by then vice president Joe Biden and his family.

After all, the Biden operation is a family business, and the Bidens are tied to CATL.

In 2013, Hunter Biden traveled to China to launch the now-notorious private equity fund BHR Partners. The company quickly became an investor in CATL. BHR then scooped up Henniges, a Michigan-based auto parts manufacturer, in partnership with a Chinese state-owned defense contractor. That deal also required federal approval.[58]

When Fisker declared bankruptcy in 2013, a Chinese company, Wanxiang, emerged as the biggest bidder for Fisker's assets, and it was Joe Biden who shepherded the company's president around America while negotiating the deal. Wanxiang also purchased A123, a major American supplier of lithium-ion batteries that received federal loans from the Obama/Biden administration.

In 2017, BHR partnered with a state-controlled mining conglomerate to purchase the Congo's Tenke Fungurume mine, one of the world's largest sources of cobalt, a critical mineral in the production of batteries. The *New York Times* described the sale as a major failure by the U.S. to prevent China's control of the global clean energy trade.[59]

The effect of this series of events is simple: Chinese supremacy in the industry. Joe Biden and Son directly participated in this transference. China controls the market for minerals that are vital to battery production. "China currently controls the processing of nearly 60% of the world's lithium, 35% of nickel, 65% of cobalt and more than 85% of rare-earth elements," according to Abigail Wulf, director of the Center for Critical Minerals Strategy at Securing America's Future Energy (SAFE).[60]

What's more, Biden has consistently banned or regulated the extraction of valuable geological material throughout his presidency.[61] This favors China, which has no qualms about drilling anywhere and everywhere on earth in order to bring the least expensive products to market.

Joe Biden has left that void, and China has filled it.

It's crystal clear how China benefits from these decisions by Joe Biden and his family. What is less clear is whether America will ever benefit from them, too.

In recent years, even Biden's beloved GM has been sustained by the Chinese.

The vast majority of GM electric vehicles are sold in China.[62]

ELECTRIC VEHICLES: THE RIGHTEOUS GRIFT

The push to make electric vehicles the centerpiece of our more sustainable future has become doctrine for Joe Biden and the American Left. The federal government has committed billions of dollars to EV investment in the last two years, primarily through the Infrastructure Investment and Jobs Act. The 2,700-page, $1.2 trillion piece of legislation was one of Biden's top legislative accomplishments of his first year as president and offered little to conservatives. The bipartisan bill was supported by nineteen Senate Republicans, including Leader Mitch McConnell, and thirteen House Republicans.

Representative Jim Banks (R-IN), who chairs the Republican Study Committee (RSC), noted that only $110 billion (or less than 10 percent) would fund roads, bridges, and other projects that fit under the traditional definition of "infrastructure." The RSC claimed the bill was in effect "Green New Deal Light," and it's hard to disagree.[63]

Included in the package was $66 billion in funding for Biden's beloved Amtrak, but as is the standard in Joe Biden's Washington, there would be no taxpayer accountability for where the funds would be allocated.[64]

The infrastructure bill actually advanced critical race theory (CRT). Not a joke. From one section: "race and gender-neutral efforts are insufficient to address" issues surrounding "disadvantaged business enterprises."[65]

This bill does more than merely create jobs and fix America's physical foundation, as its advocates argued. It also ameliorates the "racism physically built into some of our highways," according to transportation secretary Pete Buttigieg.[66] What doesn't this bill do?

Much of the bill is not even loosely related to infrastructure. One provision creates "digital equity" grants that could be based on race or ethnicity. In fact, the word "equity" is used seventy-one times in the text of the bill. Who doesn't think of "equity" when discussing repairing levies and paving roads?[67]

Though the expansion of broadband Internet access is probably a legitimate use of an infrastructure bill, the bill text indicates that minority communities will be prioritized.[68]

The wokeness doesn't stop there: "gender identity" is provided as a protected class in the bill. Why miss an opportunity such as an infrastructure bill to advance the trans agenda? The bill also encourages women to enter the field of trucking.

Though there are no specific victories for conservatives in the bill, we at Breitbart News did notice a pattern in that the U.S. Chamber of Commerce, which backed the bill, sent out checks to most of the Republicans who ended up supporting it.[69] Strange!

There were also the standard kickbacks that are ubiquitous in massive spending packages. For example, funding doubled for the Appalachian Regional Commission, which is cochaired by Gayle Manchin, wife of Senator Joe Manchin (D-WV).[70] Billions of dollars of infrastructure was allocated specifically to Kentucky, so it comes as no surprise that Senator McConnell was "delighted" by the bill's passage.[71]

He was delighted even despite an unending barrage of green policies. There was a grant for a pilot program for a vehicle miles traveled tax (VMT). There is another grant to encourage children walking to school.[72] It even mandates that states develop their own carbon-reduction plans within two years.[73] Then there was the $10 billion for "clean transit" and school buses, $5 billion for a network of EV chargers, and $7 billion for "critical minerals" and other battery components.[74]

The push for universal (or near-universal) adoption of electric vehicles comes despite the fact that the technology is obviously not yet ready. Recalls for electric vehicles are a defining characteristic of the industry. Many of them are designed to reduce risk of the engine block catching fire, which is extremely dangerous to the driver. Aside from the aforementioned Chevy Bolt fires, Tesla, for example, had more than twenty recalls in 2022 alone.[75] In December 2020, *Insider* documented a story of a Tesla driver watching in horror as another Tesla burst into flames after hitting a barrier in Los Angeles. The driver of the crashed car said he was using Autopilot (Tesla's automated driving system) at the time.[76]

It's not easy—or environmentally sustainable—to put out EV vehicle fires. It took twelve thousand gallons of water to extinguish the flames from one Tesla lithium-ion battery that ignited after hitting some debris on a Pennsylvania road in late 2022.[77] Stories like these are common.

EV charging also provides significant strain on the electrical grid. California announced its intention to ban new gas-powered cars by 2035, but in 2022, the state asked residents to limit when and where they charge their vehicles.[78] On September 6, 2020, Democrat governor Gavin Newsom issued a "Flex Alert," the oddly named signal to Californians that they ought not plug in their cars between 4 p.m. and 9 p.m., use large appliances, or set their thermostats below a sizzling 78 degrees.[79]

This is the perfect temperature for reptiles. Being a native Los Angeleno, I can attest that there are many, many lizards in the Golden State.

Two days later, Newsom's "Flex Alert" was extended to the hours of 3 p.m. and 10 p.m.[80]

The establishment media, of course, didn't fault the government or even inadequate technologies for the massive inconvenience imposed on citizens (especially those with young families), but instead blamed global warming.

(California should not be trusted on any environmental-related issues. The state is perpetually in a drought, but when it was inundated with rain in the winter of 2022–23, the state watched billions of gallons of precious water wash out into the ocean. They were unable to capture it. The state government simply lost sight of what should have been one of its most important priorities while it was distracted by the woke and trendy.[81])

"Electrical grids aren't prepared for the increasing power demands brought on by climate change, experts said," the *New York Times* reported in the summer of 2021. Yet these failures provide more reason for the government to expand even more, taxing and spending more on EV technology. It's a win-win for the oligarchy.[82]

Much of the country is lacking in adequate EV charging ports, and of the ports that are most easily accessible, many are compatible only with Teslas. All of them take hours to reach a full charge, aside from those at Direct Current Fast Charging (DCFC) stations, of which there are only six thousand in the entire country.[83] These stations are rare, cost tens of thousands of dollars per connector, and still take significantly longer than a trip to one of the nation's 150,000 gas stations.

Even on a full charge, current electric vehicles simply don't have comparable ranges to equivalent cars that run on a combustion engine. YouTuber Tyler Hoover (who also contributes to *Motor Trend*) posted a video to his channel "Hoovie's Garage" in late 2022 called "Towing with My Ford Lightning EV Pickup Was a TOTAL DISASTER!" He wasn't exaggerating. He showed that the "truck" lost ninety miles of range in what was actually a thirty-mile trip.[84]

I use scare quotes around "truck" because it was when he attempted to tow some cargo that things got truly pathetic.

"This truck can't do normal truck things. You would be stopping every hour to recharge, which would take about 45 minutes a pop, and that is absolutely not practical," Hoover said.[85]

This is especially sad, considering that Ford is arguably one of the leaders in the industry. The Mustang Mach-E was the third-bestselling EV as of July 2022 behind the Tesla Model Y and Model 3.[86]

The International Energy Agency raised concerns that the "global market value of electricity for EV charging is projected to grow over 20-fold by 2030," and "the amount of public charging infrastructure that has been announced might be insufficient to power the size of the EV market being targeted."[87]

Yet again these technological deficiencies are all the more reason for the federal government to invest in the technologies of tomorrow.

Perhaps we'll soon see another trillion-dollar infrastructure bill to further bridge the gap!

THE PARIS CLIMATE ACCORDS (AKA THE PARIS AGREEMENT)

The 2015 Paris Climate Accords, signed by the U.S. in 2016, is the document that looms large over any energy policy discussion in the Biden era. John Kerry, the former Democrat presidential nominee and secretary of state under Barack Obama, was appointed Biden's first special envoy for the climate in January 2021. He had signed the Paris Climate Accords for the U.S. in 2016.[88]

It is the green movement's Magna Carta.

The Paris Agreement set a long-term goal of limiting the global temperature increases to between 1.5 and 2 degrees Celsius, ostensibly through a worldwide effort. It was adopted by 196 parties, mostly sovereign nations, in 2015 at the United Nations Climate Change Conference. Various climate models highlighted by the U.S. government predict temperatures are on pace to rise 1.1 and 5.4 degrees Celsius by 2100.[89] That's a wide range and doesn't exactly instill a lot of faith in the supposed scientific consensus.[90] The *New York Times* suggests that number is at about 3 degrees Celsius.[91]

In order to achieve Paris's goals, it is believed that developed nations must get to "net-zero" carbon emissions by 2050. Developing nations have roughly until the 2060s to catch up. The definition of "developing" is, of course, subjective. China, for example, the world's second-most-populous nation, second-biggest economy, and by far the world's biggest polluter, still qualifies as a "developing" nation. None of this suggests that this colossally expensive plan will actually work.[92]

Less burden is placed on "developing" nations (including China) to change, and an outsized amount is placed on the "developed" West. A 2021 *Nature* study estimated that it would cost each American $1,100 per year until 2050 to get to "net zero"; that's more than $4 trillion each year, or more than we currently spend on Medicare, Medicaid, and Social Security combined.[93]

In a world where voters tolerate unfathomable levels of government spending, this has thus far proven to be too high a price tag in our current economic condition.

Typically leftist (but apparently pro-human) OxFam warned that in order to get to "net zero" on Paris's timetable, allegedly green governments and corporations would have to rely too heavily on "unreliable, unproven, and unrealistic 'carbon removal' schemes." Instead of drastically cutting pollution, wealthier nations could simply bypass emission cuts by buying carbon-offset credits, according to OxFam. The British charity produced a study in 2021 claiming that it would require more than 1.6 billion hectares of land dedicated specifically to carbon removal in order to accomplish the goal. This much land would inevitably compete with food production and could lead to an 80 percent spike in food prices, according to the study. This could lead to widespread hunger and even famine, as well as additional humanitarian crises that would come from inevitable mass migration from poorer countries to wealthier ones.[94]

In other words, the best-case scenario for Paris is that it might help the planet a little, but it would hurt humanity a lot.

It is all a virtue signal.

BIDEN'S CLIMATE CABINET

If Biden's magnificent agenda on climate policy is to be taken seriously, he will need to task the most competent figures in U.S. government to execute it. Let's meet a few of them.

John Kerry: The former secretary of state has been criticized for being an excessive polluter in his own right. For example, he has taken dozens of hours of private jet travel even after becoming Biden's climate czar.[95] The *Washington Free Beacon* reported in September 2022 that Kerry had already flown a total of 180,000 miles—or around the world more than seven times—in his role as America's top enforcer of environmentalism. This is all despite his insistence that climate change is an "existential" crisis.[96]

If he really believed it was a matter of life and death for the planet, he would have conducted more of these meetings via Skype.

Kerry, interestingly enough, has already given up on the idea of net zero by 2050. He said so in an 2021 interview with former British prime minister Tony Blair at the Science Museum Group Climate Talk.[97]

Kerry designed, with input from the Rockefeller Foundation and the Bezos Earth Fund, a plan for a carbon-trading market where businesses can buy these "offsets." This would give the wealthiest entities on earth the ability to continue polluting at their current rate, so long as they pay an extra toll that normal people and smaller businesses might not be able to afford.[98]

It is unknown how this blatant elitism will lead to climate justice.

Of all the climate alarmists in mainstream American life, Kerry is certainly among the most hysterical. In 2014, he equated climate change to a "weapon of mass destruction" in a speech in Jakarta, Indonesia.[99] The speech seemed aimed at terrifying the people of Indonesia, a country comprising a lot of small islands. "It's not an exaggeration to say that the entire way of life that you live and love is at risk," Kerry said.

Kerry isn't the only member of Obama's climate team who is back in a position of power in the Biden administration.

John Podesta: Podesta is a longtime operative for the Democrat Party, having worked as a campaign chair for Hilary Clinton, cochair of the Obama/Biden transition staff and climate counselor to Obama, and White House chief of staff to Bill Clinton. Podesta also founded the left-wing Washington think tank the Center for American Progress and was once a prolific lobbyist.[100]

Podesta is perhaps most famous for his involvement in the 2016 election interference conspiracy that was later dubbed "Russiagate," in which a Russian espionage group called Fancy Bear managed to gain access to Podesta's private Gmail account.[101] Thousands of these emails were then released through WikiLeaks and revealed multiple instances of questionable campaign practices discussed among Hillary Clinton's campaign officials as well as generally swampish behavior involving former president Bill Clinton.[102]

Recall Andrew's quote: "Fuck. You. John. Podesta."

Podesta was tapped on September 2, 2022, to serve as advisor to the president for clean energy innovation and implementation.[103] His responsibilities included the oversight of the Inflation Reduction Act, which included $369 billion worth of climate-related spending, and to chair the President's National Climate Task Force (NCTF).[104] Biden created the first-ever NCTF the first month he took office. Its leadership team is made up of twenty-five of the highest-ranking cabinet members, including Janet Yellen, Pete Buttigieg, Merrick Garland, and John Kerry.[105]

Gina Raimondo: Appointed secretary of the Commerce Department on March 3, 2021, Raimondo is another of the twenty-five cabinet members to head the NCTF. She served as governor of Rhode Island from 2015 to 2021.[106] Her tenure was an unpopular one, rife with criticisms that she weakened the competitiveness of business owners in the state, earning it the title of worst state for business.[107] This fact alone makes her perfectly suited for Biden's climate squad.

As governor in 2017, she ran afoul of environmentalists by pushing for the expansion of the Champlin Marina into the Great Salt Pond. Activists like the Conservation Law Foundation opposed the expansion because it would infringe on the pond's ecology.[108]

Jennifer Granholm: Granholm was sworn in as energy secretary on February 25, 2021.[109] From 2003 to 2011, she was the governor of Michigan and, before that, the state's attorney general. Granholm has shown no evidence that she understands the oil or gas business, which makes her a very progressive—in the woke sense of the word—choice to lead our Department of Energy. What she does know about energy is that electric vehicles can be lucrative: in May 2021, she sold $1.6 million worth of shares of the electric bus company Proterra ahead of concerns about conflicting interests with the Biden administration's agenda toward EVs.[110]

She failed to disclose stock transactions at least nine times during her tenure, blaming the issue on a clerical error.[111]

There are apparently a lot of bad clerks in Joe Biden's America.

Amos Hochstein: Antony Blinken appointed Hochstein as the State Department's senior advisor for energy security on August 10, 2021.[112] He was considered the point person for gaining the U.S. access to foreign oil markets during the Obama administration. Hochstein was tasked by Biden with mitigating risks associated with the Nord Stream 2 pipeline. He is yet another example of a not particularly diplomatic choice by Biden if he intends to keep nuclear Russia at bay: until October 2020, Hochstein was on the board of Naftogaz, Ukraine's state-owned oil and gas company.

He has been criticized for owning stock in companies that are considered to be unhumanitarian.[113]

Sam Brinton: The man who best embodies the unseriousness of Joe Biden's energy policy. In January 2022, Brinton was chosen to become deputy assistant secretary of spent fuel and waste disposition in the Energy Department's Office of Nuclear Energy. Brinton holds a nuclear engineering degree from Kansas State University and two masters of science degrees, one in nuclear science, another in engineering, from the Massachusetts Institute of Technology (MIT). Yet he seemed at the time like an incredibly odd choice for the job. He wasn't necessarily unqualified, though he apparently had "no prior federal government experience" and "no executive management or operations experience."[114] What was odd about Brinton was that he was "nonbinary," meaning he identifies as neither a man nor a woman. He wears women's clothing but sports facial hair and a bald head. In fact, he garnered notoriety and publicity as a "gender-fluid" activist by somehow getting onto the 2018 Oscars red carpet in a custom gown, Jimmy Choo stilettos, plenty of leather, and a pink mohawk perched asymmetrically atop his otherwise hairless scalp. Of course, he used the women's restroom at the event; one media report claimed that "Meryl Streep loved it."[115]

Four years later, thanks to Joe Biden, Brinton would become the first openly "gender-fluid" person in the federal government.[116] Brinton describes himself as a survivor of conversion therapy and even testified before a U.N. Convention Against Torture. (It is telling that of all the victims of atrocities on the planet, the UN took time to talk to Sam Brinton.) Prominent anti–conversion therapy activist Wayne Besen raised concerns that Brinton's claims of abuse were likely embellished and that most journalists simply found them too good to check.[117]

When he wasn't doing nuclear physics, Brinton had a busy extra-curricular life. He taught a class called Kink 101 at the University of Nebraska, Omaha.[118] He also apparently had revealed a dog-role-play fetish in a public display in the classroom.[119] Look it up. Or don't.

As has been the theme with Biden's appointments, *woke* credentials are often more important than *work* credentials.

Brinton was tasked with storing nuclear waste, particularly in Nevada's Yucca Mountain area.[120] His approach was to implement "consent-based" siting of the waste after residents of Nevada felt that the toxic by-product was being forcibly dumped on them.[121]

(Granting Sam Brinton consent sounds like a dubious proposition, regardless of the circumstances.)

At the moment Briton assumed office, the U.S. government had taken in more than $44 billion that was supposed to be allocated for a permanent nuclear waste dump, which hadn't been created yet. Brinton would not be on the job long enough to make much progress when it comes to waste disposal.[122]

In November 2022, Brinton was charged with stealing a Vera Bradley suitcase (believed to be worth more than $2,000) from the baggage claim at the Minneapolis–St. Paul Airport on September 16.[123] That led the Las Vegas police to reopen a file on a hard-case bag with more than $2,000 worth of jewelry and makeup that went missing on July 6 from Harry Reid International Airport in Las Vegas.[124] Security footage appeared to show Brinton with a woman's bag. If Brinton's physical features weren't distinctive enough, the suspect was clad in a T-shirt with an isotope on it (a symbol associated with nuclear power) set against a rainbow flag.[125]

Nothing about Sam Brinton is subtle or understated.

Soon after, the Department of Energy indicated that Brinton was no longer with the agency.

Though Brinton's stint in the federal government may have come to an end, it does not necessarily mean that he will be out of work. According to the *Daily Mail*, Brinton, or "NuclearNerd," as he is known in kink circles, delivered a hands-on "Spanking: From Calculus to Chemistry" seminar at the LA Leather Getaway conference *after* admitting to taking the bag from the Minnesota airport.[126]

After Brinton's initial arrests, Asya Khamsin, a Moroccan fashion designer living in Texas, accused Brinton of wearing clothing that she believed was stolen from Ronald Reagan Washington Airport in 2018. Khamsin claims she recognized several of her custom dresses adorning Brinton in photos posted online.[127] Following Khamsin's accusations, Brinton was again arrested in May 2023 for being a "fugitive from justice" and released from a men's jail in Maryland on bail two weeks later.[128]

His next act? Hopefully advocating for special incarceration facilities for the nonbinary and two-spirit community.

BBB AND WEF

Believe it or not, the essence of Biden's first-term domestic agenda wasn't just a jobs program for the absurd and disturbed, it was something called "Build Back Better." The "BBB" bill was introduced in October 2021 as essentially the "Green New Deal" by another name.[129] The concept was introduced during the campaign just before the Democrat National Convention in 2020.[130] It would be the signature piece of legislation of his first term, even though it would never get passed, at least in the literal sense.

Build Back Better came with the eye-popping price tag of $1.75 trillion—after it was reduced following negotiation.[131] The Wharton School of the University of Pennsylvania estimated the bill would actually cost about $3.98 trillion and would be offset by $1.56 trillion in new taxes, bringing the net total to around $2.42 trillion.[132]

At the same time, Biden was pushing the $1.8 trillion American

Families Plan, which was considered mostly a transfer of wealth from the upper classes to those with less.[133]

In December, the nonpartisan Congressional Budget Office released its "score" for BBB and determined it would likely cost as much as $4.91 trillion over ten years and recoup only a fraction of that in new taxes.[134]

The centerpiece of the bill was $555 billion in "clean energy investments" for (allegedly) reducing greenhouse gas emissions 50 percent by 2030.[135] The bulk of that money ($320 billion) would come in the form of tax credits for producers and buyers of wind, solar, and nuclear power. The bill also included a tax credit for up to $12,500 for purchasing an electric vehicle, another kickback to the stakeholder capitalists in the green industry.

Meanwhile, the congressional Democrats would also create a new Civilian Climate Corps to "work with local communities." According to NPR, it "would employ thousands of young people to address the threat of climate change."[136]

Predictably, climate activists were mostly thrilled, aside from a few who said it didn't go far enough.[137]

The original Build Back Better bill would inevitably fail, largely thanks to moderate West Virginia Democrat senator Joe Manchin, who was concerned about budgetary gimmicks used to mask costs and the effects BBB was likely to have on inflation, which was spiraling out of control at the time.

Yet like so many other bills in Washington, BBB was like a zombie, constantly rising from the dead. Manchin himself may have been playing political games as well, biding time and looking for a better bargain. Though the branding "Build Back Better" would get dropped, the spirit of it would live on and much of the bill would eventually get passed into law, especially as part of the $730 billion Inflation Reduction Act.[138]

Build Back Better doesn't have its roots in any particular set of American values. Though the first time I came across the term was in a 2015 speech to the UN by former Japanese prime minister Shinzo Abe,[139] I believe Barack Obama brought it into the American mainstream at the 2020 Democrat convention. We are currently in "dark times," Obama said, and "Joe and Kamala" can lead our country out of them and "build it back better."

The phrase has grown in usage throughout the world whenever globalist, corporatist, or leftist administrations have sought to persuade their respective societies that they need to drastically expand government to recover from or prevent disaster. Over time, the emphasis began to narrow to climate change.[140]

Rapid adoption of the term by the globalist Left began right as the 2020 campaign kicked into high gear in the United States. Whenever a past or future global disaster came up, like environmental devastation or a pandemic, *build back better!* An article posted in May 2020 to the World Economic Forum's (WEF) website uses that phraseology in its title: "'Building back better'—here's how we can navigate the risks we face after COVID-19." The article argued that recovery from the COVID era would need to include a revamping of health care systems and a focus on climate change.[141]

Biden's "Build Back Better" policy would operate in perfect tandem with the WEF's ideas of the Great Reset. The WEF was founded in the 1970s and based in a ski vacation destination, Davos, Switzerland. The Great Reset is a concept largely credited to Klaus Schwab, a German economist who leads the WEF. Though it is often referred to as a conspiracy theory, top officials from the UN, the International Monetary Fund (IMF), and other groups of unelected globalist elites have used the phrase "Great Reset" or referred to a global reboot or reset or restart.[142] There is even a Davos podcast series called "the Great Reset."[143]

The WEF claims to be "independent, impartial and not tied to any special interests," though it has for decades advanced globalism and oligarchism throughout the world. It openly tries to influence governments.[144] The WEF is focused on cultivating the next generation of politicians and bureaucrats and turning them into woke globalists, if they aren't that already. They have already had countless success stories. Schwab himself has bragged about fostering global leaders and "penetrating" governments across the world, even claiming that half of Prime Minister Justin Trudeau's cabinet in Canada were WEF mentees.[145]

Its leadership includes executives from BlackRock, the Carlyle Group, Nestlé, the European Central Bank, Bain and Company, and the IMF. But it's not just a big corporate cabal: it also includes humanitarians such as Al Gore and cellist Yo-Yo Ma, among many others.[146]

The WEF features President Biden and climate czar Kerry prominently on the "people" section of its website.[147] Brian Deese, the former global head of sustainable investing at BlackRock, negotiated the Paris Agreement on behalf of the U.S. Deese was a WEF Young Global Leader honoree in 2013. He was previously in charge of Biden's National Economic Council, making him one of the most powerful people in the White House, and a card-carrying member of the most influential globalist cabal in the world.[148]

Not coincidentally, the WEF has also been one of the largest pushers of far-left green energy policies this century. Davos launched a "Global Greenhouse Gas Register" in 2003 that promoted the disclosure of greenhouse gases in business operations as a means to display strong corporate governance.[149] Climate change has remained at the center of its agenda ever since. Alarmist articles and letters are a constant on the WEF website, stating unabashedly that "[c]limate adaptation is key to our survival."[150]

The WEF framed the COVID-19 pandemic as "the test of social responsibility" and a model for how to achieve "net-zero" emissions by enforcing "ethical" consumption standards.

This is a scary worldview—one that could lead to lockdown-like restrictions on human freedom—and it is presumably shared by members of Biden's White House. The list of WEF alumni in the Biden administration is long and growing. Deputy National Security Advisor Jonathan Finer, Assistant Administrator for International Development in Latin America and the Caribbean Marcela Escobari, and Deputy Assistant Secretary of State Joy Basu are all WEF Young Leaders, for example.[151] In early 2023, Biden appointed three individuals who are WEF members to the board of his Export Council: Farnam Jahanian, Rich Lesser, and Karen S. Lynch.[152]

The WEF's recruiting pitch is simple and ingenious: appeal to people's inner messianic complex. Win over the elites by convincing them that if they join this effort, they can save the world—and get very powerful in the process. An added perk: most of the recruiting seems to take place at lavish events in vacation destinations with celebrities and world leaders in attendance.

Of course, the best way to get to these climate change idea-fests is by private plane. Breitbart News counted more than one thousand private planes sent to Davos for a WEF confab in 2018, for example.[153]

Perhaps climate change is an existential crisis only for those who lack the means to charter aircraft.

Still, the question remains: When you're living this good, how could you possibly build back any better?

ALL THAT GREEN: BIDEN'S ECO MONEYMEN

If you want to make sense of Joe Biden's decision to spend recklessly on environmentalist fantasies, look no further than the list of the biggest donors to Joe Biden's presidential campaign.

After dropping out of the 2020 Democrat presidential primary, Michael Bloomberg famously committed to spending $100 million to get Joe Biden elected. He didn't quite live up to his promise, but he got pretty damn close. Bloomberg LP, the media mogul's company, contributed $93,848,522 in all to Joe Biden. By far the most of any entity. Like Biden, Bloomberg famously espouses radical environmentalist beliefs but takes no interest in curbing the emissions of the world's biggest polluter, the CCP. (I thoroughly documented this phenomenon in my book *Breaking the News*.)

Bloomberg was reappointed in February 2021 as the United Nations climate envoy, a position he was the first ever to hold in 2014.[154]

Bloomberg Green and other Bloomberg outlets have published extensive climate policy advice for Biden. Just days after Biden's election in November 2020, Bloomberg ran a massive feature, "41 Things Biden Should Do First on Climate Change."[155] The article is a list of proposed regulations, fines, and even social punishment recommendations for the would-be president.

The next-biggest donor to Biden's 2020 campaign was a group called Future Forward USA, which gave $61,127,271.[156] The aforementioned Future Forward USA PAC has received money from high-profile donors like Facebook billionaire Dustin Moskovitz, Google's Eric Schmidt, Kathryn Murdoch, and Sam Bankman-Fried. Since Biden's election, FFUSA has run a media campaign touting the Inflation Reduction Act (IRA) as "the most powerful climate law in U.S. history."[157] While the IRA did not reduce inflation, it did indeed ramp up spending on wind and solar energy, electric vehicles, and other green pet projects.

The third-largest donor to Biden's 2020 campaign was software company Asana, which was founded by Moskovitz. The San Francisco–based tech company focused on project management software was cofounded by another Facebook employee, Justin Rosenstein, who gave Biden's campaign $45.9 million.[158] The company is an advocate for carbon offsets, having purchased an undisclosed amount from the Garcia River Project.[159] Their website also includes language touting the numerous environmental organizations that use their software as well as promoting their ESG partnerships.[160]

In fact, all of the top donors to Biden's campaign share a similar worldview on climate policy, and Joe has seemingly done his best to satisfy them.

Another of Biden's biggest donors was the largest Democrat super PAC, Priorities USA Action. They gave almost $27 million during the 2020 presidential cycle.[161] It is headed by Bill Burton, former deputy White House press secretary from 2009 to 2011. In 2016, they spent $500,000 on attack ads against Trump for his stances on various issues including climate change.[162] In July 2021, they joined with the League of Conservation Voters to spend another $250,000 on ad buys to encourage Congress to act on the climate crisis.[163]

The Sixteen Thirty Fund, which gave Biden $21.2 million, is a left-wing lobbying and advocacy group that has propped up various other special interest groups, several of which are centered on climate change. They have also partnered with the LCV, a darling of the donor class and of the Biden White House.[164] In 2019 and 2020 they gave more than $43 million to Democrat PACs, including the NextGen Climate Action Committee. The Climate Action Fund is listed as one of their focus projects.[165]

Satisfying the global green movement gives Biden his political war chest, and as president, Biden has the key that unlocks hundreds of billions of dollars of investment into the green industry. He holds the key to the donor class's heart, and they hold the key to his.

"I want you to look at my eyes. I guarantee you, I guarantee you we're going to end fossil fuels,"[166] Joe said while fundraising in 2019. He also has called climate change the "number one issue facing humanity, and it's the number one issue for me."[167]

I don't think Biden believes that sentiment, but I do think he's smart enough to know who butters his bread.

THE NUCLEAR OPTION

One clean technology that has been adopted at a wide level is nuclear power. Even so, it seems to rarely get national media attention. (The notable exception is whenever Sam Brinton is in the news, which is fairly often.)

Nuclear is a clean, abundant energy source that has been readily available for decades. The U.S. wouldn't have to tap into national reserves to acquire it. It is more dependable than wind and solar, which generate power only intermittently. You don't even need unsightly windmills or solar panels to harvest it. Yet Greenpeace sued the European Union for daring to claim that nuclear could be part of the solution to climate change, calling the claim "greenwashing."[168]

So, what explains the hatred?

Famed researcher Bjorn Lomborg, known as the "Skeptical Environmentalist," speaks positively about nuclear, noting that "it is currently the only way to deliver 24/7, scalable, near-CO_2-free power." He told business publication *City A.M.*, "Nuclear is also one of the safest electricity technologies per kWh [kilowatt-hour] produced" when one considers the amount of radiation released and deaths caused by creating the energy.[169]

Lomborg does note that nuclear is expensive, perhaps the most expensive green technology. But when has a high price tag slowed down the modern Left, especially Joe Biden? Representative Alexandria Ocasio-Cortez's (D-NY) proposed "Green New Deal" draft that was circulated in 2019 was estimated by one study to cost upward of $90 trillion (not a typo), and it does not even include nuclear power as part of our more sustainable future.[170]

Still, Biden has quietly taken a comparatively moderate approach on the subject of nuclear power. In April 2022, he announced a $6 billion program to help power plants stay operational despite rising costs.[171]

Upon the announcement, Joe Manchin (D-WV), chairman of the Senate Energy and Natural Resources Committee, stated, "Ensuring the continued operation of our domestic nuclear fleet is essential to achieving our emission reduction goals while also maintaining reliability."

"U.S. nuclear power plants are essential to achieving President

Biden's climate goals and DOE is committed to keeping 100% clean electricity flowing and preventing premature closures," Secretary of Energy Jennifer M. Granholm said in an Energy Department press release that went along with the announcement of the new infrastructure spending.[172]

This is hardly the rhetoric of the antinuclear extremists.[173]

The World Nuclear Association notes that the U.S. is the world's largest producer of nuclear power. The U.S. got 19 percent of our total electrical output in 2019 from nuclear; we generated more than 30 percent of nuclear electricity worldwide. We have maintained roughly the same level of operable nuclear power capacity for the last thirty-five years (around 100,000 megawatts electric), so we are not regressing under Biden's watch. Yet despite his lavish spending on pretty much everything else, the allocated $6 billion that will be distributed over thirteen years[174] is significant underfunding.

Wind and solar have received respectively 17 times and 75 times more subsidies per unit of electricity generated than the average for oil, gas, coal, and nuclear between 2010 and 2019.[175] (Neither Biden nor the rest of the green movement seem to care that many of the world's solar panels are produced by Chinese slave labor.)[176]

Only two new nuclear reactors, both at a single plant in Georgia, were under construction at the time this book was drafted. This is largely due to the Nuclear Regulatory Commission's implementation of a thirty-two-step process for granting licenses for reactors that has crippled nuclear production.[177]

The limitation of nuclear's role in our allegedly sustainable future is what poker players know as a "tell." It reveals that big-government and corporate cronyism is driving our green energy policies, and not the desire to reduce emissions. Many green technologies are fashionable in the business world and among Democrat voters, but nuclear is not. Calling for more nuclear power does not score voters, and it does not provide an excuse to pump billions in government funds into the business world. Thus it has a limited constituency.

The green movement's failure to support nuclear exposes their true motives, but their man in the White House is absolutely willing to play along.

THE BIDEN PRICE HIKES (WHICH WERE BLAMED ON PUTIN)

While the Biden administration was fantasizing about technologies of tomorrow, one of the most important technologies of today (i.e., gasoline) was getting significantly more expensive. There are many contributing factors to soaring prices, but the Left quickly found an ideal scapegoat—their favorite scapegoat: Vladimir Putin. The United States and most of the West cut off supplies to Russian oil after the country invaded Ukraine, and this drove up gas prices a bit. That was good enough for the White House, which quickly branded the uptick in fuel costs the "Putin price hike."

This branding is fundamentally dishonest, ludicrous, really. Yet, Biden escalated the rhetoric even a step further. He suggested that to not support this decision to boycott Russian oil was the equivalent of supporting Putin's invasion.

The supine media failed to ask the obvious question: Why is the U.S. getting oil from Russia, a hostile country, anyway? The question seems even more urgent considering we are not tapping our own supply that is right under our feet.

"We could have turned a blind eye to Putin's murderous ways, and the price of gas wouldn't have spiked the way it has," Biden remarked in June 2022. "But the simple truth is gas prices are up almost two dollars a gallon because of Vladimir Putin's ruthless attack on Ukraine, and we wouldn't let him get away with it," he said.

The ironic and dark truth is that Putin's invasion and war on Ukraine are funded by fossil fuel revenues. Biden's refusal to do what is necessary to drive down the costs of fossil fuels allowed Putin to charge more, lining his war coffers.[178] (This is yet another reason why Biden bears much of the blame for the Russian invasion.)

Blaming it all on Putin must not have polled particularly well, because the Biden White House and others in the left-wing punditry began to split the blame between Big Bad Vlad and greedy gas station owners. They suggested that the oil industry had all of a sudden decided in the fall of 2021 that they were now going to gouge Americans at the pump. The president claimed in November of that year, without evidence, that gas companies suddenly began to overcharge customers.

Biden's logic was fallacious. He criticized gas prices for not coming down fast enough relative to declining costs of the wholesale gas market,[179] but gas prices tend to increase or decrease at a relatively slower rate than wholesale prices. This leads to slightly elevated margins when wholesale prices drop and slightly smaller margins when they increase. Biden should know this, considering that the phenomenon was explained by the Obama/Biden Department of Labor in a 2015 report.[180]

Still, his argument was parroted by others in the administration, such as energy secretary Granholm, who complained of a "disparity" between oil and gas prices.[181]

Still, Joe had his narratives that he felt justified in releasing 50 million barrels of oil from the Strategic Petroleum Reserve.

The reserve was created after the Arab oil embargo in the 1970s and was typically tapped in times of deep global supply chain interruptions.[182] In 1991, President George H. W. Bush withdrew more than 30 million barrels during the Gulf War. In 2011, Obama approved the release of 30 million barrels due to disruptions in Libya due to its civil war.[183]

So, with no new wars or crises happening, why would Joe Biden tap them in November 2021? According to PBS, it was "supply and demand." Of course this is true, but why was the demand outpacing the supply?[184]

Again, basic questions seemingly no one bothered to ask.

And if "supply and demand" is reason enough to tap our emergency oil supply, then why wouldn't we simply tap it far more often, like whenever gas prices tick up at all? Think of how low prices could go!

Biden had been waging open warfare on the oil and gas industry for his entire administration. He had stated in a Democrat debate in 2019 that he would be willing to displace hundreds of thousands of blue-collar workers in order to transition to greener energy. He canceled the Keystone XL pipeline, which would have transported 870,000 barrels of oil per day from Canada to Texas. He paused new oil and gas leases on federal land.[185]

At the precise moment the reserves were tapped, Biden's poll numbers had fallen to the lowest level of his presidency and his disapproval numbers had exceeded 50 percent for the first time.[186]

Only a fool would dismiss this as a coincidence. Even left-wing *Politico* ran a headline on November 17, 2021, "Pain at the Pump Drives Biden's Suffering in the Polls."[187]

But would this strategy work? Not necessarily. As it turned out, the tapping of the reserves in this instance had minimal impact on gas prices at first. The pain at the pump would only intensify until their Biden-era peak in June 2022.

He must have felt the walls closing in, because in April of that year, despite objections from the green Left, he finally called for more drilling on public lands, though he would simultaneously villainize the oil firms as the equivalent of war profiteers.[188]

In May 2022, gas prices rose at a torrid pace, but based on Producer Price Index data, profit margins actually decreased for gas stations. Prices continued to rise sharply in June, but profits increased only slightly. The cost of a gallon of gas topped $5.10 on June 13, more than double the price when Biden assumed office in January 2021.

It was at this point that Biden got an idea. An empty idea. Biden got a wonderful, empty idea! He would demand refiners produce more fuel.[189]

Biden said in a speech on June 21, 2022, "These are not normal times. Bring down the price you are charging at the pump to reflect the cost you are paying for the product." "Do it now. Do it today," the president ordered.[190] He repeated the sentiment in a tweet on July 2: "My message to the companies running gas stations and setting prices at the pump is simple: this is a time of war and global peril. Bring down the price you are charging at the pump to reflect the cost you're paying for the product. And do it now."[191]

This statement is pure politics. Biden is powerless to demand any industry lower prices, and he offered no incentive to do so (other than to avoid getting badgered by the POTUS). These comments display a complete lack of understanding of basic economics as well as democracy.

Additionally, the subtext of this line of attack ought not be overlooked: Biden regards the oil and gas industry as evil by nature and worthy of presidential bullying.

A July report from Reuters confirmed that significant quantities of the oil that was designed to alleviate American's pain at the pump was sent overseas to nations in Europe and Asia, including China.[192]

As my colleague John Nolte pointed out at Breitbart News, they sent us the coronavirus, then we sent them our strategic oil reserves, which are supposed to be used to protect Americans.[193]

Eventually, the prices began to come down.

Had gas station owners suddenly become less greedy? No. Their profits popped 12.3 percent that month, four times as much as June's increase. This phenomenon suggests rising gas prices do not correlate with the fleeting fancies of predatory gas station owners after all.[194]

Biden would later propose a windfall profit tax on oil companies. This public proclamation, like so many others he routinely makes, appears to be merely a virtue signal to his environmentalist voting base and allies in the renewable energy industry.[195] It has not gained traction as a public policy position. Even the pro-Biden media was immediately skeptical this could ever become law.[196] Perhaps they also were fluent enough in basic economics to know the tax would be passed on to consumers and be blatantly inflationary.

Prices began to rise again in September, particularly in some of the more pro-Biden states. In October 2022, gas was again approaching $6/gallon in California and over $7/gallon in some areas.[197] When Biden visited Los Angeles in October, he took questions from the media on the subject at a Tacos 1986 restaurant. One reporter asked, "Have you seen gas prices around here in LA? It's seven bucks a gallon almost." Biden's reply was surreal: "Well, that's always been the case here."[198]

This claim is bogus. The cost of gas in Los Angeles was under $3.46/gallon when Biden assumed office and was at $3.00/gallon as recently as 2020.[199]

Biden would tap the strategic reserves for 15 million more barrels in October, bringing the total oil pulled to more than 150 million barrels as of the end of 2022.[200]

Rounding out his interview at the taco joint, Biden was asked by a reporter what message he intended to convey to Saudi Arabia. In typical tough-guy Biden fashion, he responded with two cold, ominous words: "STAY TUNED . . ."

The scene was set, the pieces were in place: in just a few short weeks, Biden would be in an epic chess match with some of the shrewdest businessmen on the planet. The upcoming showdown with Prince Mohammed bin Salman and the Saudi royals in Riyadh would serve as the ultimate showcase of our forty-sixth president's intellectual prowess and diplomatic cunning.

Unfortunately for us, he blundered from move one.

THE FIST-BUMP SUMMIT

With just a few weeks to go until the midterm elections and gas prices still on the rise, Biden flew to Saudi Arabia. On his agenda was asking the Kingdom to postpone a planned oil supply decrease. He greeted Crown Prince Mohammed bin Salman at Al Salam Royal Palace in Jeddah with a fist bump. The White House aides discouraged him from shaking hands with "MBS." (A U.S. intelligence report concluded that MBS had approved of the assassination of *Washington Post* journalist Jamal Khashoggi in 2018, which made the prince persona non grata with much of the American public, especially the left-wing elite.)[201]

At the summit, Biden would shake hands with Saudi king Salman bin Abdulaziz.

Not only did the Saudis not honor Biden's request, but it appeared the trip backfired completely. The petroleum exporters group OPEC+, which is largely controlled by the Saudi royal family, decided to cut two million barrels of oil a day anyway.

"Saudi officials dismissed the requests," according to a *Wall Street Journal* report, with "a resounding no." The royal family believed, according to the *Journal*, that they were asked to pump more oil as part of a "political gambit by the Biden administration to avoid bad news ahead of the U.S. midterm elections."

The article also claimed that MBS was "angered" by Biden's decision to go public with private details of conversations they had.[202]

In fact, the same *Journal* report stated that the Saudis had planned to pressure OPEC+ to raise production by 500,000 barrels per day at a summit earlier that year "to please Mr. Biden," but dropped that number to 100,000 *after* a separate Biden meeting. Afterward, Biden energy envoy Amos Hochstein sent Prince Abdulaziz bin Salman an email scolding him for the mere token increase, which enraged the prince "and strengthened his resolve to forge an oil policy independent of the U.S.," according to the *Journal*'s sources.

Biden, who believes himself to be America's foremost diplomat, had bungled it. He had chaired the Senate Foreign Relations Committee and would likely have been secretary of state under Barack Obama had he not been tapped as vice president. He waxes lyrical about his diplomatic accomplishments—some real and many imagined—in interviews and in his memoirs. But in this case, he had flown halfway around the world to try to get a traditionally allied nation to help alleviate financial pressure on Americans. When it was all said and done, we would have fared better if he had stayed at the beach in Delaware, licking an ice cream cone.

Biden had stated on the campaign trail that he intended to make Saudi Arabia a global "pariah" over the killing of Khashoggi.[203] Thus far in his presidency, the opposite has happened: he has significantly increased Saudi Arabia's leverage over the U.S.

What's more, Biden had called on a foreign government to essentially do him a favor ahead of an election. This move was eerily reminiscent of the first Trump impeachment, where the then president lightly suggested the Ukrainian government reopen an investigation into Hunter Biden's business dealings.

Though the Biden administration demanded foreign oil, at this time he was still perusing a domestic policy that discouraged more production. After the unsuccessful effort to woo the Saudis and just days before the midterm, his tone suddenly changed. He complained that oil companies should actually be drilling more.[204]

Somehow, Biden's oil policy would get more embarrassing.

In November 2022, the Biden administration, via the Treasury's Office of Foreign Assets Control (OFAC), granted a license for Chevron to export oil from Venezuela and sell it in the U.S. This effectively functions as a massive handout to the brutal communist president Nicolás Maduro and his regime.

Though Venezuela sits on the largest oil reserves in the world, they have extremely heavy crude, which is difficult to refine, and their refineries are often in disrepair. In fact, soon after the Chevron deal was announced, Venezuela's largest refinery halted gasoline processing because a refining unit had broken down.[205] America, by contrast, produces much lighter crude, which is more suitable for gasoline and diesel.[206]

Venezuela wasn't the only adversarial communist regime to benefit from Joe Biden's energy policies. Russia quickly became China's main source of oil after the post-Ukraine-invasion sanctions kicked in. The CCP was able to buy up the supply at a discounted rate.[207]

Biden had gone to Saudi Arabia to give a fist bump. He came home having received a swirly.

A FRIEND TO ECOTERRORIST HEADS BLM

If you want a snapshot of Joe Biden's philosophy on environmental policy, look no further than who he appointed to head up the Bureau of Land Management (the OG BLM). The BLM manages 10 percent of the land in our country, which includes 30 percent of our minerals, and the person Biden tapped to care for it all is literally linked to ecoterrorists.

In a presidential "shock and awe" moment, Biden picked Tracy Stone-Manning for the BLM job. She was a member of a group called Earth First!, which self-identifies as a "radical environmental movement" and has engaged in a practice called "tree spiking."[208] "Tree spiking" is a sabotage technique where environmentalists hammer metal, typically rods or spikes, into trunks of trees in order to thwart logging. The spike can destroy a chain or band saw on contact, sending shards of metal flying everywhere, destroying costly machinery and posing a danger to the operator. Appropriately, this is considered ecoterrorism by the FBI. Earth First! was an influence on the Unabomber, Ted Kaczynski.[209]

While she was a graduate student at the University of Montana, Stone-Manning edited a radical environmentalist newsletter, *Wild Rockies Review*, put out by Earth First!, which advocated violence against government officials. One letter published in the Autumnal Equinox Issue of the *Review* included the comment, "Rend the entire USFS [U.S. Forest Service] limb from limb and tear out its guts. These swine are evil and must be rubbed out."

Convicted ecoterrorist and tree-spiker John P. Blount claimed that Stone-Manning knew his plans in advance and played a crucial role in his crimes.[210] In 1989, Stone-Manning sent a warning to the US Forestry Service on behalf of Blount, announcing that land they planned to sell for logging had been "spiked heavily." Hundreds of rods had been hammered into the trees, some as high as one-hundred and fifty feet up, according to the letter. Stone-Manning edited the letter, rewrote it on a rented typewriter, signed it using an alias, and dropped it in the mail.[211]

"The project required that eleven of us spend nine days in god-awful weather conditions spiking trees. We unloaded a total of five hundred pounds of spikes," the letter reads. It gets even more chilling and threatening as it goes on: "I would be more than willing to pay you a dollar for the sale, but you would have to find me first and that could be your WORST nightmare."

The letter leaves little doubt about the group's willingness to inflict harm: "P.S. You bastards go in there anyway and a lot of people could get hurt," it concluded.[212]

In Stone-Manning's graduate thesis, she argued for population control, going as far as describing a "cute baby" as an "environmental hazard." It is families, Stone-Manning argued, who are the true purveyors of "environmental horrors."[213]

I asked the BLM press secretary if Stone-Manning disavows these comments or if she still holds these beliefs, but did not receive a reply.

In the Biden administration, radical antihumanism has gone mainstream, so long as you hold chic environmental views. She was confirmed by the U.S. Senate by a 50–45 vote, along party lines.[214]

There is a perverse logic to Biden's decision to tap someone with involvement with ecoterrorists. The U.S. famously plans to help the world reach carbon neutrality by 2050, and the Biden administration regards reversing deforestation as essential to that.[215] Yet as of 2023, Stone-Manning has failed at that basic task. Conservation group Climate Forests released a report detailing how the U.S. Forest Service and BLM continue to log at "alarming rates."[216]

Upon confirmation, Stone-Manning moved senior BLM leadership from Colorado, where there is significant acreage under BLM's management, to the Washington, DC, swamp.[217]

Still, her confirmation was the proverbial 360-degree win for Biden. Not only did he get a radical nominee approved who would be seen as a hero by the environmentalist base, but any subsequent appointment put forward by Biden for the rest of his life would seem moderate by comparison.

The same goes for policy positions. Any outrageous comment or proposal would seem mild by comparison to the Stone-Manning confirmation.

For example, in November 2021, Vice President Kamala Harris asked NASA if it could use its satellites to track trees by "race" in the name of "environmental justice."[218] She implied, in the spirit of critical race theory, that warm and urban areas have fewer trees and dirtier air in contrast to cooler, less polluted, whiter areas. Her comment is indistinguishable from parody found on websites like the Babylon Bee, and it is mildly racist.

But how could anyone be shocked by any one element of the Biden/ Harris green agenda? The Overton window has shifted, and Joe Biden did the shifting.

In May 2022, the Biden-Harris administration established the "Office of Environmental Justice" for "communities of color." Again, this would have been unthinkable at any other moment in American history, but in 2022 it was created with little fanfare and housed in the Department of Health and Human Services (HHS), of all places.

Apparently the Biden administration regards climate racism as a health problem so severe it is worthy of its own office.

"The blunt truth is that many communities across our nation— particularly low-income communities and communities of color— continue to bear the brunt of pollution," HHS secretary Xavier Becerra said in a press release.[219] So not only is the Biden administration saving the planet, they are fighting racism in the process.

Antiracism by way of environmentalism.

This is cultural Marxism on full display.

But have we seen peak wokeness from the Biden administration? Probably not. After all, Biden EPA senior advisor Robin Morris Collin has pitched "environmental reparations" to compensate for the "geography of oppression."[220] We are already seeing "environmental reparations" in law via the "environmental justice" provisions in the Infrastructure Investment and Jobs Act and Inflation Reduction Act.[221]

It is yet unclear what meaningful role all of this virtue signaling and spending has played in the lives of communities of color. It certainly doesn't appear to have helped race relations at large.

While the philosophy that drove Donald Trump's energy policy was to make America energy independent, Biden's has been to push us toward a more "sustainable" future that might never arrive. But for the nation's top Democrat, these bad policies are often good politics.

Joe Biden has deeply internalized the universal desire of the Democrat moneyed-donor class and the core voter base to focus on the fight to reduce "climate change" via shifting our policies, spending, and behavior here in the United States. It appeals to their sense of moral righteousness and their business interests. He has been willing to push the agenda as far as he can until the downstream effects (such as surging gas prices) prove too great a political liability.

If there is any doubt that Biden's environmental crusade is pure, cynical politicking, look no further than his personal love for combustion engine automobiles, which have been a part of his personal narrative since he was a teenager.

"I'm an automobile buff," Biden said on Earth Day 2022. "I have a '68 Corvette that does nothing but pollute the air," he continued.[222] Later that year he was filmed making googly eyes at the latest Corvette model at a Detroit auto show as if he was witnessing an angel descend from heaven.[223] (To his credit, Biden appears to have terrific taste in gas guzzlers.)

Whether Joe Biden truly shares their ideology or not, his base and staff are composed of climate justice warriors who are pursuing an era when human flourishing is a secondary consideration, if it's even a consideration at all. They fantasize about a return to pre-humanity, a green utopia, or at least a time when there are far fewer of us around to ruin the planet.

Though their goals are grandiose and will make life worse for living, breathing Americans, Joe Biden has been their unquestioning champion.

For all of his logrolling, he has reaped substantial awards at the ballot box.

CHAPTER 10

Bidenflation, or, Everything Joe Touches Gets More Expensive

My favorite passage in George Orwell's *1984* has always been this one (slightly truncated): "It appeared that there had even been demonstrations to thank Big Brother for raising the chocolate ration to twenty grams a week. And only yesterday, he reflected, it had been announced that the ration was to be reduced to twenty grams a week. Was it possible that they could swallow that, after only twenty-four hours? Yes, they swallowed it . . . fanatically, passionately, with a furious desire to track down, denounce, and vaporize anyone who should suggest that last week the ration had been thirty grams."[1]

Big Brother (the authoritarian government) lowered chocolate rations from 30 grams to 20 grams, and then claimed they had actually *raised* rations. And the people went right along with it. Chilling.

I wonder if Joe Biden and the Democrats had just read this passage when they named the Inflation Reduction Act. If they did, they probably saw it as an inspiration.

After all, the IRA, signed by Biden in August 2022 and costing around $700 billion, will not—despite its name—reduce inflation.[2]

It passed on a party-line vote in the Senate (51–50, with Kamala Harris breaking the tie) and a party-line 220–207 vote in the House of Representatives.

The true intention of the IRA was to use a moment of national insecurity as an excuse to appropriate hundreds of billions of dollars to Democrats' legislative priorities like climate change. More than half of the cost of the bill is allocated toward energy and environmental provisions. The legislation also expanded Obamacare, with new health care spending tallying around $100 billion. IRS funding was boosted by $80 billion, making the IRS larger than the Pentagon, State Department, FBI, and Border Patrol combined. Taxes would go up on many Americans.

Some of the new IRS funding would target the working class, contrary to promises repeated by Biden and the Democrats.[3] The new taxes would hit manufacturers the hardest, according to an analysis by the nonpartisan Joint Committee on Taxation.[4]

Yet this bill also claimed to reduce the deficit.[5]

The Penn Wharton Budget Model estimated the bill would reduce inflation by only 0.1 percent over five years (the report considers this number "indistinguishable from zero").[6] Even if that number holds true to reality, it is negligible considering the rest of the blowout spending in Biden's agenda, nearly all of which is inflationary.

The Congressional Budget Office (CBO) found that the Inflation Reduction Act might actually drive inflation up.[7]

If there was any good news to come out of the passage of the IRA, it was that Americans seemed to see through the Washington spin: only 12 percent of the public believed that the bill would in fact reduce inflation.[8] Even the establishment media understood this. CBS News senior White House and political correspondent Ed O'Keefe, for example, stated that the IRA "does nothing to address short-term price hikes."[9]

Then why did we pass it? Democrats saw a crisis and didn't let it go to waste. It was their excuse to spend.

Yes, when you're Joe Biden, even inflation is an excuse to spend.

Another question is, *How* did we pass it? How is it even legal to give a bill a name that means the opposite of what it actually does?

If Orwell were alive, he might doff his cap at the brazenness of it all.

Portions of the bill might be effective in lowering drug prices, but that does not fight inflation. When the prices of prescription drugs are artificially suppressed, that increases the spending power of households, which actually drives inflation up.

The tax hikes in the bill might apply some downward pressure on inflation, but it would be marginal. Though many Americans have complained that corporate profits should be taxed at a higher rate, that money does not tend to compete for the types of goods that strain the budgets of typical American households during inflationary periods.

While Americans struggled with mounting costs, and with no hope in sight, Joe Biden had the audacity to call a bill this name when it was nothing more than a blowout taxpayer-funded shopping spree for his voters and donors.

This is how Washington works. This is how Joe Biden works.

Thanks to Orwell, we can't say that we weren't warned.

THE DEBT CLOCK IS TICKING (AND NO ONE CARES)

Joe Biden ran for president on the idea that he would have the economy roaring back after Donald Trump had ruined it with tax cuts for the rich and a suboptimal pandemic strategy. "The depth of economic devastation our nation is experiencing is not an act of God, it's a failure of presidential leadership," Biden said in a campaign statement in July 2020, referring to his presidential rival.[10] In Joe Biden's worldview, it wasn't the virus from China and ensuing lockdowns that were to blame for the economic downturn, it was the orange-hued billionaire from Queens.

When the China virus broke out, governments across the world literally commanded people to stay home and not work, and oftentimes paid them to do so. This led to the worst economic downturn in nearly a century.[11] By April, unemployment had reached 14.7 percent, a level not seen since the Great Depression.[12] It was an economic disaster.

Yet by the end of 2020, the U.S. was rebounding at a rapid clip, experiencing GDP growth of 33.1 percent in the third quarter and 4.1 percent in the fourth.[13] Overall, the economy shrank 3.5 percent for the year, but the government stimulus combined with the accelerated vaccine production had economists anticipating 2021 would be America's strongest year since Ronald Reagan was president.[14] (In terms of increased annualized GDP, which was 5.7 percent, they were correct.[15])

But by 2022, it was clear that something had gone awry. The economy had experienced two quarters of negative growth, which is the textbook definition of a "recession,"[16] and a consensus of economists believed that things were going to get worse.[17]

Upon taking office, Biden had a choice: restore fiscal responsibility, or use the pandemic emergency to justify wild spending. He chose the latter.

Biden laid out two goals for himself that would likely have conflicting solutions: shutting down the coronavirus and getting the economy to roar back. In order to stop the spread of COIVD-19, Biden's advisors believed he would need to continue various mandates that limit commerce, travel, and economic productivity and would harsh everyone's vibe. His only hope to have his cake and eat it too would be to spend, spend, spend and hope no one stopped him. That way he could stimulate the economy with government funds while maintaining his preferred coronavirus policy. That's essentially what he did.

This resulted in the defining characteristic of Biden's economy: inflation, or as we refer to it at Breitbart News, "Bidenflation."

Nearly every major decision that we examine in this chapter and in the extensive portions of this book that cover Biden's energy and environmental policy has applied upward inflationary pressure. Joe Biden simply doesn't care. His track record in Washington over the last fifty years has been that of a big-government leftist. Or to put it another way: don't just stand there, spend something.

As documented in Part I of this book, Biden has never been good with money. He hasn't made much relative to his social status, and he's never managed what he has made well.

He has been no more responsible with your money.

Throughout his career, Biden has never conveyed a clear economic philosophy. He supported the North American Free Trade Agreement (NAFTA) when he was on the Senate Foreign Relations Committee,[18] a position commonly held by establishment globalists. He has voted against tax cuts, often citing that they tend to favor corporations over citizens, a position commonly held by left-wing populists. And he has never shied away from large government expenditures, having played a significant role in Obama's mammoth $800 billion American Recovery and Reinvestment Act spending package of 2009.[19]

As president, Biden has managed to push the limits of federal spending. Projections suggest that his actions, which often go against the advice of even liberal economists, would add $4.8 trillion to the U.S. deficit between 2021 and 2031.[20]

Debt and the deficit are not priorities for Joe Biden. This statement should be obvious. In 2012, the Republican National Committee unveiled a national "debt clock" on the first day of the Republican National Convention in Tampa, Florida.[21] That week, the GOP would nominate Mitt Romney and Paul Ryan to challenge Barack Obama and Joe Biden.[22]

The number at that time on the giant digital display was just under $16 trillion.[23] The debt is double that number as of 2023.

Obama/Biden beat Romney/Ryan, making it official that fiscal responsibility is a political loser in our day. Maybe it's because we don't tend to feel the debt's effects on our daily lives; maybe it's that most Americans have a lot of personal debt themselves. It's hard to know for sure. But one thing that *is* for sure is that Americans don't treat fiscal responsibility as a political imperative. By the time he became president, Joe Biden had internalized this.

It was time to go shopping.

NEVER LET A GOOD CRISIS GO TO WASTE

Due to the China virus pandemic, Donald Trump enacted several emergency policies to help keep the economy functional. Considering that the government literally told people to stay home and not work, it's hardly a surprise that extreme measures were taken. Between vaccine development, helping states and cities with virus mitigation, loans for small businesses, paid sick leave, some foreign aid, and literal direct-deposit lump sums wired to people's bank accounts, seemingly everyone got at least one bag of cash (figuratively speaking).[24]

Biden held over many of these programs and expanded them. Every major economic move he made drove inflation up. Here are some key ones:

The Paycheck Protection Program (PPP): As of January 2021, the government had "allocated around $4 trillion of COVID relief at a net cost of over $3.4 trillion," according to the Committee for a Responsible Federal Budget.[25] The goal was ostensibly "to promote maximum employment and stable prices, along with its responsibilities to promote the stability of the financial system."[26]

According to the Federal Reserve, "The Paycheck Protection Program Liquidity Facility (PPPLF) will extend credit to eligible financial institutions that originate PPP loans."[27]

So, who qualified for the program? Virtually everyone. Our Treasury Department sums it up: "Paycheck Protection Program (PPP) borrowers may be eligible for loan forgiveness if the funds were used for eligible payroll costs, payments on business mortgage interest payments, rent, or utilities during either the 8- or 24-week period after disbursement."[28]

This was intentionally vague. It kept cash flowing but also made the program ripe for abuse. As early as June 2020, numerous reports indicated that these loans were being accessed by people who were simply not in need of additional assistance. Lax oversight and abdication of screening duties were initially blamed.[29] Third-party financial tech companies like Blueacorn, Womply, and Kabbage helped applicants get the loans, only to cash in on taxpayer-funded fees, according to a House investigations panel report.[30] The report said that billions of dollars were distributed fraudulently across hundreds of thousands of loans and that only $286 million was recovered.[31]

Even the rich and famous siphoned off funds. Here are a few notable people (names released by the U.S. Small Business Administration):

- Tax hawk Grover Norquist's Americans for Tax Reform Foundation[32]

- Joseph Kushner Hebrew School, which was named for and supported by the family of Trump senior adviser Jared Kushner[33]

- Multimillionaire real estate developer and Republican donor Joe Farrell, who reportedly received as much as $1 million[34]

- Kanye West's clothing brand, Yeezy, which received $2.3 million[35]

- Three branches of the Church of Scientology[36]

- Thirty-eight Planned Parenthood affiliates received more than $80 million.[37]

- Tom Brady, Reese Witherspoon, Khloe Kardashian, and even Paul Pelosi were among the multi-multi-multi-millionaire celebrities who took the bailout funds.[38]

- Companies owned by West Virginia governor Jim Justice, who is also the state's richest man, drew loans.[39]

- Fracking moguls and conservative financiers Dan and Farris Wilks also secured the bag of cash.[40]

The richest and most powerful person to benefit from the loans, as far as I can tell, was heiress Laurene Powell Jobs, the widow of Steve Jobs and one of the most networked women in the world. She has a reported net worth of over $13.7 billion, mostly from shares in Apple and Disney, and was perhaps the most important subject of my research in *Breaking the News*. Jobs controls a vast network of left-wing media outlets, organizations, and politicians, one of which was a start-up called Ozy Media, which obtained a PPP loan in the $2–5 million range.[41] Ozy abruptly shut down after allegations of fraud surfaced in 2021. One of the company's senior executives had impersonated a YouTube executive on a conference call in order to woo investors.[42] CEO Carlos Watson has since been arrested.[43]

Even though it was apparent that the program was being abused, Biden stuck with it. On February 22, 2021, the Biden/Harris administration enacted some light changes to the PPPLF,[44] mostly to generate an uptick in minority- and rural-owned business participation.[45] New features included marketing the program during Black History Month and Women's History Month webinars.[46] Restrictions on loan access were removed from more than 30,000 businesses that were flagged for previous loan delinquency.[47]

These reforms indicated that the problem with PPP wasn't the waste and abuse; it was that the program wasn't woke enough.

Eviction Moratorium: In March 2020, Trump's CARES Act halted landlords from evicting tenants. This was yet another means to mitigate economic hardship resulting from the pandemic. It was set to expire on July 24, 2020.[48] Under this protection, eligible tenants could submit declarations of eligibility to landlords that would prohibit landlords from evicting them.[49] On September 4, 2020, the Centers for Disease Control and Prevention (CDC) issued an extension of the order, which was to last until July 31, 2021.[50] The CDC justified the moratorium by citing a 1944 law, the Public Health Service Act, claiming that evicted people would flood shelters and increase the proliferation of the virus.[51]

Protecting people from eviction while they are locked out of their jobs sounds like a good idea, but it would assuredly have negative down-stream effects on the economy if continued over an extended period.

You see, "you can't get evicted" is synonymous with "you don't need to pay rent." That is not sustainable in a functional society. So, naturally, the Biden-Harris administration moved to extend the moratorium.[52] The Supreme Court would eventually rule that the CDC exceeded its authority with the rule.[53]

Washington infused the economy with tens of billions of dollars of emergency rental assistance funds, but not all of it was efficiently spent, due to bureaucratic red tape. Even the *New York Times* acknowledged that the funds did not prevent an eviction crisis.[54]

Following the end of the eviction moratorium, turnover in the housing market caused rent rates to balloon.[55] Some U.S. cities and states attempted to implement rent controls to stave off more evictions.[56] Economists generally consider rent controls kryptonite for an economy: as rents are capped, incumbent tenants tend to hold on to their current rentals, which lowers the supply in the market. Developers build fewer apartments, knowing that their upside is limited. St. Paul, Minnesota, for example, capped rent increases at 3 percent, which led to a 31 percent decrease in new construction permits.[57] The best way to keep prices of rental units down is supply, and rent control ensures that supply will be kept to a minimum.

Rent control is also inflationary throughout the rest of the economy because it creates a larger supply of cash in people's hands. Thus they have more purchasing power, which drives up prices.

Despite extremely low unemployment numbers, evictions rose throughout 2022 and into 2023. As Daniel Grubbs-Donovan, a researcher at the Eviction Lab at Princeton University, noted, "With inflation and the massive increases in rental prices that we've seen over the last few years, it's much worse for low-income renters than it was before the pandemic."[58]

Loan Payback Moratoria: Similar to rental tenants, borrowers who took out federal student loans were no longer expected to pay them. As of December 2021, the U.S. Department of Education owned 92 percent of student loans. About 43.5 million people owed the federal government a combined $1.63 trillion.[59] The interest rates for everyone were temporarily set to 0 percent. Putting a hold on interest payments keeps the money in the economy, which is inflationary.

Trump originally suspended student loan interest payments via executive order near the start of the pandemic;[60] Biden extended the program at least eight times.

Biden even tried to one-up Trump by outright canceling debt. He offered up to $10,000 in forgiveness for non–Pell Grant recipients and $20,000 for those with Pell Grants.[61] This was a politically dubious move. The $10,000–$20,000 total would not be enough to satisfy the Left. After all, many Americans owe ten times that or more. Senator Bernie Sanders (I-VT) noted this amount was far lower than what the average PPP loan recipient received, and we know the types of people who got those.[62] Representative Cori Bush (D-MO) suggested the policy exacerbated the "racial wealth gap" because black students tend to borrow more than their white classmates; in other words, this government giveaway wasn't equitable.[63] Conservatives saw this as an effort to buy the votes of overeducated liberals. (It is.) This program also penalizes people who never took loans, already paid back their loans, or skipped college entirely. In some instances, the program would mean wealth distribution from the lower classes to the elite, which is frowned upon by literally everyone who does not directly receive the bag of cash.

In the summer of 2023, the U.S. Supreme Court struck down Biden's student loan forgiveness program on the grounds that the president did not have the authority to cancel the debt without approval from Congress.[64]

Not to be deterred, Biden quickly made a new proposal: an income-driven repayment plan that the respected Penn Wharton budget model estimated would cost taxpayers $475 billion dollars over ten years. If the courts are unable to block this one, it will be yet another inflationary mega-handout that benefits Biden's voters.[65]

The American Rescue Plan: The first of Joe Biden's many exorbitantly expensive initiatives as president was one of the most reckless in American history. It was announced on his inauguration day and ironically called the American Rescue Plan (ARP).

It was the first major piece of Biden administration legislation: a $1.9 trillion spend when the economy was already recovering.[66] The onset of the pandemic spurred massive job losses in 2020, but by early

2021, 60 percent of those losses had already been recovered.[67] In other words, there was no need for a "rescue," and if a "rescue" was going to be imposed on us, it certainly didn't need to be one of the most expensive pieces of legislation in American history.

Piling on this level of superfluous government spending meant automatic inflation, as Larry Summers and Olivier Blanchard warned it would.[68] Summers, who was the secretary of the U.S. Treasury from 1999 to 2001 and served as the director of Obama's National Economic Council from 2009 to 2010, went as far as to call it the "least responsible" economic policy in forty years.[69] Blanchard, the former chief economist at the International Monetary Fund and maybe the most cited economist in the world, said he was concerned that the size of the plan could lead to overheating and inflation, and ultimately concluded it was a political decision by Biden and not an arithmetical one.[70]

Inflation was just over 1 percent when Joe Biden assumed office, and by July 2021, the Consumer Price Index (CPI) showed an annual increase of 5.3 percent.[71] It was then the president said, "There's nobody suggesting there's unchecked inflation on the way—no serious economist."[72]

Actually, some of the most serious economists were suggesting exactly that.

Both Jerome Powell and Treasury secretary Janet Yellen (a former Federal Reserve chair herself) had consistently described inflation as "transitory."[73] Yellen said that she didn't "think there was going to be an inflationary problem."[74] In reality, inflation continued skyward until its peak of 9.06 percent—a forty-year-high—in July 2022.[75]

John Carney, Breitbart's economics and finance editor, described the American Rescue Plan as "a lead life preserver that drowned an economy just as it was finally getting its head above water." John is not the most bombastic of my colleagues, which makes this imagery all the more vivid.

Even far-left senator Elizabeth Warren (D-MA) acknowledged the package was inflationary.[76] Senator Mark Warner (D-VA) would say in 2022 that the plan was "absolutely" too large.[77]

Wendy Edelberg, a senior fellow at the liberal Brookings Institution, agreed: "I think we can say with certainty that we would have less inflation and fewer problems that we need to solve right now if the American Rescue Plan had been optimally sized."[78]

Speaking on a panel with business leaders in July 2022, Biden told

Americans who were suffering from inflation, and in particular high gas prices, that he sent them a check for "$8,000," a number seemingly plucked at random.[79] (It is unclear where the figure came from, but my colleagues at Breitbart News concluded it was connected to the Child Tax Credit.)[80] The irony lost on Biden is that recklessly handing out checks is exactly what caused the inflation that had people upset with him.

Biden understands politics better than most, but he does not appear to comprehend basic economics. In March 2022, he said in a speech at the White House, "I'm sick of this stuff. We have to talk about it because the American people think the reason for inflation is the government is spending more money. Simply not true."[81]

Passing the buck while he simultaneously distorts the truth. The chutzpah is impressive.

Recall from the section of this book on gas prices that he tried to blame Russian president Vladimir Putin. "[T]oday's inflation report is a reminder that Americans' budgets are being stretched by price increases and families are starting to feel the impacts of Putin's price hike," Biden said.[82] This statement is absurd. Inflation was already above 7 percent when Putin invaded Ukraine on February 24, 2022,[83] and economists had projected that it would remain high before the invasion.[84] America was seeing not only inflated gas prices, but also spikes in costs of new cars, cereals, and even pets. Putin might be very powerful and very evil, but this was the first time I had heard him blamed for the price of box turtles and Count Chocula.

In a *60 Minutes* interview in September 2022, President Biden stopped playing the blame game and tried to downplay inflation instead, insisting prices were up "just an inch."[85] Journalist Scott Pelley informed him that the annual inflation rate the previous month was 8.3 percent.[86]

Simply put, the main cause of the inflation is an abundance of cash in the hands of average citizens. Even while people were not overworking, they were collecting massive amounts of government (that is, taxpayer) funds. Yes, some Americans actually would have had to take a pay cut if they went back to work instead of cashing in on the various unemployment benefits and bonuses available to them.[87] Carney estimated that in 2021, a family of five could get $92,000 a year to not work through a combination of the Child Tax Credit, enhanced unemployment benefits, and stimulus.[88]

Add these handouts to the capped rents, debt forbearance, and the wildly mismanaged pot of PPP money and America was awash with cash. Additionally, Americans were limited in how they could spend their money. Travel, restaurants, and retail shopping were severely restricted due to the pandemic. Supply chain issues made it difficult to buy automobiles.[89] Products sat in container ships off the coasts, waiting to come in. Movie theaters closed down for good.

All of this put even more money in people's pockets.

What's more, many Americans were fortunate enough to maintain or grow their earnings during 2020. The tech sector boomed during that time, for example, which drove the stock market up.[90]

Once the restrictions came off, it primed America for a massively inflationary cycle.

According to the Bureau of Labor Statistics, consumer spending rose 1.6 percent in the first quarter of 2020 compared to Q1 of 2019. It dropped 9.8 percent in Q2 as the lockdowns overwhelmed, but this quickly turned around to a 2.8 percent increase in Q3 followed by a 15.7 percent spike by Q4 compared to the year before.[91]

By May 2022, the Consumer Price Index showed that prices were up by 8.3 percent and inflation had risen more than half a percent in a single month.[92]

Inflation tends to hit the poor and working classes harder than it hits the wealthy. When food and energy prices go up, when supply chain issues reduce the supply of goods and drive up prices, when it becomes more expensive to own a home or rent one, it is the least among us who suffer the most.[93]

Biden could spin it all he wants, but Americans were living a new reality every day.

SECRETARY PETE AND THE PORT CRISIS

Though vast federal expenditures were the main cause of the Bidenflation, government incompetence and mismanagement were also contributing factors. For example, the crisis was magnified when the Biden administration let dozens of fully loaded cargo ships idle off the Southern California coast, unable to dock. The two ports, in Long Beach and San Pedro, respectively, handle about 40 percent of container traffic into the United States.[94] Dozens of fully loaded cargo ships (some of which can carry up to 24,000 crates at a time[95]) were stuck idling off the coast for weeks at a time. Considering that the U.S. economy was already experiencing inflation and there were still significant supply chain disruptions worldwide due to the coronavirus pandemic, it was a shocking oversight.

Or was it?

The person who should have been in charge was Secretary Peter P. M. Buttigieg, the former mayor of South Bend, Indiana, who was installed atop a massive bureaucracy, the Department of Transportation, presumably because he endorsed Joe Biden after ending his own presidential run in 2020. It appears Secretary Pete's best qualification for being transportation secretary was his enthusiasm for riding a bicycle to work.[96] Buttigieg's main résumé item when he got the job was that he was the mayor of a small town best known as the home of the University of Notre Dame. Thus his experiential knowledge of seaway transportation logistics was nonexistent. He was the least-qualified person to be appointed to any role in Biden's cabinet, which is itself a feat.

Murphy's law guaranteed that a major shipping crisis would occur during his first year on the job.

Yet it's not 100 percent accurate to say that Pete failed at his first big test, because he wasn't even around to try to tackle the problem.

Buttigieg is not a woman, he's not even a birthing person, but he was on a two-month paternity leave when the situation spiraled out of control. (He and his husband, Chasten Buttigieg, had adopted twins in mid-August.) Pete did convene a meeting on the budding crisis in July, but as the situation worsened, he stayed home.[97]

The White House acknowledged that no one was left in charge while Pete was away; they knew there was no "point person."[98] That fact makes it all the more negligent that Buttigieg declined to meet with Senator Chuck Grassley (R-IA) while he was taking his break, despite repeatedly saying that he would be available "24/7."[99]

Despite a number of high-profile crises (or, if you take a cup-half-full approach to life, opportunities to shine), Pete stayed out of the spotlight more than I expected. I had long wondered why this was, and I finally got my answer in May 2023 when he sat for an interview with *Wired*. Actually, saying Pete "sat for an interview" undersells it; he lent his "cathedral mind" to journalist Virginia Heffernan for the afternoon. You see, the task of overseeing America's railroads, air travel, highways, vehicle safety, and maritime transportation is far too menial for a man of Buttigieg's unfathomable intellectual abilities. "His cabinet job requires only a modest portion of his cognitive powers," Heffernan wrote, earnestly. If Pete seemed tuned out from his responsibilities, don't assume he was watching Netflix or catching a nap; he was probably boning up on "the *Iliad*, Puritan historiography, and Knausgaard's *Spring*."[100]

When Buttigieg returned to work in mid-October, there were approximately 100 ships idling off the West Coast at that time, a record.[101] The number would peak at 109 ships.[102]

He took to CNN to announce "short-term and long-term steps" he would be taking.[103] The main solution he offered was to get the ports operating 24/7.[104] It was a worthless plan, and a challenging one to execute. The supply chain holdup had nothing whatsoever to do with the hours the port was open. There were not even enough warehouse workers and truckers to maximize regular business hours, and it would be even more difficult to convince them to work in the middle of the night.[105] The International Longshore and Warehouse Union agreed to work the night shifts, but they required a large bump in pay to do it.[106]

One terminal at the Port of Long Beach opened for a week of twenty-four-hour operation in September 2021, but no trucks showed up. Then they stipulated that they would stay open only if at least twenty-five trucks made appointments to utilize those hours. That quota was met only once, and on that night a mere five trucks actually arrived (there wasn't a no-show penalty).[107] When asked about the ineffectiveness of the 24/7 model, Buttigieg flippantly stated that it's "not like flipping a switch."[108]

Apparently not.

Biden pitched in by dusting off another familiar tactic: scolding private companies. He chastised businesses for failing to make adjustments to attract enough workers.[109] *In Joe Biden's America, the beatings will continue until the economy improves!* Recall that he scolded gas station owners when prices began to rise; he also threatened a windfall profit tax on oil companies if they didn't increase drilling.[110] Not only is this obnoxious, it's counterproductive. When investors see that an industry is vulnerable to new fines, they tend to move their money elsewhere. Punishment, never mind presidential hectoring, does not encourage investment.

Another plan to fix the ports, created jointly by the DOT and the

Biden-Harris Supply Chain Disruption Task Force (which is an actual thing),[111] was to threaten the owners of the cargo crates with a "container excess dwell fee." A $100-per-day-per-container fine would be assessed for any cargo crate left on the dock; that number would bump up another $100 after nine days.[112] Yet the fees were never actually imposed, and the program was phased out entirely on January 24, 2023.[113]

Any other efforts made by Buttigieg and Biden (they did eliminate a small amount of red tape) clearly had minimal effect. Clothing, toys, cars, and other goods sat on those ships as Christmas came and went. The reduced supply sent prices climbing, if you could even get your hands on the items you wanted. Yet neither Buttigieg nor Biden did not frame the crisis as an emergency.

Stunning photos of ships waiting off the coast must have irked someone with authority, because in December the vessels were urged to wait beyond the horizon as opposed to near the shore so they would be harder to photograph.[114]

Pushing the ships back might have lessened the PR burden for Pete and Joe, but it certainly did not fix our supply chain.

Buttigieg still claimed partial victory over the port crisis, touting "heroic" efforts at a January 2022 tour of the Port of Long Beach.[115] The visit occurred ahead of a scheduled $17 billion infusion for maritime ports allotted in the Infrastructure Investment and Jobs Act.[116] Weeks later, Breitbart's California editor, Joel Pollak, reported that there were still over one hundred vessels off the shore of that very coast, all waiting to dock.[117]

It was all a stark reminder that the young man who was recently mayor of a town with a $368 million budget[118] was now in charge of a department of the federal government with a budget of over $200 billion, and he clearly had no idea what he was doing.

The backlog of ships grew into 2022.[119] Four months after Biden and Buttigieg began to tout their pointless 24/7 plan for the ports, it had not been implemented.[120]

Shipping companies began to shift some of their traffic to the East and Gulf Coasts, which added to congestion at those ports.[121] In July 2022, as many as 153 container ships were queueing up off North American coastlines at one time.[122]

The crisis finally ended in October 2022, but not because of anything

Joe or Pete did. As *Seatrade Maritime News* put it, "market reports have pointed to inflation in developed economies and low consumer confidence as negative factors for container volumes."[123]

Amid the crisis, Buttigieg said during a television appearance that America needs "not only to make sure that we have the right kind of infrastructure, but to make sure that life gets better in this country for people trying to raise children."[124] One thing that makes life easier for parents is when we can easily get the stuff we want, preferably at uninflated prices. But as a new father, Secretary Pete probably knows that.

The Department of Transportation was poised to be the cornerstone of Biden's Build Back Better agenda, but under Pete's leadership, the port fiasco has proven to be the rule and not the exception. In the winter of 2022, the nation's air travel system was brought to its knees by back-to-back glitches. First, Southwest Airlines' internal systems crumbled under the chaos wrought by a winter storm during the peak of the Christmas travel season, embarrassing both the airline industry and the DOT. Just as that catastrophe began to subside, a crucial Federal Aviation Administration (FAA) system that alerts pilots to conditions on the ground at airports across the country went down, plunging airlines into near-total chaos.[125]

The day before Biden's second State of the Union address, a train carrying volatile chemicals derailed in the small rural town of East Palestine, Ohio, spewing toxic fumes into the air. Shrapnel flew as far as a mile away. Animals dropped dead.[126] Buttigieg, again, exhibited profound levels of incompetence. He tried to blame Donald Trump for removing a regulation on trains carrying dangerous chemicals; the law would not have applied to this train.[127] Even the National Transportation Safety Board, a part of the Biden administration, said this argument was "misinformation."[128]

Chinese social media buzzed with comparisons to the Chernobyl nuclear disaster in Ukraine in 1986.[129]

The state-run *Global Times* called Buttigieg "a vanity political appointee."[130] Where's the lie?

Within the first two weeks of the derailment, Buttigieg could not be bothered to visit East Palestine, but he did speak at the National Association of Counties' 2023 Legislative Conference to discuss his commitment to building workforces that "reflect the community."[131] Woke-to-English translation: he suggested that America has too many white construction workers.

A charitable analysis of Secretary Pete's DOT tenure is that all these problems prove new infrastructure projects are essential. A more realistic take is that leadership matters, and installing someone clearly out of his or her depth at the top of a major bureaucracy—and keeping him there despite a series of failures because he is a "rising" political "star"—can cause massive problems for a society.[132]

BABY FORMULA CRISIS

In January 2022, Mrs. Dr. Marlow gave birth to our first daughter, known to my radio audience as Duchess. I nearly had to miss her birth due to a bout with the China flu, but thankfully she stayed comfy in Mama's womb long enough for me to recover in time to attend. Duchess was formula-fed. Typically, once a family picks a specific type of formula, they stick with it until the baby can subsist on solid foods and cow's milk (about a year). Changing formula during infancy can upset the baby, disturb sleep (for parents, too), and occasionally cause other complications. It is not recommended, and with our two elder children, not necessary. By April it had become difficult to acquire Duchess's preferred brand, which is designed for babies with "sensitive tummies." A formula shortage had broken out. All of a sudden the shelves were bare and rationing began.[133]

The media and Food and Drug Administration (FDA) traced the shortages to an Abbott Laboratories plant in Michigan that was shuttered in February 2022 due to contamination. The company recalled several powdered infant formulas after health officials found bacteria at the facility that could potentially cause deadly infections in small children. The FDA reported in June 2022 that nine babies had died after consuming formula produced at that particular facility. Abbott denied a link between babies who had been infected and the contaminants.[134]

Shortages got worse from there.[135] I would have to go to ten or sometimes fifteen stores to try to find the right product. My family members across the country would pick up stray cans that they spotted in the wild. For our family, this debacle was merely an irritation; if I found a stash of our preferred formula, I would stock up. Families with more financial hardship would not have been able to do that (cans run about forty dollars each). As is the case with so many of Biden's biggest blunders, the baby formula shortage hit lower-income families the hardest.[136]

Ultimately, as Duchess got toward the end of her first year, I gave up entirely and we ended up switching brands.

Soon formula started to appear on the black market.[137] Experts warned against parents making homebrew formula.[138]

Babies can typically adjust to changes in formula, but many of them have significant digestive issues that leave them in pain, at least temporarily. When babies struggle, so do their families.

Like so many other crises in the Biden era, this one could have been mitigated, if not outright avoided. A whistleblower had filed a complaint about Abbott Nutrition to the U.S. Department of Labor's Occupational Safety and Health Administration (OSHA) as far back as February 2021; the whistleblower would expand the complaint in October of that year.[139] These complaints occurred months before the plant was shut down.

The first bacterial infection that caused an infant to suffer was reported in September 2021, but the inspection of the Abbott facility did not begin until January 31, 2022.[140]

Senator Jon Tester (D-MT) said that he had become aware of the potential crisis months before it became public knowledge and had pressed the FDA commissioner on it, to no avail.[141]

In May 2022, weeks after the shortages had made front-page news across the country, Republicans said that they had not yet seen a plan from the Biden administration to resolve the ongoing issues.[142]

Biden didn't meet with formula makers to seek supply fixes until June,[143] weeks after panic had set in for many families.

As Americans struggled to feed their newborns, the news-reading public was treated to photos of pallets of formula being sent to the Mexican border to feed babies who were being brought into the country illegally.[144]

The CDC blandly attributed the formula shortages to "supply chain issues" and the "recall of several infant formula products," without much more detail.[145] The USDA is the largest purchaser of baby formula and distributes the product to low-income families via the Women, Infants, and Children program (WIC).[146] Presumably they were in touch with the nation's largest producers like Abbott, Nestlé, and Mead Johnson. Yet somehow any potential red flags were missed. Either that, or they were covered up.

Biden's first major attempt to address the problem was not made until late May 2022, when he invoked the Defense Production Act and "Operation Fly Formula."[147] Operation Fly Formula is a federal program by which crucial products are able to be imported from overseas despite regulatory barriers.[148] Sounds like a good idea, but shelves across the country were already bare.

On May 25, Dr. Jill Biden posed with the 100,000 pounds of formula flown in from Ramstein Air Base in Germany to Dulles International Airport, just outside Washington, DC.[149] That quantity of formula in the photo op was not nearly enough to feed all of America's infants for even a single feeding.[150] And how were families in California, for example, supposed to quickly get their share of this tiny haul?

The shortage intensified into July, when 30 percent of brands reportedly went out of stock.[151]

The baby formula fiasco was a 360-degree failure from the Biden administration. They ignored whistleblower warnings until it was too late, and bureaucratic red tape was insufficient to keep babies safe; in fact, formula recalls for bacterial contamination continued throughout 2022 and into 2023.[152] Quickly ramping up production or importing stock from overseas proved too difficult a task as well.[153]

As of February 2023, Biden had brought in twenty-six shipments of less-than-a-meal's-worth of formula; the program was quietly paused in October 2022.[154] I asked the White House why they jettisoned Operation Fly Formula and if they intended to revive the imports, but I did not receive a response. It looks like they simply just gave up on solving the problem and hoped no one would notice. I made a point to check stores in the summer of 2023 as I completed work on this book, and still found shelves empty.

The FDA has said no one will be fired over the fiasco,[155] though one deputy commissioner did resign.[156]

When my daughter Duchess turned one year old in January 2023 and had her last sip of formula, we were out of the woods, but countless American families were not.[157] Days later, sixteen months after the first bacterial infection was reported to the U.S. government and more than nine months after we ran our first story at Breitbart News on the formula shortage, the feds announced a criminal investigation into the shuttered Abbott Laboratories facility.[158] Biden, ever the big-government oligarch, tried to remedy the problem with a punishment carried out by the state.

This crisis isn't so much about Abbott or the FDA as it is about Joe Biden. He didn't prepare for the shortage, and he was never able to solve it. As has been the pattern, the Biden administration kept reacting to lower-than-desired production with threats.

Not enough oil? You're getting another tax!

Ports jammed? Here come some fines.

Not enough formula? A criminal investigation for you! Meanwhile, American children and families struggled to feed their babies as if they lived in the third world.

THE SPENDING IS NEVER DONE

I moved to the Beltway in the summer of 2012, I was named editor in chief of Breitbart News a few months later, and I lived there until the spring of 2021. One of the lessons I learned during my time in DC is that a Democrat is never done spending. That rule is ironclad.

You can take it to the bank. Literally.

This is how they justify their political existence. This is how they enrich their friends, this is how they ensure job security for themselves and their family members, and this is how they earn the accolades of our media. It never stops. A new program, a new package, a new deal. The gradual slide toward socialism is a feature, not a bug, of the modern Democrat Party.

On Tuesday, December 10, 2022, at 1:30 a.m., after two deadline extensions, the Senate Appropriations Committee, chaired by Senator Patrick Leahy (D-VT), released a document more than four thousand pages long. It detailed $1.7 trillion in spending that would, by claim, combat inflation, help middle-class families, and aid national security.[159]

This "omnibus" spending bill would be the last major agenda item Biden would pass before the Republicans took over the House.

Omnibus bills are cheating. Of all the things I came to detest about Washington, omnibus bills were among the worst. Theoretically, Congress is supposed to pass twelve different appropriations bills each year that allocate funds to different parts of the government. That system would ensure more transparency and less cronyism. But in modern Washington, multiple appropriations bills get packaged together in one, called an "omnibus."

Think of wanting a Bloody Mary in Las Vegas and getting served vodka and clamato with a celery stalk, a lemon wedge, a bacon slice, a crab claw, a whole jalapeño pepper, a Wagyu beef slider, a slice of pizza, a Bavarian pretzel, and a whole rotisserie chicken in it. Why can't the breakfast booze and tiny hamburger get ordered separately? Just because I want one thing doesn't mean I want all the other stuff that comes with it.

Washington's response: everyone likes pizza.

In recent years, omnibus spending packages have been costing taxpayers well north of $1 trillion each, spread out over some thousand or more pages. This shift in the approach to the appropriations process has been disastrous. First of all, reading legislation is incredibly difficult. It would take weeks if not months to actually read through bills of this length, even if you allocated time for nothing else in your life. That means literally no one in our government has read the trillion-dollar bills they pass. Second of all, since an omnibus package essentially means that multiple bills are being debated and voted on all at once, nearly anything can become a negotiating chit. The horse trading among members to get funds for their particular project(s) is limitless.

The end result is invariably unfathomably large bills that send deficits and debt to the moon.

We allocate eight-figure sums in emergency assistance to Ukraine, child nutrition programs, and FBI funding all at the same time. Ridiculous.[160]

In an epic Twitter thread, Representative Dan Bishop (R-NC) compiled a list of some of the most offensive items in the bill. Here are a few:[161]

- $65 million to restore the Pacific salmon population, and another $5 million to study salmon endangered by infrastructure projects. This is not the full extent of the salmon-based pork: the word "salmon" appears forty-eight times in the bill.

- $575 million for family planning/reproductive health, which presumably means birth control. (This section of the bill notes that population growth can "threaten biodiversity of endangered species," a manifestly antihuman sentiment.)

- $3 million to "bee-friendly" highways

- $3 million to an LGBT+ museum in New York

- $750,000 would go to modernizing the fire alarm system of the Metropolitan Opera.

- $3.6 million to the Michelle Obama Trail

- Funding for the creation of a Ukrainian Independence Park in Washington, DC

This list is seemingly endless. Much of it is laughable and pathetic, but it is also a sign of deep governmental degradation.

While Washington spent money we hadn't yet made, American households struggled with supply chain issues, Bidenflation, and collapsing household wealth.[162]

Though he may have pitched a tax on the ultra-super-mega-rich in his second State of the Union address, President Biden's tax collection scheme seemed to start with a crackdown on the unreported tips of waiters and waitresses.[163]

Biden rarely speaks deeply about his economic vision but is fond of discussing "the middle class." This is a dog whistle to remind people of his upbringing in Pennsylvania and Delaware. It is a signal to would-be voters that he is just like us. He can relate to our struggles.

But that's not true. He cannot relate. After all, he's been in the upper echelons of American politics for fifty years.

In 2023, his administration proposed higher fees for borrowers with good credit. Mortgage rates were rising thanks to skyrocketing interest rates that the Fed was deploying to fight Bidenflation, and now Joe was trying to stick it to responsible middle-class homeowners some more.[164]

This is pure exploitation of the middle class he claims to champion.

From his career in the Senate to his tenure as vice president to his budget-busting presidency, Joe Biden has rarely, if ever, resisted the temptation to expand the government, max out confiscation and redistribution of citizens' money, and reallocate those resources to best suit his political agenda and ambitions. This approach has paid dividends for him. The same can't be said for the masses. During his first year, the wealth gap between the richest and poorest Americans expanded,[165] as it had during his vice presidency.[166]

While running for president in 1987, Senator Joe falsely claimed that he "marched in the civil rights movement."[167] That isn't true. Though he never walked with Martin Luther King Jr., or any other civil rights leader for that matter, he has led America on another truly historic trek: the march toward socialism.

CHAPTER 11

The Coronavirus Power Grab

As a news person, I had long thought we were overdue to see a pandemic. In a globalized world with relatively easy and affordable travel, it was only a matter of time. We've tracked virus outbreaks at Breitbart News for as long as I've been editor. Also, considering I'm a China skeptic and a staunch advocate of more stringent border enforcement, I might have been the least surprised person that things got as bad as they did.

Everyone suffered from the coronavirus pandemic. First and foremost, there are those who died and those who lost loved ones. When Johns Hopkins University's Coronavirus Resource Center suspended tracking COVID-19 data on March 10, 2023, the global death toll was at 6,881,955. That number is probably underestimated, considering they rely on corrupt governments to supply them with the information. China, where the virus originated, allegedly lost a mere 101,056 people, according to the Hopkins data, which is less than Spain, Ukraine, South Africa, Peru, Colombia, and other such nations with a fraction of the population.

As usual, the CCP is lying to the world.

Johns Hopkins claims 1,123,836 Americans had died of the China flu when they stopped crunching the numbers, though this figure might be artificially inflated because it likely includes people who died "with COVID," and not "due to COVID." (The data likely lumps in people who were currently infected but died of a cause other than the virus itself.)

Still, this is a huge death toll, and that only partially accounts for the suffering that humanity endured due to the pandemic. People lost jobs; others became depressed and developed addictions. Others were forced by government mandate to spend prime years of their lives at home in front of screens instead of out making friends, starting families, seeing the world, or advancing careers.

I certainly have my stories. My wife, Mrs. Dr. Marlow, by the grace of God, delivered our second son, known to my radio audience as Master Marlow Jr., just days before the lockdowns kicked in. We were among the last people for years who would enjoy the freedoms of visiting a hospital for inpatient care without masks or negative tests or having to flash vaccine passports. (Those liberties were long gone by the time our daughter, Duchess, was born twenty-three months later.)

We all got home from the hospital just in time to observe the surreal, seemingly apocalyptic scenario unfold from the relative comfort of our detached single-family home (the optimal type of dwelling for social distancing).

Mama's maternity leave would soon lapse, however, and she would return to her internal medicine training, jumping into the COVID-19 fray. She would be sent to the coronavirus "front lines." Her experience wasn't as harrowing as some stories that appeared in media, but it was fraught with anxiety. Every day when she would come home from the hospital, she would have to change her clothes in the basement and thoroughly wash up before coming up to greet her children. An early COVID exposure meant we had to isolate her from the rest of the family for several days, separating her from the baby. It was a major inconvenience for what turned out to be a false alarm.

Needless to say, the grandparents were deprived of some of those magical moments with their newest family member. This is just one of many indignities "seasoned citizens" suffered during the pandemic's peak. Others suffered a far greater fate, forced to die alone in hospital rooms. Funerals were restricted, if they even happened all.

When my parents' twenty-year-old cat, Olivia, was on the brink of death, they weren't even allowed to comfort her as the vet put her to sleep. Instead, they were forced to hand her off to an anonymous vet tech in a beekeeper suit, who promptly took her inside to die. Their final goodbye took place in a nondescript strip mall parking lot.

We had become so cold so quickly. To our families, to our neighbors, to ourselves.

Master Marlow Jr. is now three years old. He is bright, beautiful, and quite loquacious (he takes after his talk-show-host dad). Yet his pediatrician also recommended we enroll him in speech therapy to help with articulation.

Scientists at the Royal College of Surgeons in Ireland found that babies born in the first few months of the pandemic saw their social development stunted. Given that masks are known to be detrimental to children's speech development, the scientists' conclusion is hardly a shock.[1]

Even left-wing, government-funded NPR would eventually admit that masks are devastating for children. Youngsters don't wear them properly, and even if they do, they are probably not high-quality or well fitting. A masked populace might even slow brain development for children, according to the NPR report.[2]

During the pandemic, children missed doctor and dentist visits. They missed seeing mental health professionals. Children from lower-income families were more likely to miss these appointments than the more affluent.[3] Pandemic babies talked, walked, and interacted later and less often.[4] Developmental delays increased for children aged three to seventeen.[5]

I don't know why, exactly, Master Marlow Jr. needed a little extra help. We kept masking to an absolute minimum, and he played with other maskless children at the park from the moment he could sit up straight. Yet I'll always wonder if he was set back by society's collective coronamania.

When I took him to his first speech lesson, the therapist was wearing a mask, but it was a style I had never seen before. This wasn't an ordinary face diaper. It had a clear plastic window in front of her mouth so that the children could read her lips.

She may not have understood the science of the virus itself, but she certainly knew that grown-ups covering their faces for years was hindering our babies' ability to learn language.

We condemned our children to this, and it turned out that the science didn't even support our decisions.

When Joe Biden came into office promising that he would "shut down the virus, not the country," it was the exact type of sentiment voters wanted to hear.[6] Despite hundreds of millions of people watching around the world, the empty promises effortlessly flew from Biden's mouth during the October 2020 debate with Trump. He would be our savior. He would give us back our freedom and vanquish the microscopic foe known as SARS-CoV-2.

At least, that's what we were told.

LIGHT AUTHORITARIANISM

We now know that Biden didn't actually have much of a plan to beat the China flu, but he did have an effective campaign strategy to blame the epidemic on Donald Trump and reap the political rewards. Joe knew his opponent was vulnerable on pandemic policy. With such a massive death toll, devastating economic fallout, and general confusion and despair sweeping the country during election season, it was going to be a political liability for any incumbent president. It was inevitable that Trump's general election opponent would declare the then POTUS a failure, claim he or she would have done a better job, and advocate that it was not too late to change course.

It was a political no-brainer for candidate Biden to tell the American people what he would have done differently and what he would do going forward. His first claim was that he would adopt a consistent scientific approach to fighting COVID that relied on experts and was driven by "the science."[7] During the campaign, Vivek Murthy, who chaired Biden's COVID-19 advisory board and would eventually be named his surgeon general, said that if Biden were elected, "You would see an approach that's driven by science and by scientists." We soon would learn that "the science" is a political term and not, ironically, a scientific one. It is used when the Left wants to limit debate.

Biden declared that the adults would be back in charge, setting national COVID policies that would be consistent across state lines and rooted in evidence and reason. By tracking the amount of viral spread within a given community, the CDC would effectively be local government's North Star, making recommendations or mandates as to when businesses could reopen, when children could go back to schools, and ultimately when America could return to normalcy.[8]

This is textbook leftism: the government usurps freedom from the people by defining parameters subjectively, possibly dishonestly, and then sets policy accordingly. The policies are always easier to implement than they are to roll back.

The credibility of the Centers for Disease Control and Prevention was critical for Biden to sell the plan to the public. The CDC's trustworthiness had fallen off a cliff in recent months. A Pew poll showed that 79 percent of Americans held a positive view of the CDC as of April 2020,[9] but a Gallup poll in September of that year showed that only 25 percent of Americans believed it had communicated a clear plan of action to tackle the pandemic.[10]

There was plenty of reason for growing skepticism. The CDC first suggested that masks were not effective at stopping the spread of COVID-19,[11] and then told Americans that masks were the most effective tool at stopping the spread,[12] and then told Americans that masks were required indoors and outdoors,[13] and then told Americans that masks really worked only indoors.[14]

The science was settled, and resettled, and resettled again, and resettled again.

Two years into the pandemic, the CDC acknowledged that many masks Americans had been wearing for years provided inadequate protection from SARS-CoV-2.[15] A major study published by the Cochrane Library in 2023 "did not show a clear reduction in respiratory viral infection with the use of medical/surgical masks."[16]

The federal government had told Americans to upend their lives, stay home from work, miss school and sports, and made them agonize over family members forced to die alone in locked-down hospital wards, all without clear scientific proof that any of it was helping. Yet we were told to comply or else lose even more liberties.

The Wuhan plague could have provided a moment for the country to come together. Biden was known to pay lip service to the concept of unity. Instead it drove a divided nation further apart. As Biden was sworn in, the China flu continued to rage, and a weary, perplexed nation endured more death.

One of the signs that Biden was not going to truly grasp the science of the pandemic was his utter lack of interest in the origins of the virus. It is as though he genuinely does not want to know the answers to what is arguably the biggest question of the century: How on earth did this pandemic happen? Why Biden is uncurious is not too difficult to ascertain: finding out the truth would no doubt further strain our relationship with China. As we have seen, Biden's personal ties to China are deep. His family famously has business entanglements with CCP-backed corporations. Biden's economic policy depends on the flow of cheap goods from China into the U.S.

The "lab leak theory"—that the SARS-CoV-2 virus was released from a lab in Wuhan, China—was once dismissed as a conspiracy but has steadily gained serious consideration throughout the pandemic.[17] By November 2022, even Dr. Anthony Fauci himself said that he was open-minded to the possibility.[18] "I have a completely open mind about that, despite people saying that I don't," he told NBC's *Meet the Press* in late 2022. In February 2023, the Energy Department revised its assessment, concluding that the pandemic most likely originated in the Wuhan lab.[19]

If the origin was a lab leak—and it probably was—it would be a compelling reason to strongly ratchet up geopolitical pressure on China. If it turned out that China was experimenting with material that could be used for biological warfare, Americans would publicly debate a hot war with another superpower.

Heavy stuff.

The true explanation for the pandemic would also likely further expose Dr. Fauci, who okayed American funds going to the Wuhan Institute of Virology to fund gain-of-function research.[20] "Gain of function" is when an organism is altered to enhance biological functions. In the case of a virus, that could mean that it becomes more contagious or more potent, for example. In October 2021, Lawrence Tabak, who would later become head of the National Institutes of Health, admitted to Congress that the NIH had funded research in the Wuhan lab from 2018 to 2019 that resulted in the SARS-related bat coronaviruses SHC014 and WIV1 becoming more infectious to humans (aka gain of function).[21]

In an epic gaslighting effort, Biden and the establishment media (which is mostly owned by conglomerates with deep ties to Communist China; see *Breaking the News*) treated the virus as if it were a spontaneous tragedy. Either that, or it was Trump's fault. It was those god-awful Republicans, not China! Fauci would get canonized while vaccine skeptics would get demonized.

All the while, the virus mutated as Americans suffered—physically, emotionally, and spiritually.

THE WINTER OF SEVERE ILLNESS AND DEATH

Rhetorically, Biden's coronavirus rhetoric was inconsistent and ineffective.

While he was on the campaign trail, Biden's public proclamations about the virus were often gibberish:

- During an interview on *The View* in March 2020, Biden was asked about lockdowns and gave a completely incoherent answer: "We have to take care of the cure, that will make the problem worse no matter what, no matter what. We know what has to be done." There were no follow-up questions to clarify whether that answer indicated he was pro-lockdown or anti-lockdown.[22]

- During an April 2020 interview on CNN about the coronavirus response, he said, "You know, there's a uh, during World War II, uh, you know, where Roosevelt came up with a thing uh, that uh, you know, was totally different than a, than the, the, it's called, he called it the, you know, the World War II, he had the war—the War Production Board."[23]

- In September 2020 he said, "COVID has taken this year, just since the outbreak, has taken more than one hundred years. . . . Look. Here's . . . The lives . . . It's just . . . I mean, think about it."[24]

In the October debate against Trump, Biden made the claim that because 220,000 Americans had died of COVID-19 under Trump's presidency, Trump should not remain as president: "If you hear nothing else I say tonight, hear this," Biden said. "Anyone that is responsible for that many deaths should not remain as president of the United States of America."[25] However, under Biden's America, deaths from COVID-19 have been much higher than under Trump, and that is with vaccines and treatments now available.

When Biden took office on January 20, 2021, U.S. deaths from COVID were at 423,945. The number of people who died from coronavirus under Biden, from January 20, 2021, to March 10, 2023, when Johns Hopkins stopped counting, was 699,891.[26]

By his own standards, Biden should have resigned from office at the end of August 2021, and two more times after that, one time for every 220,000 people who died on his watch.

At a CNN town hall event in February 2021, Biden claimed that there were no coronavirus vaccines when he assumed office. However, at that very event he contradicted himself by saying, "We came into office, there were only 50 million doses that were available."[27]

The hysteria of his words continued to increase as the death toll rose. In August 2021, Biden attacked Florida governor Ron DeSantis for allowing parents to choose whether their children would be forced to wear masks in schools. Biden told DeSantis to "get out of the way!"[28] In September 2021, Biden told Americans who had chosen not to get vaccinated that his "patience was wearing thin."[29] In December 2021, he proclaimed that it would be a "winter of severe illness and death" for the unvaccinated.[30]

The fearmongering and demonizing of under-jabbed Americans weren't a constant refrain from Biden and the Left. Given the bogus arguments behind the masking and lockdowns, it was little wonder why so many conservatives remained unconvinced about the vaccines.

Donald Trump was accused of not following the science, and occasionally he didn't, but he did tend to go with the recommendations of the leaders of the CDC, the NIH, and his COVID task force. Biden mostly kept the same people in place whom Trump had left him. The CDC was kept in the hands of Dr. Rochelle Walensky (or as she is known at Breitbart News, Dr. Hot Mess). The NIH stuck with Dr. Francis Collins (or as he is known at Breitbart, the Friendly Fascist) until he retired in December 2021 (he was succeeded by real-life dentist Lawrence Tabak). The spritely octogenarian Dr. Anthony Fauci, the director of the National Institute of Allergy and Infectious Diseases (NIAID) and the head of Trump's COVID-19 task force, was named the chief medical advisor to President Biden; he held that post for nearly two years before retiring.

The same team was put back on the field. So, it followed that things wouldn't actually get better. In fact, most of the problems that plagued Trump plagued Biden while many other elements of the virus response got worse.

One of Biden's clearest campaign promises was that the U.S. would ramp up testing.[31] The goal was abundant, reliable free tests everywhere, all the time. This policy position put him in stark contrast with President Trump, who wanted to slow down testing because all of the positive results made the country look bad.[32] Biden saw a political opening here.

Although some at-home tests were already in production, none was approved in the U.S. by the FDA. According to Biden, "It's not enough to know in seven days or five days or three days whether or not you have COVID."[33]

While rapid COVID tests were thought to be the answer to longer wait times, they were not as accurate as the PCR tests. PCR tests use a lab technique called reverse transcription polymerase chain reaction (PCR) to detect genetic material of the virus.[34] Most at-home COVID tests were antigen tests, also known as rapid tests, which do not detect the Wuhan virus as well as molecular tests do (PCR tests being the most common).[35]

Biden fell behind on his goals, so he outsourced much of the manufacturing of the tests to China in order to catch up.

Neither president ever made it clear exactly what we were supposed to do with the information that we had tested positive. Generally speaking, people would quarantine in their houses, only to pass the virus to other people with whom they lived, who could pass it to other people in their lives before they even realized they were sick.[36]

Biden's next promise was to build a national contact-tracing workforce to help track and identify those infected with COVID. Biden would supposedly organize more than 100,000 government employees to work directly with organizations in this effort. Again, the solution for the Biden administration seemed to involve a rapid and overwhelming expansion of the bureaucracy. In this case, his response would also necessitate a massive new government database of personal information.

The program would help people who had been exposed to this coronavirus contact everyone who might have been exposed because of them. Then those individuals could do the same to everyone they had exposed, and so on. Hopefully, enough of those people would quarantine in time to slow the spread.

Anyone with two brain cells to rub together would have realized this was totally absurd. While contact tracing might be recommended for something like HIV,[37] which is typically spread by sexual contact or sharing needles,[38] it was never going to make a difference for a mega-contagious respiratory virus.

Were we kidding ourselves?

Actually, we were getting tricked by our elected leaders. This "contract tracing" plan was nothing more than a massive government jobs program, and a woke one at that. According to Biden's cochair of the

COVID-19 Advisory Board and surgeon general of the United States, Vivek Murthy, the goal was not just merely to stop COVID, but also to make sure that the workforce making up this new bureaucracy was diverse enough to "look like the country that we're trying to serve."[39]

Obviously, contact tracing failed,[40] but Biden was able to score a few more woke points.

Many unscientific, unsustainable, impractical, and draconian COVID policies persisted under Biden. He continued to pay lip service to the idea of social distancing, even when a Cambridge University study from 2021 found that the "six-foot rule" did not protect against catching COVID-19, even outdoors. A person's cough, speech, and breath vary widely when it comes to spreading particles, rendering the distance arbitrary.[41] Another study from MIT found that the risk of being exposed to COVID can be as great at sixty feet as it is at six feet within a room where air is mixed.[42] Still, not everyone got the memos, as some businesses continued to recommend social distancing of six feet at least into 2023.

One frontline doctor whom I relied on as a source during the pandemic said that the main COVID exposure concern at her hospital was not the distance from the infected but time spent in a room with them. That's highly logical, but not something that was explained to most Americans. Meanwhile, we kept engaging in virtue-signal theater by pulling up our cloth masks for a one-alligator count at the precise moment we passed neighbors while we walked our dogs.

When it comes to masking, the science does seem to be quite clear: common face masks (made of cloth or paper) do not work at stopping the spread of COVID-19. N95 masks perform better but are often not a good fit or are worn improperly. There are numerous works of scholarship that show this, including a Danish study that was published in November 2020 and appears to be the most comprehensive one on this topic.[43] The randomized trial, which tracked more than 6,000 participants in Denmark, found that participants with face masks were infected at the same rate as those without face masks (the control group).[44]

In January 2023, the NIH-funded Cochrane policy institute issued a report that examined seventy-eight different high-quality studies on various COVID mitigation efforts and concluded with moderate certainty

that wearing masks in the community "probably makes little or no difference to the outcome" of the illness. (The analysis also suggested that even
the N95 masks were not particularly effective, but that conclusion was
based on low-certainty evidence.)[45]

A few weeks after the study came out, the *New York Times* published
a piece titled "The Mask Mandates Did Nothing. Will Any Lessons Be
Learned?"

Thanks, Grey Lady, but where were you in 2020 or 2021 or 2022?

The White House ignored both the Cochrane report and the *Times*
piece.[46]

Biden was slow to adjust policies but quick to demonize conservative
governors, such as Ron DeSantis, who wanted to block face-diaper mandates in schools.[47]

There was also little serious public debate on the subject of natural immunity. In October 2020, Rochelle Walensky signed the John Snow memorandum, which brazenly declared that "there is no evidence for lasting
protective immunity to SARS-CoV-2 following natural infection."[48] So, discussion over?

Media outlets immediately began to declare that the science was settled, so we should move on.[49] But not so fast. Studies including those
from the Cleveland Clinic,[50] Yale University,[51] and the Washington University School of Medicine[52] showed evidence of lasting protection from
prior infection. In 2022, Reuters reported[53] on new studies[54] that showed
prior infection was more effective at protecting against COVID-19 than
vaccination was.

One study from the CDC,[55] which analyzed data from New York and
California, found that natural immunity was six times stronger than vaccination during the Delta variant wave. Yet recent infection did not factor
into the federal government's vaccine recommendations.

Blanket policies became the norm. Masks for everyone, even children. Vaccines for everyone, even children and the recently infected. The
implication was that COVID is an equal threat to a healthy teenager who
had recently recovered from the virus and a morbidly obese septuagenar-
ian with hypertension and a weakened immune system.

Lockdowns were also ineffective. There were significant signs early
on in the virus that this would prove to be the case. The world watched
as Sweden became a success story by limiting international travel, not

with lockdowns. Among eleven wealthy neighboring countries, Sweden was the only nation with no excess mortality in 2020[56] in individuals under seventy-five. A December 2022 report from the UK government concluded that Sweden had Europe's lowest post-pandemic "proportional all-cause excess-mortality scores," tied with Norway.[57]

Comparing a country like America to Sweden is hardly apples-to-apples, but it would have been nice to talk this case study through.

China has had some of the most draconian lockdowns and appears to have suffered horribly from the virus (though it is hard to be certain because China doesn't accurately report death tolls and they do not have a free press). In late 2022, citizens were still being locked in their homes as part of the CCP's "zero Covid" policy, which was failing. China reported virtually no COVID fatalities for 2020–22, but all of a sudden they recorded tens of thousands of deaths for the first time in January 2023.[58]

Suspicious.

A recent comprehensive report from researchers at Johns Hopkins analyzed 18,000 people and found that lockdowns in the U.S. reduced mortality by only 0.2 percent on average.[59] The study only served to confirm what we all mildly observant people saw with our own two eyes.

While Trump and Biden slowly opened the country back up after initial shutdowns and slowdowns, there was never any mea culpa from the scientists, politicians, and pundits behind the failed strategy.

Trump had declared a public health emergency (PHE) near the start of the pandemic, which Biden maintained well into 2023.[60] The PHE allowed for the government to pay for vaccines, many tests, and certain treatments. To end the PHE would shrink government powers, which is something the coronavirus authoritarians were loath to do.

ENDLESS JABS

Biden repeatedly politicized the vaccine, making it about Trump and not the science, all the while claiming he was trying to defend the latter.

"Let me be clear. I trust vaccines. I trust scientists. But I don't trust Donald Trump. And at this moment, the American people can't, either," Biden proclaimed in a September 2020 speech.[61]

He was suggesting that the shots were not safe, which is anti-vax rhetoric.

He delivered the same line almost verbatim in the September 29, 2020, debate. "In terms of the whole notion of a vaccine, we're for a vaccine, but we don't trust [Trump] at all, nor do you. What we trust is a scientist," Biden said on behalf of his ticket during the chaotic first presidential debate with Trump.[62]

But those were the vaccines we got. The Trump vaccines. And now Biden was set to make one of the signature initiatives at the start of his presidency the implementation of these Trump vaccines.

In July 2021, he falsely claimed in a town hall with Don Lemon that the vaccinated cannot get COVID. "You're not going to—you're not going to get COVID if you have these vaccinations."[63]

Lemon didn't challenge Biden on this. Lemon himself was one of the media figures who most egregiously disparaged the unvaccinated, suggesting on CNN that they should be banned from supermarkets, ball games, and even work.[64]

Biden and others attacked the unvaccinated, attempting to bully them into getting the shots.

As of 2022, a consensus emerged among the scientific community that the COVID vaccines that were available to Americans were at least somewhat effective in reducing symptoms and severe infections for many people who contracted the virus.[65] The Commonwealth Fund, a health care nonprofit, estimated that between December 2020 and November 2022, the jabs prevented more than 18.5 million hospitalizations and 3.2 million additional deaths.[66]

These are huge numbers. Trump and Operation Warp Speed are to thank for it. Operation Warp Speed was President Trump's expansive effort to accelerate vaccine development and distribution through an infusion of funds and the suspension of some government regulations.

However, the vaccines were oversold to the public by Joe Biden. Biden and many of his COVID messengers/government-funded vaccine salespeople suggested the jabs would prevent infection and provide lasting immunity. Neither of those things was true.

Biden had an opportunity to show leadership and explain the truth about the masks and the vaccines. If he had done so using facts and data, perhaps he would have gotten through to vaccine skeptics.

Instead, the administration sowed further division by prioritizing vaccine "equity" as a key point of his COVID-19 strategy. Minorities and people from low-income households were prioritized. The CDC notes that they were less likely to get vaccinated, which put them at greater risk from the virus.[67] Healthy young brown people were prioritized ahead of older, at-risk whites.

That isn't science. That is racism.

Officials from Rhode Island to Montana to Washington, DC, to New York followed suit, adding elements of racial bias to the effort to beat the pandemic.[68] This certainly cost lives.

The race-based vaccine rollout set a horrific precedent and paved the way for other discriminatory woke trends when it came to allocating scarce health care resources like monoclonal antibodies.[69]

In December 2020, Biden said that he would not make COVID-19 vaccines mandatory.[70] When he became president, mandates became the centerpiece of his shut-down-the-virus strategy. Technically, Americans were not forced to inject themselves with new drugs, but nearly everyone who chose to abstain was forced to forgo some element of normal public life.

There were mandates everywhere: the military, health care workers, universities. Get the jab, or lose privileges. Businesses and employers served as Biden's vaccine enforcers. Professional athletes, the fittest people on the planet and thus at extremely low coronavirus risk, were prevented from playing against other young, healthy opponents unless they had shots.[71]

Businesses forced employees to stay home and customers to show their vax card (and sometimes mask up anyway) in order to patronize their stores.

Personally, I wouldn't have been allowed into the hospital to witness the birth of my daughter in 2022 without being current on my jabs. I had recently recovered from the virus as of the day she was born, so my antibodies were likely as high as they would ever be. That didn't matter to the vax-compliance police.

In August 2021, Biden made jabs mandatory for military troops.[72]

By November 2021, he ramped up the authoritarianism. His Department of Labor announced requirements on COVID-19 vaccines for

American workers under the department's Occupational Safety and Health Administration (OSHA).[73] Companies with more than one hundred workers would have to order employees to get the jabs by January 4, 2022, or have employees test negative once a week. All unvaccinated workers would be forced to wear antiscience masks during their work hours.

Nearly 17 million American health care employees—many of whom were frontline heroes—were forced to get vaccinated by January 4, 2022, or else lose their jobs. In the middle of a pandemic, and with America facing a perpetual shortage of physicians, Biden applied policies to further limit staffing in the health care field.[74]

In January 2022, the Supreme Court blocked vaccine mandates for most businesses but left them in place for health care workers.[75]

The administration failed again by neglecting to sponsor a program similar to Operation Warp Speed for therapeutics. This would have helped all the people who didn't want the shots at all and all the people who still got infected despite getting jabbed. Instead of following the science and the logic, Biden elected to stay the course, endlessly beating the drum about vaccines and masks and tests—and nothing else.

Finally, a legitimate reason to spend pallets of taxpayer dollars, and Biden missed it. Figures.

Meanwhile, the virus was mutating, as viruses do, and was beginning to evade the vaccines even more than it had with previous variants.[76]

A lot of fake news flooded the online space—both from the scientists and normal people. The Right became fixated on inexpensive already-FDA-approved drugs that were touted as miracle cures. For example, conservative media became enamored with ivermectin, an antiparasitic that is often used for deworming horses. It also apparently deworms humans. A study showed it is effective against COVID-19—in places where worms are prevalent, like India.[77] The best weapon against COVID-19 appears to be a strong immune system, and one of the worst things for your immune system is to have worms. Thus, taking ivermectin can restore your immune system and perhaps save you from COVID—provided that you have worms. If you don't have them, it probably won't help you very much.[78]

Still, the establishment hated ivermectin, so the Right embraced it, much like they had done with hydroxychloroquine. (The fake news about HcQ, a mostly innocuous but hardly magical option for the China flu, was discussed at length in *Breaking the News*.)

Other well-publicized treatments were effective for one variant but not the next. Regeneron, for example, seemed to work wonders against Delta, but failed against Omicron.[79] Again, most of the public probably wasn't aware of this. Regeneron, which is a cocktail that includes two monoclonal antibodies, was also quite expensive for the U.S. government, costing north of $2,000 per dose. (The vaccines cost the government about $15–$20 per dose.[80]) So, it would have been nice to have clear information on whether it was smart to take it.

Instead, the Biden administration colluded with the Silicon Valley Masters of the Universe to censor debate on the science of COVID-19 and its treatment. Andy Slavitt, senior advisor to the president on the White House's COVID-19 Pandemic Response Team, reportedly pressured Twitter to ban former *New York Times* reporter Alex Berenson for alleged COVID disinformation.[81] Berenson was canceled from the platform and eventually reinstated only after settling a lawsuit against Twitter.[82]

Berenson, who accused Pfizer of conspiring with Twitter to try to get him blacklisted, has been a relentless critic of the mRNA vaccines. However, he advocated on behalf of Pfizer-made Paxlovid,[84] an antiviral treatment that Biden himself took[83] after contracting COVID in the summer of 2022. It has a strong reputation for preventing severe complications related to the virus.[85] Did Biden make a big push to raise awareness about Paxlovid, the drug that helped him "rebound" from the illness? No. This could have been an opportunity to find common ground (that is, unity) with his harshest critics. Instead, a few months later he got another vaccine booster and touted more jabs.[86] (I asked the White House how many times President Biden was injected with the COVID-19 vaccine in total but did not receive a response.)

Biden was fond of the expression "a pandemic of the unvaccinated."[87] Presumably this connoted that the unvaccinated are dirty and getting us all sick and taking up all our hospital beds. Even the left-wing *Atlantic* acknowledged that this language only served to alienate vaccine skeptics, not convince them. It also turned out to be dead wrong. Biden himself got sick long after making that statement and having received countless jabs. He never publicly expressed remorse or regret for that horrific branding.

THE HUNTER CONNECTION

One reason Biden's coronavirus response was snakebit was because he trusted the World Health Organization (WHO).[88] The WHO failed the world on the Chinese coronavirus[89] from the jump by relying too heavily on misinformation from China; it did not declare the emerging coronavirus pandemic a "public health emergency of international concern" until March 11, 2020, weeks after it had spread globally.[90] Taiwan claimed that Tedros Adhanom Ghebreyesus, the director-general of the WHO, "mostly ignored" clear warning signs that were emerging of a potential pandemic in December 2019 and even withheld crucial information in the interim.[91] (At Breitbart News, we first reported on the "mystery pneumonia" coming out of China on January 7, 2020.[92])

The WHO, which was defunded by Trump and re-funded by Biden, has ties to the Biden family, specifically Hunter Biden.

The U.S. had engaged with the WHO on bat coronavirus in Wuhan, China, prior to the pandemic via the PREDICT project. PREDICT was an initiative of the U.S. Agency for International Development (USAID) that attempted to predict pandemics before they happened. The WHO was a PREDICT partner along with Metabiota, a company funded by Hunter Biden's firm, Rosemont Seneca, in 2014.[93]

PREDICT also regularly coordinated with Fauci's NIAID.[94]

Other PREDICT partners included the CDC, the U.S. Department of Defense, EcoHealth Alliance (the nonprofit that reportedly funneled millions of U.S. taxpayer dollars to the Wuhan Institute of Virology China), and the Wuhan Institute of Virology itself.[95] Peter Daszak, the EcoHealth president, made a "significant contribution" to the PREDICT project.[96] Daszak famously thanked Dr. Fauci in April 2020 for rejecting the lab leak theory.[97]

PREDICT supposedly was designed to discover and collect animal viruses that could infect humans as well. The program used data from the WHO to construct a digital map of where viral animal outbreaks capable of threatening humans could occur.

In 2014, Hunter Biden's Rosemont Seneca Technology Partners led Metabiota's seed and Series A funding rounds. According to emails from Hunter Biden's laptop, Hunter and his team helped Metabiota navigate the firm's early business endeavors and helped leverage Hunter's deep political connections in order to help broker deals between Meta-biota and other firms, including In-Q-Tel, which essentially functions as a venture capital arm of the CIA.[98]

A PREDICT document from 2014 revealed that the goals of the project included developing expanded surveillance for public health purposes and studying SARS-like coronavirus from Chinese horseshoe bats.

The PREDICT China team was organized by the WHO and funded by USAID.

The program died out under Trump, but in October 2021, Biden's USAID announced[99] that it would be rebooting PREDICT via a new program called the Discovery & Exploration of Emerging Pathogens—Viral Zoonoses (DEEP VZN).[100]

This news should shock only those who aren't paying attention.

THE PANDEMIC-INDUSTRIAL COMPLEX

U.S. insurance companies made a mint off COVID-19. Profit records toppled in 2020[101] and 2022[102] as more Americans avoided going to doctors and hospitals in fear of contracting the coronavirus. One poll found that 46 percent of adults who are insured are struggling to afford out-of-pocket costs; nearly 30 percent do not take prescribed medicine due to rising costs.[103] In the insurance game, it is said that the house always wins; nonetheless, it is troubling when American families are spending more on premiums and deductibles while less care is being delivered.

The insurance companies seem to have a strong preference for Joe Biden's brand of politics as well. In the 2020 campaign, Biden received $5.5 million from insurance industry PACs.[104] In retrospect, health insurers were wise to back Biden, at least from a business perspective.

According to *Business Insider*, health care executives favored Biden over Trump,[105] even though Trump had given large tax cuts to health care companies in 2017.[106] According to *Insider*'s analysis of campaign spending of executives at one hundred large health care companies, Biden raised nearly $47 million in personal donations during the 2020 election cycle, whereas Trump raised only $21 million. The $47 million in donations does not include money raised from PACs.

Donors to Biden included executives from Kaiser Permanente,

Merck, McKesson, and Independence Blue Cross. Other campaign donors included COVID-19 vaccine manufacturers such as Pfizer and Moderna.

According to data compiled by Open Secrets, Joe Biden is the top political donor recipient of both Pfizer and Moderna.[107]

The president pledged to hold health insurers accountable by cracking down on high health costs, but in actuality, he funneled billions of dollars into their coffers. His new coronavirus relief package included a provision that gave health insurance companies $61.3 billion in federal subsidies for private plans offered under the Affordable Care Act and COBRA (a program that laid-off workers can buy into after losing employer-provided insurance). This provision was a boon for the insurance companies and did only a little to help taxpaying Americans. Only 2.5 million people were added to insurance rolls after this move (there were 29 million uninsured at the time) and premiums dropped for only 11 million Americans, according to the CBO.

In the fall of 2022, Biden expanded the Affordable Care Act, which was a major benefit to the health insurance companies.[108]

He even helped spawn new industries within the health care sector. Biden had invested close to $100 million in taxpayer dollars toward "navigators" who help connect people with a health insurance plan.[109]

Call it the pandemic-industrial complex.

ONLY BIDEN WOULD TURN TO CHINA

Not only was China not held accountable for the pandemic, but they hauled in vast sums of cash from suffering Americans. The best example of this might be a $1.3 billion COVID-19 testing deal between iHealth Labs and the U.S. Department of Defense that was approved by the Biden administration. The company is owned by Chinese biotech company Andon Health.

In January 2022, Biden needed to come through on his campaign promise to make at-home testing accessible for all Americans. In order to "fulfill" that promise, Biden turned to China. Under the terms of the agreement, iHealth Labs would provide 250 million test kits to the DOD in exchange for $1.3 billion.[110] iHealth had previously received emergency use authorization from the FDA in November 2021.[111] They also struck similar agreements with local and state governments.[112]

iHealth's only investor is Xiaomi,[113] a Chinese tech company that was placed on the U.S. government's trade restriction list by the Trump administration due to its alleged links to China's government and military.[114] Not so curiously, the Biden administration removed Xiaomi from the list shortly after he assumed the presidency.[115] When a U.S. court ruled in the Chinese company's favor, Biden's DOD could have appealed the ruling. Biden himself could have changed the legal parameters of the trade restriction list to keep Xiaomi on it.[116] But that's not what happened. The DOD backed down from the fight, choosing not to appeal,[117] and instead struck a deal for COVID test kits with Xiamoi's iHealth Labs just eight months later.

iHealth's links to China's government and military don't stop at Xiaomi. The CEO of iHealth, Jack Feng, is cofounder of a Chinese-based Android app store company called Wandoujia. Wandoujia was funded by an impressive list of both Chinese and American investors and was acquired by Chinese e-commerce giant Alibaba Group for $200 million in July 2016.[118] Alibaba, like all major Chinese companies, is in effect controlled by the Chinese government. Alibaba has a partnership with Beijing Genomics Institute (now BGI Group). BGI collaborates with China's National University of Defense Technologies.[119]

In August 2020, it was reported that BGI had been using COVID-19 tests to gather genetic information on American citizens.[120] Beijing has been open about prioritizing its effort to collect genetic data from individuals around the world.

A year after Alibaba purchased Wandoujia, the company began investing in DNA testing.[121] In 2020, Alibaba worked with Chinese authorities to help build China's COVID-19 health response and enable the CCP to surveil Chinese citizens by using mobile tracking data to develop QR health applications.[122]

How quickly we went from a desperate Biden relying on China to provide coronavirus tests for Americans to the U.S. empowering Chinese military–affiliated entities that seek to collect genetic data. It's anyone's guess what they will do with the data they gathered.

BIDEN FAILS AGAINST VIRUS, WINS AGAINST REPUBLICANS

Joe Biden got nearly everything wrong about the pandemic that a president could possibly get wrong. He was too negative on the vaccines during the campaign, and too positive on them after he was sworn in. He engaged in mask theatrics as a virtue signal but never helped Americans understand the science when they failed. He fell down completely on therapeutics. He left excessive mandates in place for far too long at the expense of our health care sector, our military, and our children. He used the pandemic to pass unrelated parts of his domestic spending agenda. He failed to protect seniors and their families from horrific nursing home policies. Perhaps worst of all, he has thus far allowed China to get away with the crime of the century, all the while demonizing Americans who were skeptical of the lockdowns and the jabs.

His policies provided financial benefit to China, the WHO, and yes, the Biden family.

Biden repeatedly pinned the enduring pandemic squarely on the unvaccinated people who had reasonable (and, to be fair, occasionally unreasonable) objections to taking the shots. *They* were the ones spreading the virus. One columnist at the Biden-friendly *Washington Post* went as far as to suggest that perhaps the unvaccinated do not deserve to even get treated in the ICU.[123]

Pure evil.

At Breitbart News, we speculated that Joe Biden and the Left engaged in reverse psychology to make sure Republicans didn't get inoculated. If it was reverse psychology, it certainly seemed to work. Conservatives were not effectively sold on the jabs. The Biden administration never tapped conservative medical doctors who were pro-vax but anti-lockdown, like Senator Rand Paul (R-KY) and Representative Greg Murphy (R-NC), to try to convince Republicans to get the shots. If he had done so, maybe more Americans would have survived.

James Risen of the Intercept summed up shocking data from a September 2022 study by the National Bureau of Economic Research, in an article in October 2022:

The study found that death rates from Covid-19 were only slightly higher for Republicans than Democrats during the early days of the pandemic before vaccines became available. But by the summer of 2021 a few months after vaccines were introduced "the Republican excess death rate rose to nearly double that of Democrats and this gap widened further in the winter of 2021." The sudden increase in the gap between Republican and Democratic death rates "suggests that vaccine take-up likely played an important role" the study found.[124]

The Republican excess death rate rose to nearly double that of Democrats.

We now know that conservatives were in greater jeopardy from COVID than Biden's voter base. First of all, they skew older. According to a 2015 Gallup poll, baby boomers are more likely to identify as conservative.[125] Another Pew Research study from 2018 found that baby boomers and the Silent Generation expressed more positive views on Trump's performance than Gen Xers or millennials.[126] Young people are least susceptible to COVID and alternatively more susceptible to adverse reactions from the vaccines (myocarditis, blood clotting, etc.).[127] Older Americans are more at risk of dying from COVID and least at risk of the vaccine complications known to the public.[128]

Additionally, there is data to suggest that conservatives are more likely to have underlying health conditions that pose a risk for COVID-19. Conservatives are more likely to be overweight or obese,[129] an added risk factor to the negative effects of COVID.[130] Conservatives tend to suffer more from heart disease than Democrats do.[131]

This left Republicans the impossible decision of either getting the relatively new shots after being shamed by the Democrats and the media, or risking their health.

Quite often, we chose to suffer and even die to *own the libs*.

A month after the Intercept published that article, Republicans had a historically poor performance in the midterm elections.

This isn't entirely shocking, considering many of them were dead.

Inexplicably, vaccine mandates for foreign air travelers entering the United States were the law of the land well into 2023,[132] making the land of the free and the home of the brave one of the last countries on earth to require such antiscience totalitarian nonsense.

If Trump had maintained this policy, he no doubt would have been labeled a xenophobe. But not Biden.

Lingering vax mandates became especially odd on Monday, January 30, 2023, when Joe Biden announced that the public health emergency declared by President Trump was going to end. But not for several months. May 11, to be exact.[133]

Public policy in the age of COVID was an orgy of antiscience totalitarianism, so it is only fitting that President Joe Biden scheduled the end of the pandemic, placing it on the country's calendar months in advance like it was a dentist appointment.

CHAPTER 12

The Idea of Kamala Harris

On August 12, 2020, Kamala Harris and Joe Biden held their first campaign event together as the presumptive Democrat ticket. Harris would become the first woman, first Asian, and first black person to hold the vice presidency, breaking at least three glass ceilings all at once. In a country that survived slavery and Jim Crow and, for more than half of our history, treated women as second-class citizens without a right to vote, she certainly cut a compelling figure on the campaign stage.

"Whether I'm cheering in the bleachers at a swim meet, or setting up a college room dorm, or helping my goddaughter prepare for her school debate, or building Legos with my godson, or hugging my two baby nieces, or cooking dinner, Sunday dinner, my family means everything to me," she said in her speech that day. "I've had a lot of titles over my career. And certainly, vice president will be great. But 'Mamala' will always be the one that means the most," Harris continued.[1]

The speech was well written and well delivered.

The message sent by the DNC and "Mamala" Harris is that she's just like you.[2] She cooks, she nannies, she drives car pool, and she makes impeccable dishes. She would rather be at home right now with an apron on and a whole roasted chicken in the oven, if she weren't so busy running for office and trying to save democracy.[3]

Kamala never had children of her own, though she is stepmom to her husband Doug Emhoff's two children, who were fifteen and nineteen years old when their dad got hitched to the then attorney general of California. Harris and Emhoff, also a lawyer, met on a blind date in 2013 and wed a year later.[4]

All that is to say, the "Mamala" portion of her speech is a bit overstated. Much like "Kamala Harris" herself, it is an idea rooted in our imaginations.

Kamala Harris had been, at one point, a relatively moderate Democrat, at least by the standards of the Bay Area, the far-left region of Northern California where she cut her political teeth. Over her career, she transformed into the most radical leftist in the U.S. Senate, according to one survey.[5]

She has been tough on nonviolent criminals and also fundraised to bail out rioters.[6]

She has been hailed as one of the strongest women in the world, yet she has ridden the coattails of men to get where she is going.

All the while, she has never actually enjoyed much popularity. As I documented in great detail in my book *Breaking the News*, her 2020 presidential run was a disaster. The media dubbed the commencement of her campaign "Kamalapalooza," but any nominally informed political observer quickly realized it was anything but.[7]

She claimed that she would bring a message of unity to the campaign trail but fell for the Jussie Smollett MAGA-hat racial hate-crime hoax days later.[8]

In total, she earned zero delegates despite running for eleven months and raising an impressive $40 million before dropping out of the race.[9] (This is equal to ∞ dollars per delegate.)

Kamala Harris isn't who she says she is, or who the media says she is. In some ways, it is unclear whether "Kamala Harris" even exists. Her public persona is more like a reality TV star or a pro wrestler. You could almost convince me she's actually a deepfake. She is the ChatGPT vice president.

To be fair, whichever coder programmed Kamala Harris did a pretty good job. She can assume the persona of a smart and tough leader. She certainly looks the part, and occasionally sounds like it, too.

Except when she doesn't. And oftentimes she doesn't.

A July 2022 speech at the White House provided a quote that is more illustrative of Harris's political prowess: "You need to get to go, and you to be able to get where you need to go, to do the work, and get home."[10]

Inane utterances like these are common.

In fact, the raw quantity of Harris's gaffes nearly rivals Biden's. Take this classic from remarks she made in Louisiana when touting high-speed Internet: "We were all doing a tour of the library here and talking about the significance of the passage of time, right, the significance of the passage of time. So, when you think about it, there is great significance to the passage of time in terms of what we need to do to lay these wires. What we need to do to create these jobs. And there is such great significance to the passage of time when we think about a day in the life of our children."

Dazzling.

She repeated the phrase "significance of the passage of time" four times in thirty seconds. Additional context from the remarks did not make clear exactly what it was that she was attempting to convey with this outburst of abstract poetry. But if you watched her give the speech, particularly with the volume off, you might have been convinced she knew what she was talking about. It was delivered with crisp confidence and exemplary body language. Still, the content appeared to be written by a malfunctioning chatbot.

She certainly was not tapped by Biden for her off-the-cuff rhetoric in public settings. In fact, she was far from a perfect choice for a running mate, especially considering she had spent the last few months of her campaign excoriating Biden over his record in the Senate, stopping just short of suggesting he's a racist for his infamous busing policy[11] (she would later downplay the attack[12]).

But she did have a few strong attributes, as least politically speaking.

In August 2020, House Majority Whip Jim Clyburn (D-SC), a close confidant of Biden, along with many other prominent black members of the Democrat Party, adjured Biden to select a black woman for the job, for obvious reasons.[13] The decision was coming on the heels of "Summer of Love" race riots that followed the death of George Floyd and left the country feeling more divided than at any other time in recent memory. Choosing a black running mate would be timely.

She also was the darling of California, home to Hollywood and Silicon Valley, two of the richest fonts of Democrat crony cash in the country. Kamala championed their issues. This made her a prodigious fundraising asset. Case in point: within four hours of Biden announcing Harris as his running mate, the campaign received roughly $11 million on the ActBlue platform, a nonprofit website that enables individual donors to make contributions to left-leaning candidates. In August 2020, the month Kamala was tapped for the ticket, Amazon, Google, Facebook, and Apple donated more than $1.5 million to the campaign, more than three times what Biden had raised from those companies on his own the previous month.[14]

What quickly became apparent was that she was the donors' choice, not the people's. Joe Biden saw no bump in the polls from the selection of Harris.[15]

Kamala Harris is, in many ways, the opposite of Joe Biden. Joe is an aging white baby boomer who often comes off as creepy, but also has shared in some political victories. Kamala is younger, more vibrant, and without a noteworthy political legacy to date.

One thing they do have in common, though, is the ability to scale the political hierarchy itself. That is an important skill, and a bankable one at that, especially when her friends in Silicon Valley hold the purse strings of the Democrat Party.

Kamala does have one attribute that all of her competitors lack, the ultimate distinguishing characteristic for a Democrat politician in our woke moment: she is a multiethnic female.

No, in this case, it is not the content of her character that put Kamala Harris onto the ticket and into the vice president's mansion: it was her inherited biological traits and her ability to rake in cash.

Or perhaps it was her cooking.

THE APPLE DOESN'T FALL FAR

Kamala was born in Oakland, California, in 1964, the first of two daughters. Both of her parents, an Afro-Irish Jamaican economist and an Indian biologist, were first-generation immigrants and left-leaning professors.[16] Her mother, Shyamala Gopalan Harris, was a Tamilian biomedical researcher specializing in breast cancer. Her father, Donald Harris, was an economics professor and "Marxist scholar"[17] employed by various universities during his career. Both her parents were far-left activists. Both had impressive résumés.

Harris inherited the activist personality trait, but she took a more cautious approach than her parents. According to her contemporaries at Howard University, where she matriculated as an undergraduate, "her activism always had an institutional flavor."[18] She moved from being an "outsider to [an] insider," taking internships at the Federal Trade Commission and at the office of Democrat California senator Alan Cranston in 1983.[19]

Harris's grades in high school and college are not public, but her classmates at Howard alleged she was known for her academic intensity. Despite that, she was accepted to the University of California's Hastings law school only through an affirmative action program called the Legal Education Opportunity Program (LEOP). On their website, UC Hastings, now the University of California College of Law, San Francisco, explains that LEOP was created "to make an outstanding legal education accessible to those who come from disadvantaged educational, social, or physical backgrounds. UC Law SF understands that being subject to significant adversity may have prevented candidates from attaining numerically-measured goals. . . ."[20] She was admitted to the program despite having the privilege of being the child of accomplished academics.

This was not the last time Harris's race would benefit her career.

Harris went on to become the president of the Black Law Students Association at Hastings, graduated in 1989, and initially failed the California bar exam before passing it in 1990. She began her legal career as a deputy district attorney for Alameda County.[21] But it wasn't until five years later that the idea of Kamala Harris really began to take shape.

KAMALA HARRIS, TOP COP

Her career accelerated when she began a romantic relationship with California State Assembly Speaker Willie Brown, one of the most powerful men in the state. He was also known for being a ladies' man, to put it mildly. "The measure of his flamboyance," *Sacramento Bee* reporter James Richardson told *People* magazine in 1996, "is he'll go to a party with his wife on one arm and his girlfriend on the other." Brown and Harris took their relationship public when he was the sixty-year-old Speaker of the assembly and she was a twenty-nine-year-old assistant district attorney for Alameda County.[22]

Brown and Harris began dating in 1994. At the time, Brown had been married to his wife for thirty-five years—longer than Kamala Harris had been alive. (Brown and his wife were separated at the time.) Pictures of the new couple emerged as they became a public item at exactly the apex of Brown's career: he was running for mayorship of San Francisco, which he would win. Their relationship was juicy press fodder. One bit of gossip that made headlines was that at Brown's sixtieth-birthday party, according to one report, Clint Eastwood accidentally spilled champagne on Brown's "new steady, Kamala Harris."[23]

Harris took favors and jobs from Brown, quickly cementing her place in his "San Francisco Mafia," a moniker given by Southern Californians to the powerful Bay Area politicians who have dominated Golden State politics for decades. Big-name members of the San Francisco mob include former U.S. senator Barbara Boxer (previously a representative for Marin County), U.S. senator Dianne Feinstein (also a former mayor of San Francisco), former U.S. House Speaker and longtime San Francisco representative Nancy Pelosi, Governor Gavin Newsom (another former mayor of San Francisco), and more, including Brown.[24]

He lavished Kamala with gifts like a brand-new BMW 7 series.[25]

Brown hasn't been shy about claiming credit for her rise: "I certainly helped with her first race for district attorney in San Francisco. I have also helped the careers of House Speaker Nancy Pelosi, Gov. Gavin Newsom, Sen. Dianne Feinstein and a host of other politicians," he wrote in an article for SFGate titled "Sure, I Dated Kamala Harris. So What?"[26]

She certainly didn't squander the opportunity.

Over the next few years, Harris vaulted to the top of the California Democrat Party. She won her first race, for San Francisco district attorney, by running to be the strong arm of the law. She closed the campaign with one of her preferred tactics: playing the race card. She sent out a mailer with photos of the last ten San Francisco DAs, from 1900 to 2003, ending with incumbent Terence Hallinan. All were white men.

"It's time for a change . . ." the flyer read.[27]

And just like that, a star was born.

She ran unopposed for a second term in 2007.

During her DA tenure, Harris earned a reputation for being tough on minor drug offenses like marijuana possession. As San Francisco DA, she racked up a stunning 1,900 convictions for pot infractions.[28] She supported criminalizing prostitution and opposed criminal sentencing reform. This led to criticism that she was overcrowding jails. According to the *New York Times*, she pursued only "few on-duty cases of police force-related misconduct."[29]

Gary Delagnes, then the head of the police union, called her San Francisco's premier "pro-public safety DA" of the last two decades.

In 2011, backed by then U.S. senators Boxer and Feinstein as well as Willie Brown, she was elected attorney general of California.

Harris's pro-cop, tough-on-crime rep once again came to the fore when she refused to prosecute instances of apparent police brutality and killings. In July 2012, an unarmed twenty-five-year-old, Manny Diaz, was killed by police in Anaheim with a fatal shot to the back. There was immediate outrage from the public. Protesters swarmed City Hall. The mayor even called Harris, who refused to intervene. Not long afterward, there was another police shooting of twenty-three-year-old Mario Romero. Still, no charges were ever filed.[30]

Her positions would eventually change. Radically.

Delagnes would call her "Jekyll and Hyde" after an "extremely hard left turn."[31] The comparison was apt. In her 2009 book, *Smart on Crime*, Harris stated, "If we take a show of hands of those who would like to see more police officers on the street, mine would shoot up," adding that "virtually all law-abiding citizens feel safer when they see officers walking a beat."[32] Years later, after the death of George Floyd, she told the *New York Times*, "It is status-quo thinking to believe that putting more police on the streets creates more safety. That's wrong. It's just wrong."[33]

As attorney general of California in 2015, she was against a state initiative to relax mandatory minimums—prison sentence terms automatically applied to crimes, regardless of the specific circumstances of the offense—and sided with police unions, refusing to endorse a bill that would have assigned a prosecutor to investigate deadly police shootings, eighteen of which happened on her watch as attorney general. But as a U.S. senator, she sponsored legislation to "police" the police by banning choke holds, racial profiling, and no-knock warrants.[34]

In 2019, while running for president, she unveiled a criminal justice reform plan that called for creating a National Police Systems Review Board, which would collect police data for increased transparency.[35] She also fought for the end of mandatory minimums on a federal level and even the legalization of marijuana.[36]

While running for vice president in 2020, Harris famously tweeted a request for donations to a far-left group called the Minnesota Freedom Fund, which used the money to post bail for jailed Summer of Love rioters, including a man charged with murder.[37] When she was on the Democrat ticket running for vice president, she would call it "outdated" and "wrongheaded" to think more cops on the street makes communities safer.[38]

Long ago were the days when Kamala Harris once declared herself the "top cop."[39]

When Kamala Harris's career began, she was mostly an ally of police. When she was a national politician representing the left flank of the Democrat Party, she pursued an agenda that would make life more difficult for them. One Los Angeles Police Department Bomb Squad tech who is often assigned to Harris's detail (she maintains a home there in the ritzy Brentwood neighborhood as part of a substantial real estate portfolio) told me that she is routinely disrespectful of the time of the officers and city residents. She will maintain itineraries that keep her perpetually late, leaving roads closed to the general public and keeping officers from other responsibilities to the citizens and their families.[40]

All that matters to Kamala Harris is that she gets where she is going, literally and figuratively.

THE SENATOR HARRIS FROM SILICON VALLEY AND HOLLYWOOD

When longtime California senator Barbara Boxer announced her retirement in 2015, the San Francisco Mafia was ready. They had been preparing for this moment for some time. It was a coronation. Harris won every poll—the vast majority by double digits—and dominated fundraising. She eventually beat Democrat congresswoman Loretta Sanchez by more than twenty points before coasting past the Republican nominee in the general election in 2016.

The only significant negative attention she attracted during the campaign was for dipping into the kitty to fund first-class flights, limousines, and expensive hotels. She insisted on extravagant accommodations, racking up bills at the St. Regis, the Waldorf-Astoria, and the Four Seasons.

One ex-aide said of her, "Kamala demands a life of luxury." This would put her right at home with the other public servants of Washington.

Another strategist said, "She spent an ungodly amount" and "she wants to live the life of someone in the White House and she hasn't even won the Senate yet." Prescient. (Staffers and aides would complain about her "overspending" during her failed 2020 presidential campaign.)[41]

On January 3, 2017, Harris was sworn in, making her the first black woman to represent California in the United States Senate.[42]

She served only two-thirds of one term in the Senate, and a significant portion of that time was spent campaigning for president and vice president. It was during this time she pivoted to the left. Big league. In fact, a GovTrack analysis concluded that she was the most liberal senator in 2019, even more radical than socialist Bernie Sanders.[43]

Walking in Biden's footsteps, her signature moment in the Senate was leading a witch hunt against a conservative Supreme Court nominee. In Kamala's case, her target was then judge Brett Kavanaugh after he was tapped by President Trump in 2018. Harris smeared him as a dastardly sexual predator and perhaps a gang-rapist. It was all based on lies, but it did position her on the political hard Left and closer to the base.

The spectacle got especially absurd when Harris mockingly referred to the judge's pocket copy of the U.S. Constitution as "that book you carry."[44]

Cringe!

Kavanaugh was confirmed to the Supreme Court on October 6, 2018.

Even friendly papers like the *Los Angeles Times* knocked her approach to the hearings.[45] SFGate ran a particularly brutal headline: "Kamala Harris' Viral Grilling of Kavanaugh Ends with a Thud."[46]

Kamala's steady rise through the American political ranks hit a brief but embarrassing setback during her presidential run. The then fifty-four-year-old announced her candidacy in January 2019, having been a senator for only two years. She would drop out less than a year later without collecting a single delegate.

Kamala's campaign never picked up much momentum, even with overwhelmingly positive media attention (as documented in *Breaking the News*). The most (only?) memorable moment of her campaign was during a debate, when she attacked Joe Biden over his past positions on desegregation and busing, suggesting he might be a racist.

At one point, she even suggested Joe Biden makes women uncomfortable. When several women accused Biden of unwanted touching,

Harris said she believed them. (Harris never addressed Tara Reade's claim that Biden sexually assaulted her in 1993.)[47]

Ultimately, the attacks did not revive her campaign, but they also did not disqualify her from becoming Biden's running mate.

While he was selecting his vice presidential nominee, it would have been easy for Joe Biden and his team to fixate on Harris's embarrassing primary effort. It would also have been easy to fixate on the fact that she hailed from a deep "blue" state, so she would not be expanding Biden's electoral map. And of course, there were those awkward moments when she suggested he's a racist creeper. But Biden had another idea. First of all, she is a black woman. And second, in the age of multibillion-dollar campaigns, it helps to have as many friends with deep pockets as you can, and Harris's friends had the deepest pockets around.

Harris had been the darling of the tech oligarchy since announcing herself on the political scene. She also was one of Hollywood's most important political advocates.

This was a potent combination for a rising Democrat star.

She was championed by Democrat megadonor and media baroness Laurene Powell Jobs, the widow of Steve Jobs and one of the stars of *Breaking the News.* Jobs's publication, the *Atlantic,* hyped Harris to such an absurd degree, their coverage of her reads like satire. There was a revolving door between Harris staff and companies like Google and Amazon. She has a close relationship with former Facebook chief operating officer Sheryl Sandberg. Harris was even involved in the marketing of Sandberg's book *Lean In,* which was released in 2013—while she was California attorney general, the law enforcement agent most responsible for oversight of Facebook.[48]

Reid Hoffman, the LinkedIn billionaire who helped launch PayPal, became one of Harris's earliest bundlers. As I detail in Part I of this book, Hoffman is among the most influential—and least scrupulous—financiers in all of Democrat politics.[49]

Her former aides now work at Google, Amazon, and Airbnb.[50] One of her former speechwriters, Meghan Groob, came from the Bill & Melinda Gates Foundation; Melinda French Gates, ex-wife of Microsoft cofounder Bill Gates, has a friendly relationship with Harris. She attended the lavish wedding of former Napster and Facebook executive Sean Parker. Among Kamala's top twenty presidential donors were employees of Alphabet (Google's parent company), Microsoft, Apple, and Amazon, according to OpenSecrets.

The Silicon Valley titans—the wealthiest collection of human beings on the planet—knew that of all the possible candidates vying for a spot on either party ticket, Kamala Harris was the most likely to protect their monopolies. This meant that she would have an endless war chest at her disposal.

"Tech companies seem to like Harris' policy instincts, which are less regulatory than socialist Democrats and less tech-hostile than populist Republicans," a government professor reported to CNET. "Campaign contributions are about access. Contributors want access to a politician who will win and take their phone call."[51]

Precisely.

She also forged ties to Hollywood that were as politically valuable.

In August 2020, David Schneiderman, a Hollywood executive and major Democrat fundraiser for Hillary Clinton's 2016 campaign, commented, "Kamala has really ignited the campaign. Lit a fuse . . ." The polling shows she didn't light anything under voters, but she had the donors fired up.

Biden had been an ally of Hollywood, having opened up the Chinese market to American films, but Harris was their star. In October 2019, *Variety* reported that Hollywood "swoons for Kamala Harris." She raised $11.6 million in Hollywood in the third quarter that year from the likes of Steven Spielberg, Jason Blum, Katy Perry, Leonardo DiCaprio, Bette Midler, and J. J. Abrams. That is more than ninety times what Biden hauled in during that time ($130,000).[52] This fact is even more remarkable given Hollywood's simpatico relationship with Biden.

As California's attorney general, she targeted movie piracy.[53] She also built up what *Variety* described as a "power base in the music industry," earning a reputation as an advocate for artists and creators. In Washington, she was an advocate for the left-wing causes they tend to champion.

Harris was able to toe the line when the entertainment industry and Silicon Valley clashed over a sex-trafficking bill. No one likes trafficking, but critics argued that the proposed legislation would lead to vast new regulation of the Internet. Harris stepped in and led the effort to compromise between Big Tech and Big Hollywood.[54]

Jeffrey Katzenberg filled up the Biden campaign with millions of dollars upon Kamala's joining the ticket, and then the entertainment mogul minted a deal with Xi Jinping to create a Chinese Hollywood.[55] Synergy.

Harris was also seen as the preferred candidate of Obama World and was staffed up with members of the Clinton machine.

Biden claims he made his choice because "the person I trust most, the person I turn to when there's a hard issue is Kamala Harris."[56]

The person he trusts most? That rings hollow. The truth is, Harris was the person who brought what he needed to the ticket: money, connections, a vast network, and infinite woke points.

And lest we forget, she is a woman of color.

Trust had nothing to do with it.

DOOMED TO FAIL

Right after Joe Biden and Kamala Harris won the 2020 election, the new president put the new vice president to work—often on the most challenging elements of his policy portfolio, including immigration (which is covered in the next chapter of this book). Here are some of Harris's other tasks:

Gender Equity: In October 2021, the White House announced a $12 billion commitment to advancing gender equality and unrolled a National Strategy on Gender Equity and Equality. A large part of the strategy centered on combating climate change, which the administration believes is a major cause of gender disparity. Apart from its emphasis on increased data collection and establishment of a Gender Policy Council, Harris's plan included few concrete deliverables nor a clear implementation strategy.[57]

Jamaica: In April 2022, Harris announced that the administration would be giving $30 million in investments to Jamaica, which is also home to her father, Donald Harris.[58] Donald Harris had long since retired in 1998 but went on to serve as an economic policy consultant to the Jamaican government and an economic advisor to prime ministers in the early 2000s.[59] In October 2021, he received an Order of Merit from Jamaica for his "outstanding contributions to national development."[60] It can't possibly be a coincidence that he won this award while his daughter is the vice president of the United States, could it?

Build Back Better: Harris was instrumental in securing votes for the landmark climate/tax/health/pork bill known as the Inflation Reduction Act, which was essentially a watered-down Build Back Better bill. She even cast the tie-breaking vote in the Senate.[61] Harris and her staff complained during the first two years of Biden's presidency that constantly needing to break Senate deadlocks meant they could not leave the Beltway as often as they would have liked.[62]

Vaccines: Harris made an about-face on coronavirus vaccines after assuming office. While Trump was president, she undermined the effectiveness of Trump's Operation Warp Speed, stating that she would not take a shot based on Trump telling the public it is safe and effective.[63] "If Donald Trump tells us we should take it, I'm not taking it," she said during the vice presidential debate with Mike Pence. After blatantly politicizing the issue on the campaign trail, Harris was immediately placed in charge of selling the shots to minority communities, stumping for their effectiveness.[64] In February 2021, she threw more shade at Trump by stating that the Biden administration was "starting from scratch" on a vaccine rollout plan; even PolitiFact called that false.[65]

Voter Engagement: Harris was placed in charge of voter engagement, which is the cornerstone of the Democrat Party's agenda. In June 2021, she announced $25 million for the Democratic National Committee's plan to increase voter registration. "The Biden-Harris team will fund the largest tech team in the history of the DNC . . . to identify and contact voters affected by efforts at suppression and voter roll purges. . . ." Though details about the plan remained sparse (as is the custom with Harris), the Democrats' overperformance in the midterm elections suggests she succeeded at least to some degree.[66]

Artificial Intelligence: As if Kamala Harris didn't have enough tasks, the White House placed her in charge of AI-related risks and opportunities.

"AI is kind of a fancy thing," Harris told a group of civil rights activists, union leaders, and consumer protection advocates in 2023. "First of all, it's two letters. It means artificial intelligence, but ultimately what it is, is it's about machine learning," she continued.[67]

At least we know for certain she has no idea what she's doing in this role.

The dangers associated with under- or poorly regulated AI are far too numerous to cover for the purpose of this book, but suffice it to say, the stakes are high. So high, in fact, that I will not add a joke here about how Kamala Harris was named A.I. czar because she is, in fact, artificial intelligence herself. Elon Musk has stated that the technology "is far more dangerous than nukes."[68] In 2023, one thousand AI experts, including Apple cofounder Steve "Woz" Wozniak and Musk, signed a letter calling for a pause in developing AI systems until safeguards are developed.[69] Harris launched a new White House initiative to promote responsible AI innovation in a meeting with AI companies Alphabet, Anthropic, Microsoft, and OpenAI.[70] As Big Tech's go-to politician in DC, perhaps she was a logical choice considering that all of those companies save Microsoft are based in the Bay Area. But Harris's qualifications end there.

And, suffice it to say, placing Big Tech's top political ally in charge of regulating Big Tech elevates the risk even more.

Whether or not you're religious, now might be a good time to start praying.

So how did a person so poorly suited for the job of vice president get to the point where she is a heartbeat away from the presidency, and in a position to one day be president herself?

The answer is simple: she was well suited to get *elected* as vice president.

While Biden supplied the familiarity to the voters and the mechanical knowledge of how Washington works, particularly the executive branch, Harris was going to ensure that the Democrats' two most important constituencies, Hollywood and Silicon Valley, would be with them throughout this election and beyond. In modern Democrat politics, those are the people who matter most: the super elite, the ones with the biggest megaphones, and the country's cool kids. These are the people who control what Americanism looks like around the world. And they are all Kamala's besty friends.

And, perhaps most important, she looks like the right candidate in America's woke moment.

Kamala Harris had done everything she needed to do to put herself in a position to be vice president. Even her inherited traits gave her the right type of privilege. But as it turns out, there is more to the job than just getting it. She has few successes to speak of, and she lacks a clear path to have any in Biden's first term.

None of this is a secret, either. Though her approval rating was in the mid-50s during the first months of the Biden administration, according to FiveThirtyEight, it quickly dipped into the high 30s, where it has remained for most of the presidency as of summer 2023.[71] A June 2023 NBC News poll showed that her approval had fallen to a dismal 32 percent rating.[72] That's embarrassingly low, but it also does nothing to negate her true value to the ticket.

Yet if history is any indication, none of that that will stop her from moving ahead. So long as she is able to do what is necessary to curry favor with the country's moneyed elite, she will have her eye on the title that means the most.

And no, it's not "Mamala."

CHAPTER 13

Joe Biden's America, a Sanctuary Country

America's open southern border is her Achilles' heel.

It is our single most obvious weakness.

Leaving the border open, as we do, encourages lawlessness. It sends a message to foreigners that if you violate our rules, you might get prioritized ahead of those who abide by them.

If America still has a culture (other than the generic Western woke corporate globalism that's ubiquitous in our entertainment and news media), we certainly don't act like it's worth preserving. An open border means you don't care who takes up residence in your country. It's anti-American, and it's an intentional decision by our ruling class.

With an open border, drugs flow up and in, and organized crime is a guarantee. Organized crime, that is, the cartels, typically has two products: humans and drugs. It's morally reprehensible to tolerate either, yet we permit both.

The whole process is hideous. Families will be separated—and not by supposedly evil Republicans, but by the gangsters who know that once a child is admitted to America, any alleged "parent" will get admitted, too—even if the baby wasn't brought here by their actual parents.

"The women are warned in Mexico that they likely will be raped and assaulted during the trafficking process," human smuggling investigator Daniel Walden told Breitbart News in an interview. He also explained "rape trees," which are common along trafficking routes. Coyotes often remove an article of clothing from the trafficked female they raped and then tie it to a tree as if it were a trophy. These trees aren't only in Mexico: they're in Texas as well, as one rancher told us.[1]

The migrants' journey is dangerous, dirty, and often humiliating. They will endure all sorts of humanitarian horrors along the way, sometimes even after they've crossed into the vast deserts of America's Southwest.

Or maybe they won't suffer so much. But if they don't, that comes with a higher price, which is levied by the cartels, of course.

Freedom is never free, as the saying goes.

The cheap labor arrives in American towns and competes for low-skilled jobs, driving down the market value of American workers in our lowest classes.

Border agents are strained. Their families struggle.

The desperate foreigners are all pawns in a global game being played by the richest and most privileged people in the world.

Citizenship and national sovereignty are diminished.

The American taxpayer is left holding the bag, as always.

There is nothing good that comes from an open border.

Yet we leave it open. We can't help ourselves.

Why?

Democrats don't see the alien migrants as humans; they see them as votes. Maybe not those who cross today, but their progeny will be voters one day. The Democrats import their next generation; it's easier and faster than birthing them and raising them. The nation's "anchor baby" population keeps increasing; it may be at the highest level in U.S. history. The invaluable Center for Immigration Studies believes that nearly 400,000 children are born to illegal aliens on U.S. soil every year, including foreign tourists, foreign students, and foreign visa workers.[2]

CNN's 2016 election exit polling showed Hillary Clinton winning naturalized citizens with 64 percent support compared to Trump's 31 percent; Trump had a 49–45 percent advantage with native-born Americans.[3] Pew found that in the 2020 election, Democrats had a 14 percent party affiliation advantage with Hispanics.[4]

The Democrats portray themselves as the ones who care, the ones who are truly empathetic to the plight of migrants. This is dishonest. Their true motive is far more cynical. Their unwillingness to secure the border is the inciting incident in this horror movie: the precursor to all the humanitarian strife that follows. But who is going to refute their narrative? Republicans certainly won't. They don't even speak the language of the new arrivals. A left-wing group linked to George Soros, the Democrats' top financier, is attempting to bankroll a take-over of the Spanish-language airwaves—and not to play music.[5] Latino Media Network, which is run by Obama administration alum Stephanie Valencia and includes far-left actress Eva Longoria as a board member,[6] is gobbling up radio real estate that currently fea-tures strong conservative and anticommunist voices. The Right will gripe about this, for good reason, but they should be trying to emu-late the tactic. Buy up liberal media and rebuild it in our image. In Spanish.

Memo to the Republican donor class: the first step to reaching voters is to try to reach voters.

When it comes to the open border, Republicans aren't much better than Democrats. The GOP establishment, moneyed elite themselves, likes the idea of lower wages. This improves the bottom line for their businesses, which makes their stocks go up. Lower wages for their do-mestic employees, nannies, gardeners, etc., save them money. The com-munities devastated by the drug trade aren't their communities. For them, illegal immigration has a lot of upside.

Intellectually, Republicans understand that to have a nation, you need a border. They understand that an open-borders policy is cruel to those who play by America's rules and kind to those who play by their own. But the establishment isn't going to solve a problem if the solution is going to cost them a lot of (any?) money, even if the fate of our nation depends on it.

Unless, of course, we are talking about Ukraine's border with Russia. Then it's essential, heroic even, to have a border and defend it. After all, that border isn't keeping out cheap workers and future voters.

No, the political establishment of both parties is not eager to estab-lish a solid southern border.

Joe Biden is a creature of establishment Washington and the Demo-crat Party, so his border policy has been boilerplate. Like so many of his policies, it would be indistinguishable from most other American politi-cians' if they were in his job. Still, that doesn't make it any less devastat-ing for America and Americans.

ERASING TRUMP'S LEGACY

The first order of business for Joe Biden upon being sworn into office was to undo anything Donald Trump had done to secure our southern border. One of the primary reasons Trump was elected was as a rebuke to the Obama/Biden (open) border policy. What progress Trump made on immigration, most of which occurred during the final year of his administration, was hard-fought. Biden was eager to return things to how they were when he was the vice president, and because not much physical border wall was built during Trump's presidency, most of the reversals could be done with the stroke of a pen. (The Trump administration erected just over 450 miles of border barrier, according to U.S. Customs and Border Protection [CBP], but most of it was upgrading existing wall. In total, around 80 miles of new wall was built, of which 33 miles was secondary wall.[7])

Opening up our border would be a popular move with Biden's base for the aforementioned reasons, and the new influx of "undocumented Democrats" (Jay Leno's expression[8]) would help cement Biden's political legacy. University of Maryland researcher James Gimpel found that immigration has "remade and continues to remake the nation's electorate in favor of the Democratic Party."[9] No wonder it was priority number one for President Biden.

Even before he was sworn in, Biden indicated that he would nominate Alejandro Mayorkas to lead the Department of Homeland Security. Mayorkas, himself a Cuban immigrant, ran President Obama's U.S. Citizenship and Immigration Services (USCIS) and was eventually promoted to deputy secretary of the Department of Homeland Security. During his tenure in the Obama administration, the DHS inspector general found that he was abusing an immigration visa program to benefit wealthy Democrats like Terry McAuliffe, Ed Rendell, and Harry Reid.[10]

Immediately after being sworn into office, Biden signed an executive proclamation shutting down new construction of the border wall. He also ended the national emergency declaration at the border issued by his predecessor.[11]

Two years later, Mexican president Andrés Manuel López Obrador (AMLO) would praise Biden for this decision. "You, President Biden, you are the first president of the United States in a very long time that has not built, not even one meter, of wall," AMLO said at a 2023 summit alongside Biden and Canadian prime minister Justin Trudeau. "In that, we thank you for that, sir. Although some might not like it, although the conservatives don't like it," he added.[12]

The next open-borders policy to be implemented by Biden was a stay on the vast majority of deportations for one hundred days, even for those who had been convicted of a violent crime.[13] Mayorkas issued similar orders in September 2021 to ensure that most illegal aliens living in the U.S. are not eligible for deportation.[14]

Biden also ended "Remain in Mexico," a program that ensured border crossers who were claiming asylum were not released directly into the U.S. interior and instead were returned to Mexico to await their hearings in U.S. court.[15] This policy massively disincentivizes attempting to enter the country illegally, and in one fell swoop, Biden undid it. We examined federal data at Breitbart News and found that only about 1.6 percent of migrants subject to "Remain in Mexico" have valid asylum claims.[16] When "Remain in Mexico" ended, the default U.S. policy was "catch and release," where upon apprehension, the aliens are released into the U.S.[17]

When word got out that America would not be enforcing border laws, illegal immigration immediately skyrocketed.

With the return of "catch and release" under Biden, roughly tens of thousands of border crossers are freed into American communities every month. DHS refuses to disclose the exact monthly figures, but the Center for Immigration Studies estimates that through August 2022, Biden's DHS had released 1.3 million border crossers into the U.S. interior; many were given parole to stay in the U.S. while awaiting their asylum hearings.[18]

In February 2021, Biden's first full month in office, apprehensions at the border totaled nearly 100,000, a 170 percent increase compared to February 2020 and the highest February recorded since 2006,[19] when open-borders Republican George W. Bush was president. More apprehensions might sound like a positive thing; after all, law enforcement is doing their job. But actually, it is a telltale indicator of a big spike in people trying to cross, which means more people are presumably getting through undetected. All of those who do get apprehended need shelter, medical care, food, water, and other basics of life. The amount of paperwork is unfathomable. Big numbers are purely bad news.

The rule of thumb is that for every apprehension, one or two people make it through without getting caught. This ratio is not fixed, though, and depends on the policy of the current administration. When "catch and release" is the norm, a higher percentage of migrants will turn themselves over to law enforcement and claim asylum, even if they know their claim is bogus. They will receive a notice to appear in court and then will be freed into the country to do as they please. Needless to say, not everyone shows up in court. (This exact number is difficult to track, but about 87 percent of illegal aliens recently released by DHS into the U.S. did not show up to their asylum hearings, according to findings from one Trump-era program.)[20]

Faced with this level of adversity this early in an administration, one might expect that that a president would get decisive and devise a strategy. Declare an emergency! Build a wall! Designate the cartels terrorist organizations! Save our republic!

But not Joe Biden. He had another, simpler plan.

He was going to pass the buck.

KAMALA HARRIS, BORDER CZAR

In March 2021, President Biden gave his newly minted vice president an impossible assignment: the southern border. Harris had spent twenty-five years in law and politics in the border state of California, and she had never shown any interest in the subject. Now she was expected to lead the effort to secure about two thousand miles of border amid a surge of illegal immigration unlike anything we had ever seen.

Or was she?

The prospect was so absurd, it might have been nothing more than an effort to troll right-wingers. If that was Biden's intention, he succeeded.

Or maybe he was trolling his own vice president, intentionally giving her a task that would inevitably end in an L. She wants to be president herself, so who was she to complain?

Now for the least surprising news in this entire book: things went badly for Harris from the get-go.

By August 2021, the number of border crossers had hit a twenty-year high.[21] It was at this point that Harris finally released her strategy to address the crisis. She blamed the pandemic and "extreme weather conditions" for increased immigration. She proposed a vague five-pillar program that would ostensibly instill a "safe, orderly, and humane immigration system," without outlining specific policy actions or when they would be implemented.[22] A few months after the plan was released, anonymous White House sources complained to CNN about her "lack of follow-through" on her border assignment.[23]

None of the effective Trump policies was put back into place. A border wall was not a priority.

She drew bipartisan criticism for not visiting the border to see the problems firsthand as they developed. This too should not have been a surprise, given that Harris's public proclamations indicate that she doesn't necessarily believe there is a border at all. In 2017, she tweeted, "An undocumented immigrant is not a criminal."[24] This is a straw man argument, both dishonest and inaccurate. Occasionally undocumented migrants are not criminals, especially in the rare cases when they are deemed to have a legitimate claim to asylum, but open-borders opponents' main concern is with economic migrants and visa overstays, i.e., actual criminals.

When migration to the U.S. is up, employee pay goes down. This is an open secret in Washington. The data is in, and it has been for a long time. Steven Camarota, director of research for the Center for Immigration Studies, testified all the way back in 2010 that as immigration levels boomed, "hourly wages for those with only a high school education declined 10 percent in real terms from 1979 to 2007."[25] It took years for Washington to pay attention to this fact at all, and they have yet to do anything meaningful to address it that can't be easily undone by the next Democrat administration.

In 2016, the National Academies of Sciences, Engineering, and Medicine estimated that the recent flood of immigrants during the Obama/Biden years "lowered wages by 5.2 percent," which amounts to about a $500 billion wage cut for Americans. That is the equivalent of a half-trillion-dollar tax levied on the working class.[26]

These types of arguments—economic arguments—are frequently shared among people who don't get their news from corporate media when we discuss the open border.

Kamala Harris has also supported publicly funded, free health care for illegal aliens. "Let me just be very clear about this. I am opposed to any policy that would deny in our country any human being from access to public safety, public education, or public health. Period."[27] Sounds expensive, and a massive incentive to try to enter the country illegally. Dangling free cutting-edge health care for all who enter is the ultimate magnet for would-be migrants hoping for a better life for their families.

Harris didn't even try to right the ship as the crisis deepened. In the summer of 2022, she shifted her immigration agenda to something called the In Her Hands program, "a women's economic empowerment initiative for Central America."[28] Harris launched it in June 2022 with Laurene Powell Jobs, Christy Turlington Burns, and others.[29] Her goal was, ostensibly, to connect the private sector, the public sector, and the nonprofit world to solve this problem. She quickly was able to raise a ten-figure sum to invest in Central America's economic development.[30]

Microsoft would commit to clean energy "digital access training centers" and "clean off-grid energy" to try to make life better for those living to America's south. Mastercard would extend lines of credit to Central American microbusinesses. Nespresso would work with farmers in Guatemala, Honduras, and El Salvador.[31] This all sounds very nice, but asking American taxpayers to fund part of this corporate welfare program *while our border is still wide open* is offensive. Companies like PepsiCo, Cargill, and PriceSmart quickly jumped in.[32] Harris pooled $3.1 billion in investments from private organizations to Central America.[33] This isn't innately a bad thing, but it is far, far less efficient than simply standing up some bollard fencing between the U.S. and Mexico.

AMERICA CHOOSES CHAOS

In July 2022, an illegal alien MS-13 gang member was "caught and released" into the United States by the Biden administration as an Unaccompanied Alien Child (UAC). The seventeen-year-old El Salvadorian then allegedly raped and murdered twenty-year-old Kayla Marie Hamilton, who had autism.[34] Her mother, Angel Mom Tammy Nobles (Angel Mom is a designation for the mother of a child killed by an illegal alien), said, "He was arrested at the border, they let his aunt come and pick him up, and take him back to Fredericksburg, Maryland. . . . He raped her after she was dead and just left her on the floor on her back and then he went to lunch with his half-brother."[35] Nobles noted that the suspect smirked and laughed while he was being arrested.[36]

Every story like this is entirely unnecessary, yet they happen consistently. Murders, sexual assaults, and other crimes committed by illegal aliens do not make for pleasant reading, yet they have become a fixture on the pages of Breitbart.com since the massive influx of illegal immigration under the Obama/Biden administration.

Lawlessness spreads like a contagion; it is becoming our culture.

In January 2023, four border crossers who were bused to New York City by Texas governor Greg Abbott allegedly stole nearly $12,500 worth of merchandise from a Nassau County Macy's department store. They weren't deported, though. They all were released, two without bail.[37]

"Catch and release" isn't just our border policy; it's how we handle crime in parts of the interior of our country as well.

Biden still wasn't done erasing Trump's border agenda. He ended the agreement his predecessor forged with the "Northern Triangle" countries within his first month in office.[38] (Trump had cut aid to El Salvador, Guatemala, and Honduras for failing to stop migrant caravans that were hastily heading toward the U.S. while he tried to get the border wall construction under way.[39])

Biden also disposed of cooperative agreements that sought to eliminate asylum shopping by migrants passing through Central America. Most, if not all, migrants who cross our southern border pass through a country with similar asylum rules as ours before they reach our soil. That means that if they had a legitimate claim to asylum, they could have made it elsewhere first.

Together, Remain in Mexico and the Northern Triangle cooperative agreements represented a "legal wall" to stem the flow of illegal immigration into the country.[40]

The only border security measure that did anything to put even a mild check on illegal immigration during the first portion of Biden's administration was Title 42,[41] a measure that allows for the swift expulsion of any alien who has recently been in a country with a communicable disease, like, say, a hypercontagious respiratory virus that had killed millions of people. Trump used the rule to expel migrants without allowing them to wait in the U.S. for their day in court.

Title 42 is a highly rational policy during a pandemic. In fact, one of the absolute best reasons to have a border is to block infectious diseases from spilling into a country. Voters also happen to love it. In a Harvard/Harris Poll conducted in December 2022, nearly three years after the beginning of the pandemic emergency, 79 percent of registered voters favored using it.[42]

Biden was well aware that removing Title 42 could take an already chaotic situation at the border and make it potentially unsustainable. For the first two years of his presidency, he resisted the activist Left and did not lift it,[43] but Center for Immigration Studies director Mark Krikorian said Biden began to phase it out anyway, gradually, and without public pronouncements or fanfare. It remains a distinct possibility, however, that leaving Title 42 in place was a gift to the Democrats. Mass migration hit record levels regardless.

This final restriction has since been removed.

The good thing for Biden and the Democrats is that the cartels knew that too much border chaos doesn't help them either. They would regulate some of the influx from the Mexican side of the border so as not to attract more attention than they were already getting.

As of early 2023, more than 1.2 million illegal alien fugitives are living in the country despite receiving final deportation orders.[44]

In the first twenty-three months of Joe Biden's administration, a record 4.2 million migrants were apprehended by the Border Patrol. This did not stop Biden's U.S. Customs and Border Protection (CBP) acting commissioner Troy Miller from claiming that "our new border enforcement measures are working."[45]

Ridiculous.

Biden has set immigration enforcement priorities in such a way so as to ensure that deportations would be at a minimum. U.S. Immigration and Customs Enforcement (ICE) agents deported roughly 28,000 illegal aliens from the United States interior during fiscal year 2022.[46] Whatever the number of total illegal aliens living in the country may be (I have not seen recent data that is credible enough to cite here), this is a fraction of a percent of that. Under Biden, illegal alien convicts were arrested by ICE at the lowest rate since . . . the Obama/Biden administration.[47]

Our facilities were overwhelmed long before the cancellation of Title 42. One CBP holding facility in Donna, Texas, had a mid-pandemic capacity of 250 migrants; it was holding 4,100 migrants as of March

2021, of whom 3,200 were unaccompanied minors.[48] There is no silver lining to these numbers. This is a disaster, a humanitarian crisis, and a national disgrace.

In June 2022, police near San Antonio found an abandoned trailer that contained forty-eight dead migrants in it, as well as sixteen people clinging to life. The death toll would eventually climb to fifty-three.[49]

Biden figured out a way to blame Republicans for the invasion because they rejected a border security plan he had proposed that included amnesty for some illegal aliens, a nonstarter for any Republican who wants to be reelected.[50]

One of the most bizarre stories of Biden's border was first reported at Breitbart News: air marshals were deployed to the border to escort migrants from processing facilities to Border Patrol agents' custody before their eventual release into the country.

"The Air Marshals' whole job is to walk them 50 yards," a source told us.[51] This inexplicable decision had consequences.

Yes, there were plane flights without marshals specifically because they were diverted to the border, and major security incidents began to occur.

"Highly skilled Federal Air Marshals are being made to perform mainly non–law enforcement civilian humanitarian duties," Air Marshal National Council president David Londo wrote in a letter to DHS secretary Mayorkas and others.[52]

I asked the White House to explain the decision to deploy air marshals at the border, but I did not get a response.

For the first two years of Biden's administration, roughly 320,000 unaccompanied alien children arrived in the U.S.[53] Not so coincidentally during this time, there appears to have been a big uptick in child labor. One meatpacking cleaning service was caught in early 2023 using more than one hundred children ages thirteen to seventeen in hazardous occupations.[54] The U.S. Department of Labor touted the bust in a press release but did not reveal the national origin of the children. I am fairly certain, though, that these were mostly, if not all, unaccompanied alien teenage boys from countries to America's south, earning money in lowly jobs to pay down smuggling debts and transfer money back to their families. Left-leaning ProPublica published an extensive report in 2020 on migrants doing this exact type of work—night shifts in factories—to pay cartels and send money home.[55]

The work is often brutal.

"The authorities aren't surprised by child labor," according to Pro-Publica. "They're also not doing much about it."

No kidding. They don't want to.

FENTANYL: A WEAPON OF MASS DESTRUCTION

When the border is open, drugs comes in, and there is one drug in partic-ular that is wreaking havoc across our nation.

Fentanyl, a highly powerful synthetic opioid primarily produced in China and Mexico, has been flowing over the southern U.S. border at a torrid pace. Just two milligrams' worth, which is less than a pinch of table salt, is considered a lethal dose.[56] Six tons of it were seized by CBP in the first six weeks of 2023.[57] That is more than enough to kill every Ameri-can several times over.[58] (Isn't this reason enough to finish the border wall today?) Scarier still, just six and a half tons were seized in all of 2022, so as of early 2023, the pace at which it is being imported is on an expo-nential rise.[59]

Fentanyl smugglers are even using the U.S. government, via the U.S. Postal Service, as well as consignment carriers like FedEx, UPS, and DHL, to ship their deadly drugs. CBP seized more than five hundred pounds of it in carrier facilities during fiscal year 2022.

Overdose deaths skyrocketed in America between 2019 and 2021. The pandemic no doubt was a factor in this. With schools, sports, and church and just about every other wholesome activity suspended, lock-downs gave young people plenty of time to get into trouble and few op-tions to spend whatever money was in their pockets. Of course, illicit drug use and overdoses were going to spike under those conditions.[60] As substance abuse centers shut down and sober addicts were isolated, often under duress, relapses occurred at a nightmarish clip.[61]

Fentanyl usage played an outsized role in what became an epidemic. Here is the CDC's data:

Median monthly overdose deaths among persons aged 10–19 years (adolescents) increased 109% from July–December 2019 to July–December 2021; deaths involving illicitly manufactured fentanyls (IMFs) increased 182%. Approximately 90% of deaths involved opioids and 84% involved IMFs. Counterfeit pills were present in nearly 25% of deaths. Two thirds of decedents had one or more potential bystanders present, but most provided no overdose response. Approximately 41% of decedents had evidence of mental health conditions or treatment.[62]

Overdose deaths in America have increased nearly every year since the turn of the century, but 2021, the most recent year for which data was readily available while researching this book, was by far a record. The CDC's National Center for Health Statistics tallied 106,699 overdose deaths that year, which is five times the annual total from twenty years ago.[63]

Each one of these deaths is a tragedy. Communities are devastated. Families are forever broken. And most of the time, the drugs never should have been here in the first place.

The situation is so bad that the CDC's Dr. Debra Houry, who was acting principal deputy director, said that parents should consider having the anti-opioid overdose medication Naloxone on them at all times "to save their child's life or somebody else's life."[64] She might not be wrong, but it would also be nice if she recommended that we secured the border, too. Los Angeles schools recently updated a policy to allow students to carry Narcan, a nasal spray than can reverse an opioid overdose, in schools.[65]

Republican congressmen have pushed legislation to classify fentanyl as a "weapon of mass destruction," which would put pressure on China and Mexico to intervene to stop the flow into America.[66] I dig it, but Democrats won't support this. If they do, it is a tacit admission that the border needs to be secured, which they do not want under any circumstances.

Butler County, Pennsylvania, terminated their "sanctuary" designation over the influx of drugs being brought into the area.[67] A "sanctuary city" is one that protects illegal aliens from deportation or prosecutions that they ought to face for violating federal immigration law. It has been said that the U.S. has about 180,000 pages of federal regulations[68] (that number sounds low to me), and until recently, immigrating into the country illegally seems to have been the one law out of all of them that some cities openly disregarded. (Recently, conservative areas have claimed sanctuary from federal gun laws that infringe upon the Second Amendment,[69] a practice I applaud. I often recommend using the Left's playbook against them.)

Butler County's effort is noble, but there are over ten sanctuary states, including California, New York, and Massachusetts, and well over one hundred additional sanctuary counties and cities.[70] Thus, many more of those places will need to follow suit to truly draw attention to the crisis.

San Francisco declares on the mayor's website that "[s]ince 1989, San Francisco has proudly been a Sanctuary City. We will stand shoulder-to-shoulder with our immigrant communities and fight for the progress we've achieved in this City. We are a sanctuary city, now, to-morrow and forever."[71] There is a noteworthy exception to this: for fen-tanyl dealers. Even the city's Democrats want to drop "sanctuary" protections for illegal alien drug dealers, which would make them easier to deport.[72] Maybe San Francisco lawmakers haven't completely lost their minds just yet.

While all of these solutions have some merit, they are the proverbial Band-Aid on a gunshot wound. So long as the border remains unen-forced, the worst people in the world will try to exploit it at the expense of the health, wealth, and happiness of American citizens.

WELCOME TO MIGRANTS' VINEYARD!

In 2022, either to raise awareness about the extent of the crises or to ease pressure on existing facilities and personnel, or both, Texas governor Greg Abbott began busing migrants to sanctuary cities across the country. He favored areas where the political representatives supported open-border policies without actually having to live with their consequences every day.

By not cracking down on sanctuary cities, allowing them to blatantly disregard U.S. immigration law, America is effectually a "sanctuary" country. This is the ultimate "pull factor" for cartels and would-be mi-grants to try to make a run on our border.

In the spring of 2022, Abbott began busing some border crossers to Washington, DC, Philadelphia, Chicago, and New York City.[73] Around 130 were dropped off at Kamala Harris's vice presidential residence at the

Naval Observatory in DC on Christmas Eve.[74] The Left melted down,[75] which is certainly what Governor Abbott wanted. It became national news whenever another bus made it to its destination.[76]

Governor Ron DeSantis (R-FL) upped the ante by flying the foreign nationals to the Obamas' favorite vacation spot, the Massachusetts island of Martha's Vineyard, where they own an $11.75 million estate.[77]

New York City, which prides itself on its "sanctuary" status, got most of the busloads, receiving around 50,000 migrants in total as of February 2023.[78] Democrat mayor Eric Adams complained that it would cost billions of dollars to house, clothe, educate, and care for his new residents. That is precisely the point Abbott was trying to make. Why should Texas bear the full brunt of illegal immigration? If New Yorkers and Washingtonians want an open border, they should accept a larger share of the burden. The irony was clearly lost on Mayor Adams.[79]

The tactic was effective at raising awareness. Tom Homan, a mild-mannered former police officer who served as ICE director for President Donald Trump, summed up the situation on *Breitbart News Daily* with me: "It has helped spread the story out to people who don't know about the issue. Even CNN has covered the buses and, of course, they're attacking Gov. Abbott for doing it—but they're talking about this crisis."[80]

"You'd be surprised how many networks don't even talk about it and there are a lot of Americans out there who don't even know there is a crisis on the border," he continued.[81] Homan raises an important question: If you don't live in a border state or follow conservative media, how would you know what is truly happening?

Now that more Americans were aware of the crisis, would Biden change his approach?

Actually, yes, but only slightly.

In January 2023, border wall construction began in several small sections of Arizona where there were gaps in existing infrastructure.[82] That same month, Biden visited El Paso, Texas, to survey the border.

Just prior to the visit, Border Patrol agents began to remove and arrest aliens from El Paso streets. "The roundup appears to be an attempt to set up a Potemkin Village that paints a much different picture of the El Paso humanitarian crisis," Breitbart journalist Bob Price wrote at the time.[83]

This was Biden's first visit as president, despite White House press secretary Karine Jean-Pierre dishonestly insisting he had already been there.[84] He opted for a photo op in front of a long stretch of border fencing as opposed to barren desert terrain. Donning his signature aviator sunglasses, Joe conversed with five Border Patrol agents as he walked the length of the barrier.[85] More than a year earlier, Biden had falsely accused agents just like these of strapping migrants from horseback as they attempted to cross the Rio Grande. There was no evidence any of the migrants were strapped or whipped, according to a Department of Homeland Security investigation, and Biden never apologized.[86] Now that the border crisis had finally gotten establishment media attention, Joe needed these agents as props to show the public that he was taking charge of the situation.

If you do a simple Google search for the question "do walls work?" your first result is a DHS web page titled simply "Walls Work."[87] Click the link and at the top of the page you'll see a warning: "Archived Content . . . In an effort to keep DHS.gov current, the archive contains outdated information that may not reflect current policy or programs."

The CBP hosts a separate page also titled "Walls Work," which contains a video of a border agent explaining that border walls are a "sensible and proven" response to "terrorism, drug, trafficking, and human smuggling." "The barriers made a world of difference," she says.[88] Yet at the top there's a disclaimer again. "Archived Content . . . In an effort to keep CBP. gov current, the archive contains content from a previous administration or is otherwise outdated." The page was last modified just after Joe Biden assumed office.

So, our official government policy is that walls worked when Trump was president, but they no longer work because . . . Biden has the job now?

That sounds highly political and not at all logical, especially considering how Joe Biden behaves in his personal life.

Despite the content warnings on top of the government web pages, there is definitive evidence that Joe Biden believes walls do work. In fact, he knows they do. In 2022, DHS awarded a Delaware company a $490,000 contract, paid for by the taxpayers, for a special security project of utmost importance to the nation: a security fence for Joe Biden's Rehoboth Beach, Delaware, summer house.[89]

If only he treated the American citizens the way he treats himself and his family.

CHAPTER 14

Slouching Toward Lawlessness

A few years ago, I can't remember exactly when, I took a road trip up to the Bay Area with Mrs. Dr. Marlow. We had fond memories of this part of Northern California, even though the people there rarely shared our values. We both graduated from UC Berkeley, she in 2009, I in 2008. The college years were good years for us.

Once you make your peace with the hippie vibe, Berkeley certainly has its charms. At least back then, it was a great place to shop for music and books, to sip gourmet coffee or biodynamic wine, and waste away the days trying to answer questions that no one actually asked. At that time, Berkeley was "fully realized," meaning it had exactly the identity it was meant to have.

For us, weekends were spent in San Francisco. The restaurants were classier, if you could get in; the stores were better, if you could afford them; and movie theaters were bigger, if you remembered to get a ticket in advance. The whole city is tight quarters, but that made it seem vibrant with activity and spirit.

But this weekend, things were different. It started to dawn on me that this part of America was deeply, deeply lost. Berkeley was looking more dilapidated than when we had last left it. There was more vagrancy, more filth, and none of that college-town energy. There were always tarps and tents set up on Shattuck and Telegraph Avenues, but it seemed like full-on encampments were forming.

San Francisco was no better. The lunatics who were constantly disturbing patrons of public transit seemed angrier and more aggressive. The areas that must be avoided after dark seemed harder to avoid.

It was as if everyone had gone mad. (Even madder than usual.) I witnessed a group of nudists in novelty hats riding bicycles down the famed Embarcadero like they were in some sort of X-rated fetish Dr. Seuss parody. Of all the activities to do in the buff, what could be less appealing than riding a bicycle? (One lesson I learned from my time in the Bay: the people most likely to go nude in public are the last people you actually want to see naked.) There were cops nearby, but they seemed uninterested in the crimes against humanity I was witnessing.

One morning that weekend, Mrs. Dr. Marlow and I were waiting outside a diner on an otherwise empty street in downtown San Francisco, gray and brown buildings towering above us, looking forward to $19 breakfast burritos and $9 lemon-ginger green juices, when something caught my eye that was brand-new, yet entirely familiar at the same time.

Out in the distance, I saw a man stagger slowly around the corner. Dreadlocked and bloated, clothes tattered, mouth agape. Shuffling—limping, really—but not necessarily from an injury. Moments later, another creature emerged from around the corner. It was a variation on the same theme. Staggering, stumbling, and coming right for us. Slowly. Ever so slowly.

One more of these figures presented itself, and then another.

For a brief moment in time, we stood alone on what felt like an otherwise abandoned street in an iconic American city, in the middle of the zombie apocalypse. Or at least that's how it felt. I've always been a zombie movie guy, so I was digging it for a moment or two. But that thought was fleeting, and reality set in: these were human beings, and something had gone profoundly wrong for this precise sequence of events to take place before me.

Just like the protagonists in the third act of so many of my beloved zombie flicks, I knew I had to get out of there, though, in this case, I would wait until after our $81 breakfast.

I felt as though I had gazed into a crystal ball and seen the future of America's cities, a future where laws no longer matter, standards no longer exist, excellence and beauty are an afterthought, and taxpaying citizens are taken for granted.

So, when stories began to emerge in early 2023 that crime had officially gotten the best of the city, I wasn't exactly surprised.

Dominoes started to fall quickly, but none got more attention than the flagship Whole Foods store in the mid-Market neighborhood of San

Francisco that was shut down after just a year. Records reviewed by the *New York Times* revealed that 568 emergency calls were made in the thirteen months the store was open, an average of more than one per day. "Male with machete is back," one 911 caller reportedly said. There were food fights, fistfights, knife and gun threats against employees, security guards assaulted, and even at least one effort to defecate on the floor.[1]

The *Times* described that incident as an "attempt." Let's hope that's all it was.

A man even died of a fentanyl overdose in the bathroom.

It will not come as a shock to readers to know this behavior wasn't isolated to this particular Whole Foods market. Target had to put entire sections of products in a San Francisco store behind security glass because they were getting robbed "at least ten times a day."[2] Williams-Sonoma in Union Square was next to close, joining Nordstrom, Christian Louboutin, Ray-Ban, Lululemon, the Gap, Anthropologie, and many, many others.[3]

The *San Francisco Standard* reported that 96 out of 203 stores that were operational in the Union Square area in 2019 had shut down as of May 2023. That's a stunning 47 percent closure rate. Of course, the pandemic and economic downturn played a role, but of the mere twelve businesses that tried to open in all those newly empty storefronts, two of those already have gone out of business.[4]

One hundred stores in a downtown Westfield mall where I had many a date with Mrs. Dr. Marlow fifteen years prior had shut down as well. In the spring of 2023, the shopping center conglomerate stopped making their mortgage payments and handed the keys back to the lender.[5]

The pandemic happened everywhere, but the Bay Area had become particularly lawless. Even CNN acknowledged it, reporting that narcotic usage on the street was common without fear of prosecution.[6] The street drug "tranq," a powerful animal sedative, became fashionable. It is often mixed with fentanyl, with deadly consequences.[7]

New York magazine reporter Elizabeth Weil set out "to write a debunking-the-doom piece," only to find that the city is, in fact, in a "doom loop." "In the first three months of 2023, 200 San Franciscans OD'ed, up 41 percent from last year,"[8] she wrote.

"Doom loop (noun)—A scenario in which one negative development causes another negative development, which then makes the first problem worse. A vicious cycle. This is how San Francisco could die," began a March 2023 article in the *San Francisco Chronicle*.[9]

It's nice that the establishment media and political Left is acknowledging that there is a massive problem in the Bay—they even found a catchy way to brand it—but it would have been preferable if they had revised their priorities somewhere along the way.

In 2023, Bay Area officials spent time voting to ban gas furnaces, stoves, and water heaters (only to get slowed down by a federal court).[10] As of this writing, San Francisco—a debt-ridden city in a free state—is considering $5 million lump-sum slavery reparations checks for black citizens.[11]

The City by the Bay was lighting itself on fire, destroying itself from within. "To live in San Francisco right now, to watch its streets, is to realize that no one will catch you if you fall," Weil wrote. I could have warned them all, but who would have listened? It is a town run by the institutional Left—and now, to at least some degree, by drug-fueled mobs.

This phenomenon is not just happening in the Bay Area. It is happening in cities across the country. American cities are decaying at an alarming rate.

These streets have been abandoned by Joe Biden. Whatever his rationale may be, instead of daring to lead on the issue, he says little about crime and does less. His policies on firearms and immigration have favored criminals, and his Justice Department, led by Merrick Garland, has chosen to focus on the supposed crimes of phantom white supremacists, concerned parents who object to wokeness in schools, and, of course, the Bad Orange Man himself.

It is this precise approach that has left our metropolises in ruins.

HIDE YOUR WATER BOTTLES

On January 5, 2023, FBI director Christopher Wray wrote an opinion piece for Fox News with the headline "America's Crime Problem Is Real." Appointed by Trump but generally loathed by the MAGA faithful who (correctly, in my view) consider him a Deep State oligarch, Wray noted that violent crime rose to "alarmingly high levels" in 2020 and 2021, and that despite lacking full data for 2022, his weekly conversations with sheriffs and police chiefs across the country are evidence that "those violent crime trends have continued throughout 2022." Wray claims that local law enforcement's main concerns are "gun and gang violence" and "seeing repeat or dangerous offenders end up back on the street." In 2022 alone, the FBI and its partners "arrested more than 20,000 violent criminals and child predators—an average of 55 per day, every day." Wray also claimed the FBI had broken up 370 violent criminal gangs.[12]

This data, the data and news reports that conservative Americans read in their preferred media outlets every day, matches the reality we see in the streets. Crime, particularly violent crime, is on the rise in American cities. What is causing the increase is multifactorial. Widespread efforts to demonize cops and even celebrity-driven campaigns to "defund the police" bear much of the blame. Democrat mayors, who run nearly every major city in the country, eschew a tough-on-crime approach because it's politically unpopular among left-wing voters. Even President Trump, who tweeted critically of the Black Lives Matter riots of 2020, stopped short of cracking down on the uprisings himself.

Joe Biden rose through the political ranks as being tough on crime, as did his vice president, Kamala Harris, as I have documented in this book. Yet Biden has avoided the issue almost entirely as president. Politically, it is probably the smart approach. Taking the challenge of our deteriorating cities head-on would be tantamount to an admission that Democrats have failed their own constituencies. The Left often tries to deny this point, but our urban centers are getting more crime-ridden as they get more expensive, and they are run by Democrats. If Biden confronts this, it is a tacit attack on his political allies and his own voter base. After all, Democrats or unaffiliated liberals are in charge of twenty-two of the twenty-five biggest cities in the country.

Besides, Biden, a lifelong national politician from a small city, was not ideal casting to fix this mess.

He also must contend with a small but loud minority of constituents who believe that police are actually too tough on crime. "Defund the police," a bumper sticker slogan associated with far-left political groups and fringe political figures like Alexandria Ocasio-Cortez, is actually a wildly unpopular idea, despite all its media attention.[13] Only 17 percent of black voters, a group disproportionately affected by violent crime, want police defunded, according to an October 2022 poll.[14]

And why would they? Crime in their cities is going up as is.

On July 22, 2022, the Council on Criminal Justice (CJC) released a report titled "Pandemic, Social Unrest, and Crime in U.S. Cities; Mid-Year 2022 Update." The report, which updated and supplemented previous reports by the CJC, examined "monthly crime rates for ten violent, property, and drug offenses in 29 U.S. cities in calendar year 2021," while also providing historical crime data on these trends.[15] The monthly homicide rate in June 2022 remained "39% above the level prior to the COVID-19 pandemic (in the first half of 2019)" in these cities, despite decreasing in the first half of 2022 by 2 percent.[16]

The monthly homicide rate peaked at a historic high in July 2020 in the period of January 2018–June 2022 in the cities CJC studied. This was "amid widespread protests against police violence after George Floyd's murder in May of that year." The monthly rates for aggravated assault and gun assault were also at an all-time high the month following George Floyd's murder.[17] "Aggravated assaults (+4%) and robberies (+19%) increased in the first half of 2022 compared to the first half of 2021," according to the report. A separate report from the Department of Justice confirmed that robberies were up 19 percent during the first half of 2022 over the first half of 2021. That equates to 5,226 more robberies than the year before.[18]

Thievery was on the incline as well. "Residential burglaries (+6%), nonresidential burglaries (+8%), larcenies (+20%), and motor vehicle thefts (+15%) all increased in the first half of 2022 compared to the first six months of 2021," the study showed. There were 45,104 more larcenies in 2022 than the year before.[19]

This was not the only significant survey revealing a steady uptick in crime. The Major Cities Chiefs Association (MCCA), "a professional organization of police executives representing the largest cities in the United States and Canada," compiles and analyzes crime data for all these cities.[20] MCCA reported that since 2019, there's been a 50 percent increase in homicides and 36 percent increase in aggravated assaults.[21] From January 1 to June 30, 2022, overall violent crime spiked 4.2 percent compared to the same time period in 2021.[22]

The National Crime Victimization Survey (NCVS) found that in 2021, the violent-crime rate in urban areas was 121 percent higher than in rural ones. Urban violent crime was also 48 percent higher than suburban violent crime in 2021.[23]

The Heritage Foundation concluded that "new analysis of crime data shows that high-crime counties are governed largely by Democrats, driving up the crime rates in their otherwise red states."[24] They laid much of the blame on rogue prosecutors propped up by George Soros, the nonagenarian megadonor to left-wing causes who was the single biggest funder of Democrat politics in 2022.[25] In the American electoral system, down-ballot races are fairly easy to buy if one or more committed ideologues are willing to lay out enough cash, and Soros certainly is. For years he has tried to buy "criminal justice reform" (that is, less law enforcement and more lenient penalties) by getting handpicked prosecutors elected throughout the country. His plan is working for him and the institutional Left, but not so much for urbanites who want order in their streets.[26]

Crime did not rise in every area of the country. Florida, for example, governed by Ron DeSantis and home to an increasing conservative majority, saw its crime rate drop to a fifty-year low in 2021.[27]

Journalist Matt Palumbo, writing in the *New York Post*, calculated that Soros spent $40 million getting far-left district attorneys elected across the country. As of January 2023, seventy-five prosecutors nationwide had received Soros's support.[28]

The one condition for obtaining money from Soros's infinite coffers appears to be a willingness to not enforce the law.

The net result of installing Soros's minions in vital positions of our judicial system is fewer prosecutions, reduced sentences, and fewer bail requirements (which ensures that violent offenders will miss more court hearings).[29]

In June 2022, out of the 30 cities with the highest homicide rates, 27 have Democrat mayors; the exceptions are Jacksonville, Florida (which has since elected a Democrat); Lexington, Kentucky; and Las Vegas, Nevada (where the mayor is an Independent). "Within those cities there are at least 14 Soros-backed or Soros-inspired rogue prosecutors," according to Heritage. In America's most murderous city, New Orleans, all seven members of the City Council and the district attorney are Democrats.[30]

On September 14, 2022, Tennessee senators Marsha Blackburn and Bill Hagerty penned a letter to President Biden demanding action to stop the escalation of violent crime in our nation's cities. The letter highlights several horrific murders in the Volunteer State at the hands of criminals with violent records. "This jarring escalation in violent crime is part of a national trend," the letter states.[31] The two Republicans cite Council on Criminal Justice data showing skyrocketing murder rates across the country. "A clear cause of this undeniable deterioration of public safety is the anti-law-enforcement movement that has wrought soft-on-crime policies—from the eradication of bail and pretrial detention to prosecutors declining to prosecute or seek jail time for serious crimes—as well as emboldened criminals who are often quickly returned to the streets."[32]

President Biden did not acknowledge the letter.

He could ignore the horrifying crime numbers, but it didn't mean Americans were ignorant of what was going on. An October 28, 2022, a Gallup poll showed that a record 56 percent of U.S. adults believed crime was increasing where they live.[33]

The uptick affects more than just people's safety: it also harms businesses. When Target released its 2022 third-quarter earnings results, the big-box chain told reporters that "inventory shrinkage—or the disappearance of merchandise—has reduced its gross profit margin by $400 million so far in 2022 compared to 2021." They elaborated that "organized retail crime," specifically mass looting, was to blame.[34]

But as we know, Target was not alone. CVS said that they experienced a 300 percent uptick in theft since the beginning of the pandemic.[35] Home Depot said it has had to lock up more products. Rite Aid was hemorrhaging money from theft from its New York City stores.[36]

Most of these trends preceded Biden's presidency, but often worsened after he was sworn in. A 2022 retail security report from the National Retail Federation (NRF) claims that goods stolen from retail stores increased to $94.5 billion in losses in 2021, a nearly $4 billion increase from 2020.[37] NRF conducted a survey of its retailers, and 52.9 percent reported that organized retailed crime (ORC) had increased, while not a single company reported that they had seen crime go down.[38]

To make matters worse, 81.2 percent of retailers the NRF surveyed reported that ORC offenders got more violent in 2021 compared to a year ago; more than one-third reported drastic increases in violence.[39]

Unsurprisingly, most businesses surveyed (86.8 percent) believed a federal response was warranted to address organized retail crime.[40] Don't count on Biden to organize one on their behalf.

A series of smash-and-grab jewelry store robberies garnered headlines throughout 2022. These weren't merely dramatic anecdotes: this specific type of theft was on the rise across the country. The Jewelers Mutual Group, which has served the jewelry industry as an insurance provider since 1913, issued a news release in December 2022 reporting the disturbing trend: "Jewelry industry crime is up 14% year over year and has surpassed 50% from 2019." The Jewelers' Security Alliance reported that California saw a remarkable 200 percent increase in these robberies in the first quarter of 2022 over the first quarter of the previous year.[41]

In 2023, the Los Angeles Police Department launched a campaign called "stash it, don't flash it." In other words, hide your stuff unless you want to get robbed or mugged or both. "It could be anything from a phone charger to change in the cup holder," said Sergeant Gordon Helper, the very helpful leader of the campaign. "They're gonna break the window out and take."[42]

Captain Elaine Morales said the city's criminals will even "break a window to get a bottle of water so they can recycle its container, whether it's aluminum or plastic." At least this type of crime is environmentally sustainable.

Recycled beverage containers can fetch you either five or ten cents in California, depending on the size of the bottle.

This dystopian moment has been brought to you by Democrat mayors, George Soros's piggy bank, and Joe Biden (in absentia).

GUN TROLL

According to the *Congressional Record*, on July 9, 1985, then senator Joe Biden said that "during my 12 and a half years as a member of this body, I have never believed that additional gun control or federal registration of guns would reduce crime. I am convinced that a criminal who wants a firearm can get one through illegal, nontraceable, unregistered sources, with or without gun control."[43]

That statement was correct then and it is correct now.

Gun control takes guns out of the hands of law-abiding citizens and will leave only criminals (and the government) armed. The data backs that up. Fox News Digital did a major analysis to determine whether stricter gun laws correlate with fewer gun murders in America, and the conclusion is that they do not.[44]

At Breitbart News, we regularly report on "good guys with guns" using his or her Second Amendment right to protect themselves and avoid becoming a victim. One of the best examples of what we mean by this took place in Indiana in 2022. Surveillance video shows a twenty-year-old madman exiting a restroom at Greenwood Park Mall, guns blazing, at 5:56:48 p.m. on Sunday, July 17. A mere fifteen seconds, later, at 5:57:03, twenty-two-year-old Elisjsha Dicken, who was out shopping with his girlfriend, drew his handgun and fired ten rounds from forty yards, hitting the active shooter eight times, killing him.[45] Dicken, who had no police or military training, was carrying his gun legally under state law.[46]

Fifteen seconds was enough time for the monster to murder three innocent people. Imagine how many he would have killed had Dicken not been packing.

Another example of the same phenomenon occurred the following month in West Palm Beach, Florida, when a twenty-two-year-old armed with a shotgun threatened to "shoot up the crowd" at a family gathering. Multiple people told him to drop his weapon, but he refused. At this point, a thirty-two-year-old concealed-carry holder pulled his own gun and shot dead the man who was brandishing the shotgun.[47]

These stories aren't rare, yet they get little press compared to the ones where murderers aren't quickly stopped. In fact, a 2018 study by a pro–Second Amendment group claims that well over 90 percent of mass shootings occur in what are known as "gun-free zones."[48] Though there is no official federal data on this topic that is public, it certainly stands to reason that would-be mass murderers pick soft targets. The more people they kill, the more headlines they get, which fulfills their sick fantasies.

Here are a few of the high-profile mass murder events that occurred in "gun-free zones," from a much longer list: the Virginia Tech University attack, 32 dead (April 16, 2007); the Aurora, Colorado, movie theater attack, 12 dead (July 20, 2012); the Sandy Hook Elementary School attack in Newtown, Connecticut, 26 dead (December 12, 2014); the Pulse nightclub attack in Orlando, Florida, 49 dead (June 12, 2016); the Marjory Stoneman Douglas High School attack in Parkland, Florida, 17 dead (February 14, 2018).[49]

The lesson here is that, in actuality, these are "gun-free zones" only for the "good guys." The would-be murderers ignore the laws.

"When they say the only thing that can stop a bad guy with a gun is a good guy with a gun, they're trying to sell you two guns," antigun activist and Parkland massacre survivor David Hogg is fond of saying.[50] This argument is fallacious. Is his preference that only bad guys have guns? Because they already have them. We want the good guys to have them, too.

It has become an article of faith in Democrat circles that gun rights need to be rolled back whenever possible, regardless of who benefits in the end. It doesn't matter what the Constitution says or who will be less safe. Joe Biden, as the leader of the party, has become the de facto leader of the gun-grabbers.

I say "de facto" because it is clear Biden doesn't care all that much about guns. Whenever he discusses the matter, he appears to have no idea what he's talking about. (The same goes for other topics and issues, but he gets particularly lost when talking guns.)

Biden repeatedly states that Americans cannot own cannons, citing nonexistent bans on cannon ownership from America's earliest days. "The Second Amendment, from the day it was passed, limited the type of people who could own a gun and what type of weapon you could own," he said in remarks about gun violence in June 2021. "You couldn't buy a cannon." These claims are categorically false. He even got busted by Glenn Kessler, the leftist fact-checker at the *Washington Post*: "We have no idea where he conjured up this notion about a ban," Kessler said while chastising Biden for using a historical falsehood to push his political agenda.[51]

In his first State of the Union address in 2022, Biden called for a ban on "assault weapons" with "high-capacity magazines that hold up to 100 rounds."[52] There is no uniform definition of "assault weapon," but gun control proponents tend to use the term because it sounds more serious than "big, mean, scary rifle." The DOJ's National Institute of Justice (NIJ) concluded that the "assault weapons ban" that expired in 2004 did not reduce violence.[53] It is unclear whether a ban on hundred-round magazines would stop any crime whatsoever. A mag that size would have to take the shape of a round drum like the kind you might see in an old-timey gangster movie. They are huge, cumbersome, and rarely turn up at crime scenes.

"Do you think the deer are wearing Kevlar vests?" the president went on, rhetorically. The implication is that we should roll back our rights because certain weapons aren't necessary for hunting. This is constitutionally illiterate, and Biden knows it. He acknowledged during a speech in September 2022 that assault weapons are designed for defense.[54] The Second Amendment has many applications, hunting being one, defense being another. A check on a tyrannical government is another still.

Functionally speaking, *why* we have a Second Amendment is irrelevant. What is relevant is that the right to keep and bear arms is enshrined in the U.S. Constitution.

In October 2022, Biden claimed that he proposed legislation that said "there can be no more than eight bullets in a round."[55] Oh, Mr. President, there is but one bullet in a round.

Biden's insincerity when it comes to weapons was perfectly encapsulated in a single day in December 2022 when he released the world's most notorious arms dealer, Viktor Bout, in exchange for petty drug criminal and WNBA player Brittney Griner. That very day, he also vowed to "limit the number of bullets that can be in a cartridge"; he referred to this reform as "commonsense."[56] This statement again betrays his ignorance: cartridges have exactly one bullet in them.

Biden doesn't even understand the components of a round of ammunition, yet he felt confident releasing a warlord who makes his living dealing weapons to the worst people alive, some of whom want to kill Americans en masse.[57]

In 2023, Biden said, "There is no rationale for assault weapons and magazines that hold fifty to seventy bullets."[58] What happened to the hundred-round drum?

After the 2022 massacre of students and teachers at Robb Elementary School in Uvalde, Texas, gun control legislation was put on a fast track. Led by John Cornyn (R-TX), fifteen Republican senators joined Democrats to pass the most sweeping gun control in decades.[59] The bill, which Biden would sign, expanded background checks, broadened the list of violent offenders prohibited from purchasing firearms, and enhanced penalties for straw purchases (buying a gun for someone) and weapons trafficking. Most controversially, the bill provided taxpayer funds for states to enforce "red flag laws." Many elements of the bill have nothing to do with any of the high-profile mass school shootings that were used as political justification for the legislation.

Of all the new controls, the "red flag law" funding is the most troubling. "Red flag laws" are a mechanism to confiscate guns from people deemed to be a threat to themselves or others. Where these laws apply, a judge can empower police to confiscate firearms from citizens. The Second Amendment is a fundamental right, meaning it must be provided with the same level of due process and equal protection as any other constitutional right. If the Constitution is to be taken seriously, you can't selectively apply its laws because you really hate one of them.

Who gets "red-flagged" and who does the red-flagging? If the laws are perfectly applied, and the judges' determination is based solely on medical doctors who are making clinical diagnoses that an individual is a danger to himself or others, perhaps the laws could keep some guns out of the hands of genuinely mentally ill people. I fear, however, the laws will be selectively applied to give the government a de facto veto over who has Second Amendment rights and who does not.

The Left has made the case for years that normative conservative viewpoints are a form of psychosis or even violence. *Scientific American* published a report in 2021 titled "The 'Shared Psychosis' of Donald Trump and His Loyalists."[60] A piece published in the *New York Times* in 2017 claimed that sometimes speech is "literally a form of violence."[61] In the wake of the Black Lives Matter protests and riots following the death of George Floyd, the Left was fond of using the phrase "silence is violence."[62]

Simultaneously, the Left contends that silence is violence and speech is violence. So, no matter what you do, you're violent. *I red-flag you!*

Actually, neither speech nor silence is violence. Violence is violence. But with the shifting definition of the word, there is no objective measure by which to enforce "red flag laws." So conservatives, quite reasonably, are concerned that the laws will be abused by wannabe authoritarians to harass gun owners.

Given the political climate, I certainly don't trust that the spirit of "red flag" laws—that is, no guns for the criminally insane—will correspond with how it is applied.

Only time will tell if I'm right.

The bill marked a legislative victory for Biden—any gun control that is passed at a national level and not overturned by the courts is a big win for a Democrat.[63] By the end of 2022, he was already planning to press for more.

Given that Republicans took control of the House of Representatives, it is unlikely he will pass any additional gun control unless he is elected to a second term and the House flips blue. It is even less likely, however, that the reforms he already passed will do anything to stem the rising tide of violence in American streets.

WHY JOE BIDEN PUNCHED OUT

Joe Biden has not been tough on crime in decades. If he were, his base wouldn't like it, and Joe Biden never betrays his base. But that only partly explains his negligence. In fact, when it comes to combating criminality, Joe Biden is probably traumatized about the issue. Haunted, really. The explanation for why Biden has failed our cities lies within his record.

Some essential history:

In March of 1991, knowing Democrats were facing fierce criticism on crime going into the 1992 election, Biden sponsored a massive, two-hundred-plus-page bill called the Biden-Thurmond Violent Crime Control Act of 1991, named in honor of South Carolina senator Strom Thurmond. The resulting legislation included provisions to elevate the number of policemen on the streets, increase the number of crimes eligible for the death penalty, and allocate $3 billion in government funding for police equipment, drug testing in prisons, and training for new officers. It also proposed an "assault weapons" ban that discontented Republicans, and death penalty impositions that discontented many Democrats. This ensured a stalemate in Congress, and the threat of a veto from President Bush.[64]

But, under President Clinton, similar legislation became a major priority. Biden introduced a reworked version of the bill in the Senate that passed by a comfortable margin in the Congress and was signed into law in September 1994.[65] The 1994 crime bill devoted billions to hiring new police officers and building new prisons. It also mandated life sentences for three-time violent offenders. In more recent years, the bill has been blamed for a rapid expansion of America's prison population.[66]

But it was a lesser-known law in 1986 that Biden crafted that would truly haunt him—and America—decades later. In what the *Washington Post* would describe as a law that "came to be viewed as one of the most racially slanted sentencing policies on record,"[67] Biden's rule would treat crack cocaine as far worse than powdered cocaine, particularly when it comes to sentencing. It disproportionately penalized black men.

Perhaps that's not entirely an unintended consequence. The 1986 law was concocted with the help of Thurmond, the most notorious segregationist in the federal government at the time. In recent years, Biden has tried to downplay his support for harsher sentencing and the influence of Thurmond and the media has let him skate. Still, the fact pattern remains damning for Biden: He repeatedly worked with a segregationist on legislation that would lead to the incarceration of more black men and the 1991 bill, which was named for Thurmond, became the foundation for the infamous 1994 legislation. Biden even bragged about how he had worked with Thurmond on sentencing reform.[68]

On the campaign trail in 2019, Senator Cory Booker (D-NJ), then a presidential candidate himself, said Biden "inflicted immeasurable harm on black, brown, and low-income communities."[69]

Yet the passage of the bill also coincided with a drop in crime, which studies have linked to an increase in the number of police officers that the bill helped fund.[70] One of the main beneficiaries of this drop in crime would have largely been innocent blacks.

By the time Joe Biden was running for president in 2019, his political instincts had kicked in, and he knew his tough-on-crime past was an electoral loser. It wasn't merely time to run from some of his signature laws—he had to self-flagellate. In a speech in January 2019, he said that the powder-coke/crack sentencing disparity "trapped an entire generation."[71] Harsh, but not entirely inaccurate. "The biggest mistake in that bill in my view was making crack cocaine and powdered cocaine a different sentence, they should not be mandatory sentences," Biden told a crowd in New Hampshire later that year.[72] In a town hall with George Stephanopoulos just weeks before the 2020 general election, he said the legislation was a "mistake."[73]

On the verge of his ninth decade on earth, Joe Biden was reinventing himself before our eyes.

Back in the summer of 1976, in a Senate floor speech, Biden noted that Americans "are worried about being mugged on the subway." "Women are worried about being raped on the way to their automobiles after work," he continued. "They worry that their government does not seem to be doing much about it, and unfortunately, they appear to be right."

He was new to the government then. He is the government now. And Americans are no less worried about those things now than then.

Joe Biden ran for president in 2020 with a "criminal justice agenda [that] would reverse virtually all of his past tough-on-crime measures," according to the *Washington Post*.[74] While he has been president, crime has completely fallen off his priority list. He seems almost totally disconnected from the subject.

Even though at times Joe Biden appears to be impervious to public criticism, he clearly bears scars on this particular issue.

Perhaps that's the real reason he has abandoned our streets and left American cities to fend for themselves.

CODE ORANGE: THE THREAT OF MAGA

Even if the Biden administration isn't particularly interested in violent crime in our neighborhoods or white-collar crime carried out by allies of America's ruling class, he still has a vast law enforcement bureaucracy to train on whichever target he wants.

To lead the bureaucracy, Joe picked Merrick Garland. Garland achieved political martyrdom in 2016 when he was nominated by Barack Obama to fill the Supreme Court seat vacated by Justice Antonin Scalia upon Scalia's death in February of that year. Senate majority leader Mitch McConnell (R-KY) vowed that the Republicans would not consider filling the seat until after the presidential election. Obama tapped Garland anyway, but that nomination expired with the end of the congressional session in January 2017. Donald Trump went on to win the 2016 election and nominate Neil Gorsuch to fill the seat, and Gorsuch was confirmed.

Merrick Garland will never get to be on the Supreme Court, but he did get to be Biden's attorney general.

Given his status as the Democrats' Saint Stephen, he was guaranteed to get favorable press. The media portrays Garland as mild-mannered, thoughtful, liberal but not radically so, and very much a part of institutional Washington, which figures given that his previous job was chief judge of the United States Court of Appeals for the District of Columbia Circuit. In a lengthy profile, *Politico* depicted him as a micromanager: whereas most judges depend on clerks for research and writing, "Garland's former clerks describe him as unusually hands-on and meticulous."[75] Perhaps this makes him noble, it probably makes him a workaholic, but it is certainly an odd personality trait for someone who was being placed in charge of a bureaucracy with 115,000 employees. After all, circuit court judges manage one tiny office. The DOJ has hundreds of offices across the country, and now Garland oversaw them all.

Upon confirmation, Garland seemed to shift the focus of the DOJ to systemic discrimination and the supposed crimes of the anti-woke. He beefed up some woke bona fides by cracking down on redlining, which is when banks refuse to grant loans to people who live in financially risky areas.

In 2021, protests against mandates, critical race theory being taught in classrooms, and woke transgendered policies in schools swept the country. Met with resistance from parents, educators pushed back on those pesky moms and dads who wanted a larger say in their children's education. The National School Boards Association (NSBA) sent a letter to Joe Biden asking for law enforcement to intervene after "threats and acts of violence" endangered school board members. Shortly after the letter was received, Garland sent a memo to the FBI calling on the Bureau to help local law enforcement stop the (supposed) violence.[76]

Garland did not appear to be aware that an allegedly violent individual referenced in the NSBA's letter was Scott Smith, the father of a ninth-grade Loudon County, Virginia, girl who was brutally raped in the girls' bathroom of Stone Bridge High School by a boy who was wearing a skirt.[77] The boy would later be arrested for the sexual assault of a different girl at a different school.[78]

The NSBA would ultimately apologize for the letter, but not before the FBI's Counterterrorism Division began categorizing the threat assessments of the protesting parents.

Yes, our government was actually considering whether these concerned parents might have been terrorists.

Garland, with immeasurable resources at his disposal, never cited any data or studies or even one actual real-life example as the basis for treating normal moms and dads like violent radicals. He did, however, say "we read in the newspapers reports of threats of violence."[79] Someone should send him a copy of *Breaking the News*.

Following the leak of Justice Samuel Alito's draft majority opinion in the *Dobbs v. Jackson Women's Health Organization* case, which foreshadowed the overturning of *Roe v. Wade*, America endured a "Summer of Rage." The Family Research Council documented more than one hundred acts of violence, destruction, and harassment aimed at intimidating anti-abortion Christians and conservatives.[80] Jane's Revenge, a far-left militant group, took credit for much of the violence.[81]

These attacks generated no meaningful response from Garland or anyone else in federal law enforcement. While the feds track violence against abortion providers,[82] the same can't be said of pro-life pregnancy centers that provide resources for parents and small children, before and after birth.[83]

Ruth Sent Us, a radical pro-abortion group, organized protests at the homes of the "six extremist Catholics" on the Supreme Court. (Justices John Roberts, Samuel Alito, Clarence Thomas, Brett Kavanaugh, and Amy Coney Barrett are all Catholic; though Justice Gorsuch was raised Catholic but is said to attend Episcopal services.) The group also encouraged followers to demonstrate "at or in a local Catholic Church."

About a month after the draft opinion leaked, a man threatened to assassinate Justice Kavanaugh, showing up at his house with a gun, a knife, and zip-ties.[84] He was arrested.

Yet these very real acts of violence and intimidation apparently did not make Garland's priorities list. He had deeper concerns, like January 6th. Garland pulled personnel from other investigations to concentrate on the Capitol Riot of 2021. The FBI even sought out the public to snitch on their fellow citizens if they recognized anyone in public footage who entered the Capitol.[85] Oftentimes, the J6 protesters got arrested and held in jails with reportedly deplorable conditions, often for months at a time without bail—and zero outrage from purported social justice activists.[86]

Garland linked the deaths of five Capitol Police officers to the riots, even though the only officer whose demise was classified as "in the line of duty" was Brian Sicknick, who passed away a day later of natural causes.[87] Ashli Babbitt, a Trump supporter, was shot dead by a plainclothes officer during the riot. A DOJ investigation cleared the shooting officer.[88] None of the other three individuals who died during the riot were murdered by MAGA.

As an exercise, try to explain this cold, hard fact to someone in your life who gets their news from MSNBC.

In a March 2022 speech in Superior, Wisconsin, Joe Biden himself falsely claimed that five officers were killed by Trump supporters on January 6th. "Look, how would you feel if you saw crowds storm and break down the doors of the British Parliament, kill five cops, injure 145—or the German Bundestag, or the Italian Parliament? I think you'd wonder," he told a crowd of supporters. "Well, that's what the rest of the world saw. It's not who we are. And now, we're proving, under pressure, that we are not that country."

It is definitely "not who we are." We are literally not that country. What he said never happened. The real number of cops killed that day was zero.[89]

In July 2021, the U.S. House formed a Select Committee to Investigate the January 6th Attack on the United States Capitol. The investigators conducted more than one thousand interviews, issued more than one hundred subpoenas, and reviewed one million pages of documents.[90] Their conclusion: Donald Trump is very, very, very bad and probably guilty of something, but it's hard to pin down exactly what.

The committee even crafted a made-for-television kangaroo court to further demonize Trump and his allies. Like Biden, it falsely blamed the rioters for dead cops.[91]

As of May 2023, more than one thousand people were charged for crimes related to the riot.[92]

With Republicans on track to take over the House of Representatives after the November 2022 midterm elections, the Left knew that the January 6th committee would eventually get disbanded, thus eliminating one of the Democrats' best vehicles for planting anti-Trump content into the news cycle. This is precisely when U.S. magistrate judge Bruce Reinhart approved an FBI raid of Trump's home at his Mar-a-Lago resort in Florida.

"My beautiful home, Mar-A-Lago in Palm Beach, Florida, is currently under siege, raided, and occupied by a large group of FBI agents,"[93] Trump said in a dramatic statement on August 8, 2022.

It was a historic moment.

Reinhart's background made it clear that he was no fan of Donald Trump. He donated to Barack Obama and arch-establishmentarian Jeb Bush.[94] His personal Facebook page was a jubilee of woke: praise for far-left UC Berkeley professor Robert Reich, a video about "white privilege," and an attack on Trump. He even shared a video from a page literally called "WokeFolks."[95]

The raid took law enforcement all the way into the former First Lady's closet to look for classified documents. "FBI agents scoured Melania Trump's wardrobe and spent several hours combing through Donald Trump's private office, breaking open his safe and rifling through drawers when they raided the former First Family's Mar-a-Lago home in Florida Monday morning," according to the *New York Post*.[96]

FBI agents found more than 11,000 documents at the residence, totaling more than 200,000 pages. More than 100 were classified.[97] However, as president, Donald Trump could have declassified any document. If he had failed to do that before leaving office, then they technically became the property of the National Archives and Records Administration. That appears to be the case here, but it is a technicality.

The FBI had surveilled the Trump campaign (they used the bogus Steele dossier, which was funded by the Hillary Clinton campaign, to get the surveillance approved). Whistleblowers indicated that the FBI had worked with social media companies to suppress news about Hunter Biden's Laptop from Hell.[98] Now they had rifled through the underwear drawer of the First Lady, looking for documents the president could have declassified. Even left-leaning *Politico* called the move "unprecedented."[99]

After weeks of deliberation and preparation, Garland himself approved the raid. He must have known the controversy around it would be severe. (Biden denies having had advance notice.[100])

The real victim here, according to Director Wray, was actually the FBI. He claimed that "deplorable and dangerous" threats were made to agents. Maybe, but only after they went through Melania's intimates, looking for hidden state secrets.[101]

These are the priorities of Biden's top cops.

They are managing our decline.

Innocents and political rivals are targeted while the criminals run free.

This is our new America. Joe Biden's America.

CONCLUSION

Americans have always underestimated Joe Biden, and they've done so at their own peril. It's easy to see why. He didn't do well in college or law school, his absentmindedness is legendary, and he doesn't speak with language that dazzles the elite, or anyone else, really. His mental and physical stumbles and bumbles instantly go viral online, giving his opponents many a self-satisfied laugh. His family is not a group of overachievers—far from it. Some of the most well-known Bidens are junkies and hustlers. I don't mean that pejoratively. They are literal junkies and hustlers. How do you build a dynasty with people like that?

Yet they're winning. Or at least Joe is winning, and the rest are reaping the spoils.

How? Why?

As of 2023, the Right has not figured out how to break Joe Biden. We've decided to declare that he is stupid and a puppet of a powerful and shadowy network of people. We have assumed he's physically frail, maybe even on the brink of death.

We're comfortable with that analysis, and we've moved on to other foes, both real and imagined.

Well, how's that approach going for us?

How's it going for the country?

In case you decided to skip ahead to the conclusion (by all means, go back and enjoy the entire book!), the answer is a resounding "not well."

Perhaps we got a few things wrong about Lunchbucket Joe over all these years.

First of all, he's not stupid, and never has been. He says stupid things, but he has a fastball. And he has other things going for him as well. His persona is a throwback to traditional masculinity, he never acts fearful, he's well tailored, and he doesn't indulge in petty squabbles with people who help him get stuff done. His most important skill is the one that is the most obvious: he seems to know what Democrat voters want, and he's all too happy to give it to them.

Combine all that with a lifelong belief that nothing is too good for a Biden and a freakish ability to take a punch, and lo and behold, you have the makings of a politician who has, as Richard Ben Cramer might put it, *what it takes*.

How did we miss all that?

Now in his eighties, he is presiding over a struggling America.

There is no way to sugarcoat it: fifty years into the Joe Biden era, America is on a descent.

Gallup reported in May 2023 that depression rates are at an all-time high.[1] Young Americans are dying at an alarming pace, largely from suicides and overdoses, reversing years of steady progress.[2] New York City police are resigning at a record rate.[3] LA County is handing out crack pipes to the homeless to prevent fentanyl deaths.[4] Hundreds of students in Chicago's public school system were raped or sexually assaulted in 2022.[5] Viral videos of hordes of zombified drug users, airport brawlers, and ransacked storefronts dot front pages and social media feeds every day.[6]

Train derailments, unusable schools, and filthy cities are everywhere.

Our border remains open, and we are releasing thousands of convicted criminals into our interior.[7]

More than a dozen cancer drugs were in short supply as of May 2023.[8]

Only 50 percent of us have a favorable view of our FBI.[9]

Only 20 percent of the country has faith in our election system.[10]

Half of Americans believe the news media are intentionally trying to mislead them—and they are.[11]

Median home prices rose more than a third between 2020 and 2022,[12] yet wages ticked up only a modest 4 percent per year.[13]

No one has held China accountable for the pandemic.

No one has been held accountable for the antiscience masking, lockdowns, and mandates.

And worst of all, perhaps, America is less fun.

All of this is causing we the people to punch out.

Everywhere you look, you're sure to see Americans with their heads down, staring at their phones, scrolling, scrolling, always scrolling.

We waste our money on meal delivery, Bubble Kush, Funko Pops!, OnlyFans subscriptions, and of course, infinite government programs.

What's happening to us? Why are we doing this to ourselves?

We've been demoralized, but we've also been distracted.

While Barack Obama wanted to fundamentally transform America, Joe Biden is *transitioning* it to some debased version of her former self.

Sometimes literally. He abruptly decided in his late seventies that the LGBTQQIAAP2S+ agenda is at the top of his priority list. His assistant secretary of health and human services has said that helping children change genders is supported at the "highest levels" of the administration.[14] First Lady Dr. Jill gave a "Women of Courage" award—to a biological man.[15] The U.S. Navy now has a drag queen digital ambassador to recruit "a wide range of potential candidates."[16] Apparently, it just recently dawned on Joe Biden after all his time in Washington that it is important to have trans people in the military.[17]

Joe Biden even flew the "Progress Pride" flag from the White House during June 2023 in clear violation of U.S. Flag Code §7. (For those of you who have no access to the Internet and never leave your house, America celebrates Ls, Gs, Bs, Ts, Qs, 2-spirit, and 3-spirit Americans throughout the entire month of June.) The "Progress Pride" flag is more than your typical rainbow flag: it has extra pink and blue stripes as a nod to the transgenders. Biden flew it in the center of a group of flags that included the American flag, which is prohibited, theoretically. It doesn't matter how many children are coerced into taking life-altering drugs or undergoing gruesome surgeries, or how many women have to lose to men in sports, Joe Biden wants America to know that he "stans" for the trans.

That same day, a trans influencer flashed *his* breasts on the White House lawn. And posed for a picture with the president, of course.

One of my editors at Breitbart News asked me, "Why does Biden do this?" I told him the answer is simple: this is what his base wants, and he delivers. It's one reason he keeps getting elected. He's mobilizing a new coalition of voters. In this case, they happen to be gender confused.

What we are experiencing is hyperwokeness inflation: a race to see who can signal their virtue, that is, their social justice warrior values, the fastest and the loudest. It is happening in our corporations and at the highest levels of our government, and it is moving the Overton window in terms of what are mainstream American values. It seems like just yesterday that we were debating same-sex marriage; now we're arguing over whether allowing adults to twerk on children in a public library is a civil right.

Did we even stop to discuss whether this is a net benefit for society?

There are so many battles ahead, yet none of them will matter if conservatives can't figure out one important thing: how to get more ballots into ballot boxes. This is the essence of community organizing. Elections are now less about the best slogans, the most accurate polling, the best policies, or even the best candidates; they're all about the ground game. Whatever party does the best job getting voters to turn in ballots for their candidates and causes is going to win. Just ask Joe Biden. In 2021, Biden issued "Executive Order on Promoting Access to Voting," which effectively allows him to use every bureaucratic agency to get out the vote.[18]

Advantage: Democrats.

Conservatives need to confront this reality. We cannot shine this on.

While we build up our army of volunteers, we have another massive obstacle in our path that we have to surmount: the new era of blacklisting. The U.S. government, social media companies, and the Democrat Party are all working together to censor content that could damage their electoral prospects. The aforementioned executive order on voting access declares that it is the reasonability of the federal government "to combat misinformation," which seems to be defined as anything the Democrats want censored. The Biden White House even pressured Facebook to crack down on Tucker Carlson.[19] They are playing to win, no matter what civil rights they trample upon in the process.

Conservatives have some wonderful spokespeople, reporters, and media outlets. We are even starting to build our own platforms. But nothing compares to what the political Left can do. The power of Google alone is incalculable. The Left writes Google's algorithm, controls Facebook's boardroom, and will no doubt program most popular first-gen AI in their image.

If Republicans think that complaining that Joe Biden spends too much time in his "basement" is going to negate that type of clout, they are living in a dream world.

Advantage: Democrats.

The Democrats designed the system, Joe Biden as much as anyone, and they are positioned to use it to dominate politics over the next several decades. If they do, they will institutionalize wokeness at a rapid rate, our institutions will be politicized even more than they are now, the collapse of our cities will accelerate, tax rates will rise, and our energy policy will place ideology above practical realities. If we are not asked to fight in more foreign wars, we'll certainly be paying for them.

Maybe even the end of Americanism as we know it is in the offing. The stakes are high, and things could get pretty bleak pretty fast.

Unless . . .

Unless, of course, other emerging trends win out.

Joe Biden is the last of a dying breed. Though his public persona is that of the moderate, working-class Democrat, he has governed like a member of the Squad. Democrats have come full circle during his fifty years in Washington. When he arrived in the Senate, he worked with segregationists in his own party. He even praised their "civility," noting that together they "got things done."[20] Now the modern Left is trying to reinstitutionalize racism in parts of society. Biden is a fitting person to link previous generations of Democrats to the race-obsessives who run the party today.

Diversity, equity, and inclusion rules put identity and inherited traits over merit in school admissions and the job market.

Discussions of slavery reparations have been a constant in recent years, particularly in the free state of California.[21] When I grew up there in the 1990s and 2000s, there was almost no discussion of race, positive or negative. Now here we are. Basic standards of professionalism are now considered white supremacy.[22] Punctuality is white supremacy. Speaking "perfect English" is white supremacy.[23] These are the new rules of the modern Left, the same group of people who run the Democrat establishment.

The America I know is not obsessed with race, gender, and identity. This is an opportunity for conservatives to reach new people who reject the premise that everything must be viewed through the prism of an oppressor/oppressed dichotomy.

As of now, Biden is set to leave his party without a clear heir. At this point in his narrative arc, he was supposed to pass the torch to Beau, who would have had a glide path to the White House. The machine would have made it so, and the Republicans would have been powerless to stop it. Now the best bets to succeed Joe Biden within his own administration are empty suits: Kamala Harris and Pete Buttigieg, both of whom have, to put it mildly, failed in their current administration jobs.

Outside the White House, radical Democrats within the House of Representatives provide ample social media energy that fires up base voters, but they offer little to Americans who don't think that Twitter is real life. California leftists Gavin Newsom and Eric Garcetti see themselves in the Oval Office, but Newsom squandered the chance of a lifetime: a rare budget surplus in a semi-socialist blue state. Former mayor Garcetti was caretaker of the City of Angels as it transformed into the city of looting and tent cities. Compelling but offbeat outsiders like Robert F. Kennedy Jr. will be disenfranchised by the corporate media establishment who don't want their system disrupted.

The wokeness inflation has also caused at least a bit of a backlash. As of June 2023, more Americans identified as social conservatives than at any other point in the last decade.[24]

In this case, advantage: conservatives, provided they can find the right message and the right messengers.

What Biden will leave behind to be sure is a playbook on how a powerful family can sell access to the American government—and do so without necessarily breaking the law. This stain on our republic isn't just on the Bidens: it's on our entire country, and it's time to close these loopholes the moment we get the chance.

Biden's legacy will also age like a slice of avocado toast. It is no secret that Democrat-controlled megacities are crime-ridden, filthy, and way too expensive. Their residents are fleeing to red states like Florida and Texas in droves, proving beyond a doubt the undeniable appeal of the conservative vision for the country.

The Left employs constant censorship, politicized investigations, and character assassinations to get what they want; these are all signs of a movement that lacks confidence in its own arguments and its own people. Besides, why would they be confident? As their constituents get older, they often switch parties, which means they have to keep the border open to ensure replacement voters flow in. The public is coming to the knowledge that our foreign policy has served the defense industry more than the American people, our energy policies are antihuman, and authoritarian pandemic responses did not serve their stated intent of shutting down the virus.[25]

Once again, advantage: conservatives.

What's more, while Joe Biden and the American oligarchs (sounds like an eighties band) have not delivered on their promises to U.S. citizens, our competition around the world has been struggling as well. Russia has become the poster child for an empire in decline, having proven itself to be almost comically weak in their war on Ukraine. China is beset by economic woes, raucous protests against the communist regime, and widespread apathy among their own people. The ruling class appears to be giving up on anticommunist millennials, who seem thoroughly uninterested in participating in the Chinese-style colonialism pushed by the CCP.[26] Though their cheap goods and Belt and Road debt trap diplomacy mean China is deeply intertwined with nations around the globe, affording it a substantial level of geopolitical security, it no longer seems inevitable that it will surpass America as the world's preeminent superpower.

I am heartened that some conservatives are finally externalizing Andrew Breitbart's immortal words that "politics is downstream from culture" in various media.[27] Yet we need a much more robust effort to disrupt the culture if we want to defeat juggernauts like Hollywood, Silicon Valley, and increasingly woke Wall Street. We can make all the excuses we want as to why we are behind, but if we want to keep our republic, we have to persevere.

We have to do whatever it takes to reach voters. We have to crave "the connect," the same way Joe Biden did. Messaging is key, outreach is key, but ultimately, the goal is clear: get the ballots into the ballot boxes. Pockets of California and Florida[28] proved in the 2022 election that it is possible to beat the Democrats at their own game, but it won't be easy, and they will be honing their tactics and expanding their arsenal while we try to catch up. It will take time to master this game, but we have to play it nonetheless.

If we stand down, we turn the country over to Joe Biden and the hidden forces and secret money machine that made him possible. Americanism will be replaced by a cross section of Deep State semi-authoritarianism and woke globalist leftism.

But it doesn't have to be this way. We can choose a different path.

It is said that the price of liberty is eternal vigilance. It is time to renew that bond with one another.

This is America. Land of the free and home of the brave. Now let's act like it.

EPILOGUE

In 2018, the federal government began investigating Hunter Biden over the millions he was making from deals with overseas entities. The investigation began as a tax case: the DOJ alleged that he had owed taxes on more than seven figures in income. The investigation unveiled a slew of apparent violations, the most eye-popping being that a former investigator claimed that Hunter was deducting payments to prostitutes as a business expense.[1] (Is Hunter running a bordello?) The probe expanded into money laundering, foreign lobbying, as well as a gun charge.[2]

Interestingly, what set off the IRS investigation was not Hunter's foreign business activities, lavish spending, or association with various white-collar criminals and unsavory international characters. No, the investigation spun out of an IRS probe into a foreign amateur porn platform.[3]

Hunter's penis had gotten him into trouble yet again.

In June of 2023, Hunter admitted to not paying taxes on more than $1.5 million each in 2017 and 2018 and signed a deal with the US Attorney in Delaware, pleading guilty to two charges of tax evasion. He also agreed to a pretrial diversion program over the gun charge; Hunter had lied about his drug use while purchasing a firearm, as detailed earlier in this book.

He has escaped prosecution and jail time thus far, giving Biden and Democrats reason to rejoice. The message to the world is that there is nothing more to see. All of this resolved a comfy seventeen months from the next election. Rep. Daniel Goldman (D-NY) even suggested that "[Hunter] should be commended for taking accountability and accepting responsibility for what he did. He has paid off the taxes that he was delinquent in paying long ago. And he's now accepting responsibility."[4]

He should be *commended*. They're trolling us again.

Simultaneously, Hunter was skating on his personal delinquencies. The same week he settled with federal prosecutors, he also settled his long running child-support dispute with his former girlfriend and baby mama Lunden Roberts. Hunter would pay only an inexplicably low $5,000, down from the $20,000 per month Roberts had initially demanded.

Hunter had done it again. He had gotten away with everything.

It was time to celebrate and live deliciously, and it just so happened that he had an invite to the marquee social event of the summer: the White House state dinner. Yes, Hunter Biden's first public appearance after the deal was at a black-tie banquet hosted by President Pop honoring Indian Prime Minister Narendra Modi. Hunter, flaunting a mouth full of custom toilet bowl-tinted dentures to match his dad's, hob-knobbed with a who's who of Hollywood, tech, politics, and diplomacy. Uncle James and sister, Ashley, were in attendance as well, among other Bidens.[5]

Also on the guest list was Attorney General Merrick Garland, who had appointed the special counsel that had indicted former president Trump less than two weeks prior for mishandling classified documents. Garland brazenly selected Jack Smith to head up the investigation into the Republican standard bearer despite the fact that Smith's wife donated thousands of dollars to Joe Biden's campaign.[6]

Joe Biden got to watch his degenerate son living his best life at the exact moment his chief political rival was getting pressurized by his own Department of Justice. Joe himself has yet to face any consequences for keeping classified documents at his home in Wilmington, Delaware, that could have been easily accessed by the likes of Hunter, an admitted criminal.

In the figurative sense, this is all wildly unjust. In the legal sense, it is all appears to be permissible. The Bidens were using the system to their advantage yet again. Without any accountability of consequences, the influence peddling will continue or even intensify. And if the heat gets turned up on the Bidens, look for them to sharpen their tactics.

Attorney Kevin Morris, who has emerged as Hunter's new fixer and a central player in the Biden Business, got control over the LLC through which Hunter owns his stake in BHR Partners, the Chinese equity fund. That stake is potentially worth tens of millions of dollars. It was Morris, in fact, who paid off the delinquent tax bill that landed Hunter in hot water, lending him $2 million.[7] Now Morris in a position to bag commie cash, thanks to and/or on behalf of the First Family.

Yet it is unlikely that Hunter's legal woes are entirely resolved. In a press release announcing the deal over the tax and gun charges, the U.S. Attorney for Delaware noted that, nonetheless, the investigation was still "ongoing."[8]

So, perhaps, there will be more to this story after all. To quote Joe, STAY TUNED. . . .

As I am completing work on this book, House Oversight Committee chairman James Comer (R-KY) is conducting what is likely the deepest investigation ever into Hunter Biden. Comer revealed that the FBI knew that Burisma had attempted to bribe Hunter and Joe Biden, among other details previously mentioned in this book, such as that Hunter wrote off payments to hookers and that the White House intervened to shield his art business from public scrutiny.

Presumably there will be more revelations to follow.

In a testimony before the House Ways and Means Committee, a whistleblower who had overseen the Hunter Biden investigation at the IRS claimed that the Department of Justice, especially U.S. Attorney for Delaware David Weiss, impeded aspects of the case.

The IRS also handed over a 2017 WhatsApp message Hunter had sent to Henry Zhao, one of his associates at BHR Partners, the Chinese private equity fund in which he is a partner. The message speaks volumes:

> I am sitting here with my father, and we would like to understand why the commitment made has not been fulfilled. Tell the director that I would like to resolve this now before it gets out of hand, and now means tonight. And, Z, if I get a call or text from anyone involved in this other than you, Zhang, or the chairman, I will make certain that between the man sitting next to me and every person he knows and my ability to forever hold a grudge that you will regret not following my direction. I am sitting here waiting for the call with my father.[9]

Seriously, is Scorsese on the Biden payroll to punch up their text messages?

Photographs from Hunter's laptop showed he was at Joe's house the day he sent his threatening message to Zhao.[10] Was Joe literally sitting with his son at the time? It's impossible to know, but what difference does it make? He was certainly there in spirit.

In response to questions about this particular text message, the White House narrowed their language from the fundamentally dishonest claim that Joe "never discussed" business with his family to the much more lawyerly assertion that the president is "not in business" with his son.[11]

So much for that "absolute wall" between Hunter and Joe.

Biden World has thrived off of the intermingling of government and business—foreign business, no less. That is their bailiwick. The family capitalizes on the family name, and they can finally attain the social status Joe aspired to achieve for them since he was a boy. The revolving door of consultants, lobbyists, and activists that surround Biden are all part of the machine.

The true history of the Bidens reads like a political thriller. Drugs, sex, death, money, power, deceit, and treachery are at the essence of their family history. For better or worse—usually for worse, I believe—they have charted their own unique course. Yet, the Democrats argue that it is Joe and the Bidens who are the victims of politicized attacks. Their suggestion is that if the Bidens are so bad, point to all the laws that they have broken.

But that's precisely the point. It's not that the Bidens have broken so many laws, it is that they have seemingly broken so few. And when they do break them, they never lose their freedoms.

That's the system. That's their system. That's how it was designed.

ACKNOWLEDGMENTS

There are many people who made *Breaking Biden* possible.

Whenever I've written anything, I've written it for my family. Every time I sit down to my keyboard, the goal is to make the world a slightly better place for them. Every time I complete a major project like this book, it is because I had their support. Mrs. Dr. Marlow, Master Marlow, Master Marlow Jr., Duchess Marlow, Molly Marlow, Robert Marlow, Wynn Marlow, Lauren Wilson, and Francesco Federico are my people. This is their book, too.

One of the best parts about writing *Breaking Biden* was having another chance to work with my editor, Natasha Simons, who is a literary force multiplier, and my agent, Tom Flannery. I wouldn't have started this book, much less completed it, had they not believed in me and in this project. Also thank you to super-agent David Vigliano for his wisdom and support. Many thanks to the team at Simon & Schuster for doing the thankless work of putting the book together.

I was fortunate enough to recruit a team of researchers who all have more experience working on bestsellers than I have. They helped me unearth details, organize thoughts, tell stories, and, most important, maintain the highest degree of accuracy possible. My head of research, Jacob McCleod, and my associate researchers, Mark Hoekenga, Price Sukhia, Peggy Sukhia, and Jedd McFatter, deserve immense credit.

As if I wasn't already fortunate enough, Breitbart News' John Binder, John Carney, and the one and only Emma-Jo Morris supplied essential research for this book as well. They are brilliant and generous. My colleagues bless me every day. Our CEO, Larry Solov, to whom I owe a debt of gratitude, has set me up to succeed.

I completed this book with the support of the Government Accountability Institute (GAI) and its president, Peter Schweizer. Peter is a badass with a heart of gold. His research changes the world, and his insight helps me walk in his footsteps. Having the rest of GAI in my corner, particularly Stuart Christmas, has been an ace up my sleeve.

Finally, I would like to thank Corn Pop for not sticking Joe Biden with his jagged rusty straight razor that summer at the Wilmington, Delaware, municipal pool. Had he done so, *Breaking Biden* might never have been written.

And to Andrew, thank you for everything.

NOTES

INTRODUCTION

1 "Vice President cited Irish-American mom's influence," *Irish Echo*, February 17, 2011, https://group.irishecho.com/2011/02/vice-president -cited-irish-american-moms-influence-2/.

2 Brandi Kruse, "CHOP: Seattle mayor walks back 'summer of love' comment," Fox 13 Seattle, June 22, 2020, https://www.q13fox.com/news/chop-seattle -mayor-walks-back-summer-of-love-comment.

3 "More Than 2,000 Officers Injured in Summer's Protests and Riots," *Police Magazine*, December 3, 2020, https://www.policemag.com/585160/more -than-2-000-officers-injured-in-summers-protests-and-riots.

4 David Propper, "Stephan Cannon gets life for killing ex-St. Louis Police Capt. David Dorn amid 2020 riots," *New York Post*, https://nypost.com/2022/10/05 /stephan-cannon-gets-life-sentence-in-killing-of-david-dorn/.

5 Ben Shreckinger, *The Bidens* (New York: Hachette Book Group, 2021), 45–47.

6 John Hendrickson, "What Joe Biden Can't Bring Himself to Say." *Atlantic*, January 2020, https://www.theatlantic.com/magazine/archive/2020/01/joe -biden-stutter-profile/602401/.

7 Meredith Newman, "How Joe Biden went from 'Stutterhead' to senior class president," Delaware Online, June 24, 2019, https://www.delaware online.com/story/news/2019/06/24/how-joe-biden-overcame-stutter-class -president-archmere-high-school/1261174001/.

8 Kate Sullivan, "Biden offers words of encouragement to young girl with stut-ter," CNN, November 29, 2011, https://www.cnn.com/2021/11/29/politics /biden-stutter-encouragement-video/index.html.

9 Newman, "How Joe Biden went from . . ." https://www.delawareonline.com /story/news/2019/06/24/how-joe-biden-overcame-stutter-class-president -archmere-high-school/1261174001/.

10 Schreckinger, *The Bidens*.

11 Untitled article (Biden's law school record and plagiarism accusations), Associ-ated Press, https://apnews.com/article/cd977f7ff301993f7976974ba07c5495.

12 Jenni Fink, "Joe Biden, Elected to Tame the Virus Sees His VOCID Death Toll Surpass Donald Trump's," *Newsweek*, January 14, 2022, https://www.newsweek

.com/joe-biden-elected-tame-virus-sees-his-covid-death-toll-surpass
-donald-trumps-1654136.

13 Read Pickert, "Core US Inflation Rises to 40-Year High, Securing Big Fed
Hike," *Bloomberg News*, October 13, 2022, https://www.bloomberg.com
/news/articles/2022-10-13/core-us-inflation-rises-to-40-year-high
-securing-big-fed-hike#:~:text=The%20core%20consumer%20price%20
index,Labor%20Department%20data%20showed%20Thursday.

14 Emma Kinery, "Biden blames extreme MAGA Republicans for intimidating voters and election officials, calling it 'corrosive' to democracy," CNBC,
November 2, 2022, https://www.cnbc.com/2022/11/02/biden-blames-ex
treme-maga-republicans-for-intimidating-voters-election-officials.html

15 Mike McIntire and Serge Kovaleski, "An Everyman on the Trail, With
Perks at Home," *New York Times*, October 1, 2008, https://www.nytimes
.com/2008/10/02/us/politics/02finances.html.

16 Miranda Devine, "Kathleen Buhle, Hunter Biden's ex, married a total sleaze-
ball," *New York Post*, June 12, 2022, https://nypost.com/2022/06/12
/kathleen-buhle-married-a-biden-sleazeball/.

17 "When Joe Biden Plagiarized Bobby Kennedy," *BuzzFeed News*, July 15, 2012,
https://www.buzzfeednews.com/article/buzzfeedpolitics/when-joe-biden
-plagiarized-bobby-kennedy.

18 Alex Thompson, "'The President Was Not Encouraging': What Obama Really
Thought About Biden," *Politico*, August 14, 2020, https://www.politico.com
/news/magazine/2020/08/14/obama-biden-relationship-393570.

19 Patrick Reilly, "Biden recalls 'the old days' of grabbing lunch with 'real
segregationists' in Senate," *New York Post*, May 7, 2022, https://nypost
.com/2022/05/07/biden-recalls-eating-lunch-with-senate-segregationists
-james-eastland-strom-thurmond/.

20 John Harwood, "Institutional racism the problem, not '94 crime bill: Biden,"
CNBC, April 19, 2016, https://www.cnbc.com/2016/04/19/institutional
-racism-the-problem-not-crime-bill-biden.html.

21 Justin Jouvenal, "Biden helped usher in an era of mass incarceration. Can
he now end it?," *Washington Post*, January 11, 2021, https://www.washington
post.com/politics/2021/01/11/biden-mass-incarceration/.

22 Hannah Bleau, "Joe Biden Admits 1994 Crime Bill Was a 'Mistake' During
Town Hall," Breitbart News, October 15, 2020, https://www.breitbart.com
/law-and-order/2020/10/15/joe-biden-admits-1994-crime-bill-was-mistake
-during-town-hall/.

23 Charlie Spiering, "Joe Biden Brain Freeze: 'Let Me Start Off with Two Words
– Made in America,'" Breitbart News, October 7, 2022, https://www.breitbart
.com/politics/2022/10/07/joe-biden-brain-freeze-let-me-start-off-with-two
-words-made-in-america/.

24 Charlie Spiering, "'A Pound of Ukrainian People'? 10 Brain Freezes in Joe
Biden's State of the Union Delivery," Breitbart News, March 1, 2022, https://
www.breitbart.com/politics/2022/03/01/joe-bidens-stumbles-through-state
-of-the-union/.

25 Amy Sherman, "Joe Biden's Pants on Fire claim about his arrest in South Africa," *Politifact*, March 4, 2020, https://www.politifact.com/factchecks/2020
/mar/04/joe-biden/joe-bidens-pants-fire-claim-about-his-arrest-south/.

26 Sherman, "Joe Biden's Pants on Fire."

27 John Nolte, "Biden Uses Jewish Slur 'Shylock,'" *Breitbart News,* September 17, 2014, https://www.breitbart.com/politics/2014/09/17/biden-shylock/.

28 Astead Herndon and Katie Glueck, "Biden Apologizes for Saying Black Voters 'Ain't Black' if They're Considering Trump," *New York Times,* May 22, 2020, https://www.nytimes.com/2020/05/22/us/politics/joe-biden-black-breakfast -club.html.

29 Paul Bois, "Watch: Joe Biden Incorrectly Claims His Son Beau 'Lost His Life in Iraq,'" Breitbart News, October 12, 2022, https://www.breitbart.com /politics/2022/10/12/watch-joe-biden-incorrectly-claims-his-son-beau-lost -his-life-in-iraq/.

30 Tamar Lapin, "Joe Biden calls woman 'lying dog-faced pony soldier' at campaign event," *New York Post,* February 9, 2020, https://nypost.com/2020/02/09 /joe-biden-calls-woman-lying-dog-faced-pony-soldier-at-campaign-event/.

31 "'I'd beat the hell out of him' says Joe Biden of Trump—video," *Guardian,* March 22, 2018, https://www.theguardian.com/us-news/video/2018/mar/22 /id-beat-the-hell-out-of-him-says-joe-biden-of-trump-video.

32 "1988 Road to the White House with Sen. Biden," YouTube video, 2:38, posted by "C-Span," August 23, 2008, https://www.youtube.com/watch?v=D 1j0FS0Z6ho.

33 James Dickenson, "Biden Academic Claims 'Inaccurate,'" *Washington Post,* September 22, 1987, https://www.washingtonpost.com/archive /politics/1987/09/22/biden-academic-claims-inaccurate/932 eaeed-9071-47a1-aeac-c94a51b668e1/; "Biden's 'mistakes' caught up with him," *Tampa Bay Times,* October 3, 2002, https://www.tampabay.com /archive/2002/10/03/biden-s-mistakes-caught-up-with-him/.

34 Peter Wade, "Obama Ethics Chief Scoffs at White House Plan to Keep Hunter Biden Art Sales Anonymous," *Rolling Stone,* July 11, 2021, https://www .rollingstone.com/politics/politics-news/obama-hunter-biden-art-sales -anonymous-1195623/.

35 Tim Hains, "Peter Schweizer: Hunter Biden Paid for a Private Global Cell Phone for Joe Biden While He Was Vice President," RealClearPolitics, June 25, 2023, https://www.realclearpolitics.com/video/2023/06/25/peter _schweizer_oversight_committee_must_subpoena_records_of_cell_phone _hunter_got_for_joe_biden.html.

PART I: THE BIDEN BUSINESS

CHAPTER 1: JOE BIDEN CAN DO ANYTHING

1 Richard Ben Cramer, *What It Takes* (New York: Random House, 1992), 262.

2 Adam Entous, "The Untold History of the Biden Family," *New Yorker,* August 22, 2022, https://www.newyorker.com/magazine/2022/08/22/the -untold-history-of-the-biden-family.

3 Entous, "The Untold History."

4 Cramer, *What It Takes,* 251–52.

5 Cramer, *What It Takes,* 251–52.

6 Allan Smith and Mike Memoli, "Biden calls Iowa voter who pushed him

on Ukraine 'a damn liar,' challenges him to pushup contest," NBC News, December 5, 2019, https://www.nbcnews.com/politics/2020-election/biden-calls-iowa-voter-who-pushed-him-ukraine-damn-liar-n1096646.

7   Entous, "The Untold History." https://www.newyorker.com/magazine/2022/08/22/the-untold-history-of-the-biden-family.

8   Schreckinger, *The Bidens.*

9   Joe Biden, *Promises to Keep* (New York: Random House, 2007).

10   Hendrickson, "What Joe Biden Can't." Janet Hook, "Joe Biden's childhood struggle with a stutter: How he overcame it and how it shaped him," *Los Angeles Times,* September 15, 2019, https://www.latimes.com/politics/story/2019-09-15/joe-bidens-childhood-struggle-with-a-stutter.

11   Newman, "How Joe Biden went from 'Stutterhead' "; Lochlahn March, "A look back at Joe Biden's days as an athlete," *Daily Pennsylvanian,* August 20, 2020, https://www.thedp.com/article/2020/08/joe-biden-penn-athletics-football-archmere-2020-election-delaware.

12   Jay Busbee, "The story of Joe Biden, football star," Yahoo, January 18, 2021, https://www.yahoo.com/video/the-story-of-joe-bidens-high-school-football-heroics-202613291.html.

13   Brad Myers, "White House visit with Biden thrills Archmere football team," Delaware Online, July 11, 2022, https://www.delawareonline.com/story/sports/high-school/2022/07/11/president-biden-hosts-archmere-football-team-at-white-house/65369710007/.

14   March, "A look back at Joe Biden's days."

15   "Biden's Law School Ranking Not as He Said," *Los Angeles Times,* September 21, 1987, https://www.latimes.com/archives/la-xpm-1987-09-21-mn-6104-story.html.

16   Mark Weiner, "Joe Biden's Syracuse law school professor: 'This guy will do what is right,' " Syracuse.com. January 20, 2021, https://www.syracuse.com/politics/2021/01/joe-bidens-syracuse-law-school-professor-this-guy-will-do-what-is-right.html.

17   Weiner, "Joe Biden's Syracuse law school professor."

18   E. J. Dionne Jr., "Biden Admits Plagiarism in School But Says It was Not 'Malevolent,' " *New York Times,* September 18, 1987, https://www.nytimes.com/1987/09/18/us/biden-admits-plagiarism-in-school-but-says-it-was-not-malevolent.html; Paul Taylor, "Biden Admits Plagiarizing In Law School," *Washington Post,* September 18, 1987, https://www.washingtonpost.com/archive/politics/1987/09/18/biden-admits-plagiarizing-in-law-school/53047c90-c16d-4f3a-9317-a106be8f6102/; Jack Dutton, "Did Joe Biden Cheat in Law School? What He Has Said About 'Stupid' Mistake," *Newsweek,* May 20, 2022, https://www.newsweek.com/did-joe-biden-cheat-law-school-what-he-has-said-about-stupid-mistake-1708548.

19   Sean Kirst, "Syracuse homecoming bittersweet for Biden: 'Sometimes it just overwhelms me,' " Syracuse.com, June 1, 2002, https://www.syracuse.com/kirst/2002/05/syracuse_homecoming_bitterswee.html.

20   Henry Gomez, "Joe Biden's Time As A Public Defender Was A Brief Line On His Résumé. Now It's A Virtue Signal For His Campaign," *BuzzFeed News,* July 25, 2019, https://www.buzzfeednews.com/article/henrygomez/joe

-biden-public-defender; Steven Levingston, "Joe Biden: Life Before the Presidency," University of Virginia Miller Center, accessed June 12, 2023, https://millercenter.org/joe-biden-life-presidency.

21 Levingston, "Joe . . . Before Presidency."

22 Shreckinger, *The Bidens*, 28.

23 Matt Viser, "Biden's sister, Valerie, at his side for 74 years—and for one final goal," *Washington Post*, August 30, 2020, https://www.washingtonpost.com /politics/valerie-joe-biden-sister/2020/08/28/7d6998a8-e22c-11ea-8dd2 -d07812bf00f7_story.html.

24 Cramer, *What It Takes*, 266.

25 Rob Crilly, "Jill Biden's ex-husband paid hitman Frank 'The Irishman' Sheeran $3K to set up a strike and stop the delivery of Delaware newspapers with anti-Biden ads before Joe's shock 1972 Senate win, book claims," *Daily Mail*, September 10, 2021, https://www.dailymail.co.uk/news/article-9971555/Jill-Bidens-ex-husband -claims-paid-Frank-Irishman-Sheeran-3-000-help-Joe-win-1972.html.

26 Joe Biden, *Promises to Keep*, quote accessed via Good Reads on June 12, 2023, https://www.goodreads.com/quotes/133759-my-own-father-had-always -said-the-measure-of-a.

27 Kitty Kelley, "Death and the All-American," *Washingtonian*, June 1, 2974, https://www.washingtonian.com/1974/06/01/joe-biden-kitty-kelley-1974 -profile-death-and-the-all-american-boy/.

28 Max Cohen, "Biden says he thought about suicide after 1972 death of his wife and daughter," *Politico*, August 17, 2020, https://www.politico.com /news/2020/08/17/biden-contemplated-suicide-after-1972-deaths-wife -daughter-397487.

29 David Wilcox, "Hunter Dinerant in Auburn closes," *Auburn Pub*, December 31, 2022, https://auburnpub.com/news/local/hunter-dinerant-in -auburn-closes/article_4d4d3b0f-b61d-57a1-ac86-869d51547ce2.html.

30 Michael Kruse, "How Grief Became Joe Biden's 'Superpower,' " *Politico*, January 25, 2019, https://www.politico.eu/article/how-grief-became-joe -bidens-superpower-vice-president-2020/.

31 Seth Abramovitch, "Kitty Kelley, Queen of the Unauthorized Biography, Spills Her Own Secrets," *Hollywood Reporter*, March 3, 2022, https:// www.hollywoodreporter.com/lifestyle/arts/kitty-kelley-interview -unauthorized-biographies-1235101933/.

32 Abramovitch, "Kitty Kelley, Queen."

33 Kruse, "How Grief Became Joe Biden's 'Superpower.' "

34 Karen Travers, "Vice President Biden and Wife Defend Washington Marriages," ABC News, https://abcnews.go.com/GMA/Valentine/vice-president -joe-biden-wife-jill-biden-marriage/story?id=9812470.

35 Schreckinger, *The Bidens*, 28.

36 Schreckinger, *The Bidens*, 53–56.

37 Byron York, "The Senator from MBNA," *National Review*, August 23, 2008, https://www.nationalreview.com/2008/08/senator-mbna-byron-york/; Chiana Dickson, "Joe Biden's houses—explore the real estate portfolio of the POTUS," *Homes & Gardens*, November 9, 2022, https://www .homesandgardens.com/news/joe-biden-house.

38 E. J. Dionne Jr., "Biden Joins Campaign for the Presidency," *New York*

Times, June 10, 1987, https://www.nytimes.com/1987/06/10/us/biden-joins-campaign-for-the-presidency.html.

39 Cramer, *What It Takes,* 364, 367.

40 Maureen Dowd, "Biden's Debate Finale: An Echo From Abroad," *New York Times,* September 12, 1987, https://www.nytimes.com/1987/09/12/us/biden-s-debate-finale-an-echo-from-abroad.html.

41 Dowd, "Biden's Debate Finale."

42 Jon Margolis and Elaine Povich, "September 24, 1987: Biden admits errors, drops out," *Chicago Tribune,* September 24, 1987, accessed via Wayback Machine on June 12, 2023, https://web.archive.org/web/20230208204811/https://www.chicagotribune.com/news/ct-xpm-1987-09-24-8703120482-story.html.

43 Taylor, "Biden Admits Plagiarizing"; Olivia Waxman, "Why Joe Biden's First Campaign for President Collapsed After Just 3 Months," *Time,* August 2, 2019, https://time.com/5636715/biden-1988-presidential-campaign/.

44 Associated Press, "Biden Resting After Surgery For Second Brain Aneurysm," *New York Times,* May 4, 1988, https://www.nytimes.com/1988/05/04/us/biden-resting-after-surgery-for-second-brain-aneurysm.html.

45 Meredith Newman, "What Joe Biden learned from his life-threatening brain aneurysms," *Delaware Online,* March 18, 2019, https://www.delawareonline.com/story/news/politics/joe-biden/2019/03/18/joe-biden-2020-how-then-senator-overcame-life-threatening-brain-aneurysms/3002961002/.

46 Marc Caputo, "We talked to experts on aging about the 2020 field. Here's what they told us," *Politico,* August 20, 2019, https://www.politico.com/story/2019/08/20/joe-biden-old-age-1468635.

47 Newman, "What Joe Biden learned from his."

48 "Valerie Biden Owens," biography, Harvard Kennedy School Institute of Politics, Fall 2014, accessed June 12, 2023, https://iop.harvard.edu/fellows/valerie-biden-owens.

49 Alex Thompson and Tyler Pager, "They failed spectacularly in '88. Now, these Biden aides are getting sweet redemption.," *Politico,* January 19, 2021, https://www.politico.com/news/2021/01/19/joe-biden-1988-campaign-redemption-460332.

50 William Safire, "ESSAY; Upgrade the Court," *New York Times,* August 12, 1987, https://www.nytimes.com/1987/08/12/opinion/essay-upgrade-the-court.html.

51 George Will, "Biden v. Bork," *Washington Post,* July 2, 1987, https://www.washingtonpost.com/archive/opinions/1987/07/02/biden-v-bork/be124295-d2a5-4353-ad3a-a05c20ee0c32/; Tamara Keith, "Joe Biden, 1987 Brought Triumph in the Wake of Political Setback," NPR, December 21, 2019, https://www.npr.org/2019/12/21/789323826/for-joe-biden-1987-brought-triumph-in-the-wake-of-political-setback.

52 Quint Forgey, "5 landmark Justice Kennedy opinions," *Politico,* June 27, 2018, https://www.politico.com/story/2018/06/27/anthony-kennedy-retirement-supreme-court-opinions-680044.

53 Ron Elving, "A Refresher On Anita Hill And Clarence Thomas," NPR, December 10, 2017, https://www.npr.org/2017/12/10/569716802/a-refresher-on-anita-hill-and-clarence-thomas.

54 Jane Meyer, "What Joe Biden Hasn't Owned Up To About Anita Hill," *New*

Yorker, April 27, 2019, https://www.newyorker.com/news/news-desk/what
-joe-biden-hasnt-owned-up-to-about-anita-hill; Sarah Gray, "Joe Biden says
he regrets not getting Anita Hill 'the kind of hearing she deserved,' " *Business
Insider,* March 26, 2019, https://www.businessinsider.com/joe-biden-regrets
-1991-anita-hill-hearings-metoo-movement-2019-3.

CHAPTER 2: THE BIDEN DYNASTY

1 "#BREAKING: Joe Biden holds press conference for first time in months |
Full Event Q&A," YouTube video, posted by *The Hill,* June 30, 2020, https://
www.youtube.com/watch?v=GeAYelRbs1E&t=21s.

2 Holmes Lybrand, "Fact check: Biden says he hasn't taken a cognitive test. Is
he flip-flopping?," CNN, August 5, 2020, https://www.cnn.com/2020/08/05
/politics/joe-biden-donald-trump-jr-cognitive-test-fact-check/index.html.

3 Marc Caputo, "We talked to experts on aging about the 2020 field. Here's
what they told us," *Politico,* August 20, 2009, https://www.politico.com
/story/2019/08/20/joe-biden-old-age-1468635.

4 Michael Shear, "Biden Has Begun Using a CPAP Machine for Sleep Apnea,"
New York Times, June 28, 2023, https://www.nytimes.com/2023/06/28/us
/politics/biden-cpap-sleep-apnea.html.

5 Linda Wells, "Eye of the Beholder," *Airmail,* July 23, 2022, https://airmail
.news/issues/2022-7-23/eye-of-the-beholder.

6 Wells, "Eye of the Beholder."

7 "Joe Biden 'Corn Pop' Story Full Segment," YouTube video, posted by WITN
Channel 22, September 17, 2019, https://www.youtube.com/watch?v=
oihV9yrZRHg.

8 "Joe Biden 'Corn Pop' Story Full Segment."

9 "Roach," The Racial Slur Database, accessed June 12, 2023, http://www
.racialslurs.net/slur/roach.

10 "Foot-in-Mouth Disease: Diversity in Delaware?," *Time,* June 17,
2006, https://content.time.com/time/specials/packages/article/0,28804,1895
156_1894977_1643323,00.html.

11 Ted Barrett and Xuan Thai, "Biden's description of Obama draws scrutiny,"
CNN, February 9, 2007, https://www.cnn.com/2007/POLITICS/01/31/biden
.obama/.

12 "Biden 'put you all back in chains' remark causes stir," YouTube video,
posted by CBS News, August 14, 2012, https://www.youtube.com/watch?v=
5gII8D-lzbA.

13 Colby Itkowitz, "Biden: 'Make sure the record player is on at night' so kids
hear more words," *Washington Post,* September 12, 2019, https://www
.washingtonpost.com/politics/2019/live-updates/election-2020/third
-democratic-debate-analysis-and-fact-checking/biden-make-sure-the
-record-player-is-on-at-night-so-kids-hear-more-words/.

14 "BIDEN GAFFE: 'Chuck, Stand Up, Let Them See Ya!,'" YouTube video, posted
by BlazeTV, August 26, 2015, https://www.youtube.com/watch?v=Rkr-le
Pr7jA.

15 Tristan Justice, "Joe Biden Says Campaign Lawyers Are Going To 'Voter
Registration Physicians,' " *Federalist,* July 21, 2020, https://thefederalist

.com/2020/07/21/joe-biden-says-campaign-lawyers-are-going-to-voter
-registration-physicians/.

16 Julie Fine, "NBC 5 Exclusive: Biden Talks Oil, Pandemic and Chances in
Texas," NBC, October 26, 2020, https://www.nbcdfw.com/news/politics/nbc
-5-exclusive-biden-talks-oil-pandemic-and-chances-in-texas/2467130/.

17 Joey Garrison, " 'Where's Jackie?' President Biden calls out dead congresswoman during speech," Yahoo News, September 29, 2022, https://www
.yahoo.com/news/wheres-jackie-president-biden-calls-163720517.html.

18 Joseph R. Biden, "Remarks by President Biden Marking the 30th Anniversary of the Family and Medical Leave Act" (speech), February 2, 2023,
The White House, https://www.whitehouse.gov/briefing-room/speeches
-remarks/2023/02/02/remarks-by-president-biden-marking-the-30th
-anniversary-of-the-family-and-medical-leave-act/#:~:text=But%20
here's%20what%20matters.,%2C%20that's%20across%20the%20
board.%E2%80%9D.

19 Adam Sabes, "Biden slammed for laughing while discussing mom who lost
two children to fentanyl: 'Shameful,' " Fox News, March 1, 2023, https://www
.foxnews.com/politics/biden-criticized-laughing-discussing-mom-lost-two
-children-fentanyl.

20 Wendell Husebo, "Joe Biden's Top 3 Gaffes and Awkward Moments in Ireland:
'Go Lick the World,' " Breitbart News, April 14, 2023, https://www.breitbart
.com/politics/2023/04/14/joe-bidens-top-3-gaffes-and-awkward-moments
-in-ireland-go-lick-the-world/.

21 Natasha Korecki (@natashakorecki) "Oops: Biden says 'we choose truth
over facts,' " Twitter, August 8, 2019, https://twitter.com/natashakorecki
/status/1159537956912336896.

22 "Joe Biden Answers the Web's Most Searched Questions," YouTube video,
posted by Wired, May 21, 2020, https://www.youtube.com/watch?v=
nGrB-5ieeMU.

23 Alexandra Jaffe, "Senator's daughter doesn't think Biden's 'creepy,' " CNN,
January 12, 2015, https://www.cnn.com/2015/01/12/politics/biden-maggie
-coons-creepy/index.html.

24 Charlie Spiering, "Joe Biden's Awkwardly Long Hug with Hillary Clinton," Breitbart News, August 15, 2016, https://www.breitbart.com
/politics/2016/08/15/joe-bidens-awkwardly-long-hug-hillary-clinton/.

25 Jordan Dixon-Hamilton, "Watch: Joe Biden Nibbles Toddler's Shoulder on
Final Day of European Trip," Breitbart News, July 14, 2023, https://www.bre
itbart.com/politics/2023/07/14/watch-joe-biden-nibbles-toddlers-shoulder
-on-final-day-of-european-trip/.

26 Lisa Lerer, Jim Rutenberg, Stephanie Saul, "Tara Reade's Tumultuous Journey to the 2020 Campaign," New York Times, June 5, 2020, www.nytimes
.com/2020/05/31/us/politics/tara-reade-joe-biden.html.

27 Michael Barbaro, host, "Examining an Allegation Against Joe Biden," New
York Times: The Daily (podcast), April 14, 2020, https://www.nytimes
.com/2020/04/14/podcasts/the-daily/joe-biden-sexual-assault-allegation.html.

28 Jack Shafer, "Opinion: No, the Media Isn't Burying the Biden Allegations," Politico, April 29, 2020, https://www.politico.com/news/magazine/2020/04/29
/no-the-media-isnt-burying-the-biden-allegations-221920.

29 Asma Khalid, "On The Record: A Former Biden Staffer's Sexual Assault Allegation," NPR, April 19, 2020, https://www.npr.org/2020/04/19/837966525/on-the-record-a-former-biden-staffers-sexual-assault-allegation.

30 Asma Khalid, "On The Record: A Former Biden Staffer's."

31 Barbaro, "Examining an Allegation Against Joe Biden."

32 Natasha Korecki, "'Manipulative, deceitful, user': Tara Reade left a trail of aggrieved acquaintances," Politico, May 15, 2020, https://www.politico.com/news/2020/05/15/tara-reade-left-trail-of-aggrieved-acquaintances-260771.

33 United States Department of Justice, "United States of America v. Aimee Harris and Robert Kurlander," https://www.justice.gov/usao-sdny/press-release/file/1528671/download.

34 Andrew Rice, "Will Ashley Biden's Diary Take Down Project Veritas? After a decade of punking liberals with hidden-camera stings, James O'Keefe becomes the story," New York Intelligencer, January 16, 2023, https://nymag.com/intelligencer/article/project-veritas-james-okeefe-ashley-biden-diary.html.

35 Adam Goldman and Michael S. Schmidt, "How Ashley Biden's Diary Made Its Way to Project Veritas," New York Times, December 16, 2021, www.nytimes.com/2021/12/16/us/politics/ashley-biden-project-veritas-diary.html; Karen Compton, "President Joe Biden's daughter reportedly writes of alleged abuse in diary," WTRF News, June 28, 2022, https://www.wtrf.com/top-stories/alleged-showers-with-my-dad-president-joe-bidens-daughter-reportedly-writes-of-abuse-in-diary/.

36 Adam Goldman and Michael S. Schmidt, "Florida Pair Pleads Guilty in Theft of Biden's Daughter's Diary," New York Times, August 15, 2022, https://www.nytimes.com/2022/08/25/us/politics/ashley-biden-diary-project-veritas-guilty.html.

37 Josh Gerstein, "Two plead guilty to trafficking Ashley Biden's diary, property," Politico, August 25, 2022, https://www.politico.com/news/2022/08/25/guilty-trafficking-ashley-biden-diary-00053770.

38 Jesse O'Neill, "Project Veritas founder's apartment raided as part of probe into Ashley Biden's stolen diary: report," New York Post, November 6, 2021, https://nypost.com/2021/11/06/james-okeefe-apartment-raided-as-part-of-probe-into-ashley-bidens-stolen-diary/.

39 Josh Gerstein, "FBI raid on Project Veritas founder's home sparks questions about press freedom," Politico, November 13, 2021, https://www.politico.com/news/2021/11/13/raid-veritas-okeefe-biden-press-521307; Ryan Grim, "A Project Veritas Employee Leaked Ashley Biden's Diary, Intercept, September 7, 2022, https://theintercept.com/2022/09/07/project-veritas-ashley-biden-diary-leak/.

40 Mike Hogan, "Ashley Biden, Drugs, and the Real Cause for Outrage," Vanity Fair, March 30, 2009, https://www.vanityfair.com/news/2009/03/ashley-biden-drugs-and-the-real-cause-for-outrage; Brad Hamilton, "'Friend' of Biden's Daughter Shopping Tape of Her Allegedly Doing Cocaine," New York Post, March 28, 2009, https://nypost.com/2009/03/28/friend-of-bidens-daughter-shopping-tape-of-her-allegedly-doing-cocaine/.

41 Savannah Walsh, "All About Ashley Biden, Joe's Youngest Daughter Who Has A Civically-Minded Fashion Label," Elle, November 2, 2020, https://www.elle.com/culture/career-politics/a33645978/who-is-ashley-biden-joe-biden-daughter/.

42 Peter Schweizer, *Profiles in Corruption* (New York: HarperCollins, 2020).

43 "Joe Biden: If I'm elected, we're going to cure cancer," CNN, June 12, 2019, https://www.cnn.com/videos/politics/2019/06/12/joe-biden-cure-cancer-campaign-richmond-bolduan-sot-ath-vpx.

44 StartUp Health (@startuphealth) "@VP Biden continuing his #cancermoonshot tour with @Pontifex and our Chief Medical Officer @KreinMD. #endcancernow," Twitter, April 30, 2016, 11:51 a.m., https://twitter.com/startuphealth/status/726484130033242114.

45 Dr. Howard Krein (@KreinMD), "In Davos with @VP @Toby CosgroveMD @BillRMcDermott and other transformers changing the face of cancer," Twitter, January 20, 2016, https://twitter.com/KreinMD/status/689741053897871361?s=20.

46 Ben Schreckinger, "Biden's son-in-law advises campaign on pandemic while investing in Covid-19 startups," *Politico,* October 13, 2020, https://www.politico.com/news/2020/10/13/howard-krein-covid-startups-biden-429123.

47 "StartUp Health," Crunchbase.com, accessed June 12, 2023, https://www.crunchbase.com/organization/startup-health/investor_financials.

48 Jen Frost, "COVID led to a telemedicine fraud explosion?" *Insurance Business,* November 28, 2022, https://www.insurancebusinessmag.com/us/news/healthcare/has-covid-led-to-a-telemedicine-fraud-explosion-428828.aspx.

49 CK Tan, "Ping An Good Doctor's first-half revenue jumps amid pandemic," Nikkei Asia, August 20, 2020, https://asia.nikkei.com/Business/Health-Care/Ping-An-Good-Doctor-s-first-half-revenue-jumps-amid-pandemic.

50 Henry Schein, "Henry Schein Awarded Strategic National Stockpile Contract for PPE Storage and Distribution," May 26, 2021, https://investor.henryschein.com/news-releases/news-release-details/henry-schein-awarded-strategic-national-stockpile-contract-ppe.

51 Jen Psaki, "Press Briefing by Press Secretary Jen Psaki, February 9, 2021," February 9, 2021, The White House, https://www.whitehouse.gov/briefing-room/press-briefings/2021/02/09/press-briefing-by-press-secretary-jen-psaki-february-9-2021/.

52 "StartUp Health Launches Health Equity Moonshot at Clinton Global Initiative (CGI)," *Medium* (blog), September 19, 2022, https://healthtransformer.co/startup-health-launches-health-equity-moonshot-at-clinton-global-initiative-cgi-f5020dd34d0c.

53 Joel B. Pollak, "'We Ended Cancer': White House Buries Biden Gaffe in Transcript," Breitbart News, July 26, 2023, https://www.breitbart.com/politics/2023/07/26/we-ended-cancer-white-house-buries-biden-gaffe-in-transcript/.

54 Fatos Bytyci, "Kosovo Honors Beau Biden, Late Son of US President," VOA News, August 1, 2021, https://www.voanews.com/a/europe_kosovo-honors-beau-biden-late-son-us-president/6209033.html.

55 Matt Bittle, "Delaware law firm hires Beau Biden," *Delaware State News,* January 12, 2015, https://web.archive.org/web/20150602210427/http://delaware.newszap.com/centraldelaware/137604-70/delaware-law-firm-hires-beau-biden.

56 Paul Bois, "Report: President Biden Yet Again Incorrectly Claims Son Beau Died in Iraq," Breitbart News, May 23, 2023, https://www.breitbart.com

/politics/2023/05/23/president-biden-yet-again-incorrectly-claims-son
-beau-died-in-iraq/.

57 Mark Silva, "Beau Biden takes a pass on a Senate," *Los Angeles Times,*
January 25, 2010, https://web.archive.org/web/20100128205156/http://
latimesblogs.latimes.com/dcnow/2010/01/beau-biden-takes-a-pass-on-a
-senate-run.html.

58 Robert Kraychick, "'The Biden Five': The Definitive Breakdown of One
of America's Most Corrupt Families," Breitbart News, October 28, 2020,
https://www.breitbart.com/clips/2020/10/28/the-biden-five-the-definitive
-breakdown-of-one-of-americas-most-corrupt-families/.

59 Valeriebidenowens.com, "About Valerie," accessed June 12, 2023, https://
www.valeriebidenowens.com/about.

60 Michael Sherer, "Potential family conflicts arise for Joe Biden and aides as his administration drafts new ethics rules," *Washington Post,* December 14, 2020, https://
www.washingtonpost.com/politics/biden-transition-ethics-trump/2020/12/13
/dcee6e3e-3b2d-11eb-9276-ae0ca72729be_story.html; Stephanie Saul, "Politics, Money, Siblings: The Ties Between Joe Biden and Valerie Biden Owens,"
New York Times, February 25, 2020, https://www.nytimes.com/2020/02/25/us
/politics/valerie-joe-biden-sister.html.

61 Saul, "Politics, Money, Siblings."

62 Houston Keene, "Biden niece worked in Coca-Cola government relations
as company lobbied against Uyghur forced labor bill," Fox Business, April 9,
2021, https://www.foxbusiness.com/politics/biden-niece-coca-cola.

63 Casey Owens Castello (@CaseyCastello), Twitter profile, accessed June 12,
2023, https://twitter.com/caseycastello?lang=en; LinkedIn profile, s.v. "Casey
Owens Castello," accessed June 12, 2023, https://www.linkedin.com/in
/casey-owens-castello-90540b1/.

64 Shannon Raphael, "Meghan King Reveals the Real Reason She Married
Cuffe Biden Owens After Only 5 Weeks of Dating," Yahoo, March 28, 2023,
https://www.yahoo.com/entertainment/meghan-king-reveals-real-reason
-153016616.html.

65 Schweizer, *Profiles in Corruption,* 72.

66 Schweizer, *Profiles in Corruption,* 72.

67 Schweizer, *Profiles in Corruption,* 72–73.

68 Hill International, "James B. Biden Joins Hill International Subsidiary as Executive Vice President," November 23, 2010, https://www.globenewswire.com
/news-release/2010/11/23/434923/207583/en/James-B-Biden-Joins-Hill
-International-Subsidiary-as-Executive-Vice-President.html.

69 Schweizer, *Profiles in Corruption,* 73.

70 Schweizer, *Profiles in Corruption,* 73.

71 Schweizer, *Profiles in Corruption,* 74

72 Josh Boswell, "EXCLUSIVE: Jim Biden admitted he was hired to negotiate
with Saudis over a secret $140million deal 'because of his position and re-
lationship' to his VP brother Joe—who would be 'instrumental to the deal,'
bombshell affidavit claims," *Daily Mail,* February 14, 2023, https://www
.dailymail.co.uk/news/article-11731831/Jim-Biden-negotiated-deal
-Saudis-relationship-Joe.html.

73 Josh Boswell, "EXCLUSIVE: Jim Biden admitted."

74 Joseph N. Distefano, "Joe Biden's Friends and Backers Come Out on Top—at the Expense of the Middle Class," *Nation*, November 9, 2017, https://www.thenation.com/article/archive/biden-delaware-way-graft/; Ben Schreckinger, "Donor with deep Ukraine ties lent $500,000 to Biden's brother," *Politico*, August 15, 2019, https://www.politico.com/story/2019/08/15/james-biden-bungalow-ukraine-donor-1463645.

75 Joseph N. Distefano, "Joe Biden's Friends and Backers."

76 Brian Schwartz, "Biden brother touts relationship with president in Inauguration Day ad for law firm," CNBC, January 27, 2021, https://www.cnbc.com/2021/01/27/biden-brother-touts-relationship-with-president-in-inauguration-day-ad-for-law-firm.html.

77 "Francis Biden, Senior Advisor (Non-Attorney)," Bermanlawgroup.com, accessed June 12, 2023, https://www.bermanlawgroup.com/meet-our-team/government-relations/francis-biden/.

78 Schweizer, *Profiles in Corruption*, 77.

79 Madison Dibble, "Biden's brother Frank dodged paying $1M to daughters orphaned in crash," *Washington Examiner*, February 6, 2020, https://www.washingtonexaminer.com/news/bidens-brother-frank-dodged-paying-1m-to-daughters-orphaned-in-crash.

80 Josh Boswell, Alan Butterfield, and Ryan Parry, "EXCLUSIVE: Joe Biden's brother Frank owes dead man's family $1 MILLION for 80mph car crash - but has never paid a cent in 20 years and the Democratic candidate did NOTHING to help," *Daily Mail*, February 6, 2020, https://www.dailymail.co.uk/news/article-7908559/Joe-Bidens-brother-Frank-owes-1-million-dead-mans-family-2020-Democrat-did-help.html.

81 Schweizer, *Profiles in Corruption*, 78.

82 Josh Boswell, Alan Butterfield, and Ryan Parry, "'It's no coincidence!' Joe Biden's brother Frank finally agrees to pay some of the $1M he owes family of young father killed in a horrific car crash 20 years ago as election draws near - after dodging creditors for decades," *Daily Mail*, October 2, 2020, https://www.dailymail.co.uk/news/article-8770121/Joe-Bidens-brother-Frank-finally-agrees-pay-1M-owes-family-killed-father.html.

83 Schweizer, *Profiles in Corruption*, 80–82.

84 Josh Boswell, Alan Butterfield, and Ryan Parry, "Meet Frank Biden, Joe's 'penniless' brother who has snubbed mourning family he owes $1m—but who dined at the White House, boasts of his links to the former VP and vacations at $1,000-a-night ranch" *Daily Mail*, February 6, 2020, https://www.dailymail.co.uk/news/article-7961825/Meet-Frank-Biden-Joes-brother-place-inner-circle-resume-raises-questions.html..

85 Schweizer, *Profiles in Corruption*, 83–89.

86 Schweizer, *Profiles in Corruption*, 83–89.

87 Bob Norman, "The Sheriff's Criminal Association," *New Times*, October 15, 1998, https://www.browardpalmbeach.com/news/the-sheriffs-criminal-association-6331789; Select Committee on Narcotics Abuse and Control, House of Representatives, "Financial Investigation of Drug Trafficking," October 9, 1981,

88 Schweizer, *Profiles in Corruption*, 83–89.

89 Schweizer, *Profiles in Corruption*, 83–89.

90 Patrick Svitek, "Biden makes first Texas trip as a 2020 presidential candidate, pitching new education plan," *Texas Tribune,* May 28, 2019, https://www .texastribune.org/2019/05/28/joe-biden-first-texas-trip-2020-candidate -pitches-education-plan/.

91 Schweizer, *Profiles in Corruption,* 83–89.

92 Emily Jacobs, "Biden calls son Hunter 'smartest guy I know' as brother refuses to talk business deals," *New York Post,* October 29, 2020, https://nypost .com/2020/10/29/biden-calls-hunter-smartest-guy-i-know-in-virtual-event -with-oprah/.

CHAPTER 3: HUNTER BIDEN AND THE CLASSIFIED DOCUMENTS

1 Breitbart News, articles tagged "Hunter Biden," accessed June 11, 2023, https://www.breitbart.com/tag/hunter-biden/.

2 Adam Entous, "The Untold History of the Biden Family," *New Yorker,* August 15, 2022, https://www.newyorker.com/magazine/2022/08/22/the -untold-history-of-the-biden-family.

3 Ben Schreckinger, "Biden Inc.," *Politico,* August 2, 2019, https://www.politico .com/magazine/story/2019/08/02/joe-biden-investigation-hunter-brother -hedge-fund-money-2020-campaign-227407/.

4 Emma Schwartz, "My Son, The Lobbyist: Biden's Son a Well-Paid DC Insider," ABC News, August 24, 2008, https://abcnews.go.com/Blotter /story?id=5640118&page=1.

5 Schreckinger, "Biden Inc."

6 Schreckinger, "Biden Inc."

7 Schreckinger, "Biden Inc."

8 Schreckinger, "Biden Inc."

9 Alexander Marlow, " 'Breaking the News' Reveals: Secret Service Records Show Hunter Biden Took at Least 23 flights Through Joint Base Andrews, Home of Air Force One and Two," Breitbart News, May 22, 2021, https:// www.breitbart.com/the-media/2021/05/22/breaking-the-news-reveals -secret-service-records-show-hunter-biden-took-at-least-23-flights -through-joint-base-andrews-home-of-air-force-one-and-two/.

10 Robert Farley, "Trump's Claims About Hunter Biden in China," FactCheck .org, October 10, 2019, https://www.factcheck.org/2019/10/trumps-claims -about-hunter-biden-in-china/.

11 Chuck Grassley United States Senator for Iowa, "Grassley Raises Concerns Over Obama Admin Approval of U.S. Tech Company Joint Sale to Chinese Government and Investment Firm Linked To Biden, Kerry Families," August 15, 2019, TK.

12 Burisma, "Hunter Biden joins the team of Burisma Holdings," May 12, 2014, https://docs.house.gov/meetings/JU/JU00/20191211/110331/HMKP-116 -JU00-20191211-SD984.pdf; Miranda Devine, "Hunter Biden's Ukraine salary was cut two months after Joe Biden left office," *New York Post,* May 26, 2021, https://nypost.com/2021/05/26/hunter-bidens-ukraine-salary-was-cut -after-joe-biden-left-office/.

13 Dave Michaels and Theo Francis, "Hunter Biden's Name Was Used as Selling Point in Fraudulent Bond Scheme," *Wall Street Journal,* October 24, 2019,

https://www.wsj.com/articles/hunter-bidens-name-was-used-as-selling
-point-in-fraudulent-bond-scheme-11571863676.

14 Laura Strickler and Rich Schapiro, "Hunter Biden's legal work in Romania raises new questions about his overseas dealings," NBC News, October 24, 2019, https://www.nbcnews.com/politics/politics-news/hunter-biden-s-legal-work-romania-raises-new-questions-about-n1071031; Alexandra Stevenson, David Barboza, Matthew Goldstein, and Paul Mozur, "A Chinese Tycoon Sought Power and Influence. Washington Responded.," *New York Times,* December 12, 2018, https://www.nytimes.com/2018/12/12/business/cefc-biden-china-washington-ye-jianming.html; Jenni Marsh, "The rise and fall of a Belt and Road billionaire," CNN, https://www.cnn.com/interactive/2018/12/asia/patrick-ho-ye-jianming-cefc-trial-intl/; Shu Zhang and Chen Aizhu, "China's CEFC founder Ye named in corruption case - state media," Reuters, October 12, 2019, https://www.reuters.com/article/china-corruption-cefc/chinas-cefc-founder-ye-named-in-corruption-case-state-media-idUSL4N1WS26I.

15 Colleen McCain Nelson and Julian E. Barnes, "Biden's Son Hunter Discharged From Navy Reserve After Failing Cocaine Test," *Wall Street Journal,* October 16, 2014, https://www.wsj.com/articles/bidens-son-hunter-discharged-from-navy-reserve-after-failing-cocaine-test-1413499657?mod=WSJ_hppMIDDLENexttoWhatsNewsSecond.

16 Eric Bradner, "Biden's son discharged from Navy after testing positive for cocaine," CNN, October 17, 2014, https://www.cnn.com/2014/10/16/politics/hunter-biden-discharged-from-navy/index.html.

17 Sarah Fitzpatrick, Tom Winter, Ken Dilanian, and Michael Kosnar, "Federal prosecutors have considered four possible charges against Hunter Biden," NBC News, April 20, 2023, https://www.nbcnews.com/politics/justice-department/federal-prosecutors-hunter-biden-taxes-gun-charge-rcna80692; Mark Moore, "Hunter Biden raged at sister-in-law-turned-lover Hallie after she tossed his gun in trash: report," *New York Post,* June 15, 2022, https://nypost.com/2022/06/15/hunter-biden-raged-at-hallie-after-she-trashed-his-gun-report/; Andrew C. McCarthy, "Hunter Biden should be charged for lying on his gun application," *New York Post,* March 29, 2021, https://nypost.com/2021/03/29/hunter-biden-should-be-charged-for-lying-on-gun-application/.

18 Steven Nelson, "Hallie Biden revealed as 'new' Biden family member who got China cash," *New York Post,* March 16, 2023, https://nypost.com/2023/03/16/comer-reveals-new-biden-family-member-who-got-china-cash-prez-dined-with-her-friday/; Emma Jo-Morris, "BOMBSHELL: Biden Family Scored $31 Million from Deals with Individuals with Direct Ties to the Highest Levels of Chinese Intelligence," Breitbart News, January 24, 2022, https://www.breitbart.com/politics/2022/01/24/bombshell-biden-family-scored-31-million-from-deals-with-individuals-with-direct-ties-to-the-highest-levels-of-chinese-intelligence/.

19 Henry Rodgers and Kay Smythe, "Hunter Biden Told Brother's Widow To Get HIV Screening During Affair," *Daily Caller,* April 25, 2022, https://dailycaller.com/2022/04/25/hunter-biden-hiv-hallie-biden/.

20 Samuel Chamberlain, "Hunter Biden's ex-stripper baby mama was on his payroll while pregnant: texts," *New York Post,* June 2, 2021, https://nypost

.com/2021/06/02/hunter-bidens-ex-stripper-baby-mama-was-on-his
-payroll-while-pregnant-texts/; Morgan Phillips, "Lawyer of stripper who had
Hunter Biden's daughter says he expects the President's son to be INDICTED
in his criminal tax probe in Delaware and hands prosecutors MORE financial
documents," *Daily Mail*, March 18, 2022, https://www.dailymail.co.uk/news
/article-10627297/Lawyer-stripper-Hunter-Bidens-daughter-says-expects
-Presidents-son-INDICTED.html.

21 Danielle Wallace, "Hunter Biden child support case: Who is Lunden Roberts?," Fox News, May 2, 2023, https://www.foxnews.com/politics/hunter
-biden-child-support-case-who-lunden-roberts.

22 Steven Vago and Emily Crane, "Hunter Biden appears in court for baby mama
showdown, lawyer says he's already paid $750k child support," *New York Post*,
May 1, 2023, https://nypost.com/2023/05/01/hunter-biden-in-court-for
-baby-mama-lunden-roberts-paternity-case/.

23 Amy Furr, "Report: Hunter Biden Claimed He Was Broke at Child Support
Hearing After Flying on Private Jet," Breitbart News, May 21, 2023, https://
www.breitbart.com/politics/2023/05/21/report-hunter-biden-claimed
-broke-child-support-hearing-after-flying-private-jet/.

24 Michael Levenson, "Hunter Biden's Child Support Dispute Touches on
Political Discord," *New York Times*, May 2, 2023, https://www.nytimes
.com/2023/05/02/us/hunter-biden-child-arkansas.html.

25 Joe Biden, "Remarks by President Biden on Take Your Child to Work Day,"
The White House, April 27, 2023, https://www.whitehouse.gov/briefing-room
/speeches-remarks/2023/04/27/remarks-by-president-biden-on-take-your
-child-to-work-day/.

26 Joe Schoffstall, "Biden again refuses to acknowledge Hunter's out-of-wedlock
daughter while speaking about grandchildren," Fox News, April 27, 2023,
https://www.foxnews.com/politics/biden-again-refuses-acknowledge-hunt
ers-out-of-wedlock-daughter-while-speaking-about-grandchildren.

27 Ben Ashford, "EXCLUSIVE: Callous Joe Biden REFUSES to provide security
for Hunter's mini-me lovechild Navy despite being 'made aware' his three-
year-old granddaughter and her mom Lunden Roberts were threatened
by angry cage fighter ex," *Daily Mail*, June 6, 2022, https://www.dailymail
.co.uk/news/article-10882957/Joe-Biden-REFUSES-provide-security
-Hunters-lovechild-Navy-Joan.html.

28 Jessie O'Neil, "Hunter Biden's out-of-Wedlock Daughter Left out of White
House Christmas Display," *New York Post*, December 1, 2021, https://nypost
.com/2021/12/01/bidens-stocking-display-excludes-hunters-daughter-born
-out-of-wedlock/.

29 Brandon Gillespie, "Critics shred Biden for claiming 'our nation's children are
all our children': 'Absolutely wrong,'" Fox News, April 24, 2023, https://www
.foxnews.com/politics/critics-shred-biden-claiming-our-nations-children
-are-all-our-children.

30 Josh Boswell, "EXCLUSIVE: Hunter gone wild! Unhinged videos show the president's son dancing shirtless, slipping down a waterslide naked and entertain-
ing hookers at debauched pool party in $4,140-per-night Malibu rental," *Daily
Mail*, September 22, 2022, https://www.dailymail.co.uk/news/article-11228367
/Wild-videos-Hunter-Biden-going-waterslide-naked-entertaining-hookers.html.

31 Joe Biden (@JoeBiden), "I've had a rule my entire life: No matter what's happening, no matter how important the meeting, I'll always answer a call from
my grandchildren.," Twitter, October 18, 2020, 7:10 p.m., https://twitter.com
/joebiden/status/1317966186907226113.

32 Emma-Jo Morris and Gabrielle Fonrouge, "Hunter Biden emails show leveraging connections with his father to boost Burisma pay," *New York Post*,
October 14, 2020, https://nypost.com/2020/10/14/hunter-biden-emails
-show-leveraging-connections-with-dad-to-boost-burisma-pay/; Emma-Jo
Morris and Gabrielle Fonrouge, "Obama conference call leaked to Burisma: Biden emails," *New York Post*, October 14, 2020, https://nypost
.com/2020/10/14/obama-conference-call-leaked-to-burisma-biden-emails/;
Emma-Jo Morris and Gabrielle Fonrouge, "Smoking-gun email reveals how
Hunter Biden introduced Ukrainian businessman to VP dad," *New York
Post*, October 14, 2020, https://nypost.com/2020/10/14/email-reveals-how
-hunter-biden-introduced-ukrainian-biz-man-to-dad/.

33 Morris and Fonrouge, "Smoking-gun email reveals."

34 Emma-Jo Morris and Gabrielle Fonrouge, "Emails reveal how Hunter
Biden tried to cash in big on behalf of family with Chinese firm," *New York
Post*, October 15, 2020, https://nypost.com/2020/10/15/emails-reveal-how
-hunter-biden-tried-to-cash-in-big-with-chinese-firm/.

35 Natasha Bertrand, "Hunter Biden story is Russian disinfo, dozens of former intel officials say," *Politico*, October 19, 2020, https://www.politico.com
/news/2020/10/19/hunter-biden-story-russian-disinfo-430276.

36 Bertrand, "Hunter Biden story is Russian disinfo."

37 Ebony Bowden and Steven Nelson, "Hunter's ex-partner Tony Bobulinski: Joe
Biden's a liar and here's the proof," *New York Post*, October 22, 2020, https://nypost
.com/2020/10/22/hunter-ex-partner-tony-bobulinski-calls-joe-biden-a-liar/.

38 Steven Nelson, "Trump and Biden clash over Hunter corruption claims at final
debate," *New York Post*, October 22, 2020, https://nypost.com/2020/10/22
/trump-and-joe-biden-debate-hunter-corruption-claims-at-final-debate/.

39 Ashley Oliver, "Testimony Reveals Blinken—As Adviser to Biden Campaign—
Spurred Letter from 51 Intel Officials Discrediting Hunter Laptop Story," Breitbart News, April 20, 2023, https://www.breitbart.com/politics/2023/04/20
/testimony-reveals-blinken-as-adviser-to-biden-campaign-spurred-letter
-from-51-intel-officials-discrediting-hunter-laptop-story/.

40 Emma-Jo Morris, "Morris: Twitter Files Reveal 'Laptop from Hell' Censorship Was Orchestrated by Security State," Breitbart News, December 19,
2022, https://www.breitbart.com/tech/2022/12/19/morris-twitter-files-reveal
-laptop-from-hell-censorship-was-orchestrated-by-security-state/.

41 Edward-Isaac Dovere, *Battle for the Soul: Inside the Democrats' Campaigns to
Defeat Trump* (New York: Penguin Books, 2021).

42 Tara Palmeri and Ben Schreckinger, "Sources: Secret Service inserted itself into case of Hunter Biden's gun," *Politico*, March 25, 2021, https://www
.politico.com/news/2021/03/25/sources-secret-service-inserted-itself-into
-case-of-hunter-bidens-gun-477879.

43 Emily Smith and Bruce Golding, "Hunter Biden sells five art prints for $75K
each as NYC show pushed back," *New York Post*, https://nypost.com/2021/10/07
/hunter-biden-sells-five-prints-for-75k-each-as-nyc-show-pushed-back/.

44 Tina Sfondeles and Alex Thompson, "We asked art critics about Hunter's paintings," *Politico*, July 27, 2021, https://www.politico.com/newsletters /west-wing-playbook/2021/07/27/we-asked-art-critics-about-hunters -paintings-493751.

45 Graham Bowley and Robin Pogrebin, "A Gallery Sells Hunter Bidens. The White House Says It Won't Know Who's Buying," *New York Times*, August 13, 2021, https://www.nytimes.com/2021/08/13/arts/design/hunter-biden-art -white-house.html.

46 Isabel Vincent, "Hunter Biden's art dealer refuses to give buyer names to House committee," *New York Post*, February 7, 2023, https://nypost.com/2023/02/07 /hunter-biden-art-dealer-refuses-to-give-names-to-house-committee/.

47 John Bowden, "Former White House ethics chief knocks Bidens over ethics of Hunter's private art sale," *Independent*, July 9, 2021, https://www .independent.co.uk/news/world/americas/us-politics/hunter-biden-art-sale -shaub-b1880858.html.

48 Matthias Schwartz, "Exclusive: Hunter Biden's Gallery Sold His Art to a Democratic Donor 'Friend' Who Joe Biden Named to a Prestigious Commission", Business Insider, July 24, 2023, https://www.businessinsider.com/hunter -biden-joe-artwork-berges-gallery-elizabeth-hirsh-naftali-2023-7.

49 Elizabeth Hirsh Naftali, "Hunter Biden's Art Patron Visited White House Over a Dozen Times", *The Washington Free Beacon*, July 25, 2023, https:// freebeacon.com/biden-administration/hunter-bidens-art-patron-visited -white-house-over-a-dozen-times/ 1m.

50 Matthias Schwartz, "Exclusive: Hunter Biden's Gallery Sold His Art to a Democratic Donor 'Friend' Who Joe Biden Named to a Prestigious Commission", Business Insider, July 24, 2023, https://www.businessinsider.com/hunter -biden-joe-artwork-berges-gallery-elizabeth-hirsh-naftali-2023-7.

51 Josh Margolin, John Santucci and Soo Rin Kim, "Secret Service paying over $30K per month for Malibu mansion to protect Hunter Biden," ABC News, April 4, 2022, https://abcnews.go.com/US/secret-service -paying-30k-month-malibu-mansion-protect/story?id=83821498.

52 University of Pennsylvania Annenberg School for Communication, "Joe R. Biden Jr.," profile, accessed via Wayback Machine on June 8, 2023, https:// web.archive.org/web/20180217183607/https://www.asc.upenn.edu/people /faculty/joseph-r-biden-jr.

53 University of Pennsylvania Penn Global, "Penn Biden Center for Diplomacy & Global Engagement," accessed June 8, 2023, https://global.upenn.edu /penn-biden-center.

54 Alana Goodman, "Across Biden Charitable Organizations, A Refusal to Disclose Funding," *Washington Free Beacon*, May 21, 2020, https://freebeacon .com/elections/watchdog-raises-questions-about-china-influence-as-penn -biden-center-wont-disclose-donors/.

55 Alana Goodman, "Since Biden Inauguration, Anonymous Chinese Donors Poured Millions Into University That Houses His Think Tank," *Washington Free Beacon*, January 18, 2023, https://freebeacon.com/biden-administration /since-biden-inauguration-anonymous-chinese-donors-poured-millions -into-university-that-houses-his-think-tank/.

56 Seamus Bruner and Jedd McFatter, "Exclusive—Secret China Donations

to University of Delaware Soared After the Opening of the Biden Institute," Breitbart News, February 14, 2023, https://www.breitbart.com/politics/2023/02/14/exclusive-secret-china-donations-to-university-of-delaware-soared-after-the-opening-of-the-biden-institute/.

57 "Biden Institutes mission is to tackle nations difficult domestic problems," University of Delaware Biden School of Public Policy & Administration, accessed on June 9, 2023, https://www.bidenschool.udel.edu/news/Pages/Biden-Institute-at-UD-Launched.aspx.

58 Michela Tindera and Eric Fan, "Biden Has Brought More People Into Government From His Nonprofits Than Trump Did From His Business," *Forbes,* December 23, 2021, https://www.forbes.com/sites/michelatindera/2021/12/23/biden-has-brought-more-people-into-government-from-his-nonprofits-than-trump-did-from-his-business/?sh=61b634d8b554.

59 Peter Schweizer, *Red-Handed* (New York: HarperCollins, 2022), 40–42.

60 Schweizer, *Red-Handed,* 40–42.

61 Schweizer, *Red-Handed,* 40–42.

62 Peter Flaherty, Chair of the National Legal and Policy Center, "Re: Investigation of University of Pennsylvania and the Penn Biden Center for Diplomacy and Global Engagement for Failing to Disclose Anonymous Gifts and Contracts from China in violation of Section 117 of the Higher Education Act and Referral to the Department of Justice for Enforcement Action and Payment of Investigation Costs," to Betsy Devos, Secretary of the United States Department of Education, May 20, 2020, accessed via Scribd on June 12, 2023, https://www.scribd.com/document/462458499/NLPC-Complaint-vs-University-of-Pennsylvania-Biden-Center-for-Undisclosed-China-Donations.

63 Hunter Biden, email to 'hurricane5155' January 18, 2017, https://media.Breitbart.com/media/2023/02/HB-Email-2-REDACTED.jpg.

64 Hunter Biden laptop, email.

65 Hunter Biden laptop, Valerie text.

66 Dionissios (Dennis) Assanis, n.d. "Curriculum Vitae," University of Delaware, November 2020, accessed June 12, 2023, https://www.udel.edu/content/dam/udelImages/president/communications/Assanis_CV_November2020.pdf.

67 Assanis, "Curriculum Vitae."

68 China Defence Universities Tracker, s.v. "Shanghai Jiao Tong University," accessed June 9, 2023, https://unitracker.aspi.org.au/universities/shanghai-jiaotong-university/.

69 Ballotpedia, s.v. "Mike Donilon," accessed June 9, 2023, https://ballotpedia.org/Mike_Donilon.

70 Dan Diamond, "Biden's top doctor nominee made more than $2 million doing pandemic consulting, speeches," *Washington Post,* February 20, 2021, https://www.washingtonpost.com/health/2021/02/20/vivek-murthy-surgeon-general-coronavirus-consulting/.

71 Yusra Asif, "UD president appointed to president's national advisory council," Delaware Online, May 20, 2022, https://www.delawareonline.com/story/news/2022/05/20/biden-appoints-university-delaware-president-dennis-assanis/9840790002/.

72 United States Department of Education: College Foreign Gift and Contract Reporting, s.v. "University of Delaware," via Microsoft Excel sheet,

"Section-117_Public-Records_complete_2023-04-06," accessed June 9, 2023, https://sites.ed.gov/foreigngifts/.

73 Yael Halon, "Reports of Chinese donations to second Biden-linked university prompt new calls for investigation: 'Absurd,' " Fox News, https://www.foxnews.com/media/reports-chinese-donations-second-biden-linked-university-prompts-calls-investigation-absurd.

74 University of Delaware, Institute for Global Studies, "International Partnerships," accessed June 8, 2023, https://www.udel.edu/content/dam/udelImages/global/pdf/Partnerships.20.pdf.

75 Marco Rubio, United States Senator, to Dennis Assanis, University of Delaware President, February 8, 2022, https://www.rubio.senate.gov/public/_cache/files/6abac22c-e7bb-4559-85e2-2ef65b535801/1541C9BE9E1390BA090C71CDA24DF03.02.08.22—-smr-letter-to-u.-of-delaware-re-mcf.pdf.

76 Kate O'Keefe, "Huawei Executive Accused by U.S. Startup of Involvement in Trade-Secrets Theft," *Wall Street Journal,* May 23, 2019, https://www.wsj.com/articles/huawei-executive-is-accused-of-involvement-in-trade-secrets-theft-u-s-startup-said-in-court-filings-11558550468.

77 China Defence Universities Tracker, s.v. "Shandong University," accessed June 10, 2023, https://unitracker.aspi.org.au/universities/shandong-university/.

78 Jessica Chamar and Joe Schoffstall, "Hunter Biden, China, classified documents: Mystery swirls around Penn Biden Center," Fox News, January 12, 2023, https://www.foxnews.com/politics/hunter-biden-china-classified-documents-mystery-swirls-penn-biden-center

79 "Clinton Global Initiative," Clinton Foundation, accessed on June 11, 2023, https://www.clintonfoundation.org/programs/leadership-public-service/clinton-global-initiative/.

80 Jerome Hudson, "Clinton Foundation Donations Plummeted by 37 Percent," Breitbart News, November 20, 2016, https://www.breitbart.com/politics/2016/11/20/clinton-foundation-donations-plummeted-by-37-percent/.

81 Paul Bois, "Clinton Global Initiative Reactivated After Long Hiatus," Breitbart News, March 6, 2022, https://www.breitbart.com/politics/2022/03/06/clinton-global-initiative-reactivated-long-hiatus/.

82 Robert Farley, "Timeline of Biden's Classified Documents," FactCheck.org, January 19, 2023, https://www.factcheck.org/2023/01/timeline-of-bidens-classified-documents/.

83 Jamie Gangel, Marshall Cohen, Evan Perez, and Phil Mattingly, " Classified documents from Biden's time as VP discovered in private office," CNN, January 9, 2023, https://www.cnn.com/2023/01/09/politics/joe-biden-classified-documents-upenn/index.html.

84 "Key dates in discovery of classified records tied to Biden," AP News, January 14, 2023, https://apnews.com/article/biden-politics-united-states-government-barack-obama-merrick-garland-def4c44c23229671e1e50bf170dc67d2.

85 Glenn Thrush and Charlie Savage, "Biden 'Surprised' to Learn Classified Documents Were Found in Private Office," *New York Times,* January 10, 2023, https://www.nytimes.com/2023/01/10/us/politics/biden-documents-classified-foreign-countries.html.

86 Simon Kent, "Joe Biden Blames Sloppy Staffers for Classified Document Debacle," *Breitbart News*, February 9, 2023, https://www.breitbart.com /politics/2023/02/09/joe-biden-blames-sloppy-staffers-for-classified -document-debacle/.

CHAPTER 4: AMERICAN CORPORATISM: THE BIDEN BENEFICIARIES

1 Theodoric Meyer, "Biden Swears off Lobbyists' Money, but K Street Likes Him Anyway." *Politico*, April 25, 2019, https://www.politico.com/story/2019/04/25 /biden-swears-off-lobbyists-money-but-k-street-likes-him-anyway -1290333.

2 David McCabe, and Jim Tankersley, "Biden Urges More Scrutiny of Big Businesses, Such as Tech Giants," *New York Times*, July 9, 2021, https://www .nytimes.com/2021/07/09/business/biden-big-business-executive-order.html.

3 Zachary Crockett, "Why Delaware Is the Sexiest Place in America to Incorporate a Company," *The Hustle*, April 10, 2021, https://thehustle.co/why -delaware-is-the-sexiest-place-in-america-to-incorporate-a-company/.

4 Delaware Division of Corporations, "Annual Report Statistics," July 20, 2022, https://corp.delaware.gov/stats/.

5 Walter Rugaber, "Nader Study Says Du Pont Runs Delaware," *New York Times*, November 30, 1971, https://www.nytimes.com/1971/11/30/archives/nader -study-says-du-pont-runs-delaware.html.

6 Casey Michel, "How Delaware Became the World's Biggest Offshore Haven," *Foreign Policy*, November 19, 2021, https://foreignpolicy.com/2021/11 /19/delaware-illicit-finance-corruption-offshore-wealth-american -kleptocracy-book-excerpt/; Alan Livsey, "Lifting the Lid on Delaware — Corporate America's Tax Haven," *Financial Times*, December 5, 2022, https:// www.ft.com/content/6b28d569-cdb4-4f9f-865b-0b6346912cbb.

7 Tim Murphy, "House of Cards," *Mother Jones*, November 11, 2019, https:// www.motherjones.com/politics/2019/11/biden-bankruptcy-president/.

8 Philip Rucker, "Mitt Romney Says 'Corporations Are People,'" *Washington Post*, August 11, 2011, https://www.washingtonpost.com/politics/mitt-rom ney-says-corporations-are-people/2011/08/11/gIQABwZ38I_story.html.

9 Hal Weitzman, "Delaware: The State Where Companies Can Vote," ProMarket, May 19, 2022, https://www.promarket.org/2022/05/23/delaware-the -state-where-companies-can-vote/. Karl Baker, "Newark, Delaware, Where Some People Can Vote More than Once," Delaware Online, July 5, 2018, https://www.delawareonline.com/story/news/2018/06/29/newark-delaware -where-some-people-can-vote-more-than-once/735314002/.

10 Byron York, "The Senator from MBNA," *National Review*, July 29, 2020, https://www.nationalreview.com/2008/08/senator-mbna-byron-york/; Arijeta Lajka, "Property That False Post Calls 'Biden's House' Was Sold by Him in 1996," AP News, October 18, 2020, *https://apnews.com/article/fact -checking-afs:Content:9571784771*; Cris Barrish, "Analysis: How Biden Made a Large Profit on the Sale of His House (News Journal Archives)," Delaware Online, October 20, 2020, https://www.delawareonline.com/story/news /politics/joe-biden/2020/10/20/analysis-how-biden-made-large-profit-sale -his-house-2008-archive-article/5996458002/.

11 "MBNA Paid Biden's Son as Biden Backed Bill," CBS News, August 25, 2008, https://www.cbsnews.com/news/mbna-paid-bidens-son-as-biden-backed -bill/.

12 Alex Gangitano, "Biden Signs Executive Order Invoking 2-Year Lobbying Ban for Appointees," *The Hill*, January 21, 2021, https://thehill.com/business -a-lobbying/535176-biden-signs-executive-order-invoking-2-year -lobbying-ban-for-appointees/.

13 Chad Day, "Unions, Pfizer and a Record Label Helped Biden Inaugural Committee Raise $61.8 Million," *Wall Street Journal*, April 21, 2021, https://www .wsj.com/articles/unions-pfizer-and-a-record-label-helped-biden-inaugural -committee-raise-61-8-million-11619006767.

14 Open Secrets, "Lobbying Data Summary," accessed May 28, 2023, https:// www.opensecrets.org/federal-lobbying.

15 Open Secrets, "Lobbying Data Summary."

16 Open Secrets, "Ricchetti Inc," 2021 lobbying profile, accessed May 28, 2023, https://www.opensecrets.org/federal-lobbying/firms/summary?cycle =2021&id=D000037088; Open Secrets, "Ricchetti Inc," 2019 lobbying profile, accessed May 28, 2023, https://www.opensecrets.org/federal-lobbying/firms /summary?cycle=2019&id=D000037088.

17 Open Secrets, "Ricchetti Inc," 2021 lobbying profile.

18 Michael Scherer, and Sean Sullivan, "Lobbyist Brother of Top Biden Adviser Poses Challenge to President's Ethics Promises," *Washington Post*, June 15, 2021, https://www.washingtonpost.com/politics/biden-lobbying-ethics -ricchetti/2021/06/13/1f2f0826-c864-11eb-81b1-34796c7393af_story .html; Sean Sullivan, and Michael Scherer, "A Family Affair: Children and Other Relatives of Biden Aides Get Administration Jobs," *Washington Post*, June 19, 2021, https://www.washingtonpost.com/politics/biden-aides-relatives -jobs/2021/06/17/ab504a22-cea4-11eb-8cd2-4e95230cfac2_story.html.

19 Caitlyn Oprysko, "Biden-Tied Lobbying Firms Raked in the Dough during His First Year," *Politico*, accessed May 28, 2023. https://www.politico.com /news/2022/01/21/its-a-gold-rush-for-lobbying-firms-with-biden-ties-527635.

20 "Michèle Flournoy and Tony Blinken Form Global Strategic Advisory Firm with Former Senior National Security Officials—WESTEXEC Advisors," WestExec Advisors, February 15, 2018, https://www.westexec .com/michele-flournoy-and-tony-blinken-form-global-strategic -advisory-firm-with-former-senior-national-security-officials/.

21 Rob Galbraith, "Biden Draws Foreign Policy Team from Military-and Tech-Tied Consulting and Private Equity Firms," *Eyes on The Ties*, December 7, 2020, https://news.littlesis.org/2020/12/07/biden-draws-foreign-policy-team -from-military-and-tech-tied-consulting-and-private-equity-firms/.

22 Yuichiro Kakutani, "Biden-Linked Firm Westexec Scrubs China Work from Website," *Washington Free Beacon*, December 2, 2020, https://freebeacon.com /elections/biden-linked-firm-westexec-scrubs-china-work-from-website/.

23 Jigsaw (website), accessed June 6, 2023, https://jigsaw.google.com/.

24 "Pine Island Capital Partners (website)," Pine Island Capital Partners, accessed June 6, 2023, https://pineislandcp.com/.

25 Pine Island Acquisition Corp, November 19, 2020 Form 8-K (filed November 25, 2020), United States Securities and Exchange Commission,

accessed June 6, 2023, https://www.sec.gov/Archives/edgar/data/1822835/000110465920129527/tm2037104d1_8k.htm.

26 Peter Schweizer and Jacob McLeod, "The Defense-Industry Swamp Is Eager to Engulf the Biden Administration," *New York Post*, December 12, 2020, https://nypost.com/2020/12/11/the-defense-industry-swamp-is-eager-to-engulf-the-biden-administration/.

27 Natasha Bertrand, "The Inexorable Rise of Jake Sullivan," *Politico*, November 27, 2020, https://www.politico.com/news/2020/11/27/jake-sullivan-biden-national-security-440814; Jonathan Guyer, "How a Biden Adviser Got a Gig with Uber," *American Prospect*, July 8, 2020, https://prospect.org/world/biden-adviser-jake-sullivan-gig-with-uber/.

28 Soo Rin Kim and Lucien Bruggmen, "Watchdogs Concerned about Some Biden Appointees' Opaque Consulting Work," ABC News, February 1, 2021, https://abcnews.go.com/US/watchdogs-concerned-biden-appointees-opaque-consulting-work/story?id=75563844.

29 Kim and Bruggmen, "Watchdogs Concerned about Some Biden Appointees."

30 "Teneo Acquires Majority Stake in WestExec Advisors," Teneo, accessed May 28, 2023, https://www.teneo.com/teneo-acquires-majority-stake-in-westexec-advisors/.

31 The White House, "Executive Order on Ethics Commitments by Executive Branch Personnel," January 20, 2021, https://www.whitehouse.gov/briefing-room/presidential-actions/2021/01/20/executive-order-ethics-commitments-by-executive-branch-personnel/.

32 Bryan Bender and Theodoric Meyer, "The Secretive Consulting Firm That's Become Biden's Cabinet in Waiting," *Politico*, November 23, 2020, https://www.politico.com/news/2020/11/23/westexec-advisors-biden-cabinet-440072.

33 Anthony Capaccio, "US to Provide Ukraine with JDAM-Er Long-Range Version of GPS-Guided Bomb," *Bloomberg News*, February 21, 2023, https://www.bloomberg.com/news/articles/2023-02-21/boeing-to-provide-ukraine-long-range-version-of-gps-guided-bomb#xj4y7vzkg.

34 Alan Levin and Julie Johnsson, "Antony Blinken Recuses Himself on Boeing (BA) Foreign Policy Discussions," *Bloomberg News*, May 20, 2021, *https://www.bloomberg.com/news/articles/2021-05-20/blinken-recuses-himself-on-boeing-foreign-policy-discussions*; Tim Hepher and David Shepardson, "Boeing CEO Hints at Higher Jet Output, Optimistic on China," Reuters, January 31, 2023, https://www.reuters.com/business/aerospace-defense/boeing-ceo-hints-higher-jet-output-optimistic-china-2023-01-31/.

35 Dan Alexander, "Inside the $10 Million Fortune of Antony Blinken, Biden's Secretary of State," *Forbes*, July 26, 2021, https://www.forbes.com/sites/danalexander/2021/06/17/inside-the-10-million-fortune-of-antony-blinken-bidens-secretary-of-state/?sh=63130e565376.

36 Dan Alexander, "Inside the $10 Million Fortune"; Executive Branch Personnel Public Financial Disclosure Report (OGE form), accessed May 28, 2023, https://extapps2.oge.gov/201/Presiden.nsf/PAS+Index/411F57AEF2A7AE7485258884002ECCD8/$FILE/Antony-J-Blinken-2022-278.pdf.

37 Kenneth P. Vogel and Eric Lipton, "Washington Has Been Lucrative for Some on Biden's Team," *New York Times*, January 2, 2021, https://www.nytimes.com/2021/01/01/us/politics/yellen-speaking-fees-disclosure.html.

38 "Select Committee on Intelligence United States Senate," Senate Intelligence Committee, accessed May 28, 2023, https://www.intelligence.senate.gov/sites /default/files/documents/qfr-ahaines-011921.pdf.

39 United States Office of Government Ethics, *Executive Branch Personnel Public Financial Disclosure Report*, July 2020, https://extapps2.oge.gov/201 /Presiden.nsf/PAS+Index/00CB412D4BCCFDF58525864F00810563/$FILE /Haines,%20Avril%20%20final%20278.pdf.

40 Caitlyn Oprysko, "Anita Dunn Finally Discloses Her Corporate Clients," *Politico*, accessed May 28, 2023, https://www.politico.com/newsletters/politi co-influence/2022/08/12/anita-dunn-discloses-corporate-clients-00051541; Brian Schwartz, "Biden Senior Advisor Anita Dunn Has to Divest Investment Portfolio Worth between $16.8 Million and $48.2 Million to Avoid Con-flicts," CNBC, August 12, 2022. https://www.cnbc.com/2022/08/12/biden -senior-advisor-anita-dunn-has-to-divest-investment-portfolio-to-avoid -conflict.html.

41 The White House, "President Biden Announces Senior Clean Energy and Climate Team," September 2, 2022, https://www.whitehouse.gov/brief ing-room/statements-releases/2022/09/02/president-biden-announces -senior-clean-energy-and-climate-team/; Ben Geman, "White House Taps John Podesta to Oversee Clean Energy Spending," *Axios*, September 2, 2022, https://www.axios.com/2022/09/02/biden-john-podesta-clean-energy -spending; Lisa Friedman, "Biden, Remaking Climate Team, Picks John Po-desta to Guide Spending," *New York Times*, September 2, 2022, https://www .nytimes.com/2022/09/02/climate/john-podesta-climate-biden.html; Zack Colman, "Podesta-Led White House Team Tagged to Execute Climate Law," *Politico*, September 12, 2022, https://www.politico.com/news/2022/09/12 /white-house-climate-law-00056192.

42 "Andrew Breitbart: 'Fuck You John Podesta!,'" YouTube video, posted by "Nando Jivatman," May 9, 2020, 0:31, https://www.youtube.com/watch?v=o3hhja2O9JE.

43 Jerome Hudson, "Report: John Podesta May Have Violated Federal Law by Not Disclosing 75,000 Shares in Putin-Linked Company," Breitbart News, March 27, 2017, https://www.breitbart.com/politics/2017/03/27/report -podesta-may-have-violated-federal-law-not-disclosing-75000-shares-putin -linked-company/.

44 Jerome Hudson, "Wikileaks: Podesta Daughter Got His Shares in Putin-Linked Joule," Breitbart News, October 20, 2016, https://www.breitbart .com/politics/2016/10/20/wikileaks-bombshell-john-podestas-daughter -received-75000-shares-putin-connected-energy-company/.

45 Andrew Kerr, "John Podesta Made a Fortune Consulting for Green Energy Billionaires. He Now Oversees a Federal Fund That Could Make Them Rich," *Washington Free Beacon*, December 15, 2022, https://freebeacon .com/biden-administration/john-podesta-earned-thousands-consulting -for-green-energy-billionaires-he-now-oversees-a-federal-fund-that-could -make-them-rich/.

46 "Tom Steyer and Katie Hall, "Tom Steyer and Katie Hall Launch Galva-nize Climate Solutions," *Philanthropy News Digest*, September 13, 2021, https://philanthropynewsdigest.org/news/tom-steyer-and-katie-hall-launch -galvanize-climate-solutions; Kerr, "John Podesta Made"; https://freebea

con.com/biden-administration/john-podesta-earned-thousands-consulting
-for-green-energy-billionaires-he-now-oversees-a-federal-fund-that-could
-make-them-rich/; United States Office of Government Ethics, "Executive Branch Personnel Public Financial Disclosure Report," *Free Beacon,*
November 2021, https://freebeacon.com/wp-content/uploads/2022/12/john
-podestas-personal-financial-disclosure-statement-oct-28-2022-1-1.pdf.

47 United States Office of Government Ethics, "Executive Branch."

48 Kenneth P. Vogel and Katie Robertson, "Top Bidder for Tribune Newspapers
Is an Influential Liberal Donor," *New York Times,* April 13, 2021, https://www
.nytimes.com/2021/04/13/business/media/wyss-tribune-company-buyer
.html?smid=tw-share.

49 Alana Goodman, "Swiss Billionaire Bankrolling Dark Money Group Pushing
for Biden Climate Initiative," *Washington Free Beacon,* November 12, 2021,
https://freebeacon.com/policy/swiss-billionaire-bankrolling-dark-money
-group-pushing-for-biden-climate-initiative/.

50 Joel B. Pollock, "NYT: Swiss Billionaire behind 'hub Project' to Influence
U.S. Media, Politics; Bids for Tribune Co.," Breitbart News, April 14, 2021,
https://www.breitbart.com/the-media/2021/04/13/nyt-swiss-billionaire-be
hind-hub-project-to-influence-u-s-media-politics-tribune/?utm_medium
=social&utm_source=facebook&fbclid=IwAR2QhCOed4cbQRJ4RkggqOx
TwMAcS9poqAYQntBVfGNBNOk3JmHhsWmFUIU.

51 Brian Slodysko, "Group Steers Swiss Billionaire's Money to Liberal
Causes," AP News, April 4, 2023, https://apnews.com/article/dark-money
-democrats-wyss-politics-elections-601d40cd01569190559d545418afe396.

52 Alexandra Alper and Jarrett Renshaw, "Huawei Paid Democratic Power-
broker Podesta $1 Million to Lobby -Sources," Reuters, October 28, 2021,
https://www.reuters.com/business/media-telecom/huawei-paid-washington
-lobbyist-podesta-1-million-sources-2021-10-28/. Demetri Sevastopulo
and Kathrin Hille, "Washington Halts Licences for US Companies to Export to Huawei," *Financial Times,* January 31, 2023, https://www.ft.com
/content/23433f43-8d81-4a24-9373-fc0ac18f948a.

53 Bill Allison, "'Dark Money' Helped Pave US President Joe Biden's Path
to White House," *Business Standard,* January 24, 2021, https://www
.business-standard.com/article/international/dark-money-helped-pave-us
-president-joe-biden-s-path-to-white-house-121012500052_1.html;
"'Dark Money' Helped Pave Joe Biden's Path to the White House," *Infobae,*
January 23, 2021, https://www.infobae.com/en/2021/01/23/dark-money
-helped-pave-joe-bidens-path-to-the-white-house/..

54 Jim Rutenberg, "Obama Yields in Marshaling of 'Super Pac,'" *New York Times,*
February 7, 2012, https://www.nytimes.com/2012/02/07/us/politics/with-a
-signal-to-donors-obama-yields-on-super-pacs.html.

55 *Forbes,* "George Soros," profile, accessed May 29, 2023, https://www.forbes
.com/profile/george-soros/?sh=167c501d2024.

56 "Who We Are," Open Society Foundations, accessed May 29, 2023, https://
www.opensocietyfoundations.org/who-we-are.

57 *Forbes,* "George Soros."

58 Joe Schoffstall, "Top George Soros Director Has Frequent Biden White House
Access, Records Show," Fox News, January 26, 2023, https://www.foxnews

.com/politics/top-george-soros-director-frequent-biden-white-house
-access-records-show.

59 Joe Schoffstall and Cameron Cawthorne, "George Soros' Son Has Visited
the White House at Least 17 Times Since Biden Took Office, Records Show,"
Fox News, May 31, 2023, https://www.foxnews.com/politics/george-soros
-son-visited-white-house-at-least-17-times-since-biden-took-office-records
-show.

60 Forbes, "George Soros."

61 Brian Schwartz, "Nonprofit Financed by Billionaire George Soros Quietly
Donated $140 Million to Political Causes in 2021," CNBC, January 4, 2023,
https://www.CNBC.com/2023/01/04/nonprofit-financed-by-billionaire
-george-soros-donated-140-million-to-political-groups-in-2021.html.

62 Open Secrets "Soros Fund Management," top recipients, accessed May 29,
2023, https://www.opensecrets.org/orgs/soros-fund-management/summary?
toprecipcycle=2022&contribcycle=2022&lobcycle=2022&out
spendcycle=2022&id=D000000306&topnumcycle=2020.

63 OpenSecrets, "Soros Fund Management."

64 Open Secrets, "Priorities USA Action PAC Donors," individual donors, accessed June 6, 2023, https://www.opensecrets.org/political-action-committees
-pacs/priorities-usa-action/C00495861/donors/2016

65 "George Soros—Agenda Contributor," World Economic Forum, accessed
May 29, 2023, https://www.weforum.org/agenda/authors/georgesoros.

66 Forbes, "Thomas Steyer," profile, accessed June 6, 2023, https://www.forbes
.com/profile/thomas-steyer/?sh=16f6c64373f5

67 Michela Tindera, "Here's Where Tom Steyer Is Donating His Money Now
That He's Not Running for President," Forbes, November 20, 2022, https://
www.forbes.com/sites/michelatindera/2021/11/20/heres-where-tom-steyer
-is-donating-his-money-now-that-hes-not-running-for-president/?sh=e72c
6c33dc08.

68 Penny Starr, "Clinton/Obama Official, Tom Steyer to Advise Biden on Climate Change," Breitbart News, July 7, 2020, https://www.breitbart.com/2020
-election/2020/07/07/joe-biden-enlists-clinton-obama-loyalist-tom-steyer
-to-advise-on-climate-change/.

69 Tom Steyer (@Tomsteyer), "Big Wins for Our Planet This Week with
Courts Halting Permits and Progress on the Dakota Access Pipeline and
the Atlantic Coast Pipeline," Twitter, July 6, 2020, 12:43 p.m., https://twit
ter.com/TomSteyer/status/1280225809475796994?ref_src=twsrc%5Etf
w%7Ctwcamp%5Etweetembed%7Ctwterm%5E1280225809475796994%7
Ctwgr%5E530daf187a2c8dd90b295ff06ead0703ccfc8e1c%7Ctwco
n%5Es1_&ref_url=https%3A%2F%2Fwww.breitbart.com%2F2020-elec
tion%2F2020%2F07%2F07%2Fjoe-biden-enlists-clinton-obama-loyalist
-tom-steyer-to-advise-on-climate-change%2F.

70 Michael Barbaro and Coral Davenport, "Aims of Donor Are Shadowed by Past
in Coal," New York Times, July 5, 2014, https://www.nytimes.com/2014/07/05
/us/politics/prominent-environmentalist-helped-fund-coal-projects.html?_r=1.

71 "Organization—Fahr LLC—Biden's Basement," Inside Biden's Basement, Accessed May 29, 2023, https://www.insidebidensbasement.org/organizations
/fahr-llc.

72 "Laurene Powell Jobs & Family" profile, *Forbes,* accessed May 29, 2023, https://www.forbes.com/profile/laurene-powell-jobs/?sh=42046383704f.

73 Open Secrets, "Atlantic Media," total contributions by party of recipient, accessed May 29, 2023, https://www.opensecrets.org/orgs/totals? cycle=A&id=D000031688; "Emerson Collective," World Economic Forum, accessed May 29, 2023, https://www.weforum.org/organizations/emerson -collective.

74 "Today, Laurene Powell Jobs Accepted the Medal of Freedom from President Biden on Behalf of Her Late Husband, Steve Jobs," Patently Apple, accessed May 29, 2023, https://www.patentlyapple.com/2022/07/today-laurene -powell-jobs-accepted-the-medal-of-freedom-from-president-biden -on-behalf-of-her-late-husband-steve-jobs.html; Jesse Hollington, "Steve Jobs Awarded the Presidential Medal of Freedom at White House," iDrop News, July 8, 2022, https://www.idropnews.com/news/steve-jobs-awarded-the -presidential-medal-of-freedom/191465/#:~:text=In%20a%20ceremony%20 held%20yesterday,in%20striving%20to%20end%20cancer.

75 "Photo: Guest Arrivals for State Dinner at the White House— Wasp20221001127," UPI, accessed May 29, 2023, https://www.upi.com/News _Photos/view/upi/300374725ee3f64107f27c7b8752a825/Guest-Arrivals -for-State-Dinner-at-the-White-House/.

76 *Forbes,* "Reid Hoffman" profile, accessed May 29, 2023, https://www.forbes .com/profile/reid-hoffman/?sh=7a1a13251849

77 MIT Initiative on the Digital Economy (website) "Reid Hoffman," accessed June 12, 2023, https://ide.mit.edu/people/reid-hoffman/#:~:text=Reid%20 Hoffman%20has%20been%20called,PayPal%2C%20Facebook%20and%20 many%20others.

78 Open Secrets, "Greylock Partners," contributions, accessed May 29, 2023, https:// www.opensecrets.org/orgs/greylock-partners/summary?id=D000034198.

79 Open Secrets, "LinkedIn Corp," total contributions by party of recipient, accessed May 29, 2023, https://www.opensecrets.org/orgs/linkedin-corp /totals?id=D000067159; Open Secrets, "Microsoft Corp," top recipients, accessed May 29, 2023, https://www.opensecrets.org/orgs/microsoft-corp /summary?id=D000000115.

80 Scott Shane and Alan Blinder, "Secret Experiment in Alabama Senate Race Imitated Russian Tactics," *New York Times,* December 19, 2018, https://www .nytimes.com/2018/12/19/us/alabama-senate-roy-jones-russia.html.

81 Scott Shane, "LinkedIn Co-Founder Apologizes for Deception in Alabama Senate Race," *New York Times,* December 26, 2018, https://www.nytimes .com/2018/12/26/us/reid-hoffman-alabama-election-disinformation.html.

82 Nathan Gardels and Bijian Zheng, "21st Century Council—Our Work," *Berggruen Institute,* April 1, 2022, https://www.berggruen.org/work/the -planetary/twenty-first-century-council/.

83 Evelyn M. Rusli, "A King of Connections Is Tech's Go-to Guy," *New York Times,* November 6, 2011, https://www.nytimes.com/2011/11/06/business /reid-hoffman-of-linkedin-has-become-the-go-to-guy-of-tech.html.

84 Alexander Marlow, "Marlow: LinkedIn Billionaire Reid Hoffman's Dark Money behind Clandestine 'Good Information Foundation'; Group Accused of Election Meddling," Breitbart News, October 5, 2022, https://

www.breitbart.com/politics/2022/10/05/marlow-linkedin-billionaire
-reid-hoffmans-dark-money-behind-clandestine-good-information
-foundation-group-accused-of-election-meddling/.

85 Katherine Hamilton, "Formal IRS Complaint Filed against Good Information
Foundation," Breitbart News, September 26, 2022, https://www.breitbart.com
/politics/2022/09/26/formal-irs-complaint-filed-good-information
-foundation-whistleblower-claims-election-activity/.

86 Brian Chappatta, Tom Maloney, Jack Witzig, Pei Yi Mak, and Andrew Heath-
cote, "Bloomberg Billionaires Index," Bloomberg, March 1, 2017, https://
www.bloomberg.com/billionaires/profiles/laurene-p-jobs/#xj4y7vzkg.

87 Nikhil Kumar and Oliver Wright, "Google Boss: I'm Very Proud of Our
Tax Avoidance Scheme," Independent, December 13, 2012, https://www
.independent.co.uk/news/uk/home-news/google-boss-i-m-very-proud-of
-our-tax-avoidance-scheme-8411974.html.

88 Richard Nieva, "Eric Schmidt, Who Led Google's Transformation into a Tech
Giant, Has Left the Company," CNET, May 9, 2020, https://www.cnet.com
/tech/tech-industry/eric-schmidt-who-led-googles-transformation-into-a
-tech-giant-has-left-the-company/.

89 Schmidt Futures, "Eric Braverman-CEO" biography, accessed June 06, 2023,
https://www.schmidtfutures.com/person/eric-braverman/.

90 Alex Thompson, "A Google Billionaire's Fingerprints Are All over Biden's
Science Office," Politico, March 28, 2022, https://www.politico.com
/news/2022/03/28/google-billionaire-joe-biden-science-office-00020712.

91 Abacus.Ai (website), "About," accessed June 6, 2023, https://abacus.ai/about.

92 Thompson, "A Google Billionaire's."

93 Andy Greenberg, "Inside Google's Internet Justice League and Its AI-Powered
War on Troll," Wired, September 19, 2016, https://www.wired.com/2016/09
/inside-googles-internet-justice-league-ai-powered-war-trolls/; "TTP - Eric
Schmidt's Hidden Influence over US Defense Spending," Tech Transparency
Project, May 25, 2022, https://www.techtransparencyproject.org/articles/eric
-schmidts-unseen-influence-over-us-defense-spending.

94 Open Secrets, "Google Inc," top recipients, accessed June 6, 2023, https://
www.opensecrets.org/orgs/google-inc/summary?topnumcycle=A&contrib
cycle=2014&lobcycle=2014&outspendcycle=2014&id=D000022008&topre
cipcycle=2014.

95 Open Secrets, "Alphabet Inc," top recipients, accessed June 6, 2023, https://www
.opensecrets.org/orgs/alphabet-inc/summary?toprecipcycle=2022&contrib
cycle=2022&lobcycle=2022&outspendcycle=2022&id=d000067823&to
pnumcycle=A.

96 Forbes, "Dustin Moskovitz" profile, accessed May 29, 2023, https://www
.forbes.com/profile/dustin-moskovitz/?sh=3d6a574e1dd3.

97 Open Secrets, "Who Are the Biggest Donors?," 2020 election overview,
accessed June 6, 2023, https://www.opensecrets.org/elections-overview
/biggest-donors?cycle=2020.

98 Theodore Schleifer, "Silicon Valley Megadonors Unleash a Last-Minute,
$100 Million Barrage of Ads against Trump," Vox, October 20, 2020,
https://www.vox.com/recode/2020/10/20/21523492/future-forward
-super-pac-dustin-moskovitz-silicon-valley.

199 Open Secrets, "PAC Profile: Future Forward USA," PAC summary data, 2019-2020, accessed May 29, 2023, https://www.opensecrets.org/political -action-committees-pacs/future-forward-usa/C00669259/summary/2020.

100 Will Greenberg, "Dustin Moskovitz's Transformation into a Democratic Mega-Donor," Blue Tent, February 9, 2021, https://bluetent.us/articles /campaigns-elections/dustin-moskovitz-cari-tuna-democratic-donor-2020/.

101 Open Secrets, "Asana," top recipients, accessed May 29, 2023, https://www .opensecrets.org/orgs/asana/summary?id=D000068517.

102 Theodore Schleifer, "Tech Billionaires Are Plotting Sweeping, Secret Plans to Boost Joe Biden," Vox, May 27, 2020, https://www.vox.com /recode/2020/5/27/21271157/tech-billionaires-joe-biden-reid-hoffman -laurene-powell-jobs-dustin-moskovitz-eric-schmidt.

103 Luis Melgar and Chris Alcantara, "Analysis | Meet the Mega-Donors Pump-ing Millions into the 2022 Midterms," Washington Post, October 24, 2022, https://www.washingtonpost.com/politics/interactive/2022/top-election -donors-2022/#; Brian Schwartz, "How Former Crypto King Sam Bankman-Fried and Friends Quietly Donated to Political Groups and Relatives," CNBC, December 19, 2022, https://www.cnbc.com/2022/12/19/how-ftx-founder -sbf-and-friends-quietly-donated-to-political-groups-and-relatives.html.

104 Michela Tindera, "Here's Where Mike Bloomberg, the Biggest Spender in the 2020 Election, Has Donated This Year," Forbes, November 5, 2021, https://www .forbes.com/sites/michelatindera/2021/11/05/heres-where-mike-bloomberg-the -biggest-spender-in-the-2020-election-has-donated-this-year/?sh=2d7f7e995a10.

105 Alex Samuels, "Michael Bloomberg to Spend $15 Million on TV Ads for Biden in Texas and Ohio after Seeing Tight Polling," Texas Tribune, October 27, 2020, https://www.texastribune.org/2020/10/27/michael-bloomberg-biden-texas/.

106 Capital Research Center, "The Left Has a $500 Million Dark Money 'ATM Machine' Called Arabella," Breitbart News, September 4, 2019, https://www .breitbart.com/politics/2019/09/04/the-left-has-a-500-million-dark-money -atm-machine-called-arabella/; Thomas Catenacci, "Major Eco Group Saw Large Funding Uptick Fueled by Liberal Dark Money Network: 'Best Year Ever,' " Fox News, December 20, 2022, https://www.foxnews.com/politics/major-eco-group -saw-large-funding-uptick-fueled-liberal-dark-money-network-best-year-ever.

107 Hayden Ludwig, "Examining Arabella Advisors Dark Money Lobby-ing Power," Tablet Magazine, September 13, 2022, https://www.tablet mag.com/sections/news/articles/for-profit-dc-firm-staging-americas -grassroots-movements-arabella-advisors.

108 Scott Bland, "Liberal 'Dark-Money' Behemoth Funneled More than $400m in 2020," Politico, November 17, 2021, https://www.politico.com /news/2021/11/17/dark-money-sixteen-thirty-fund-522781.

109 Kenneth P. Vogel, "Swiss Billionaire Quietly Becomes Influential Force among Democrats," New York Times, May 3, 2021, https://www.nytimes .com/2021/05/03/us/politics/hansjorg-wyss-money-democrats.html.

110 Catenacci, "Major Eco Group."

111 "Moskovitz, Tuna Pledge $20 Million to Democratic PACS, Groups," Philos-ophy News Digest, September 11, 2016, https://philanthropynewsdigest.org /news/moskovitz-tuna-pledge-20-million-to-democratic-pacs-groups.

112 Schleifer, "Tech Billionaires Are."

PART II: THE BIDEN DOCTRINE: SPEAK LOUDLY AND CARRY A SMALL STICK

CHAPTER 5: WITHDRAWN, BUT NOT FORGOTTEN: THE AFGHANISTAN CALAMITY

1 Martin Pengelly, "Joe Biden advised against Osama bin Laden raid, Barack Obama writes," *Guardian,* November 12, 2020, https://www.theguardian.com /us-news/2020/nov/12/barack-obama-memoir-joe-biden-bin-laden-raid.

2 Kristina Wong, "A Hijacking, Secret Extractions, Taliban Executions: Troops Braved Biden's Botched Afghanistan Withdrawal," Breitbart News, October 19, 2021, https://www.breitbart.com/politics/2021/10/19/a-hijacking-secret-extractions -taliban-executions-troops-braved-bidens-botched-afghanistan-withdrawal/.

3 John Nolte, "Nolte: 9 Ways Biden's Afghanistan Catastrophe Is Much Worse than Saigon," Breitbart News, August 20, 2021, https://www.breitbart.com /politics/2021/08/20/nolte-9-ways-bidens-afghanistan-catastrophe-much -worse-saigon/; Katharine Hamilton, "Rep. Elise Stefanik on Fall of Afghan- istan: 'This Is Joe Biden's Saigon,' " Breitbart News, August 15, 2021, https:// www.breitbart.com/politics/2021/08/15/rep-elise-stefanik-fall-afghanistan -this-joe-bidens-saigon/; Gordon Lubold, Saeed Shah, and Yaroslav Trofi- mov, "Violence Erupts at Kabul Airport as Afghans Try to Flee Taliban," *Wall Street Journal,* August 16, 2021, https://www.wsj.com/articles/three-killed-in -kabul-airport-as-afghans-scramble-to-escape-taliban-11629096273.

4 Ruby Mellen, "Two weeks of chaos: A timeline of the U.S. pullout of Afghan- istan," *Washington Post,* August 15, 2022, https://www.washingtonpost.com /world/2022/08/10/afghanistan-withdrawal-timeline/.

5 Kristina Wong, "Confusion, Chaos, War Crimes: Inside the Harrowing First Days of Biden's Botched Afghanistan Withdrawal," Breitbart News, October 6, 2021, https://www.breitbart.com/politics/2021/10/06/confusion -chaos-war-crimes-inside-the-harrowing-first-days-of-bidens-botched -afghanistan-withdrawal/.

6 Wong, "Confusion, Chaos, War Crimes."

7 Wong, "A Hijacking, Secret Extractions, Taliban Executions."

8 Wong, "A Hijacking, Secret Extractions, Taliban Executions."

9 Wong, "A Hijacking, Secret Extractions, Taliban Executions."

10 Michael McCaul, "House Republican Interim Report: A 'Strategic Failure': Assessing the Administration's Afghanistan Withdrawal," August 14, 2022, https://gop-foreignaffairs.house.gov/wp-content/uploads/2022/08/HFAC -Republican-Interim-Report-A-22Strategic-Failure22-Assessing-the -Administrations-Afghanistan-Withdrawal.pdf.

11 McCaul, "House Republican Interim Report."

12 Barbara Marcolini, Sanjar Sohail, and Alexander Stockton, "The Taliban Promised Them Amnesty. Then They Executed Them," *New York Times,* April 12, 2022, https://www.nytimes.com/interactive/2022/04/12/opinion /taliban-afghanistan-revenge.html.

13 John Hayward, "Biden State Department Falsely Denies Taliban, Terror- ist Haqqani Network Ties," Breitbart News, August 27, 2021, https://www .breitbart.com/politics/2021/08/27/biden-state-department-falsely -denies-taliban-terrorist-haqqani-network-ties/.

14 Stanford Center for International Security and Cooperation (CISAC), "Map-

ping Militant Organizations: Haqqani Network," n.d., https://web.stanford
.edu/group/mappingmilitants/cgi-bin/groups/print_view/363.

15 Eric Garcia, "Pentagon admits 'thousands' of Isis-K militants released from US
prisons by Taliban," *Independent*, August 27, 2021, https://www.independent
.co.uk/news/world/americas/us-politics/isis-k-us-prisons-taliban-b1910021.html.

16 Francis Martel, "U.N.: ISIS Present in Every Province of Afghanistan After
Only 3 Months of Taliban Rule," Breitbart News, November 19, 2021, https://
www.breitbart.com/asia/2021/11/19/u-n-isis-afghanistan-taliban-rule/.

17 Mellen, "Two weeks of chaos."

18 Mellen, "Two weeks of chaos."

19 McCaul, "House Republican Interim Report."

20 C. Todd Lopez, "'Over-the Horizon' Air Strike Kills 2 High-Profile ISIS-K
Targets," *DOD News*, August 28, 2021, https://www.defense.gov/News
/News-Stories/Article/Article/2756029/over-the-horizon-air-strike-kills-2
-high-profile-isis-k-targets/.

21 Sophie Reardon, "Afghanistan drone strike the Pentagon previously described as 'righteous' killed as many as 10 civilians, officials say," CBS News,
September 17, 2021, https://www.cbsnews.com/news/afghanistan-drone
-strike-mistake-civilians-killed-pentagon/.

22 Howard Altman, "CENTCOM IDs man it says was ISIS-K facilitator killed
in Aug. 27 drone strike," *Military Times*, September 23, 2021, https://www
.militarytimes.com/flashpoints/afghanistan/2021/09/23/centcom-ids-man
-it-says-was-isis-k-facilitator-killed-in-aug-27-drone-strike/.

23 U.S. House Committee on Oversight and Reform, "Comer: Biden Administration Will Be Held Accountable for Botched Afghanistan Withdrawal," press release, December 7, 2022, https://oversight.house.gov/release
/comer-biden-administration-will-be-held-accountable-for-botched
-afghanistan-withdrawal/.

24 U.S. House Committee on Oversight and Reform, "Comer: Biden Administration Will Be Held Accountable for Botched Afghanistan Withdrawal."

25 "The Report on Human Rights Violations in the United States in 2021," State
Council Information Office, People's Republic of China, February 28, 2022,
http://english.scio.gov.cn/m/scionews/2022-02/28/content_78076572.htm.

26 Domenico Montanaro, "Biden's Approval Rating Hits a New Low After the
Afghanistan Withdrawal," NPR, September 2, 2021, https://www.npr.org
/2021/09/02/1033433959/biden-approval-rating-afghanistan-withdrawal.

27 Ellen Knickmeyer, "Costs of the Afghanistan war, in lives and dollars," AP
News, August 17, 2021, https://apnews.com/article/middle-east-business
-afghanistan-43d8f53b35e80ec18c130cd683e1a38f.

28 Watson Institute of International & Public Affairs, Cost of War Project,
"Human and Budgetary Costs to Date of the U.S. War in Afghanistan, 2001–
2022," n.d., https://watson.brown.edu/costsofwar/figures/2021/human-and
-budgetary-costs-date-us-war-afghanistan-2001-2022.

29 McCaul, "House Republican Interim Report."

30 Aaron Blake, "Biden says the 'buck stops with me'—while pinning blame on
Trump and many Afghans," *Washington Post*, August 16, 2021, https://www
.washingtonpost.com/politics/2021/08/16/biden-says-buck-stops-with-me
-while-pinning-blame-trump-lots-afghans/.

31 U.S. Department of State, "Agreement for Bringing Peace to Afghanistan," February 29, 2020, PDF file, accessed June 13, 2023, https://www.state.gov/wp-content/uploads/2020/02/Agreement-For-Bringing-Peace-to-Afghanistan-02.29.20.pdf.

32 Matthew Lee and Eric Tucker, "Was Biden handcuffed by Trump's Taliban deal in Doha?," AP News, August 19, 2021, https://apnews.com/article/joe-biden-middle-east-taliban-doha-e6f48507848aef2ee849154604aa11be.

33 Natasha Anderson, James Gordon, and James Robinson, "State Department confirms ALL staff working at the US Embassy in Kabul have been evacuated to chaotic airport where thousands gather on the tarmac desperate to escape Taliban forces tightening grip on capital," Daily Mail, August 16, 2021, https://www.dailymail.co.uk/news/article-9895741/US-ambassador-flees-Kabul-embassy-flag-Americans-shelter-place.html?ito=social-twitter_dailymailus.

34 McCaul, "House Republican Interim Report."

35 Blake, "Biden says the 'buck stops with me.'"

36 Lolita C. Baldor, "Watchdog: US troop pullout was key factor in Afghan collapse," AP News, May 17, 2022, https://apnews.com/article/afghanistan-biden-government-and-politics-donald-trump-7cef514c6cc96848f61a9e8b7fcdf263.

37 Madiha Afzal, "Order from Chaos: Biden was wrong on Afghanistan," Brookings Institution, November 9, 2021, https://www.brookings.edu/blog/order-from-chaos/2021/11/09/biden-was-wrong-on-afghanistan/.

38 Karl Rove, "The Afghanistan Withdrawal Debacle Didn't Have to Happen," Wall Street Journal, August 17, 2022, https://www.wsj.com/articles/the-afghan-debacle-I-have-to-happen-michael-mccaul-report-kabul-isis-marines-withdrawal-taliban-preparation-anniversary-biden-trump-11660761159; William A. Galston, "Anger, betrayal, and humiliation: How veterans feel about the withdrawal from Afghanistan," Brookings Institution, November 12, 2021, https://www.brookings.edu/blog/fixgov/2021/11/12/anger-betrayal-and-humiliation-how-veterans-feel-about-the-withdrawal-from-afghanistan/; Matthew Lee and Eric Tucker, "Was Biden handcuffed by Trump's Taliban deal in Doha?," AP News, August 19, 2021, https://apnews.com/article/joe-biden-middle-east-taliban-doha-e6f48507848aef2ee849154604aa11be.

39 Zeke Miller and Nomaan Merchant, "Biden review of chaotic Afghan withdrawal blames Trump," AP News, April 6, 2023, https://apnews.com/article/joe-biden-afghanistan-withdrawal-congress-war-5ff87c14ffd4f7daaa6675e52d3bba1c.

40 David E. Sanger, "For Biden, Images of Defeat He Wanted to Avoid," New York Times, August 31, 2021, https://www.nytimes.com/2021/08/15/us/politics/afghanistan-biden.html.

41 McCaul, "House Republican Interim Report."

42 Jared Keller, "Watch the Secretary of State say Afghanistan can't fall from 'Friday to Monday,'" Task & Purpose, August 16, 2021, https://taskandpurpose.com/news/afghanistan-kabul-blinken-video/.

43 Jeff Schogol, "Taliban capture Kabul, marking final victory as Afghanistan collapses," Task & Purpose, August 15, 2021, https://taskandpurpose.com/news/taliban-victory-kabul-afghanistan/.

44 Kawoon Khamoosh (@KawoonKhamoosh), Afghan ambassador in Tajiki-
stan says Ashraf Ghani escaped with bags full of 169 million US dollars when
Kabul was falling," Twitter, August 18, 2021, 1:18 a.m., https://twitter.com
/KawoonKhamoosh/status/1427907632040398849.

45 John Hayward, "Ashraf Ghani Declares: 'I Am Still President of Afghanistan,' " Breitbart News, August 12, 2022, https://www.breitbart.com/national
-security/2022/08/12/ashraf-ghani-declares-i-am-still-president-of
-afghanistan/.

46 McCaul, "House Republican Interim Report."

47 Saeed Ahmed, "A Watchdog Group Had Been Sounding the Warning About
Afghanistan's Meltdown for Years," NPR, August 16, 2021, https://www.gpb
.org/news/2021/08/16/watchdog-group-had-been-sounding-the-warning
-about-afghanistans-meltdown-for-years.

48 John F. Sopko, "SIGAR Quarterly Report to the United States Congress," Special Inspector General for Afghanistan Reconstruction, July 30, 2020, https://
www.sigar.mil/pdf/quarterlyreports/2020-07-30qr-intro-section1.pdf.

49 Joseph R. Biden, "Remarks by President Biden on Afghanistan" (speech),
August 16, 2021, The White House, https://www.whitehouse.gov/briefing
-room/speeches-remarks/2021/08/16/remarks-by-president-biden-on
-afghanistan/.

50 Natasha Bertrand, Andrew Desiderio, Lara Seligman, and Nahal Toosi, "How
Biden's team overrode the brass on Afghanistan," Politico, April 14, 2021,
https://www.politico.com/news/2021/04/14/pentagon-biden-team-overrode
-afghanistan-481556.

51 "Full transcript of ABC News' George Stephanopoulos' interview with
President Joe Biden," ABC News, August 19, 2021, https://abcnews.go.com
/Politics/full-transcript-abc-news-george-stephanopoulos-interview
-president/story?id=79535643.

52 McCaul, "House Republican Interim Report."

53 McCaul, "House Republican Interim Report."

54 Robert Kraychik, "Exclusive—Sen. Tom Cotton: Disaster in Afghanistan 'Totally Avoidable,' Will Be Used by Our Enemies 'for Years to Come,' " Breitbart
News, August 17, 2021, https://www.breitbart.com/radio/2021/08/17/exclu
sive-tom-cotton-disaster-afghanistan-totally-avoidable/.

55 Joseph R. Biden, "Remarks by President Biden on the End of the War in
Afghanistan" (speech), August 31, 2021, The White House, https://www
.whitehouse.gov/briefing-room/speeches-remarks/2021/08/31/remarks-by
-president-biden-on-the-end-of-the-war-in-afghanistan/.

56 Kristina Wong, "Republicans Expose 3 Blatant Biden Afghanistan Lies in
Contentious Hearing with Military Leaders," Breitbart News, September 28,
2021,   https://www.breitbart.com/politics/2021/09/28/republicans-expose
-three-blatant-biden-afghanistan-lies-military-leaders/.

57 Sahil Kapur, "Joe Biden bets a war-weary America will reward him for leaving Afghanistan," NBC News, August 19, 2021, https://www.nbcnews.com
/politics/white-house/joe-biden-bets-war-weary-america-will-reward-him
-leaving-n1277104.

58 Joseph R. Biden, "Remarks by President Biden on Evacuations in Afghanistan" (speech), August 20, 2021, The White House, https://www

.whitehouse.gov/briefing-room/speeches-remarks/2021/08/20
/remarks-by-president-biden-on-evacuations-in-afghanistan/.

59 McCaul, "House Republican Interim Report."

60 Mark Landler, "Biden Rattles U.K. with His Afghanistan Policy," *New York
    Times,* August 18, 2021, https://www.nytimes.com/2021/08/18/world
    /europe/britain-afghanistan-johnson-biden.html.

61 McCaul, "House Republican Interim Report."

62 McCaul, "House Republican Interim Report."

63 McCaul, "House Republican Interim Report"; Andrew Desiderio, Lara Se-
    ligman, and Alexander Ward, "800 Americans evacuated from Afghanistan
    since Taliban takeover," *Politico,* August 14, 2022, https://www.politico.com
    /news/2022/08/14/afghanistan-800-evacuated-taliban-00051525.

64 McCaul, "House Republican Interim Report."

65 Jennifer Smith, "Defense officials say they'll save 5,000 a day from Kabul but
    'up to 40,000' Americans remain stranded: Taliban fighters close in on airport
    after taking ALL access points which forces US troops to negotiate with them
    on who gets in," *Daily Mail,* August 17, 2021, https://www.dailymail.co.uk
    /news/article-9901361/Up-40-000-Americans-stranded-Afghanistan.html.

66 Sawsan Morrar and Jason Pohl, "Nearly 50 Sacramento-area students remain
    trapped in Afghanistan. When will they be rescued?," *Sacramento Bee,* Sep-
    tember 26, 2021, https://www.sacbee.com/news/local/article254412638.html.

67 McCaul, "House Republican Interim Report."

68 McCaul, "House Republican Interim Report."

69 United States Senate Committee on Foreign Relations, *A Brief Assessment of
    the Biden Administration's Strategic Failures during the Afghanistan Evacua-
    tion,* minority report (February 2022), https://www.foreign.senate.gov/imo
    /media/doc/Risch%20Afghanistan%20Report%202022.pdf.

70 McCaul, "House Republican Interim Report."

71 McCaul, "House Republican Interim Report."

72 Ellie Kaufman, "First on CNN: US left behind $7 billion of military equipment
    in Afghanistan after 2021 withdrawal, Pentagon report says," CNN, April 28,
    2022, https://www.cnn.com/2022/04/27/politics/afghan-weapons-left-behind
    /index.html.

73 Eileen Guo and Hikmat Noori, "Crisis in Kabul: This is the real story of the
    Afghan biometric databases abandoned to the Taliban," *MIT Technnology
    Review,* August 30, 2021, https://www.technologyreview.com/2021/08/30
    /1033941/afghanistan-biometric-databases-us-military-40-data-points/;
    McCaul, "House Republican Interim Report"; Struan Stevenson, "Taliban's
    windfall from U.S. withdrawal: $83B in weapons," United Press International,
    September 20, 2021, https://www.upi.com/Voices/2021/09/20/Afghanistan
    -withdrawal-US-weapons-left-behind/7181632140222/.

74 Idrees Ali, Patricia Zengerle, and Jonathan Landay, "Planes, guns, night-vision
    goggles: The Taliban's new U.S.-made war chest," Reuters, August 19, 2021,
    https://www.reuters.com/business/aerospace-defense/planes-guns-night
    -vision-goggles-talibans-new-us-made-war-chest-2021-08-19/.

75 "Taliban to create Afghanistan 'grand army' with old regime troops," Al
    Jazeera, February 22, 2022, https://www.aljazeera.com/news/2022/2/22
    /taliban-create-grand-army-afghanistan-old-regime-troops.

76 Ruhullah Khapalwak and David Zucchino, "For Sale Now: U.S.-Supplied Weapons in Afghan Gun Shops," *New York Times,* October 15, 2021, https://www.nytimes.com/2021/10/05/world/asia/us-weapons-afghanistan.html.

77 McCaul, "House Republican Interim Report."

78 Kathy Gannon, "US left Afghan airfield at night, didn't tell new commander," Associated Press, July 6, 2021, https://apnews.com/article/bagram-afghanistan-airfield-us-troops-f3614828364f567593251aaaa167e623.

79 Gannon, "US left Afghan airfield at night, didn't tell new commander."

80 Ian Thomas, "A former US intelligence officer breaks down the mistakes in Afghanistan," *Northeastern Global News,* August 19, 2021, https://news.northeastern.edu/2021/08/19/a-former-us-intelligence-officer-breaks-down-the-mistakes-in-afghanistan/.

81 McCaul, "House Republican Interim Report."

82 Nick Paton Walsh and Sandi Sidhu, "Al Qaeda and Taliban members among thousands of prisoners left under Afghan control in jail next to deserted US air base," CNN, July 6, 2021, https://www.cnn.com/2021/07/06/world/al-qaeda-taliban-prisoners-us-air-base-intl/index.html.

83 David Zucchino, "At an Abandoned American Base, a Notorious Prison Lies Empty," *New York Times,* December 21, 2021, https://www.nytimes.com/2021/12/21/world/asia/afghanistan-taliban-bagram-prison.html.

84 McCaul, "House Republican Interim Report."

85 McCaul, "House Republican Interim Report."

86 McCaul, "House Republican Interim Report."

87 The White House, "Press Briefing by Press Secretary Jen Psaki, August 31, 2021," August 31, 2021, https://www.whitehouse.gov/briefing-room/press-briefings/2021/08/31/press-briefing-by-press-secretary-jen-psaki-august-31-2021/.

88 Watson Institute of International & Public Affairs, Cost of War Project, "Afghanistan before and after 20 years of war (2001–2021)," n.d., https://watson.brown.edu/costsofwar/Afghanistanbeforeandafter20yearsofwar.

89 Christopher Helman and Hank Tucker, "The War in Afghanistan Cost America $300 Million Per Day for 20 Years, with Big Bills Yet to Come," *Forbes,* August 16, 2021, https://www.forbes.com/sites/hanktucker/2021/08/16/the-war-in-afghanistan-cost-america-300-million-per-day-for-20-years-with-big-bills-yet-to-come/?sh=7f152ed97f8d.

90 Helman and Tucker, "The War in Afghanistan Cost."

91 Watson Institute of International & Public Affairs, Cost of War Project, "Corporate Power, Profiteering, and the 'Camo Economy,' " n.d., https://watson.brown.edu/costsofwar/costs/social/corporate.

92 Watson Institute, "Corporate Power."

93 William D. Hartung, "Profits of War: Corporate Beneficiaries of the Post-9/11 Pentagon Spending Surge," Watson Institute of International & Public Affairs, September 12, 2021, https://watson.brown.edu/costsofwar/files/cow/imce/papers/2021/Profits%20of%20War_Hartung_Costs%20of%20War_Sept%2013%2C%202021.pdf.

94 Graig Graziosi, "Why did US leave Afghanistan and how much did America

spend?," *Independent,* August 18, 2021, https://www.independent.co.uk/news/world/americas/us-politics/us-leave-afghanistan-america-spend-b1904289.html.

95 Neta C. Crawford, "The U.S. Budgetary Costs of the Post-9/11 Wars," Watson Institute of International & Public Affairs, September 1, 2021, https://watson.brown.edu/costsofwar/files/cow/imce/papers/2021/Costs%20of%20War_U.S.%20Budgetary%20Costs%20of%20Post-9%2011%20Wars_9.1.21.pdf.

96 Helman and Tucker, "The War in Afghanistan Cost."

97 Watson Institute, "Afghanistan before and after."

98 Watson Institute, "Afghanistan before and after."

99 Watson Institute, "Afghanistan before and after."

100 Michele Geraci, "For Afghanistan, the Silk Road is better than the Tank Road," *Global Times,* August 19, 2021, https://www.globaltimes.cn/page/202108/1232006.shtml.

101 "China can contribute to Afghan development—Taliban spokesman," Reuters, August 19, 2021, https://www.reuters.com/world/asia-pacific/taliban-spokesman-says-china-can-contribute-afghanistans-development-state-media-2021-08-19/.

102 Mohammad Yunus Yawar, "Afghanistan's Taliban administration in oil extraction deal with Chinese company," Reuters, January 5, 2023, https://www.reuters.com/business/afghanistans-taliban-administration-oil-extraction-deal-with-chinese-company-2023-01-05/.

103 Jonathan Landay, "Profits and poppy: Afghanistan's illegal drug trade a boon for Taliban," Reuters, August 16, 2021, https://www.reuters.com/world/asia-pacific/profits-poppy-afghanistans-illegal-drug-trade-boon-taliban-2021-08-16/.

104 Frances Martel, "Starving Afghans Sell Young Girls to Old Men for as Little as $1000," Breitbart News, November 3, 2021, https://www.breitbart.com/asia/2021/11/03/starving-afghans-sell-young-girls-to-old-men-for-as-little-as-1000/.

105 Rob Picheta and Zahid Mahmood, "Taliban tell Afghan women to stay home from work because soldiers are 'not trained' to respect them," CNN, August 25, 2021, https://www.cnn.com/2021/08/25/asia/taliban-women-workplaces-afghanistan-intl/index.html.

106 Sophie Tanno, "The Taliban pledged to honor women's rights in Afghanistan. Here's how it eroded them instead," CNN, December 23, 2022, https://www.cnn.com/2022/12/23/asia/taliban-women-freedoms-intl/index.html.

107 "Death in slow motion: Women and girls under Taliban rule," Amnesty International, July 7, 2022, https://www.amnesty.org/en/documents/asa11/5685/2022/en/.

108 McCaul, "House Republican Interim Report."

109 Michael T. McCaul, "Letter to Secretary Blinken, Secretary Yellen, and Administrator Power," December 1, 2022, https://gop-foreignaffairs.house.gov/wp-content/uploads/2022/12/SIGAR-Obstruction-Letter-Final.pdf.

110 McCaul, "House Republican Interim Report."

CHAPTER 6: JOE BIDEN'S UNDENIABLE ROLE IN UKRAINE'S INVASION OF RUSSIA

1 Edmund DeMarche, "Gates Seems to Double Down on Claim That Biden's Been Wrong on Top Foreign Policy Issues for Decades," Fox News, October18,2021,https://www.foxnews.com/politics/gates-seems-to-double-down -on-claim-that-bidens-been-wrong-on-top-foreign-policy-issues-for-decades.

2 Georgiy Kasianov, "War Over Ukrainian Identity," *Foreign Affairs*, May 4, 2022, https://www.foreignaffairs.com/articles/ukraine/2022-05-04/war-over -ukrainian-identity; Kremlin, "Working visit to Volgograd," President of Russia, July 12, 2021, http://en.kremlin.ru/events/president/news/66181.

3 Paul Stronski, "What Is Russia Doing in the Black Sea?," Carnegie Endowment for International Peace, May 20, 2021, https://carnegieendowment .org/2021/05/20/what-is-russia-doing-in-black-sea-pub-84549.

4 Geir Moulson, "German Parliament Labels 1930s Soviet Famine in Ukraine as Genocide," *PBS NewsHour*, November 30, 2022, https://www.pbs.org /newshour/world/german-parliament-labels-1930s-soviet-famine-in -ukraine-as-genocide; Ambassador Michael Carpenter, statement, "On the 90th Anniversary of the Holodomor Genocide of 1932 and 1933 in Ukraine," U.S. Mission to the OSCE, November 24, 2022, https://osce.usmission.gov /on-the-90th-anniversary-of-the-holodomor-genocide-of-1932-and-1933 -in-ukraine/; European Parliament, "Holodomor: Parliament Recognises Soviet Starvation of Ukrainians as Genocide," *European Parliament News*, December 15, 2022, https://www.europarl.europa.eu/news/en/press -room/20221209IPR64427/holodomor-parliament-recognises-soviet -starvation-of-ukrainians-as-genocide.

5 Guy Faulconbridge, "Ukraine war: Already with up 354,000 casualties, it is likely to drag on, U.S. documents say," Reuters, April 12, 2023, https://www .reuters.com/world/europe/ukraine-war-already-with-up-354000-casualties -likely-drag-us-documents-2023-04-12/.

6 Faulconbridge, "Ukraine war."

7 "Germany to pull plug on three of its last six nuclear plants," Reuters, December 30, 2021, https://www.reuters.com/world/europe/germany-pull -plug-three-its-last-six-nuclear-plants-2021-12-30/#:~:text=The%20last%20 three%20nuclear%20power,targets%20and%20rising%20power%20prices.

8 Bojan Pancevski, "How Germany Is Curing Its Dependence on Russian Energy," *Wall Street Journal*, May 17, 2022, https://www.wsj.com/articles/how -germany-is-curing-its-dependence-on-russian-energy-11652801958.

9 "Blinken seeks to revitalize NATO alliance," *DW News*, March 23, 2021, https:// www.dw.com/en/blinken-seeks-to-revitalize-nato-alliance/a-56957728.

10 "Ukrainian official: Biden's answer gives Putin 'green light' to invade," YouTube video, 8:49, posted by "CNN" January 20, 2022, https://www.youtube .com/watch?v=c67eB14OWJc.

11 Tracy Wilkinson, "Biden's 'minor incursion' comment roils diplomatic efforts to halt Russian invasion of Ukraine," *Los Angeles Times*, January 20, 2022, https://www.latimes.com/politics/story/2022-01-20/bidens-minor-incursion -comment-roils-diplomatic-efforts-to-halt-russian-invasion-of-ukraine.

12 Mark Landler, "Trump Abandons Iran Nuclear Deal He Long Scorned," *New York Times*, May 8, 2018, https://www.nytimes.com/2018/05/08/world

/middleeast/trump-iran-nuclear-deal.html. Ian Mason, "Trump Supporters Elated as President Ends Iran Nuclear Deal," Breitbart News, May 8, 2018, https://www.breitbart.com/politics/2018/05/08/trump-supporters-elated -president-ends-iran-nuclear-deal/.

13 Carol Morello, "Retired generals and admirals urge Congress to reject Iran nu-clear deal," *Washington Post,* August 26, 2015, https://www.washingtonpost.com /world/national-security/retired-generals-and-admirals-urge-congress-to-re ject-iran-deal/2015/08/26/8912d9c6-4bf5-11e5-84df-923b3ef1a64b_story.html.

14 Mason, "Retired generals and admirals urge Congress."

15 "Obama Thanks Putin for Russia's Role in Iran Nuclear Deal," Reuters, July 16, 2015, https://www.nbcnews.com/storyline/iran-nuclear-talks/obama -thanks-putin-russias-role-iran-nuclear-deal-n392976.

16 Andrew C. Mccarthy, "Russia and Iran Taunt Biden in Humiliating Revival of Nuclear Deal," *National Review,* March 5, 2022, https://www.nationalreview .com/corner/russia-and-iran-taunt-biden-in-humiliating-revival-of-nuclear -deal/.

17 "Biden: Putin is a 'butcher,'" YouTube, 0:37, posted by Reuters, March 26, 2022, https://www.youtube.com/watch?v=ZNiEsTKUT5o.

18 Joel B. Pollak, "Report: Biden's Iran Deal Gives Regime Access to $90 Bil-lion, $7 Billion for Ransom, Sanctions Relief to Terrorists," Breitbart News, March 8, 2022, https://www.breitbart.com/politics/2022/03/08/report-bidens -iran-deal-gives-regime-access-to-90-billion-7-billion-for-ransom -sanctions-relief-to-terrorists/; Joel B. Pollak, "Russia: Biden Has Caved on Our Iran Deal Demands, Talks May Resume," Breitbart News, March 16, 2022, https://www.breitbart.com/national-security/2022/03/16/russia-biden -has-caved-on-our-iran-deal-demands-talks-may-resume/.

19 Nahal Toosi and Stephanie Liechtenstein, "Russia may do Biden a favor by killing the Iran deal," *Politico,* March 14, 2022, https://www.politico.com /news/2022/03/14/russia-biden-killing-iran-deal-00017113.

20 Toosi and Liechtenstein, "Russia may do Biden a favor."

21 Aresu Eqbali, "Iran Acknowledges Supplying Drones to Russia," *Wall Street Journal,* November 5, 2022, https://www.wsj.com/articles/iran-acknowledges -supplying-drones-to-russia-11667650978?mod=article_inline.

22 Barak Ravid and Hans Nichols, "Biden in newly surfaced video: Iran nuclear deal is 'dead,'" Axios, December 20, 2022, https://www.axios.com/2022/12/20 /biden-iran-nuclear-deal-dead-video.

23 Mike McDaniel, "Why Paul Whelan Wasn't Included in Deal for Brittney Griner, per Report," *Sports Illustrated,* December 8, 2022, https://www.si.com /wnba/2022/12/08/why-paul-whelan-wasnt-included-deal-for-brittney -griner-russia-release-report.

24 Duncan Mackay, "American double Olympic basketball gold medallist ar-rested on drugs charges in Moscow," Inside the Games, March 6, 2022, https://www.insidethegames.biz/articles/1120148/us-olympic-gold-medallist -drugs-moscow.

25 Jacob Sullum, "Brittney Griner's 9-Year Sentence Highlights Stark Differences Between Russian and U.S. Pot Penalties," *Reason,* August 5, 2022, https:// reason.com/2022/08/05/brittney-griners-9-year-sentence-highlights-stark -differences-between-russian-and-u-s-pot-penalties/.

26 Althea Legaspi, "Brittney Griner Testifies That She Packed Vape Cartridges Accidentally in Russian Drug Trial," *Rolling Stone,* July 27, 2022, https://www.rollingstone.com/culture/culture-news/brittney-griner-to-testify-russian-trial-1388224/.

27 Jim Heintz, "WNBA's Griner convicted at drug trial, sentenced to 9 years," AP News, August 4, 2022, https://apnews.com/article/brittney-griner-trial-verdict-live-updates-40eccfc427da65b3c02eeabc8a7410ff.

28 "Frequently Asked Questions," VictorBout.com, accessed via Wayback Machine on May 28, 2023, https://web.archive.org/web/20090607041502/http://www.victorbout.com/FAQ.htm; "Meet Viktor Bout, the Real-Life 'Lord of War,' " *Mother* Jones, accessed via Wayback Machine on May 28, 2023, https://web.archive.org/web/20180612184639/https://www.motherjones.com/politics/2007/09/meet-viktor-bout-real-life-lord-war/.

29 "Viktor Bout: 'The Merchant of Death,' " YouTube video, 12:54, posted by CBS News on November 21, 2010, https://www.youtube.com/watch?v=XvPGIcVRKco; "The charges against Charles Taylor," BBC News, February 8, 2011, https://www.bbc.com/news/world-africa-12391507.

30 "Viktor Bout: 'The Merchant of Death.' "

31 "How 9/11 Changed the Game for Arms Dealer Viktor Bout," YouTube video, posted by Smithsonian Channel on April 25, 2020, https://www.youtube.com/watch?v=6q4jY7_0Hh4.

32 " 'Nazi'-inspired US prison guards, American 'revolution' and Ukraine conflict: Highlights from Viktor Bout's RT interview," RT News, December 10, 2022 https://www.rt.com/russia/568022-viktor-bout-rt-interview/.

33 Patrick Reevell, "Ex-Marine Paul Whelan sentenced to 16 years in Russian jail," ABC News, June 15, 2020, https://abcnews.go.com/International/us-marine-paul-whelan-sentenced-16-years-jail/story?id=71251643.

34 Joel B. Pollak, "Biden Leaves Marine Paul Whelan Behind in Russia in Brittney Griner Swap; Family: 'Catastrophe,' " Breitbart News, December 8, 2022, https://www.breitbart.com/national-security/2022/12/08/biden-leaves-marine-paul-whelan-behind-in-russia-brittney-griner-swap-family-catastrophe/.

35 Jennifer Hansler, "Exclusive: Paul Whelan tells CNN he is 'disappointed' that more has not been done to secure his release," CNN, December 8, 2022, https://www.cnn.com/2022/12/08/politics/paul-whelan-CNN-interview-brittney-griner/index.html.

36 Paul Kirby, "Brittney Griner: Russia frees US basketball star in swap with arms dealer Viktor Bout," BBC News, December 9, 2022, https://www.bbc.com/news/world-europe-63905112.

37 Kirby, "Brittney Griner."

38 "Diplomat: Russia might discuss swap for jailed US reporter," AP News, April 13, 2023, https://apnews.com/article/russia-detained-wall-street-journal-reporter-d3a51b09c1db6b1d5b8012367bff51c4; "Report: Russia charges Journal reporter with espionage," *Politico,* April 7, 2023, https://www.politico.com/news/2023/04/07/report-russia-formally-charges-wall-street-journal-reporter-00091026.

39 Ann M. Simmons, "Russia Could Consider Swap for WSJ Reporter Evan Gershkovich After Trial Ends," *Wall Street Journal,* April 13, 2023, https://www

.wsj.com/articles/russia-could-consider-swap-for-evan-gershkovich
-after-trial-ends-80d74783.

40 Peter Spiegel, "Biden Says Weakened Russia Will Bend to U.S.," *Wall Street Journal,* July 25, 2009, https://www.wsj.com/articles/SB124848246032580581.

41 Peter Baker, "Obama Offered Deal to Russia in Secret Letter," *New York Times,* March 2, 2009, https://www.nytimes.com/2009/03/03/washington/03prexy.html.

42 Baker, "Obama Offered Deal."

43 Baker Spring, "Twelve Flaws of New START That Will Be Difficult to Fix," Heritage Foundation, September 16, 2010, https://www.heritage.org /arms-control/report/twelve-flaws-new-start-will-be-difficult-fix.

44 Charles Digges, "Russian-US 123 agreement comes into force, bringing possible nuclear hazards for Russia," Bellona, January 13, 2011, https://bellona .org/news/nuclear-issues/radioactive-waste-and-spent-nuclear-fuel/2011 -01-russian-us-123-agreement-comes-into-force-bringing-possible-nuclear -hazards-for-russia.

45 Jo Becker and Mike McIntire, "Cash Flowed to Clinton Foundation Amid Russian Uranium Deal," *New York Times,* April 23, 2015, https://www .nytimes.com/2015/04/24/us/cash-flowed-to-clinton-foundation-as -russians-pressed-for-control-of-uranium-company.html.

46 Andrew C. Mccarthy, "Remembering Obama's 'Russia Reset': Hillary and the 'Skolkovo' Misadventure," *National Review,* February 22, 2022, https:// www.nationalreview.com/corner/remembering-obamas-russia-reset -hillary-and-the-skolkovo-misadventure/; Peter Schweizer, "The Clinton Foundation, State and Kremlin Connections," *Wall Street Journal,* July 31, 2016, https://www.wsj.com/articles/the-clinton-foundation-state-and -kremlin-connections-1469997195.

47 "Russia GDP Annual Growth Rate," Trading Economics, accessed May 29, 2023, https://tradingeconomics.com/russia/gdp-growth-annual.

48 Seamus Bruner, "Obama Administration's Botched 'Russia Reset' Enriched Political Class and Set the Stage for Chaos in Ukraine," *The Drill Down with Peter Schweizer,* March 24, 2022, https://thedrilldown.com/newsroom /botched-reset-enriched-political-class-set-stage-for-ukraine-chaos

49 United States Congress, Senate, Committee on Foreign Relations, *The Debate on NATO Enlargement: Hearings Before the Committee on Foreign Relations,* 105th Cong., 1st sess., 1997, 105–285, https://www.govinfo.gov/content/pkg /CHRG-105shrg46832/html/CHRG-105shrg46832.htm.

50 "Rice deputy says outside pressure could be used to influence Russian politics," *Canadian Press,* February 15, 2005, https://advance.lexis.com /document/?pdmfid=1519360&crid=03a6700d-a147-45a4-8946 -abc30bf9bd50&pddocfullpath=%2fshared%2fdocument%2fnews %2furn%3acontentItem%3a4FGW-Y8K0-01G6-91GR-00000-00&pdco ntentcomponentid=253760&pdteaserkey=sr3&pditab=allpods&ecomp= zxmyk&earg=sr3&prid=b028bb31-fc56-47cc-855f-e0e34edd 8abc&aci=la&cbc=0&lnsi=a602d9d5-830a-4b7e-93ca-cb06e1a41a05&rm flag=0&sit=1674981244335.355.

51 Marcy Oster, "Russia Doesn't Want Ukraine to Join NATO. Is That a Reason to Invade?" The Medialine, February 28, 2022, https://themedialine.org /news/russia-doesnt-want-ukraine-to-join-nato-is-that-a-reason-to-invade/.

52 North Atlantic Treaty Organization, "Bucharest Summit Declaration," press release, July 5, 2022, https://www.nato.int/cps/en/natolive/official _texts_8443.htm.

53 Stephen F. Larrabee and Bernard Gwertzman, "Russia's Offensive in Georgia a Signal to NATO to Stay Away from Its 'Space,' " Council on Foreign Relations, August 25, 2008, https://www.cfr.org/interview/russias-offensive-georgia -signal-nato-stay-away-its-space.

54 Larrabee and Gwertzman, "Russia's Offensive in Georgia."

55 Andrew Roth, "Ukraine's ex-president Viktor Yanukovych found guilty of trea-son," *Guardian,* January 25, 2019, https://www.theguardian.com/world/2019 /jan/25/ukraine-ex-president-viktor-yanukovych-found-guilty-of-treason.

56 Alastair Macdonald, "Moscow accuses U.S. of fomenting Ukraine coup; re-cordings leaked," Reuters, February 6, 2014, https://www.reuters.com/article /ukraine-russia-us/moscow-accuses-u-s-of-fomenting-ukraine-coup -recordings-leaked-idINDEEA1602A20140207.

57 John J. Mearsheimer, "Why the Ukraine Crisis Is the West's Fault," *For-eign Affairs,* August 18, 2014, https://www.foreignaffairs.com/articles /russia-fsu/2014-08-18/why-ukraine-crisis-west-s-fault.

58 Robert Parry, "Did the U.S. Carry Out a Ukrainian Coup?" Real News Net-work, March 4, 2014, https://therealnews.com/rparry0303ukraine.

59 Parry, "Did the U.S. Carry Out a Ukrainian Coup?"

60 Oksana Grytsenko, "Ukrainian protesters flood Kiev after president pulls out of EU deal," *Guardian,* November, 24, 2013, https://www.theguardian.com /world/2013/nov/24/ukraine-protesters-yanukovych-aborts-eu-deal-russia.

61 Victoria Nuland gives food for demonstration people in Ukraine," YouTube video, 1:41, posted by "FrontNews Ge," December 11, 2013, https://www .youtube.com/watch?v=fbjNJbjEy04.

62 "Maidan Puppets," YouTube video, 4:10, posted by "Re Post," February 4, 2014, https://www.youtube.com/watch?v=MSxaa-67yGM.

63 "Ukraine crisis: Transcript of leaked Nuland-Pyatt call," BBC News, February 7, 2014, https://www.bbc.com/news/world-europe-26079957.

64 William Nattrass, "Russia and Ukraine named as Europe's most corrupt countries," UnHerd, February 3, 2023, https://unherd.com/thepost/russia -and-ukraine-named-as-europes-most-corrupt-countries/; "Corruption Per-ceptions Index 2018," Transparency International, accessed May 29, 2023, https://www.transparency.org/en/cpi/2022.

65 Rob Young, "Bribes and bureaucrats: Doing business in Ukraine," BBC News, March 7, 2011, http://news.bbc.co.uk/2/hi/programmes/direct /ukraine/9406824.stm.

66 Paul D'Anieri, "Power and Institutions: Overview of the Argument," in *Understanding Ukrainian Politics: Power, Politics, and Institutional De-sign* (Armonk, NY: M. E. Sharpe, 2006), 63, https://books.google.com /books?id=Wp7VKL4p7kQC&pg=PA63&dq=vote+rigging+Ukraine&hl= nl&ei=phVxTqClNIGdOqDkmJMJ&sa=X&oi=book_result&ct=result& resnum=1&ved=0CCsQ6AEwADgK#v=onepage&q=vote%20rigging%20 Ukraine&f=false; "Regions Party declares current government corrupt," *Kyiv Post,* accessed via Wayback Machine on May 29, 2023, https://web .archive.org/web/20110605125708/http://www.kyivpost.com/news/politics

/detail/56404/; "Ukrainska Pravda exposes presidential estate scandal," *Kyiv Post*, accessed via Wayback Machine on May 29, 2023, https://web.archive.org /web/20120614060200/http://www.kyivpost.com/news/nation/detail/91317/.

67 "Jackpot," *Kyiv Post*, accessed via Wayback Machine on May 29, 2023, https:// web.archive.org/web/20120614030839/http://www.kyivpost.com/news /nation/detail/62564/; "In Ukraine, scales of justice often imbalanced," *Kyiv Post*, accessed via Wayback Machine on May 29, 2023, https://web.archive.org /web/20120504072130/http://www.kyivpost.com/news/nation/detail/125714/.

68 Vladislava Batyrgareieva, Andriy Babenko, and Sandra Kaija, "Corruption in medical sphere of Ukraine: Current situation and ways of prevention," *Wiadomosci lekarskie* 72, no. 9 (2019): 1814–21, https://pubmed.ncbi.nlm.nih .gov/31622272/.

69 Iulia Mendel, "In Ukraine's universities, trading bribes for diplomas," *Politico*, January 30, 2016, https://www.politico.eu/article/trading-bribes-for-diplomas -in-ukraines-universities-taxes-transparency-education-corruption/.

70 Emma-Jo Morris, " 'My Son Hunter' True Fact: Hunter Biden Took a Salary of $83K per Month from Ukrainian Energy Co. Burisma," Breitbart News, September 13, 2022, https://www.breitbart.com/entertainment/2022/09/13 /my-son-hunter-true-fact-hunter-biden-took-a-salary-of-83k-per-month -from-burisma/.

71 Emma-Jo Morris, " 'My Son Hunter' True Fact: Joe Biden Threatened to Withhold $1 Billion from Ukraine Unless They Fired the Prosecutor Investigating the Company That Hired Hunter," Breitbart News, September 16, 2022, https://www.breitbart.com/entertainment/2022/09/16/my-son-hunter -true-fact-joe-biden-threatened-to-withhold-1-billion-from-ukraine-to -protect-company-hunter-was-working-with/.

72 Steven Pifer, "The Biden presidency and Ukraine," Brookings Institution, January 28, 2021, https://www.brookings.edu/blog/order-from -chaos/2021/01/28/the-biden-presidency-and-ukraine/.

73 Mark Episkopos, "Joe Biden's Pick of Victoria Nuland Means Relations with Russia Could Get Worse," *National Interest*, January 15, 2021, https:// nationalinterest.org/feature/joe-biden%E2%80%99s-pick-victoria -nuland-means-relations-russia-could-get-worse-176516.

74 Abby Ohlheiser, "State Department Official Caught on Tape Saying 'F-ck the EU,' " *Atlantic*, February 6, 2014, https://www.theatlantic.com/politics/archive /2014/02/state-department-official-caught-tape-saying-f-eu/357812/.

75 John Hudson, "The Undiplomatic Diplomat," *Foreign Policy*, June 18, 2015, https://foreignpolicy.com/2015/06/18/the-undiplomatic-diplomat/.

76 "Victoria Nuland is not allowed into the territory of Russia," Top War, May 23, 2019, https://en.topwar.ru/158201-viktoriju-nuland-ne-pustili-na -territoriju-rossii.html.

77 United States Department of State, "Undersecretary for Political Affairs," accessed May 30, 2023, https://www.state.gov/bureaus-offices/under -secretary-for-political-affairs/.

78 "Biden administration announces $125M military aid package for Ukraine," NBC News, March 2, 2021, https://www.nbcnews.com/politics/national -security/biden-administration-announces-125m-military-aid-package -ukraine-n1259254.

79 U.S. Embassy in Ukraine, "Defense Department Announces $125M for Ukraine," March 1, 2021, https://ua.usembassy.gov/defense-department -announces-125m-for-ukraine/.

80 "Blinken seeks to 'revitalize' NATO alliance," DW News, March 23, 2021, https://www.dw.com/en/blinken-seeks-to-revitalize-nato-alliance/a -56957728.

81 United States Embassy & Consulates in Russia, " 'Reaffirming and Reimagining America's Alliances,' " March 24, 2021, https://ru.usembassy.gov/reaffirming -and-reimagining-americas-alliances-speech-by-secretary-blinken-at -nato-headquarters/.

82 The White House, "Readout of President Joseph R. Biden, Jr. Call with President Volodymyr Zelenskyy of Ukraine," April 02, 2021, https://www .whitehouse.gov/briefing-room/statements-releases/2021/04/02/readout-of -president-joseph-r-biden-jr-call-with-president-volodymyr-zelenskyy-of -ukraine/.

83 "Defense Ministry announces NATO plans to concentrate 40 thousand military personnel near Russian borders," Interfax, April 13, 2021, https://www .interfax.ru/russia/760993.

84 Alexander Smith and Matthew Bodner, "Russia amasses troops near U.S. ally Ukraine. But what is Putin's goal?," NBC News, April 14, 2021, https://www .nbcnews.com/news/world/russia-amasses-troops-near-u-s-ally-ukraine -what-putin-n1263894.

85 Andrea Shalal, Timothy Gardner, and Steve Holland, "U.S. waives sanctions on Nord Stream 2 as Biden seeks to mend Europe ties," Reuters, May 19, 2021, https://www.reuters.com/business/energy/us-waive-sanctions-firm-ceo -behind-russias-nord-stream-2-pipeline-source-2021-05-19/.

86 Jonathan Swan and Dave Lawler, "Exclusive: Zelensky 'surprised' and 'disappointed' by Biden pipeline move," Axios, June 6, 2021, https://www.axios .com/2021/06/06/zelensky-biden-ukraine-russia-nord-stream-pipeline.

87 Steven Nelson, "Biden denies Ukraine prez's claim that NATO 'confirmed' his country can join," New York Post, June 14, 2021, https://nypost .com/2021/06/14/biden-denies-ukraine-prezs-claim-that-nato-confirmed -ukraine-can-join/.

88 "Biden on NATO Supporting Ukraine: 'School's Out on That Question,' " YouTube video, 2:21, posted by NBC News on June 14, 2021, https://www .youtube.com/watch?v=_b_Bcruv6Wk.

89 Joel B. Pollak, "Pollak: Joe Biden Got Nothing in Geneva Summit with Russia's Vladimir Putin," Breitbart News, June 16, 2021, https://www.breitbart.com /national-security/2021/06/16/pollak-joe-biden-got-nothing-in-geneva -summit-with-russia-vladimir-putin/.

90 Associated Press, "Putin praises summit result, calls Biden a tough negotiator," Tampa Bay Times, June 17, 2021, https://www.tampabay .com/news/nation-world/2021/06/17/putin-praises-summit-result-calls -biden-a-tough-negotiator/.

91 Lauren Egan, "Biden, Zelensky meet at White House amid Ukraine-Russia conflict," NBC News, September 1, 2021, https://www.nbcnews.com/politics /white-house/biden-zelensky-meet-white-house-amid-ukraine-russia -conflict-n1278232.

92 The White House, "Joint Statement on the U.S.-Ukraine Strategic Partnership," September 1, 2021, https://www.whitehouse.gov/briefing-room/statements-re leases/2021/09/01/joint-statement-on-the-u-s-ukraine-strategic-partnership/.

93 "Kremlin says NATO expansion in Ukraine is a 'red line' for Putin," Reuters, September 27, 2021, https://www.reuters.com/world/kremlin-says-nato -expansion-ukraine-crosses-red-line-putin-2021-09-27/

94 Pavel Felgenhauer, "A War and Peace Visit to Moscow," Jamestown Foundation, October 14, 2021, https://jamestown.org/program/a-war-and-peace -visit-to-moscow/.

95 United States Department of State, "U.S.-Ukraine Charter on Strategic Partnership," November 10, 2021, https://www.state.gov/u-s-ukraine-charter-on -strategic-partnership/.

96 Vladimir Soldatkin and Andrew Osborn, "Putin warns Russia will act if NATO crosses its red lines in Ukraine," Reuters, November 30, 2021, https:// www.reuters.com/markets/stocks/putin-warns-russia-will-act-if-nato -crosses-its-red-lines-ukraine-2021-11-30/.

97 Shane Harris, Karen DeYoung, Isabelle Khurshudyan, Ashley Parker, and Liz Sly, " Road to war: U.S. struggled to convince allies, and Zelensky, of risk of invasion," Washington Post, August 16, 2022, https://www.washingtonpost .com/national-security/interactive/2022/ukraine-road-to-war/.

98 Isabelle Khurshudyan and Paul Sonne, "Putin expected to demand guarantee in Biden call that NATO won't expand east," Washington Post, December 6, 2021, https://www.washingtonpost.com/world/europe/biden-putin-meeting-nato -ukraine/2021/12/06/71225812-5677-11ec-8396-5552bef55c3c_story.html.

99 Paul D. Shinkman, "U.S. Threatens 'Extreme' Sanctions if Russia Invades Ukraine," U.S. News & World Report, December 7, 2021, https://www.usnews .com/news/world-report/articles/2021-12-07/u-s-threatens-extreme -sanctions-if-russia-invades-ukraine.

100 Scott Neuman, "The U.S. and Russia are talking, and Ukraine's fate hangs in the balance," NPR, January 21, 2022, https://www.npr .org/2022/01/21/1074684145/us-russia-ukraine-talks-lavrov-blinken.

101 "Russia invades Ukraine live updates: Biden announces new sanctions," NPR, February 24, 2022, https://www.npr.org/live-updates/russia -invades-ukraine-putin.

102 The White House, "Statement by President Biden on Nord Stream 2," February 23, 2022, https://www.whitehouse.gov/briefing-room/statements -releases/2022/02/23/statement-by-president-biden-on-nord-stream-2/; Zolan Kanno-Youngs and Edward Wong, "New U.S. Sanctions Target Russian Company Behind Lucrative Pipeline," New York Times, February 23, 2022, https://www.nytimes.com/2022/02/23/us/politics/biden-russia-sanctions -nord-stream-2.html.

103 Alan Cole, "There's a Giant Loophole in Biden's Sanctions Against Russia," Slate, February 25, 2022, https://slate.com/business/2022/02/biden-left-a -giant-loophole-in-his-sanctions-against-russias.html.

104 Nick Wadhams and Bloomberg, "Many of Biden's own aides didn't think his Russia sanctions plan would work," Fortune, February 24, 2022, https:// fortune.com/2022/02/24/biden-aides-doubt-russia-sanctions-plan-change -putin-behavior-ukraine/.

105 Paddy Hirsch, "Why sanctions against Russia aren't working—yet," NPR, December 6, 2022, https://www.npr.org/sections/money/2022/12/06/1140120 485/why-the-sanctions-against-russia-arent-working-yet.

106 Agathe Demarals, "Sanctions on Russia Are Working. Here's Why," *Foreign Policy*, December 1, 2022, https://foreignpolicy.com/2022/12/01/ukraine -russia-sanctions-economy-war-putin-embargo-technology-financial -energy/; Vladimir Milov, "The Sanctions on Russia Are Working," *Foreign Policy*, January 18, 2023, https://www.foreignaffairs.com/russian-federation /sanctions-russia-are-working.

107 "Volodymyr Zelensky. Big interview for CNN (2022) News of Ukraine," You-Tube video, 36:13, posted by Odesa Film Studio on March 21, 2022, https:// www.youtube.com/watch?v=cQO7ij2IIxE&t=362s.

108 Tony Ward, "Army of Thieves: Putin's Military Weakness Follows Long His-tory of Corrupt Russian Regimes," *Milwaukee Independent*, June 18, 2022, https://www.milwaukeeindependent.com/syndicated/army-thieves-putins -military-weakness-follows-long-history-corrupt-russian-regimes/; Alexey Kovalev, "As War Hits the Homefront, Russia's Defeat Inches Closer," *Foreign Policy*, October 19, 2022, https://foreignpolicy.com/2022/10/19 /russia-ukraine-war-putin-defeat-retreat-mobilization-military-corruption/; "Disastrous troop management compounds Russia's missteps," Breitbart News, September 16, 2022, https://www.breitbart.com/news/disastrous-troop -management-compounds-russias-missteps/.

109 Sean Moran, "11 Senate Conservatives Defy Establishment to Vote Against $40 Billion Boondoggle in Aid to Ukraine," Breitbart News, May 19, 2022, https://www.breitbart.com/politics/2022/05/19/11-senate-conservatives -defy-establishment-to-vote-against-40-billion-boondoggle-in-aid-to -ukraine/.

110 Jacob Bliss, "Exclusive—Sen. Vance, Rep. Bishop Lead Letter Demand-ing Biden Administration Produce Report on All Ukraine-Related Appro-priations," Breitbart News, January 19, 2023, https://www.breitbart.com /politics/2023/01/19/exclusive-sen-vance-rep-bishop-lead-letter-demanding -biden-admin-produce-report-all-ukraine-related-appropriations/.

111 Kristina Wong, "Biden's Remarks on Paying Ukrainian Pensions Resurfaces, Stoking Anger," Breitbart News, February 19, 2023, https://www.breitbart .com/politics/2023/02/19/bidens-remarks-on-paying-ukrainian-pensions -resurfaces-stoking-anger/.

112 Heinz Strubenhoff, "The War in Ukraine Triggered a Global Food Short-age," Brookings Institution, June 14, 2022, https://www.brookings.edu/blog /future-development/2022/06/14/the-war-in-ukraine-triggered-a-global -food-shortage/.

113 Strubenhoff, "The War in Ukraine Triggered."

114 David Gaffen, "How the Russia-Ukraine war accelerated a global energy cri-sis," Reuters, December 15, 2022, https://www.reuters.com/business/energy /year-russia-turbocharged-global-energy-crisis-2022-12-13/.

115 "Russian Invasion of Ukraine Impedes Post-Pandemic Economic Recov-ery in Emerging Europe and Central Asia," World Bank, October 4, 2022, https://www.worldbank.org/en/news/press-release/2022/10/04/russian -invasion-of-ukraine-impedes-post-pandemic-economic-recovery-in

-emerging-europe-and-central-asia#:~:text=According%20to%20recent%20
World%20Bank,pre%2Dwar%20economy%20in%202021.

116 Jim Garamone, United States Department of Defense, "Biden Signs National
Defense Authorization Act Into Law," December 23, 2022, https://www
.defense.gov/News/News-Stories/Article/Article/3252968/biden-signs
-national-defense-authorization-act-into-law/.

117 Eric Lipton, Michael Crowley, and John Ismay, "Military Spending Surges,
Creating New Boom for Arms Makers," *New York Times,* December 18,
2022, https://www.nytimes.com/2022/12/18/us/politics/defense-contractors
-ukraine-russia.html.

118 Nick Turse and Alex Emmons, "Biden Defense Secretary Nominee
Lloyd Austin Comes Under Fire for Industry Connections," *Intercept,*
December 8, 2020, https://theintercept.com/2020/12/08/biden-defense
-secretary-lloyd-austin-raytheon/.

119 Larry Fink, "To our shareholders," BlackRock, March 24, 2022 https://www
.blackrock.com/corporate/investor-relations/larry-fink-chairmans-letter.

120 Sydney Maki, "Pimco, BlackRock See Opportunity in Emerging Market Selloff," Bloomberg, February 24, 2022, https://www.bloomberg.com
/news/articles/2022-02-25/pimco-blackrock-see-opportunity-in-russia
-fueled-em-selloff.

121 Elliot Smith, "Zelenskyy, BlackRock CEO Fink agree to coordinate Ukraine
investment," CNBC, December 28, 2022, https://www.cnbc.com/2022/12/28
/zelenskyy-blackrock-ceo-fink-agree-to-coordinate-ukraine-investment.html.

122 Dominic Culverwell, "Ukraine could be a 'beacon about the power of capitalism,' says Larry Fink, CEO of BlackRock," bne Intellinews, January 22, 2023,
https://www.intellinews.com/ukraine-could-be-a-beacon-about-the-power
-of-capitalism-says-larry-fink-ceo-of-blackrock-267557/.

123 Helene Cooper, Eric Schmitt, and Thomas Gibbons-Neff, "Soaring Death Toll
Gives Grim Insight Into Russian Tactics," *New York Times,* February 2, 2023,
https://www.nytimes.com/2023/02/02/us/politics/ukraine-russia-casualties
.html.

124 Helene Cooper, "Russia and Ukraine each have suffered over 100,000 casualties, the top U.S. general says," *New York Times,* November 10, 2022,
https://www.nytimes.com/2022/11/10/world/europe/ukraine-russia-war
-casualties-deaths.html.

125 Samuel Stebbins, "How much money does your state receive from the federal
government? Check out this list," *USA Today,* March 20, 2019, https://www
.usatoday.com/story/money/economy/2019/03/20/how-much-federal
-funding-each-state-receives-government/39202299/.

126 Lolita Baldor and Tara Copp, "Pentagon accounting error provides extra
$6.2 billion for Ukraine military aid," AP News, June 20, 2023, https://
apnews.com/article/ukraine-russia-war-weapons-surplus-funding
-72eeb6119439146f1939d5b1973a44ef.

127 Conor Finnegan, "Zelenskyy's emotional call for American resolve: ANAL-
YSIS," ABC News, December 2, 2022, https://abcnews.go.com/International
/zelenskyys-emotional-call-american-resolve-analysis/story?id=95699194.

128 Jim Garamone, United States Department of Defense, "U.S. Announces $2.98
Billion in Aid to Ukraine," August 24, 2022, https://www.defense.gov/News

/News-Stories/Article/Article/3138602/us-announces-298-billion-in-aid-to
-ukraine/#:~:text=Since%20January%202021%2C%20the%20United,the%20
Javelin%20and%20Stinger%20systems.

129 Andrew Restuccia and Burgess Everett, "Longest shutdown in history ends
after Trump relents on wall," *Politico*, January 25, 2019, https://www.politico
.com/story/2019/01/25/trump-shutdown-announcement-1125529.

CHAPTER 7: CHINA JOE AND THE BEIJING BIDENS

1   Emma-Jo Morris, "BOMBSHELL: Biden Family Scored $31 Million from
Deals with Individuals with Direct Ties to the Highest Levels of Chinese
Intelligence," Breitbart News, January 24, 2022, https://www.breitbart.com
/politics/2022/01/24/bombshell-biden-family-scored-31-million-from
-deals-with-individuals-with-direct-ties-to-the-highest-levels-of-chinese
-intelligence/.

2   Michael Schuman, "When Biden Went to China," *Atlantic*, August 11, 2022,
https://www.theatlantic.com/international/archive/2022/08/joe-biden
-china-cold-war-1979-visit/671053/.

3   Edward Wong, Michael Crowley, and Ana Swanson, "Joe Biden's China
Journey," *New York Times*, September 6, 2020, https://www.nytimes
.com/2020/09/06/us/politics/biden-china.html.

4   Wong, Crowley, and Swanson, "Joe Biden's China Journey."

5   Kenneth Rapoza, "China Trade in Really Bad Shape, Says Government Official," *Forbes*, September 21, 2020, https://www.forbes.com/sites
/kenrapoza/2016/09/21/china-trade-in-really-bad-shape-says-government
-official/?sh=1c7fa4572b4b.

6   Julie Wernou, "Forced Tech Transfers Are on the Rise in China, European Firms Say," *Wall Street Journal*, https://www.wsj.com/articles/forced
-tech-transfers-are-on-the-rise-in-china-european-firms-say-11558344240.

7   David Leonhardt, "The Real Problem with China," *New York Times*,
January 11, 2011, https://www.nytimes.com/2011/01/12/business/economy
/12leonhardt.html.

8   Bill Bostock, "Secretary of State Antony Blinken says he stands by Mike
Pompeo's designation that China committed genocide against the Uighurs,"
Business Insider, January 28, 2021, https://www.businessinsider.com/ant
ony-blinken-agrees-china-uighur-genocide-pompeo-designation-2021-1.

9   Carlyle Thayer, "China's New Wave of Aggressive Assertiveness in the South
China Sea," Center for Strategic & International Studies, June 30, 2011, https://
www.files.ethz.ch/isn/130696/Thayer%20CSIS%20South%20China%20Sea.pdf.

10 Peter Schweizer, *Red-Handed* (New York: HarperCollins, 2022).

11 Peter Schweizer, *Secret Empires* (New York: HarperCollins, 2018), 37–44.

12 Peter Schweizer, "Chinese elite have paid some $31 million to Hunter and
the Bidens," *New York Post*, January 27, 2022, https://nypost.com/2022/01/27
/chinese-elite-have-paid-some-31m-to-hunter-and-the-bidens/.

13 Select Committee on U.S. National Security and Military/Commer-
cial Concerns with the People's Republic of China, H.R. Rep. No. 105-851
(1999), https://www.govinfo.gov/content/pkg/GPO-CRPT-105hrpt851/pdf
/GPO-CRPT-105hrpt851.pdf.

14 Schweizer, "Chinese elite have paid."

15 China Institute of Navigation, "COSCO Acquires 10% Shares of CCCC Dredging Group," January 9, 2020, https://www.cinnet.cn/en/news_e/4837 -cosco-acquires-10-shares-cccc-dredging-group.htm.

16 United States Department of Commerce, "Commerce Department Adds 24 Chinese Companies to the Entity List for Helping Build Military Islands in the South China Sea," August 26, 2020, https://2017-2021.commerce.gov /news/press-releases/2020/08/commerce-department-adds-24-chinese -companies-entity-list-helping-build.html; Walt Bogdanich and Michael Forsythe, "How McKinsey Has Helped Raise the Stature of Authoritarian Governments," *New York Times*, December 15, 2018, https://www.nytimes .com/2018/12/15/world/asia/mckinsey-china-russia.html.

17 Schweizer, "Chinese elite have paid."

18 Schweizer, *Red-Handed*, 19–20.

19 Leandra Bernstein, "Will foreign money dominate 2020? Author explains Biden's family ties to China, Ukraine," CBS Austin, June 7, 2019, https:// cbsaustin.com/news/nation-world/will-foreign-money-dominate-2020 -author-explains-bidens-family-ties-to-china-ukraine.

20 Bernstein, "Will foreign money dominate 2020?"

21 Morris, "Bombshell: Biden Family Scored $31 million."

22 Morris, "Bombshell: Biden Family Scored $31 million."

23 "China's new leaders," CNN, accessed May 18, 2023, https://www.cnn.com /interactive/2012/11/world/china-new-leadership/index.html.

24 "Liu Yunshan sworn in as president of Central Party School," *Want China Times*, January 18, 2013, accessed via WayBackMachine on May 18, 2023, https://web.archive.org/web/20141110165121/http://www.wantchinatimes .com/news-subclass-cnt.aspx?id=20130118000081&cid=1601.

25 Morris, "Bombshell: Biden Family Scored $31 million."

26 Morris, "Bombshell: Biden Family Scored $31 million."

27 Schweizer, *Red-Handed*, 34.

28 Schweizer, "Chinese elite have paid."

29 Morris, "Bombshell: Biden Family Scored $31 million."

30 Schweizer, "Chinese elite have paid."

31 Emma-Jo Morris and Gabrielle Fonrouge, "Emails reveal how Hunter Biden tried to cash in big on behalf of family with Chinese firm," *New York Post*, October 15, 2020, https://nypost.com/2020/10/15/emails-reveal-how-hunter -biden-tried-to-cash-in-big-with-chinese-firm/.

32 Emma-Jo Morris, " 'My Son Hunter' True Fact: Hunter Biden Gifted $80K Diamond by Chinese Energy Co. Partner," Breitbart News, September 13, 2022, https://www.breitbart.com/entertainment/2022/09/13/my-son-hunter -true-fact-hunter-biden-gifted-80k-diamond-by-chinese-energy-co-part ner/.

33 Peter Schweizer, *Red-Handed*, 39.

34 Tim Hains, "Leaked Audio: Hunter Biden Discussing Business Deals With The "Spy Chief of China," RealClearPolitics, October 28, 2020, https://www .realclearpolitics.com/video/2020/10/28/leaked_audio_hunter_biden _discussing_business_deals_with_the_spy_chief_of_china.html.

35 Schweizer, "Chinese elite have paid."

36　Schweizer, "Chinese elite have paid."

37　Morris, "Bombshell: Biden Family Scored $31 million."

38　"'China is going to eat our lunch?': Joe Biden dismisses Beijing as threat to US," *South China Morning Post,* May 2, 2019, https://www.scmp.com/news /world/united-states-canada/article/3008505/china-going-eat-our-lunch -joe-biden-dismisses.

39　Laura Silver, "Some Americans' views of China turned more negative after 2020, but others became more positive," Pew Research Center, September 28, 2022, https://www.pewresearch.org/fact-tank/2022/09/28/some-americans -views-of-china-turned-more-negative-after-2020-but-others-became -more-positive/.

40　Jennifer Conrad, "A Year In, Biden's China Policy Looks a Lot Like Trump's," *Wired,* December 30, 2021, https://www.wired.com/story/biden-china -policy-looks-like-trumps/.

41　Conrad, "A Year In, Biden's China."

42　Adriana Belmonte, "Biden faces increasing calls for rolling back China tariffs amid inflation," Yahoo Finance, July 23, 2022, https://finance.yahoo.com /news/biden-faces-increasing-calls-for-rolling-back-china-tariffs-amid -inflation-195948221.html?guccounter=1.

43　David Lawder, "Biden administration to maintain China tariffs while review continues," Reuters, September 2, 2022, https://www.reuters.com /markets/us/biden-administration-maintain-china-tariffs-while-review -continues-2022-09-02/.

44　United States Department of the Treasury, Committee on Foreign Investment in the United States (CFIUS), accessed May 19, 2023, https://home.treasury .gov/policy-issues/international/the-committee-on-foreign-investment -in-the-united-states-cfius.

45　Ignacio Sanchez, Christine Daya, Melanie Garcia, and Jan Zhan, "Congress ramps up pressure on outbound investments and 'strategic competition' with China," DLA Piper, January 17, 2023, https://www.dlapiper.com/en-us /insights/publications/2023/01/congress-ramps-up-pressure-on-outbound -investments-and-strategic-competition-with-china.

46　Jihye Lee, "'We are not decoupling': G-7 leaders agree on approach to 'de-risk' from China," CNBC, May 21, 2023, https://www.cnbc.com/2023/05/22/g-7 -leaders-de-risk-china.html.

47　Michael Forsythe, Eric Lipton, and Dionne Searce, "How Hunter Biden's Firm Helped Secure Cobalt for the Chinese," *New York Times,* November 20, 2021, https://www.nytimes.com/2021/11/20/world/hunter-biden-china-cobalt.html.

48　Take-Profit.org, "China Wages Data: Minimum and Average," accessed May 19, 2023, https://take-profit.org/en/statistics/wages/china/.

49　World Population Review, "Manufacturing by Country 2023," accessed May 19, 2023, https://worldpopulationreview.com/country-rankings/manu facturing-by-country.

50　David Lynch, "Biden's 'Buy America' bid runs into manufacturing woes it aims to fix," *Washington Post,* February 18, 2023, https://www.washingtonpost .com/us-policy/2023/02/18/biden-buy-america-roads-bridges/.

51 Joel Pollak, "China Rebukes Biden's Foreign Policy Team; Cites 'Black Lives Matter' on U.S. Human Rights Abuses," Breitbart News, March 18, 2021, https://www.breitbart.com/national-security/2021/03/18/china-rebukes -bidens-foreign-policy-team-cites-black-lives-matter-on-u-s-human-rights -abuses/.

52 Pollak, "China Rebukes."

53 Robert Kraychik, "Exclusive—Charlie Hurt: China Gave Blinken a 'Swirly' in Anchorage," Breitbart News, March 22, 2021, https://www.breitbart.com /radio/2021/03/22/exclusive-charlie-hurt-china-gave-blinken-a-swirly-in -anchorage/.

54 Kraychik, "Exclusive—Charlie Hurt."

55 Allan Stein, "National Security Concerns Mount as Chinese Company with Ties to China Continuing," Epoch Times, July 19, 2022, https://www .theepochtimes.com/company-with-ties-to-china-continuing-with-corn -mill-project-near-airbase-in-north-dakota_4605916.html.

56 John Feng, "Chinese-Owned Farmland in U.S. Comes Under Scrutiny," Newsweek, July 19, 2022, https://www.newsweek.com/us-china-farmland -ownership-national-security-1725939.

57 Meghan Arbegast, "Path opens for Fufeng project after federal agencies determine land deal was 'not covered' by CFIUS," Grand Forks Herald, December 13, 2022, https://www.grandforksherald.com/news/north-dakota /path-opens-for-fufeng-project-after-federal-agencies-determine-land-deal -was-not-covered-by-cfius.

58 Sydney Mook, "Grand Forks UAS company General Atomics comes out against Fufeng project," Grand Forks Herald, September 21, 2022, https:// www.grandforksherald.com/news/north-dakota/grand-forks-uas-company -general-atomics-comes-out-against-fufeng-project?ajs_aid=723acafd-3f76 -482b-b157-153dfd8c895d.

59 Lauren Greenwood, China's Interests in U.S. Agriculture: Augmenting Food Security through Investment Abroad, special report prepared by the United States–China Economic and Security Review Commission, May 26, 2022, https://www.uscc.gov/sites/default/files/2022-05/Chinas_Interests_in_U.S. _Agriculture.pdf.

60 Greenwood, China's Interests in U.S. Agriculture.

61 Andrew Ewing, "Smithfield and Shuanghui: Implications on the American Agricultural System and the Government's Flawed Review Process," Drake Journal of Agricultural Law 20, no. 1, https://aglawjournal.wp.drake.edu /wp-content/uploads/sites/66/2018/10/110315EwingFinalMacro.pdf.

62 Greenwood, China's Interests in U.S. Agriculture.

63 U.S. Department of Justice Office of Public Affairs, "Chinese National Pleads Guilty to Economic Espionage Conspiracy," January 6, 2022, https://www .justice.gov/opa/pr/chinese-national-pleads-guilty-economic-espionage -conspiracy.

64 Greenwood, China's Interests in U.S. Agriculture.

65 Greenwood, China's Interests in U.S. Agriculture.

66 United States Department of Justice, "Chinese National Pleads Guilty to Eco-

nomic Espionage Conspiracy," January 6, 2022, https://www.justice.gov/opa
/pr/chinese-national-pleads-guilty-economic-espionage-conspiracy.

67 Greenwood, *China's Interests in U.S. Agriculture.*

68 "China to cut gasoline, diesel retail prices," Xinhua Net, August 9, 2022,
https://english.news.cn/20220809/2735ed51137d4d94a81977f95f0c2e48/c
.html.

69 Clifford Krauss and Michael Shear, "Biden will tap oil reserve, hoping to
push gasoline prices down," *New York Times,* March 31, 2022, https://www
.nytimes.com/2022/03/31/business/energy-environment/biden-oil-strategic
-petroleum-reserve.html.

70 Chen Aizhu and Dmitry Zhdannikov, "EXCLUSIVE China boosts oil reserves, ignoring U.S. push for global release," Reuters, February 25, 2022,
https://www.reuters.com/business/energy/exclusive-china-boosts-oil
-reserves-ignoring-us-push-global-release-2022-02-25/.

71 Collin Anderson, "Biden Sold a Million Barrels From US Strategic Petroleum Reserve to China-Owned Gas Giant," *Washington Free Beacon,* July 7,
2022, https://freebeacon.com/national-security/biden-sold-a-million-barrels
-from-us-strategic-petroleum-reserve-to-china-owned-gas-giant/.

72 "Report on the Biden LapTop, Marco Polo, accessed May 18, 2023, https://
bidenlaptopreport.marcopolousa.org/report_viewer/index.html#p=103.

73 Andrew Kerr, "Hunter Biden still listed as part owner of Chinese firm despite divestment claim," *Washington Examiner,* March 9, 2022, https://www
.washingtonexaminer.com/news/hunter-biden-still-listed-as-part-owner-of
-chinese-firm-despite-divestment-claim.

74 Jordan Dixon-Hamilton, "House Democrats Block Motion to Prohibit Biden
from Selling U.S. Oil to China," Breitbart News, July 20, 2022, https://www
.breitbart.com/politics/2022/07/20/house-democrats-block-motion-to
-prohibit-biden-from-selling-u-s-oil-to-china/.

75 Chase Doak, "Video of Chinese spy satellite hovering over Billings Wednesday," *Billings Gazette,* February 4, 2023, https://billingsgazette.com/news
/video-of-chinese-spy-satellite-hovering-over-billings-Wednesday/article
_e647fbee-a34f-11ed-94a4-fb08447d073b.html.

76 Peter Martin, Jenny Leonard, and Jennifer Jacobs, "From China to Big Sky:
The Balloon That Unnerved the White House," Bloomberg News, February 4,
2023, https://www.bloomberg.com/news/articles/2023-02-04/from-china-to
-big-sky-the-balloon-that-unnerved-the-white-house#xj4y7vzkg.

77 Martin, Leonard, and Jacobs, "From China to Big Sky."

78 *Encyclopedia of the Great Plains,* s.v. "Missile Silos," accessed May 19, 2023,
http://plainshumanities.unl.edu/encyclopedia/doc/egp.ii.042.

79 Andrew Buncombe, "Could the China 'spy' balloon be linked to Montana's
nuclear missile sites?," *Independent UK,* https://www.independent.co.uk
/news/world/americas/montana-explosion-nuclear-missile-chinese-spy
-balloon-b2276108.html.

80 Bernd Debusmann Jr., "Suspected Chinese spy balloon was 200ft tall—US
defence official," BBC News, February 6, 2023, https://www.bbc.com/news
/world-us-canada-64548140.

81 Aaron Rupar (@atrupar), "Biden 'On the balloon, I ordered the Pentagon to
shoot it down on Wednesday as soon as possible [for safety] . . . they suc-

cessfully took it down,' " Twitter, February 4, 2023, 12:19 p.m., https://twitter
.com/atrupar/status/1621966810366050311.

82 Ian Hanchett, "Panetta: Chinese Spy Balloon 'Gathering Intelligence' on U.S.,
I'd 'Really Be Concerned' if We Didn't Intercept It or Shoot It down," Breitbart
News, February 3, 2023, https://www.breitbart.com/clips/2023/02/03/panetta
-chinese-spy-balloon-gathering-intelligence-on-u-s-id-really-be-concerned-if
-we-didnt-intercept-it-or-shoot-it-down/.

83 Center for American Political Studies, "Approval and Mood of Country:
February 15–16, 2023," accessed May 19, 2023, https://harvardharrispoll
.com/wp-content/uploads/2023/02/HHP_Feb2023_KeyResults.pdf.

84 Kristina Wong, "Joe Biden: Three Objects Shot Down Were 'Most Likely Balloons' Not Tied to Chinese Surveillance," Breitbart News, February 16, 2023,
https://www.breitbart.com/politics/2023/02/16/biden-three-objects-shot
-down-were-most-likely-balloons-not-tied-chinese-surveillance/.

85 Paul Bertorelli, "The Amazing Technology of Pico Balloons," AV Web,
February 19, 2023, https://www.avweb.com/multimedia/votw/the-amazing
-technology-of-pico-balloons/.

86 Steve Trimble, "Hobby Club's Missing Balloon Feared Shot Down by USAF,"
Aviation Week, February 16, 2023, https://aviationweek.com/defense-space
/aircraft-propulsion/hobby-clubs-missing-balloon-feared-shot-down-usaf.

87 Nick Mordowanec, " 'Sidewinder' Missile Biden Used Over Lake Huron Cost
Over $450K," *Newsweek*, February 13, 2023, https://www.newsweek.com/
sidewinder-missile-biden-used-lake-huron-cost-450k-1780900.

88 John Hayward, "Canada Ends Search for 'Suspected Balloon' Debris with
No Findings," Breitbart News, February 21, 2023, https://www.breitbart
.com/latin-america/2023/02/21/canada-ends-search-suspected-balloon
-debris-no-findings/.

CHAPTER 8: HOW JOE BIDEN SOLD HOLLYWOOD TO CHINA

1 Statista, "Global box office revenue from 2005 to 2021," chart, accessed
May 12, 2023, https://www.statista.com/statistics/271856/global-box-office
-revenue/.

2 Box Office Mojo, "Domestic Yearly Box Office," IMDbPro, accessed May 12,
2023, https://www.boxofficemojo.com/year/?ref_=bo_nb_di_secondarytab.

3 Douglas McIntyre, "This Is the Price of a Movie Ticket in the Pas 25 Years,"
24/7 Wall St, March 29, 2021, https://247wallst.com/media/2021/03/29/this
-is-the-price-of-a-movie-ticket-in-the-past-25-years/.

4 Box Office Mojo, "Spider-Man: No Way Home (2021)," IMDbPro, accessed
May 31, 2023, https://www.boxofficemojo.com/title/tt10872600/?ref_=bo_
cso_table_3; Box Office Mojo, "Top Gun: Maverick (2022)," IMDb-
Pro, accessed May 31, 2023, https://www.boxofficemojo.com/title
/tt1745960/?ref_=bo_cso_table_5; Box Office Mojo, "Avatar: The Way of
Water (2022)," IMDbPro, accessed May 31, 2023, https://www.boxofficemojo
.com/title/tt1630029/?ref_=bo_cso_table_7.

5 Jonathan Papish, "Foreign Films in China: How Does it Work?," China Film
Insider, March 2, 2017, https://chinafilminsider.com/foreign-films-in-china
-how-does-it-work/.

6 Peter Nicholas and Erica Orden, "Movie Mogul's Starring Role in Raising Funds for Obama," *Wall Street Journal*, September 30, 2012, https://www.wsj .com/articles/SB10000872396390443571904577630430778711196.

7 "Obama finds friends in Hollywood, and money too!," Reuters, February 21, 2007, https://www.reuters.com/article/us-obama/obama-finds-friends-in -hollywood-and-money-too-idUSN2145471520070221.

8 Nicole Sperling, "Obama's Hollywood fundraiser: Who was guest list?," *Entertainment Weekly*, September 18, 2008, https://ew.com/article/2008/09/18 /obamas-fundrais/.

9 "Kung Fu Panda breaks Chinese box-office records," *Telegraph*, July 8, 2008, https://www.telegraph.co.uk/news/worldnews/asia/china/2268139/Kung -Fu-Panda-breaks-Chinese-box-office-records.html.

10 Chengdu Municipal Government Information Office, "Kung Fu Panda 2 Art Director Comes to China," PR Newswire, May 24, 2011, https://www .prnewswire.com/news-releases/kung-fu-panda-2-art-director-comes-to -china-122496058.html.

11 Chengdu Municipal Government Information Office, "Kung Fu Panda 2 Art Director"; Jeroen Jacobs, "Pandas Home Town Chengdu in Kung Fu Panda 2," Giant Panda Global, May 25, 2011, https://www.giantpandaglobal.com /giant-panda-news/pandas-home-town-in-kung-fu-panda-2/; Sascha, "Defending Chinese Culture & Kung Fu Panda," Chengdu Living, June 17, 2011, https://www.chengduliving.com/defending-chinese-culture/.

12 Huang Zhiling, "Chengdu has starring role in Kung Fu Panda 2," *China Daily*, June 17, 2011, https://usa.chinadaily.com.cn/epaper/2011-06/17 /content_12722016.htm; Yang Xin, "Chengdu elements stand out in Kung Fu Panda 2," *China Culture*, June 27, 2011; http://en.chinaculture.org/info/2011 -06/27/content_418083.htm.

13 Bayles, "Dream Factory, Propaganda Machine?"

14 "'Kung Fu Panda 2' incorporates more Chinese elements," Thinking Chinese, accessed May 10, 2023, http://thinkingchinese.com/index.php?page_id=291.

15 Box Office Mojo, "Kung Fu Panda 2 (2011)," IMDbPro, accessed May 31, 2023, https://www.boxofficemojo.com/title/tt1302011/?ref_=bo_se_r_1.

16 Box Office Mojo, "Kung Fu Panda 3," IMDbPro, accessed May 31, 2023, https://www.boxofficemojo.com/release/rl2468710145/weekend/.

17 Doug Palmer, "U.S. winning WTO ruling on China's film barriers," Reuters, June 24, 2009, https://www.reuters.com/article/us-usa-china-films-wto/u-s -winning-wto-ruling-on-chinas-film-barriers-idUSTRE55O0OG20090625.

18 Keith Bradsher, "W.T.O. Rules Against China's Limits on Imports," *New York Times*, August 12, 2009, https://www.nytimes.com/2009/08/13/business /global/13trade.html.

19 Obama Administration Pledges Anti-Piracy Help," *Billboard*, December 15, 2009, https://www.billboard.com/music/music-news/obama-adminstration -pledges-anti-piracy-help-1261726/.

20 Art Brodsky, "Public Knowledge Disappointed with White House Piracy Meeting," Public Knowledge, December 15, 2009, accessed via WayBack-Machine May 12, 2023, https://web.archive.org/web/20110601214511/http: /www.publicknowledge.org/node/2817.

21 Mike Masnick, "Biden Convenes 'Piracy Summit' That Appears To Be En-

tirely One-Sided," Tech Dirt, December 15, 2009, https://www.techdirt.com /2009/12/15/biden-convenes-piracy-summit-that-appears-to-be-entirely -one-sided/; Brodsky, "Public Knowledge Disappointed."

22 David Barboza, "Billions in Hidden Riches for Family of Chinese Leader," *New York Times*, October 25, 2012, https://www.nytimes.com/2012/10/26 /business/global/family-of-wen-jiabao-holds-a-hidden-fortune-in-china.html.

23 Paul Eckert, "Special Report: Cables show U.S. sizing up China's next leader," Reuters, February 17, 2011, https://www.reuters.com/article/us-wiki -china-xi/special-report-cables-show-u-s-sizing-up-chinas-next-leader -idUSTRE71G5WH20110217; Mu Chunshan, "WikiLeaks, Hollywood and GDP," The Diplomat, December 15, 2010, https://thediplomat.com/2010/12 /wikileaks-hollywood-and-gdp/.

24 The White House, *The China State Visit*, overview, January 19, 2011, https:// obamawhitehouse.archives.gov/sites/default/files/China_State_Visit.pdf.

25 "China State Dinner GUEST LIST: Barbra Streisand, Vera Wang, Anna Wintour & More," *Huffington Post*, January 19, 2011, https://www.huffpost.com /entry/china-state-dinner-guest_n_811278.

26 Peter Schweizer and Peter Boyer, "The Illegal Donor Loophole," Daily Beast, July 14, 2017, https://www.thedailybeast.com/the-illegal-donor-loophole; Eliana Johnson, "Who is Robert Roche?," *National Review*, October 8, 2012, https://www.nationalreview.com/corner/who-robert-roche-eliana-johnson/.

27 Ministry of Foreign Affairs of the People's Republic of China, "Chinese Vice President Xi Jinping Holds Talks with U.S. Vice President Biden," August 18, 2011, https://www.fmprc.gov.cn/mfa_eng/zxxx_662805/201108 /t20110822_418180.html.

28 Ministry of Foreign Affairs, "Chinese Vice President Xi Jinping Holds Talks."

29 The White House, "Remarks by the Vice President at Sichuan University," August 24, 2011, https://obamawhitehouse.archives.gov/the-press-office /2011/08/21/remarks-vice-president-sichuan-university.

30 Sascha, "Defending Chinese Culture," https://www.chengduliving.com/ defending-chinese-culture/; "Dreamworks crew visits panda in Chengdu," China.org, May 28, 2011, http://www.china.org.cn/video/2011-05/28/content _22662584.htm.

31 "Remarks by the Vice President at Sichuan University."

32 Clifford Coonan, "DMG invests big in China theater," *Variety*, September 30, 2011, https://variety.com/2011/film/news/dmg-invests-big-in-china-theaters -1118043646/.

33 Joshua Weinstein, "Exclusive: Chinese Media Conglomerate DMG Shopping $300M Film Fund," Reuters, August 11, 2011, https://www.reuters.com /article/idUS352854198120110811.

34 "Xu Qing, Bruce Willis lingering in 'Looper,' " *China Daily*, July 23, 2012, https:// www.chinadaily.com.cn/entertainment/2012-07/23/content_15609470.htm.

35 "Relativity Media Launches Strategic Partnership in China," *Hollywood Reporter*, August 14, 2011, https://www.hollywoodreporter.com/news/general -news/relativity-media-launches-strategic-partnership-222940/.

36 Matt Goldberg, "IRON MAN 3 to Be Co-Financed by Chinese Company DMG Entertainment; Filming Begins in Five Weeks," *Collider*, April 16, 2012, https://collider.com/iron-man-3-sequel-china-dmg-entertainment/.

37 https://www.thewrap.com/dmg-entertainment-to-invest-300-million-in
    -entertainment-media-tech/.

38 Rand Paul (@RandPaul), "I oppose #SOPA & #PIPA have pledged to fil-
    ibuster and do everything I can to stop gov't censorship of the Inter-
    net," Twitter, January 18, 2012, 9:52 a.m., https://twitter.com/RandPaul
    /status/159694610719969281.

39 The White House, Macon Phillips, Victoria Espinel, Aneesh Chopra, and
    Howard Schmidt, "Obama Administration Responds to We the People Peti-
    tions on SOPA and Online Piracy," January 14, 2012, https://obamawhitehouse
    .archives.gov/blog/2012/01/14/Obama-administration-responds-we-people
    -petitions-sopa-and-online-piracy.

40 Tina Daunt, "Jeffrey Katzenberg Sets Spring Hollywood Fundraiser for Presi-
    dent Obama (Exclusive)," *Hollywood Reporter,* February 2, 2012, https://www
    .hollywoodreporter.com/news/politics-news/obama-fundraiser-jeffrey
    -katzenberg-dreamworks-286702/.

41 Dan Eggen, "George Clooney fundraiser could be a $12 million blockbuster
    for Obama," *Washington Post,* May 4, 2012, https://www.washingtonpost
    .com/politics/george-clooney-fundraiser-could-be-a-12-million-blockbuster
    -for-obama/2012/05/04/gIQARwwn1T_story.html?tid=a_inl_manual.

42 Jennifer Rubin, "Biden's role in U.S. companies' deals with China," *Washington
    Post,* June 1, 2012, https://www.washingtonpost.com/blogs/right-turn/post/
    bidens-role-in-us-companies-deals-with-china/2012/06/01/gJQAEcSz7U_
    blog.html.

43 Rubin, "Biden's Role."

44 Rubin, "Biden's Role."

45 "China Film: Quota? What Quota?," Harris Bricken, June 19, 2018, https://
    harrisbricken.com/chinalawblog/china-film-quota-what-quota/.

46 Bill Allison, "Stealthy Wealthy: Did Katzenberg's support for Obama fast-
    track movie deal with China?," Sunlight Foundation, April 18, 2012, https://
    sunlightfoundation.com/2012/04/18/katzenberg/.

47 Sharon Waxman, "Legendary secures $220 mln for China movie venture,"
    Reuters, August 21, 2011, https://www.reuters.com/article/industry-us
    -legendary-china/legendary-secures-220-mln-for-china-movie-venture
    -idUSTRE77K2YR20110821.

48 Rubin, "Biden's Role."

49 Chris Peters and Kanika Sikka, "Walt Disney, Shanghai Media Group to de-
    velop Disney-branded movies," Reuters, March 6, 2014, https://www.reuters
    .com/article/us-disney-shanghaimediagroup-idUSBREA2605220140307
    #tVQJkRY4bB1hgyW9.97.

50 "Amblin Partners and Alibaba Pictures Announce Comprehensive Strate-
    gic Partnership," *Businesswire,* October 9, 2016, https://www.businesswire
    .com/news/home/20161008005088/en/Amblin-Partners-and-Alibaba
    -Pictures-Announce-Comprehensive-Strategic-Partnership; "Alibaba Pic-
    tures, Amblin to co-produce films for global, Chinese audi-
    ences," Reuters, October 9, 2016, https://www.reuters.com/article/us
    -ali-pictures-amblin-partnership/alibaba-pictures-amblin-to-co-pro
    duce-films-for-global-chinese-audiences-idUSKCN129072.

51 Humeyra Pamuk and David Brunnstrom, "Pompeo says U.S. designates six

more Chinese media firms as foreign missions," Reuters, October 21, 2020, https://www.reuters.com/article/us-usa-china-pompeo-idUSKBN2762D0; China Business News, "China Business News Celebrates Fifth Anniversary," PR Newswire, November 17, 2009, accessed via WayBackMachine on May 31, 2023, https://web.archive.org/web/20180620182631/https:/www.prnewswire.com/news-releases/china-business-news-celebrates-fifth-anniversary-70273192.html.

52 Xinyan Fu, "No Ghost Land: Chinese Horror Growing Under Strict Censorship," *Independent Magazine,* October 21, 2021, https://independent-magazine.org/2021/10/21/no-ghost-land-chinese-horror-growing-under-strict-censorship/.

53 James Griffiths, "Banned on Chinese TV: 'Western lifestyles,' cleavage and time travel," CNN, August 31, 2016, https://www.cnn.com/2016/08/31/asia/china-banned-on-tv-censorship/index.html#.

54 Louise Watt, "'Cloud Atlas' loses 40 minutes of love scenes to Chinese censors," *Toronto Star,* January 24, 2013, https://www.thestar.com/news/world/2013/01/24/cloud_atlas_loses_40_minutes_of_love_scenes_to_chinese_censors.html.

55 John Nolte, "'Godzilla vs. Kong' Review: Monstrously Stupid and Tedious," Breitbart News, April 1, 2021, https://www.breitbart.com/entertainment/2021/04/01/godzilla-vs-kong-review-monstrously-stupid-and-tedious/.

56 Matilda Battersby, "Prostitution and torture censored from Skyfall to appease Chinese market," *Independent,* January 17, 2013, https://www.independent.co.uk/arts-entertainment/films/news/prostitution-and-torture-censored-from-skyfall-to-appease-chinese-market-8455547.html.

57 Watt, "'Cloud Atlas' loses 40 minutes."

58 Beth Elkderkin, "Gay Kiss Cut from Chinese Version of *Alien: Covenant,*" Gizmodo, June 18, 2017, https://gizmodo.com/gay-kiss-cut-from-chinese-version-of-alien-covenant-1796204589.

59 Eduardo Baptista, "Six LGBT moments cut from 'Bohemian Rhapsody' in China," CNN, March 25, 2019, https://www.cnn.com/2019/03/25/asia/bohemian-rhapsody-censorship-china-intl/index.html.

60 Josh Horwitz, "Chinese censors change ending of latest 'Minions' movies," Reuters, August 22, 2022, https://www.reuters.com/world/china/chinese-censors-change-ending-latest-minions-movie-2022-08-22/.

61 Terry Gross, "Hollywood relies on China to stay afloat. What does that mean for movies?," NPR, https://www.npr.org/2022/02/21/1081435029/china-hollywood-movies-censorship-erich-schwartzel.

62 Chris Fuchs, "Tibet Supporters Protest Marvel's 'Doctor Strange' over Changed Character," NBC News, November 3, 2016, https://www.nbcnews.com/news/asian-america/tibet-supporters-protest-marvel-s-dr-strange-over-changed-character-n677706.

63 James Tager, *Made in Hollywood, Censored by Beijing* (New York: PEN America, 2020), https://pen.org/wp-content/uploads/2020/09/Made_in_Hollywood_Censored_by_Beiing_Report_FINAL.pdf.

64 David Ng, "Disney's 'Mulan' Thanks City Running Uyghur Concentration Camps in Its Credits," Breitbart News, September 7, 2020, https://www

.breitbart.com/entertainment/2020/09/07/disneys-mulan-under-fire-for
-filming-in-chinese-city-running-uyghur-concentration-camps/.

65 "'Fast & Furious' Star John Cena Apologizes for Calling Taiwan a Country," Breitbart News, May 25, 2021, https://www.breitbart.com /entertainment/2021/05/25/fast-furious-star-john-cena-apologises-for-call ing-taiwan-a-country/.

66 Zack Sharf, "Tarantino Tells Critics of Bruce Lee Scene to 'Suck a D*ck': He 'Had No Respect for American Stuntmen,'" *IndieWire*, June 30, 2021, https://www.indiewire.com/features/general/tarantino-bruce-lee-hollywood -scene-critics-1234647709/.

67 Tager, *Made in Hollywood.*

68 Nancy Tartaglione, "China Film Industry to Be Regulated by Communist Party Propaganda Department," *Deadline*, March 21, 2018, https://deadline .com/2018/03/china-film-industry-regulation-communist-party -propaganda-department-1202350328/.

69 Ralph Jennings, "Censorship of Hollywood Blockbuster Films Intensifies in China," *VOA News*, May 4, 2022, https://www.voanews.com/a/censorship -of-hollywood-blockbuster-films-intensifies-in-china-/6557850.html.

70 Lucas Shaw, "How China Used Hollywood To Build The World's Biggest Film Market," Bloomberg, February 13, 2022, https://www.bloomberg.com/news /newsletters/2022-02-13/how-china-used-hollywood-to-build-the-world-s -biggest-film-market.

71 Zen Soo, "China's Original Force hires DreamWorks veterans, heads to Holly- wood to make 'major' CGI film every 18 months," *South China Morning Post*, August 17, 2015, https://www.scmp.com/tech/enterprises/article/1849596 /chinas-original-force-hires-dreamworks-veterans-heads-hollywood.

72 Box Office Mojo, "Chinese Box Office For 2016," IMDbPro, accessed on June 13, 2023, https://www.boxofficemojo.com/year/2016/?area=CN.

73 Will Seaton, "The tragic romance of China and Hollywood," China Proj- ect, November 21, 2022, https://thechinaproject.com/2022/11/21/the-tragic -romance-of-china-and-hollywood/.

74 Tager, *Made in Hollywood;* Ben Kaye, "China Banned Spider-Man: No Way Home Because of Statue of Liberty Scene," Consequence Film, May 2, 2022, https://consequence.net/2022/05/china-spider-man-no-way-home-banned -statue-of-liberty/.

75 Ralph Jennings, "Censorship of Hollywood Blockbuster Films Inten- sifies in China," *VOA News*, May 4, 2022, https://www.voanews.com/a /censorship-of-hollywood-blockbuster-films-intensifies-in-china-/655 7850.html.

76 "Killing of 'Winnie the Pooh,' Flick in Hong Kong and Macau Raises Chinese Censorship Concerns," *Time*, March 22, 2023, https://time.com/6264991/win nie-the-pooh-movie-hong-kong-censorship/; Ben Kew, "Winnie the Pooh Banned in China Over Comparisons to President Xi Jinping," Breitbart News, July 17, 2017, https://www.breitbart.com/national-security/2017/07/17/win nie-pooh-banned-china-over-comparisons-president/.

77 Steve Balestrieri, "Chinese Rip Off Hollywood for Their Own Propa- ganda Films," SOFREP, September 22, 2020, https://sofrep.com/news /chinese-theft-hollywood-propaganda-military-bombers/.

78 Ted Johnson, "Jeffrey Katzenberg, George Clooney & Byron Allen Among L.A. Hosts Of Post-Convention Joe Biden-Kamala Harris Fundraiser," *Deadline,* August 18, 2020, https://deadline.com/2020/08/joe-biden-kamala -harris-george-clooney-jeffrey-katzenberg-1203016883/.

79 Alexi McCammond, "Biden team launches fundraiser series, starting with Tom Hanks," *Axios,* November 25, 2020, https://www.axios.com/2020/08/18 /biden-fundraiser-series-tom-hanks.

80 Gene Maddaus, "Katzenberg-Clooney Fundraiser Nets $7 Million for Joe Biden," *Variety,* August 21, 2020, https://variety.com/2020/politics/news /katzenberg-clooney-biden-fundraiser-1234743953/.

81 James Politi, "Hollywood mogul pledges 'all the resources' Joe Biden needs to win in 2024," *Financial Times,* May 11, 2023, https://www.ft.com /content/43bf35f8-e000-41a4-848e-272dd71f3930.

82 Nick Spake, "Top 20 Movie Flops of the Last Decade," Watch Mojo, accessed May 31, 2023, https://www.watchmojo.com/articles/top-20-movie-flops -of-the-last-decade; https://www.breitbart.com/entertainment/2022/06/27 /nolte-woke-lightyear-second-weekend-box-office-hits-record-pixar -low/?utm_source=facebook&utm_medium=social; John Nolte, "Nolte: Steven Spielberg's Woke 'West Side Story' Bombs with $10M Opening," Breitbart News, December 11, 2021, https://www.breitbart.com/entertainment /2021/12/11/nolte-steven-spielbergs-woke-west-side-story-bombs-with -10m-opening/; John Nolte, "Nolte: The Biggest, Dumbest, Woketard Plot Hole in 'Terminator: Dark Fate,' " Breitbart News, November 3, 2019, https:// www.breitbart.com/entertainment/2019/11/03/biggest-dumbest-woketard -plot-hole-in-terminator-dark-fate/.

83 John Nolte, "Nolte: Woke 'Shazam 2' Could Lose Up To $150 Million," Breitbart News, April 4, 2023, https://www.breitbart.com/entertainment/2023/04/04 /nolte-woke-shazam-2-could-lose-up-to-150-million/.

84 John Nolte, "Nolte: Homophobia? Math Proves 95% of Gays Avoided Billy Eichner's 'Bros,' " Breitbart News, October 3, 2022, https://www.breitbart .com/entertainment/2022/10/03/nolte-homophobia-math-proves-95-of -gays-avoided-billy-eichners-bros/; Rotten Tomatoes, "Bros," ratings, accessed May 31, 2023, https://www.rottentomatoes.com/m/bros_2022.

85 Peter Kiefer and Peter Savodnik, "Hollywood's New Rules," *Free Press,* January 11, 2022, https://www.thefp.com/p/hollywoods-new-rules.

86 Tom Brueggemann, "Theater Audiences Shrank by Half in the Last 4 Years. Can Movies Get Them Back?," *IndieWire,* January 5, 2023, https://www .indiewire.com/features/general/2022-box-office-2023-1234795871/.

87 Box Office Mojo, "Spider-Man: No Way Home (2021)," IMDbPro, accessed May 31, 2023, https://www.boxofficemojo.com/title/tt10872600/?ref_=bo_ cso_table_3; Box Office Mojo, "The Super Mario Bros. Movie," IMDbPro, accessed May 31, 2023, https://www.boxofficemojo.com/release /rl1930593025/?ref_=bo_yld_table_1; Box Office Mojo, "John Wick 4," IMDbPro, accessed May 31, 2023, https://www.boxofficemojo.com/release /rl1644725761/?ref_=bo_yld_table_5.

PART III: AMERICA TRANSITIONS: JOE BIDEN'S MANAGED DECLINE
CHAPTER 9: SNEAKY JOE'S LOW-ENERGY ENERGY POLICY

1 "9 Key Elements of Joe Biden's Plan for a Clean Energy Revolution," JoeBiden .com, accessed via WayBackMachine on May 28, 2023, https://web.archive .org/web/20230111150614/https://joebiden.com/9-key-elements-of-joe -bidens-plan-for-a-clean-energy-revolution/#.

2 Alejandra Borunda, "The origins of environmental justice—and why it's finally getting the attention it deserves," *National Geographic*, February 24, 2021, https://www.nationalgeographic.com/environment/article/environmental -justice-origins-why-finally-getting-the-attention-it-deserves.

3 U.S. Department of Health and Human Services, "Biden-Harris Administration Establishes HHS Office of Environmental Justice," May 31, 2022, https://www.hhs.gov/about/news/2022/05/31/biden-harris-administration -establishes-hhs-office-of-environmental-justice.html.

4 "Joe's Plan for a Clean Energy Future and Environmental Justice," JoeBiden .com, accessed via WayBackMachine on May 28, 2023, https://web.archive .org/web/20200807092657/https://joebiden.com/climate-plan/#.

5 Kassie Perlongo, "Greening of the Earth Mitigates Surface Warming," NASA, November 23, 2020, https://www.nasa.gov/feature/greening-of-the-earth -mitigates-surface-warming; Chi Chen, Dan Li, Yue Li, Shilong Piao, Xuhui Wang, Maoyi Huang, Pierre Gentine, Ramakrishna, Nemani, and Ranga Myneni, "Biophysical impacts of Earth greening largely controlled by aerodynamic resistance," *Science Advances* 6, no. 47 (November 20, 2023), 10.1126 /sciadv.abb1981.

6 Penny Starr, "Andrew Yang: 'Too Late' to Stop Global Warming; Move to 'Higher Ground,'" Breitbart News, July 31, 2019, https://www.breitbart .com/2020-election/2019/07/31/andrew-yang-too-late-to-stop-global -warming-move-to-higher-ground/.

7 "What is the optimal human population? An eminent economist weighs in," Overpopulation Project, March 8, 2021, https://overpopulation-project.com /what-is-the-optimal-human-population-an-eminent-economist-weighs-in/; "A Planet of 3 Billion: Mapping Humanity's Long History of Ecological Destruction and Finding Our Way to a Resilient Future—A Global Citizen's Guide to Saving the Planet," review of *A Planet of 3 Billion,* September 9, 2019, *Kirkus Reviews,* https:// www.kirkusreviews.com/book-reviews/christopher-tucker/planet-of-3-billion/.

8 Pew Research Center, "Election 2020: Voters Are Highly Engaged, but Nearly Half Expect to Have Difficulties Voting," August 13, 2020, https://www .pewresearch.org/politics/2020/08/13/important-issues-in-the-2020 -election/.

9 Joel Pollak, "Rule by Decree: Joe Biden Sets Record for Executive Orders in First Week," Breitbart News, January 25, 2021, https://www.breitbart.com /politics/2021/01/25/rule-by-decree-joe-biden-sets-record-for-executive -orders-in-first-week/.

10 "EPA to Tighten Rules on Oil and Gas Production to Reduce Methane," NACS, November 3, 2021, https://www.convenience.org/Media/Daily/2021 /Nov/3/2-EPA-Tighten-Rules-Oil-Gas-Production-Methane_GR.

11 U.S. Environmental Protection Agency, *Overview of Greenhouse Gases,* April 13, 2003, https://www.epa.gov/ghgemissions/overview-greenhouse-gases.

12 Keith Nunes, "Biden administration to invest in US meat processing capacity," *Food Business News,* January 4, 2022, https://www.foodbusinessnews.net /articles/20338-biden-administration-to-invest-in-us-meat-process ing-capacity; Eric Bradner and Arlette Saenz, "Joe Biden's climate plan targets net-zero emissions by 2050," CNN, June 4, 2019, https://www.cnn .com/2019/06/04/politics/joe-biden-2020-climate-plan/index.html; Bill Barrow, "Joe Biden's $5T climate plan: Net zero emissions by 2050," AP News, June 4, 2019, https://apnews.com/article/climate-donald-trump-ap-top -news-joe-biden-environment-2ad4e1c11f89436890748a137feff930.

13 Todd Spangler, "Biden wants funds to electrify federal vehicle fleet in next budget," *Detroit Free Press,* April 9, 2021, https://www.freep.com/story /money/cars/2021/04/09/joe-biden-electric-vehicles/7154870002/; Robert Walton, "Biden's infrastructure plan goes big on EVs, but his first budget starts small, analysts say," Utility Dive, April 14, 2021, https://www.utilitydive .com/news/bidens-infrastructure-plan-goes-big-on-evs-but-his-first-budget -starts-sm/598264/#:~:text=The%20U.S.%20Department%20of%20Trans portation,his%20%242.25%20trillion%20infrastructure%20proposal; The White House, "FACT SHEET: The American Jobs Plan," March 31, 2021, https://www.whitehouse.gov/briefing-room/statements-releases/2021/03/31 /fact-sheet-the-american-jobs-plan/; Robert Walton, "American Jobs Plan: Transportation Infrastructure Proposals," Industry Dive, accessed May 28, 2023, https://www.documentcloud.org/documents/20613787-transportation -details-1.

14 The White House, "Biden-?Harris Administration Launches American Innovation Effort to Create Jobs and Tackle the Climate Crisis," February 11, 2021, https://www.whitehouse.gov/briefing-room/statements-releases/2021/02/11 /biden-harris-administration-launches-american-innovation-effort-to-cre ate-jobs-and-tackle-the-climate-crisis/; The White House, "President Biden's FY 2023 Budget Reduces Energy Costs, Combats the Climate Crisis, and Advances Environmental Justice," March 28, 2022, https://www.whitehouse.gov /omb/briefing-room/2022/03/28/president-bidens-fy-2023-budget-reduces -energy-costs-combats-the-climate-crisis-and-advances-environmental-justice/; Emma Newburger, "Biden's budget proposal calls for more than $36 billion to fight climate change," CNBC, May 28, 2021, https://www.CNBC.com/2021/05/28 /bidens-budget-proposal-calls-for-36-billion-to-fight-climate-change.html.

15 Kevin McGill and Matthew Brown, "Ruling clears Joe Biden's 2021 pause on new oil, gas leases," *PBS NewsHour,* August 17, 2022, https://www.pbs.org /newshour/politics/ruling-clears-joe-bidens-2021-pause-on-new-oil-gas -leases#:~:text=Biden%20had%20signed%20an%20executive,states%20op posed%20to%20Biden's%20move; United States Department of the Interior, "Interior Department Announces Significantly Reformed Onshore Oil and Gas Lease Sales," press release, April 15, 2022, https://content.govdelivery .com/accounts/USDOI/bulletins/313a817.

16 Associated Press, "Biden Admin Halts Oil Drilling in Alaska Wildlife Refuge," *VOA News,* June 2, 2021, https://www.voanews.com/a/economy-business _biden-admin-halts-oil-drilling-alaska-wildlife-refuge/6206510.html#:~:

text=US%20President%20Joe%20Biden's%20administration,Donald%20 Trump%20to%20allow%20drilling; Joel Pollak, "Report: Biden to Cancel Oil, Gas Leases in Arctic National Wildlife Refuge (ANWR), Despite High Gas Prices," Breitbart News, June 1, 2021, https://www.breitbart.com /politics/2021/06/01/report-biden-to-cancel-oil-gas-leases-in-arctic-national -wildlife-refuge-anwr-despite-gas-prices/.

17 Emma Newburger, "Biden announces standards to make electric vehicle charging stations accessible," CNBC, June 9, 2022, https://www .cnbc.com/2022/06/09/biden-announces-standards-for-electric-vehicle -charging-stations.html#:~:text=Kevin%20Lamarque%20%7C%20Reu ters-,The%20Biden%20administration%20this%20week%20proposed%20 new%20standards%20for%20its,the%20country's%20c.

18 "9 Key Elements of Joe Biden's Plan for a Clean Energy," JoeBiden.com, https://web.archive.org/web/20201203011850/https://joebiden.com/9-key -elements-of-joe-bidens-plan-for-a-clean-energy-revolution/.

19 David Gura, "The SEC wants companies to disclose how climate change is affecting them," NPR, March 21, 2022, https://www.npr.org/2022/03/21/1087832674 /the-s-e-c-climate-change-disclosures-companies.

20 BlueGreen Alliance, "9 Million Jobs from Climate Action: The Inflation Reduction Act," Political Economy Research Institute, accessed April 10, 2023, https://www.bluegreenalliance.org/site/9-million-good-jobs-from-climate -action-the-inflation-reduction-act/.

21 "President Biden & Michael Powell Race Corvettes, Jay Leno's Garage Season 7 Rewind," YouTube video, 4:17, posted by CNBC Prime, November 4, 2022, https://www.youtube.com/watch?v=2hW0xmnp4Ys.

22 Ryan Dagostino, "Things My Father Taught Me: An Interview with Joe and Hunter Biden," Popular Mechanics, November 9, 2020, https://www .popularmechanics.com/home/a20655/things-my-father-taught-me/.

23 Valerie Biden Owens, Growing Up Biden (New York: Celadon Books, 2022).

24 Mariah Espada, "President Biden, His Corvette, and the Latest Stash of Classified Documents," Time, January 12, 2023, https://time.com/6246994 /biden-classified-documents-delaware-corvette/.

25 "Oops! GM Bailout Cost Taxpayers Almost $1B More Than Estimated," NBC News, April 30, 2014, https://www.nbcnews.com/business/autos/oops -gm-bailout-cost-taxpayers-almost-1b-more-estimated-n93816.

26 Ralph Nader, "General Motors could buy Delaware if DuPont were willing to sell it," AZ Quotes, accessed May 28, 2023, https://www.azquotes.com/quote/1206950.

27 Ronnie Green, "Electric cars and the Department of Energy: Two giant loans, two different paths," Florida Bulldog, May 23, 2013, https://www.florida bulldog.org/2013/05/electric-cars-and-the-department-of-energy-two -giant-loans-two-different-paths/.

28 Matt Degen, "Irvine's Fisker makes it official, buys old GM plant," Orange County Register, October 27, 2009, https://www.ocregister.com/2009/10/27 /irvines-fisker-makes-it-official-buys-old-gm-plant/.

29 Joel Pollak, "Hunter Biden's Business Partners Invested in Failed Fisker Automotive," Breitbart News, September 29, 2020, https://www.breitbart .com/economy/2020/09/29/hunter-bidens-business-partners-invested -in-failed-fisker-automotive/.

30 Allison Stone, "The 2011, 2012, and 2021 Fisker Karma's Changes Over the Years," Jerry Insurance, July 7, 2022, https://getjerry.com/electric -vehicles/2011-2012-and-2021-fisker-karmas-changes-over-years; Aruna Viswanatha, Sadie Gurman, and James Areddy, "Prosecutors Advance Tax Probe of Hunter Biden," *Wall Street Journal,* March 28, 2022, https://www.wsj .com/articles/prosecutors-advance-tax-probe-of-hunter-biden-11648465200.

31 Stone, "The 2011, 2012, and 2021 Fisker."

32 Sean O'Kane, "Fisker and Karma raise millions of dollars following wave of Tesla optimism," *The Verge,* July 9, 2020, https://www.theverge .com/2020/7/9/21319273/fisker-inc-karma-automotive-fundraising-public -evs-tesla-nikola.

33 Jon Fingas, "GM plans to build a military vehicle based on the Hummer EV," Engadget, November 11, 2021, https://www.engadget.com/gm -hummer-ev-military-vehicle-elrv-181909646.html.

34 Peter Johnson, "US Department of Defense embracing electric military vehicles using GM's Ultium Platform," Electrek, October 7, 2022, https://electrek .co/2022/10/07/us-department-of-defense-embracing-electric-military -vehicles/.

35 United States Department of Energy, "U.S. Department of Energy Announces $2.5 Billion Loan to Ultium Cells for Three Domestic Battery Cell Manufacturing Facilities," December 12, 2022, https://www.energy.gov/articles /us-department-energy-announces-25-billion-loan-ultium-cells-three -domestic-battery-cell.

36 Joey Klender, "Toyota will join Tesla, GM in losing EV tax credit after it reaches sales cap," Teslarati, April 7, 2022, https://www.teslarati.com/toyota-will -join-tesla-gm-in-losing-ev-tax-credit-after-it-reaches-sales-cap/; Kalea Hall, "GM hires Biden niece, former Obama aide to head environment, sustainability and governance policy," *Detroit News,* February 9, 2022, https:// www.detroitnews.com/story/business/autos/general-motors/2022/02/09 /biden-niece-former-obama-aide-joins-general-motors-washington /6720560001/.

37 Ari Natter, "GM, Ford Extra EV Credits At Risk in Senate Review," Bloomberg News, December 8, 2021, https://www.bloomberg.com/news /articles/2021-12-08/extra-tax-credit-for-ev-s-put-at-risk-by-parliamentar ian-review#:~:text=A%20Biden%2Dbacked%20proposal%20to,nearly%20 %242%20trillion%20economic%20package; Ari Natter and Keith Laing, "More EVs Will Qualify for Tax Credits After US Reverses Course," Bloomberg News, February 3, 2023, https://www.bloomberg.com/news /articles/2023-02-03/more-evs-to-qualify-for-tax-credits-after-us-reverses -course#xj4y7vzkg.

38 Open Secrets, "General Motors," Annual Lobbying Totals: 1998–2022, accessed May 29, 2023, https://www.opensecrets.org/orgs/general-motors /lobbying?id=D000000155; Open Secrets, "General Motors," Top Recipients 2022, accessed May 29, 2023, https://www.opensecrets.org/orgs /general-motors/summary?topnumcycle=2022&contribcycle=2022&lob cycle=2022&outspendcycle=2022&id=D000000155&toprecipcycle=2022; Open Secrets, "General Motors," Top Recipients 2020, accessed May 29, 2023, https://www.opensecrets.org/orgs/general-motors/summary?topnum

cycle=2022&contribcycle=2022&lobcycle=2022&outspendcycle=
2022&id=D000000155&toprecipcycle=2020.

39 Michael Wayland, "General Motors plans to exclusively offer electric vehicles by 2034," CNBC, January 28, 2021, https://www.cnbc.com/2021/01/28
/general-motors-plans-to-exclusively-offer-electric-vehicles-by-2035
.html#:~:text=GM%20plans%20to%20exclusively%20offer,its%20global%20
products%20and%20operations.

40 Ryan King, "Inflation Reduction Act promises $7,500 electric vehicle credits
after Ford and GM raised prices," *Washington Examiner*, August 16, 2022,
https://www.washingtonexaminer.com/news/democrats-extended-credits
-evs-ford-gm-prices.

41 Chuck Ross, "Easy Access: Top Biden Adviser Hosted Lobbyist Brother's Clients at White House," *Washington Free Beacon*, July 8, 2022, https:/
/freebeacon.com/biden-administration/easy-access-biden-adviser-hosted
-lobbyist-brothers-clients-at-white-house/.

42 Ballotpedia, s.v. "Steve Richetti," accessed May 29, 2023, https://ballotpedia
.org/Steve_Ricchetti.

43 Alex Thompson and Theodoric Meyer, "The Ricchetti administration?,"
Politico, June 14, 2021, https://www.politico.com/newsletters/west-wing
-playbook/2021/06/14/the-ricchetti-administration-493243.

44 Stephen Jones, "Americans are paying $54,000 on average for an electric
vehicle. A year ago, they were paying closer to $44,000," Business Insider,
June 27, 2022, https://www.businessinsider.com/electric-vehicle-prices-rise
-22-percent-fossil-fuel-14-percent-2022-6; Andrew Hawkins, "EV prices
are going in the wrong direction," *The Verge*, August 24, 2022, https://
www.theverge.com/2022/8/24/23319794/ev-price-increase-used-cars
-analysis-iseecars; Mike Colias, "Tesla, Ford and GM Raise EV Prices as
Costs, Demand Grow," *Wall Street Journal*, June 26, 2022, https://www.wsj
.com/articles/tesla-ford-and-gm-raise-ev-prices-as-costs-demand-grow
-11656241381?mod=business_lead_pos1.

45 "President Biden Test Drives New Electric Hummer During GM Factory
Tour," YouTube video, 0:48, posted by "The Hill," November 17, 2021, https://
www.youtube.com/watch?v=JLcWpZzgNxo.

46 Brian Silvestro, "GMC Hummer EV Sold Out for Two Years or More, Company Says," *Road & Track*, November 1, 2022, https://www.roadandtrack
.com/news/a41830106/gmc-hummer-ev-sold-out-for-two-years/#:~:text
=More%2C%20Company%20Says-,GMC%20Hummer%20EV%20Sold%20
Out%20for%20Two%20Years%20or%20More,sitting%20around%20wait
ing%20until%202025.&text=If%20you're%20waiting%20for,be%20pre
pared%20to%20keep%20waiting;   https://www.motortrend.com/cars/gmc
/hummer-ev/2022/.

47 United States Department of Energy, "Saving Money with Electric Vehicles,"
September 28, 2022, https://www.energy.gov/energysaver/articles/saving
-money-electric-vehicles.

48 Anderson Economic Group, "Gas-Powered Cars Cheaper to Fuel than Electric in Late 2022," January 24, 2023, https://www.andersoneconomicgroup
.com/cars-gas-powered-cheaper-to-fuel-than-electric-in-late-2022/.

49 Paul Van Osdol, "Chevy Bolt owners frustrated by slow response to re-

call of fire-prone batteries," WTAE, June 30, 2022, https://www.wtae.com /article/chevy-bolt-owners-frustrated-by-slow-response-to-recall-of-fire -prone-batteries/40476126#:~:text=General%20Motors%20recalled%20 140%2C000%20Chevrolet%20Bolts%20after%20some%20batteries%20 caught%20fire.,-But%20Action%20News.

50 Josh Hendrickson, "Don't Park Your Chevy Bolt Inside Where It Might Burn Down your Home," Review Geek, July 17, 2021, https://www.reviewgeek .com/92305/dont-park-your-chevy-bolt-inside-where-it-might-burn-down -your-home/.

51 Cris Barrish, "Amazon hiring blitz for fulfillment center at former GM plant in Del. includes $3,000 bonuses," WHYY, August 28, 2021, https://whyy.org/articles/amazon-hiring-blitz-for-fulfillment-center-at -former-gm-plant-in-del-includes-3000-bonuses/#:~:text=Amazon's%20 creation%20of%20the%20820%2C000,assembly%20plant%20on%20Box wood%20Road; Brandon Holveck, "Delaware losing bragging rights for big-gest Amazon warehouse. Who's claiming the title?," Delaware Online, August 1, 2022, https://www.delawareonline.com/story/money/business/2022/08/01 /amazon-warehouse-on-boxwood-road-will-no-longer-be-largest -in-u-s/65385285007/.

52 Gavin Maguire, "Column: Europe eats into China's lead as top EV growth mar-ket," Reuters, October 5, 2022, https://www.reuters.com/markets/commodities /europe-eats-into-chinas -lead-top-ev-growth-market-2022-10-05/.

53 Takashi Kawakami, Yohei Muramatsu, and Saki Shirai, "China led world with 500,000 electric car exports in 2021," Nikkei Asia, March 8, 2022, https://asia .nikkei.com/Spotlight/Electric-cars-in-China/China-led-world-with-500 -000-electric-car-exports-in-2021.

54 Gavin Maguire, "Column: Europe eats into China's lead as top EV growth mar-ket," Reuters, October 5, 2022, https://www.reuters.com/markets/commodities /europe-eats-into-chinas-lead-top-ev-growth-market-2022-10-05/.

55 Daniel Shvartsman, "Tesla Growth and Production Statistics: How Many Vehicles Are Sold Across the Globe?," Investing, May 26, 2023, https://www .investing.com/academy/statistics/tesla-facts/.

56 Colin McKerracher, "China Has Shot at Seizing 60% Share of Global EV Sales This Year," Bloomberg News, November 15, 2022, https://www.bloomberg .com/news/articles/2022-11-15/china-has-shot-at-seizing-60-share-of -global-ev-sales-this-year#xj4y7vzkg.

57 Henry Sanderson, "China's Electric Vehicle Battery King," Time, September 29, 2022, https://time.com/6217992/china-electric-vehicle-catl/; https://www .nytimes.com/2021/12/22/business/china-catl-electric-car-batteries.html.

58 Keith Bradsher and Michael Forsythe, "Why a Chinese Company Dominates Electric Car Batteries," New York Times, November 20, 2021, https://www .nytimes.com/2021/11/20/world/hunter-biden-china-cobalt.html.

59 Eric Lipton and Dionne Searcey, "How the U.S. Lost Ground to China in the Contest for Clean Energy," New York Times, November 21, 2021, https://www .nytimes.com/2021/11/21/world/us-china-energy.html.

60 Roger Schreffler, "Shots on EV Battery Materials," Wards Auto, December 8, 2021, https://www.wardsauto.com/industry-news/expert-warns-china-calling -shots-ev-battery-materials.

61 Steve Karnowski, "Biden administration move could block Minnesota copper mine," Associated Press, October 20, 2021, https://apnews.com /article/business-environment-and-nature-minnesota-environment -cbc661943924283f639251df7d1c808d; House Committee on Natural Resources, "Biden Administration Blocks Development of World-Class Mineral Deposit," January 26, 2023, accessed via WayBackMachine on May 29, 2023, https://web.archive.org/web/20230211203905/https://naturalresources .house.gov/newsroom/documentsingle.aspx?DocumentID=412737.

62 Sam Mceachern, "General Motors Sold Over 200,000 EVs in 2020," GM Authority, May 4, 2021, https://gmauthority.com/blog/2021/05/general-motors -sold-over-200000-evs-in-2020/#:~:text=While%20the%20automaker%20 still%20has,202%2C488%20electric%20vehicles%20in%202020.

63 Jacob Bliss, "Jim Banks Slams the Democrat 'Infrastructure' Bill: 'Essentially A Green New Deal Lite,' " Breitbart News, August 2, 2021, https://www .breitbart.com/politics/2021/08/02/jim-banks-slams-the-democrat -infrastructure-bill-essentially-green-new-deal-lite/.

64 The White House, "Fact Sheet: The Bipartisan Infrastructure Deal," November 6, 2021, https://www.whitehouse.gov/briefing-room/statements -releases/2021/11/06/fact-sheet-the-bipartisan-infrastructure-deal/#:~: text=The%20legislation%20positions%20rail%20to,the%20northeast%20 and%20mid%2DAtlantic.

65 U.S. Congress, House, "Infrastructure Investment and Jobs Act," HR 3684, 117th Cong., 1st Sess., became Public Law No. 117-58 November 15, 2021, https://www.congress.gov/bill/117th-congress/house-bill/3684/text.

66 Steven Malanga, "The Agenda Behind Buttigieg's Claim That Highways Are 'Racist,' " Wall Street Journal, April 19, 2011, https://www.wsj.com/articles/the -agenda-behind-buttigiegs-claim-that-highways-are-racist-11618847867.

67 U.S. Congress, House, "Infrastructure Investment and Jobs Act."

68 John Binder, "So-called 'Infrastructure' Bill Includes Racial Quotas for Broadband," Breitbart News, August 2, 2021, https://www.breitbart.com /politics/2021/08/02/so-called-infrastructure-bill-includes-racial-quotas -for-broadband/.

69 John Binder, "Republicans Voted for Biden's Infrastructure Bill After Securing Cash from Chamber of Commerce," Breitbart News, November 10, 2021, https://www.breitbart.com/politics/2021/11/10/republicans-voted-for-bidens -infrastructure-bill-after-securing-cash-from-chamber-of-commerce/.

70 Haris Alic, "Biden's infrastructure bill doubles annual funding for commission run by Manchin's wife," Washington Times, August 1, 2021, https://www.washingtontimes .com/news/2021/aug/1/gayle-manchin-led-commission-sees-funding-double-u/.

71 Sean Moran, "Mitch McConnell 'Delighted' Congress Passed $1.2 Trillion So-Called Bipartisan Infrastructure Bill," Breitbart News, November 8, 2021, https://www.breitbart.com/politics/2021/11/08/mitch-mcconnell-delighted -congress-passed-1-2-trillion-so-called-bipartisan-infrastructure-bill/.

72 Robert Bowman, "Can a VMT Tax Solve the Infrastructure Funding Dilemma?," Supply Chain Brain, October 4, 2021, https://www.supplychain brain.com/blogs/1-think-tank/post/33846-can-a-vmt-tax-solve-the -infrastructure-funding-dilemma.

73 Sean Moran and Matthew Boyle, "Exclusive: Bipartisan So-Called 'Infrastruc-

ture' Bill 2,700 Pages Long," Breitbart News, August 1, 2021. https://www
.breitbart.com/politics/2021/08/01/exclusive-bipartisan-so-called
-infrastructure-bill-2700-pages-long/.

74 The White House, "FACT SHEET: President Biden's Economic Plan Drives
America's Electric Vehicle Manufacturing Boom," September 14, 2022,
https://www.whitehouse.gov/briefing-room/statements-releases/2022/09/14
/fact-sheet-president-bidens-economic-plan-drives-americas-electric-ve
hicle-manufacturing-boom/; United States Department of Transportation,
Federal Highway Administration, "President Biden, USDOT and USDOE
Announce $5 Billion over 5 Years for National EV Charging Network,
Made Possible by Bipartisan Infrastructure Law," February 10, 2022, https://
highways.dot.gov/newsroom/president-biden-usdot-and-usdoe-announce
-5-billion-over-five-years-national-ev-charging.

75 Cody Carlson, "TOTAL RECALL: Tesla recalls 435,000 vehicles over 'defective' feature that can increase crash risk," *U.S. Sun,* December 1, 2022, https://
www.the-sun.com/motors/6813941/tesla-recalls-defective-position-lights/.

76 Sam Tabahriti, "A Tesla driver watched in horror as another Tesla burst into
flames after hitting a barrier," *Business Insider,* December 26, 2022, https://
www.businessinsider.com/tesla-driver-watched-in-horror-tesla-crashed
-burst-into-flames-2022-12.

77 Debra Worley, "Tesla disintegrates in fire along the interstate," WBTV 3,
November 17, 2022, https://www.wbtv.com/2022/11/17/tesla-disintegrates
-fire-along-interstate/#.

78 State of California Air Resources Board, *Advanced Clean Cars II Resolution,
Resolution 22-12,* August 25, 2022, https://ww2.arb.ca.gov/sites/default/files
/barcu/board/books/2022/082522/prores22-12.pdf.

79 Alana Mastrangelo, "Don't Plug It In! California Man's Tesla Implores Him
Not to Charge Vehicle," Breitbart News, September 8, 2022, https://www
.breitbart.com/tech/2022/09/08/dont-plug-it-in-california-mans-tesla
-implores-him-not-to-charge-vehicle/.

80 "California ISO extends Flex Alert to today from 3–10 p.m.," California ISO,
September 8, 2022, https://www.flexalert.org/news/126-california-iso-ex
tends-flex-alert-to-today-from-3-10-pm.

81 Ralph Vartabedian, "In a Drought, California Is Watching Water Wash
Out to Sea," *New York Times,* January 13, 2023, https://www.nytimes
.com/2023/01/13/us/california-drought-storms-water-storage.html.

82 Jill Cowan, "Turn off your lights and turn up the heat, all of California is told
in a plea for power conservation," *New York Times,* July 28, 2021, https://www
.nytimes.com/2021/07/28/us/flex-alert-california.html.

83 Andrew Moseman, "The U.S. only has 6,000 fast charging stations for EVs.
Here's where they all are," *MIT Technology Review,* June 28, 2022, https://www
.technologyreview.com/2022/06/28/1053908/electric-vehicle-charging
-stations/.

84 Tyler Hoover, "Towing with my Ford Lightning EV Pickup was a TOTAL DI-
SASTER!," YouTube video, 0:30, posted by "Hoovies Garage," September 23,
2022, https://www.youtube.com/watch?v=3nS0Fdayj8Y&t=14s.

85 Alana Mastrangelo, "'Complete and Total Disaster: Ford Electric Truck Utterly Fails YouTuber's Towing Test," Breitbart News, September 27, 2022,

https://www.breitbart.com/tech/2022/09/27/complete-and-total-disaster
-ford-electric-truck-utterly-fails-youtubers-towing-test/.

86 Ben Stewart, "10 Most Popular Electric Cars," *Kelley Blue Book,* July 27, 2022, https://www.kbb.com/best-cars/most-popular-electric-cars/.

87 IEA, *Global EV Outlook 2022 Executive Summary,* 2022, https://www.iea.org /reports/global-ev-outlook-2022/executive-summary.

88 The White House, Tanya Somanader, "President Obama: The United States Formally Enters the Paris Agreement," September 3, 2016, https://obama whitehouse.archives.gov/blog/2016/09/03/president-obama-united -states-formally-enters-paris-agreement; Natasha Geiling, "Alongside 174 Nations and Holding His Granddaughter, John Kerry Signs Paris Climate Accord," Think Progress, April 22, 2016, https://web.archive.org/web/20160720132703 /http://thinkprogress.org/climate/2016/04/22/3771889/paris-agreement -signing/; Justin Fishel, "John Kerry Signs Climate Deal with Granddaughter Seated in His Lap," ABC News, April 22, 2016, https://abcnews.go.com /International/john-kerry-signs-climate-deal-granddaughter-seated-lap /story?id=38600097.

89 U.S. National Oceanic and Atmospheric Administration, David Herring, *Climate Change: Global Temperature Projections,* March 6, 2012, https://www .climate.gov/news-features/understanding-climate/climate-change-global -temperature-projections.

90 U.S. National Aeronautics and Space Administration, *Scientific Consensus: Earth's Climate Is Warning,* accessed April 10, 2023, https://climate.nasa.gov /scientific-consensus/.

91 Henry Fountain, "Failure to Slow Warming Will Set Off Climate 'Tipping Points,' Scientists Say," *New York Times,* September 8, 2022, https://www .nytimes.com/2022/09/08/climate/global-warming-climate-tipping-point .html?smid=tw-share.

92 Caleb Silver, "The Top 25 Economies in the world," Investopedia, September 1, 2022, https://www.investopedia.com/insights/worlds-top -economies/; "Which countries are the world's biggest carbon polluters?," Climate Trade, https://climatetrade.com/which-countries-are-the-worlds-big gest-carbon-polluters/.

93 Bjorn Lomborg (@BjornLomborg), "New Nature study shows net-zero will cost each American more than $11,000 every year by 2050. That's ~100x more expensive than what Americans are willing to pay." Twitter, August 28, 2021, 5:48 a.m., https://twitter.com/BjornLomborg/sta tus/1431599612616445958; Bjorn Lomborg (@BjornLomborg), "New Nature study shows net-zero will cost the US more than 12% of its GDP every year by 2050 For comparison, Social Security today costs 5% of US GDP and Medicare." Twitter, August 28, 2021, 5:48 a.m., https://twitter.com/BjornLomborg /status/1431599618115219456?s=20&t=0V34JN7bhxcYjR-pTYCxDg.

94 OxFam International, " 'Net zero' carbon targets are dangerous distractions from the priority of cutting emissions says new Oxfam report," press release, August 3, 2021, https://www.oxfam.org/en/press-releases/net-zero-carbon -targets-are-dangerous-distractions-priority-cutting-emissions-says.

95 Thomas Catenacci, "John Kerry's family private jet emitted over 300 metric tons of carbon since Biden took office," Fox News, July 19, 2022, https://www

.foxnews.com/politics/john-kerrys-family-private-jet-emitted-300-metric
-tons-carbon-biden-took-office.

96 Collin Anderson, "As Biden's Climate Czar, John Kerry Has Flown More Than 180,000 Miles, Emitting 9.5 Million Pounds of Carbon," *Washington Free Beacon,* September 8, 2022, https://freebeacon.com/biden-administration /as-bidens-climate-czar-john-kerry-has-flown-more-than-180000-miles -emitting-9-5-million-pounds-of-carbon/.

97 John Kerry and Tony Blair, "John Kerry: It's 'too late' to reach net zero carbon emissions by 2050," *Fortune* video, 2:20, July 30, 2021, https://fortune .com/videos/watch/John-Kerry-Its-too-late-to-reach-net-zero-carbon -emissions-by-2050/afaedd3c-f8de-4e65-bbeb-ed3c1384b0d8.

98 Paige Bennett, "U.S. Climate Envoy Kerry Launches Controversial Carbon Offset Plan," EcoWatch, November 16, 2022, https://www.ecowatch.com /us-voluntary-carbon-trading-market.html.

99 Arshad Mohammed, "Kerry calls climate change 'weapon of mass destruction,'" Reuters, February 16, 2014, https://www.reuters.com/article /us-kerry-climate/kerry-calls-climate-change-weapon-of-mass-destruction -idUSBREA1F0BP20140216.

100 Ballotpedia, "John Podesta," accessed on April 23, 2023, https://ballotpedia. org/John_Podesta; Lynn Sweet, "All-business Obama begins transition to White House," *Chicago Sun-Times,* November 10, 2008, accessed via Web Archive on April 23, 2023, https://web.archive.org/web/20081210025245 /http:/www.suntimes.com/news/sweet/1264016,CST-NWS-sweet06.ar ticle; Obama White House, "John Podesta," accessed on April 23, 2023, https://obamawhitehouse.archives.gov/blog/author/john-Podesta; Clinton White House, "Meet Chief of Staff, John Podesta," Fall 1999, https://clinton whitehouse4.archives.gov/WH/kids/inside/html/fall99/html/podesta .html; Center for American Progress, "John Podesta," biography, accessed on April 24, 2023, https://www.americaNPRogress.org/people/podesta-john/.

101 "The phishing email that hacked the account of John Podesta," CBS News, October 28, 2016, https://www.cbsnews.com/news/the-phishing-email-that -hacked-the-account-of-john-podesta/.

102 "18 revelations from Wikileaks' hacked Clinton emails," BBC News, October 27, 2016, https://www.bbc.com/news/world-us-canada-37639370.

103 The White House, "President Biden Announces Senior Clean Energy and Climate Team," September 2, 2022, https://www.whitehouse.gov/briefing -room/statements-releases/2022/09/02/president-biden-announces-se nior-clean-energy-and-climate-team/.

104 United States Senate Democratic Caucus, *Summary: The Inflation Reduction Act of 2022,* accessed on April 24, 2023, https://www.democrats.senate.gov /imo/media/doc/inflation_reduction_act_one_page_summary.pdf.

105 President Joseph Biden, "Executive Order on Tackling the Climate Crisis at Home and Abroad," January 27, 2021, The White House, https://www .whitehouse.gov/briefing-room/presidential-actions/2021/01/27/executive -order-on-tackling-the-climate-crisis-at-home-and-abroad/.

106 United States Department of Commerce, "Gina Raimondo," biography, accessed on April 26, 2023, https://www.commerce.gov/about/leadership /gina-m-raimondo.

107 "Biden's Choice for Commerce Secretary Gina Raimondo Has Failed Rhode Island's Business Owners," Republican Governors Association, January 8, 2021, https://www.rga.org/bidens-choice-commerce-secretary-gina-raimo ndo-failed-rhode-islands-business-owners/; "Top States 2019: Overall Ranking—50: Rhode Island," CNBC, July 10, 2019, https://www.CNBC .com/2019/07/09/top-states-for-business-rhode-island.html.

108 Jake O'Neill, "RI Supreme Court Denies Block Island Marina Expansion," Conservation Law Foundation, October 14, 2022, https://www.clf.org/ newsroom/ri-supreme-court-denies-block-island-marina-expansion/.

109 United States Department of Energy, "Jennifer M. Granholm Sworn in as 16th Secretary of Energy," February 25, 2021, https://www.energy.gov/articles /jennifer-m-granholm-sworn-16th-secretary-energy.

110 Gregory Wallace, "Energy Secretary sells off Proterra stock for $1.6 mil- lion," CNN Politics, May 27, 2021, https://www.cnn.com/2021/05/27/politics /jennifer-granholm-proterra-stock/index.html.

111 Christina Wilkie, "Energy Secretary Jennifer Granholm violated a stock dis- closure law nine times last year," CNBC, January 20, 2022, https://www.cnbc .com/2022/01/20/energy-secretary-jennifer-granholm-violated-stock -disclosure-law-9-times.html.

112 United States Department of State, Antony J. Blinken, Secretary of State, "Se- nior Advisor for Energy Security Press Statement," August 10, 2021, https:// www.state.gov/senior-advisor-for-energy-security/.

113 Max Moran, "Biden Oil Envoy Advised Emirati Gas Firm and Owns Stock in Human Rights–Violating Companies," Sludge, September 1, 2021, https:// readsludge.com/2021/09/01/biden-oil-envoy-advised-emirati-gas-firm-and -owns-stock-in-human-rights-violating-companies/.

114 Avery Thompson, "The Alexandria Ocasio-Cortez 'Green New Deal' Wants to Get Rid of Nuclear Power. That's a Great Idea," Popular Mechanics, February 8, 2019, https://www.popularmechanics.com/science/energy /a26255413/green-new-deal-nuclear-power/; Gabe Kaminsky, "'Em- barrassment': House GOP fuming over Biden administration ever hir- ing nonbinary alleged thief," Washington Examiner, December 13, 2022, https://www.washingtonexaminer.com/news/house/gop-fumes-biden -administration-sam-brinton.

115 Nico Lang, "This Genderfluid Activist Used the Women's Bathroom at the Oscars—And Meryl Streep Loved It," Into Magazine, May 28, 2018, https:// www.intomore.com/culture/this-genderfluid-activist-used-the-womens -bathroom-at-the-oscarsand-meryl-streep-loved-it/.

116 Brittany Jones-Cooper and Jacquie Cosgrove, "Sam Brinton on becoming the first openly genderfluid person in federal government: 'I am given the oppor- tunity to serve my country as I am,'" Yahoo News, October 26, 2022, https:// www.yahoo.com/lifestyle/sam-brinton-first-openly-genderfluid-person -federal-government-174428142.html?guccounter=1.

117 Wayne Besen, "Has Sam Brinton's story always been too good to be true," LGBTQ Nation, December 7, 2022, https://www.lgbtqnation.com/2022/12 /sam-brintons-story-always-good-true/.

118 Jennifer Smith, "REVEALED: Biden's 34-year-old pick for top nuclear waste job endured conversion therapy 'torture' at hands of Southern Baptist mission-

ary parents and is now non-binary drag queen who enjoys 'pup play' and worships 'Daddy Fauci,' " *Daily Mail,* February 17, 2022, https://www.dailymail .co.uk/news/article-10523529/Bidens-pick-nuclear-waste-job-Southern -Baptists-son-turned-drag-queen-Sister-Ray-Dee-OActive.html.

119 Jeremiah Poff, "Biden unleashes dog-role-playing fetishist on key nuclear post," *Washington Examiner,* February 11, 2022, https://www .washingtonexaminer.com/policy/biden-administration-installs-dog-role -playing-fetish-advocate-to-nuclear-post.

120 Nico Portuondo, "Meet the DOE official helping solve the nuclear waste impasse," E&E News Greenwire, October 13, 2022, https://www.eenews.net /articles/meet-the-doe-official-helping-solve-the-nuclear-waste-impasse/; Beth Wallis, "Where should we put our country's nuclear waste? StateImpact Oklahoma goes underground to find out," State Impact Oklahoma NPR, September 15, 2022, https://stateimpact.npr.org/oklahoma/2022/09/15 /to-see-what-oklahoma-could-do-with-nuclear-waste-stateimpact-goes -underground/.

121 United States Department of Energy, Office of Nuclear Energy, *Consent-Based Siting: Request for Information Comment Summary and Analysis,* report, September 2022, https://www.energy.gov/sites/default/files/2022-09/Consent -Based%20Siting%20RFI%20Summary%20Report%200915.pdf.

122 Catherine Clifford, "The feds have collected more than $44 billion for a permanent nuclear waste dump—here's why we still don't have one," CNBC, December 18, 2021, https://www.cnbc.com/2021/12/18/nuclear-waste-why -theres-no-permanent-nuclear-waste-dump-in-us.html.

123 Anthony Gockowski, "Controversial energy official charged with stealing woman's luggage at MSP," Alpha News, November 28, 2022, https://alphanews .org/controversial-energy-official-charged-with-stealing-womans-luggage -at-msp/.

124 Thomas Catenacci, "Former Biden official Sam Brinton's mug shot released after bail set at $15,000," Fox News, December 14, 2022, https://www.foxnews .com/politics/former-biden-official-sam-brintons-mug-shot-released-bail -set-15000.

125 Victor Nava, "Non-binary Biden nuclear official Sam Brinton fired after multiple luggage theft charges: reports," *New York Post,* December 12, 2022, https://nypost.com/2022/12/12/non-binary-biden-nuclear-official-sam -brinton-fired-after-multiple-luggage-theft-charges-reports/.

126 Paul Farrell, "EXCLUSIVE: Biden's married, non-binary nuclear waste guru who stole woman's $2,325 bag from airport hosted SPANKING seminar at kink conference just weeks later—under 'NuclearNerd' nickname that's still in use on fetish hookup website," *Daily Mail,* November 30, 2022, https:// www.dailymail.co.uk/news/article-11487033/Sam-Brinton-Bidens-nuclear -waste-guru-spoke-spanking-seminar-weeks-bag-theft.html; Geneva Sands, Maegan Vazquez, and Jeremy Diamond, "Top Energy Department official no longer employed after luggage theft accusations," CNN, December 13, 2022, https://www.cnn.com/2022/12/13/politics/sam-brinton-department-of -energy/index.html.

127 Patrick Reilly, "Fashion designer claims Sam Brinton wore her clothes that were stolen from DC airport in 2018," *New York Post,* February 22, 2023,

https://nypost.com/2023/02/22/fashion-designer-claims-sam-brinton-wore-her-stolen-clothes/; Ashley Carnahan, "Fashion designer says ex-Biden official Sam Brinton likely stole her clothes: 'What I need is justice,' " Fox News, March 14, 2023, https://www.foxnews.com/media/fashion-designer-biden-official-sam-brinton-stole-clothes-what-need-justice.

128　Marjorie Hernandez, "Non-binary ex-nuclear Biden official Sam Brinton out on bond after 2 weeks in jail over suitcase theft," *New York Post,* June 1, 2023, https://nypost.com/2023/06/01/sam-brinton-free-after-bonding-out-of-virginia-jail/; Marjorie Hernandez, "Non-binary, ex-Biden official Sam Brinton to be held in men's jail over suitcase theft charges: sheriff," *New York Post,* May 23, 2023, https://nypost.com/2023/05/23/non-binary-sam-brinton-will-be-placed-in-mens-jail/.

129　The White House, "President Biden announces the Build Back Better Framework," October 28, 2021, https://www.whitehouse.gov/briefing-room/statements-releases/2021/10/28/president-biden-announces-the-build-back-better-framework/.

130　Asma Khalid and Barbara Sprunt, "Biden Counters Trump's 'America First' with 'Build Back Better' Economic Plan," NPR, July 9, 2020, https://www.npr.org/2020/07/09/889347429/biden-counters-trumps-america-first-with-build-back-better-economic-plan.

131　Melissa Quinn and Kathryn Watson, "What's in Democrats' $1.75 trillion social spending and climate bill?," CBS, November 28, 2021, https://www.cbsnews.com/news/bill-build-back-better-spending-bill-contents/.

132　Wendell Husebø, "Wharton Study: Build Back Better Will Not Be Free; Net Cost $2.42 Trillion," Breitbart News, November 4, 2021, https://www.breitbart.com/politics/2021/11/04/wharton-study-build-back-better-will-not-be-free-net-cost-2-42-trillion/.

133　The White House, "FACT SHEET: The American Families Plan," April 28, 2021, https://www.whitehouse.gov/briefing-room/statements-releases/2021/04/28/fact-sheet-the-american-families-plan/.

134　"Build Back Better Cost Would Double with Extensions," Committee for a Responsible Federal Budget, November 15, 2021, https://www.crfb.org/blogs/build-back-better-cost-would-double-extensions.

135　Coral Davenport and Lisa Friedman, " 'Build Back Better' Hit a Wall, but Climate Action Could Move Forward," *New York Times,* January 20, 2022, https://www.nytimes.com/2022/01/20/climate/build-back-better-climate-change.html.

136　U.S. Congress, Senate, Civilian Climate Corps for Jobs and Justice Act, S1244, 117th Cong., 1st Sess., introduced in Senate April 20, 2021, https://www.congress.gov/bill/117th-congress/senate-bill/1244; Nathan Rott and Scott Detrow, "Reaching Back to the New Deal, Biden Proposes a Civilian Climate Corps," NPR, May 11, 2021, https://www.npr.org/2021/05/11/993976948/reaching-back-to-the-new-deal-biden-proposes-a-civilian-climate-corps.

137　Paul Bois, "Biden's Build Back Better Bill Gives $555 Billion in 'Clean Energy Investments,' " Breitbart News, October 28, 2021, https://www.breitbart.com/politics/2021/10/28/bidens-build-back-better-bill-555-billion-clean-energy-investments/.

138　Lisa Mascaro, "Sinema gives her nod, and influence, to Democrats' big bill," AP News, August 5, 2022, https://apnews.com/article/biden-politics

-kyrsten-sinema-joe-manchin-congress-c0d40a6f2490b2613a690995da
ca7e11.

139 Shunichi Koshimura and Nobuo Shuto, "Response to the 2011 Great East
     Japan Earthquake and Tsunami disaster," *Philosophical Transactions of the
     Royal Society A* 373, no. 2053, https://doi.org/10.1098/rsta.2014.0373.

140 United Nations Office for Disaster Risk Reduction, "Now is the time to do
     bold things," March 19, 2019, https://www.undrr.org/news/now-time-do
     -bold-things.

141 "'Building back better'—here's how we can navigate the risks we face after
     COVID-19," World Economic Forum, May 20, 2020, https://www.weforum
     .org/agenda/2020/05/covid-19-risks-outlook-saadia-zahidi.

142 Mark Hay, "As the coronavirus crisis shows (some) signs of waning, the peo-
     ple who tried to argue it was all part of a sinister government plot are pivoting
     a new boogeyman," Daily Beast, April 30, 2022, https://www.thedailybeast
     .com/conspiracy-theorists-are-already-freaking-out-about-the-next
     -pandemic-as-part-of-the-so-called-great-reset.

143 Radio Davos, *The Great Reset,* World Economic Forum, https://podcasts
     .apple.com/us/podcast/the-great-reset/id1517364006.

144 World Economic Forum, "Reskilling Revolution Champions," initiatives,
     accessed May 29, 2023, https://initiatives.weforum.org/reskilling-revolution
     /about.

145 James Melville (@JamesMelville), "But what we are very proud of now is the
     young generation like Prime Minister Trudeau. . . . We penetrate the cab-
     inets," Twitter, March 24, 2022, 1:50 a.m., https://twitter.com/jamesmelville
     /status/1506916359174770694.

146 World Economic Forum, "Leadership and Governance," About page, accessed on
     April 23, 2023, https://www.weforum.org/about/leadership-and-governance.

147 World Economic Forum, "Joseph R. Biden Jr.," bio, accessed on April 25,
     2023, https://www.weforum.org/people/joseph-r-biden.

148 Trevor Hunnicutt, Valerie Volcovivci, and Andrea Shalal, "Biden names top eco-
     nomic adviser Deese to fight climate change, jobs crisis," Reuters, December 3,
     2020, https://www.reuters.com/article/usa-biden-deese-idINKBN28E099.

149 "World Economic Forum Creates Global Greenhouse Gas Register," *Green-
     Biz,* December 9, 2003, https://www.greenbiz.com/article/world-economic
     -forum-creates-global-greenhouse-gas-register.

150 Gim Huay Neo, "It's time to get serious about climate adaptation. Here's how,"
     World Economic Forum, November 15, 2022, https://www.weforum.org
     /agenda/2022/11/cop27-time-to-get-serious-climate-adaptation/.

151 World Economic Forum, "Jonathan Finer," biography, accessed on April 25,
     2023, https://www.weforum.org/people/jonathan-finer; Natasha Bertrand,
     Tyler Pager, and Lara Seligman, "Biden to tap more Obama vets to fill key
     national security roles," *Politico,* January 5, 2021, https://www.politico.com
     /news/2021/01/05/biden-national-security-roles-455062; World Economic
     Forum, "Marcela Escobari," bio, accessed on April 25, 2023, https://www
     .weforum.org/people/marcela-escobari; The White House, "White House Ap-
     points 2021–2022 Class of White House Fellows," October 18, 2021, https://
     www.whitehouse.gov/briefing-room/statements-releases/2021/10/18/white
     -house-appoints-2021-2022-class-of-white-house-fellows/.

152 The White House, "President Biden Announces Key Appointments to Boards and Commissions," February 28, 2023, https://www.whitehouse.gov /briefing-room/statements-releases/2023/02/28/president-biden-announces -key-appointments-to-boards-and-commissions-18/.

153 Virginia Hale, "Irony Alert: A Thousand Private Jets Deliver Globalist Elite to Davos for Climate Change Summit," Breitbart News, January 24, 2018, https:// www.breitbart.com/europe/2018/01/24/private-jets-davos-climate-change/.

154 United Nations, "Mr. Michael R. Bloomberg of the United States—Special Envoy on Climate Ambition and Solutions," February 5, 2021, https://www .un.org/sg/en/content/sg/personnel-appointments/2021-02-05/mr-michael -r-bloomberg-of-the-united-states%C2%A0-special-envoy-climate -ambition-and-solutions%C2%A0-%C2%A0%C2%A0%C2%A0.

155 "The 41 Things Biden Should Do First on Climate Change," Bloomberg News, November 12, 2020, https://www.bloomberg.com/features/2020-biden -climate-change-advice/?leadSource=uverify%20wall.

156 Open Secrets, "Joe Biden," Top Contributors, federal election data for Joe Biden, 2020 cycle, accessed May 29, 2023, https://www.opensecrets .org/2020-presidential-race/joe-biden/contributors?id=N00001669.

157 League of Conservation Voters, "Climate Power, LCV, and Future Forward Launch $10 Million Inflation Reduction Act Education Campaign," press release, August 18, 2022, https://www.lcv.org/media-center/climate-power -lcv-and-future-forward-launch-10-million-inflation-reduction-act -education-campaign/.

158 Stephen Overly, "Why this Facebook co-founder is donating big money to Hillary Clinton," Washington Post, October 24, 2016, https://www .washingtonpost.com/news/innovations/wp/2016/10/24/why-this-face book-co-founder-is-donating-big-money-to-hillary-clinton/; Open Secrets, "Joe Biden," Top Contributors, 2020 cycle, https://www.opensecrets .org/2020-presidential-race/joe-biden/contributors?id=N00001669.

159 Jenny Thai, "On this Earth Day, Asana is going carbon neutral," The Work-Back, April 22, 2019, https://theworkback.com/asana-carbon-offsets/# close.

160 Asana, Environmental and Social Governance (website), accessed on May 29, 2023, https://asana.com/esg/environmental/.

161 Open Secrets, "Joe Biden," Top Contributors, 2020 cycle, https://www.open secrets.org/2020-presidential-race/joe-biden/contributors?id=N00001669.

162 Eliza Collins, "Progressive groups team up to hit Trump with 6 new ads," USA Today, July 12, 2016, https://www.usatoday.com/story/news/politics /onpolitics/2016/07/12/priorities-usa-action-planned-parenthood-emi lys-list-trump/86998692/.

163 Priorities USA, "Priorities USA and the League of Conservation Voters Launch Joint NH Digital Ad Buy," press release, July 29, 2021, https:// priorities.org/press/priorities-usa-and-the-league-of-conservation-voters -launch-joint-nh-digital-ad-buy/.

164 Sixteen Thirty Fund (website), accessed May 29, 2023, https://www.sixteen thirtyfund.org.

165 Influence Watch, s.v. "Sixteen Thirty Fund (1630 Fund)," accessed May 29, 2023, https://www.influencewatch.org/non-profit/sixteen-thirty-fund/.

166 Jude Clemente, "Joe Biden's 'Alternative Energy' Fantasy," RealClearPolitics, November 11, 2022, https://www.realclearenergy.org/articles/2022/11/11/joe_bidens_alternative_energy_fantasy_864009.html.

167 Emma Newburger, "Joe Biden calls climate change the 'number one issue facing humanity'," CNBC, October 24, 2020, https://www.cnbc.com/2020/10/24/joe-biden-climate-change-is-number-one-issue-facing-humanity.html.

168 Saphora Smith, "Greenpeace to sue European Union for 'gas and nuclear greenwashing,'" Independent, September 19, 2022, https://www.independent.co.uk/climate-change/news/greenpeace-european-union-sue-taxonomy-gas-nuclear-greenwashing-b2168267.html; Saphora Smith, "EU parliament decision to label gas and nuclear investments climate-friendly 'catastrophic,'" Independent, July 6, 2022, https://www.independent.co.uk/climate-change/news/eu-parliament-gas-nuclear-energy-b2117009.html.

169 Michiel Williams, "Exclusive: 'Nuclear has a lot going for it while net zero will simply not happen,' says skeptical environmentalist Bjorn Lomborg," City A.M., February 22, 2022, https://www.cityam.com/exclusive-nuclear-has-a-lot-going-for-it-while-net-zero-will-simply-not-happen-says-sceptical-environmentalist-bjorn-lomborg/.

170 Sean Moran, "Study: Green New Deal Would Cost $93 Trillion, Over Four Times the National Debt," Breitbart News, February 25, 2019, https://www.breitbart.com/politics/2019/02/25/study-green-new-deal-would-cost-93-trillion-over-four-times-the-national-debt/; Avery Thompson, "The Alexandria Ocasio-Cortez 'Green New Deal' Wants to Get Rid of Nuclear Power. That's a Great Idea," Popular Mechanics, February 8, 2019, https://www.popularmechanics.com/science/energy/a26255413/green-new-deal-nuclear-power/.

171 Jennifer McDermott and Matthew Daly, "Biden launches $6B effort to save distressed nuclear plants," Associated Press, April 19, 2022, https://apnews.com/article/climate-business-environment-nuclear-power-us-department-of-energy-2cf1e633fd4d5b1d5c56bb9ffbb2a50a#.

172 United States Department of Energy, "DOE Establishes $6 Billion Program to Preserve America's Clean Nuclear Infrastructure," February 11, 2022, https://www.energy.gov/articles/doe-establishes-6-billion-program-preserve-americas-clean-nuclear-energy-infrastructure.

173 Ashutosh Jogalekar, "Top 5 reasons why intelligent liberals don't like nuclear energy," Scientific American, February 6, 2013, https://blogs.scientificamerican.com/the-curious-wavefunction/top-5-reasons-why-intelligent-liberals-dont-like-nuclear-energy/.

174 "Nuclear Power in the USA," World Nuclear Association, April 2023, https://world-nuclear.org/information-library/country-profiles/countries-t-z/usa-nuclear-power.aspx.

175 Brent Bennett, Karl Schmidt, and Gary Faust, "The Siren Song That Never Ends: Federal Energy Subsidies and Support from 2010 to 2019," Texas Policy Institute, July 2020, https://www.texaspolicy.com/wp-content/uploads/2020/04/Bennett-LP-Federal-Energy-Subsidies-2.pdf.

176 Ana Swanson and Chris Buckley, "Chinese Solar Companies Tied to Use of Forced Labor," New York Times, January 8, 2021, https://www.nytimes.com/2021/01/08/business/economy/china-solar-companies-forced-labor-xinjiang.html.

177 Tim Cavanaugh, "Why does Biden continue to hold back the nuclear energy industry?," *The Hill,* October 1, 2022, https://thehill.com/opinion/energy-environment/3662300-why-does-biden-continue-to-hold-back-the-nuclear-energy-industry/.

178 Andrei Ilas, Hubert Thieriot, Isaac Levi, Jan Lietava, Lauri Myllyvirta, Meri Pukarinen, "One year on, who is funding Russia's war in Ukraine?," Center for Research on Energy and Clean Air, February 24, 2023, https://energyandcleanair.org/publication/one-year-on-who-is-funding-russias-war-in-ukraine/.

179 "Biden calls out oil refiners over 'unprecedented' profits and urges them to produce more gasoline," Associated Press, June 16, 2022, https://www.cbsnews.com/news/biden-oil-companies-unprecedented-profits/.

180 John Carney, "Fact-Check: Biden Says Gas Companies Are Overcharging Americans at the Pump," Breitbart News, November 24, 2021, https://www.breitbart.com/economy/2021/11/24/biden-gasoline-gouging/.

181 Ian Hanchett, "Granholm: There's 'Disparity' Between Oil and Gas Prices, but 'Not Saying That Everybody Is Gouging,' " Breitbart News, May 10, 2022, https://www.breitbart.com/clips/2022/05/10/granholm-theres-disparity-between-oil-and-gas-prices-but-not-saying-that-everybody-is-gouging/.

182 United States Department of State, Office of the Historian, *Oil Embargo, 1973-1974,* accessed on May 10, 2023, https://history.state.gov/milestones/1969-1976/oil-embargo#:~:text=During%20the%201973%20Arab%2DIsraeli,the%20post%2Dwar%20peace%20negotiations.

183 United States Department of Energy, *History of the Strategic Petroleum Reserve,* July 1, 2015, https://www.energy.gov/articles/history-strategic-petroleum-reserve.Brad.

184 William Brangham and Harry Zahn, "How tapping strategic oil reserve will affect U.S. gas prices, OPEC+," PBS SoCal, November 23, 2021, https://www.pbs.org/newshour/show/how-tapping-strategic-oil-reserve-will-affect-u-s-gas-prices-opec.

185 Adam Sabes, "US energy producers roast Biden for demanding 'companies running gas stations' lower pump prices," Fox Business, July 3, 2023, https://www.foxbusiness.com/politics/u-s-energy-roast-biden-demanding-companies-running-gas-stations-lower-pump-prices.

186 FiveThirtyEight, "How popular/unpopular is Joe Biden," poll, accessed on May 10, 2023, https://projects.fivethirtyeight.com/biden-approval-rating/.

187 Ben Lefebvre, "Pain at the pump drives Biden's suffering in the polls," *Politico,* November 17, 2021, https://www.politico.com/news/2021/11/17/gas-prices-biden-inflation-522777.

188 Libby Cathey, "Infuriating climate activists, Biden expands oil drilling on public land," ABC News, April 18, 2022, https://abcnews.go.com/Politics/infuriating-climate-activists-biden-expands-oil-drilling-public/story?id=84148098; Zeke Miller and Seung Min Kim, "WATCH: Biden compares oil firms to war profiteers, talks of windfall tax," *PBS NewsHour,* October 31, 2022, https://www.pbs.org/newshour/politics/watch-biden-makes-statement-on-oil-company-profits-in-the-face-of-high-gas-prices-at-the-pump.

189 "Biden calls out oil refiners," Associated Press.

190 Charlie Spiering, "Joe Biden Demands Gas Stations Lower Prices: 'Do It

Now,' " Breitbart News, June 22, 2022, https://www.breitbart.com/politics /2022/06/22/joe-biden-demands-gas-stations-lower-prices-do-it-now/.

191 President Biden (@POTUS), "My message to the companies running gas stations and setting prices at the pump is simple: this is a time of war and global peril. Bring down the price you are charging at the pump to reflect the cost you're paying for the product. And do it now," Twitter, July 2, 2022, 9:00 a.m., https://twitter.com/POTUS/status/1543263229006254080.

192 Arathy Somasekhar, "Oil from U.S. reserves sent overseas as gasoline prices stay high," Reuters, July 5, 2022, https://news.yahoo.com/oil-u-reserves -head-overseas-110438513.html.

193 John Nolte, "Nolte: Joe Biden Ships U.S. Oil Reserves to Foreign Countries," Breitbart News, July 6, 2022, https://www.breitbart.com/politics/2022/07/06 /nolte-joe-biden-ships-u-s-oil-reserves-to-foreign-countries/.

194 John Carney, "Breitbart Business Digest: Gas Station Profits Rose While Prices Crashed, a Big Greedflation Fail," Breitbart News, August 11, 2022, https://www.breitbart.com/economy/2022/08/11/bbd-greedflation-theory -detroyed-by-rising-gas-station-margins/.

195 Peter Baker and Clifford Krauss, "Biden Accuses Oil Companies of 'War Profiteering' and Threatens Windfall Tax," New York Times, October 31, 2022, https://www.nytimes.com/2022/10/31/us/politics/biden-oil-windfall-tax.html.

196 Timothy Gardner and Andrea Shalal, "Analysis: Biden's threatened windfall oil tax unlikely to pass U.S. Congress," Reuters, November 2, 2022, https:// www.reuters.com/business/energy/bidens-threatened-windfall-oil-tax -unlikely-pass-us-congress-2022-11-02/.

197 Y Charts, "California Retail Gas Price," overview, accessed on May 10, 2023, https://ycharts.com/indicators/california_retail_price_of_gasoline_monthly.

198 The White House, "Remarks by President Biden in Press Gaggle," October 13, 2022, https://www.whitehouse.gov/briefing-room/speeches -remarks/2022/10/13/remarks-by-president-biden-in-press-gaggle-6/.

199 Y Charts, "Los Angeles Retail Premium Gas Price, overview, accessed on May 10, 2023, https://ycharts.com/indicators/los_angeles_retail_price_of _premium_gasoline_monthly.

200 Dustin Jones, "Biden is releasing 15 million barrels from the strategic oil reserve to tame prices," NPR, October 19, 2022, https://www .npr.org/2022/10/18/1129788081/biden-to-release-another-15m-barrels -from-strategic-reserve#:~:text=Biden%20is%20releasing%2015%20mil lion,oil%20reserve%20to%20tame%20prices&text=Evan%20Vucci% 2FAP-,President%20Joe%20Biden%20announced%20Wednesday%20 that%20he%20is%20authorizing%20the,from%20the%20Strategic%20Petro leum%20Reserve.

201 Julian Barnes and David Sanger, "Saudi Crown Prince Is Held Responsible for Khashoggi Killing in U.S. Report," New York Times, February 26, 2021, https://www.nytimes.com/2021/02/26/us/politics/jamal-khashoggi-kill ing-cia-report.html.

202 Summer Said, Benoit Faucon, Dion Nissenbaum, and Stephen Kalin, "Saudi Arabia Defied U.S. Warnings Ahead of OPEC+ Production Cut," Wall Street Journal, October 11, 2022, https://www.wsj.com/articles/saudi-arabia-defied -u-s-warnings-ahead-of-opec-production-cut-11665504230.

203 Alex Emmons, Aida Chavez, and Akela Lacy, "Joe Biden, in Departure from Obama Policy, Says He Would Make Saudi Arabia a Pariah," *Intercept,* November 21, 2019, https://theintercept.com/2019/11/21/democratic -debate-joe-biden-saudi-arabia/.

204 Charlie Spiering, "Joe Biden Complains Oil Companies 'Should Be Drilling More' After Vowing to End Fossil Fuels," Breitbart News, November 3, 2022, https://www.breitbart.com/politics/2022/11/03/oe-biden-complains-oil -companies-should-be-drilling-more-after-vowing-to-end-fossil-fuels/.

205 Mircely Guanipa and Deisy Buitrago, "Venezuela's biggest refinery halts gasoline production," Reuters, December 2, 2022, https://www.reuters .com/world/americas/venezuelas-biggest-refinery-halts-gasoline-production -sources-2022-12-03/.

206 Kimray Inc., "Types of Crude Oil: Heavy vs Light. Sweet vs Sour, and TAN count," training and demos, https://kimray.com/training/types-crude-oil -heavy-vs-light-sweet-vs-sour-and-tan-count.

207 Agence France-Presse, "Sanctioned Russia Becomes China's Main Source of Oil, Customs Data Show," *VOA News,* June 23, 2022, https://www.voanews .com/a/sanctioned-russia-becomes-china-s-main-source-of-oil-customs -data-show-/6630543.html.

208 Earth First! (website), Biocentric Media Inc., accessed May 10, 2023, https:// earthfirstjournal.news/about/.

209 R.H. Lossin, "What We're Still Getting Wrong about the Unabomber," *Nation,* March 15, 2022, https://www.thenation.com/article/society/ted-kaczynski -unabomber-technology/; Ashley Oliver, "Joe Manchin Backs Biden Nomi- nee Involved in Ecoterrorist Plot," Breitbart News, July 20, 2021, https://www .breitbart.com/environment/2021/07/20/joe-manchin-backs-biden-nominee -involved -ecoterrorist-plot/; Ashley Oliver and Rebecca Monsour, "Un- abomber Praised Ecoterrorist Group Linked to Biden BLM Nominee," Breit- bart News, July 7, 2021, https://www.breitbart.com/environment/2021/07/07 /unabomber-praised -ecoterrorist-group-linked-to-biden-blm-nominee/.

210 Scott Streater and Jennifer Yachnin, "Convicted tree spiker: Stone-Manning knew plans in advance," E&E News Greenwire, July 17, 2021, https://www .eenews.net/articles/convicted-tree-spiker-stone-manning-knew-plans-in -advance/.

211 Joshua Partlow and Dino Grandoni, "As a student, Tracy Stone-Manning sent a letter on behalf of eco-saboteurs. It's now complicating her chance to lead the Bureau of Land Management.," *Washington Post,* July 4, 2021, https:// www.washingtonpost.com/climate-environment/2021/07/04/student-tracy -stone-manning-sent-letter-behalf-eco-saboteurs-its-now-complicating-her -chance-lead-bureau-land-management/.

212 Ibid.

213 Andrew Kerr, "'Stop at Two': Biden BLM Nominee Argued for Population Control in Graduate Thesis," Daily Caller, June 23, 2021, https://dailycaller .com/2021/06/23/joe-biden-bureau-of-land-management-forest-service/.

214 Ashley Oliver, "Senate Confirms Joe Biden's Ecoterrorist Nominee to Lead Bureau of Land Management," Breitbart News, September 30, 2021, https://www.breitbart.com/politics/2021/09/30/senate-confirms-joe-biden -ecoterrorist-nominee-lead-bureau-land-management/.

215 United States Department of State, "U.S. Center at COP27," https://www
.state.gov/u-s-center-at-cop27/; U.S. Center at UNFCCC (@US_Cen-
ter), "9:00-10:00am EET, Getting to Zero-Deforestation by 2030," Twitter, November 13, 2022, 10:05 p.m., https://twitter.com/US_Center/status
/1592035910249766913?ref_src=twsrc%5Etfw%7Ctwcamp%5Eembed
dedtimeline%7Ctwterm%5Escreen-name%3AUS_Center%7Ctwcon%5Es1.

216 Climate Forests Coalition, *America's Vanishing Climate Forests: How the U.S.
Is Risking Global Credibility on Forest Conservation,* November 2022, https://
drive.google.com/file/d/1gs65Jcc6ok9HYXajV9WM77_zbH0t454d/vie.w;
Climate Forests Coalition, "America's Vanishing Climate Forests," accessed
May 10, 2023, https://www.climate-forests.org/worth-more-standing.

217 Scott Streater. "BLM details plans for HQ move," *E&E News,* September 8,
2022, https://www.eenews.net/articles/blm-details-plans-for-hq-move/.

218 Joshua Klein, "'Black Trees Matter'—VP Kamala Harris Asks NASA if It Can
Track Trees by Race for 'Environmental Justice,'" Breitbart News, November 7,
2021, https://www.breitbart.com/politics/2021/11/07/black-trees-matter-vp
-kamala-harris-asks-nasa-can-track-trees-race-environmental-justice/.

219 United States Department of Health and Human Services, "Biden-Harris Administration Establishes HHS Office of Environmental Justice," May 31, 2022,
https://www.hhs.gov/about/news/2022/05/31/biden-harris-administration
-establishes-hhs-office-of-environmental-justice.html.

220 Robin Morris Collin, "The Geography of Injustice and the Ecology of Reparations," YouTube video, 1:09:00, posted by Oregon Humanities Center, December 8,
2020,https://www.youtube.com/watch?v=zUZ-wPSHTAI&t=4s;JacobBliss,"EPA
Senior Adviser for Environmental Justice Wants 'Environmental Reparations'
to Heal Relationship with Nature," Breitbart News, May 9, 2022, https://www
.breitbart.com/politics/2022/05/09/epa-senior-adviser-for-environmental
-justice-wants-environmental-reparations-to-heal-relationship-with-nature/.

221 The White House, "FACT SHEET: Inflation Reduction Act Advances
Environmental Justice," August 17, 2022, https://www.whitehouse.gov
/briefing-room/statements-releases/2022/08/17/fact-sheet-inflation
-reduction-act-advances-environmental-justice/.

222 Steven Nelson, "Jet-set Biden vows 'climate-friendly' military, flexes gas
-guzzling Corvette," *New York Post,* April 22, 2022, https://nypost.com
/2022/04/22/biden-calls-for-climate-friendly-military-fleet-on-earth-day/.

223 Charlie Spiering, "Joe Biden Drools over Gas-Powered Corvette During Detroit Trip to Showcase Electric Cars," Breitbart News, September 14, 2022,
https://www.breitbart.com/politics/2022/09/14/joe-biden-drools-over-gas
-powered-corvette-during-detroit-trip-to-showcase-electric-cars/.

CHAPTER 10: BIDENFLATION, OR,
EVERYTHING JOE TOUCHES GETS MORE EXPENSIVE

1 George Orwell, "It appears that there had been demonstrations to thank Big
Brother for raising the chocolate ration. . . ." In *1984,* quoted on GoodReads,
accessed May 31, 2023, https://www.goodreads.com/quotes/8887641-it
-appeared-that-there-had-even-been-demonstrations-to-thank.

2 Sean Moran, "Congress Passes $700 Billion 'Inflation Reduction' Act," Breit-

bart News, August 12, 2022, https://www.breitbart.com/politics/2022/08/12
/congress-passes-700-billion-inflation-reduction-act/.

3 John Binder, "Janet Yellen Begs IRS Not to Target Middle-Class Americans
   After Democrats Greenlight Audits," Breitbart News, August 11, 2022, https://
   www.breitbart.com/politics/2022/08/11/janet-yellen-begs-irs-not-to-target
   -middle-class-americans-after-democrats-greenlight-audits/.

4 Sean Moran, "Democrat Tax Hikes to Hit Manufacturers Hardest," Breitbart
   News, August 1, 2022, https://www.breitbart.com/politics/2022/08/01/demo
   crat-tax-hikes-hit-manufacturers-hardest/.

5 Wharton School, University of Pennsylvania, *Senate-Passed Inflation Reduction Act: Estimates of Budgetary and Macroeconomic Effects,* August 12, 2022,
   https://budgetmodel.wharton.upenn.edu/issues/2022/8/12/senate-passed
   -inflation-reduction-act.

6 Wharton, *Senate-Passed Inflation Reduction Act.*

7 United States Senate Committee on the Budget, "CBO Confirms to Graham: Dems' 'Inflation Reduction Act' Won't Reduce Inflation," August 4,
   2022, https://www.budget.senate.gov/ranking-member/newsroom/press/cbo
   -confirms-to-graham-dems-inflation-reduction-act-wont-reduce
   -inflation#:~:text=CBO%20found%3A,would%20reduce%20incentives%20
   to%20work.

8 John Carney, "The Big Lie Failed: Just 12% of Americans Think the Inflation Reduction Act Will Reduce Inflation," Breitbart News, August 15, 2022,
   https://www.breitbart.com/economy/2022/08/15/the-big-lie-failed-just-12
   -of-americans-think-the-inflation-reduction-act-will-reduce-inflation/.

9 Ian Hanchett, "CBS' O'Keefe: Biden Celebrated Inflation Act That 'Does Nothing to Address Short-Term Price Hikes,' " Breitbart News, September 15, 2022,
   https://www.breitbart.com/clips/2022/09/15/cbs-okeefe-biden-celebrated
   -inflation-act-that-does-nothing-to-address-short-term-price-hikes/.

10 Tucker Higgins, "Joe Biden says Trump's failure to lead is responsible
   for historic economic slump," CNBC, July 30, 2020, https://www.cnbc
   .com/2020/07/30/biden-says-trump-is-responsible-for-historic-economic
   -slump.html.

11 Gita Gopinath, "The Great Lockdown: Worst Economic Downturn Since
   the Great Depression," International Monetary Fund, April 14, 2020, https://
   www.imf.org/en/Blogs/Articles/2020/04/14/blog-weo-the-great-lockdown
   -worst-economic-downturn-since-the-great-depression.

12 United States Bureau of Labor Statistics, "Unemployment Rate [UNRATE],"
   FRED, Federal Reserve Bank of St. Louis, accessed May 31, 2023, https://
   fred.stlouisfed.org/series/UNRATE; "Great Depression," economic data,
   FRED, Federal Reserve Bank of St. Louis, accessed May 31, 2023, https://
   fredaccount.stlouisfed.org/public/dashboard/440?&utm_source=fred.stlou
   isfed.org&utm_medium=referral&utm_term=related_resources&utm
   _content=&utm_campaign=dashboard.

13 Jeff Cox, "U.S. GDP booms at 33.1% rate in Q3, better than expected,"
   CNBC, October 29, 2020, https://www.cnbc.com/2020/10/29/us-gdp-report
   -third-quarter-2020.html; Associated Press, "Anticipating a 2021 boom,
   fourth-quarter GDP is revised up slightly to 4.1%," CNBC, February 25, 2021,
   https://www.cnbc.com/2021/02/25/us-gdp-q4-2020.html.

14 Associated Press, "Anticipating a 2021 boom."

15 Jeff Cox, "GDP grew at a 6.9% pace to close out 2021, stronger than expected despite omicron spread," CNBC, January 27, 2022, https://www.cnbc.com/2022/01/27/gdp-grew-at-a-6point9percent-pace-to-close-out-2021-stronger-than-expected-despite-omicron-spread.html.

16 Robert Barro, "Yes, the US Economy Is Likely in Recession," Project Syndicate, August 1, 2022, https://www.project-syndicate.org/commentary/two-consecutive-quarters-negative-us-growth-predict-recession-since-1948-by-robert-j-barro-2022-07?barrier=accesspaylog.

17 Dion Rabouin, "Big Banks Predict Recession, Fed Pivot in 2023," Wall Street Journal, January 2, 2023, https://www.wsj.com/articles/big-banks-predict-recession-fed-pivot-in-2023-11672618563?mod=economy_lead_story; https://www.bbc.com/news/business-64142662; John Carney, "Breitbart Business Digest: Nearly Everyone Expects a Recession in 2023," Breitbart News, January 3, 2023, https://www.breitbart.com/economy/2023/01/03/Breitbart-business-digest-nearly-everyone-expects-a-recession-in-2023/.

18 Holly Otterbein, "Democrats itching to take down Biden over free-trade past," Politico, May 2, 2019, https://www.politico.com/story/2019/05/02/joe-biden-nafta-2020-1296786.

19 Asma Khalid, "A Look Back at How Joe Biden Managed the 2009 Stimulus Package," NPR, April 6, 2020, https://www.npr.org/2020/04/06/828303824/a-look-back-at-how-joe-biden-managed-the-2009-stimulus-package.

20 "The Biden Administration Has Approved $4.8 Trillion of New Borrowing," Committee for a Responsible Federal Budget, September 13, 2022, https://www.crfb.org/blogs/biden-administration-has-approved-48-trillion-new-borrowing.

21 Meghashyam Mali, "RNC to unveil 'national debt clock' at convention," The Hill, August 27, 2012, https://thehill.com/conventions-2012/gop-convention-tampa/123446-rnc-to-unveil-national-debt-clock-at-convention/.

22 Mali, "RNC to unveil 'national debt clock.'"

23 Mali, "RNC to unveil 'national debt clock.'"

24 United States Congress, House, Coronavirus Preparedness and Response Supplemental Appropriations Act, 2020, HR 6074, 116th Cong., Sess. 2, became Public Law No: 116-123 on March 6, 2020, https://www.congress.gov/bill/116th-congress/house-bill/6074; United States Congress, House, Families First Coronavirus Response Act, HR 6201, 116th Cong., Sess. 2, became Public Law No: 116-127 on March 18, 2020, https://www.congress.gov/bill/116th-congress/house-bill/6201; "United States: President Signs Law to Provide New Economic Stimulus to Address Pandemic Hardships," Library of Congress, December 28, 2020, https://www.loc.gov/item/global-legal-monitor/2020-12-28/united-states-president-signs-law-to-provide-new-economic-stimulus-to-address-pandemic-hardships/.

25 "Breaking Down $3.4 Trillion in COVID Relief," Committee for a Responsible Federal Budget, January 7, 2021, https://www.crfb.org/blogs/breaking-down-34-trillion-covid-relief.

26 Board of Governors of the Federal Reserve System, "Federal Reserve takes additional actions to provide up to $2.3 trillion in loans to support the econ-

omy," press release, April 9, 2020, https://www.federalreserve.gov/newsevents/pressreleases/monetary20200409a.htm.

27 Board of Governors, "Federal Reserve takes additional actions."

28 United States Department of Treasury, Small Business Administration, *Paycheck Protection Program Loan Forgiveness*, accessed May 31, 2023, https://home.treasury.gov/system/files/136/PPP-Forgiveness-Factsheet-508.pdf.

29 Fatima Hussein, "House panel says lax screening helped facilitate PPP fraud," Associated Press, December 1, 2022, https://apnews.com/article/biden-technology-health-small-business-33d0cb5acc8357e14efd8e30f09b5199.

30 United States House, Select Subcommittee on the Coronavirus Crisis, *How FinTechs Facilitated Fraud in the Paycheck Protection Program*, December 1, 2022, accessed via WayBackMachine on May 31, 2023, https://web.archive.org/web/20230131040524/https://coronavirus.house.gov/sites/democrats.coronavirus.house.gov/files/2022.12.01%20How%20Fintechs%20Facilitated%20Fraud%20in%20the%20Paycheck%20Protection%20Program.pdf.

31 Fatima Hussein, "Secret Service recovers $286M in stolen pandemic loans," Associated Press, August 26, 2022, https://apnews.com/article/covid-health-small-business-us-secret-service-ed482641a658543f4db9e2ec5121153e.

32 Jordan Weissman, "Grover Norquist's Anti-Tax Group Took Money From the Paycheck Protection Program," *Slate*, July 6, 2020, https://slate.com/news-and-politics/2020/07/grover-norquist-ppp-coronavirus.html.

33 Taylor Borden, "15 of the most surprising companies that the Small Business Administration listed as paycheck protection loan recipients," *Business Insider*, July 7, 2020, https://www.businessinsider.com/surprising-coronavirus-ppp-loan-recipients-2020-7.

34 Ben Popken, "Here are some of the billionaires who got PPP loans while small businesses went bankrupt," NBC News, July 6, 2020, https://www.nbcnews.com/business/business-news/here-are-some-billionaires-who-got-ppp-loans-while-small-n1233041.

35 Popken, "Here are some of the billionaires."

36 Popken, "Here are some of the billionaires."

37 Kate Smith, "Planned Parenthoods received $80 million in PPP loans. Now, the SBA wants it back," CBS News, May 22, 2020, https://www.cbsnews.com/news/planned-parenthood-paycheck-protection-program-loan-controversy/.

38 Steve Goldstein, "The rich and famous including Tom Brady, Reese Witherspoon and Jared Kushner had their PPP loans forgiven. Is that a scandal or a success?," MarketWatch, August 19, 2022, https://www.marketwatch.com/story/scandal-or-success-ultra-wealthy-including-tom-brady-kanye-west-jared-kushner-and-nancy-pelosis-husband-had-ppp-loans-forgiven-11660898994.

39 Ken Ward Jr., "Companies Owned by This Billionaire Governor Received up to $24 Million in Bailout Loans," ProPublica, July 6, 2020, https://www.propublica.org/article/companies-owned-by-this-billionaire-governor-received-up-to-24-million-in-bailout-loans.

40 Deniz Cam, "Kanye West, West Virginia's Governor Jim Justice and 16 Other Billionaires' Businesses Got PPP Loans," *Forbes*, July 6, 2020, https://www.forbes.com/sites/denizcam/2020/07/06/kanye-west-west-virginias-governor-jim-justice-and-13-other-billionaires-businesses-got-ppp-loans/?sh=574dd50b4f0d.

41 Cam, "Kanye West."

42 Ben Smith, "Goldman Sachs, Ozy Media and a $40 Million Conference Call Gone Wrong," *New York Times,* September 26, 2021, https://www.nytimes .com/2021/09/26/business/media/ozy-media-goldman-sachs.html.

43 United States Attorney's Office, Eastern District of New York, "Ozy Media and Its Founder Carlos Watson Indicted in a Years-Long Multi-Million Dollar Fraud Scheme," February 23, 2023, https://www.justice.gov/usao-edny/pr /ozy-media-and-its-founder-carlos-watson-indicted-years-long-multi-mil lion-dollar-fraud.

44 The White House, "FACT SHEET: Biden-?Harris Administration Increases Lending to Small Businesses in Need, Announces Changes to PPP to Further Promote Equitable Access to Relief," February 22, 2021, https:// www.whitehouse.gov/briefing-room/statements-releases/2021/02/22 /fact-sheet-biden-harris-administration-increases-lending-to-small -businesses-in-need-announces-changes-to-ppp-to-further-promote -equitable-access-to-relief/.

45 United States Small Business Administration, "Fact Sheet: Changes to Paycheck Protection Program by Biden-Harris Administration Increase Equitable Access to Relief," March 9, 2021, https://www.sba.gov/article/2021 /mar/09/fact-sheet-changes-paycheck-protection-program-biden-harris -administration-increase-equitable-access.

46 United States Small Business Administration, "Fact Sheet: Changes to Paycheck Protection Program."

47 United States Small Business Administration, "Fact Sheet: Changes to Paycheck Protection Program."

48 United States Department of Agriculture, "Biden-Harris Administration Extends Eviction Moratorium for Homeowners," July 30, 2021, https://www .federalregister.gov/documents/2020/09/04/2020-19654/temporary-halt-in -residential-evictions-to-prevent-the-further-spread-of-covid-19.

49 The White House, "President Donald J. Trump Is Working to Stop Evictions and Protect Americans' Homes During the COVID-19 Pandemic," September 1, 2020, https://trumpwhitehouse.archives.gov/briefings-state ments/president-donald-j-trump-working-stop-evictions-protect-ameri cans-homes-covid-19-pandemic/.

50 Centers for Disease Control and Prevention and United States Department of Health and Human Services, *Temporary Halt in Residential Evictions to Prevent the Further Spread of COVID-19,* agency order, September 4, 2020, https://s3.amazonaws.com/public-inspection.federalregister.gov/2020 -19654.pdf.

51 Adam Liptak and Glenn Thrush, "Supreme Court Ends Biden's Eviction Moratorium," *New York Times,* August 26, 2021, https://www.nytimes .com/2021/08/26/us/eviction-moratorium-ends.html.

52 United States Department of Agriculture, "Biden-Harris Administration Extends Eviction Moratorium for Homeowners," July 30, 2021, https://www .usda.gov/media/press-releases/2021/07/30/biden-harris-administration -extends-eviction-moratorium-homeowners.

53 Liptak and Thrush, "Supreme Court."

54 Glenn Thrush and Conor Dougherty, "Why $46 Billion Couldn't Prevent an

Eviction Crisis," *New York Times,* September 10, 2021, https://www.nytimes.com/2021/09/10/business/evictions-rental-assistance.html.

55 "Evictions spike with inflation rising and little help left for tenants," The Real Deal, November 12, 2022, https://therealdeal.com/2022/11/12/evictions-spike-with-inflation-rising-and-little-help-left-for-tenants/.

56 Jason Lalljee, "The 6 cities and states trying to stop landlords from jacking up rent prices," *Business Insider,* March 15, 2022, https://www.businessinsider.com/states-cities-rent-control-stop-landlords-raising-prices-tenants-evictions-2022-3.

57 Ryan Bourne, "Freezing Rents Offers No Answer to Inflation and Only Creates More Trouble," Cato Institute, September 22, 2022, https://www.cato.org/commentary/freezing-rents-offers-no-answer-inflation-only-creates-more-trouble#.

58 Shannon Pettypiece, "Evictions are piling up across the U.S. as Covid-era protections end and rents climb," NBC News, November 5, 2022, https://www.nbcnews.com/politics/politics-news/evictions-are-piling-us-covid-era-protections-end-rents-climb-rcna54798.

59 Anna Helhoski, Ryan Lane, and Eliza Haverstock, "Student Loan Debt Statistics: 2023," NerdWallet, May 2, 2023, https://www.nerdwallet.com/article/loans/student-loans/student-loan-debt#citation-list.

60 Annie Nova, "Trump gives people with student loans a break amid coronavirus," CNBC, March 13, 2023, https://www.cnbc.com/2020/03/13/mnuchin-may-suspend-student-loan-repayments-amid-coronavirus-outbreak.html.

61 The White House, "FACT SHEET: President Biden Announces Student Loan Relief for Borrowers Who Need It Most," August 24, 2022, https://www.whitehouse.gov/briefing-room/statements-releases/2022/08/24/fact-sheet-president-biden-announces-student-loan-relief-for-borrowers-who-need-it-most/.

62 Hannah Bleau, "Student Loan Forgiveness Doesn't Satisfy All Democrats: It's Not Enough, 'Cancel All Student Debt,' " Breitbart News, August 24, 2022, https://www.breitbart.com/politics/2022/08/24/student-loan-forgiveness-doesnt-satisfy-all-democrats-not-enough-cancel-all-student-debt/.

63 Bleau, "Student Loan Forgiveness."

64 Lawrence Hurley, "Supreme Court kills Biden student loan relief plan," NBC News, June 30, 2023, https://www.nbcnews.com/politics/supreme-court/supreme-court-rule-bidens-student-loan-forgiveness-plan-friday-rcna76874.

65 Tim Doescher and David Ditch, "$1.9 Trillion COVID 'Relief' Package," Heritage Foundation, https://www.heritage.org/budget-and-spending/heritage-explains/19-trillion-covid-relief-package.

66 Wharton School, University of Pennsylvania, *Biden's New Income-Driven Repayment ("SAVE") Plan: Budgetary Cost Estimate Update,* July 17, 2023, https://budgetmodel.wharton.upenn.edu/issues/2023/7/17/biden-income-driven-repayment-budget-update.

67 Alison Aughinbaugh and Donna Rothstein, "How did employment change during the COVID-19 Pandemic? Evidence from a new BLS survey supplement," *United States Bureau of Labor Statistics* 11, no. 1 (January 2022), https://www.bls.gov/opub/btn/volume-11/how-did-employment-change-during-the-covid-19-pandemic.htm#_edn1.

68 John Carney, "Breitbart Business Digest: The Great Biden Inflation Disaster," Breitbart News, March 10, 2022, https://www.breitbart.com/economy/2022/03/10/Breitbart-business-digest-the-great-biden-inflation-disaster/.

69 Jordan Williams, "Larry Summer blasts $1.9 T stimulus as 'least responsible' economic policy in 40 years," *The Hill*, March 20, 2021, https://thehill.com/policy/finance/544188-larry-summers-blasts-least-responsible-economic-policy-in-40-years/.

70 John Carney, "Breitbart Business Digest: The Great Biden Inflation Disaster," Breitbart News, March 10, 2022, https://www.breitbart.com/economy/2022/03/10/Breitbart-business-digest-the-great-biden-inflation-disaster/.

71 United States Department of Labor, Bureau of Labor Statistics, *Consumer Price Index 2021,* August 11, 2021, https://www.bls.gov/news.release/archives/cpi_08112021.pdf.

72 President Joe Biden, "Remarks by President Biden on the Economy," The White House, July 19, 2021, https://www.whitehouse.gov/briefing-room/speeches-remarks/2021/07/19/remarks-by-president-biden-on-the-economy-3/.

73 Jeff Cox, "Yellen says the administration is fighting inflation, admits she was wrong that it was 'transitory,'" CNBC, June 1, 2022, https://www.cnbc.com/2022/06/01/yellen-says-the-administration-is-fighting-inflation-admits-she-was-wrong-that-it-was-transitory.html.

74 Ann Saphir and David Lawder, "Yellen says she sees no inflation problem after rate hike comments roil Wall Street," Reuters, May 4, 2021, https://www.reuters.com/article/usa-fed-yellen-idINKBN2CM072.

75 Tobias Burns, "Inflation eases in July but remains near 40-year highs," *The Hill,* August 10, 2022, https://thehill.com/business/3595518-inflation-eases-in-july-but-remains-near-40-year-highs/.

76 Ian Hanchett, "Warren: Spending in American Rescue Plan Was a Factor in Inflation," Breitbart News, April 20, 2022, https://www.breitbart.com/clips/2022/04/20/warren-spending-in-american-rescue-plan-was-a-factor-in-inflation/.

77 Ian Hanchett, "Dem Sen. Warner: Rescue Plan Was Too Big, It Hasn't 'Been the Sole Driving Force' of Inflation," Breitbart News, October 10, 2022, https://www.breitbart.com/clips/2022/10/19/dem-sen-warner-rescue-plan-was-too-big-it-hasnt-been-the-sole-driving-force-of-inflation/.

78 Andrew Prokop, "Biden's American Rescue Plan worsened inflation. The question is how much," Vox, May 12, 2022, https://www.vox.com/23036340/biden-american-rescue-plan-inflation.

79 Charlie Spiering, "Joe Biden: Americans Complaining About Inflation Forgot We Sent Them a Check for $8,000," Breitbart News, July 28, 2022, https://www.breitbart.com/politics/2022/07/28/joe-biden-americans-complaining-about-inflation-forgot-we-sent-them-a-check-for-8000/.

80 Spiering, "Joe Biden."

81 President Joe Biden, "Remarks by President Biden at the House Democratic Caucus Issues Conference," Philadelphia, Hilton Philadelphia at Penn's Landing, March 11, 2022, https://www.whitehouse.gov/briefing-room/speeches-remarks/2022/03/11/remarks-by-president-biden-at-the-house-democratic-caucus-issues-conference/.

82 Charlie Spiering, "Joe Biden Falsely Blames 'Putin's Price Hike' for February Inflation," Breitbart News, March 10, 2022, https://www.breitbart.com /politics/2022/03/10/joe-biden-falsely-blames-putins-price-hike-for -february-inflation/.

83 Trading Economics, "United States Inflation Rate," accessed May 31, 2023, https://tradingeconomics.com/united-states/inflation-cpi.

84 Paul Wiseman, "Explainer: Why US inflation is so high, and when it may ease," Associated Press, February 10, 2022, https://apnews.com/article/corona virus-pandemic-business-health-prices-inflation-bd71ae9e491907a51956c 1d4eb07fb90.

85 Scott Pelley, "President Joe Biden: The 2022 60 Minutes Interview," CBS News, September 18, 2022, https://www.cbsnews.com/news/president -joe-biden-60-minutes-interview-transcript-2022-09-18/.

86 Pelley, "President Joe Biden."

87 Brian Riedl, "The worst spending bill ever: Democrats' $1.9T 'rescue' is drowning us," New York Post, December 8, 2021, https://nypost.com/2021/12/08 /dems-1-9t-spending-bill-likely-most-expensive-bill-of-past-50-years/.

88 John Carney, "Carney: Biden's Covid Relief Could Pay Families $92,000 This Year for Not Working," Breitbart News, March 11, 2021, https://www .breitbart.com/economy/2021/03/11/carney-bidens-covid-relief-could-pay -families-92000-a-year-for-not-working/.

89 Luke Vidovic, "Industries Most and Least Impacted by COVID-19 from a Probability of Default Perspective—January 2022 Update," S&P Global, February 11, 2022, https://www.spglobal.com/marketintelligence/en/news -insights/blog/industries-most-and-least-impacted-by-covid-19-from-a -probability-of-default-perspective-january-2022-update.

90 MarketWatch, "Tech stocks surged along with COVID-19. Don't expect the same in 2021," December 30, 2020, https://www.marketwatch.com/story /tech-stocks-covid-19-surge-could-face-turbulence-in-2021-11609341239.

91 United States Department of Labor, Bureau of Labor Statistics, "Changes to consumer expenditures during the COVID-19 Pandemic," May 3, 2022, https://www.bls.gov/opub/ted/2022/changes-to-consumer-expenditures -during-the-covid-19-pandemic.htm.

92 "U.S. Inflation Report: Prices Continued to Rise in April, but Gains Slowed a Little: Live Updates," New York Times, May 11, 2022, https://www.nytimes .com/live/2022/05/11/business/inflation-cpi-report-april.

93 John Nolte, "Nolte: Biden White House Spreads Lie That Inflation Is 'High Class Problem,'" Breitbart News, October 14, 2022, https://www.breitbart.com/poli tics/2021/10/14/nolte-biden-white-house-spreads-lie-inflation-high-class-prob lem/.

94 John Carney, "Biden's Plan to Relieve Backlog at Port of Los Angeles Is Not Working," Breitbart News, October 20, 2021,https://www.breitbart.com /economy/2021/10/20/bidens-plan-to-relieve-backlog-at-port-of-los -angeles-is-not-working/.

95 Niraj Chokshi, "Why the World's Container Ships Grew So Big," New York Times, March 20, 2021, https://www.nytimes.com/2021/03/30/business /economy/container-ships-suez-canal.html.

96 Jon Levine, "Pete Buttigieg mocked for 'phony' Cabinet meeting bike stunt,"

New York Post, April 3, 2021, https://nypost.com/2021/04/03/pete-buttigieg-mocked-for-phony-bike-stunt/.

97 Charlie Spiering, "WATCH: White House Admits No 'Point Person' During Buttigieg Paternity Leave, Cargo Crisis," Breitbart News, October 19, 2021, https://www.breitbart.com/politics/2021/10/19/watch-white-house-admits-no-point-person-during-buttigieg-paternity-leave-cargo-crisis/.

98 Spiering, "WATCH: White House Admits No 'Point Person.' "

99 Alex Schemmel, "Emails show Buttigieg declined meeting with senator while on paternity leave," National Desk, January 13, 2023, https://wpde.com/news/nation-world/emails-show-buttigieg-declined-meeting-with-senator-while-on-paternity-leave-pete-transportation-security-chuck-grassley.

100 Virginia Heffernan, "Pete Buttigieg Loves God, Beer, and His Electric Mustang," *Wired,* May 18, 2023, https://www.wired.com/story/pete-buttigieg-interview-god-beer-electric-mustang/.

101 "New Record: 100 Vessels Are Waiting to Berth at LA/Long Beach," *Maritime Executive,* October 19, 2021, https://maritime-executive.com/article/new-record-100-vessels-are-waiting-to-berth-at-la-long-beach.

102 Carl Quintanilla (@carlquintanilla), "Number of ships waiting to unload at Ports of LA/Long Beach: *in January: 109; *this week: 4," Twitter, October 21, 2022, 4:38 a.m., https://twitter.com/carlquintanilla/status/1583422352771387393?ref_src=twsrc%5Etfw%7Ctwcamp%5Etweetembed%7Ctwterm%5E15834 22352771387393%7Ctwgr%5Ee54bc81e43546d4fd3931f0efe9a097e8b 9f995a%7Ctwcon%5Es1_&ref_url=https%3A%2F%2Fwww.breitbart.com %2Feconomy%2F2022%2F10%2F23%2Fl-a-cargo-crisis-ends-as-u-s-imports-crash%2F.

103 Devan Cole and Jason Hoffman, "Buttigieg says US supply chain issues will 'certainly' continue into 2022," CNN, October 17, 2021, https://www.cnn.com/2021/10/17/politics/pete-buttigieg-supply-chain-issues-CNNtv/index.html.

104 Carney, "Biden's Plan."

105 Carney, "Biden's Plan."

106 Charlie Spiering, "Joe Biden Blames Private Companies for Port Delays," Breitbart News, October 13, 2022, https://www.breitbart.com/politics/2021/10/13/joe-biden-blames-private-companies-for-port-delays/.

107 Paul Berger, "Truckers Steer Clear of 24-Hour Operations at Southern California Ports," *Wall Street Journal,* November 17, 2021, https://www.wsj.com/articles/truckers-steer-clear-of-24-hour-operations-at-southern-california-ports-11637173872.

108 Carney, "Biden's Plan."

109 Carney, "Biden's Plan."

110 Peter Baker and Clifford Krauss, "Biden Accuses Oil Companies of 'War Profiteering' and Threatens Windfall Tax," *New York Times,* October 31, 2022, https://www.nytimes.com/2022/10/31/us/politics/biden-oil-windfall-tax.html.

111 Port of Los Angeles, "San Pedro Bay Announces New Cargo," October 25, 2021, https://www.portoflosangeles.org/references/2021-news-releases/news_102521_jointclearcargo.

112 Port of Los Angeles, "San Pedro Bay."

113 Sarah Zimmerman, "Port of Los Angeles, Long Beach to end terminal dwell

fee," Supply Chain Dive, December 18, 2022, https://www.supplychaindive .com/news/ports-los-angeles-long-beach-terminal-dwell-fee-ends/639051/? mod=djemlogistics_h.

114 Grace Kay, "This image shows the port's backlogs haven't decreased—the problem's just lurking over the horizon," Business Insider, December 12, 2021, https://www.businessinsider.com/port-backlogs-california-havent-dec reased-boat-line-over-horizon-2021-12.

115 Port of Long Beach, "Transportation Secretary Tours Port of Long Beach," January 11, 2022, https://polb.com/port-info/news-and-press/transportation -secretary-buttigieg-tours-port-of-long-beach-01-11-2022/.

116 Port of Long Beach, "Transportation Secretary."

117 Joel Pollak, "As Pete Buttigieg Declared Victory, Shipping Backlog Continued, and Spread," Breitbart News, January 28, 2022, https://www.breitbart.com /economy/2022/01/28/as-pete-buttigieg-declared-victory-shipping-backlog -continued-and-spread/.

118 City of South Bend, Indiana, "City Celebrates Passage of 2019 Budget," accessed May 31, 2023. https://southbendin.gov/city-celebrates-passage-of-2019-budget/.

119 Paul Berger, "Imports Drop at Southern California Ports as Ship Backup Grows," Wall Street Journal, January 25, 2022, https://www.wsj.com/articles/imports -drop-at-southern-california-ports-as-ship-backup-grows-11643143742.

120 Joel Pollak, "Biden's Plan Fails to Move Long Beach Port Operations to 24/7 After 4 Months," Breitbart News, February 10, 2022, https://www.breitbart .com/economy/2022/02/10/bidens-plan-fails-to-move-long-beach-port -operations-to-24-7-after-4-months/.

121 City of South Bend, "City Celebrates Passage of 2019 Budget."

122 Greg Miller, "Record container ship traffic backlog continues to build," Freight Waves, July 28, 2022, https://www.freightwaves.com/news/traffic -jam-of-waiting-container-ships-is-now-as-bad-as-ever?p=451268.

123 Gary Howard, "Drop in US inbound container volumes accelerates," Seatrade Maritime News, October 20, 2022, https://www.seatrade-maritime.com /containers/drop-us-inbound-container-volumes-accelerates.

124 U.S. Transportation Secretary Pete Buttigieg and Rep. Adam Kinzinger (R-IL), interview by Jon Stewart, CNN, transcript, October 17, 2021, https:// transcripts.cnn.com/show/sotu/date/2021-10-17/segment/01.

125 Mark Walker, "Air Travel Debacles Put a Star of Biden's Cabinet in the Hot Seat," New York Times, January 20, 2023, https://www.nytimes.com/2023/01/20/us /politics/pete-buttigieg-southwest-faa.html.

126 Paul LeBlanc, "A freight train derailment in Ohio puts US infrastructure back in a bruising spotlight," CNN Politics, February 6, 2023, https://www.cnn .com/2023/02/06/politics/ohio-train-derailment-infrastructure-what-mat ters/index.html; "Fears for human safety after animals drop dead at Ohio train crash site," 9 News, February 14, 2023, https://www.9news.com.au /world/animals-dropping-dead-near-site-of-train-crash-in-east-palestine -ohio-usa/9123915d-22db-4a38-93c2-55fe1d5ebfd0.

127 Jason Wulfsohn, "WaPo fact-checker says Trump-era policies 'can't be blamed' for Ohio train derailment," Fox News, February 27, 2023, https://www .foxnews.com/media/wapo-fact-checker-says-trump-era-policies-cant -blamed-ohio-train-derailment.

128 Corey Walker, "Pete Buttigieg Slammed by Biden Administration Official Over 'Misinformation' on East Palestine Train Derailment," *Daily Caller*, February 17, 2023, https://dailycaller.com/2023/02/17/pete-buttigieg-east -palestine-misinformation-train-ntsb/.

129 John Hayward, "China Blasts 'Vanity Political Appointee' Pete Buttigieg over Ohio Train Catastrophe," Breitbart News, February 15, 2023, https:// www.breitbart.com/asia/2023/02/15/china-blasts-vanity-political-appointee -pete-buttigieg-ohio-train-catastrophe/.

130 Bradley Blankenship, "Ohio train explosion reveals extremem corruption at the highest levels," *Global Times*, February 14, 2023, Bradley Blankenship, https://www.globaltimes.cn/page/202302/1285419.shtml.

131 Cullen McCue, "Buttigieg Complains That There Are Too Many White Construction Workers," National File, February 15, 2023, https://nationalfile.com /buttigieg-complains-that-there-are-too-many-white-construction-workers/.

132 Dan Avery, "Pete Buttigieg's star continues to rise, from presidential front-run ner to Cabinet member," NBC News, June 1, 2021, https://www.nbcnews .com/feature/nbc-out/pete-buttigieg-s-star-continues-rise-presidential -frontrunner-cabinet-member-n1269133.

133 Amy Furr, "Report: Walgreens Rationing Baby Formula amid Supply Chain Woes," Breitbart News, April 9, 2022, https://www.breitbart.com /economy/2022/04/09/report-walgreens-rationing-baby-formula-supply -chain-woes/.

134 Laura Reiley, "New documents show more claims of baby formula illness and death," *Washington Post*, June 10, 2022, https://www.washingtonpost.com /business/2022/06/10/baby-formula-deaths-abbott/.

135 "US faces baby formula 'crisis' as shortage worsens," BBC News, May 9, 2022, https://www.bbc.com/news/business-61387183.

136 Simon Kent, "Report: Low Income Families Hit Hardest by Baby Formula Shortage," Breitbart News, May 13, 2022, https://www.breitbart.com /health/2022/05/13/report-low-income-families-hit-hardest-by-baby -formula-shortage/.

137 "US parents turn to black market due to formula shortage," BBC News, June 19. 2022, https://www.bbc.com/news/business-61752799.

138 Catherine Pearson, "Why Doctors Don't Recommend Homemade Baby Formula," *New York Times*, May 11, 2022, https://www.nytimes.com/2022/05/11 /well/homemade-baby-formula.html.

139 Katherine Dillinger, "Former employee filed whistleblower complaint about Abbott's Sturgis facility eight months before previously known," CNN, June 9, 2022, https://www.cnn.com/2022/06/08/health/abbott-whistleblower-com plaints/index.html.

140 Anne Flaherty, "Baby formula timeline: Plant posed a risk last fall," ABC News, May 13, 2022, https://abcnews.go.com/Politics/baby-formula-timeline -plant-posed-risk-fall/story?id=84703748; Department of Health and Human Services, Food and Drug Administration, "Abbott Laboratories Inspection Results," https://www.fda.gov/media/157073/download?utm_medium=email &utm_source=govdelivery.

141 Ian Hanchett, "Tester: 'I Pushed the FDA Commissioner Months Ago' on Formula Issue," Breitbart News, May 13, 2022, https://www.breitbart.com

/clips/2022/05/13/tester-i-pushed-the-fda-commissioner-months-ago-on
-formula-issue/.

142 Trent Baker, "GOP Rep. Stefanik Calls Out Biden over Baby Formula
Shortage—'We Have Seen No Plan,'" Breitbart News, May 11, 2023, https://www
.breitbart.com/clips/2022/05/11/gop-rep-stefanik-calls-out-biden-over
-baby-formula-shortage-we-have-seen-no-plan/.

143 Baker, "GOP Rep. Stefanik Calls Out Biden."

144 John Nolte, "Nolte: GOP Rep Says Illegal Immigrants Receiving 'Pallets of Baby
Formula,'" Breitbart News, https://www.breitbart.com/politics/2022/05/12
/nolte-gop-rep-says-illegal-immigrants-receiving-pallets-baby-formula/.

145 Centers for Disease Control and Prevention, "Information for Families
During the Infant Formula Shortage," accessed May 31, 2023, https://www
.cdc.gov/nutrition/infantandtoddlernutrition/formula-feeding/infant
-formula-shortage.html.

146 Saranac Hale Spencer, "Fact Check: Baby Formula Shortage Fuels Misleading
Partisan Claims" NBC Boston, May 13, 2022, https://www.nbcboston.com
/news/national-international/fact-check-baby-formula-shortage-fuels
-misleading-partisan-claims/2719906/.

147 United States Department of Health and Human Services, "HHS Secretary
Becerra Invokes Defense Production Act to Accelerate Delivery of Raw
Materials and More Needed to Manufacture Infant Formula," press release,
May 5, 2022, https://www.hhs.gov/about/news/2022/05/22/hhs-secretary
-becerra-invokes-defense-production-act-accelerate-delivery-of-raw-materi
als-more-needed-manufacture-infant-formula.html.

148 Adam Korzeniewski, "Ending the Baby-Formula Crisis," American Conservative, July 6, 2022, https://www.theamericanconservative.com/ending-the
-baby-formula-crisis/.

149 Charlie Spiering, "Jill Biden Stages Airport Baby Formula Photo-Op as
Shelves Remain Empty," Breitbart News, May 25, 2022, https://www.breitbart
.com/politics/2022/05/25/jill-biden-stages-airport-baby-formula-photo-op
-as-shelves-remain-empty/.

150 "Advisory: First Lady Jill Biden and U.S. Surgeon General Dr. Vivek Murthy to
Greet Second Shipment Under 'Operation Fly Formula,'" American Presidency
Project, May 24, 2022, https://www.presidency.ucsb.edu/documents/advisory
-first-lady-jill-biden-and-us-surgeon-general-dr-vivek-murthy-greet-second;
Centers for Disease Control and Prevention, "U.S. Births and Natality," accessed
May 31, 2023, https://www.cdc.gov/nchs/fastats/births.htm.

151 Natasha Anderson, "Baby formula crisis WORSENS as out-of-stock levels hit
30%: Parents accuse Biden of forgetting about them and mom struggling to
feed twins says 'I'm sure these politicians' babies eat,'" Daily Mail, July 30, 2022,
https://www.dailymail.co.uk/news/article-11063829/Baby-Formula-crisis
-starts-getting-WORSE-parents-accuse-Biden-forgetting-them.html.

152 "Baby formula recalled after third-party testing finds Cronobacter," Food
Safety News, December 12, 2022, https://www.foodsafetynews.com/2022/12
/baby-formula-recalled-after-third-party-testing-finds-cronobacter/; Abbott
Laboratories, "RECALL NOTICE: October 2022—Abbott 2 fl oz Ready-to
-Feed Liquid Products," accessed May 31, 2023, https://www.similacrecall
.com/us/en/home.html.

153 Natalie Kenzie, "Importing Baby Formula to USA: Overcoming the Challenges," USA Customs Clearance, May 25, 2022, https://usacustomsclearance.com/process/importing-baby-formula-to-usa/.

154 The White House, "President Biden Announces Twenty-Sixth Operation Fly Formula Mission," October 5, 2022, https://www.whitehouse.gov/briefing-room/statements-releases/2022/10/05/president-biden-announces-twenty-sixth-operation-fly-formula-mission/.

155 Chris Pandolfo, "FDA will not fire anyone over baby formula fiasco, chief says," Fox News, February 1, 2023, https://www.foxnews.com/politics/fda-will-not-fire-anyone-over-baby-formula-fiasco-chief-says.

156 Meredith Hull, "Senior FDA official resigns following baby formula crisis, turmoil in agency," *Politico*, January 25, 2023, https://www.politico.com/news/2023/01/25/senior-fda-official-resigns-baby-formula-crisis-00079502; Reagan Udall Foundation for the FDA, *Operational Evaluation of the FDA Human Foods Program*, December 2022, https://reaganudall.org/sites/default/files/2022-12/Human%20Foods%20Program%20Independent%20Expert%20Panel%20Final%20Report%20120622.pdf.

157 Richa Naidu, "Exclusive: Reckitt expects U.S. infant formula shortage until spring," Reuters, December 1, 2022, https://www.reuters.com/business/healthcare-pharmaceuticals/enfamil-maker-reckitt-sees-formula-shortage-continuing-until-spring-2022-12-01/.

158 Madeline Halpert, "US investigating baby formula plant after national shortage," BBC News, January 21, 2022, https://www.bbc.com/news/world-us-canada-64347165.

159 Elizabeth Nolan Brown, "Why Does Funding Government Take $1.7 Trillion and 4,000 Pages?," *Reason*, December 20, 2022, https://reason.com/2022/12/20/why-does-funding-government-take-1-7-trillion-and-4000-pages/; Nikki Carvajal, "Biden signs $1.7 trillion government spending bill into law," CNN, December 29, 2022, https://www.cnn.com/2022/12/29/politics/joe-biden-omnibus/index.html.

160 Brown, "Why Does Funding Government."

161 Representative Dan Bishop (@Rep.DanBishop), "This omnibus bill spends $6+ billion per day, $250+ million per hour, $4+ million per MINUTE . . . until Sept. 30th, when we start the process all over again," Twitter, December 23, 2022, 7:38 a.m., https://twitter.com/RepDanBishop/status/1606313247107424256; Sean Moran, "$1.7 Trillion Omnibus Would Establish Ukrainian Independence Park in Washington, DC," Breitbart News, December 20, 2022, https://www.breitbart.com/politics/2022/12/20/1-7-trillion-omnibus-would-establish-ukrainian-independence-park-in-washington-dc/.

162 Rex Nutting, "Opinion: Household wealth dropped by $13.5 trillion from January to September, second-worst destruction on record," *MarketWatch*, December 9, 2022, https://www.marketwatch.com/story/household-wealth-down-by-13-5-trillion-in-2022-second-worst-destruction-on-record-11670623787#:~:text=Nominal%20net%20worth%20fell%204.6,wealth%20for%20most%20American%20families.

163 Kristen Altus, "Biden's IRS slammed over plan to dip into tip jars: 'Already struggling to survive,' " Fox News, February 9, 2023, https://www.foxbusiness.com/economy/biden-irs-slammed-plan-tip-struggling-survive.

164 Carlos Granda, "Higher fees for borrowers with good credit? Inside Biden's new rules on mortgage fees," *ABC 7 Eyewitness News,* April 28, 2023, https://abc7.com /joe-biden-mortgage-fees-policy-homeowners-first-time-buyer/13190960/.

165 Alexandre Tanzi, "US Income Inequality Rose to Record During Biden's First Year," Bloomberg News, September 13, 2022, https://www.bloomberg.com /news/articles/2022-09-13/us-income-inequality-rose-to-record-during -biden-s-first-year.

166 Statista, "Household income distribution according to the Gini Index of income inequality in the United States from 1990 to 2021," accessed May 31, 2023, https://www.statista.com/statistics/219643/gini-coefficient-for-us-in dividuals-families-and-households/.

167 Matt Flegenheimer, "Biden's First Run for President Was a Calamity. Some Missteps Still Resonate," *New York Times,* June 3, 2023, https://www.nytimes .com/2019/06/03/us/politics/biden-1988-presidential-campaign.html.

CHAPTER 11: THE CORONAVIRUS POWER GRAB

1 David Lewkowicz, "Masks Can Be Detrimental to Babies' Speech and Language Development," *Scientific American,* February 11, 2021, https:// www.scientificamerican.com/article/masks-can-be-detrimental-to -babies-speech-and-language-development1/.

2 Anya Kamenetz, "After 2 years, growing calls to take masks off children in school," NPR, January 28, 2022, https://www.npr.org/2022/01/28/1075842341 /growing-calls-to-take-masks-off-children-in-school.

3 Elizabeth Williams and Patrick Drake, "Headed Back to School: A Look at the Ongoing Effects of COVID-19 on Children's Health and Well-Being," Kaiser Family Foundation, August 5, 2022, https://www.kff.org/coronavirus -covid-19/issue-brief/headed-back-to-school-a-look-at-the-ongoing-effects -of-covid-19-on-childrens-health-and-well-being/.

4 Karen D'Souza, "Pandemic babies show developmental delays, more research shows," Ed Source, June 17, 2022, https://edsource.org/updates/pandemic -babies-show-developmental-delays-more-research-shows#:~:text =Born%20during%20or%20shortly%20before,physical%20aggression%20 and%20separation%20anxiety.

5 Benjamin Zablotsky, Lindsey Black, Matthew Maenner, Laura Schieve, Melissa Danielson, Rebecca Bitsko, Stephen Blumberg, Michael Kogan, and Coleen Boyle, "Prevalence and Trends of Developmental Disabilities among Children in the United States: 2009–2017," *Pediatrics* 144, no. 4 (October 8, 2019), https:// doi.org/10.1542/peds.2019-0811, https://pubmed.ncbi.nlm.nih.gov/31558576/.

6 "Joe Biden: I'm going to 'shut down the virus,' not the US," YouTube video, 1:00, posted by *Guardian News,* October 23, 2020, https://www.youtube.com /watch?v=nekvd4iw6Hg.

7 Allison Aubrey, "Coronavirus Is a Key Campaign Issue: What's Joe Biden's Plan?," NPR, October 28, 2020, https://www.npr.org/sections/health-shots /2020/10/28/928392673/coronavirus-is-a-key-campaign-issue-whats-joe -biden-s-plan.

8 Aubrey, "Coronavirus Is a Key Campaign Issue."

9 "Public Holds Broadly Favorable Views of Many Federal Agencies, In-

cluding CDC and HHS," Pew Research Center, April 9, 2020, https://www
.pewresearch.org/politics/2020/04/09/public-holds-broadly-favorable-views
-of-many-federal-agencies-including-cdc-and-hhs/.

10 Jeffrey Jones, "Americans' Ratings of CDC Communication Turn Negative,"
Gallup, September 7, 2021, https://news.gallup.com/poll/354566/americans
-ratings-cdc-communication-turn-negative.aspx.

11 Elizabeth Buchwald, "U.S. health officials say Americans shouldn't wear
face masks to prevent coronavirus—here are 3 other reasons not to wear
them," MarketWatch, March 2, 2020, https://www.marketwatch.com/story
/the-cdc-says-americans-dont-have-to-wear-facemasks-because-of-corona
virus-2020-01-30.

12 Centers for Disease Control and Prevention, "CDC calls on Americans to
wear masks to prevent COVID-19 spread," July 14, 2020, https://www.cdc
.gov/media/releases/2020/p0714-americans-to-wear-masks.html.

13 Centers for Disease Control and Prevention et al., "Summary of Guidance for
Public Health Strategies to Address High Levels of Community Transmission
of SARS-CoV-2 and Related Deaths, December 2020," *Morbidity and Mortality Weekly Report* 69, no. 49 (December 4, 2020): 1860–67, http://dx.doi
.org/10.15585/mmwr.mm6949e2.

14 Centers for Disease Control and Prevention, "Guidance for Adult Day Services
Centers: Summary of Recent Changes," July 14, 2021, https://www.cdc.gov
/ncbddd/humandevelopment/covid-19/adult-day-care-service-centers.html.

15 Apoorva Mandavilli, "The C.D.C. concedes that cloth masks do not protect
against the virus as effectively as other masks," *New York Times,* January 14, 2022,
https://www.nytimes.com/2022/01/14/health/cloth-masks-covid-cdc.html.

16 Tom Jefferson et al., "Physical interventions to interrupt or reduce the spread of
respiratory viruses," *Cochrane Database of Systematic Reviews* 1, no.CD006207
(January 30, 2023), https://doi.org/10.1002/14651858.CD006207.pub6.

17 Ivan Oransky, "Question the 'Lab Leak' Theory. But Don't Call It a Conspiracy,"
Medscape, November 29, 2021, https://www.medscape.com/viewarticle/963762;
Faye Flam, "The Search for Covid's Origins Is as Important as Ever," Bloomberg,
https://www.bloomberg.com/opinion/articles/2022-11-12/where-did-covid
-come-from-the-china-lab-leak-theory-persists; Maria Cheng and Jamey
Keaten, "WHO: COVID origins unclear but lab leak theory needs study," AP
News, June 9, 2022, https://apnews.com/article/covid-science-health-world-or
ganization-government-and-politics-8662c2bc1784d3dea33f61caa6089ac2;
Jacob Bliss, "Republicans Release 'Unclassified' Report of COVID Origins
Before Taking Over House Majority," Breitbart News, December 15, 2022,
https://www.breitbart.com/politics/2022/12/15/republicans-release-unclassi
fied-report-of-covid-origins-before-taking-over-house-majority/; Colin Butler
and Delia Randolph, "There has been a suppression of the truth, secrecy and
cover-ups on an Orwellian scale over the origin of Covid-19 in China," *Daily
Mail,* January 28, 2023, https://www.dailymail.co.uk/news/article-11687597/
There-suppression-truth-secrecy-cover-ups-origin-Covid-19-China.html; Steven Quay and Richard Muller, "The Science Suggests a Wuhan Lab Leak," *Wall
Street Journal,* June 6, 2021, https://www.wsj.com/articles/the-science-suggests
-a-wuhan-lab-leak-11622995184.

18 Olivia Olander, "Fauci on Covid lab leak theory: 'I have a completely

open mind,'" *Politico,* November 27, 2022, https://www.politico.com /news/2022/11/27/fauci-china-covid-lab-leak-theory-00070867.

19 Michael Gordon and Warren Strobel, "Lab Leak Most Likely Origin of Covid-19 Pandemic, Energy Department Now Says," *Wall Street Journal,* February 26, 2023, https://www.wsj.com/articles/covid-origin-china-lab -leak-807b7b0a.

20 Sharon Lerner, Mara Hvistendahl, and Maia Hibbet, "NIH Documents Provide New Evidence U.S. Funded Gain-of-Function Research in Wuhan," *Intercept,* September 9, 2021, https://theintercept.com/2021/09/09/covid -origins-gain-of-function-research/.

21 Steven Nelson, "NIH director confirms agency hid early COVID genes at request of Chinese scientists," *New York Post,* May 11, 2022, https://nypost .com/2022/05/11/nih-director-tabak-confirms-agency-hid-covid-genes-per -chinese/.

22 Bruce Haring, "Joe Biden Gaffe Alert: Stuns 'The View' by Claiming Coronavirus Cure Will Make the Problem Worse," *Deadline,* March 24, 2020, https:// deadline.com/2020/03/joe-biden-gaffe-alert-stuns-the-view-by-claiming -coronavirus-cure-will-make-the-problem-worse-1202891856/.

23 "Joe Biden Stupid Quotes," All Great Quotes, accessed on March 24, 2023, https://www.allgreatquotes.com/authors/joe-biden-stupid/.

24 Chris Pleasance, "Gaffe-prone Joe Biden stumbles his words while describing the impact of COVID, saying it has 'uh, taken more lives than any year in the past 100 years,'" *Daily Mail,* September 2, 2020,https://www.dailymail.co.uk /news/article-8688775/Gaffe-prone-Joe-Biden-struggles-impact-COVID .html.

25 Mitch Kokai, "Biden's COVID Campaign Promises Fell Flat," John Locke Foundation, December 3, 2021, https://www.johnlocke.org/bidens-covid -campaign-promises-fell-flat/.

26 Institute for Health Metrics and Evaluation, *COVID-19 Projections,* accessed on March 24, 2023, https://covid19.healthdata.org/united-states-of-america ?view=cumulative-deaths&tab=trend.

27 Zachary Evans, "Biden Claims 'We Didn't Have' a COVID Vaccine When He Took Office," *National Review,* February 17, 2021, https://www.nation alreview.com/news/biden-claims-we-didnt-have-a-covid-vaccine-when-he -took-office/; Lori Robertson, Eurgene Kiely, and D'Angelo Gore, "Biden's Misleading Vaccine Boasts," FactCheck.org, February 23, 2021, https://www .factcheck.org/2021/02/bidens-misleading-vaccine-boasts/.

28 "'I am standing in your way': DeSantis blasts Biden after president tells him to 'get out of the way' on COVID," Wesh 2, August 4, 2021, https://www.wesh .com/article/watch-live-gov-desantis-and-deo-secretary-provide-update-on -state-of-floridas-economy/37223004.

29 Joseph Biden, "Biden message to unvaccinated. Our patience is wearing thin," BBC video, 0:55, September 9, 2021, https://www.bbc.com/news/av/world -us-canada-58510013.

30 Allie Malloy and Maegan Vazquez, "Biden warns of winter of 'severe illness and death' for unvaccinated due to Omicron," CNN, December 16, 2021, https://www.cnn.com/2021/12/16/politics/joe-biden-warning-winter/index .html.

31 "Joe and Kamala's Plan to Beat COVID," JoeBiden.com, accessed via Way-BackMachine on May 30, 2023, https://web.archive.org/web/20201111164957/https:/joebiden.com/covid19/.

32 Maegan Vazquez, "Trump now says he wasn't kidding when he told officials to slow down coronavirus testing, contradicting staff," CNN, June 23, 2020, https://www.cnn.com/2020/06/22/politics/donald-trump-testing-slow-down-response/index.html.

33 Allison Aubrey, "President-Elect Biden Has a Plan to Combat COVID-19. Here's What's in It," NPR, November 8, 2020, https://www.npr.org/sections/health-shots/2020/11/08/930887069/hold-president-elect-biden-has-a-plan-to-combat-covid-19-heres-what-s-in-it.

34 Cleveland Clinic, "COVID-19 and PCR Testing," August 24, 2021, https://my.clevelandclinic.org/health/diagnostics/21462-covid-19-and-pcr-testing.

35 U.S. Food and Drug Administration, "At-Home COVID-19 Antigen Tests—Take Steps to Reduce Your Risk of False Negative Results: FDA Safety Communication," https://www.fda.gov/medical-devices/safety-communications/home-covid-19-antigen-tests-take-steps-reduce-your-risk-false-negative-results-fda-safety; Samuel Yang and Richard Rothman, "PCR-based diagnostics for infectious diseases: Uses, limitations, and future applications in acute-care settings," *Lancet Infectious Diseases* 4, no. 6 (June 2004): 337–48, https://doi.org/10.1016/S1473-3099(04)01044-8.

36 Sandee LaMotte and Virginia Langmaid, "Household spread of Covid-19 is common and quick, a new CDC study finds," CNN, October 30, 2020, https://www.cnn.com/2020/10/30/health/household-spread-covid-19-wellness/index.html.

37 Bohdan Nosyk, Wendy Armstrong, and Carlos Del Rio, "Contact Tracing for COVID-19: An Opportunity to Reduce Health Disparities and End the Human Immunodeficiency Virus/AIDS Epidemic in the United States," *Clinical Infectious Diseases* 71, no. 16 (October 15, 2020): 2259–61, https://doi.org/10.1093/cid/ciaa501.

38 Centers for Disease Control and Prevention, "Ways HIV Can Be Transmitted," accessed on May 30, 2023, https://www.cdc.gov/hiv/basics/hiv-transmission/ways-people-get-hiv.html.

39 Aubrey, "Coronavirus Is a Key Campaign Issue."

40 Eva Clark, Elizabeth Chiao, and Susan Amirian, "Why Contact Tracing Efforts Have Failed to Curb Coronavirus Disease 2019 (COVID-19) Transmission in Much of the United States," *Clinical Infectious Diseases* 72, no. 9 (May 4, 2021): 415–19, https://doi.org/10.1093/cid/ciaa1155.

41 Mark Waghorn, "6-foot social distancing rule doesn't protect from COVID-19 whether indoors or outdoors," Study Finds, November 29, 2021, https://studyfinds.org/6-foot-rule-doesnt-protect-covid/.

42 Martin Bazant and John Bush, "A guideline to limit indoor airborne transmission of COVID-19," *Proceedings of the National Academy of Sciences* 118, no. 17 (April 27, 2021), https://doi.org/10.1073/pnas.201899511; Rich Mendez, "MIT researchers say time spent indoors increases risk of Covid at 6 feet or 60 feet in new study challenging social distancing policies," CNBC, April 23, 2021, https://www.cnbc.com/2021/04/23/mit-researchers-say-youre-no-safer-from-covid-indoors-at-6-feet-or-60-feet-in-new-study.html.

43 Henning Bundgaard et al., "Effectiveness of Adding a Mask Recommendation to Other Public Health Measures to Prevent SARS-CoV-2 Infection in Danish Mask Wearers," *Annals of Internal Medicine* 174, no. 3 (March 2021): 335–43, https://www.acpjournals.org/doi/10.7326/m20-6817.

44 "Denmark trial measures effectiveness of adding a mask recommendation to other public health measures for preventing SARS-CoV-2 infection," American College of Physicians, November 18, 2020, https://www .acponline.org/acp-newsroom/denmark-trial-measures-effectiveness -of-adding-a-mask-recommendation-to-other-public-health-measures.

45 Tom Jefferson et al., "Physical interventions to interrupt or reduce the spread of respiratory viruses," *Cochrane Database of Systematic Reviews,* no. 1 (January 30, 2023), https://doi.org/10.1002/14651858.CD006207.pub6.

46 Bret Stephens, "The Mask Mandates Did Nothing. Will Any Lessons Be Learned?," *New York Times,* February 21, 2023, https://www.nytimes .com/2023/02/21/opinion/do-mask-mandates-work.html.

47 Sheryl Stolberg and Erica Green, "The Biden administration will use a federal civil rights office to deter states from banning universal masking in classrooms," *New York Times,* August 18, 2021, https://www.nytimes .com/2021/08/18/us/politics/biden-masks-schools-civil-rights.html.

48 John Snow Memorandum (website), accessed May 30, 2023, https://www .johnsnowmemo.com/john-snow-memo.html.

49 William Haseltine, "Why We Can't Rely on Natural Immunity to Protect Us from Covid-19," *Forbes,* September 18, 2020, https://www.forbes.com/sites /williamhaseltine/2020/09/18/why-we-cant-rely-on-natural-immunity-to -protect-us-from-covid-19/?sh=4d0ef1a31ff2; Christie Aschwanden, "The False Promise of Herd Immunity for COVID-19," *Nature,* October 21, 2020, https://www.nature.com/articles/d41586-020-02948-4.

50 Sanchari Sinha Dutta, "No point vaccinating those who've had COVID-19: Cleveland Clinic study suggests," News-Medical, April 12, 2023, https:// www.news-medical.net/news/20210608/No-point-vaccinating-those -whoe28099ve-had-COVID-19-Findings-of-Cleveland-Clinic-study.aspx.

51 "New research: Exposure to common cold virus can help fight Covid-19," Indian Express News Service, August 18, 2021, https://indianexpress.com/article /explained/exposure-to-common-cold-virus-can-help-fight-covid-19-7364207/.

52 Tamara Bhandari, "Good news: Mild COVID-19 induces lasting antibody protection," Washington University School of Medicine, May 24, 2021, https://medicine.wustl.edu/news/good-news-mild-covid-19-induces-lasting -antibody-protection/.

53 Julie Steenhuysen and Manas Mishra, "Prior COVID infection more protective than vaccination during Delta surge—U.S. study," Reuters, January 19, 2022, https://www.reuters.com/business/healthcare-pharmaceu ticals/prior-covid-infection-more-protective-than-vaccination-during -delta-surge-us-2022-01-19/.

54 John Ley, "Natural immunity gets another boost from two new U.S. studies," Clark County Today, January 31, 2022, https://www.clarkcountytoday.com /news/natural-immunity-gets-another-boost-from-two-new-u-s-studies/.

55 Priscilla Kim, Steven Gordon, Megan Sheehan, and Michael Rothberg, "Duration of Severe Acute Respiratory Syndrome Coronavirus 2 Natural Im-

munity and Protection Against the Delta Variant: A Retrospective Cohort Study," *Clinical Infectious Diseases* 75, no. 1 (July 2022): 185–90, https://doi .org/10.1093/cid/ciab999.

56 Krutika Amin and Cynthia Cox, "COVID-19 pandemic-related excess mortality and potential years of life lost in the U.S. and peer countries," Peterson-KFF Health System Tracker, April 7, 2021, https://www.healthsystemtracker.org /brief/covid-19-pandemic-related-excess-mortality-and-potential-years-of -life-lost-in-the-u-s-and-peer-countries/.

57 United Kingdom Office for National Statistics and Government Office for Science, *Comparing different international measures of excess mortality,* December 20, 2022, ONS Website, https://www.ons.gov.uk/peoplepopu lationandcommunity/birthsdeathsandmarriages/deaths/articles/comparing differentinternationalmeasuresofexcessmortality/2022-12-20.

58 World Health Organization, "China," COVID data, accessed May 30, 2023, https://covid19.who.int/region/wpro/country/cn.

59 Roger Stark, "Comprehensive Research Finds That Lockdowns Don't Work," Washington Policy Center, February 3, 2022, https://www.washingtonpolicy.org /publications/detail/comprehensive-research-finds-that-lockdowns-dont-work.

60 The White House, "Proclamation on Declaring a National Emergency Concerning the Novel Coronavirus Disease (COVID-19) Outbreak," March 13, 2020, https://trumpwhitehouse.archives.gov/presidential-actions/proclama tion-declaring-national-emergency-concerning-novel-coronavirus-dis ease-covid-19-outbreak/.

61 "Biden Says Americans Can't Trust Trump on Vaccine," *New York Times,* September 17, 2020, accessed via WayBackMachine on March 19, 2023, https://web.archive.org/web/20210114010826/https:/www.nytimes.com /live/2020/09/16/us/trump-vs-biden.

62 Cassidy Morrison, "Biden does not trust Trump to deliver a safe vaccine," *Washington Examiner,* September 29, 2020, https://www.washingtonexaminer .com/news/biden-does-not-trust-trump-to-deliver-a-safe-vaccine.

63 Joseph Biden, "Remarks by President Biden in a CNN Town Hall with Don Lemon," July 21, 2021, Mount St. Joseph University, Cincinnati, Ohio, transcript, https://www.whitehouse.gov/briefing-room/speeches-remarks/2021/07/22/re marks-by-president-biden-in-a-CNN-town-hall-with-don-lemon/.

64 Pam Key, "CNN's Lemon: Unvaccinated Should Not Be Allowed in Supermarkets, Ball Games, Work," Breitbart News, July 26, 2021, https://www .breitbart.com/clips/2021/07/26/CNNs-lemon-unvaccinated-should-not-be -allowed-in-supermarkets-ball-games-work/.

65 Amit Bahl, Steven Johnson, Gabriel Maine, Martha Hernandez Garcia, Srininavasa Nimmagadda, and Lihua Qu, "Vaccination reduces need for emergency care in breakthrough COVID-19 infections: A multicenter cohort study," *Lancet,* September 9, 2021, https://www.thelancet.com/journals lanam/article/PIIS2667-193X(21)00061-2/fulltext; Sumathi Reddy, "New Study Shows Vaccination Reduces Long Covid Risk, but Modestly," *Wall Street Journal,* May 25, 2022; https://www.wsj.com/articles/can-vaccines -prevent-long-covid-new-details-on-risks-and-symptoms-11653492114; Seyed Moghadas et al., " The Impact of Vaccination on Coronavirus Disease 2019 (COVID-19) Outbreaks in the United States," *Clinical Infectious Dis-*

. *eases* 73, no. 12 (December 15, 2021): 2257–64, https://doi.org/10.1101/202
0.11.27.20240051.

66 Meagan Fitzpatrick, Seyed Moghadas, Abhishek Pandey, and Alison Galvani, "Two Years of U.S. COVID-19 Vaccines Have Prevented Millions of Hospitalizations and Deaths," Commonwealth Fund, December 13, 2022, https://www.commonwealthfund.org/blog/2022/two-years-covid-vaccines-prevented-millions-deaths-hospitalizations#:~:text=on%20our%20methods.-,Findings,and%203.2%20million%20additional%20deaths.

67 Centers for Disease Control and Prevention, "COVID-19 Vaccine Equity for Racial and Ethnic Minority Groups," March 29, 2022, https://www.cdc.gov/coronavirus/2019-ncov/community/health-equity/vaccine-equity.html.

68 Candice Norwood, "Biden has a plan to address COVID-19 disparities. Here's what experts recommend," *PBS NewsHour,* February 5, 2021, https://www.pbs.org/newshour/politics/biden-has-a-plan-to-address-covid-19-disparities-heres-what-experts-recommend; DC Office of Planning, "DC Office of Planning's Commitment to Racial Equity," accessed May 30, 2023, https://planning.dc.gov/racialequity; Montana State University, "Health Equity & Health Disparities," accessed May 30, 2023, https://healthinfo.montana.edu/cheg/health-equity/index.html.

69 Erin Alberty, "Utah eliminates race and sex as factors in monoclonal antibody COVID treatments after 'legal concerns,' " *Salt Lake Tribune,* January 21, 2022, https://www.sltrib.com/news/2022/01/21/utah-eliminates-race-sex/.

70 "Joe Biden: Covid vaccination in US will not be mandatory," BBC News, December 5, 2020, https://www.bbc.com/news/world-us-canada-55193939; Michelle Miller and Nikole Killion, "Biden says he would not make coronavirus vaccine mandatory," news broadcast, filmed on December 5, 2020, in New York City and Wilmington, Delaware, *CBS Mornings,* video, 2:53, December 5, 2020, https://www.youtube.com/watch?v=ob3ER7fKeDs; Joseph Biden, "COVID-19 vaccine should not be mandatory: Remarks by President-Elect filmed on December 4, 2020, in Wilmington, Delaware," Reuters, video, 1:05, December 4, 2020,https://www.youtube.com/watch?v=e6QNsNMFH5s; Isobel Asher Hamilton, "Biden said the COVID-19 vaccine will not be mandatory in the US—but he will encourage people to 'do the right thing,' " Business Insider, December 5, 2020, https://www.businessinsider.com/biden-covid-19-vaccine-will-not-be-mandatory-in-us-2020-12; Joseph Biden, "COVID-19 vaccine should not be mandatory: Remarks by President-Elect, filmed on December 4, 2020, in Wilmington, Delaware," Reuters, video, 1:06, December 4, 2020, https://www.reuters.com/video/watch/idOVD7LKPUN.

71 Wilton Jackson, "Report: Unvaccinated Players in Some Cities Won't Be Allowed to Play in Home Games," *Sports Illustrated,* September 9, 2021, https://www.si.com/nba/2021/09/01/unvaccinated-nba-players-several-markets-not-allowed-team-activities.

72 Jim Garamone, United States Department of Defense, "Biden to Approve Austin's Request to Make COVID-19 Vaccine Mandatory for Service Members," August 9, 2021, https://www.defense.gov/News/News-Stories/Article

/Article/2724982/biden-to-approve-austins-request-to-make-covid-19
-vaccine-mandatory-for-service/.

73 Tom Porter, "Video shows President-elect Biden saying 10 months ago he wouldn't
make vaccines mandatory," *Business Insider,* September 10, 2021,https://www
.businessinsider.com/video-biden-said-december-2020-wouldnt-make-vaccine
-mandatory-2021-9; Hannah Knowles, Annie Linskey, Annabelle Timsit, Bryan
Pietsch, Paulina Firozi, Lenny Bernstein, Laurie McGinley, and Maria Luisa Paul,
"What to know about Biden's pandemic plan and vaccine mandates," *Washington
Post,* September 9, 2021, https://www.washingtonpost.com/nation/2021/09/09/
covid-delta-variant-live-updates/; Annie Linskey, Yasmeen Abutaleb, Seung Min
Kim, and Lisa Rein, "Biden administration extends vaccine mandate to large
U.S. companies," *Texas Tribune,* September 9, 2021, https://www.texastribune
.org/2021/09/09/covid-vaccine-requirement-businesses/; Ivy Baer, "Biden Administration Issues Vaccine Requirement Rules," Association of American
Medical Colleges, September 10, 2021, https://www.aamc.org/advocacy-policy
/washington-highlights/president-biden-announces-covid-19-action-plan
-new-vaccine-mandates.

74 Andis Robeznieks, "Doctor shortages are here—and they'll get worse if we
don't act fast," American Medical Association, April 13, 2022, https://www
.ama-assn.org/practice-management/sustainability/doctor-shortages-are
-here-and-they-ll-get-worse-if-we-don-t-act.

75 Kevin Breuninger and Spencer Kimball, "Supreme Court blocks Biden Covid
vaccine mandate for businesses, allows health-care worker rule," CNBC,
January 13, 2022, https://www.cnbc.com/2022/01/13/supreme-court-ruling
-biden-covid-vaccine-mandates.html.

76 Gretchen Vogel, "New versions of Omicron are masters of immune evasion,"
Science, May 10, 2022, https://www.science.org/content/article/new-versions
-omicron-are-masters-immune-evasion.

77 Priyamadhaba Behera et al., "Role of ivermectin in the prevention of
SARS-CoV-2 infection among healthcare workers in India: A matched case
-control study," *PLoS One* 16, no. 2 (February 16, 2021): e0247163, https://doi
.org/10.1371/journal.pone.0247163.

78 "Ivermectin may help covid-19 patients—but only those with worms,"
Economist, November 27, 2021, https://www.economist.com/graphic
-detail/2021/11/18/ivermectin-may-help-covid-19-patients-but-only-those
-with-worms.

79 Kevin Dunleavy, "Regeneron's COVID antibody loses effectiveness against
omicron, so it's working on a new version," Fierce Pharma, December 16, 2021,
https://www.fiercepharma.com/pharma/regeneron-working-new-covid
-19-antibody-treatment-could-be-ready-for-trials-first-quarter.

80 Jacob Jarvis, "Fact Check: Regeneron Monoclonal Antibody Costs Government $2,100 Per Dose," *Newsweek,* October 12, 2021, https://www
.*Newsweek.*com/fact-check-regeneron-regen-cov-covid-monoclonal-anti
body-cost-1637526.

81 Alex Berenson (@AlexBerenson), "Yes, I am 'openly shilling' a drug made by
a company that conspired to ban me from Twitter. Because when it comes to

Covid, I don't care about anything except what works." Twitter, January 23, 2023, 6:49 p.m., https://twitter.com/AlexBerenson/status/161771615123212 2880.

82 Susannah Luthi, "Twitter loses bid to toss Alex Berenson lawsuit," *Politico,* April 30, 2022, https://www.politico.com/news/2022/04/30/twitter-loses-bid -to-toss-alex-berenson-lawsuit-00029131.

83 Katherine Ellen Foley and David Lim, "Biden experiences a Covid rebound after treatment with one course of Paxlovid," *Politico,* July 30, 2022, https://www.politico.com/news/2022/07/30/biden-covid-rebound-pax lovid-00048349.

84 Berenson, "Yes, I am 'openly shilling' "; Avie Schneider, "Biden is still feeling well after testing positive for COVID again, his doctor says," NPR, July 31, 2022, https://www.npr.org/2022/07/30/1114716874/president-biden-covid -positive.

85 Kristina Sauerwein, "Paxlovid reduces risk of long-term health problems, death from COVID-19," Washington University School of Medicine, March 23, 2023, https://medicine.wustl.edu/news/paxlovid-reduces-risk-of -long-term-health-problems-death-from-covid-19/.

86 "President Biden Receives His Updated COVID-19 Vaccine and Delivers Remarks," YouTube video, 13:58, posted by The White House, October 25, 2022, https://www.youtube.com/watch?v=f-ehCTw_oCc.

87 Yasmin Tayag, "Stop Calling It a 'Pandemic of the Unvaccinated,' " *Atlantic,* September 16, 2021, https://www.theatlantic.com/ideas/archive/2021/09 /persuade-unvaccinated-protect-unvaccinated/620091/.

88 Frances Martel, "Joe Biden Admin 'Committed' to W.H.O. Pandemic Accord," Breitbart News, March 1, 2023, https://www.breitbart.com/asia/2023/03/01 /joe-biden-admin-committed-w-h-o-pandemic-accord/.

89 Stephen Buranyi, "The WHO v coronavirus: Why it can't handle the pandemic," *Guardian,* April 10, 2020, https://www.theguardian.com/news/2020 /apr/10/world-health-organization-who-v-coronavirus-why-it-cant-han dle-pandemic; Salvatore Babones, "Yes, Blame WHO for Its Disastrous Coronavirus Response," *Foreign Policy,* May 27, 2020, https://foreignpolicy .com/2020/05/27/who-health-china-coronavirus-tedros/.

90 Dr. Tedros Ghebreyesus, "WHO Director-General's opening remarks at the media briefing on COVID-19," speech, Geneva, Switzerland, March 11, 2020, World Health Organization, https://www.who.int/director-general/speeches /detail/who-director-general-s-opening-remarks-at-the-media-briefing-on -covid-19—-11-march-2020.

91 Frances Martel, "Taiwan: World Health Organization 'Mostly Ignored' Coronavirus Warnings in December," Breitbart News, March 23, 2020, https://www.breitbart.com/asia/2020/03/23/taiwan-world-health-organiza tion-mostly-ignored-coronavirus-warnings-in-december/.

92 Frances Martel, "Hong Kong Expands Power to Isolate Individuals to Fight Chinese 'Mystery Pneumonia,' " Breitbart News, January 7, 2020, https:// www.breitbart.com/asia/2020/01/07/hong-kong-expands-power-to-iso late-individuals-to-fight-chinese-mystery-pneumonia/.

93 Price Sukhia, "The Truth about Ukrainian Biolabs," Government Accountability Institute, September 2022, https://thedrilldown.com/wp-content

/uploads/2022/09/PDF-GAI-Report-The-Truth-About-Ukrainian-Biolabs
-DD-Clean.pdf.

94 United States Agency for International Development, PREDICT Consortium,
One Health Institute, University of California, Davis, *Reducing Pandemic Risk,
Promoting Global Health,* December 2014, https://pdf.usaid.gov/pdf_docs
/PBAAF347.pdf.

95 United States Agency for International Development, *PREDICT 2 Factsheet,*
November 2014, accessed via Wayback Machine on March 25, 2023, https://
web.archive.org/web/20220123053352/http://www.usaid.gov/sites/default
/files/documents/1864/Predict2-factsheet.pdf.

96 United States Agency for International Development, *Reducing Pandemic
Risk,* https://pdf.usaid.gov/pdf_docs/PBAAF347.pdf.

97 Charlie Spiering, "Researcher Tied to Wuhan Lab Thanked Dr. Fauci for
Dismissing Lab-Leak Theory," Breitbart News, June 2, 2021, https://www
.breitbart.com/politics/2021/06/02/researcher-tied-to-wuhan-lab-thanked
-dr-fauci-for-dismissing-lab-leak-theory/.

98 Andrew Huff (@AGHuff), "It get's [*sic*]better in-Q-Tel, the CIA venture capital firm invested in Metabiota. It's all in Hunter Biden's laptop emails," Twitter,
January 31, 2023, 3:55 p.m., https://twitter.com/AGHuff/status/16205714618
90224128?lang=en.

99 United States Agency for International Development, "USAID Announces
New $125 Million Project to Detect Unknown Viruses with Pandemic Poten-
tial," press release, October 5, 2021, https://www.usaid.gov/news-information
/press-releases/oct-5-2021-usaid-announces-new-125-million-project
-detect-unknown-viruses-pandemic-potential.

100 Donald McNeil and Thomas Kaplan, "U.S. Will Revive Global Virus
-Hunting Effort Ended Last Year," *New York Times,* August 30, 2020, https://
www.nytimes.com/2020/08/30/health/predict-pandemic-usaid.html.

101 Amanda Holpuch, "Pandemic profits: Top US health insurers make billions
in second quarter," *Guardian,* August 6, 2021, https://www.theguardian.com
/us-news/2021/aug/06/us-healthcare-insurance-covid-19-coronavirus.

102 "Health insurance companies make record profits as costs soar in US," CNN,
February 3, 2022, https://www.live5news.com/2022/02/03/health-insurance
-companies-make-record-profits-costs-soar-us/.

103 "Health insurance companies make record profits," CNN.

104 Andrew Simpson, "How Much Insurance Groups Have Given to Trump,
Biden and House, Senate Candidates," *Insurance Journal,* October 29, 2020,
https://www.insurancejournal.com/news/national/2020/10/29/588600.htm.

105 Kimberley Leonard, "We combed through records of 100 healthcare companies to see who their top executives are donating to in the 2020 election. They
reveal a surprising trend," Business Insider, October 30, 2020, https://political
accountability.net/hifi/files/CPA—-Business-Insider—-We-combed-through
-records-of-100-healthcare-companies-L-L——10-30-20—-CPA-quoted.pdf.

106 Paige Cunningham, "The Health 202: Health industry giants get tax windfall. But it's unclear how it will be used," *Washington Post,* April 18, 2018,
https://www.washingtonpost.com/news/powerpost/paloma/the-health
-202/2018/04/18/the-health-202-health-industry-giant-get-tax-windfall
-but-it-s-unclear-how-it-will-be-used/5ad6083c30fb046acf7bccc1/.

107 Open Secrets, "Pfizer, Inc.," 2020 Top Recipients, accessed April 4, 2023, https://www.opensecrets.org/ORGS/toprecips.php?id=D000000138&cycle=A; Open Secrets, "Moderna, Inc.," 2020 money to congressional candidates, accessed April 4, 2023, https://www.opensecrets.org/ORGS/toprecips.php?id=D000073555&cycle=2020.

108 Kimberley Leonard, "Biden promised to go after insurance companies for their high costs. Instead, his administration gave them an additional $61 billion via the stimulus plan," Business Insider, March 15, 2021, https://www.businessinsider.com/biden-stimulus-health-insurance-companies-obamacare-2021-2.

109 Tony Pugh, "Obamacare Sign-Up Helpers to Get Funding of Nearly $100 Million," Bloomberg Law, August 26, 2022, https://news.bloombergtax.com/health-law-and-business/obamacare-sign-up-helpers-to-get-funding-of-nearly-100-million?context=search&index=6.

110 Nick Paul Taylor, "iHealth Lab gets DoD order for additional 104M home COVID-19 tests," MedTechDive, January 31, 2022, https://www.medtechdive.com/news/dod-orders-covid-19-tests-ihealth-lab/618000/.

111 Namandjé N. Bumpus, Chief Scientist, U.S. Food and Drug Administration to Jack Feng, iHealth Labs, February 10, 2023, FDA website, https://www.fda.gov/media/153925/download.

112 Roxanne Liu and Meg Shen, "China's Andon Health to supply at-home COVID-19 tests to U.S.," Reuters, January 13, 2022, https://www.reuters.com/business/healthcare-pharmaceuticals/chinas-andon-health-supply-at-home-covid-19-tests-us-2022-01-14/.

113 Josh Nathan Kazis and Tanner Brown, "Why the U.S. Contracted with a Chinese Covid Test-Kit Maker You've Never Heard Of," Barron's, March 3, 2022, https://www.barrons.com/articles/covid-19-test-maker-ihealth-andon-health-51646318989.

114 Jack Lee and Jennifer Zeng, "The Chinese Military Network Behind the World's Third-Largest Cell Phone Maker," Epoch Times, February 11, 2021, https://www.theepochtimes.com/the-chinese-military-network-behind-the-worlds-third-largest-cell-phone-maker_3691545.html?utm_medium=social&utm_source=twitter&utm_campaign=digitalsub.maker_3691545.html?utm_medium=social&utm_source=twitter&utm_campaign=digitalsub.

115 Aakriti Bhalla, "U.S. will remove Xiaomi from blacklist, reversing jab by Trump," Reuters, May 11, 2021, https://www.reuters.com/world/china/us-defense-department-xiaomi-agree-resolve-litigation-court-filing-2021-05-12/.

116 Jimmy Quinn, "The Biden Administration Is Letting a Dangerous Chinese Company Off the U.S. Government's Investment Blacklist," National Review, June 11, 2021, https://www.nationalreview.com/2021/06/the-biden-administration-is-letting-a-dangerous-chinese-company-off-the-u-s-governments-investment-blacklist/.

117 Xiaomi Corporation, Q1 2021 Results Announcement, March 2021, https://ir.mi.com/static-files/9f0e2af7-4564-4540-a52f-b85ab64ef6d0.

118 Jon Russell, "Alibaba snaps up Chinese Android app store Wandoujia," TechCrunch, July 6, 2016, https://techcrunch.com/2016/07/06/alibaba-snaps-up-chinese-android-app-store-wandoujia/.

119 Inspur Electronic Information Industry Co. Ltd., "Intel, Inspur, BGI and Alibaba Cloud Jointly Launched the GATK Chinese Association for Precision Med-

icine," PR Newswire, June 27, 2017, https://www.prnewswire.com/news-re
leases/intel-inspur-bgi-and-alibaba-cloud-jointly-launched-the-gatk-chi
nese-association-for-precision-medicine-300480903.html.

120 Julian Barnes, "U.S. Warns of Efforts by China to Collect Genetic Data," *New York Times,* October 22, 2021, https://www.nytimes.com/2021/10/22/us/poli tics/china-genetic-data-collection.html.

121 Steven Millward, "Alibaba goes in on $40m boost for DNA-testing startup Prenetics," Tech in Asia, October 17, 2017, https://www.techinasia.com /dna-testing-startup-prenetics-series-b-funding-alibaba.

122 Line Heidenheim Juul, "How big tech helped battle Covid-19 in China," China Experience, November 5, 2020, https://www.china-experience.com /china-experience-insights/how-big-tech-is-helping-battle-corona-in-china.

123 Nancy Gibbs, "Do the unvaccinated deserve scarce ICU beds?," *Washington Post,* September 1, 2021, https://www.washingtonpost.com/opin ions/2021/09/01/do-unvaccinated-deserve-scarce-icu-beds/.

124 James Risen, "The Right's Anti-Vaxxers are Killing Republicans," *Intercept,* accessed via WayBackMachine on April 10, 2023, https://web.archive.org /web/20221012000502/https:/theintercept.com/2022/10/10/covid-republi can-democrat-deaths/.

125 Jeffrey Jones, "U.S. Baby Boomers More Likely to Identify as Conservative," Gallup, January 29, 2015, https://news.gallup.com/poll/181325/baby-boom ers-likely-identify-conservative.aspx.

126 "The Generation Gap in American Politics," Pew Research, March 1, 2018, https://www.pewresearch.org/politics/2018/03/01/the-generation-gap -in-american-politics/.

127 Ian Sample, "Boys more at risk from Pfizer jab side-effect than Covid, suggests study," *Guardian,* September 1, 2021, https://www.theguardian.com /world/2021/sep/10/boys-more-at-risk-from-pfizer-jab-side-effect-than -covid-suggests-study; Jennifer Couzin-Frankel, "Heart risks, data gaps fuel debate over COVID-19 boosters for young people," *Science,* October 17, 2022, https://www.science.org/content/article/heart-risks-data-gaps-fuel-de bate-covid-19-boosters-young-people; Loanne Silberner, "COVID Vaccines in Teens and Myocarditis: What You Need to Know," NPR, June 23, 2021, https://www.npr.org/sections/health-shots/2021/06/17/1007447098/pfiz er-covid-vaccine-teens-symptoms-myocarditis.

128 Centers for Disease Control and Prevention, "Risk for COVID-19 Infection, Hospitalization, and Death By Age Group," April 25, 2023, https://www.cdc .gov/coronavirus/2019-ncov/covid-data/investigations-discovery/hospital ization-death-by-age.html.

129 Nigel Barber, "Why Red States Suffer Greater Obesity," *Psychology Today,* November 10, 2020, https://www.psychologytoday.com/us/blog/the-human -beast/202011/why-red-states-suffer-greater-obesity; Michael Shin and William McCarthy, "The association between county political inclination and obesity: Results from the 2012 presidential election in the United States," *National Library of Medicine* 57, no. 5 (August 28, 2013): 721–24, https://doi .org/10.1016/j.ypmed.2013.07.026; Ben Chapman, "Who's Healthier: Republicans or Democrats," Medium, September 28, 2017, https://extranewsfeed .com/whos-healthier-republicans-or-democrats-21dce4811bfa.

130 Centers for Disease Control and Prevention, *Obesity, Race/Ethnicity, and COVID-19*, accessed on April 15, 2023, https://www.cdc.gov/obesity/data/obesity-and-covid-19.html; Meredith Wadman, "Why COVID-19 is more deadly in people with obesity—even if they're young," *Science*, September 8, 2020, https://www.science.org/content/article/why-covid-19-more-deadly-people-obesity-even-if-theyre-young#:~:text=The%20biology%20of%20obesity%20includes,which%20can%20worsen%20COVID%2D19.

131 Benjamin Fearnow, "Conservative concern? Study finds Americans in 'red states' more likely to die early," StudyFinds, October 31, 2022, https://study finds.org/conservative-red-states-die-early/.

132 David Shepardson, "U.S. House plans vote to end foreign air traveler COVID vaccine mandate," Reuters, February 3, 2023, https://www.reuters.com /world/us/us-house-plans-vote-end-foreign-air-traveler-covid-vaccine-man date-2023-02-03/.

133 Spencer Kimball, "Biden administration plans to end Covid public health emergency in May," CNBC, January 30, 2023, https://www.cnbc .com/2023/01/30/biden-administration-plans-to-end-covid-public-health -emergency-on-may-11.html.

CHAPTER 12: THE IDEA OF KAMALA HARRIS

1 "Joe Biden and Kamala Harris Speech Transcript August 12: First Campaign Event as Running Mates," *Rev*, August 12, 2020, https://www.rev.com/blog /transcripts/joe-biden-and-kamala-harris-speech-transcript-august-12-first -campaign-event-as-running-mates.

2 Jessica Bennett, "What's It Like to Have Kamala Harris as 'Momala'? We Asked Her Stepkids," *New York Times*, January 17, 2021, https://www.nytimes .com/2021/01/17/us/politics/kamala-harris-stepmom-cole-ella-emhoff.html.

3 Mura Dominko, "Here's What Kamala Harris Likes to Eat (and Cook)," Yahoo News, October 19, 2020, https://www.yahoo.com/video/heres-kamala -harris-likes-eat-151030062.html.

4 Andrea Wurzburger, "Kamala Harris and Doug Emhoff's Relationship Timeline," *People*, September 18, 2022, https://people.com/politics/kamala -harris-doug-emhoff-relationship-photos/.

5 "Our ideology score placed Kamala Harris as the most liberal senator in 2019; what kinds of bills has she introduced?," GovTrack Insider, August 14, 2020, https://govtrackinsider.com/our-ideology-score-placed-kamala-harris-as -the-most-liberal-senator-in-2019-bbd25493ca72.

6 John Binder, "Report: Kamala Harris Promoted Bail Fund That Freed Six Domestic Abusers," Breitbart News, September 23, 2020, https://www .breitbart.com/law-and-order/2020/09/23/report-kamala-harris-promoted -bail-fund-freed-six-domestic-abusers/.

7 Alex Marlow, *Breaking the News* (New York: Simon & Schuster, 2021), 51.

8 Asma Khalid, "Democratic Sen. Kamala Harris Enters 2020 Presidential Race with a Call for Unity," NPR, January 21, 2019,https://www.npr .org/2019/01/21/687255705/democratic-sen-kamala-harris-enters-2020 -presidential-race-with-a-call-for-unity.

9 Open Secrets, "Kamala Harris," Fundraising Details for 2020 Election Cycle,

accessed June 13, 2023, https://www.opensecrets.org/2020-presidential-race
/kamala-harris/candidate?id=N00036915.

10 Elizabeth Elkind, "'You need to get to go and need to be able to get where
you need to go to do the work and go home': More word salad from Kamala in job development speech after her rambling answer on Dems abortion failure," *Daily Mail*, July 13, 2022, https://www.dailymail.co.uk/news/arti
cle-11011107/Kamala-Harris-stumbles-transportation-remark-job-develop
ment-speech-gaffe.html.

11 "Kamala Harris attacks Joe Biden's record on race in Democratic debate,"
YouTube video, 0:19, posted by Guardian News, June 28, 2019, https://www
.youtube.com/watch?v=S6-UC8yr0Aw.

12 Ali Swenson, "Kamala Harris did not call Joe Biden a racist on the debate stage," AP News, August 11, 2020, https://apnews.com/article
/fact-checking-9244041620; Devon Link, "Fact check: Video lacks context about Harris' debate criticism of Biden's record on race," *USA Today*,
February 17, 2021, https://www.usatoday.com/story/news/factcheck/2021
/02/17/fact-check-video-biden-harris-relationship-misses-vital-con
text/6769848002/; Philip Bump, "No, Kamala Harris didn't call Joe Biden a
racist," *Washington Post*, August 11, 2020, https://www.washingtonpost.com
/politics/2020/08/11/no-kamala-harris-didnt-call-joe-biden-racist/; Saranac Spencer, "Harris Hasn't Called Biden a 'Racist or a 'Rapist,' " FactCheck,
August 14, 2020, https://www.factcheck.org/2020/08/harris-hasnt-called
-biden-a-racist-or-a-rapist/.

13 Caroline Kelly, "Rep. Jim Clyburn says he urged Biden to choose a Black
woman as his running mate," CNN, November 7, 2020, https://www.cnn
.com/2020/11/07/politics/clyburn-biden-black-woman-running-mate-CN
Ntv/index.html.

14 Dara Kerr and Richard Nieva, "Vice President–elect Kamala Harris walks
a fine line with tech industry," CNET, November 7, 2020, https://www.cnet
.com/news/politics/vice-president-elect-kamala-harris-walks-a-fine-line
-with-tech-industry/.

15 RealClearPolitics, "General Election: Trump vs. Biden," polls, accessed
May 21, 2023, https://www.realclearpolitics.com/epolls/2020/president/us
/general_election_trump_vs_biden-6247.html.

16 Danny Hakim, Stephanie Saul, and Richard Oppel Jr., "'Top Cop' Kamala
Harris's Record of Policing the Police," *New York Times*, August 9, 2020,
https://www.nytimes.com/2020/08/09/us/politics/kamala-harris-policing
.html.

17 Donald Harris, *Capital Accumulation and Income Distribution* (Stanford, CA:
Stanford University Press, 1978), https://web.stanford.edu/~dharris/papers
/Capital%20Accumulation%20and%20Income%20Distribution.pdf; Ellen
Barry, "Kamala Harris's Father, a Footnote in Her Speeches, Is a Prominent
Economist," *New York Times*, November 7, 2020, https://www.nytimes.com
/article/kamala-harris-dad-don-harris.html.

18 Jesús Rodríguez, "What Kamala Harris' Law School Years Reveal About Her
Politics," *Politico*, August 18, 2021, https://www.politico.com/news/maga
zine/2021/08/18/kamala-harris-law-school-politics-503924.

19 Kamala Harris, "Kamala Harris: Serving as California's senator has been an

honor, but this is not a goodbye," *San Francisco Chronicle,* January 18, 2021, https://www.sfchronicle.com/opinion/openforum/article/Serving-as-Cali fornia-s-senator-has-been-an-15878708.php; Astead Herndon, "What Ka mala Harris Learned About Power at Howard," *New York Times,* October 14, 2020, https://www.nytimes.com/2020/10/14/us/politics/kamala-harris-how ard.html.

20 University of California College of Law, San Francisco, "LEOP Admissions," ac cessed May 14, 2023, https://www.uchastings.edu/admissions/leop-admissions/.

21 Kirsten Rogers, "A timeline of Kamala Harris' career," Ignite, November 7, 2020, https://ignitenational.org/blog/a-timeline-of-kamala-harris-career.

22 Ben Ashford, "How 29-year-old Kamala Harris began an affair with powerful San Francisco politician Willie Brown, then 60 and married, who appointed her to two lucrative positions only to dump her after he was voted first black mayor of the city," *Daily Mail,* August 13, 2020, https://www.dailymail.co.uk /news/article-8623781/Kamala-Harris-affair-San-Franciscos-black-may or-Willie-Brown.html.

23 Ben Christopher, "What California Knows About Kamala Harris," *North Coast Journal of Politics, People & Art,* August 11, 2020, https://www.northcoastjour nal.com/NewsBlog/archives/2020/08/11/what-california-knows-about-ka mala-harris.

24 David Horsey, "Willie Brown warns Villaraigosa 'Don't crowd Kamala!,' " *Baltimore Sun,* February 3, 2015, https://www.baltimoresun.com/opinion/bal -willie-brown-warns-villaraigosa-dont-crowd-kamala-20150202-story.html.

25 Katherine Rodriguez, "Peter Schweizer: Kamala Harris Gained 'Job Pro motions' and BMW 7 Series During Willie Brown Affair," Breitbart News, January 30, 2020, https://www.breitbart.com/clips/2020/01/30/peter-sch weizer-kamala-harris-gained-job-promotions-bmw-7-series-willie-brown -affair/.

26 Willie Brown, "Willie Brown: Sure, I dated Kamala Harris. So what?," SF Gate, January 25, 2019, https://www.sfgate.com/politics/article/Sure-I-dated -Kamala-Harris-So-what-13562972.php?t=c1bc437ba8&f.

27 David Siders, " 'Ruthless': How Kamala Harris Won Her First Race," *Po litico Magazine,* January 24, 2019, https://www.politico.com/magazine /story/2019/01/24/kamala-harris-2020-history-224126/.

28 Casey Tolan, "Campaign fact check: Here's how Kamala Harris really prose cuted marijuana cases," *Mercury News,* September 11, 2019, https://www.mer curynews.com/2019/09/11/kamala-harris-prosecuting-marijuana-cases/.

29 Hakim, Saul, and Oppel, " 'Top Cop' Kamala Harris."

30 Hakim, Saul, and Oppel, " 'Top Cop' Kamala Harris."

31 Hakim, Saul, and Oppel, " 'Top Cop' Kamala Harris."

32 David Mikkelson, "Did Kamala Harris Make These Contrasting Statements About Police?," Snopes, August 12, 2020, https://www.snopes.com/fact -check/kamala-harris-police-statements/.

33 Hakim, Saul, and Oppel, " 'Top Cop' Kamala Harris."

34 Hakim, Saul, and Oppel, " 'Top Cop' Kamala Harris."

35 Christopher Cadelago, "Kamala Harris rolls out broad plan for crimi nal justice reform," *Politico,* September 9, 2019, https://www.politico.com /story/2019/09/09/kamala-harris-criminal-justice-reform-1485443.

36 Cadelago, "Kamala Harris rolls out broad plan."

37 Houston Keene, "Minnesota bail fund promoted by Kamala Harris freed convict now charged with murder," Fox News, August 30, 2022, https://www.foxnews.com/politics/minnesota-bail-fund-promoted-kamala-harris-freed-convict-now-charged-murder.

38 Hannah Bleau, "Kamala Harris: It Is 'Outdated' and 'Wrongheaded' to View More Police as Only Way to Make Communities Safer," Breitbart News, September 23, 2020, https://www.breitbart.com/law-and-order/2020/09/23/kamala-harris-it-is-outdated-wrongheaded-view-more-police-only-way-make-communities-safer/.

39 David Lightman, "She once called herself California's 'top cop.' Where is Kamala Harris on police reform now?," Sacramento Bee, August 11, 2020, https://www.sacbee.com/article243906742.html.

40 Leena Kim, "A Look at All of Kamala Harris's Homes," Town & Country, January 22, 2021, https://www.townandcountrymag.com/leisure/real-estate/a33825054/kamala-harris-homes-real-estate-photos/.

41 Christopher Cadelago, " 'No discipline. No plan. No strategy': Kamala Harris campaign in meltdown," Politico, November 25, 2019, https://www.politico.com/news/2019/11/15/kamala-harris-campaign-2020-071105.

42 "Kamala Harris Sworn in to U.S. Senate," KPBS News, January 3, 2017, https://www.kpbs.org/news/politics/2017/01/03/kamala-harris-sworn-us-senate.

43 Jesse Rifkin, "Our ideology score placed Kamala Harris as the most liberal senator in 2019; what kinds of bills has she introduced?," GovTrack Insider, August 14, 2020, https://govtrackinsider.com/our-ideology-score-placed-kamala-harris-as-the-most-liberal-senator-in-2019-bbd25493ca72.

44 Joel Pollak, "Kamala Harris Led Smear Campaign Against Brett Kavanaugh," Breitbart News, August 12, 2020, https://www.breitbart.com/politics/2020/08/12/kamala-harris-led-smear-campaign-against-brett-kavanaugh/.

45 "Readers React: Sen. Feinstein was polite but effective in questioning Kavanaugh; Sen. Harris was just a bully," Los Angeles Times, September 11, 2018, https://www.latimes.com/opinion/readersreact/la-ol-le-feinstein-harris-kavanaugh-20180911-story.html.

46 Joe Garofoli and John Wildermuth, "Kamala Harris' viral grilling of Kavanaugh ends with a thud," SFGate, September 6, 2018, https://www.sfgate.com/politics/article/GOP-tries-to-help-Kavanaugh-after-tough-13210347.php?t=2f1850b55e.

47 John Nolte, "Nolte: 16 Reasons Why I Believe Joe Biden Sexually Assaulted Tara Reade," Breitbart News, April 26, 2020, https://www.breitbart.com/politics/2020/04/26/nolte-16-reasons-why-i-believe-joe-biden-sexually-assaulted-tara-reade/.

48 Max Moran, "Vice president candidate Sen. Kamala Harris (D-Calif.) has gone easy on Facebook and tech giants for years, and in her 2020 presidential bid she was rewarded with many maxed-out contributions from Silicon Valley executives," Sludge, July 21, 2020, https://readsludge.com/2020/07/21/kamala-harris-deep-history-of-letting-facebook-off-the-hook/.

49 Max Moran, "Kamala Harris' Deep History of Letting Facebook off the Hook," Sludge, July 21, 2020, https://readsludge.com/2020/07/21/kamala-harris-deep-history-of-letting-facebook-off-the-hook/.

50 Christopher Cadelago and Carla Marinucci, "Key Kamala Harris polit-ical consultant heads to top Airbnb post," *Politico,* September 4, 2020, https://www.politico.com/news/2020/09/04/kamala-harris-political-consultant-airbnb-409154;https://www.cnet.com/news/politics/vice-president-elect-kamala-harris-walks-a-fine-line-with-tech-industry/.

51 Dara Kerr and Richard Nieva, "Vice President–elect Kamala Harris walks a fine line with tech industry," CNET, November 7, 2020, https://www.cnet.com/news/politics/vice-president-elect-kamala-harris-walks-a-fine-line-with-tech-industry/.

52 Itay Hod, "Kamala Harris Has Hollywood Donors Fired up," Spectrum News 1, August 19, 2020, https://spectrumnews1.com/ca/la-west/politics/2020/08/19/kamala-harris-has-hollywood-donors-fired-up-; Gene Mad-daus, "Biden? Warren? Nope. Hollywood Swoons for . . . Kamala Harris," *Variety,* October 30, 2019, https://variety.com/2019/politics/news/kamala-harris-hollywood-contributions-1203384381/.

53 Richard Verrier, "California Attorney General Harris targets movie piracy ring," *Los Angeles Times,* June 14, 2013, https://www.latimes.com/entertainment/envelope/la-xpm-2013-jun-14-la-et-ct-mpaa-piracy-20130614-story.html.

54 Kim Hart and David McCabe, "Why Google and Facebook folded on sex-trafficking bill," *Axios,* November 8, 2017, https://www.axios.com/2017/12/15/why-google-and-facebook-folded-on-sex-trafficking-bill-1513306739.

55 Ted Johnson, "Hollywood Figures Help Raise $7 Million For Joe Biden–Kamala Harris Post-Convention Event; Jeffrey Katzenberg, George Cloo-ney Among Hosts," *Deadline,* August 21, 2020, https://deadline.com/2020/08/joe-biden-kamala-harris-fundraiser-george-clooney-jeffrey-katzenberg-1203020148/; Hod, "Hollywood Donors Fired up."

56 Lauren Egan, Gabe Gutierrez, and Dareh Gregorian, "Biden tasks Harris with 'stemming the migration' on southern border," NBC News, March 24, 2021, https://www.nbcnews.com/politics/white-house/biden-taps-harris-lead-coordination-efforts-southern-border-n1261952.

57 The White House, *National Strategy on Gender Equity and Equality,* accessed April 24, 2023, https://www.whitehouse.gov/wp-content/uploads/2021/10/National-Strategy-on-Gender-Equity-and-Equality.pdf.

58 Lester Hinds, "Kamala Harris pledges US $30m in funding for Jamaica," *Gleaner,* April 1, 2022, https://jamaica-gleaner.com/article/news/20220401/kamala-harris-pledges-us30m-funding-jamaica; Derrick Scott, "PM Holness: Jamaica Can Be an Economic Powerhouse with Help from US," *Caribbean Today,* April 8, 2022, https://www.caribbeantoday.com/sections/business-blog/pm-holness-jamaica-can-be-an-economic-powerhouse-with-help-from-us.

59 "Planning Institute of Jamaica hires growth expert," *Gleaner,* November 24, 2010, http://jamaica-gleaner.com/gleaner/20101124/business/business4.html; Wikipedia, s.v. "Donald J. Harris," last modified March 15, 2023 at 02:53, https://en.wikipedia.org/wiki/Donald_J._Harris#cite_note-4.

60 "Prof Donald Harris, father of US vice president, to receive Jamaica's third highest honour," *Jamaica Observer,* August 6, 2021, https://www.jamaicaobserver.com/latest-news/prof-donald-harris-father-of-us-vice-president-to-receive-jamaicas-third-highest-honour/.

61 Alexander Bolton, "Harris breaks 50-50 deadlock to advance landmark climate, tax, health bill," *The Hill,* August 6, 2022, https://thehill.com/homenews /senate/3591216-harris-breaks-50-50-deadlock-to-advance-landmark-climate-tax-health-bill/.

62 Eugene Daniels, "Kamala Harris wants to get out of D.C. more. But she literally can't," *Politico,* May 17, 2022, https://www.politico.com/news/2022/05/17 /kamala-harris-senate-ties-00032949.

63 Raphael Satter, "Kamala Harris says Trump not credible on possible COVID-19 vaccine," Reuters, September 15, 2020, https://www.reuters.com/article /health-coronavirus-usa-politics/kamala-harris-says-trump-not-credible -on-possible-covid-19-vaccine-idUSKBN25X01L.

64 Emily Cadei, "Kamala Harris emerges as voice of immigrant advocates," McClatchy DC, January 14, 2018, https://www.mcclatchydc.com/news/pol itics-government/white-house/article250143109.html; Edmund DeMarche, "Harris started 'politicization' of COVID-19 vaccines, Christie says," Fox News, September 12, 2021, https://www.foxnews.com/politics/harris-started -politicization-of-covid-19-vaccines-christie-says; Eugene Daniels, "Call in Kamala: Biden turns to the veep to sell Covid vax to communities of color," *Politico,* February 1, 2021, https://www.politico.com/news/2021/02/01/kamala -harris-vp-coronavirus-vaccine-464165.

65 Wendell Huesbø, "Kamala Harris Contradicts Fauci: 'We're Starting from Scratch' on COVID Vaccinations," Breitbart News, February 15, 2021, https:// www.breitbart.com/politics/2021/02/15/kamala-harris-contradicts-fauci -were-starting-from-scratch-on-covid-vaccinations/.

66 Allum Bokhari, "'Kind of a Fancy Thing:' 'AI Czar' Kamala Harris Meets with Civil Rights Leaders on 'Machine Learning Fairness,'" Breitbart News, July 13, 2023, https://www.breitbart.com/tech/2023/07/13/kind-of-a-fancy-thing-ai -czar-kamala-harris-meets-with-civil-rights-leaders-on-machine-learning -fairness/.

67 Brian Schwartz, "Vice President Harris announces $25 million for DNC voter registration efforts ahead of midterms," CNBC, July 8, 2021, https:// www.cnbc.com/2021/07/08/kamala-harris-to-announce-25-million-dnc-vot ing-program-investment.html.

68 Catherine Clifford, "Elon Musk: 'Mark my words—A.I. is far more dangerous than nukes," CNBC, March 13, 2018, https://www.cnbc.com/2018 /03/13/elon-musk-at-sxsw-a-i-is-more-dangerous-than-nuclear-weap ons.html.

69 Lucas Nolan, "1,000 AI Experts and Tech Leaders Call for Temporary Halt in Advanced AI Development," Breitbart News, March 29, 2023, https://www .breitbart.com/tech/2023/03/29/1000-ai-experts-and-tech-leaders-call-for -temporary-halt-in-advanced-ai-development/.

70 The White House, "FACT SHEET: Biden-?Harris Administration Announces New Actions to Promote Responsible AI Innovation that Protects Americans' Rights and Safety," May 4, 2023, https://www.whitehouse.gov/ostp /news-updates/2023/05/04/fact-sheet-biden-harris-administration-an nounces-new-actions-to-promote-responsible-ai-innovation-that-protects -americans-rights-and-safety/.

71 FiveThirtyEight, "Do Americans approve or disapprove of Kamala Harris?,"

poll data, accessed April 23, 2023, https://projects.fivethirtyeight.com/polls /approval/kamala-harris/.

72 Paul Hennessey, "DeSantis' GOP Support Declining in New NBC Poll," NBC-News, June 26, 2023, https://www.nbcnews.com/meet-the-press/first-read /desantis-gop-support-declining-new-nbc-poll-rcna91102.

CHAPTER 13: JOE BIDEN'S AMERICA, A SANCTUARY COUNTRY

1 Brandon Darby and Bob Price, "Rape Trees, Dead Migrants and the Consequences of an Unsecured Border," Breitbart News, April 25, 2016, https://www.breitbart.com/border/2016/04/25/rape-trees-dead-migrants-consequences-open-border/.

2 John Binder, "Analysis: Nearly 400K Anchor Babies Born Across U.S. Last Year, Exceeding Population of Cleveland," Breitbart News, January 5, 2023, https://www.breitbart.com/politics/2023/01/05/analysis-nearly-400k-anchor-babies-born-across-u-s-last-year-exceeding-population-of-cleveland/.

3 "Exit Polls 2016," CNN, 2016, accessed February 27, 2023, https://edition.cnn .com/election/2016/results/exit-polls.

4 Abby Budiman, Luis Noe-Bustamante, and Mark Hugo Lopez, "Naturalized Citizens Make Up One-in-Ten U.S. Eligible Voters in 2020," Pew Research Center, February 26, 2020, https://www.pewresearch.org/his panic/2020/02/26/naturalized-citizens-make-up-record-one-in-ten-u-s-eli gible-voters-in-2020/.

5 Brian Flood, "Soros takeover: FCC clears path for liberal group to buy Spanish-language conservative talk radio stations," Fox News, November 22, 2022, https://www.foxnews.com/media/soros-takeover-fcc-clears-path-liberal -group-buy-spanish-language-conservative-talk-radio-stations.

6 Latino Media Network, "Leadership," accessed May 31, 2023, https://lati nomedianetwork.com/leadership/; United States Department of Commerce, "Stephanie Valencia, Deputy Chief of Staff to the Secretary," accessed May 31, 2023, https://2010-2014.commerce.gov/About%20Commerce /Commerce%20Leadership/Stephanie%20Valencia,%20Deputy%20 Chief%20of%20Staff%20to%20the%20Secretary.html.

7 Chris Guiles, "Trump's wall: How much has been built during his term?," BBC News, January 12, 2021, https://www.bbc.com/news/world-us-can ada-46748492.

8 Alex Seitz-Wald, "Jay Leno: Call them 'undocumented democrats,'" Salon, April 3, 2013, https://www.salon.com/2013/04/03/jay_leno_call_them_un documented_democrats/.

9 Center for Immigration Studies, James Gimpel, "Immigration's Impact on Republican Political Prospects, 1980 to 2012," Backgrounder, April 15, 2014, https://cis.org/Immigrations-Impact-Republican-Political-Prospects -1980-2012.

10 Caroline May, "Sen. Grassley: DHS Must Hold Top Official Accountable for Acts of Democrat Favoritism," Breitbart News, March 27, 2015, https://www .breitbart.com/politics/2015/03/27/sen-grassley-dhs-must-hold-top-official -accountable-for-acts-of-democrat-favoritism/.

11 Proclamation No. 10142, 86 Fed. Reg. 7225 (Jan. 20, 2021), "Procla-

mation on the Termination of Emergency with Respect to the Southern Border of the United States and Redirection of Funds Diverted to Border Wall Construction," https://www.whitehouse.gov/briefing-room /presidential-actions/2021/01/20/proclamation-termination-of-emergency -with-respect-to-southern-border-of-united-states-and-redirection-of -funds-diverted-to-border-wall-construction/.

12 John Binder, "Mexican President AMLO Praises Biden for Halting Border Wall: 'Thank You,'" Breitbart News, January 10, 2023, https://www.breitbart.com /politics/2023/01/10/mexican-president-amlo-praises-biden-for-halting-bor der-wall-thank-you/; President Joseph Biden, Prime Minister Justin Trudeau, and President López Obrador, "Remarks by President Biden, Prime Minister Trudeau, and President López Obrador in Joint Conference," Mexico City, Mexico, National Palace, January 10, 2023, https://www.whitehouse.gov/brief ing-room/speeches-remarks/2023/01/10/remarks-by-president-biden-prime -minister-trudeau-and-president-lopez-obrador-in-joint-press-conference/.

13 Exec. Order No. 13, 993, 86 Fed. Reg. 7051 (Jan. 25, 2021), "Revision of Civil Immigration Enforcement Policies and Priorities," https://www.whitehouse .gov/briefing-room/presidential-actions/2021/01/20/executive-order-the-re vision-of-civil-immigration-enforcement-policies-and-priorities/; Rebecca Morin, "Biden administration to halt deportations for 100 days for undoc umented immigrants," USA Today, January 21, 2021, https://www.usatoday .com/story/news/politics/2021/01/21/biden-administration-halts-deporta tions-some-undocumented-immigrants-100-days/6663021002/.

14 Department of Homeland Security, "Secretary Mayorkas Announces New Immigration Enforcement Priorities," September 30, 2021, https://www.dhs .gov/news/2021/09/30/secretary-mayorkas-announces-new-immigra tion-enforcement-priorities.

15 Jaclyn Diaz, "Biden Suspends Deportations, Stops 'Remain in Mex ico' Policy," NPR, January 21, 2021, https://www.npr.org/sections /president-biden-takes-office/2021/01/21/959074750/biden-suspends-de portations-stops-remain-in-mexico-policy.

16 John Binder, "Data: Only 1.6% of 'Remain in Mexico' Migrants Have Valid Asylum Claims," Breitbart News, June 30, 2022, https://www.breitbart.com /politics/2022/06/30/data-only-1-6-of-remain-in-mexico-migrants-have -valid-asylum-claims/.

17 Binder, "Data: Only 1.6% of 'Remain in Mexico' Migrants."

18 Andrew Arthur, "CBP Document Details Mass Release of Illegal Aliens under Biden," Center for Immigration Studies, September 27, 2022, https://cis.org /Arthur/CBP-Document-Details-Mass-Release-Illegal-Aliens-under-Biden.

19 Bob Price, "100K Migrants Apprehended Last Month—Highest Feb. Total Since 2006," Breitbart News, March 10, 2021, https://www.breitbart.com/bor der/2021/03/10/100k-migrants-apprehended-last-month-highest-feb-total -since-2006/.

20 John Binder, "Nearly 9-in-10 Illegal Aliens Recently Released into U.S. Not Showing Up to Court Hearings," Breitbart News, May 30, 2019, https://www .breitbart.com/politics/2019/05/30/nearly-nine-in-ten-illegal-aliens-recently -released-into-u-s-not-showing-up-to-court-hearings/.

21 "Rising Border Encounters in 2021: An Overview and Analysis," Ameri-

can Immigration Council, March 4, 2022, https://www.americanimmigra
tioncouncil.org/rising-border-encounters-in-2021.

22 Annika Kim Constantino, "Vice President Kamala Harris unveils strategy to
address illegal immigration at the border," CNBC, July 29, 2021, https://www
.cnbc.com/2021/07/29/vice-president-kamala-harris-unveils-strategy-to-add
ress-illegal-immigration.html; Sara Schonhardt, "Climate change drives migrants
to U.S. border, Harris says," E&E News, May 6, 2021, https://www.eenews.net
/articles/climate-change-drives-migrants-to-u-s-border-harris-says/.Edward-

23 Isaac Dovere and Jasmine Wright, "Exasperation and dysfunction: Inside
Kamala Harris' frustrating start as vice president," CNN, November 18,
2021, https://www.cnn.com/2021/11/14/politics/kamala-harris-frustrating
-start-vice-president.

24 Michelle Lee, "Sen. Kamala Harris's claim that an 'undocumented immigrant is not a criminal,'" Washington Post, April 26, 2017, https://www
.washingtonpost.com/news/fact-checker/wp/2017/04/26/sen-kamala-har
riss-claim-that-an-undocumented-immigrant-is-not-a-criminal/.

25 Hearing on the Role of Immigration in Strengthening America's Economy
Before the Subcommittee on Immigration, Citizenship, Refugees, Border Security, and International Law, 111th Cong. 32 (2010) (statement of Steven
Camarota, Director of Research, Center for Immigration Studies), C-SPAN
video, 36:40, Center for Immigration Studies, September 30 2010, https://cis
.org/Testimony/Immigration-and-US-Economy.

26 George Borjas, "A User's Guide to the 2016 National Academy Report on 'The
Economic and Fiscal Consequences of Immigration,'" Harvard Kennedy
School, September 22, 2016, https://scholar.harvard.edu/files/gborjas/files
/nas2016.pdf.

27 Cameron Cawthorne, "Harris: 'Any Human Being' in U.S. Should Have Access
to Health Care, Public Education," Washington Free Beacon, May 12, 2019,
https://freebeacon.com/politics/harris-any-human-being-in-u-s-should
-have-access-to-health-care-public-education/.

28 "The Partnership for Central America Launches in Her Hands with Remarks
from Vice President Kamala Harris Alongside Summit of the Americas," Partnership for Central America, June 7, 2022, accessed via WayBackMachine on
May 31, 2023, https://web.archive.org/web/20220619082123/https://www
.centampartnership.org/mediacoverage/the-partnership-for-central-america
-launches-in-her-hands-with-remarks-from-vice-president-kamala-harris
-alongside-summit-of-the-americas.

29 "The Partnership for Central America Launches."

30 The White House, "Vice President Kamala Harris Announces New Commitments as Part of the Call to Action for the Private Sector to Deepen Investment
in Central America, Now Totaling Over $1.2 Billion," December 13, 2021,
https://www.whitehouse.gov/briefing-room/statements-releases/2021/12/13
/vice-president-kamala-harris-announces-new-commitments-as-part-of
-the-call-to-action-for-the-private-sector-to-deepen-investment-in-central
-america-now-totaling-over-1-2-billion/.

31 White House, "Vice President Kamala Harris Announces New Commitments."

32 White House, "Vice President Kamala Harris Announces New Commitments."

33 Manas Joshi, "US VP Kamala Harris announces USD 3.2 billion migration fund for Central American countries," Wion News, June 8, 2022, https://www.wionews.com/world/us-vp-kamala-harris-announces-usd-32-billion-migration-fund-for-central-american-countries-486093.

34 Emma Colton, "MS-13 gang member arrested for murder of 20-year-old Maryland woman with autism," Fox News, January 21, 2023, https://www.foxnews.com/us/ms-13-gang-member-arrested-murder-20-year-old-maryland-woman-autism?intcmp=tw_fnc.

35 John Binder, "Angel Mom: Illegal Alien MS-13 Gang Member Was Freed into U.S. at Border Before Murdering, Raping My Daughter," Breitbart News, February 5, 2023, https://www.breitbart.com/politics/2023/02/05/angel-mom-illegal-alien-ms-13-gang-member-was-freed-into-u-s-at-border-before-murdering-raping-my-daughter/.

36 Binder, "Angel Mom."

37 Bernadette Hogan and Craig McCarthy, "Four migrants bused to NYC arrested for shoplifting $12K from Macy's," New York Post, January 23, 2023, https://nypost.com/2023/01/23/four-migrants-arrested-for-shoplifting-12k-from-ny-macys/.

38 U.S. Department of State, "Press Statement by Secretary of State Antony K. Blinken: Suspending and Terminating the Asylum Cooperative Agreements with the Governments El Salvador, Guatemala, and Honduras," February 6, 2021, https://www.state.gov/suspending-and-terminating-the-asylum-cooperative-agreements-with-the-governments-el-salvador-guatemala-and-honduras/; John Binder, "Joe Biden to Dismantle Trump's Legal Wall, Inviting Central Americans to Southern Border," Breitbart News, December 22, 2020, https://www.breitbart.com/politics/2020/12/22/joe-biden-to-dismantle-trumps-legal-wall-inviting-central-americans-to-southern-border/.

39 John Hayward, "Trump Halts Aid to El Salvador, Guatemala, Honduras as Flood of Migrants Overwhelms Border Patrol," Breitbart News, March 31, 2019, https://www.breitbart.com/national-security/2019/03/31/trump-halts-aid-to-el-salvador-guatemala-honduras-as-flood-of-migrants-overwhelms-border-patrol/.

40 Neil Munro, "Donald Trump Creates Border Wall in Guatemala," Breitbart News, January 23, 2020, https://www.breitbart.com/politics/2020/01/23/donald-trump-creates-border-wall-in-guatemala/.

41 Spencer Lindquist, "Title 42 Is the 'Only Functioning Policy Preventing Illegal Immigration,' Border Advocates Say," Breitbart News, December 20, 2022, https://www.breitbart.com/immigration/2022/12/20/title-42-is-the-only-functioning-policy-preventing-illegal-immigration-border-advocates-say/.

42 Mark Penn, Dritan Nesho and Stephen Ansolabehere, "Most Voters Support Continuing Title 42," Harvard Capps Harris Poll, 41, December 14-15, 2022, https://harvardharrispoll.com/wp-content/uploads/2022/12/HHP_Dec2022_KeyResults.pdf.

43 Ian Hanchett, "Dem Rep. Gonzalez: Biden's 'Been Under a Lot of Pressure' from Activists to Lift Title 42, 'And Allow People In—They Don't Have a Plan," Breitbart News, December 20, 2022, https://www.breitbart.com/clips/2022/12/20/dem-rep-gonzalez-bidens-been-under-a-lot-of-pressure-from-activists-to-lift-title-42-and-allow-people-in-they-dont-have-a-plan/.

44 John Binder, "More than 1.2M Fugitive Illegal Aliens Remain Living Across U.S. Despite Having Final Deportation Orders," Breitbart News, January 3, 2023, https://www.breitbart.com/politics/2023/01/03/more-than-1-2m-fugitive-illegal-aliens-remain-living-across-u-s-despite-having-final-deportation-orders/.

45 Bob Price, "4.2 Million Migrants Apprehended Along Southwest Border Under Biden Admin," Breitbart News, January 21, 2023, https://www.breitbart.com/border/2023/01/21/4-2-million-migrants-apprehended-along-southwest-border-under-biden-admin-policies/.

46 John Binder, "Biden's Sanctuary Country: Fewer than 30K Illegal Aliens Deported from American Communities in 2022," Breitbart News, January 2, 2023, https://www.breitbart.com/politics/2023/01/02/bidens-sanctuary-country-fewer-30k-illegal-aliens-deported-american-communities-2022/.

47 John Binder, "Illegal Alien Convicts Arrested at Lowest Rate in Over Half a Decade," Breitbart News, January 2, 2023, https://www.breitbart.com/politics/2023/01/02/illegal-alien-convicts-arrested-at-lowest-rate-in-half-a-decade/.

48 Mireya Villareal, Nicole Sganga, and Camilo Montoya-Galvez, "Inside a Border Patrol facility holding 16 times more migrants than capacity," CBS News, March 31, 2021, https://www.cbsnews.com/news/immigration-border-patrol-migrant-holding-facility-over-capacity/.

49 Bob Price and Randy Clark, "53 Migrants Died in Abandoned Trailer in Texas Smuggling Incident," Breitbart News, June 27, 2022, https://www.breitbart.com/border/2022/06/27/42-migrants-found-dead-in-abandoned-trailer-in-texas-18-taken-to-hospital/.

50 Wendell Husebø, "Joe Biden Blames Republicans for Border Invasion, Claims Partisan Hostility Is Problem," Breitbart News, January 5, 2023, https://www.breitbart.com/politics/2023/01/05/joe-biden-blames-gop-border-invasion-claims-partisan-hostility-problem/.

51 John Binder, "Exclusive: Biden Using Air Marshals to Escort Border Crossers Ahead of Release into American Communities," Breitbart News, July 31, 2022, https://www.breitbart.com/politics/2022/07/31/exclusive-air-marshals-escorting-border-crossers-biden/.

52 John Binder, "Biden Warned to Stop Redirecting Air Marshals to Border as 'Major Security Incidents' Occur on Recent U.S. Flights," Breitbart News, December 1, 2022, https://www.breitbart.com/politics/2022/12/01/biden-warned-to-stop-redirecting-air-marshals-to-border-as-major-security-incidents-occur-on-recent-u-s-flights/.

53 Neil Munro, "GOP Rep. Pushes Bill to End Democrats' 'Cruel' Use of Migrant Workers," Breitbart News, March 22, 2023, accessed via United States Congressman Michael Burgess's website on June 1, 2023, https://burgess.house.gov/news/documentsingle.aspx?DocumentID=403660.

54 Steve Karnowski, "Meat plant cleaning service fined $1.5M for hiring minors," AP News, February 17, 2023, https://apnews.com/article/grand-island-us-department-of-labor-health-business-children-3afa3ace009791b8cf29fa91f2a8e6e4; Michael Levenson, "Food Safety Company Employed More Than 100 Children, Labor Officials Say," New York Times, February 17, 2023, https://www.nytimes.com/2023/02/17/business/child-labor-packers-sanitation.html.

55 Melissa Sanchez, "Inside the Lives of Immigrant Teens Working Dangerous Night Shifts in Suburban Factories," ProPublica, November 19, 2020, https://www.propublica.org/article/inside-the-lives-of-immigrant-teens-working-dangerous-night-shifts-in-suburban-factories.

56 Anne Zheng and Sean Tseng, "China's Role in Illicit Fentanyl Running Rampant on US Streets," *Epoch Times,* January 8, 2023, accessed via Congressman David Trone's website on June 1, 2023, https://trone.house.gov/2023/01/08/chinas-role-in-illicit-fentanyl-running-rampant-on-us-streets/#:~:text=Just%20two%20milligrams%20of%20the,in%20a%20pill%20or%20powder.

57 Bob Price, "CBP Seizes 6 Tons of Fentanyl in 2023, Nearly Matches 2022 Total," Breitbart News, February 21, 2023, https://www.breitbart.com/border/2023/02/21/cbp-seizes-6-tons-of-fentanyl-in-2023-nearly-matches-2022-total/.

58 Adam Shaw, "Border Patrol seizes enough fentanyl to kill 100 million Americans in under five months," Fox News, February 17, 2023, https://www.foxnews.com/politics/border-patrol-seizes-enough-fentanyl-kill-100-million-americans-under-five-months.

59 Price, "CBP Seizes 6 Tons of Fentanyl."

60 Senate Republican Policy Committee, "Substance Use Has Risen During Covid-19 Pandemic," March 15, 2022, https://www.rpc.senate.gov/policy-papers/substance-use-has-risen-during-covid-19-pandemic#:~:text=The%20COVID%2D19%20pandemic%20led,30%25%20from%20the%20year%20before.

61 Emma Goldberg, "'Relapsing Left and Right': Trying to Overcome Addiction in a Pandemic," *New York Times,* January 4, 2021, https://www.nytimes.com/2021/01/04/nyregion/addiction-treatment-coronavirus-new-york-new-jersey.html.

62 Centers for Disease Control and Prevention, Lauren Tanz, Amanda Dinwiddie, Christine Mattson, Julie O'Donnell, and Nicole Davis, "Drug Overdose Deaths Among Persons Aged 10–19 Years—United States, July 2019–December 2021," *Morbidity and Mortality Weekly Report* 71 (December 16, 2022): 1576–82, http://dx.doi.org/10.15585/mmwr.mm7150a2.

63 National Institute on Drug Abuse, *Drug Overdose Death Rates,* February 9, 2023, https://nida.nih.gov/research-topics/trends-statistics/overdose-death-rates.

64 Ian Hanchett, "CDC: Parents 'Should Consider Carrying Naloxone Around' to Reverse Overdoses," Breitbart News, September 28, 2022, https://www.breitbart.com/clips/2022/09/28/cdc-parents-should-consider-carrying-naloxone-around-to-reverse-overdoses/.

65 Emily Reyes, "L.A. students will be able to carry Narcan in schools under updated policy," *Los Angeles Times,* February 1, 2023, https://12ft.io/proxy?q=https%3A%2F%2Fwww.latimes.com%2Fcalifornia%2Fstory%2F2023-02-01%2Fl-a-students-will-be-able-to-carry-narcan-in-schools.

66 John Binder, "Exclusive: Ohio Rep. Brad Wenstrup Issues Plan Declaring Fentanyl a WMD Against American Citizens," Breitbart News, October 6, 2022, https://www.breitbart.com/politics/2022/10/06/exclusive-ohio-rep-brad-wenstrup-issues-plan-declaring-fentanyl-a-wmd-against-american-cit

izens/; United States Congress, House, Fentanyl Is a WMD Act, HR 8030, 117th Cong., Sess. 2, introduced in House June 14, 2022, https://www.con gress.gov/bill/117th-congress/house-bill/8030/text?r=7&s=1.

67 Tom Garris, "Butler County terminates 'sanctuary county' designation," WTAE Pittsburgh, February 21, 2023, https://www.wtae.com/article/but ler-county-terminates-sanctuary-county-designation/43009697.

68 Patrick McLaughlin and Jonathan Nelson, "There's nothing biblical about 180,000 pages of federal regulations," *The Hill,* December 15, 2017, https:// thehill.com/opinion/white-house/365122-theres-nothing-biblical-about -180000-pages-of-federal-regulations/.

69 Awr Hawkins, "AP: At Least 1,200 Second Amendment Sanctuaries Across Country," Breitbart News, July 14, 2021, https://www.breitbart.com/poli tics/2021/07/14/ap-at-least-1200-second-amendment-sanctuaries-across -country/.

70 Jessica Vaughan and Bryan Griffith, "Map: Sanctuary Cities, Counties, and States," Center for Immigration Studies, https://cis.org/Map-Sanctuary-Cit ies-Counties-and-States.

71 San Francisco Office of the Mayor, "We Are a Sanctuary City," accessed June 1, 2023, https://sfmayor.org/sanctuary-city.

72 Trisha Thadani, "Undocumented fentanyl dealers in S.F. could be easier to de-port under new proposal," *San Francisco Chronicle,* February 14, 2023, https:// www.sfchronicle.com/sf/article/fentanyl-dealers-crime-sf-deport-immigra tion-17782315.php.

73 Joe Rubino and Nick Coltrain, "Nearly 150 migrants unexpectedly dropped in downtown Denver, prompting city to open emergency shelter," *Denver Post,* accessed via Archive.today on March 13, 2023, https://archive.vn/olG2y.

74 John Binder, "Watch: Busloads of Migrants Arrive at Kamala Harris's Home on Christmas Eve," Breitbart News, December 26, 2022, https://www.breit bart.com/politics/2022/12/26/watch-busloads-migrants-arrive-kamala-har ris-s-home-christmas-eve/.

75 John Binder, "Democrats: 'Piece of Sh*t' Greg Abbott 'Belongs in Prison' for Busing Migrants to VP Kamala Harris's Home in Freezing Cold," Breitbart News, December 26, 2022, https://www.breitbart.com/politics/2022/12/26 /democrats-greg-abbott-busing-migrants-christmas-eve/.

76 Pam Key, "CNN's Jake Tapper: Are Abbott, DeSantis 'Trolling' by Bussing Migrants?," Breitbart News, September 18, 2022, https://www.breitbart.com /clips/2022/09/18/CNNs-jake-tapper-are-abbott-desantis-trolling-by-bus sing-migrants/.

77 Jordan Dixon-Hamilton, "Florida Gov. Ron DeSantis Sends Planes Full of Il-legal Immigrants to Obama's Vacation Spot in Martha's Vineyard," Breitbart News, September 14, 2023, https://www.breitbart.com/politics/2022/09/14 /florida-gov-ron-desantis-sends-planes-illegal-immigrants-obamas-vaca tion-spot-marthas-vineyard/; Monique Valeris and Leena Kim, "President Obama Has Canceled His 60th Birthday Bash at His Martha's Vineyard Man-sion," *Town & Country,* August 4, 2021, https://www.townandcountrymag .com/leisure/real-estate/a30169311/barack-michelle-obama-buy-marthas -vineyard-house/.

78 John Binder, "Data: Majority of Migrants in NYC Still in Shelters After Arriv-

ing on Buses," Breitbart News, February 15, 2023, https://www.breitbart.com /politics/2023/02/15/data-majority-of-migrants-in-nyc-still-in-shelters-af ter-arriving-on-buses/.

79 Binder, "Data: Majority of Migrants."

80 Neil Munro, "Tom Homan: Gov. Abbott's Buses Expose Biden's Open Borders," Breitbart News, August 20, 2022, https://www.breitbart.com /economy/2022/08/20/tom-homan-gov-abbotts-bussing-strategy-spotlights -bidens-open-border/.

81 Munro, "Tom Homan: Gov. Abbott's Buses."

82 Bob Price, "Construction to Begin on Border Barrier in Arizona," Breitbart News, January 10, 2023, https://www.breitbart.com/border/2023/01/10/con struction-to-begin-on-border-barrier-in-arizona/.

83 Bob Price, "Potemkin Village: Officials Clear Homeless Migrants from El Paso Streets Ahead of Biden Visit," Breitbart News, January 8, 2023, https://www .breitbart.com/border/2023/01/08/potemkin-village-officials-clear-home less-migrants-from-el-paso-streets-ahead-of-biden-visit/.

84 Joel Pollak, "Fact Check: Karine Jean-Pierre Falsely Claims Biden Has Vis- ited Border," Breitbart News, November 30, 2022, https://www.breitbart.com /politics/2022/11/30/fact-check-karine-jean-pierre-falsely-claims-biden -has-visited-border/.

85 Joel Pollak, "Biden Chooses 'Wall' for Photo of First Border Visit—After End- ing Trump's Project," Breitbart News, January 9, 2023, https://www.breitbart .com/politics/2023/01/09/biden-chooses-wall-for-photo-of-first-border-vis it-after-ending-trumps-project/.

86 Bob Price and Randy Clark, "No Apology from Biden One Year After Falsely Accusing Horse-Mounted Border Patrol Agents of 'Strapping' Mi- grants," Breitbart News, September 25, 2022, https://www.breitbart.com /border/2022/09/25/no-apology-from-biden-one-year-after-falsely-accus ing-horse-mounted-border-patrol-agents-of-strapping-migrants/.

87 United States Department of Homeland Security, "Walls Work," December 12, 2018, https://www.dhs.gov/news/2018/12/12/walls-work.

88 United States Customs and Border Protection, "Walls Work," updated February 3, 2021, https://www.cbp.gov/newsroom/video-gallery/video-li brary/walls-work.

89 Jessica Chasmar, "Biden heads back to Delaware beach house, where he's building $500K taxpayer-funded security fence," Fox News, August 19, 2022, https://www.foxnews.com/politics/biden-heads-back-delaware-beach -house-building-500k-taxpayer-funded-security-fence.

CHAPTER 14: SLOUCHING TOWARD LAWLESSNESS

1 Thomas Fuller and Sharon LaFraniere, "In San Francisco, a Troubled Year at a Whole Foods Market Reflects a City's Woes," New York Times, April 30, 2023, https://www.nytimes.com/2023/04/30/us/san-francisco-whole-foods-crime -economy.html.

2 Sean Moran, "San Francisco Target Puts Inventory on Lockdown amid Crime Spree," Breitbart News, April 24, 2023, https://www.breitbart.com /crime/2023/04/24/san-francisco-target-puts-inventory-lockdown-crime-spree/.

3 Caroline McCaughey, "Williams-Sonoma to Close at San Francisco, as Residents Debate Whether the City Is in a 'Doom Loop,'" *New York Sun*, May 22, 2023, https://www.nysun.com/article/williams-sonoma-to-close-in -san-francisco-as-residents-debate-whether-the-city-is-in-a-doom-loop.

4 McCaughey, "Williams-Sonoma to Close."

5 Mike Murphy, "Westfield surrenders keys to downtown San Francisco shopping mall to lender," *Market Watch*, June 12, 2023, https://www.marketwatch .com/story/westfield-surrenders-keys-to-downtown-san-francisco-shop ping-mall-to-lender-80348f71.

6 Ian Hanchett, "CNN's Sidner: Drug Users Come to San Francisco Because of Lax Laws, COVID Shutdowns a Factor in Homeless Problem," Breitbart News, May 13, 2023, https://www.breitbart.com/clips/2023/05/13/CNNs -sidner-drug-users-come-to-san-francisco-because-of-lax-laws-covid-shut downs-a-factor-in-homeless-problem/.

7 Trisha Thadani and Kevin Fagan, "Horrific new street drug 'tranq' found in S.F. overdose victims, showing dangerous shift in supply," *San Francisco Chronicle*, February 16, 2023, https://www.sfchronicle.com/sf/article/horrif ic-new-street-drug-tranq-found-s-f-17787084.php.

8 Elizabeth Weil, "Spiraling in San Francisco's Doom Loop: What it's like to live in a city that no longer believes its problems can be fixed," *Curbed*, May 10, 2023, https://www.curbed.com/2023/05/san-francisco-doom-loop.html.

9 Roland Li, Noah Arroyo, "Cities are struggling. San Francisco could be in for the biggest 'doom loop' of all," *San Francisco Chronicle*, March 30, 2023, https://www.sfchronicle.com/sf/article/city-economy-doom-loop-17846412 .php.

10 Terry Castleman, "Federal court slows a California ban on natural gas appliances," *Los Angeles Times*, April 17, 2023, https://www.latimes.com /california/story/2023-04-17/natural-gas-debate-heats-up-as-federal-appeals -courtstrikes-down-berkeley-ban.

11 Annie Gaus, "San Francisco's Deficit Swells to $780M in Latest Sign of Budget Distress," *San Francisco Standard*, March 31, 2023, https://sfstandard.com /politics/city-hall/san-franciscos-deficit-swells-to-780m-in-latest-sign-of -budget-distress/.

12 Christopher Wray, "America's crime problem is real. Tackling it requires respect for cops," Fox News, January 5, 2023, https://www.foxnews.com/opin ion/america-crime-problem-real-tackling-requires-respect-cops.

13 Arah Elbeshbishi and Mabinty Quarshie, "Fewer than 1 in 5 support 'defund the police' movement, *USA Today*/Ipsos Poll finds," *USA Today*, March 7, 2021, https://www.usatoday.com/story/news/politics/2021/03/07/usa-today -ipsos-poll-just-18-support-defund-police-movement/4599232001/.

14 Emily Jacobs, "Only 17% of black voters support defunding the police: Poll," *Washington Examiner*, October 30, 2022, https://www.washingtonexaminer .com/news/crime/thegrio-kff-survey-black-voters-17-percent-support-de funding-police.

15 Richard Rosenfeld, Bobby Boxerman, and Ernesto Lopez, *Pandemic, Social Unrest, and Crime in U.S. Cities: Mid-Year 2022 Update* (Washington, DC: Council on Criminal Justice, 2022), https://counciloncj.org/mid-year-2022-crime-trends/.

16 Rosenfeld, Boxerman, and Lopez, *Pandemic, Social Unrest, and Crime.*

17 Rosenfeld, Boxerman, and Lopez, *Pandemic, Social Unrest, and Crime.*

18 Jenifer Warren, "Homicides, Gun Assaults Fall Modestly in Major U.S. Cities as Robberies Spike," Council on Criminal Justice, July 28, 2022, https:// counciloncj.org/mid-year-2022-crime-pr/; United States Department of Justice, Office of Justice Programs, Alexandra Thompson and Susannah Tapp, *Criminal Victimization, 2021,* September 2022, https://bjs.ojp.gov/content /pub/pdf/cv21.pdf.

19 Warren, "Homicides, Gun Assaults Fall Modestly; United States Department of Justice, *Criminal Victimization, 2021.*

20 Major Cities Chiefs Association (website), Philadelphia Web Design, accessed May 14, 2023, https://majorcitieschiefs.com/.

21 Jorge L. Ortiz, "Homicides down but violent crime increased in major US cities, midyear survey says," *USA Today,* September 11, 2022, https://www .usatoday.com/story/news/nation/2022/09/11/united-states-major-cities-vi olent-crime-homicides-survey/8060734001/.

22 Laura Cooper, "Violent Crime Survey—National Totals, Midyear Comparison January 1 to June 30, 2022, and 2021," accessed May 21, 2023, https:// majorcitieschiefs.com/wp-content/uploads/2022/08/MCCA-Violent-Crime -Report-2022-and-2021-Midyear.pdf.

23 Jeffrey Anderson, "Criminal Neglect," *City Journal,* October 4, 2022, https:// www.city-journal.org/violent-crime-in-cities-on-the-rise.

24 Charles Stimson, Zack Smith, and Kevin Dayaratna, "The Blue City Murder Problem," Heritage Foundation, November 4, 2022, https://www.heritage .org/crime-and-justice/report/the-blue-city-murder-problem.

25 Open Secrets, "Who are the Biggest Donors?," accessed May 24, 2023, https:// www.opensecrets.org/elections-overview/biggest-donors.

26 "George Soros' quiet overhaul of the U.S. justice system," *Politico,* August 30, 2016, https://www.politico.com/story/2016/08/george-soros-criminal-justice -reform-227519.

27 Ashley Harding and Brie Isom, "Florida crime rate drops for record 50-year low: Report," News4Jax, December 1, 2022, https://www.news4jax.com/news /local/2022/12/01/florida-crime-rate-drops-for-record-50-year-low-report/.

28 Matt Palumbo, "George Soros spent $40M getting lefty district attorneys, officials elected all over the country," *New York Post,* January 22, 2023, https:// nypost.com/2023/01/22/george-soros-spent-40m-getting-lefty-district-at torneys-officials-elected-all-over-the-country/.

29 Stimson, Smith, and Dayaratna, "The Blue City Murder Problem."

30 Stimson, Smith, and Dayaratna, "The Blue City Murder Problem."

31 United States Senator Marsha Blackburn and United States Senator Bill Hagerty to United States President Joseph Biden, September 14, 2022, https:// www.blackburn.senate.gov/services/files/1315770B-6C35-4023-BF39 -2BD1E5DDA99C.

32 Andy Sher, "Tennessee Senators Urge Biden to Tackle Crime Epidemic," Governing, September 15, 2022, https://www.governing.com/now/tennes see-senators-urge-biden-to-tackle-crime-epidemic.

33 Megan Brenan, "Record-High 56% in U.S. Perceive Local Crime Has Increased," Gallup, October 28, 2022, https://news.gallup.com/poll/404048/re cord-high-perceive-local-crime-increased.aspx.

34 Brian Sozzi, "Target: 'Organized retail crime' has driven $400 million in extra profit loss this year," Yahoo Finance, November 16, 2022, https://finance.yahoo.com/news/target-organized-retail-crime-400-million-profits-113006396.html.

35 Jennifer Kingson, "Shoplifting reaches crisis proportions," *Axios,* February 11, 2022, https://www.axios.com/2022/02/11/shoplifting-retail-crisis-online-resale.

36 John Carney, "Biden Crime Wave: Target Reports $400 Million in Looting Losses," Breitbart News, November 16, 2022, https://www.breitbart.com/economy/2022/11/16/biden-crime-wave-target-reports-400-million-in-looting-losses/.

37 National Retail Federation and Loss Prevention Research Council, "2022 Retail Security Survey," Appriss Retail, accessed May 27, 2023, https://cdn.nrf.com/sites/default/files/2022-09/National%20Retail%20Security%20Survey%20Organized%20Retail%20Crime%202022.pdf.

38 "2022 Retail Security Survey."

39 "2022 Retail Security Survey."

40 "2022 Retail Security Survey."

41 Jessica VandenHouten, "Jewelers Mutual Group Spearheads Movement to Reduce Jewelry Crime," Jewelers Mutual, December 1, 2022,?https://www.jewelersmutual.com/newsroom/partner-for-protection-movement.

42 John Phillips, "Can LAPD Chief Michel Moore finally get serious about crime in Los Angeles?," *Los Angeles Daily News,* February 16, 2023, https://www.dailynews.com/2023/02/16/can-lapd-chief-michel-moore-finally-get-serious-about-crime-in-los-angeles/.

43 Awr Hawkins, "Joe Biden Admitted in 1985 Criminals Will Get Firearms 'With or Without Gun Control,' " Breitbart News, June 3, 2022, https://www.breitbart.com/politics/2022/06/03/joe-biden-admitted-in-1985-criminals-will-get-firearms-with-or-without-gun-control/.

44 Michael Lee and Emma Colton, "States with higher rate of gun ownership do not correlate with more gun murders, data show," Fox News, June 30, 2022, https://www.foxnews.com/us/states-higher-rate-gun-ownership-not-correlate-more-gun-murders-data-show.

45 Evan Simko-Bednarski, "Indiana mall hero Elisjsha Dicken returned fire just 15 seconds into mass shooting," *New York Post,* July 19, 2022, https://nypost.com/2022/07/19/indiana-mall-hero-elisjsha-dicken-returned-fire-just-15-seconds-into-shooting/; NRA (@NRA), "NEW DETAILS[.] The Greenwood Park Mall shooter began firing at 5:56:48PM. 15 SECONDS LATER, at 5:57:03, 22-year-old Eli Dicken carrying under the new NRA-BACKED Constitutional Carry law, fired 10 rounds from 40 yards, hitting the shooter 8 times. The shooter collapsed & died," Twitter, July 19, 2022, 3:56 p.m., https://twitter.com/NRA/status/1549528645231943686.

46 Allie Griffin, "Police identify 3 victims, their killer and 'hero' bystander in Indiana mall shooting," *New York Post,* July 19, 2022, https://nypost.com/2022/07/19/elisjsha-dicken-killed-indiana-mall-shooter-jonathan-sapirman/.

47 Danielle Scruggs and Tara Jakeway, "Man shot, killed after threatening to open fire at party in West Palm Beach," 24WPBF, August 9, 2022, https://

www.wpbf.com/article/florida-west-palm-beach-man-shot-at-party-investigation/40839497.

48 Awr Hawkins, "FACT CHECK: Gun Owners of America Spokeswoman Claims '94 Percent of Mass Shootings Occur in Gun-Free Zones,' " Breitbart News, July 27, 2022, https://www.breitbart.com/politics/2022/07/27/fact-check-gun-owners-america-spokeswoman-claims-94-percent-mass-shootings-occur-gun-free-zones/.

49 Hawkins, "FACT CHECK."

50 Haley Lerner, "David Hogg talks gun control at the Boston Public Library," Boston University News Service, October 19, 2018, https://bunewsservice.com/david-hogg-talks-gun-control-at-the-boston-public-library/; Trent Baker, "David Hogg: Saying Good Guy with a Gun Stops Bad Guy with a Gun Is Utilized to Sell You Two Guns," Breitbart News, October 28, 2022, https://www.breitbart.com/clips/2018/10/28/david-hogg-saying-good-guy-with-a-gun-stops-bad-guy-with-a-gun-is-utilized-to-sell-you-two-guns/.

51 Glenn Kessler, "Biden's false claim that the 2nd Amendment bans cannon ownership," Washington Post, June 28, 2021, https://www.washingtonpost.com/politics/2021/06/28/bidens-false-claim-that-2nd-amendment-bans-cannon-ownership/.

52 Rob Crilly, " 'You think the deer are wearing a Kevlar vest?' Biden goes off script as he calls for a ban on assault rifles and high-capacity magazines in State of the Union speech," Daily Mail, March 2, 2022, https://www.dailymail.co.uk/news/article-10567773/Biden-goes-script-calls-ban-assault-rifles-high-capacity-magazines.html.

53 "Ban on assault weapons didn't reduce violence," Washington Times, August 16, 2004, https://www.washingtontimes.com/news/2004/aug/16/20040816-114754-1427r/.

54 The Post Millennial (@TPostMillennial), "Biden: "What in God's name do you need an assault weapon for? It's an assault weapon designed to kill people, to defend America, to defend people," Twitter, September 23, 2022, 10:31 a.m., https://twitter.com/TPostMillennial/status/1573364406112632832?

55 Awr Hawkins, "Joe Biden Pushing to Limit Gun Owners to 'Eight Bullets in a Round,' " Breitbart News, October 24, 2022, https://www.breitbart.com/politics/2022/10/24/joe-biden-pushing-limit-gun-owners-eight-bullets-round/.

56 Awr Hawkins, "Biden Quotes Scripture, Vows to 'Limit the Number of Bullets That Can Be in a Cartridge,' " Breitbart News, December 7, 2022, https://www.breitbart.com/politics/2022/12/07/biden-quotes-scripture-vows-limit-number-bullets-cartridge/.

57 Awr Hawkins, "Biden Pushes Gun Control, Releases Convicted Arms Dealer in Prisoner Swap, All in Same Day," Breitbart News, February 15, 2023, https://www.breitbart.com/politics/2022/12/08/biden-pushes-gun-control-releases-convicted-arms-dealer-prisoner-swap-all-same-day/.

58 Hawkins, "Biden Pushes."

59 Awr Hawkins, "The 15 GOP Senators Who Caved and Voted 'Yes' on Gun Control," Breitbart News, June 24, 2022, https://www.breitbart.com/politics/2022/06/24/15-gop-senators-who-caved-voted-yes-gun-control/; Awr Hawkins, "Senate Unveils Language of Gun Control Deal: Expands Background Checks, Expands Prohibited Purchasers," Breitbart News, June 21,

2022,https://www.breitbart.com/politics/2022/06/21/senate-unveils-lan guage-gun-control-deal-expands-background-checks/.

60 Tanya Lewis, "The 'Shared Psychosis' of Donald Trump and His Loyalists," *Scientific American,* January 11, 2021, https://www.scientificamerican.com /article/the-shared-psychosis-of-donald-trump-and-his-loyalists/.

61 Lisa Feldman Barrett, "When Is Speech Violence?," *New York Times,* July 14, 2017, https://www.nytimes.com/2017/07/14/opinion/sunday/when -is-speech-violence.html.

62 "Silence is Violence: Black Lives Matter," Global Integrity, June 5, 2020, https:// www.globalintegrity.org/2020/06/05/blacklivesmatter/.

63 Charlie Spiering, "Joe Biden Celebrates Republican Cave on Gun Control: 'We've Finally Moved that Mountain,' " Breitbart News, July 11, 2022, https:// www.breitbart.com/politics/2022/07/11/joe-biden-celebrates-republican -cave-on-gun-control-weve-finally-moved-that-mountain/.

64 "Biden-Thurmond Violent Crime Control Act of 1991," S.1241 – 102nd congress, 1st session, congressional record 169, (1991-1992), H.R. 3371, https://www.congress.gov/bill/102nd-congress/senate-bill/1241/text; Clifford Krauss, "Bush Threatens to Veto Crime Bill, Saying It's Too Soft on Defendants," *New York Times,* November 26, 1991, https://www.nytimes .com/1991/11/26/us/bush-threatens-to-veto-crime-bill-saying-it-s-too-soft -on-defendants.html.

65 "Violent Crime Control and Law Enforcement Act of 1993," S.1488 – 103rd Congress, 1st session, congressional record 113 (1993-1994), https://www .congress.gov/bill/103rd-congress/senate-bill/1488.

66 Udi Ofer, "How the 1994 Crime Bill Fed the Mass Incarceration Crisis," American Civil Liberties Union, June 4, 2019, https://www.aclu.org/news /smart-justice/how-1994-crime-bill-fed-mass-incarceration-crisis.

67 Elise Viebeck, "How an early Biden crime bill created the sentencing disparity for crack and cocaine trafficking," *Washington Post,* July 28, 2019, https://www.washingtonpost.com/politics/how-an-early-biden-crime -bill-created-the-sentencing-disparity-for-crack-and-cocaine-trafficking /2019/07/28/5cbb4c98-9dcf-11e9-85d6-5211733f92c7_story.html.

68 Clifford Krauss, "Bush Threatens to Veto Crime Bill, Saying It's Too Soft on Defendants," *New York Times,* November 26, 1991, https://www.nytimes .com/1991/11/26/us/bush-threatens-to-veto-crime-bill-saying-it-s-too-soft -on-defendants.html.

69 Viebeck, "How an early Biden crime bill."

70 Lauren-Brooke Eisen and Inimai Chettiar, "Analysis: The complex history of the controversial 1994 crime bill," MSNBC, April 14, 2016, https://www .msnbc.com/msnbc/analysis-the-complex-history-the-controversial-1994 -crime-bill-msna832401.

71 Viebeck, "How an early Biden crime bill."

72 Charlie Spiering, "Joe Biden: 'Mistakes Were Made' in My Nineties-Era Anti-Crime Bills," Breitbart News, May 14, 2019, https://www.breitbart.com /politics/2019/05/14/joe-biden-mistakes-were-made-in-my-nineties-era-an ti-crime-bills/.

73 Hannah Bleau, "Joe Biden Admits 1994 Crime Bill Was a 'Mistake' During Town Hall," Breitbart News, October 15, 2020, https://www.breitbart.com

/law-and-order/2020/10/15/joe-biden-admits-1994-crime-bill-was-mistake
-during-town-hall/.

74 Matt Viser and Sean Sullivan, "Biden announces criminal justice policy
    sharply at odds with his '94 crime law," *Washington Post,* July 23, 2019, https://
    www.washingtonpost.com/politics/biden-announces-criminal-justice-poli
    cy-sharply-at-odds-with-his-94-crime-law/2019/07/23/950e7eb0-acc2-11e9
    -a0c9-6d2d7818f3da_story.html.

75 Ankush Khardori, "The Merrick Garland You Don't Know," *Politico,*
    January 15, 2023, https://www.politico.com/news/magazine/2023/01/15/mer
    rick-garland-donald-trump-00066769.

76 Sadie Gurman and Aruna Viswanatha, "FBI Tracks Threats Against Teachers,
    School-Board Members," *Wall Street Journal,* November 16, 2021, https://www
    .wsj.com/articles/fbi-tracks-threats-against-teachers-school-board-mem
    bers-11637092957?st=nuzewliq1bd6wps&reflink=desktopwebshare_twitter.

77 Luke Rosiak, "Loudoun County Schools Tried to Conceal Sexual Assault
    Against Daughter in Bathroom, Father Says," *Daily Wire,* accessed May 24,
    2023,   https://www.dailywire.com/news/loudoun-county-schools-tried-to
    -conceal-sexual-assault-against-daughter-in-bathroom-father-says.

78 Rosiak, "Loudoun County Schools."

79 Mary Olohan, "3 Takeaways from AG Garland's House Panel Testimony on
    Virginia School Rape Case," *Daily Signal,* October 21, 2021, https://www
    .dailysignal.com/2021/10/21/3-takeaways-from-ag-garlands-house-panel
    -testimony-on-virginia-school-rape-case-conflict-of-interest/.

80 "Attacks on Churches, Pro-Life Organizations, Property, and People Since the
    Dobbs Leak on May 2, 2022 (as of 5/19/23)," Family Research Council, ac-
    cessed May 25, 2023, https://downloads.frc.org/EF/EF22F17.pdf.

81 Jessica Chasmar, "More than 100 pro-life orgs, churches attacked since Dobbs
    leak," Fox News, October 20, 2022, https://www.foxnews.com/politics/100
    -pro-life-orgs-churches-attacked-dobbs-leak.

82 United States Department of Justice, "Recent Cases on Violence Against Re-
    productive Health Care Providers," accessed May 24, 2023, https://www.justice
    .gov/crt/recent-cases-violence-against-reproductive-health-care-providers.

83 Alexander Marlow, "Summer of Rage, Part VI: Biden Administration Ignores
    Systematic Attack on Religious Communities in Wake of Dobbs Leak," Breit-
    bart News, August 20, 2022, https://www.breitbart.com/politics/2022/08/20
    /summer-of-rage-part-vi-biden-administration-ignores-systematic-attack
    -on-religious-communities-in-wake-of-dobbs-leak/.

84 Mark Sherman, Michael Balcamo, and Michael Kunzelman, "Armed man ar-
    rested for threat to kill Justice Kavanaugh," AP News, June 8, 2022, https://
    apnews.com/article/us-supreme-court-brett-kavanaugh-district-of-co
    lumbia-maryland-government-and-politics-179d18e7f933b3decbaddb
    542ceb0b29.

85 Haven Orecchio-Egresitz, "The FBI is asking for the public's help to identify
    the Capitol insurrectionists in one of the most well-documented crimes in US
    history, and the internet thinks it's laughable," *Insider,* January 7, 2021, https://
    www.insider.com/internet-slams-fbi-ask-for-help-identifying-mob-2021-1.

86 Eric Flack and Eliana Block, "VERIFY: Yes, some Capitol Riot defendants are
    being held without bond before their trials," WUSA9, July 26, 2021, https://

www.wusa9.com/article/news/verify/why-capitol-riot-defendants-being
-held-without-bond-before-trial-january-6-congress/65-1e4d4dd6-eded
-4187-85f1-d4dfcc3a9519.

87 Joel Pollak, "Merrick Garland Links 5 Capitol Police Deaths to January
6 Riot," Breitbart News, January 5, 2023, https://www.breitbart.com/poli
tics/2023/01/05/merrick-garland-links-5-capitol-police-deaths-to-january
-6-riot/; United States Capitol Police, "Medical Examiner Finds USCP Officer Brian Sicknick Died of Natural Causes," April 19, 2021, https://www.uscp
.gov/media-center/press-releases/medical-examiner-finds-uscp-officer-bri
an-sicknick-died-natural-causes.

88 Ellen Barry, Nicholas Bogel-Burroughs, and Dave Philipps, "Woman Killed
in Capitol Embraced Trump and QAnon," New York Times, January 7, 2021,
https://www.nytimes.com/2021/01/08/us/who-was-ashli-babbitt.html.

89 Charlie Spiering, "Joe Biden Falsely Claims Five Police Officers Killed by
Trump Supporters on January 6," Breitbart News, March 3, 2022, https://
www.breitbart.com/politics/2022/03/03/joe-biden-falsely-claims-five-police
-officers-killed-in-january-6-protests/.

90 Luke Broadwater and Maggie Haberman, "Jan. 6 Panel Issues Final Report,
Placing Blame for Capitol Riot on 'One Man,' " New York Times, December 22,
2022, https://www.nytimes.com/2022/12/22/us/politics/jan-6-committee-re
port.html.

91 Joel Pollak, "Merrick Garland Links 5 Capitol Police Deaths to January 6
Riot," Breitbart News, January 5, 2023, https://www.breitbart.com/politics
/2023/01/05/merrick-garland-links-5-capitol-police-deaths-to-january-6-riot/.

92 Madison Hall, Skye Gould, Rebecca Harrington, Jacob Shamsian, Azmi
Haroun, Taylor Ardrey, and Erin Snodgrass, "At least 1,003 people have been
charged in the Capitol insurrection so far. This searchable table shows them
all," Insider, February 16, 2023, https://www.insider.com/all-the-us-capitol
-pro-trump-riot-arrests-charges-names-2021-1.

93 Kaitlan Collins, Kevin Liptak, Katelyn Polantz, Sara Murray, Evan Perez,
Gabby Orr, and Dan Berman, "FBI executes search warrant at Trump's Mar-
a-Lago in document investigation," CNN, August 9, 2022, https://www.cnn
.com/2022/08/08/politics/mar-a-lago-search-warrant-fbi-donald-trump
/index.html.

94 Natalie Winters, "REPORT: Judge Behind Mar A Lago Raid Is Epstein-Linked,
Obama Donor," National Pulse, August 9, 2022, https://thenationalpulse
.com/2022/08/09/mar-a-lago-warrant-authorized-by-epstein-lawyer/.

95 Allum Bokhari, "Facebook Posts Reveal Epstein-Linked Magistrate Bruce
Reinhart's Woke, Anti-Trump Attitudes," Breitbart News, August 10, 2022,
https://www.breitbart.com/tech/2022/08/10/facebook-posts-reveal-epstein
-linked-magistrate-bruce-reinharts-woke-anti-trump-attitudes/.

96 Miranda Devine, "FBI searched Melania's wardrobe, spent hours in Trump's private office during Mar-a-Lago raid," New York Post, August 9, 2022, https://ny
post.com/2022/08/09/fbi-even-searched-melanias-wardrobe-in-trump-raid/.

97 Dan Mangan, "FBI seized almost 200,000 pages of documents from Trump
at Mar-a-Lago, his lawyers say in new court filing," CNBC, September 29,
2022, https://www.cnbc.com/2022/09/29/fbi-seized-nearly-200000-pages-of
-trump-documents-at-mar-a-lago.html.

98 Emma-Jo Morris, "Morris: Multiple Indications FBI, Intelligence Agencies Guided Censorship of the Laptop from Hell," Breitbart News, December 6, 2022, https://www.breitbart.com/tech/2022/12/06/morris-multiple-indica tions-fbi-intelligence-agencies-guided-censorship-of-the-laptop-from -hell/.

99 Jonathan Lemire, Kyle Cheney, and Nicholas Wu, "Trump's Mar-a-Lago home searched by FBI in unprecedented move," *Politico*, August 8, 2022, https://www.politico.com/news/2022/08/08/trump-fbi-maralago -search-00050442.

100 Acyn (@Acyn), "Doocy: How much advance notice did you have of the FBI's plan to search Mar-A-Lago? Biden: None. Zero," Twitter, August 24, 2022, 12:11 p.m., https://twitter.com/Acyn/status /1562518048581373952?ref_src=twsrc%5Etfw%7Ctwcamp%5Etwee tembed%7Ctwterm%5E1562518048581373952%7Ctwgr%5E b50ad9fc33f7cc9d766fccdd80830505ecb1086a%7Ctwcon%5Es1_c10&ref_ url=https%3A%2F%2Fwww.thedailybeast.com%2Fjoe-biden-says-he-had -zero-advance-notice-of-fbis-raid-of-donald-trumps-mar-a-lago.

101 Paul Bois, "'Deplorable': FBI Director Christopher Wray Claims 'Threats' Against Agency," Breitbart News, August 10, 2022, https://www.breitbart .com/politics/2022/08/10/deplorable-fbi-director-christopher-wray-de nounces-threats-after-mar-a-lago-raid/.

CONCLUSION

1 Dan Witters, "U.S. Depression Rates Reach New Highs," Gallup, May 17, 2023, https://news.gallup.com/poll/505745/depression-rates-reach-new-highs .aspx.

2 Janet Adamy, "Young Americans Are Dying at Alarming Rates, Reversing Years of Progress," *Wall Street Journal*, May 17, 2023, https://www.wsj.com /articles/death-rate-children-teens-guns-drugs-54c604f4.

3 Dean Balsamini, Joe Marino, Craig McCarthy and Steven Vago, "NYPD cops resigning in new year at record-breaking pace — with a 117% jump from 2021 numbers," *New York Post*, March 10, 2023, https://nypost.com/2023/03/10 /nypd-cops-resigning-from-force-in-2023-at-record-pace/.

4 Gale Holland, "L.A. County wants to curb riskier fentanyl use. Its approach worries some activists," *Los Angeles Times*, May 30, 2023, https://www.latimes .com/california/story/2023-05-30/desperate-to-stop-fentanyl-deaths-offi cials-are-distributing-drug-pipes.

5 Breccan Thies, "Hundreds of Chicago Teachers Raped, Sexually Assaulted, Groomed Students in 2022," Breitbart News, January 9, 2023, https://www .breitbart.com/politics/2023/01/09/hundreds-chicago-teachers-raped-sexu ally-assaulted-groomed-students-2022/.

6 Jacob Geanous, "Horrific footage shows devastation of Philadelphia's 'tranq' epidemic," *New York Post*, May 27, 2023, https://nypost.com/2023/05/27 /horrific-footage-shows-devastation-of-philadelphias-tranq-epidemic/; Allie Griffin, "Wild brawl involving at least a dozen breaks out at Chicago O'Hare Airport: video: *New York Post*, May 24, 2023, https://nypost.com/2023/05/24/ two-travelers-arrested-after-wild-brawl-at-chicago-ohare-airport-video/;

Zachary Rogers, "'Flash mob' takeover of LA street leads to ransacking of store, video shows," Dayton 24/7 Now, August 19, 2022, https://dayton 247now.com/news/nation-world/flash-mob-takeover-of-la-street-leads-to -ransacking-of-store-video-shows.

7   John Binder, "Biden's DHS Frees 2.3K Illegal Alien Convicted Criminals into U.S. in Five Months," Breitbart News, May 25, 2023, https://www.breitbart .com/politics/2023/05/25/bidens-dhs-frees-2-3k-illegal-alien-convicted -criminals-into-u-s-in-five-months/; Neil Munro, "Biden Opens Border to 1 Million+ Illegals Per Year," Breitbart News, June 1, 2023, https://www.breit bart.com/immigration/2023/06/01/biden-opens-border-to-1-million-ille gals-per-year/.

8   Marina Kopf and Catie Beck, "As cancer drug shortages grow, some doctors are forced to ration doses or delay care," NBC News, May 26, 2023, https:// www.nbcnews.com/health/cancer/cancer-drug-shortages-14-medicines -now-short-supply-fda-says-rcna86106.

9   "'Biden's Gestapo'? Trump Raid Hurts Voter Trust in FBI," Rasmussen Reports, August 18, 2022, https://www.rasmussenreports.com/public_content /politics/public_surveys/biden_s_gestapo_trump_raid_hurts_voter_trust _in_fbi.

10 Brittany Shepherd, "Americans' faith in election integrity drops: POLL," ABC News, January 6, 2022, https://abcnews.go.com/Politics/americans-faith-elec tion-integrity-drops-poll/story?id=82069876.

11 David Bauder, "Trust in media is so low that half of Americans now believe that news organizations deliberately mislead them," Fortune, February 15, 2023, https://fortune.com/2023/02/15/trust-in-media-low-misinform-mis lead-biased-republicans-democrats-poll-gallup/.

12 Jack Caporal and Lyle Daly, "Average House Price by State in 2023," The Ascent, May 11, 2023, https://www.fool.com/the-ascent/research/aver age-house-price-state/#:~:text=Average%20home%20price%20in%20 the,when%20the%20median%20was%20%24329%2C000.&text=ME DIAN%20SALES%20PRICE%20OF%20HOMES%20IN%20THE%20U.S.

13 Jessica Semega and Melissa Kollar, Income in the United States: 2021, Report Number P60-276, United States Census Bureau, September 13, 2022, https:// www.census.gov/library/publications/2022/demo/p60-276.html#:~:text =The%20real%20median%20earnings%20of,4.1%20percent%20(Fig ure%204).

14 Aneeta Bhole, "Transgender Assistant Secretary of Health Rachel Levine says changing kids' genders has the 'highest support' of the Biden administration and is key to the mental health of minors," Daily Mail, March 17, 2023, https:// www.dailymail.co.uk/news/article-11871045/Dr-Rachel-Levine-says-gen der-affirming-care-minors-Biden-administrations-highest-support.html.

15 Anna Allen, "Jill Biden Gives International Women of Courage Award to Biological Man," Washington Free Beacon, March 9, 2023, https://freebeacon. com/biden-administration/jill-biden-gives-international-women-of-cour age-award-to-biological-man/; Simon Kent, "Rachel Levine Nominated as One of USA TODAY's 'Women of The Year,' " Breitbart News, March 15, 2022, https://www.breitbart.com/politics/2022/03/15/rachel-levine-nominat ed-as-one-of-usa-todays-women-of-the-year/

16 Kristina Wong, "Navy Confirms Using Drag Queen Influencer as a 'Digital Ambassador' to Attract Recruits," Breitbart News, May 3, 2023, https://www .breitbart.com/politics/2023/05/03/navy-confirms-using-drag-queen-influ encer-as-digital-ambassador-to-attract-recruits/.

17 Dan De Luce and Shannon Pettypiece, "Biden admin scraps Trump's restrictions on transgender troops," NBC News, March 31, 2021, https://www .nbcnews.com/news/military/biden-admin-scraps-trump-s-restrictions -transgender-troops-n1262646.

18 Joel Pollak, "Joe Biden's Executive Order on Voting Tells Agencies to Push Vote-by-Mail, 'Combat Misinformation,'" Breitbart News, March 7, 2021, https://www.breitbart.com/politics/2021/03/07/joe-bidens-executive-or der-on-voting-promotes-vote-by-mail-combat-misinformation/.

19 Allum Bokhari, "Biden White House Pressured Facebook to Censor Tucker Carlson," Breitbart News, January 9, 2023, https://www.breitbart.com /tech/2023/01/09/biden-white-house-pressured-facebook-to-censor-tucker -carlson/.

20 Katie Glueck, "Biden, Recalling 'Civility' in Senate, Invokes Two Segregationist Senators," New York Times, June 19, 2019, https://www.nytimes .com/2019/06/19/us/politics/biden-segregationists.html.

21 Taryn Luna, "Is California giving reparations for slavery? Here's what you need to know," Los Angeles Times, May 6, 2023, https://www.latimes.com /california/story/2023-05-06/californias-reparations-task-force-recommen dations-heres-what-you-need-to-know.

22 https://ssir.org/articles/entry/the_bias_of_professionalism_standards#.

23 H. Samy Alim and Geneva Smitherman, ' "Perfect English" and White Supremacy," in Language in the Trump Era: Scandals and Emergencies, ed. Janet McIntosh and Norma Mendoza-Denton (Cambridge: Cambridge University Press, 2020), https://www.cambridge.org/core/books/abs/language-in-the-trump-era/per fect-english-and-white-supremacy/8704FAA92F598319245A53DA1D2A5FBC.

24 Jeffrey Jones, "Social Conservatism in U.S. Highest in About a Decade," Gallup, June 8, 2023, https://news.gallup.com/poll/506765/social-conserva tism-highest-decade.aspx.

25 Thomas Franck, "Biden disapproval hits new high as voters give him bad grades on economy, new CNBC/Change poll says," CNBC, January 4, 2022, https://www.cnbc.com/2022/01/04/biden-disapproval-rating-high-voters -blame-him-on-economy-CNBC-poll.html; "Biden warns China will 'eat our lunch' on infrastructure spending," BBC News, February 12, 2021, https:// www.bbc.com/news/business-56036245.

26 Gabrielle Reyes, "China Gives Up on Anti-Communist Millennials, Turns to Gen Z," Breitbart News, July 9, 2021, https://www.breitbart.com /asia/2021/07/09/china-gives-up-on-anti-communist-millennials-turns-to -gen-z/

27 Derek Robertson, "Politics is downstream from (virtual) culture," Politico, March 14, 2023, https://www.politico.com/newsletters /digital-future-daily/2023/03/14/politics-are-downstream-from-virtual -culture-00087041.

28 Jenny Goldsberry, "Stacey Abrams spent $1.2 million on private security since campaign launch: Report," Washington Examiner, October 10, 2022, https://

www.washingtonexaminer.com/news/campaigns/stacey-abrams-securi
ty-executive-protections-agencies-georgia-midterms.

EPILOGUE

1 Jordan Dixon-Hamilton, "Whistleblower: Hunter Biden Deducted Payments
to Sex Club, Hookers on His Taxes," Breitbart News, June 23, 2023, https://
www.breitbart.com/politics/2023/06/23/whistleblower-hunter-biden-de
ducted-payments-to-sex-club-hookers-on-his-taxes/.

2 Katie Benner, Kenneth Vogel and Michael Schmidt, "Hunter Biden Paid
Tax Bill, but Broad Federal Investigation Continues," New York Times,
March 16, 2022, https://www.nytimes.com/2022/03/16/us/politics/hunter
-biden-tax-bill-investigation.html.

3 Joel Pollak, "Hunter Biden Investigation Began as 'Offshoot' of Inquiry into
Foreign Adult Platform," Breitbart News, https://www.breitbart.com/pol
itics/2023/06/22/hunter-biden-investigation-began-as-offshoot-of-inqui
ry-into-foreign-adult-platform/; Interview before the Committee on Ways
and Means, House of Representatives, 118th Cong. (2023) (interview of
Gary A. Shapley, Jr.), https://waysandmeans.house.gov/wp-content/up
loads/2023/06/Whistleblower-1-Transcript_Redacted.pdf.

4 Ian Hanchett, "Dem Rep. Goldman: Hunter Biden 'Should Be Commended
for' 'Accepting Responsibility' by Taking a Plea Deal on Felony Gun Crime,"
Breitbart News, June 21, 2023, https://www.breitbart.com/clips/2023/06/21
/dem-rep-goldman-hunter-biden-should-be-commended-for-accepting-re
sponsibility-by-taking-a-plea-deal-on-felony-gun-crime/.

5 Emily Goodin and Nikki Schwab, "Hunter Biden makes first public appearance since 'sweetheart' tax crimes deal at glamorous White House
state dinner with India: President turns lavish Modi event into a family
affair by inviting scandal-hit son, daughter and granddaughter," Daily
Mail, June 22, 2023, https://www.dailymail.co.uk/news/article-12224793
/Joe-Biden-turns-state-dinner-Indias-Modi-family-affair-Hunter-Naomi
.html.

6 United States Federal Election Commission, "Katy Chevigny," Individual
contributions, accessed June 26, 2023, https://www.fec.gov/data/receipts
/individual-contributions/?contributor_name=Katy+Chevigny+.

7 Aaron Kliegman, "Hunter Biden's 'sugar brother' keeps the first son afloat
amid multiple scandals," Fox News, May 29, 2023, https://www.foxnews.com
/politics/hunter-bidens-sugar-brother-keeps-first-son-afloat-amid-multiple
-scandals.

8 Department of Justice United States Attorney's Office, District of Delaware,
"Tax and Firearm Charges Filed Against Robert Hunter Biden," press release,
June 20, 2023, https://www.justice.gov/usao-de/pr/tax-and-firearm-charges
-filed-against-robert-hunter-biden.

9 Interview before the Committee on Ways and Means, House of Representatives, 118th Cong. (2023) (interview of [redacted whistleblower name]),
https://waysandmeans.house.gov/wp-content/uploads/2023/06/Whistleblow
er-2-Transcript_Redacted.

10 Chuck Ross and Andrew Kerr, "Photos Place Hunter Biden At Father's House

The Day He Invoked Dad's Name to Threaten Chinese Business Partner," *Washington Free Beacon*, June 22, 2023, https://freebeacon.com/biden-ad ministration/photos-place-hunter-biden-at-fathers-house-the-day-he-in voked-dads-name-to-chinese-business-partner/.

11 Joel Pollak, "Biden WH Changes Story: From 'Never Discussed' to 'Not in Business' with Hunter," June 23, 2023, https://www.breitbart.com/poli tics/2023/06/23/biden-wh-changes-story-from-never-discussed-to-not-in -business-with-hunter/.

INDEX